AP® PSYCHOLOGY
PREMIUM PREP

21st Edition

The Staff of The Princeton Review

PrincetonReview.com

| Penguin
Random
House |

The Princeton Review
110 East 42nd St, 7th Floor
New York, NY 10017

Published in the United States by Penguin Random House LLC, New York.

ISBN: 978-0-593-51723-9
eBook ISBN: 978-0-593-51724-6
ISSN: 2690-652X

AP is a trademark registered and owned by the College Board, which is not affiliated with, and does not endorse this product.

The Princeton Review is not affiliated with Princeton University.

The material in this book is up-to-date at the time of publication. However, changes may have been instituted by the testing body in the test after this book was published.

If there are any important late-breaking developments, changes, or corrections to the materials in this book, we will post that information online in the Student Tools. Register your book and check your Student Tools to see whether there are any updates posted there.

Editor: Aaron Riccio
Production Editors: Ali Landreau and Becky Radway
Production Artist: Amanda Shurgin
Content Contributors: Jerry Dresner, Anthony Krupp, Christine Lindwall, and Toni Scorsese

Printed in the United States of America.

10 9 8 7 6 5 4 3 2 1

21st Edition

The Princeton Review Publishing Team
Rob Franek, Editor-in-Chief
David Soto, Senior Director, Data Operations
Stephen Koch, Senior Manager, Data Operations
Deborah Weber, Director of Production
Jason Ullmeyer, Production Design Manager
Jennifer Chapman, Senior Production Artist
Selena Coppock, Director of Editorial
Orion McBean, Senior Editor
Aaron Riccio, Senior Editor
Meave Shelton, Senior Editor
Chris Chimera, Editor
Patricia Murphy, Editor
Laura Rose, Editor
Isabelle Appleton, Editorial Assistant

Penguin Random House Publishing Team
Tom Russell, VP, Publisher
Alison Stoltzfus, Senior Director, Publishing
Brett Wright, Senior Editor
Emily Hoffman, Assistant Managing Editor
Ellen Reed, Production Manager
Suzanne Lee, Designer
Eugenia Lo, Publishing Assistant

For customer service, please contact **editorialsupport@review.com**, and be sure to include:

- full title of the book

- ISBN

- page number

Acknowledgments

The Princeton Review would like to give special thanks to Jerry Dresner, Anthony Krupp, Christine Lindwall, and Toni Scorsese for their valuable contributions to the latest edition of this book.

Additionally, thank you to Ali Landreau, Becky Radway, and Amanda Shurgin for their time and attention to each page.

Contents

Get More (Free) Content
at PrincetonReview.com/prep

As easy as 1·2·3

1 Go to PrincetonReview.com/prep or scan the **QR code** and enter the following ISBN for your book: **9780593517239**

2 Answer a few simple questions to set up an exclusive Princeton Review account. *(If you already have one, you can just log in.)*

3 Enjoy access to your **FREE** content!

Once you've registered, you can...

- Access your fifth, full-length practice AP Psychology Exam, plus an answer key and detailed explanations

- Get our take on any recent or pending updates to the AP Psychology Exam

- Take a full-length practice SAT and/or ACT

- Get valuable advice about the college application process, including tips for writing a great essay and where to apply for financial aid

- If you're still choosing between colleges, use our searchable rankings of *The Best 389 Colleges* to find out more information about your dream school

- Access comprehensive study guides and a variety of printable resources, including: Key Terms lists, score conversion tables for the Practice Tests, and bubble sheets

- Check to see whether there have been any corrections or updates to this edition

Need to report a potential **content** issue?

Contact **EditorialSupport@review.com** and include:

- full title of the book
- ISBN
- page number

Need to report a **technical** issue?

Contact **TPRStudentTech@review.com** and provide:

- your full name
- email address used to register the book
- full book title and ISBN
- Operating system (Mac/PC) and browser (Chrome, Firefox, Safari, etc.)

Look For These Icons Throughout The Book

 ONLINE ARTICLES

 PROVEN TECHNIQUES

 APPLIED STRATEGIES

 ONLINE PRACTICE TESTS

Part I
Using This Book to Improve Your AP Score

- Preview: Your Knowledge, Your Expectations
- Your Guide to Using This Book
- How to Begin

PREVIEW: YOUR KNOWLEDGE, YOUR EXPECTATIONS

Your route to a high score on the AP Psychology Exam depends a lot on how you plan to use this book. To help you determine your approach, respond to the following questions.

Looking for More Help with Your APs?

We now offer specialized AP tutoring and course packages that guarantee a 4 or 5 on the AP. To see which courses are offered and available, and to learn more about the guarantee, visit PrincetonReview.com/college/ap-test-prep.

1. Rate your level of confidence about your knowledge of the content tested by the AP Psychology Exam:

    A. Very confident—I know it all

    B. I'm pretty confident, but there are topics for which I could use help

    C. Not confident—I need quite a bit of support

    D. I'm not sure

2. Circle your goal score for the AP Psychology Exam:

    5 4 3 2 1   I'm not sure yet

3. What do you expect to learn from this book? Circle all that apply to you.

    A. A general overview of the test and what to expect

    B. Strategies for how to approach the test

    C. The content tested by this exam

    D. I'm not sure yet

YOUR GUIDE TO USING THIS BOOK

This book is organized to provide as much—or as little—support as you need, so you can use this book in whatever way will be most helpful to improving your score on the AP Psychology Exam.

*   The remainder of **Part I** will provide guidance on how to use this book and help you determine your strengths and weaknesses.

*   **Part II** of this book contains Practice Test 1, the Diagnostic Answer Key, answers and explanations for each question, and a scoring guide. (Bubble sheets can be found in the very back of the book for easy tear-out.) We strongly recommend that you take this test before going any further, in order to realistically determine:

    o   your starting point right now
    o   which question types you're ready for and which you might need to practice
    o   which content topics you are familiar with and which you will want to carefully review; our Diagnostic Answer Key will assist you with this process

Once you have nailed down your strengths and weaknesses with regard to this exam, you can focus your test preparation, build a study plan, and be efficient with your time.

- **Part III** of this book will:
  - provide information about the structure, scoring, and content of the AP Psychology Exam
  - help you to make a study plan
  - point you toward additional resources

- **Part IV** of this book will explore various strategies, including the following:
  - how to solve multiple-choice questions
  - how to write effective essays
  - how to manage your time to maximize the number of points available to you

- **Part V** of this book covers the content you need for the AP Psychology Exam.

- **Parts VI and VII** of this book contain Practice Tests 2, 3, and 4, their answers and explanations, and scoring guides. (Bubble sheets can be found in the very back of the book for easy tear-out.) If you skipped Practice Test 1, we recommend that you do all four (with at least a day or two between them) so that you can compare your progress. Additionally, this will help to identify any external issues: if you answer a certain type of question wrong all four times, you probably need to review it. If you answered it incorrectly only once, you may have run out of time or been distracted by something. In either case, comparing the four exams will allow you to focus on the factors that caused the discrepancy in scores and to be as prepared as possible on the day of the test.

You may choose to use some parts of this book over others, or you may work through the entire book. Your approach will depend on your needs and how much time you have. Let's now look at how to make this determination.

HOW TO BEGIN

1. **Take a Test**
   Before you can decide how to use this book, you need to take a practice test. Doing so will give you insight into your strengths and weaknesses, and the test will also help you make an effective study plan. If you're feeling test-phobic, remind yourself that a practice test is a tool for diagnosing yourself—it's not how well you do that matters but how you use information gleaned from your performance to guide your preparation.

Don't Forget!
To take Practice Test 5, be sure to register your book online following the instructions on pages viii–ix. You'll also gain access to a bunch of other helpful Student Tools, including study guides and a list of key terms!

Score Conversion Sheets

After each practice test in this book, you'll find conversion sheets that can help you approximate what you would score if it were an actual AP exam. Don't be alarmed if it's lower than you expected; use your score on the first practice test to help you better improve on the second practice test!

Key Concepts

Want an extended list of concepts broken down by course units? Log onto your online Student Tools! You'll also find digital copies of the key term lists at the end of each content chapter in this book.

So, before you read further, take Practice Test 1 starting on page 9 of this book. Be sure to do so in one sitting, following the instructions that appear before the test.

2. **Check Your Answers**
   Using the Diagnostic Answer Key on page 30, follow our three-step process to identify your strengths and weaknesses with regard to the tested topics. This will help you determine which content review chapters to prioritize when studying this book. Don't worry about the explanations for now, and don't worry about missed questions. We'll get to that soon.

3. **Reflect on the Test**
   After you take your first test, respond to the following questions:

   • How much time did you spend on the multiple-choice questions?

   • How much time did you spend on each essay?

   • How many multiple-choice questions did you miss?

   • Do you feel you had the knowledge to address the subject matter of the essays?

   • Do you feel you wrote well-organized, thoughtful essays?

4. **Read Part III of This Book and Complete the Self-Evaluation**
   Part III will provide information on how the test is structured and scored. It will also list areas of content that are tested.

   As you read Part III, reevaluate your answers to the questions above. At the end of Part III, you will revisit and refine your answers to these questions. You will then be able to make a study plan, based on your needs and time available, that will allow you to use this book most effectively.

5. **Engage with Parts IV and V as Needed**
   Notice the word *engage*. You'll get more out of this book if you use it intentionally than if you read it passively, hoping for an improved score through osmosis. Strategy chapters in Part IV will help you think about your approach to the question types on this exam. This part opens with a reminder to think about how you approach questions now and then closes with a reflection section asking you to think about how/whether you will change your approach in the future.

   The content chapters in Part V are designed to provide a review of the content tested on the AP Psychology Exam, including the level of detail you need to know and how the content is tested. You will have the opportunity to assess your proficiency of the content of each chapter through test-appropriate questions and a reflection section.

6. **Take Practice Test 2 and Assess Your Performance**

   Once you feel you have developed the strategies you need and gained the knowledge you lacked, you should take Practice Test 2, which starts on page 343 of this book. You should do so in one sitting, following the instructions at the beginning of the test.

   When you are done, check your answers to the multiple-choice sections. See whether a teacher will read your essays and provide feedback.

   Once you have taken the test, reflect on what areas you still need to work on, and revisit the chapters in this book that address those deficiencies. Through this type of reflection and engagement, you will continue to improve. Use the rest of your practice tests to measure your progress along the way.

7. **Keep Working**

   As we'll discuss in Part III, there are other resources available to you, including a wealth of information on the section of the College Board's AP website called AP Students. You can continue to explore areas that can stand to improve and engage in those areas right up to the day of the test.

Part II
Practice Test 1

Practice Test 1

AP® Psychology Exam

SECTION I: Multiple-Choice Questions

DO NOT OPEN THIS BOOKLET UNTIL YOU ARE TOLD TO DO SO.

Instructions

Section I of this exam contains 100 multiple-choice questions. Fill in only the ovals for numbers 1 through 100 on your answer sheet.

Indicate all of your answers to the multiple-choice questions on the answer sheet. No credit will be given for anything written in this exam booklet, but you may use the booklet for notes or scratch work. After you have decided which of the suggested answers is best, completely fill in the corresponding oval on the answer sheet. Give only one answer to each question. If you change an answer, be sure that the previous mark is erased completely. Here is a sample question and answer.

At a Glance

Total Time
1 hour and 10 minutes
Number of Questions
100
Percent of Total Score
66.6%
Writing Instrument
Pencil required

Sample Question   Sample Answer

Omaha is a

(A) state
(B) city
(C) country
(D) continent
(E) village

Use your time effectively, working as quickly as you can without losing accuracy. Do not spend too much time on any one question. Go on to other questions and come back to the ones you have not answered if you have time. It is not expected that everyone will know the answers to all of the multiple-choice questions.

About Guessing

Many candidates wonder whether or not to guess the answers to questions about which they are not certain. Multiple-choice scores are based on the number of questions answered correctly. Points are not deducted for incorrect answers, and no points are awarded for unanswered questions. Because points are not deducted for incorrect answers, you are encouraged to answer all multiple-choice questions. On any questions you do not know the answer to, you should eliminate as many choices as you can, and then select the best answer among the remaining choices.

GO ON TO THE NEXT PAGE.

This page intentionally left blank.

GO ON TO THE NEXT PAGE.

PSYCHOLOGY
Section I
Time—1 hour and 10 minutes
100 Questions

Directions: Each of the questions or incomplete statements below is followed by five answer choices. Select the one that is best in each case and then completely fill in the corresponding oval on the answer sheet.

1. Which of the following is an example of habituation?

   (A) The first time Ilene wears high-heeled shoes, she finds them extremely uncomfortable.
   (B) Ilene can only tolerate wearing high-heeled shoes for a few hours because they hurt.
   (C) Ilene wore high-heeled shoes for the first time two weeks ago; now she wears them every day.
   (D) High-heeled shoes always hurt Ilene's feet, but she forces herself to wear them because they are fashionable.
   (E) When Ilene wears high-heeled shoes all day her feet usually only hurt for the first few minutes.

2. Which of the following is NOT a symptom of major depressive disorder?

   (A) Loss of appetite
   (B) Mania
   (C) Social withdrawal
   (D) Prolonged feelings of sadness
   (E) Suicidal ideation

3. Joe's psychotherapist often asks him to recount his dreams, discuss his early childhood, and explore possible feelings and motivations of which he is unaware. His therapist would best be described as

   (A) behavioral
   (B) psychodynamic
   (C) client-centered
   (D) cognitive-behavioral
   (E) eclectic

4. Which of the following groups of quiz scores has the highest standard deviation?

   (A) 80, 80, 80, 82, 85
   (B) 90, 91, 93, 95, 98
   (C) 50, 53, 54, 54
   (D) 60, 65, 75, 84, 98
   (E) 70, 70, 79

5. Jill commits a minor criminal offense. Consequently, a judge orders her to perform community service: picking up garbage along the side of the highway. This scenario is best described as

   (A) positive reinforcement
   (B) negative punishment
   (C) shaping
   (D) negative reinforcement
   (E) positive punishment

6. On a public street, Dave is accosted by a stranger who proceeds to rob him. According to social psychological theory, his chances of receiving help from someone are greatest if how many people witness the incident?

   (A) 0
   (B) 1
   (C) 2
   (D) 3
   (E) 4

7. Which of the following scientists is most closely associated with the "collective unconscious"?

   (A) Sigmund Freud
   (B) Carl Jung
   (C) B.F. Skinner
   (D) Ivan Pavlov
   (E) William James

8. A drug counselor observes that her client is extremely lethargic and his pupils are constricted. Which of the following illegal drugs is the client most likely to have taken?

   (A) Cocaine
   (B) Heroin
   (C) LSD (lysergic acid diethylamide)
   (D) Methamphetamine
   (E) Ecstasy (methylenedioxymethamphetamine)

GO ON TO THE NEXT PAGE.

9. A researcher reads the following list of words to a group of subjects in this order: horse, nose, book, dog, lamp, mind, train, glass, ice, paint, hat, and chair. Then he asks the subjects to write down all the words they remember. On average, the group will

   (A) be more likely to remember the word "horse" than the word "chair," owing to the recency effect
   (B) be more likely to remember the word "nose" than the word "mind," owing to the recency effect
   (C) be more likely to remember the words "horse" and "chair" than the word "train," owing to serial position effects
   (D) be more likely to remember the words in the middle of the list than those at the beginning, owing to the primacy effect
   (E) be more likely to remember certain words randomly than to recall any of the words based on serial position

10. Robert sees an angry bear approach him and runs as fast as he can to escape. Which of the following bodily changes would be most likely to occur as Robert is running from the bear?

    (A) Increased parasympathetic activity
    (B) Decreased respiration
    (C) Decreased sympathetic activity
    (D) Increased epinephrine levels
    (E) Decreased adrenaline levels

11. Linda gives all employees of her company a 2% raise every January. She rewards her employees on which type of schedule?

    (A) Fixed-interval
    (B) Variable-ratio
    (C) Fixed-variable
    (D) Fixed-ratio
    (E) Variable-interval

12. Sue is shy, works exclusively from home, and has very few friends. While she would like to be socially accepted, she generally avoids contact with others for fear that they will reject her. Which personality disorder best describes Sue?

    (A) Antisocial
    (B) Narcissistic
    (C) Borderline
    (D) Schizotypal
    (E) Avoidant

13. Mary just turned seventeen. Which of Erikson's developmental stages is she working on at this point in her life?

    (A) Trust vs. mistrust
    (B) Autonomy vs. shame and doubt
    (C) Identity vs. role confusion
    (D) Generativity vs. stagnation
    (E) Integrity vs. despair

14. During Jack's first two years in college, he took one history class every semester and found each professor extremely entertaining. This prompted him to take European History with Professor Smith, whom he found terribly boring. After dropping the class, Jack concluded that history teachers are not all entertaining. The fact that he changed his mind based on this recent experience is best described as

    (A) cognitive dissonance
    (B) schema
    (C) accommodation
    (D) assimilation
    (E) archetype

15. Ever since Jane sustained a head injury in a car accident, she has been unable to form new memories. Which part of her brain has been damaged?

    (A) The hippocampus
    (B) The hypothalamus
    (C) The occipital lobe
    (D) The temporal lobe
    (E) The medulla

16. Which of the following is the best example of the psychotherapeutic technique known as "mirroring"?

    (A) Dr. Jones challenges her client's explanation of his hostile behavior.
    (B) Dr. Jones is empathic and caring towards her client when he recounts traumatic experiences.
    (C) Dr. Jones praises her client when he abstains from alcohol and withholds her praise when he does not.
    (D) Dr. Jones points out how her client's behavior resembles that of his father.
    (E) Dr. Jones summarizes her client's concerns about losing his job and states that he seems worried and upset about it.

GO ON TO THE NEXT PAGE.

17. Louis is thirty years old with an IQ of 65. He can dress and groom himself, make small purchases independently, and work in a restaurant clearing tables with some assistance. He lives with his parents, whom he relies on for help with major life decisions. Which of the following best describes Louis's intellectual functioning?

    (A) No disability
    (B) Mild disability
    (C) Moderate disability
    (D) Severe disability
    (E) Profound disability

18. Which of the following scenarios best exemplifies the just-world hypothesis?

    (A) Laura is the prettiest and most popular girl in school. Her peers unanimously elect her class president, despite her lack of relevant experience and qualifications.
    (B) Fred is serving a life sentence for a serious crime; crowds of people protest, asserting that he was falsely convicted.
    (C) Phil feels bad about ridiculing a fellow student, but he does it because all his friends are doing it.
    (D) Roy is mugged at gunpoint; the community believes he brought the attack upon himself by bragging about how much cash he carries.
    (E) Julia is fired from her job and her coworkers support her claim of gender discrimination.

19. Zachary, who loves sugary carbonated drinks, reads a magazine article about how bad such beverages are for one's health. According to cognitive dissonance theory, Zachary is LEAST likely to do which of the following after reading the article?

    (A) Substantially reduce his consumption of sugary carbonated drinks
    (B) Eliminate sugary carbonated drinks from his diet altogether
    (C) Question the medical accuracy of the statements in the magazine article
    (D) Decide that enjoying oneself is more important than maintaining perfect health
    (E) Accept the article's conclusions and continue to consume the same number of sugary carbonated drinks

20. Jennifer finally goes to bed after staying up for 24 hours straight in order to cram for a test. She remains asleep even though a fire alarm goes off in her dormitory, requiring her roommate to shake her a few times in order to wake her up. Which of the following brainwaves were likely dominant in Jennifer's brain while she slept through the alarm?

    (A) Alpha and beta
    (B) Theta
    (C) Beta and theta
    (D) Delta
    (E) Delta and beta

21. In John Watson's "Little Albert" experiment, fear of white rats was the

    (A) unconditioned response
    (B) conditioned stimulus
    (C) unconditioned stimulus
    (D) conditioned response
    (E) primary punisher

22. A professional dancer is warming up before a show by performing some elementary dance moves. If he is suddenly joined by several other dancers who perform the same moves, his performance will most likely

    (A) improve
    (B) worsen substantially due to the bystander effect
    (C) worsen slightly due to social loafing
    (D) remain unaffected
    (E) improve substantially due to the mere-exposure effect

23. Which of the following is an example of chunking?

    (A) Reciting a telephone number as follows: the area code first followed by a pause, then the first three digits followed by a pause, then the last four digits
    (B) Preparing for an exam by studying a different subject each day
    (C) Repeating a license plate number over and over out loud until it can be written down
    (D) Using the scent of roses to trigger a childhood memory of being in a rose garden
    (E) Teaching children the alphabet through the use of the "ABC's" song

GO ON TO THE NEXT PAGE.

24. Margaret stores tomatoes together with apples and oranges, rather than together with carrots and celery. This is most likely an example of which Gestalt principle?

    (A) Proximity
    (B) Similarity
    (C) Figure and ground
    (D) Continuity
    (E) Closure

25. Falsely concluding that research findings are statistically significant is called

    (A) a null hypothesis
    (B) a Type I error
    (C) a regression toward the mean
    (D) a random error
    (E) a Type II error

26. The brain's occipital lobe controls

    (A) impulse inhibition
    (B) hearing and language processing
    (C) planning and goal-setting
    (D) pain recognition
    (E) visual processing

27. Kerri didn't bother to study much for her medical school entrance exam. She believed that, if she was meant to be a doctor, she would do well on the test and ultimately get accepted to medical school. Which of the following is most likely to be true based on this information?

    (A) She has an external locus of control.
    (B) She suffers from learned helplessness.
    (C) She has an internal locus of control.
    (D) She has a self-serving bias.
    (E) She lacks self-esteem.

28. A psychology professor examining the effects of teacher praise on academic performance randomly assigns each of her students to one of two groups: high praise or low praise. She praises her students accordingly and then administers a test: the "high praise" students perform an average of 13% better than they did on the last exam, while the "low praise" students perform only 6% better on average. The independent variable in this study is

    (A) the test scores earned by the two groups
    (B) how well the teacher expected the two groups to perform
    (C) how well the students performed on the last test prior to the experiment
    (D) the amount of praise given to the students
    (E) the difference between the average improvement rates demonstrated by the "high praise" and "low praise" groups

29. Fred received a score of 120 on a standardized college entrance exam, which places him in the 68th percentile. This means that

    (A) he answered 68% of the questions correctly
    (B) 32% of the students who took that test scored lower than he did
    (C) he scored higher than 68% of the students who took that test
    (D) 68% of the students who took that test scored higher than he did
    (E) a score of 120 is below average for that test

30. One evening Carol wears clothing that she herself thinks is appropriate, but is sharply criticized by her community for dressing in that manner. Upon learning of the criticism, Carol is overcome with shame and guilt and swears never to wear clothing of that type again. According to Kohlberg, Carol is most likely at which level/stage of moral development?

    (A) Preconventional morality
    (B) Stage 8: Integrity vs. despair
    (C) Conventional morality
    (D) Stage 6: Universal ethical principles
    (E) Stage 1: Punishment and obedience orientation

31. According to Freudian theory, a lifelong criminal with no regard for others' rights has probably failed to develop a(n)

    (A) id
    (B) ego
    (C) superego
    (D) Oedipal complex
    (E) fixation

32. Delirium tremens is associated with withdrawal from which of the following substances?

    (A) Caffeine
    (B) Tobacco
    (C) Morphine
    (D) Amphetamines
    (E) Alcohol

33. The word "unhappiness" has how many morphemes?

    (A) 0
    (B) 1
    (C) 2
    (D) 3
    (E) 4

GO ON TO THE NEXT PAGE.

34. Jenny is diagnosed with aphasia after a severe blow to the head. She will most likely be unable to perform which of the following activities?

    (A) Standing unaided for several minutes
    (B) Recognizing human faces
    (C) Forming new memories
    (D) Digesting large amounts of food
    (E) Conversing with a group of friends

35. Dennis is an extremely aggressive eleven-year-old boy who is frequently in trouble for physically assaulting other children. According to the research and theories of Albert Bandura, Dennis probably

    (A) finds at least some of the consequences of his aggressive behavior desirable
    (B) is genetically predisposed to violence
    (C) is fixated at an earlier stage of psychosexual development
    (D) has observed adults in his life behaving violently
    (E) would have had a distinct survival advantage had he lived in a prehistoric era

36. Which of the following is an example of secondary drive-reduction?

    (A) Veronica pulls her car off the road for a quick nap because she's afraid she might fall asleep at the wheel.
    (B) Veronica purchases a new coat, despite living in a warm climate, because an unusually cold winter has been predicted.
    (C) Veronica works exhausting double shifts at her job all month in order to receive a large paycheck.
    (D) Veronica eats her dessert before dinner has been served because she cannot resist chocolate cake.
    (E) Veronica spends several hundred dollars on a new air-conditioning system for her car.

37. Which part of the eye contains the cells that sense light?

    (A) The pupil
    (B) The retina
    (C) The lens
    (D) The cornea
    (E) The iris

38. Sandra tells her therapist, who has been trained in rational emotive behavior therapy (REBT), that she feels depressed, guilty, and unwanted since her divorce. The therapist would be most likely to do which of the following?

    (A) Empathize with her feelings
    (B) Ask her about her relationship with her father
    (C) Put her on a behavior modification program
    (D) Have her lie on a couch and say whatever comes to mind
    (E) Help her understand that her negative beliefs about herself are false

39. Which of the following is an example of the door-in-the-face technique?

    (A) Liz's boss grants her request to leave 30 minutes early one day, even though leaving early is against company rules. The next week she asks to leave several hours early, and her boss allows it.
    (B) Every time Liz's boss lets her leave early, she showers him with praise and thanks.
    (C) Liz pesters her boss to allow her to leave early one day, constantly complaining that she feels ill-treated, until he finally gives in. Then she stops bothering him.
    (D) Liz asks her boss to let her leave four hours early one day and he flatly refuses. She then asks him to let her leave 30 minutes early, and he agrees.
    (E) Liz's boss never lets her leave early, no matter how much she pleads.

40. Which of the following is a projective test?

    (A) The Wechsler Adult Intelligence Scale
    (B) The Rorschach
    (C) The Minnesota Multiphasic Personality Inventory (MMPI)
    (D) The *DSM-5*
    (E) A clinical intake interview

41. Instead of throwing away an empty wine bottle, Julie paints it and uses it as a vase to display flowers. Julie has overcome which of the following?

    (A) Conformity
    (B) The fundamental attribution error
    (C) The mere exposure effect
    (D) Functional fixedness
    (E) Learned helplessness

GO ON TO THE NEXT PAGE.

42. Conversion disorder (or "functional neurological symptom disorder") might cause an individual to complain of which one of the following problems?

   (A) A debilitating fear of heights
   (B) A fear of germs
   (C) Paralysis for which there is no apparent medical explanation
   (D) A compulsion to inflict self-harm
   (E) Delusions of grandeur

43. A child who has mastered conservation understands that

   (A) objects still exist even though they can't be seen
   (B) human law is fallible and subject to a higher morality
   (C) abstract ideas can be represented by symbols
   (D) a given amount of liquid remains the same despite being poured into a smaller container
   (E) outward expression of aggressive impulses will displease authority figures

44. Which of the following best exemplifies the halo effect?

   (A) Louise is the best student in her algebra class, so her teacher praises her constantly in front of the other students.
   (B) Louise has won the annual skiing competition for the past three years, so everyone assumes she'll win again this year.
   (C) Louise has the highest GPA in her class, so everyone assumes she'll be the best cheerleader on the new team and votes to make her captain.
   (D) Louise is the most obedient child out of all her siblings, so her parents reward her with special privileges.
   (E) Louise is such an exceptionally talented dancer that the others in her class seem mediocre in comparison, even though some are quite good.

45. Which of the following is true of Wernicke's area?

   (A) It is largely responsible for language comprehension.
   (B) It is located in the frontal lobe.
   (C) It is responsible for speech production.
   (D) It controls balance and movement.
   (E) It is associated with memory formation.

46. Which of the following is characteristic of FDIA (factitious disorder imposed on another, also known as Munchausen syndrome by proxy)?

   (A) Ignoring one's child
   (B) Committing suicide
   (C) Verbally abusing one's child in public
   (D) Physically abusing one's spouse in public
   (E) Contaminating food to keep a family member ill

47. Biofeedback training would be LEAST likely to benefit a person who suffers from which of the following?

   (A) Severe anxiety
   (B) Hypertension
   (C) Tumors
   (D) Migraine headaches
   (E) Mild pain

48. Which of the following statements is true about hypnosis?

   (A) While hypnotized, subjects can be forced to violate their personal moral codes.
   (B) Hypnosis has proven beneficial in treating some physical conditions.
   (C) Most people can be hypnotized against their will.
   (D) All people are equally susceptible to hypnosis.
   (E) Post-hypnotic suggestion is not used in therapeutic settings.

49. A longitudinal study would be most appropriate to examine which of the following research issues?

   (A) The rate of remission for institutionalized schizophrenics vs. non-institutionalized schizophrenics
   (B) The relationship between race, divorce, and income in the United States
   (C) The effects of age and gender on conformity
   (D) The efficacy of a new experimental drug for hypertension
   (E) The extent to which single-parent households are impoverished in urban vs. rural areas

50. Approximately what percentage of the population has an IQ score of 130 or above?

   (A) 0.05%
   (B) 2%
   (C) 10%
   (D) 15%
   (E) 20%

GO ON TO THE NEXT PAGE.

51. Cindy's therapist tells her that her debilitating fear of dogs likely stems from an unconscious fear of her parents, who were abusive to Cindy when she was a young child. The therapist prescribes sedatives for Cindy to calm her nerves. He then begins to gradually expose Cindy to dogs during therapy, beginning with stimuli that Cindy finds least frightening (e.g., a picture of a tiny dog). This therapist is best described as

   (A) behavioral
   (B) psychodynamic
   (C) client-centered
   (D) eclectic
   (E) cognitive-behavioral

52. Which of the following best exemplifies confirmation bias?

   (A) Victor holds no definitive views on alcohol consumption, so he avoids discussing the topic with others.
   (B) Victor believes drinking alcohol is morally wrong, although he remains open to thoughtful debate on the subject.
   (C) Victor used to drink heavily, but, after suffering alcohol-related health problems, firmly believes that drinking is wrong.
   (D) Victor has never believed that drinking alcohol is harmful; he continues to drink on occasion.
   (E) Victor believes that drinking alcohol leads to serious health problems; he subscribes to several newsletters and podcasts that address the dangers of alcohol.

53. Which of the following statements is NOT true regarding hormones and neurotransmitters?

   (A) Neurotransmitters are primarily found in the nervous system.
   (B) Hormones transmit signals faster than neurotransmitters do.
   (C) Hormones are transmitted through the bloodstream.
   (D) Neurotransmitters are transmitted across the synaptic cleft.
   (E) Hormones are produced by the endocrine system.

54. Which of the following tests appears to have predictive validity?

   (A) 97% of high school students who take a certain college entrance exam a second time will score within 3 points of their first score on that exam.
   (B) A questionnaire designed to assess the severity of tobacco addiction asks a variety of questions about how often the subject smokes, the circumstances under which the subject smokes, the severity of withdrawal symptoms, etc.
   (C) Scores on a law school entrance exam are very highly correlated with first-year law school GPAs.
   (D) A certain narcissism scale has very little overlap with most sociopathy scales: those who are determined to be narcissistic are typically NOT determined to be sociopathic.
   (E) Scores on a newly developed depression scale correlate highly with scores on a well-established depression scale.

55. A psychologist wishes to examine the relationship between age and career satisfaction among Americans. Which of the following research methods would be the best choice?

   (A) A case study
   (B) Naturalistic observation
   (C) A controlled laboratory experiment
   (D) A quasi-experiment
   (E) A cross-sectional study

56. In the Milgram obedience experiments, subjects ("teachers") were instructed by the experimenter to administer shocks to confederates ("learners") as punishment for wrong answers on a memory test. Which of the following variations did NOT lead to a decrease in obedience?

   (A) Conducting the experiment in a run-down office instead of a prestigious university
   (B) Allowing the teacher to instruct an assistant to administer the shocks
   (C) Moving the experimenter farther from the teacher
   (D) Having other teachers present who refused to obey
   (E) Moving the learner closer to the teacher

GO ON TO THE NEXT PAGE.

57. Jerry (15 months old), Jimmy (17 months old), Jana (22 months old), and Jason (24 months old) do not yet walk. Which of the children, if any, can be considered developmentally delayed?

    (A) None of the children
    (B) Jason only
    (C) Jason and Jana only
    (D) Jason, Jana, and Jimmy only
    (E) Jason, Jana, Jimmy, and Jerry

58. Short-term memory lasts for approximately

    (A) 5 to 15 seconds
    (B) 20 to 30 seconds
    (C) 60 to 75 seconds
    (D) 75 to 90 seconds
    (E) 90 to 120 seconds

59. Scores on a certain standardized essay test range from 1 to 6: 1 to 2 is below average, 3 to 4 is average, and 5 to 6 is above average. Layla received a score of 3, as one grader gave her a 1 and another grader gave her a 5—with 3 being the arithmetic mean. After challenging her score, Layla requested that another grader review her essay, and this third individual gave Layla a score of 3. Based on this information alone, the essay test in question might have

    (A) high parallel-forms reliability
    (B) high inter-rater reliability
    (C) high test-retest reliability
    (D) low inter-rater reliability
    (E) low split-half reliability

60. Which of the following groups, charged with the task of making a collective decision, would be most likely to fall victim to a groupthink process?

    (A) A nationwide television audience voting online for their favorite performers on a talent-competition reality show
    (B) Residents of a sparsely populated state voting to elect a new governor
    (C) Members of two rival sororities required to plan campus charity events together
    (D) A close-knit extended family whose members must decide where to go on vacation
    (E) A group of commuters on a subway attempting to render first aid to an injured woman

61. On a snowy day, the *Eta Pi* fraternity members miss an important meeting with the dean of students, as do members of their rival fraternity. Which of the following would best exemplify the ultimate attribution error?

    (A) The *Eta Pi* members blame the snowstorm for causing both fraternities to miss the meeting.
    (B) The *Eta Pi* members admit that they didn't attend because they really don't care about administrative meetings; they assume their rival fraternity felt the same way.
    (C) The rival fraternity assumes that *Eta Pi* didn't attend because of the snowstorm.
    (D) The rival fraternity assumes that the *Eta Pi* members were just too lazy and irresponsible to attend the meeting.
    (E) The *Eta Pi* members believe that the snowstorm prevented them from getting to the meeting, but that the rival fraternity members were too lazy to attend.

62. Tim, an animal trainer, wanted to teach his seal to clap its flippers whenever Tim said the seal's name. Which manner of training the seal would be LEAST effective?

    (A) Rewarding the seal with a fish every time it claps at the sound of its name
    (B) Rewarding the seal with a fish every five minutes, regardless of its behavior
    (C) Rewarding the seal with a fish every other time it claps at the sound of its name
    (D) Rewarding the seal with a fish every third time it claps at the sound of its name
    (E) Rewarding the seal with a fish for claps at the sound of its name, on average once every five times (sometimes every three times, sometimes every seven times, etc.)

63. Which of the following is NOT a problem with the Stanford prison experiment conducted by Philip Zimbardo?

    (A) The treatment of the subjects, some of whom suffered extreme distress, was unethical.
    (B) The demand characteristics were prominent and problematic.
    (C) The study improperly inferred causality from correlation.
    (D) The subjects were all young males of college age.
    (E) The mock prison setting differed significantly from a real one.

GO ON TO THE NEXT PAGE.

64. Dr. Jackson gives Louie, his three-year-old patient, a painful shot and Louie screams and cries. The next four times Louie visits Dr. Jackson, Louie screams and cries at the sight of him, even though no shot is given. On the fifth visit no shot is given and Louie shows no signs of distress. Which of the following best describes ALL of Louie's abovementioned reactions to Dr. Jackson?

   (A) Louie was conditioned to cry at the sight of Dr. Jackson through negative reinforcement.
   (B) Dr. Jackson became a conditioned stimulus for Louie's screaming and crying response.
   (C) Through shaping, Louie was conditioned not to scream and cry at the sight of Dr. Jackson.
   (D) Louie was classically conditioned to respond fearfully to Dr. Jackson; then that conditioned response was extinguished.
   (E) Louie was positively reinforced for crying and screaming in Dr. Jackson's presence, then positively reinforced for remaining calm in his presence.

65. Which of the following individuals, each of whom suffers from severe anxiety, would be LEAST likely to benefit from systematic desensitization?

   (A) A young mother who developed debilitating generalized anxiety after giving birth
   (B) A combat veteran who began experiencing crippling symptoms of post-traumatic stress disorder after an intense battle
   (C) A CEO who is so afraid of flying that she panics at the mere sight of an airplane
   (D) A college student who developed a mild fear of dogs after having been attacked by one
   (E) A housebound man who is terrified to step outside his home

66. Of the following research studies, which one would be the most likely to be compromised by a ceiling effect?

   (A) A study measuring the effects of professional tutoring on third-graders' standardized test scores
   (B) A study measuring the effects of monetary rewards on college students' ability to solve simple arithmetic problems
   (C) A study measuring the effects of praise on middle school students' test scores in advanced algebra
   (D) A study measuring the effects of parental encouragement on toddlers' ability to learn new words
   (E) A study measuring the effects of health food consumption on high school students' SAT scores

67. The Asch conformity experiments involved asking subjects to identify the longest of several lines in the context of a "vision test." Which of the following is true regarding this series of experiments?

   (A) Subjects were as likely to conform when they delivered written responses in private as they were when they voiced their responses aloud.
   (B) Most subjects conformed even when one of the confederates opposed the group by giving the correct response.
   (C) The study was representative in that it included roughly equal numbers of males and females, as well as adult subjects of all ages.
   (D) The number of confederates present affected the rate at which the subjects conformed.
   (E) Making the lines more similar in length decreased conformity on the part of the subjects.

68. Billy's mother takes him out of the crib in his bedroom and carries him away for a bath, leaving his favorite stuffed toy behind. While being taken down the hallway Billy cries and reaches out in the direction of the bedroom for the toy. According to Piaget, Billy most likely

   (A) has reached the formal operations stage because he used logic in his attempt to regain the toy
   (B) has reached the concrete operations stage
   (C) has achieved object permanence
   (D) is in the sensorimotor stage because he has mastered conservation
   (E) is in the preoperational stage because he can think symbolically

69. Alice had always included two teaspoons of salt in her gravy recipe until her husband, Ralph, recently complained that it was too bland. The next six times Alice made gravy, she added an additional teaspoon of salt, but Ralph only noticed this increase on two of those six occasions. Which of the following statements is accurate regarding Ralph and Alice's gravy?

   (A) His absolute threshold for salt is two teaspoons.
   (B) His difference threshold (JND) for salt is one teaspoon.
   (C) His absolute threshold for salt is greater than his difference threshold (JND) for salt.
   (D) His difference threshold (JND) for salt is three teaspoons.
   (E) His difference threshold (JND) for salt is greater than one teaspoon.

GO ON TO THE NEXT PAGE.

70. A double-blind design is preferable for an experimental drug trial because it will likely eliminate which of the following?

    (A) The placebo effect
    (B) Demand characteristics
    (C) Random error
    (D) The need for informed consent
    (E) Serious side effects of the drugs ingested

71. According to Freudian theory, an individual who is fixated at the oral stage of psychosexual development is likely to

    (A) be verbally abusive to others
    (B) have a rigid sense of gender roles
    (C) be preoccupied with cleanliness
    (D) have an overly obsessive personality
    (E) have difficulties with romantic partners

72. Annie is very late for an important interview and there are few empty parking spaces nearby. When a woman attempts to park her car in a spot that Annie had planned to park in, an argument develops and insults are exchanged. According to attribution theory, Annie will most likely

    (A) assume that the other woman was also late for an interview
    (B) attribute the other woman's hostile behavior to the fact that Annie was herself hostile
    (C) consider the argument to be the result of her own character flaws and feel guilty
    (D) believe that the unpleasant exchange occurred because both women were feeling stressed
    (E) conclude that the other woman is a rude and aggressive individual

73. A psychology professor visits a certain kindergarten classroom, which is known for being especially rowdy, in order to study the effects of a token economy on disruptive behavior. Half the students were put on a token economy and the other half were not, with students being randomly assigned to the "token" and "control" groups. If disruptive behavior decreased significantly for both groups, but the reduction was much greater for the "token" group, which concepts would, respectively, best explain these two findings?

    (A) Social facilitation and operant conditioning
    (B) The Hawthorne effect and the placebo effect
    (C) The placebo effect and the Hawthorne effect
    (D) The Hawthorne effect and operant conditioning
    (E) Operant conditioning and social facilitation

74. Randy is a new patient at a psychiatric facility and his doctor suspects that he might have antisocial personality disorder. Which of the following would be the best way to assess Randy for this disorder?

    (A) Have him fill out a psychopathy questionnaire
    (B) Rely on whatever relevant information is available from third parties, such as family accounts and police reports, and have staff monitor his behavior closely
    (C) Interact with him for several hours in order to get an intuitive sense of his character
    (D) Go over each of the *DSM-5* criteria for antisocial personality disorder with him during the clinical intake interview in order to determine which, if any, apply
    (E) Administer a Rorschach test

75. Frank helped his father paint their house on Saturday and did an excellent job. To show his gratitude for his son's efforts, Frank's father gave him a big hug, took him out for ice cream, and gave him $20. The hug, the ice cream, and the $20 are, respectively

    (A) a primary reinforcer, a secondary reinforcer, and a secondary reinforcer
    (B) a secondary reinforcer, a primary reinforcer, and a secondary reinforcer
    (C) a secondary reinforcer, a secondary reinforcer, and a primary reinforcer
    (D) a primary reinforcer, a primary reinforcer, and a primary reinforcer
    (E) a primary reinforcer, a primary reinforcer, and a secondary reinforcer

76. Bobby is furious with his teacher for failing him in math. When he gets home, he immediately hits his younger brother, whom he dislikes intensely, shouting "don't give me that mean look!" For the next few hours, Bobby constantly gives his brother treats and tells him how much he loves him. Bobby's behavior suggests all the following defense mechanisms EXCEPT

    (A) displacement
    (B) projection
    (C) reaction formation
    (D) undoing
    (E) intellectualization

GO ON TO THE NEXT PAGE.

77. A researcher wanted to examine the effects of vitamin intake on standardized test scores. One hundred local high school students were randomly assigned to receive either a potent vitamin pill, an inert tablet that they were told was a potent vitamin, or no pill at all each morning. The test scores of the students who received the vitamins increased by 20% on average, the scores of those who received the inert tablet increased by 9% on average, and the scores of the remaining students increased by 3% on average. Which of the following is true regarding this study?

(A) It uses a within-subjects design.
(B) Its findings can all be explained by the placebo effect.
(C) It is a quasi-experiment, so causation cannot properly be inferred.
(D) It uses a between-subjects design.
(E) It is methodologically flawed because the sample size is too small.

78. Shaun's behavior is extremely erratic and he is prone to frequent mood swings. He is self-destructive, highly emotional, overly concerned with his physical appearance, and never comfortable unless he is the center of attention. In terms of a differential diagnosis, Shaun's psychologist should consider which of the following personality disorders?

(A) Histrionic and antisocial
(B) Antisocial and avoidant
(C) Borderline and paranoid
(D) Paranoid, borderline, and antisocial
(E) Histrionic, borderline, and narcissistic

79. Paul Ekman identified 6 basic human emotions that are universal across cultures. These emotions are

(A) happiness, disgust, jealousy, sadness, fear, and anger
(B) disgust, anger, fear, happiness, surprise, and sadness
(C) fear, love, happiness, sadness, surprise, and disgust
(D) surprise, sadness, happiness, disgust, shame, and jealousy
(E) shame, sadness, disgust, anger, fear, and happiness

80. Which of the following statistics, if true, would provide the most support for the assertion that alcoholism causes depression?

(A) 78% of alcoholics are depressed.
(B) 85% of depressed people are alcoholics.
(C) 72% of alcoholics are depressed, and for 85% of those individuals, a diagnosis of alcoholism preceded a diagnosis of depression by a minimum of three years.
(D) Whenever rates of alcoholism increase among the population, rates of depression increase proportionately.
(E) Whenever rates of depression decrease among the population, rates of alcoholism decrease proportionately.

81. Which of the following accurately states a critical difference between PTSD and Generalized Anxiety Disorder?

(A) PTSD, not Generalized Anxiety Disorder, emerges following exposure to the threat of death, injury, or sexual assault.
(B) PTSD affects older individuals more than Generalized Anxiety Disorder.
(C) Generalized Anxiety Disorder is more likely than PTSD to involve hypervigilance.
(D) Unlike Generalized Anxiety Disorder, PTSD does not usually involve intrusive thoughts.
(E) Unlike PTSD, Generalized Anxiety Disorder does not usually involve avoidance behaviors.

82. According to Maslow's humanistic theory of motivation, which of the following is at the very top of the pyramid of human needs?

(A) Physical safety
(B) Food and water
(C) Self-actualization
(D) Esteem
(E) Love and a sense of belonging

83. Tonya, a very shy three-year-old girl, falls and skins her knee. She runs to her mother crying, but then runs away when her mother attempts to comfort her. Based on the research and theories of Mary Ainsworth, it is likely that

(A) Tonya has a "secure" attachment to her mother
(B) Tonya's mother has never attempted to comfort her daughter before
(C) Tonya has an "insecure ambivalent/resistant" attachment to her mother
(D) Tonya has a more secure attachment to her father than to her mother
(E) Tonya has an "insecure avoidant" attachment to her mother

84. A police officer conducts a traffic stop, suspecting that the driver is under the influence of alcohol. She instructs him to close his eyes and touch his nose with his right finger. She is primarily testing the driver's

(A) short-term memory
(B) proprioception
(C) attention span
(D) reaction time
(E) visual acuity

GO ON TO THE NEXT PAGE.

85. Which of the following scenarios provides the most support for the theory that antisocial personality traits are genetic?

    (A) Dizygotic twins are reared together; both are antisocial.
    (B) Monozygotic twins are reared apart; neither is antisocial.
    (C) Monozygotic twins are reared together; both are antisocial.
    (D) Dizygotic twins are reared apart; only one is antisocial.
    (E) Monozygotic twins are reared apart; both are antisocial.

86. Which of the following survey findings are most likely to accurately reflect what they purport to measure?

    (A) Jeffrey stands outside an upscale grocery store and asks the first 100 people who walk by whom they intend to vote for in the upcoming senatorial election (they all answer his question). Based on the results, he concludes that candidate X will win.
    (B) On orientation day at Jeffrey's college, he passes out a survey about attitudes towards capital punishment. Based on the 100 responses he collects (everyone present responds), he concludes that young people in America disapprove of capital punishment.
    (C) Jeffrey mails a survey about environmental issues to 500 people randomly selected from the local phone book. Based on the 100 responses he receives, he concludes that most people in his county of residence believe that more money should be spent on conservation efforts.
    (D) At an elementary school, Jeffrey chooses three of the four sixth-grade classes at random and distributes a survey about which field trips the children desire. All 100 children complete the survey and, based on the results, he concludes that the overwhelming majority of sixth-graders at that school want to visit a science museum.
    (E) Jeffrey visits a community meeting at the Town Hall, shows a film about the plight of the poor, and passes out a political survey (all 100 people present complete it). Based on the results, he concludes that most local citizens believe that the government should be doing more to eliminate poverty in their area.

87. Edward and Elsie are siblings who grew up with highly critical parents. Edward lacks confidence in his abilities to make significant life decisions and relies extensively on his wife to guide him. He similarly requires a great deal of help from his coworkers to perform routine tasks at his job. In contrast, Elsie is a wealthy, powerful, and fiercely competitive executive who strives to dominate everyone around her. According to the theories of Alfred Adler, which of the following statements best characterizes Edward and Elsie's behavior?

    (A) Edward harbors unconscious feelings of inferiority, but Elsie does not.
    (B) Elsie harbors unconscious feelings of inferiority, but Edward does not.
    (C) Edward and Elsie are both overcompensating for unconscious feelings of inferiority.
    (D) Elsie is overcompensating for unconscious feelings of inferiority, while Edward is undercompensating for such feelings.
    (E) Edward is compensating for unconscious feelings of inferiority in a negative way, while Elsie is compensating for such feelings in a positive way.

88. The external ear is separated from the middle ear by the

    (A) tympanic membrane
    (B) cochlea
    (C) semicircular canals
    (D) incus
    (E) malleus

89. Which of the following is NOT a symptom of fetal alcohol syndrome?

    (A) Intellectual disability
    (B) Low birth weight
    (C) A large head
    (D) Poor social skills
    (E) Poor coordination

90. Which of the following is true about efferent neurons?

    (A) They are sensory neurons.
    (B) They transmit impulses between other neurons.
    (C) They carry neural impulses away from the central nervous system to the muscles.
    (D) They carry neural impulses from sensory stimuli towards the central nervous system.
    (E) They enable communication between sensory and motor neurons.

GO ON TO THE NEXT PAGE.

91. Brad is highly sociable and loves to attend large parties, although when he does he often gets into physical altercations or other legal trouble. He is quick to anger and unpredictable, often jeopardizing his safety and that of others. According to Hans Eysenck, which of the following is probably true of Brad?

    (A) He falls towards the "stability" end of the stability/neuroticism continuum and the high end of the psychoticism scale.
    (B) He falls towards the low end of the psychoticism scale and towards the "neuroticism" end of the stability/neuroticism continuum.
    (C) He is biologically predisposed to avoid stimulation.
    (D) He falls towards the "introversion" end of the introversion/extraversion continuum.
    (E) He falls towards the high end of the psychoticism scale and towards the "extraversion" end of the extraversion/introversion continuum.

92. Which of the following is the best example of top-down processing?

    (A) Ned reaches into his bag for his French book but mistakenly grabs his English book instead, as the books are about the same size.
    (B) Ned sees an object lying in the road but can't identify it at such distance; when he gets closer he realizes that it is a discarded bag of groceries.
    (C) Ned sees a woman standing outside a store, then notices that she is wearing a uniform, then notices that she is holding a plate of food; he then realizes that the woman is a salesperson offering free samples of the store's merchandise.
    (D) Ned is color blind, so he differentiates between oranges and grapefruits by size, not color.
    (E) Ned is trying to read a cookie recipe that has been partially torn. He sees the letters "b" and "u" and correctly concludes that the word is "butter."

93. Mr. Reynolds, an elderly jewelry store owner, is looking to hire a new manager. He interviews Candy, a very attractive twenty-five-year-old blond woman, who has excellent references. Mr. Reynolds likes Candy but doesn't hire her; he believes that someone with her looks wouldn't be "taken seriously" as an authority figure. He is also afraid that a "flighty blonde" would spend more time flirting with customers than attending to her managerial duties. Which of the following does NOT characterize Mr. Reynold's actions?

    (A) Prejudice
    (B) Self-serving bias
    (C) Out-group homogeneity
    (D) Discrimination
    (E) Stereotype

94. Which of the following research studies is probably the LEAST ethically problematic?

    (A) An experiment about social loafing in which the researcher lies about the purpose of the study, telling subjects it's about short-term memory
    (B) A drug trial in which prisoners are required to participate in order to retain important privileges within the correctional facility
    (C) A study involving treatment for depression in which subjects' names are published along with the data pertaining to them
    (D) An experiment measuring the extent to which subjects are willing to administer a lethal electric shock to a stranger (although, unbeknownst to the subject, the shocks are fake)
    (E) A nutritional study in which kindergarteners are given vitamin supplements without their parents' knowledge

95. Allie is surprised to learn that her family and friends find her use of her new floral perfume excessive and overwhelming. The most likely explanation is that Allie is experiencing which of the following?

    (A) Anosmia
    (B) Olfactory fatigue
    (C) Cocktail party syndrome
    (D) Ageusia
    (E) Aphasia

96. Which of the following pairs of symptoms probably warrants a diagnosis of schizophrenia, as opposed to schizotypal personality disorder?

    (A) Social isolation and social anxiety
    (B) Marked eccentricities and odd behavior
    (C) Delusions and hallucinations
    (D) Paranoia and distorted perceptions
    (E) Flat affect and inappropriate emotional responses

GO ON TO THE NEXT PAGE.

97. Which of the following is the best example of the availability heuristic?

    (A) Greg thinks that good-looking people are more likely to commit murder than they really are because the media tends to focus on such cases.

    (B) Greg believes that his next child will definitely be a girl because he and his wife already have five boys.

    (C) Greg assumes that his daughter is a bad driver because she has had four accidents in the last month.

    (D) Greg is worried about his car breaking down because that model is associated with a disproportionate number of online consumer complaints.

    (E) Greg adopts a German shepherd, although he would have preferred a golden retriever, because there were no golden retrievers available for adoption.

98. Vera's cat, Fluffy, meows excitedly whenever Vera opens a can of tuna (Fluffy's favorite food); Vera almost always shares the tuna with Fluffy. Fluffy also behaves this way when Vera opens a can of corn (which Fluffy does not eat), but not when she opens a can of mushrooms (which Fluffy also does not eat). Vera didn't share her last two cans of tuna with Fluffy. Based on this information, which of the following is most likely true?

    (A) Stimulus discrimination caused Fluffy to meow at the can of corn.

    (B) Stimulus generalization caused Fluffy not to meow at the mushrooms.

    (C) The sound of the tuna can opening is more similar to that of the corn can opening than that of the mushroom can opening.

    (D) Fluffy's conditioned response has been extinguished.

    (E) If Fluffy meows at any more cans of tuna, this will be due to spontaneous recovery.

99. In a research experiment, only inmates on "Block A" of a certain prison participated in an anger-management program. Daily staff reports showed that there was an average of only five violent incidents on Block A that year—73% fewer than average in that prison. Which of the following, if true, would NOT cast doubt on the study's finding that anger management reduces prison violence?

    (A) Only Block A inmates were given a special diet intended to promote well-being.

    (B) Security is much stricter on Block A than in other areas of the prison.

    (C) Only highly violent prisoners were studied.

    (D) Block A staff created the anger-management program and wanted it to succeed.

    (E) All Block A inmates received the same basic treatment.

100. Several patients on a psychiatric unit report symptoms to the head nurse. Which one is most likely to be diagnosed with factitious disorder?

    (A) A thirty-year-old woman hospitalized for bipolar disorder who reports suicidal thoughts

    (B) A twenty-five-year-old man hospitalized for schizophrenia who reports hearing voices

    (C) A sixteen-year-old girl hospitalized for an eating disorder who reports thoughts of self-harm

    (D) A seventy-five-year-old woman hospitalized for Parkinson's disease who reports difficulty breathing

    (E) A twenty-five-year-old woman hospitalized for abdominal pain who reports sudden vision loss

END OF SECTION I

IF YOU FINISH BEFORE TIME IS CALLED, YOU MAY CHECK YOUR WORK ON THIS SECTION. DO NOT GO ON TO SECTION II UNTIL YOU ARE TOLD TO DO SO.

PSYCHOLOGY
Section II
Time—50 minutes

Percent of total score—$33\frac{1}{3}$

Directions: You have 50 minutes to answer BOTH of the following questions. It is not enough to answer a question by merely listing facts. You should present a cogent argument based on your critical analysis of the question posed, using appropriate psychological terminology.

1. Simon's fourth grade teacher has become increasingly concerned about his behavior. He is extremely fidgety in class and he cannot stay on task for more than a few minutes. Also, if not immediately praised for the work he is doing, he becomes dejected and uncommunicative. She calls in Simon's parents for a conference. The parents have not noticed these specific behaviors at home; there, Simon spends a great deal of time seemingly focused on his laptop, but his parents are not sure how much time he spends on any given site or what he might be doing that is productive. However, they have noticed that his school notebook is very disorganized and he has difficulty planning ahead; specifically, he often misses due dates to turn in work that the teacher has assigned. The parents are very resistant to having a diagnostic label attached to Simon or to having him medicated. Rather, they agree with the teacher on an intervention program: whenever Simon completes a fifteen minute period exclusively on task, he will be rewarded with additional time on the school computer, his favorite activity, during "free time." If, after a verbal warning from the teacher, he continues with behavior that is too fidgety or off task, he will receive "timeout": this means that he will sit by himself in an adjoining room for ten minutes; he'll be able to hear what is happening in class, but not participate. After Simon is doing better, the time necessary for him to earn a reward will gradually increase from 15 minutes, by five minute intervals, until it gets to a full class period.

Address the following concepts and explain how they may be involved in Simon's situation:

- ADHD
- Executive function
- Erik Erikson's Theory of Psychosocial Development
- Behaviorism
- Fixed-interval schedule
- Negative punishment
- Shaping

GO ON TO THE NEXT PAGE.

2. Researchers at State University had a theory that people have an underlying core of "emotionality" that constitutes a personality trait. To test out this theory, they designed a study. They placed an advertisement in the student newspaper seeking study participants who had vivid memories of the day that their parents dropped them off at college. Students who responded to the ad were then administered a questionnaire that asked them, among other things, to rate the emotion they felt on the day their parents dropped them off on a scale of one to ten, one being utterly miserable and ten being elated. Elsewhere in the questionnaire, the students were asked about their most significant interpersonal relationship during college and they were asked to rate their most recent feelings about that relationship on the same one-to-ten scale. Researchers categorized scores of 1, 2, 9, or 10 as "high emotionality," and scores of 3 to 8, inclusive, as "low to moderate emotionality." They found that students who had "high emotionality" scores for moving-in day were five times more likely to have "high emotionality" scores about their relationships as students who had "low to moderate emotionality" scores for moving-in day. Believing that their theory has been validated, they hope to publish an article in the journal *Psychology of Emotions* detailing their findings.

Part A

Respond to the following questions about the nature of this study:

- What is the study design, and, specifically, is this an experiment?
- Where does statistical significance fit into an analysis of this study?
- What is the significance of peer review in the future assessment of this theory?

Part B

Indicate how the following concepts relate to this study:

- Subject selection and exclusion
- Episodic memory
- Trait theory
- Confirmation bias

STOP

END OF EXAM

Practice Test 1: Diagnostic Answer Key and Explanations

PRACTICE TEST 1: DIAGNOSTIC ANSWER KEY

Let's take a look at how you did on Practice Test 1. Follow the three-step process in the Diagnostic Answer Key below and go read the explanations for any questions you got wrong or you struggled with but got correct. Once you finish working through the answer key and the explanations, go to the next chapter to make your study plan.

STEP 1 » Check your answers and mark any correct answers with a ✔ in the appropriate column.

Section I: Multiple Choice							
Q #	Ans.	✔	Chapter #, Section Title	Q #	Ans.	✔	Chapter #, Section Title
1	E		10, Nonassociative Learning	26	E		7, The Forebrain
2	B		16, Depressive Disorders	27	A		15, Social-Cognitive Theories
3	B		17, Psychoanalysis	28	D		6, Experimental Design
4	D		6, Descriptive Statistics	29	C		6, Descriptive Statistics
5	E		10, Operant Conditioning	30	C		13, Development Theories
6	B		18, Altruism and Helping Behavior	31	C		15, Psychoanalytic Theories
7	B		15, Psychoanalytic Theories	32	E		8, Psychoactive Drug Effects
8	B		8, Psychoactive Drug Effects	33	D		11, Language
9	C		11, Short-Term Memory (STM)	34	E		7, The Forebrain
10	D		7, Functional Organization of the Nervous System	35	D		10, Social Learning
11	A		10, Operant Conditioning	36	C		14, Biological Bases
12	E		16, Personality Disorders	37	B		9, Visual Mechanisms
13	C		13, Social Development	38	E		17, Treatment Approaches
14	C		13, Cognitive Development	39	D		18, Conformity
15	A		7, Neuroanatomy	40	B		12, Types of Tests
16	E		17, Treatment Approaches	41	D		11, Problem-Solving and Creativity
17	B		12, Human Diversity	42	C		16, Somatic Symptom and Related Disorders
18	D		18, Attribution	43	D		13, Cognitive Development
19	E		18, Cognitive Dissonance	44	C		18, Attraction
20	D		8, Sleep and Dreaming	45	A		7, Neuroanatomy
21	D		10, Classical Conditioning	46	E		16, Somatic Symptom and Related Disorders
22	A		18, Group Dynamics	47	C		17, Behavioral Therapy
23	A		11, Short-Term Memory (STM).	48	B		8, Hypnosis
24	B		9, Perceptual Processes	49	A		6, Experimental Design
25	B		6, Inferential Statistics	50	B		6, Descriptive Statistics

Section I: Multiple Choice (Continued)

Q #	Ans.	✔	Chapter #, Section Title	Q #	Ans.	✔	Chapter #, Section Title
51	D		**17,** Treatment Approaches	76	E		**15,** Psychoanalytic Theories
52	E		**11,** Problem-Solving and Creativity	77	D		**6,** Clinical Research
53	B		**7,** Neural Transmission and Endocrine System	78	E		**16,** Personality Disorders
54	C		**6,** Experimental Design	79	B		**14,** Theories of Emotion
55	E		**6,** Experimental Design	80	C		**6,** Experimental Design
56	B		**18,** Conformity	81	A		**16,** Anxiety Disorders
57	C		**13,** Physical Development	82	C		**14,** Theories of Motivation
58	B		**11,** Short-Term Memory (STM)	83	C		**13,** Social Development
59	D		**6,** Experimental Design	84	B		**9,** Other Sensory Mechanisms
60	D		**18,** Group Dynamics	85	E		**7,** Heredity and Environment: Behavioral Genetics
61	E		**18,** Attribution	86	D		**6,** Experimental Design
62	B		**10,** Operant Conditioning	87	D		**15,** Psychoanalytic Theories
63	C		**6,** Correlation and Causation	88	A		**9,** Auditory Mechanisms
64	D		**10,** Classical Conditioning	89	C		**13,** Developmental Theories
65	A		**17,** Behavioral Therapy	90	C		**7,** Functional Organization of the Nervous System
66	B		**6,** Descriptive Statistics	91	E		**15,** Trait Theory Assessments
67	D		**18,** Obedience	92	E		**9,** Perceptual Processes
68	C		**13,** Piaget	93	B		**18,** Identities and Groups
69	E		**9,** Thresholds	94	A		**6,** Ethics in Research
70	B		**6,** Clinical Research	95	B		**9,** Other Sensory Mechanisms
71	A		**13,** Sex Differences	96	C		**16,** Schizophrenia Spectrum and Other Psychotic Disorders
72	E		**18,** Attribution	97	A		**11,** Problem-Solving and Creativity
73	D		**18,** Organizational Psychology and Operant Conditioning	98	C		**10,** Classical Conditioning
74	B		**16,** Cluster B	99	C		**6,** Clinical Research
75	E		**10,** Operant Conditioning	100	E		**16,** Bipolar Disorders

Section II: Free Response

Q #	Ans.	✔	Chapter #, Section Title
1	See Explanation		**16,** Neurodevelopmental Disorders
2	See Explanation		**6,** Experimental Design

 **STEP 2** » Tally your correct answers from Step 1 by chapter. For each chapter, write the number of correct answers in the appropriate box. Then, divide your correct answers by the number of total questions (which we've provided) to get your percent correct.

CHAPTER 6 TEST SELF-EVALUATION

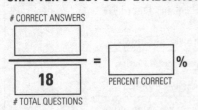

CHAPTER 7 TEST SELF-EVALUATION

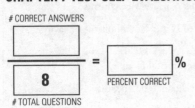

CHAPTER 8 TEST SELF-EVALUATION

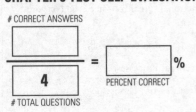

CHAPTER 9 TEST SELF-EVALUATION

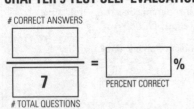

CHAPTER 10 TEST SELF-EVALUATION

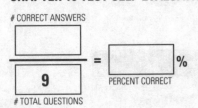

CHAPTER 11 TEST SELF-EVALUATION

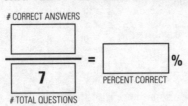

CHAPTER 12 TEST SELF-EVALUATION

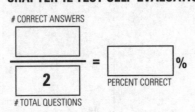

CHAPTER 13 TEST SELF-EVALUATION

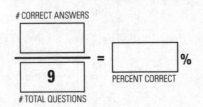

CHAPTER 14 TEST SELF-EVALUATION

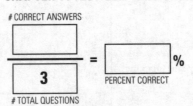

CHAPTER 15 TEST SELF-EVALUATION

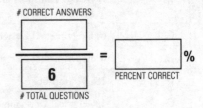

CHAPTER 16 TEST SELF-EVALUATION

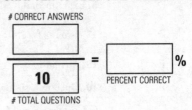

CHAPTER 17 TEST SELF-EVALUATION

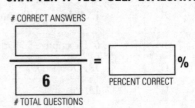

CHAPTER 18 TEST SELF-EVALUATION

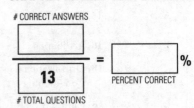

STEP 3 » Use the results above to customize your study plan. You may want to start with, or give more attention to, the chapters with the lowest percents correct.

PRACTICE TEST 1: ANSWERS AND EXPLANATIONS

Section I: Multiple Choice

Note: The explanations in this section make use of the smart-tester strategies introduced in Part IV. Please refer to pages 67–84 first in order to make the most of this section.

1. **E** *Understand the Question/Key Words:* Here we're asked to identify an example of *habituation*—the process whereby a stimulus has less effect after repeated or continuous exposure. *Predict the Answer*: Look for the scenario in which somebody is less affected by something because she gets used to it. Choice (A) simply states that Ilene wore high heels once and found them uncomfortable (eliminate (A)). Choice (B) states that Ilene can only stand wearing high heels for a few hours, suggesting that there is no habituation (eliminate (B) too). Choice (C) states that Ilene wore heels for the first time two weeks ago and now wears them every day. Who cares? There's no information about discomfort or her response to it. This trick answer choice describes the development of a "habit" in the ordinary sense of the word, not "habituation" as a technical term (eliminate (C)). Similarly, (D) tells us that Ilene forces herself to wear heels because they're fashionable, even though they hurt. There's nothing to suggest that she has habituated to the discomfort. Choice (E) is exactly what we need here. When Ilene wears heels they only hurt for the first few minutes (because she gets used to them).

2. **B** *Understand the Question/Key Words:* This is a straightforward question testing your knowledge of major depressive disorder. Since it's a "NOT" question, all the *wrong* answers will be symptoms of severe depression. *Predict the Answer*: Don't be afraid to use common sense here. Mania, a symptom of bipolar disorder, obviously doesn't fit in with the rest of the depressive symptoms listed ((B) is correct).

3. **B** *Understand the Question/Key Words*: Joe's therapy deals with *dreams*, his *early childhood*, and motivations and feelings *he's not aware of* (i.e., "unconscious"). Yep—gotta be Freud! These are the hallmarks of psychodynamic (Freudian-based) therapy and are not generally associated with any of the other three schools of thought listed ((A), (C), and (D) can be eliminated). Choice (E) is wrong because there's nothing to suggest that Joe's therapist is eclectic (i.e., that they borrow different techniques from various schools of thought). Every aspect of the therapy mentioned is associated with psychodynamic theory; (B) is correct.

4. **D** *Understand the Question/Key Words*: *Highest standard deviation* means that the scores are spread out from the mean (arithmetic average) more than in the other choices. *Predict the Answer*: Look for the group of numbers with the widest range. Here that would clearly be (D).

5. **E** *Understand the Question/Key Words*: Circle *a judge orders*. Students often get these answer choices confused. Remember that "reinforcement" always means you're trying to *increase* behavior that you want to see more of, while "punishment" always means that you're trying to *decrease* behavior that you want to eliminate. You can get rid of (A) and (D) on this basis; the judge obviously doesn't want Jill to commit more crimes. Don't get confused by the words "positive" and "negative" in this context: they don't mean *good* or *bad*. "Positive punishment" simply means that you're *administering*

an unpleasant or undesirable stimulus to the subject to decrease the unwanted behavior, while "negative punishment" means that you're *removing* a pleasant or desirable stimulus in order to do so. If the judge had fined Jill, thereby taking away her money (which everybody likes!), that would be an instance of negative punishment. Since she's being forced to pick up nasty garbage on the road instead, the punishment is "positive" ((B) is wrong and (E) is correct). Choice (C), shaping, refers to the process of rewarding successive approximation to a target goal. If Jill were having difficulty meeting her daily garbage quota, so her supervisor praised her every time she picked up a piece of garbage, emptied her bucket properly, etc., that would be considered shaping.

6. **B** *Understand the Question/Key Words:* Circle the words *help* and *witness. Predict the Answer:* Based on the key words, we're dealing with the bystander effect. Research has repeatedly shown that people are more likely to render assistance to a stranger when they are the only ones present. The more people around at the time, the greater the tendency to assume somebody else will intervene (i.e., there is diffusion of responsibility; (B) is correct). If you didn't know this information, you can still use Process of Elimination (POE) to narrow it down. Choice (A) defies common sense (if nobody is there, nobody can help!). Clever analysis can get rid of (C) and (D) as well. A relevant theory would probably make one of two predictions: it's better to have *fewer* people present, or it's better to have *more* people present. For exactly two or three people to be the ideal scenario would seem less likely ((C) and (D) can be eliminated). Now you have it narrowed down to two. Remember that well-known social psychological theories are, if not always counterintuitive, at least interesting or significant in some way. If the likelihood of being helped increased as the number of people available to help increased (which would make perfect sense), then why even call it an "effect"? Accordingly, (B) would be a better guess than (E) here.

7. **B** *Understand the Question/Key Words*: The term *"collective unconscious,"* which refers to images and beliefs that all humans share, is associated with Carl Jung ((B) is correct). Freud (who taught Jung) developed the idea of the unconscious and Jung expanded on it in this way ((A) is wrong). Pavlov, (D), and Skinner, (C), are both known for their respective seminal experiments in behaviorism (so neither dealt with the realm of the unconscious). William James, (E), is known as the father of American psychology.

8. **B** *Understand the Question/Key Words:* If you didn't know how various drugs affect the pupils, the phrase "extremely lethargic" should be enough to get you through this question. Which drugs make you extremely lethargic? *Predict the Answer*: Opiates like heroin (certainly not stimulants like cocaine and methamphetamine!). Eliminate (A) and (D). Serotonergic hallucinogens like LSD may put some people into a bit of a daze as they react to nonexistent stimuli, but they don't make you extremely tired ((C) is out). Neither does ecstasy, which acts as both a stimulant and a hallucinogen ((E) is out as well). All the other drugs on this list except heroin actually cause mydriasis (dilation of the pupils), while opiates cause miosis (constriction of the pupils).

9. **C** *Understand the Question/Key Words:* Here you're being asked to anticipate which words in a list people will be more likely to recall. The answer choices all deal with serial position effects: the "primacy effect" (we're more likely to remember words at the beginning of a list) and the "recency effect" (we're more likely to remember words at the end of a list). *Predict the Answer:* The words

at the beginning and end of the list are more likely, on average, to be recalled ((C) is the correct answer). The other choices are all inconsistent with serial position effects; (E) is particularly unlikely, as it seems to deny that order has any effect whatsoever on recall.

10. **D** *Understand the Question/Key Words:* Robert is hightailing it away from an angry bear and is undoubtedly scared out of his wits. *Predict the Answer:* The "fight or flight" response! You can eliminate (B) and (E) through common sense and basic knowledge: respiration and adrenaline *increase* when we are extremely frightened. As for the remaining choices, remember this idea: in a crisis, the nervous system that is "sympathetic" responds (it's a bit corny, but it works; eliminate (C)). The *parasympathetic* nervous system is the one that helps return the body to homeostasis *after* the emergency is over (so (A) is wrong and (D) must be the answer). *Epinephrine* is just another name for adrenaline, which is triggered during fight or flight.

11. **A** *Understand the Question/Key Words:* Here you're asked what type of reward/reinforcement schedule is being used. Linda rewards her employees every January, and there's no mention of output or required behavior on the part of the employees. *Predict the Answer:* A fixed-interval schedule, (A). If you forgot your reinforcement schedules, you can use POE here. Since there's no variation in this scenario (the reward *always* comes in January), you can eliminate any choice beginning with the word "variable"—(B) and (E). Since *time* is the factor that determines reinforcement here, not output, "interval" is a better bet than "ratio" ((D) is out and (A) is correct). There is no such thing as a fixed-variable schedule, (C), and, since nothing varies in this scenario and "interval" indicates time, (A) is clearly the better choice for a guess.

12. **E** *Understand the Question/Key Words:* Sue is shy and *avoids* contact with others for fear of rejection. *Predict the Answer:* If you're up on the diagnostic categories, you'll recognize these signs of an avoidant personality disorder, (E). If you didn't know the term, the word "avoids" in the question should highlight (E) as a strong possibility. Beware, however, of (A)—it's a trap! Being antisocial in *DSM-5* terms does *not* mean that you avoid people; it means you basically have no regard for societal rules. Many antisocial people love the company of other people (all the better to manipulate and abuse them!). If you're familiar with the other disorders on the list, you can use POE to narrow down the choices here. Choice (B) can easily be eliminated; we all know that *narcissistic* means self-centered and grandiose. *Borderline* individuals are unstable and impulsive (with behavior sometimes "bordering" on the psychotic). Even if you didn't know that, the word "borderline" doesn't seem to fit here (on the border between what and what?)—so you can eliminate (C). Schizotypal individuals (D) display oddities in speech or behavior that are less extreme than those seen in full-blown schizophrenia.

13. **C** *Understand the Question/Key Words:* Here you're being asked which of Erikson's stages applies to teenagers. *Predict the Answer:* You should recall that identity vs. role confusion is the stage that deals with adolescent developmental struggles. If you forgot that, common sense and POE can narrow it down. "Trust" should have been achieved way before age 17 (as an infant, according to Erikson)—eliminate (A). "Stagnation" and "integrity" sound like issues that much older people would be dealing with, not a seventeen-year-old—eliminate (D) and (E). That leaves only (B) and (C). Teenagers do try to achieve "autonomy," but so do younger kids (although the milestones are

obviously different). The key challenge during adolescence is to develop an *identity* and find your way in the world, so (C) is a better choice than (B).

14. **C**   *Understand the Question/Key Words*: Jack had a bunch of interesting history professors, so he got the idea that they were all fun and entertaining (until Professor Smith bored him to tears and he changed this perception). You should be looking for the term that involves changing your mind to fit new experiences: that would be accommodation, (C)! Every time Jack perceived a history teacher to be a total blast, this idea was assimilated into his general conceptual framework (or "schema") about history teachers. So a schema in which history teachers are entertaining was the product of assimilation ((D) and (B) are wrong). In contrast, accommodation is the process whereby our existing ideas about the world are changed in order to incorporate new information. Jack's conclusion that not all history teachers are in fact entertaining, based on his experience with Professor Smith, was the result of accommodation ((C) is correct). If you didn't recall these psychological terms, simply remembering that "assimilate" means "to absorb" and "accommodate" means "to adapt" would help you here. Cognitive dissonance refers to the mental tension or discomfort that we experience when we hold inconsistent beliefs or when our beliefs are inconsistent with our behavior. Jack would have experienced dissonance when his ideas about how boring Professor Smith was conflicted with his established schema about history teachers ((A) is wrong). An archetype, (E), is an image or idea that all human beings have in common, so this term doesn't apply here.

15. **A**   Be sure to know the parts of the brain and their functions! Jane's anterograde amnesia would be due to an injury to the hippocampus, which is responsible for forming new memories ((A) is correct). The hypothalamus, (B), largely regulates the pituitary gland and endocrine activity. The occipital lobe, (C), is responsible for vision. The temporal lobe, (D), is associated with auditory processing. The medulla, (E), controls basic functions such as breathing, heart rate, swallowing, etc.

16. **E**   *Understand the Question/Key Words: "Mirroring"* is the therapeutic technique most closely associated with client-centered ("Rogerian") therapy: the therapist repeats or paraphrases what the client says, focusing on the emotions involved. *Predict the Answer*: The only technique that resembles mirroring here is (E). Mirroring doesn't involve challenging the client's stated motivations or telling him that he acts like his father (a psychodynamic therapist would be more likely to go that route; eliminate (A) and (D)). Mirroring doesn't involve giving and withholding praise according to the client's behavior (this is more of a behavioral technique; eliminate (C)). Choice (B) is the trap answer here: while Rogerian therapists *are* very empathic and caring, mirroring, as a technique, involves more than empathy. Choice (E) is correct.

17. **B**   *Understand the Question/Key Words*: Circle *an IQ of 65*. *Predict the Answer*: His IQ places Louis in the mildly disabled range, and his basic level of functioning is consistent with this diagnosis. While the *DSM-5* places more emphasis on overall level of functioning than did previous versions of the manual (as opposed to simply using the IQ to categorize people), here the IQ and the functioning level both point to a mild disability. Louis is somewhat independent in that he can hold down a simple job with some help, make small purchases, etc. However, he still requires assistance from family to manage his personal financial matters and make important decisions ((B) is correct).

18. **D** *Understand the Question/Key Words:* The gist of the *just-world hypothesis* is that we all generally deserve what happens to us. *Predict the Answer*: Look for the scenario in which people believe that somebody basically got what was coming to them. Choices (B) and (E) contradict the just-world hypothesis: in both cases a person was "punished" and others consider what happened unfair ((B) and (E) are out). In (A), an unqualified person was elected class president, but there's no indication of whether people believed she deserved it or not. Choice (A) actually illustrates the "halo effect": people who are viewed as having positive qualities, especially beauty, are viewed as having unrelated positive qualities (such as the ability to be a good class president; (A) is out). Choice (C) is simply a case of *conformity*: Phil picks on another kid because his peers are doing it (who deserves what is never addressed; (C) is out). Choice (D) is the answer: Roy is clearly victimized, but his community blames him because he was "asking for it."

19. **E** *Understand the Question/Key Words:* This question concerns dissonance theory and tells us the source of Zachary's cognitive dissonance: he loves sugary carbonated drinks, but has just acquired some pesky knowledge that they're bad for his health. Keep in mind that this is a "LEAST" question, so we're looking for a response that will NOT reduce Zachary's dissonance. *Predict the Answer*: Remember that cognitive discomfort occurs when our behaviors conflict, our beliefs conflict, or our behaviors conflict with our beliefs. In order to reduce the dissonance, we either change our behavior, change our beliefs, or reduce the importance of the beliefs that are causing the dissonance. Choice (A) has him substantially reducing his intake of these drinks, which would at least reduce the tension (eliminate (A) too). Choice (B) has Zachary eliminating these drinks from his diet, which would also eliminate the tension, so (B) is out. Choice (C) has him questioning the accuracy of the troublesome information, which would reduce dissonance as well. (If whoever wrote the article doesn't know what he's talking about, then who cares?) Choice (D) has Zachary downplaying the importance of good health by adopting a "YOLO" attitude; this would relieve the tension as well. Choice (E), however, has him accepting the article's conclusions, but not changing his sugary-carbonated-beverage-drinking behavior in any way ((E) is correct).

20. **D** *Understand the Question/Key Words:* When Jennifer was in a very deep sleep, which brain waves were dominant in her brain? *Predict the Answer:* The deep sleep that occurs during stages 3 and 4 is dominated by slow, high-amplitude delta waves, (D). Beta and alpha waves are associated with waking states and REM sleep ((A), (C), and (E) are wrong). Theta waves dominate the lighter sleep that occurs in stages 1 and 2, and also occur during REM sleep ((B) is wrong as well).

21. **D** *Understand the Question/Key Words:* Watson (quite unethically!) used classical conditioning techniques to get Little Albert to fear white rats, which the child had no problem with before. *Predict the Answer:* Watson paired a loud noise (the unconditioned stimulus) with the white rat (a neutral stimulus that became the conditioned stimulus). Albert's unconditioned response to the loud noise was fear, so, when the noise was paired with the rat, the conditioned response was fear of the rat. If you weren't sure of these terms, you could have used POE effectively. Fear is a response, not a stimulus (so eliminate (B) and (C)). *Primary punisher* is an operant conditioning term and inapplicable here (eliminate (E)). Now you have to choose between (A) and (D). If you remember that Albert didn't initially fear the rat, you know that this fear response was *conditioned* and that (D) must be the correct answer.

22.   **A**   *Understand the Question/Key Words:* This scenario involves a dancer doing some routine moves who is then joined by other dancers performing the same moves. You are asked how the presence of the others should affect the first dancer's performance. *Predict the Answer*: This question is testing your knowledge of social facilitation (the phenomenon whereby individuals engaged in simple tasks, or ones with which they are very familiar, perform better when in the presence of others ((A) is correct). However, if you didn't remember that concept but remembered other social psychological theories, you could still use POE. Choice (C) is the trap answer here. Social loafing occurs when individuals working in a group exert less effort than if working alone because there is a diffusion of responsibility among the group members (think "tug of war"). This doesn't apply here because social loafing occurs when people are working in a concerted effort to complete a task or reach a common goal (not working on their own tasks or goals in a group setting). The bystander effect, (B), may sound relevant but is inapplicable here: it deals with the likelihood of receiving assistance in an emergency. The mere-exposure effect, (E), is also inapplicable: it refers to the tendency to rate stimuli more positively after you've been exposed to them.

23.   **A**   *Understand the Question/Key Words*: You're being asked to identify an example of *chunking*: a method of aiding short-term memory by grouping bits of information into "chunks." *Predict the Answer*: Look for the situation wherein somebody is trying to remember something better in the short term by dividing information into groups. Choice (A) fits the bill; the way we recite phone numbers (3-3-4) helps us remember them and is a classic example of chunking. Choice (B) involves dividing information into groups in that different academic subjects are studied on different days, but this is not a short-term memory process. Choice (C), saying a license plate number over and over, involves simple repetition; the question does not indicate that any numbers or letters were divided into groups. Choice (D), triggering olfactory memory with a scent, involves retrieving long-term memories—not aiding short-term memory. Choice (E), teaching information by setting it to music, is a different mnemonic device.

24.   **B**   *Understand the Question/Key Words:* We're being asked to identify which Gestalt principle applies to a situation wherein tomatoes are grouped with apples and oranges, rather than together with carrots and celery. *Predict the Answer:* Ask yourself why Margaret would put tomatoes with apples and oranges. While it is true that all three are fruits, the answer choices have nothing to do with such a logical categorical reason. But, tomatoes, apples, and oranges are all round, and thus may appear similar to Margaret. So, the Gestalt principle of similarity, (B), in which similar items are grouped together, is the correct answer. Choice (A), proximity, is wrong because the tomatoes were not already found next to the apples and oranges. Figure-ground organization refers to the tendency to view objects as either in the background or the foreground ((C) is wrong). Continuity, (D), refers to the tendency to perceive lines as continuous and uninterrupted. Closure, (E), refers to the tendency to perceive whole objects despite a break in the pattern.

25.   **B**   *Understand the Question/Key Words:* This question is testing your knowledge of statistics terminology; it's asking what we call the mistake we make when we wrongly conclude that our findings are statistically significant. *Predict the Answer*: Ideally you'll remember that this mistake is called a Type I error. If you forgot that bit of information, you could use POE effectively here.

Regression toward the mean, (C), is a statistical phenomenon (not an error) whereby scores tend to average out. Similarly, the null hypothesis, (A), is not an error but rather a hypothesis (hence, the name!). It hypothesizes that the findings are merely due to chance and are not statistically significant. A random error, (D), is an error that is unexplained and essentially random (hence, the name!); this wouldn't make sense here either. The most appealing wrong choice would be a Type II error, (E), which involves making the opposite mistake (wrongly concluding that your findings are NOT statistically significant). Choice (B) is correct.

26. **E** *Understand the Question/Key Words:* This question is simply testing your knowledge of the *occipital lobe* (which controls visual processing). *Predict the Answer:* You could use POE to eliminate the other choices if you know the various lobe functions. The frontal lobe largely controls planning, goal-setting, and impulse inhibition ((A) and (C)). Hearing and language processing (B) are controlled by the temporal lobe. Pain recognition (D) is controlled by the parietal lobe. Choice (E) is correct.

27. **A** *Understand the Question/Key Words:* This scenario involves a woman who doesn't really study for a medical school entrance exam because she thinks that, if she was meant to become a doctor, she would do well on the test and it would all work out. *Predict the Answer:* You should realize that this woman seems to have an external locus of control, (A); she believes that what happens to her is largely controlled by outside forces. Learned helplessness, (B), is a deceptively attractive answer here because Kerri is sort of acting like she can't control what happens to her. However, there's no evidence that she believes that she will *fail*; she may very well think the universe, so to speak, will be kind to her. An internal locus of control, (C), is simply the opposite phenomenon (i.e., we believe that we ourselves control what happens to us). A self-serving bias, (D), involves taking credit for our own successes but blaming our failures on situational factors; this couldn't be the answer because Kerri hasn't succeeded or failed at anything yet. Choice (E) is wrong because we have no evidence to suggest that Kerri has low self-esteem.

28. **D** *Understand the Question/Key Words:* This question presents the basics of an experiment and asks you to identify the independent variable (the variable that the experimenter changes in order to measure its effect on the dependent variable). *Predict the Answer:* Choose the variable that the researcher intentionally manipulates (not the one that is measured). Here that would be the amount of praise given to each of the two groups ((D) is correct). The test scores, (A), is the dependent variable.

29. **C** *Understand the Question/Key Words:* This is a straightforward question for which you need to understand the concept of *percentile rank*. *Predict the Answer:* If Fred scored in the 68th percentile on the entrance exam, that means that he scored better than 68% of the people who took that exam ((C) is correct).

30. **C** *Understand the Question/Key Words:* The question asks how far Carol appears to have progressed in terms of Kohlberg's stages of moral development. *Predict the Answer:* Carol views her behavior as bad if other people view it as bad, feeling shame and guilt when others criticize her. She is clearly at the "conventional" level of morality. More specifically, she is probably in stage 3 (the "good boy/girl" stage) in which morality is determined by others' approval ((C) is correct). If you didn't remember

Kohlberg so well, you can use POE to eliminate some of the choices. Carol seems to be past stage 1: the preconventional level of moral development, in which good = avoidance of punishment (this is common among very young children). Carol genuinely feels guilty and ashamed because she believes she did something wrong; she's not simply conforming in order to escape some punishment meted out by an authority figure (eliminate (A) and (E)). Stage 6: *universal ethical principles*, (D), wouldn't seem to fit here either. Carol sees an action as "wrong" because others see it that way, not because it violates some higher universal moral code that she's developed (as the name would seem to imply). Integrity vs. despair, (B), is one of Erikson's developmental stages and is inapplicable here.

31. **C** *Understand the Question/Key Words:* The key words here are *criminal with no regard for others' rights* and *Freudian theory*. *Predict the Answer:* Ask yourself which Freudian concept deals basically with the conscience? That would have to be the superego, (C), which is correct here. The id, (A), refers to our primal, pleasure-seeking impulses, and the ego, (B), is the part of our psyche that mediates between the outside world, the demands of the id, and the dictates of the superego. The Oedipal complex, (D), is an early childhood conflict involving the same-sex parent. A fixation, (E), occurs when a child fails to successfully negotiate a particular psychosexual stage and gets psychologically "stuck," unable to move on.

32. **E** *Understand the Question/Key Words:* This question is asking you which substance causes *delirium tremens* (the DT's) when you suddenly stop taking it. *Predict the Answer:* As the name might suggest, delirium tremens is a dangerous syndrome that can cause disorientation, hallucinations, irregular heartbeat, etc. It is associated with withdrawal from alcohol ((E) is correct).

33. **D** *Understand the Question/Key Words:* Here you simply need to know what a *morpheme* is. *Predict the Answer:* Since a morpheme is the smallest unit of meaning in language, dissect the word into the smallest units that convey linguistic meaning and then count how many you have. Here we have "happi" ("happy")—an adjective meaning "glad." Further, the prefix "un" means "not" and the suffix "ness" indicates state or quality, so altogether we have three morphemes ((D) is correct).

34. **E** *Understand the Question/Key Words:* Here you need to know what *aphasia* is. *Predict the Answer:* Aphasia involves the loss of expressive or receptive language skills, so look for the scenario that involves language impairment of some sort (it's clearly (E)). If you didn't remember what aphasia is, knowing some other terms would help you with POE here. The inability to form new memories is anterograde amnesia (eliminate (C)) and the inability to recognize faces is prosopagnosia (eliminate (B)). Common sense would probably allow you to eliminate (D) here as well (a digestive disorder resulting from a blow to the head would seem unlikely).

35. **D** *Understand the Question/Key Words:* This question asks about *Albert Bandura* and *aggressive* behavior. *Predict the Answer:* You should definitely be thinking "Bobo doll experiment: social learning"! Find the scenario that suggests that Dennis is aggressive because he observes others (especially significant adults) behaving aggressively ((D) is the answer). For this type of question, you're at a disadvantage if you don't recognize the name. You would need to understand that the other theories of aggression are behavioral, (A), genetic, (B), psychoanalytic, (C), and evolutionary, (E), and take your best guess.

36. **C** *Understand the Question/Key Words:* This question tests your ability to distinguish *secondary* drives from primary ones in accordance with drive-reduction theory. *Predict the Answer*: Primary drives are innate biological needs such as sleep, (A); a normal body temperature, (B) and (E); and food, (D). Secondary drives are the product of conditioning; they are desirable only because they are associated with primary drives (e.g., money; (C) is correct).

37. **B** *Understand the Question/Key Words:* This is a straightforward test of your knowledge of eye structure and function. Be sure to read carefully and note that the question asks specifically about the *cells* that sense light. *Predict the Answer*: Light-sensing cells, or photoreceptors, are located in the retina ((B) is correct). Light enters the eye through the cornea, (D), and travels through the pupil, (A). The iris, (E), controls the amount of light that enters the eye. The lens, (C), located behind the iris, focuses light onto the retina.

38. **E** *Understand the Question/Key Words:* The question discusses a patient with negative self-views and asks you to identify what a therapist trained in *REBT* (which focuses on getting rid of irrational beliefs) might do. *Predict the Answer*: Look for the scenario that involves eliminating self-defeating cognitions ((E) is the only response that fits). Choice (A) is a client-centered technique, (B) and (D) are psychodynamic, and (C) is classic behaviorism.

39. **D** *Understand the Question/Key Words:* Here you're asked to identify an example of the *door-in-the-face technique*: someone makes a large or unreasonable request, which is refused, then makes a smaller or more reasonable request, which is more likely to be granted because it fares well in the comparison. *Predict the Answer*: Choose the scenario wherein a second, comparatively reasonable request is granted. Choice (A) is actually an example of the foot-in-the-door technique: one makes a small request, which is granted, then makes a larger one, which is more likely to be granted because a precedent has been established. Choice (B) is simply positive reinforcement and (C) is simply negative reinforcement (there are no second requests involved). Choice (D) fits here: the request to leave only thirty minutes early seems much more reasonable in light of the previous request. Choice (E) doesn't exemplify any particular psychological phenomenon—just a mean boss.

40. **B** *Understand the Question/Key Words:* Here you need to understand the concept of a *projective test* in order to identify one. *Predict the Answer*: Ideally you'll remember (or at least guess) that a projective test entails presenting the subject with ambiguous stimuli. Then the subject *projects* emotions, conflicts, etc. onto the situation for the clinician to interpret. So pick whichever assessment tool has ambiguous elements. Choice (A) is a straightforward IQ test, so get rid of it. The Rorschach, (B), is the quintessential projective test, involving projection of one's psyche onto ambiguous inkblots (definitely keep (B)). The MMPI is a personality assessment, but it involves answering true/false questions; there's nothing ambiguous about it and there's no projection involved (get rid of (C) too). Choices (D) and (E) can be eliminated (even if you don't know what a projective test is) because neither is a "test" per se: the *DSM-5* is a diagnostic manual and an *intake interview* simply gathers information about the client. Choice (B) is the answer.

41. **D** *Understand the Question/Key Words:* Here we have a situation wherein someone is using an object in an unusual way and we're asked what the person has *overcome* by doing so. *Predict the Answer*:

What tendency would prevent someone from using an object in a novel way? Functional fixedness! ((D) is correct). Conformity, (A), is an appealing wrong choice here in that Julie's use of the wine bottle is atypical. However, conformity deals more with social pressure to behave and think as others do with respect to significant matters; there's no evidence that others would disapprove of her unusual vase. The fundamental attribution error, (B), deals with others' behavior and the mere exposure effect, (C), deals with the tendency to like what is familiar. Learned helplessness, (E), deals with the effects of repeated failure and is also inapplicable.

42. **C** *Understand the Question/Key Words:* This question asks you to identify an example of *conversion disorder* (FNSD). *Predict the Answer:* Look for the situation wherein somebody has a neurological symptom, such as paralysis or loss of one of the senses, with no medical explanation or other psychological disorder that could account for this ((C) fits perfectly). The remaining choices are unrelated psychological symptoms.

43. **D** *Understand the Question/Key Words:* Here you'll need to choose the statement that reflects what a child who has mastered *conservation* (according to Piaget) would understand. *Predict the Answer:* Mastering conservation means that the child grasps that a physical quantity remains the same even though its physical appearance can change ((D) is clearly correct). Choices (A) and (C), respectively, describe the Piagetian ideas of *object permanence* and *symbolic thinking*. Choice (B) describes one of Kohlberg's moral stages and (E) alludes to Freudian psychosexual development.

44. **C** *Understand the Question/Key Words:* To answer this question correctly you'll need to know (or guess) what the *halo effect* is in order to identify an example. *Predict the Answer:* Choose the scenario in which a positive assessment of Louise in one area generalizes to a (perhaps unwarranted) positive assessment of her in another unrelated area. Choice (C) is the only scenario that fits. Just because Louise has a stellar GPA doesn't mean that she'll be the best cheerleader, as different skill sets are involved.

45. **A** *Understand the Question/Key Words:* Here you're being asked to pick out a true statement about Wernicke's area—which is responsible for language comprehension. *Predict the Answer:* If you didn't remember that (A) is right on point, ideally you'd be able to use POE here. The most attractive wrong choice would be (C), which deals with speech *production*, not comprehension (the former is associated with *Broca's* area).

46. **E** *Understand the Question/Key Words:* Here you're being asked to identify behavior that is characteristic of *FDIA (factitious disorder imposed on another)*. *Predict the Answer:* Look for a case in which somebody, especially a parent, is intentionally making someone in their care ill (or greatly exaggerating symptoms of an existing illness) in order to get attention. Choice (A) can be eliminated; these parents don't ignore their children (if anything they are overly "attentive")! Choice (B) is wrong because there's no "proxy" involved in a suicide. Choices (C) and (D) can be eliminated because they involve abuse in public; those with FDIA act like loving caregivers in front of others and are sure to keep any abuse a secret. Choice (E) makes sense here: contaminating food to keep someone ill is a common pattern seen with this disorder.

47. **C** *Understand the Question/Key Words:* Note that this is a "LEAST" question; you're being asked which ailment biofeedback would be *least* likely to help. *Predict the Answer:* Biofeedback is a technique that attempts to control involuntary bodily functions (e.g., breathing, heart rate, blood pressure, etc.) through auditory or visual feedback. With this in mind, look for the medical condition that probably couldn't be helped in any way by relaxation, lowering your stress levels, etc. Tumors, (C), are much less likely to get better as the result of a relaxation technique than would anxiety, (A), hypertension, (B), headaches, (D), or mild pain, (E). Common sense would suggest that surgery (or another serious medical intervention) would probably be required to get rid of a tumor!

48. **B** *Understand the Question/Key Words:* Here you're being asked to evaluate the truth of various statements about *hypnosis*. *Predict the Answer:* Keep in mind that answer choices with extreme language (e.g., none, all, never, etc.) are always suspect. They *can* be true, but are much harder to support than are moderate statements. Compare (D): "all people are equally susceptible to hypnosis" with (B): "hypnosis has proven beneficial in treating some physical conditions." It's hard to argue with the second one because it's pretty conservative (and it's the correct answer here). On the other hand, if just ONE person is more susceptible than another to hypnosis, (D) can be disproved. Choices (A) and (C) are completely incorrect (hypnosis does not cause people to violate their moral codes, nor can people be hypnotized against their will). Moreover, *post-hypnotic suggestion* is often used in therapeutic settings ((E) is wrong as well).

49. **A** *Understand the Question/Key Words:* This question asks which research issue would be best suited to a *longitudinal study* (a design wherein the same subjects are studied over a long period). *Predict the Answer:* Ask yourself which scenario would require keeping track of the *same people* for a pretty long time in order to get the data you need. A study about remission rates in institutionalized vs. non-institutionalized schizophrenics would probably require keeping track of the same folks for a while to see whether they relapsed, etc. ((A) looks pretty good). Choices (B) and (E) need a *cross-sectional* design: we want to find correlations between and among different factors such as race, divorce, poverty, etc. There's no need to study the same individuals over a long period to see how those factors are linked (eliminate (B) and (E)). Studying the effects of age and gender on conformity, (C), would seem to require some sort of *quasi-experimental* manipulation: otherwise, what "conformity" could we measure? At any rate, we wouldn't need years to get our data. Similarly, a drug trial for a new blood pressure medication would require the standard experimental design involving stringent controls. Blood pressure, moreover, can be assessed right away; there's no need to follow the same subjects over an extended period. Choice (A) is correct.

50. **B** *Understand the Question/Key Words:* This question asks approximately what percentage of people have an IQ of 130 or above. *Predict the Answer:* An IQ of 130 is obviously very high, so you can easily eliminate (C), (D), and (E). Understanding that intelligence is normally distributed (picture a bell-shaped curve) will allow you to conclude that 2%, (B), is the correct answer. Approximately 95% of the population has an IQ between 70 and 130, with those above 130 falling at the very high end of the distribution (approximately 2.5% of the population).

51. **D** *Understand the Question/Key Words:* Here you're being asked to describe Cindy's therapist. The information given indicates that he uses different techniques from various theoretical schools of thought (e.g, Freudian interpretation, behavioral systematic desensitization, medication). *Predict the Answer*: Clinicians who "borrow" ideas and techniques from different schools of thought are best described as eclectic, (D).

52. **E** *Understand the Question/Key Words:* This question asks you to identify an example of *confirmation bias* (the tendency to seek out information that confirms our biases and established beliefs). *Predict the Answer*: Look for the scenario in which Victor is focusing on facts that support his preconceived notions. Choice (E) is the only answer that fits: Victor believes that drinking is bad for you, so he subscribes to newsletters and podcasts that promote that viewpoint.

53. **B** *Understand the Question/Key Words:* Here you're being asked to evaluate the truth of various statements about hormones and neurotransmitters (keep in mind you're looking for the one that's false). *Predict the Answer:* You'll need to know your basics for this question (but a bit of common sense will help too). Hormones do NOT transmit faster than neurotransmitters do; the latter typically take only milliseconds, while hormones can take up to days for transmission ((B) is correct). All the remaining statements are true.

54. **C** *Understand the Question/Key Words:* Here you're being asked to identify an example of a test with *predictive validity*. *Predict the Answer*: Look for the test that predicts *future* scores, behavior, etc. with respect to the construct at issue. Choice (A) might seem like it fits because it deals with future scores, but it's actually just an example of *reliability*, not validity. Students who take that same test again simply get a very similar score; there's no indication as to whether that test is accurately measuring what it's supposed to measure. The test score is only "predicting" a future score on that same test, which could be measuring anything. Choice (B) is an example of *face validity*; the test appears on the surface to be measuring what it claims to measure. Choice (C) is the classic example and is correct here: a law school entrance exam accurately predicts first-year law school GPAs. Choice (D) is an example of *construct validity*. A narcissism scale should measure narcissism— and *only* narcissism, *not* a closely related disorder such as sociopathy. Choice (E) is an example of *concurrent validity*; the test correlates highly with an established test of the same construct (in this case depression).

55. **E** *Understand the Question/Key Words:* "Relationship between age and career satisfaction" and "among Americans" are the key phrases here. *Predict the Answer*: We're looking for a method whereby we can assess career satisfaction at different ages and then generalize the findings to Americans (who are a very large group!). A case study, (A), wouldn't make any sense here: it's an in-depth analysis of a single individual, small group, or event. Naturalistic observation, (B), whereby researchers closely scrutinize behavior in a natural setting, wouldn't make any sense here either. There's no ongoing behavior that needs to be observed (and you can only naturistically observe so many people!). Choice (C) might be tempting because a controlled laboratory experiment is usually the preferred research method because it allows you to infer causality, etc. However, an experiment wouldn't make any sense here either. You can't randomly assign people to different age groups (or levels of career satisfaction). Moreover, an experiment wouldn't involve enough subjects to conclude

anything about Americans in general. A quasi-experiment, (D), is just an experiment without random assignment and would be equally inappropriate here. Choice (E), a cross-sectional study, would be perfect. This design involves assessing, at a single point in time, similar individuals who differ on a key characteristic (like how Americans of different age groups view their jobs!). These studies often deal with correlations among large samples.

56. **B** *Understand the Question/Key Words:* Make sure that you truly understand what this type of complicated and convoluted question is asking before you proceed! You are being asked which variation in the Milgram experiments did NOT lead to a DECREASE in obedience (i.e., all the *wrong* answer choices will have led to *less* shocking by the teacher). *Predict the Answer:* If you recall the experiments, you'll know (B) is the answer. Allowing an assistant to administer the shocks relieved the teacher of some personal responsibility—and led to a greater willingness to hurt the learner. While research findings aren't always predictable or consistent with common sense, if you didn't remember the study you would simply have had to guess here based on reasonable assumptions. A run-down office, (A), diminished the authority of the experimenter, and physically removing the experimenter from the scene, (C), similarly diminished his authoritative presence. The presence of other teachers who refused to shock, (D), emboldened the teacher to also refuse, and moving the learner closer to the teacher, (E), emphasized the suffering of the learner and the personal responsibility of the teacher.

57. **C** *Understand the Question/Key Words:* Here you'll need to know what the normal developmental parameters for walking are. *Predict the Answer:* Most children walk by 14 or 15 months and 18 months is considered delayed. Choice (C), Jason and Jana only, is the answer. Remember to use POE effectively if you're not sure.

58. **B** *Understand the Question/Key Words:* This question is asking how long we can keep information stored in short-term memory. *Predict the Answer:* Short-term memory lasts approximately 20 to 30 seconds ((B) is correct).

59. **D** *Understand the Question/Key Words:* Don't be fooled by the fact that Layla got a 3 on her test, challenged her score, and then got a 3 again. The scores for this essay test are all over the place and something is clearly wrong. *Predict the Answer:* Inter-rater reliability means that different people who score the same test will come up with approximately the same score. Given that three graders gave Layla three very different scores, this test may lack this kind of reliability ((D) is correct). You could pretty much have eliminated (A), (B), and (C) right off the bat here: no type of reliability has been established through this information. Choice (E) deals with split-half reliability, which would be more applicable to a multiple-choice exam (the score on one half of an exam should correlate highly with the score on the other half of the exam).

60. **D** *Understand the Question/Key Words:* Remember that the key factor that triggers a groupthink process (which is an undesirable phenomenon) is the *cohesiveness* of the group. Members censor their own dissenting opinions, and those of others, in order to preserve the unity and harmony of the group (which can lead to some pretty bad decisions!). *Predict the Answer:* The group most likely to fall victim to this phenomenon will be the most close-knit bunch of people. You can eliminate (A) and

(B) right off the bat. Are nationwide TV audiences and state voting electorates close-knit groups? Clearly not! Moreover, the "decisions" these groups make are made privately. Are the members of two rival sororities a close-knit group? Nope—they're just the opposite (eliminate (C)). Are the members of a close-knit extended family a close-knit group? I'm gonna say "yeah" (save (D)). Are a bunch of good Samaritan commuters on a subway a close-knit group? Nope—get rid of (E). Don't be lured by the fact that the decisions to be made in that last scenario are more urgent and important. The key to groupthink is group cohesiveness, not the critical nature of the situation.

61. **E** *Understand the Question/Key Words:* Here you're being asked to evaluate a scenario in terms of the *ultimate attribution error* (which deals with situational vs. dispositional attributions regarding "in" and "out" groups). You should have noticed that the fraternities were described as "rivals" (i.e., each likely considers the other an "out" group). You should also have noted the "snowy day" (an obvious situational factor that will probably come into play). Remember that this question is asking for the *best* example of the ultimate attribution error in this context; beware of answer choices that are correct but simply not as good as another choice. *Predict the Answer:* A scenario that exemplifies the ultimate attribution error here will have the fraternity members attribute their own failure to show up to the meeting to situational factors (probably the bad weather), but attribute the failure of the rival group (the "out" group) to negative personal traits. Choice (D) has the one group thinking that the other group was just too lazy and irresponsible to show up (good so far)! However, those guys don't also attribute their own failure to show up to the snowy day (or some situational factor like that). Choice (E) is correct.

62. **B** *Understand the Question/Key Words:* This scenario involves a trainer who wants to condition his seal to clap at the sound of its name. We're asked to identify which behavior on the part of the trainer would make it LEAST likely that he could so train the seal (i.e., which reinforcement schedule would be least effective). *Predict the Answer:* In general, ratio schedules are the MOST effective, so you can already eliminate (C) and (D), which are fixed-ratio schedules, as well as (E), which is a variable-ratio schedule. Continuous reinforcement is initially good for teaching a new behavior, so eliminate (A). Giving the seal a fish every five minutes, no matter what it is doing, is a fixed-interval schedule. Skinner found that this tends to produce superstitious behaviors in animals and in humans. The seal might believe it is being rewarded for throwing its head back, rather than clapping, and so it will now constantly throw its head back when it wants a fish. Thus, (B) is correct.

63. **C** *Understand the Question/Key Words:* You should know the basic facts about the famous (and highly questionable) Zimbardo prison experiment. Even if you forgot some of them, a bit of common sense and POE can narrow down the choices here. *Predict the Answer:* Remember that this is a NOT question, so any aspect of the study that was basically okay will be the answer. Choice (A) can be eliminated pretty easily; causing subjects extreme distress is always an ethical problem. For (B), you need to remember what demand characteristics are; they are the cues (sometimes very subtle) that let research subjects know that they're expected to act a certain way. Many believe that the Zimbardo "guards" who behaved abusively were simply adopting the role they knew they were expected to play. Choice (C) looks good! Zimbardo never inferred causation from correlation, as you might when dealing with survey results or other large numbers. This was an experiment

involving a handful of subjects (keep (C)). It's always an issue when the results of a study are used to draw conclusions about people in general, yet the subjects are not representative of the larger population. College-age males might differ from females or older males in terms of aggression (eliminate (D)). The fact that the mock prison setting differed significantly from a real prison is absolutely a problem (eliminate (E)); it's very difficult to generalize the study's results to the real world.

64. **D** *Understand the Question/Key Words:* Here we have a scenario about little Louie and how he seemed to develop a fear of the doctor after he received a shot from him. You're being asked to choose the best description of what occurred. Note that the word "all" is capitalized; you can be sure that there will be at least one wrong choice that only addresses some of Louie's behavior! *Predict the Answer*: You should identify the type of conditioning that occurred here before proceeding to the answer choices. Note that there are no rewards or punishments, so this must be classical conditioning— *not* operant conditioning. Also note that Louie's fear response to the doctor seemed to die out (i.e., it was *extinguished*). Choice (A) deals with negative reinforcement, (C) deals with shaping, and (E) deals with positive reinforcement; all three can be eliminated because they involve operant conditioning concepts. That leaves us with (B) and (D). Choice (B) is accurate but incomplete because it doesn't address the fact that the behavior was ultimately extinguished. Choice (D) accurately describes all of Louie's reactions.

65. **A** *Understand the Question/Key Words:* The key to getting this question right is understanding how systematic desensitization works (and not getting confused by all the red herrings)! The technique involves exposing the individual (sometimes virtually or only in the person's mind) to increasingly frightening aspects of whatever it is they fear (imagine a snake across the room, now imagine the snake a few feet away, now imagine the snake about to bite you, etc.). The fear must have a *specific focus*—otherwise you can't use the technique. The intensity of the fear, and how it came about, aren't the critical factors here. *Predict the Answer*: Choose the scenario in which the fear is generalized (remember that this is a LEAST question, so we're looking for the case in which desensitization *won't* work). Choice (A) describes a young mother suffering from *generalized* anxiety since the birth of her child (this one looks good)! Dogs are a specific source of fear (eliminate (D)), as is flying (eliminate (C)). The combat veteran with PTSD, (B), isn't afraid of a specific animal or activity, but rather a series of traumatic memories. However, the therapist can still "expose" him to these memories gradually as he confronts the source of his fear in the safe therapeutic environment. The agoraphobic man can also benefit from desensitization therapy: he might be asked to imagine himself going outside, then actually putting his coat on to go outside, then placing one foot outside, etc. (eliminate (E) and choose (A)).

66. **B** *Understand the Question/Key Words*: Here you're being asked to identify the data that would be most likely to suffer a ceiling effect (i.e., the dependent variable measures are so high that the independent variable can't really affect them much). *Predict the Answer:* Look for the test (or other assessment) that's too easy for the group of people taking it. Choice (B) fits: most college students can easily solve simple arithmetic problems.

67. **D** *Understand the Question/Key Words*: Here you'll need to assess the truth of various statements about the Asch conformity experiments. *Predict the Answer*: If you don't remember this series of experiments, then simply make an educated guess. Allowing private responses, (A), and introducing a non-conforming confederate, (B), *decreased* conformity (which makes perfect sense). Choice (C) is also incorrect: one of the problems with this study is that all subjects were college-age males. Choice (E) is incorrect because making the lines more similar (and the task harder) *increased* conformity—and predictably so; when we're less sure of ourselves, we're less likely to openly challenge the consensus. Choice (D) is correct; the number of confederates present did affect conformity rates (conformity was maximized at 3 to 5 people; additional confederates had no significant effect).

68. **C** *Understand the Question/Key Words*: The question refers to Piaget, so you should be thinking in terms of his developmental stages. It appears that Billy is an infant and that he understands that the toy is still there even though he can no longer see it. *Predict the Answer*: You should be thinking—sensorimotor stage (birth to 2 yrs.), with object permanence achieved ((C) is correct). If you forgot some or all of Piaget's stages, you could still use POE and common sense to narrow down the choices. Choice (A) makes no sense because babies aren't capable of "logic," which involves a sophisticated thought process. If you didn't know what the "concrete operations" stage is, you might not be able to eliminate (B) yet. Choice (D) is the trap answer here because it lists the correct stage, but the wrong milestone; conservation occurs many years later in the concrete operations stage (remember that "half right" is *all* wrong!). Since (E) can be eliminated through common sense (there's no "symbolism" here: Billy simply understands that the toy is still there), you would still have it narrowed down to three even if you didn't remember the stages. Choice (C) is the only one that mentions objects, so that would be your best bet for a guess.

69. **E** *Understand the Question/Key Words*: This question seems to be focusing on Ralph's ability to detect when more salt has been added to the gravy, so you should be thinking "difference threshold (or JND)"! *Predict the Answer*: If you knew the definition of the JND (the smallest difference between two stimuli that can be detected 50% of the time), then it's clear that we don't actually know what the JND is here (but it *must* be greater than one teaspoon). Ralph only noticed the extra teaspoon of salt two out of six times, so you can eliminate (B) and (D). If you didn't know how to define JND you could still eliminate (A) because we know nothing about Ralph's *absolute* threshold for salt in gravy (i.e., the lowest level at which he can detect salt at all). Choice (C) makes no sense because the level at which Ralph can detect an *increase* in salt can't be lower than his ability to detect *any* salt whatsoever. Choice (E) is correct.

70. **B** *Understand the Question/Key Words*: Here you need to know what a *double-blind* experiment (i.e., neither the experimenter nor the subjects know who is in which group) is designed to *eliminate*. *Predict the Answer*: The correct answer will be something negative that you could plausibly eliminate by not telling the experimenter which subjects are receiving which treatment. Choice (D) is out (informed consent is a good thing). Choice (C) makes no sense: random error can't be eliminated so easily (it's random). Choice (E) is implausible as well; if a drug has serious side effects, research methodology can't change that. Choice (A), the placebo effect, might seem like an attractive answer, but it doesn't fit either. If one group gets a drug and the other gets a placebo,

the second group might demonstrate a placebo effect. It doesn't matter that the experimenter doesn't know which group received the actual drug (not knowing might actually make a placebo effect more likely). Choice (B) is the answer. Demand characteristics are subtle cues given by the researcher to the subjects that let them know how they're supposed to behave. In a double-blind scenario, the experimenter doesn't *know* how each group is supposed to behave.

71.   **A**   *Understand the Question/Key Words:* Here you're being tested on your knowledge of the Freudian theories of psychosexual development and what happens when somebody gets fixated, or psychologically "stuck," at the oral stage. *Predict the Answer*: Choose the scenario that involves some sort of oral gratification or "infantile" dependency. Choices (C) and (D) both involve an anal-retentive fixation, (B) seems to involve trouble during the phallic stage, and (E) indicates trouble during the genital phase, which could have various causes. Although chewing gum, drinking, and overeating are classic examples of a passive oral fixation, Freud also described using one's voice to control or harass others as an active oral fixation from a time when one didn't get one's needs met by crying. Choice (A) is the correct answer.

72.   **E**   *Understand the Question/Key Words:* The question asks how Annie would view the hostile incident in terms of *attribution theory* (the ways in which we all try to explain everybody's behavior). *Predict the Answer*: You should be thinking in terms of *attribution biases*, such as the *fundamental attribution error*. We know that we tend to overestimate dispositional factors (and underestimate situational factors) when interpreting the behavior of others. However, when we're interpreting our *own* behavior, we tend to do the opposite. So Annie would probably assume that the other woman fought with her because she's simply a hostile and unpleasant person, not because the woman was stressed out, etc. In contrast, she would attribute her own hostile behavior to the stressful situation in which she found herself. Choices (A), (B), (C), and (D) are wrong; (E) is the only answer consistent with this theory.

73.   **D**   *Understand the Question/Key Words*: We have a scenario wherein *both* groups of children showed a significant reduction in disruptive behavior, even though only one group was placed on a token economy. However, the "token" group did show a much greater decrease than did the control group. *Predict the Answer:* The concept that best accounts for the substantial decrease in disruptive behavior in the "token" group is simply operant conditioning: good behavior is rewarded with something the child wants (nothing extraordinary here). In terms of the decrease in disruptiveness in the *control* group, however, you'd be at an advantage if you remembered the Hawthorne effect: this involves a change in the behavior being assessed simply as the result of the fact that the subjects are being observed. In this case, the kids are on their best behavior with an authoritative adult stranger in the room ((D) is correct). The placebo effect is inapplicable here (no children were falsely told they were receiving treatment). Social facilitation refers to one's ability to perform simple tasks when observed and is also inapplicable.

74.   **B**   *Understand the Question/Key Words*: Here you're being asked to identify the best way to assess an antisocial personality. *Predict the Answer:* Eliminate any answer choice that relies on information provided by Randy himself (psychopaths are deceptive, manipulative, and adept at hiding their negative traits)! Get rid of (A) and (D). The information gained from a projective test like the

Rorschach is harder to fake and will be more accurate. However, it won't be specific or thorough enough to warrant a diagnosis (eliminate (E)). While skilled clinicians often have good intuition about patients, the doctor's own feelings about Randy are not an adequate basis for a diagnosis (eliminate (C)). The doctor's best bet is to rely on what others say about Randy (especially documented incidents of antisocial conduct) and watch his behavior closely ((B) is correct).

75. **E** *Understand the Question/Key Words*: We need to consider each of the three rewards given here (a hug, ice cream, and $20) and determine whether it is a primary or secondary reinforcer. *Predict the Answer*: Remember that a primary reinforcer is something that is inherently pleasant or rewarding on a biological level (e.g., food and drink), with no need to pair it with another reinforcer. A secondary reinforcer, in contrast, has no biological significance; it gains its reward value through association with a primary reinforcer (e.g., a winning raffle ticket). Is a hug inherently rewarding on a biological level? Absolutely—human affection and physical contact are basic needs (you can eliminate (B) and (C)). Is ice cream inherently rewarding on a biological level? There's no doubt about that! Eliminate (A). Is twenty dollars inherently rewarding on a biological level? Nope! No matter how much we humans like our cash, money has no inherent value for us. Getting twenty dollars is only rewarding because we can exchange it for something else ((D) is wrong and (E) is correct).

76. **E** *Understand the Question/Key Words*: Bobby was evidently really mad at his teacher, took it out on his younger brother (sort of claiming that the brother was the one who was hostile), then tried to make it up by being especially nice to the little brother he abused. This is an EXCEPT question, so look for the defense mechanism that doesn't fit in anywhere in this scenario. *Predict the Answer*: Bobby's behavior is a classic example of displacement, in which impulses or feelings, often aggressive ones, are transferred from their original object to one perceived as less threatening (eliminate (A)). His behavior is also classic projection; he attempts to disown his own unacceptable feelings and impulses by falsely attributing them to his brother (accusing his brother of giving him a "mean look"; eliminate (B)). A reaction formation occurs when we behave in a manner that is directly opposed to an underlying impulse that we consider unacceptable. Bobby was nice to his brother and told him that he loved him, even though he really doesn't like him (eliminate (C)). Undoing involves an attempt to negate or reverse an act that the individual has committed, but considers unacceptable, by doing its opposite. Bobby is clearly trying to make up for his bad behavior towards his brother by being overly nice to him (eliminate (D)). Intellectualization involves an attempt to protect ourselves from anxiety by engaging in abstract reasoning or excessive intellectual activity (this one doesn't apply; (E) is the answer).

77. **D** *Understand the Question/Key Words*: This question describes an experiment and then asks which statement is true about that experiment. Make sure you understand the experimental scenario before proceeding. *Predict the Answer*: Choice (A) is wrong because it states that a within-subjects design was used. That would mean that all subjects experienced all the conditions or manipulations, but here one group was given a vitamin, another was given a placebo, etc. Choice (B) is wrong because the placebo effect (i.e., students improved because they thought they took a helpful pill) can't explain ALL the findings: it wouldn't explain why the "vitamin" group seriously outperformed the "placebo" group. Choice (C) is wrong because a quasi-experiment lacks random assignment, which this study has.

Choice (D) is correct: in a between-subjects design there is more than one condition or manipulation, but each subject is only exposed to one, so the subjects are divided into groups (vitamin vs. placebo vs. no pill). Choice (E) is wrong because 100 subjects is a high number for a controlled experiment.

78. **E** *Understand the Question/Key Words:* To make a *differential diagnosis*, Shaun's therapist must distinguish between or among various diagnoses (which may have overlapping symptoms) and determine which labels, if any, are appropriate. *Predict the Answer*: Shaun's list of symptoms, traits, and behaviors suggest that he *might* have borderline, histrionic, and narcissistic personality disorders ((E) is correct). There is nothing to suggest that he is paranoid or avoidant ((B), (C), and (D) can be eliminated on that basis alone). While antisocial personality disorder might be a tempting answer, Shaun shows no telltale signs of sociopathy (lying, cheating, hurting people, etc.).

79. **B** *Understand the Question/Key Words:* Here you're being asked to identify Ekman's six basic emotions. *Predict the Answer*: Be sure to use POE effectively here and eliminate any answer that doesn't include an emotion that you know for sure is on the list—or includes one that you know is wrong. The six basic emotions are disgust, anger, fear, happiness, surprise, and sadness ((B) is correct).

80. **C** *Understand the Question/Key Words:* The word *causes* is critical here; you need to identify the statistic that shows that alcoholism actually *causes* depression, not just that the two phenomena are associated. To answer this question correctly, you'll need to understand the difference between causation and correlation! *Predict the Answer*: Any answer choice that simply shows that alcoholism and depression tend to occur together is wrong; you can eliminate (A), (B), (D), and (E) on this basis. If these two phenomena are only correlated, then maybe depression actually causes alcoholism (people feel sad, so they drink in order to cope). Alternatively, maybe some third factor that's not even mentioned (such as poverty) is correlated with both factors and is what's actually causing depression—and maybe even alcoholism too! Choice (C) is the answer because it's the only statistic that tends to eliminate one of these alternative explanations. If most alcoholics are depressed, and the vast majority of those people were diagnosed with alcoholism *before* being diagnosed with depression, that would make it unlikely that depression causes alcoholism. If (C) were true (these figures are all made up, by the way), it wouldn't *prove* that alcoholism is the causal factor, but, of the five choices, it would offer the most support for that conclusion.

81. **A** *Understand the Question/Key Words:* Here you're being asked to distinguish PTSD from Generalized Anxiety Disorder. *Predict the Answer:* Both PTSD and Generalized Anxiety Disorder share the symptoms mentioned in (C), (D), and (E). There is no research supporting (B). And, it is true that PTSD, not Generalized Anxiety Disorder, emerges following exposure to the threat of death, injury, or sexual assault. Thus, (A) is the correct answer.

82. **C** *Understand the Question/Key Words:* This question concerns Maslow's hierarchy of needs (remember that the needs at the very tippy top of the pyramid are the ones achieved last—*after* all the others have been satisfied). *Predict the Answer:* The more basic the need, the *lower* on the pyramid it should go (eliminate (A) and (B) right off the bat). Recall that Maslow spoke of self-actualization, including the need for creative self-expression, as the ultimate human goal and driving force (higher on the pyramid than even love or esteem). Choice (C) is the answer.

83. **C** *Understand the Question/Key Words:* Here we're asked to evaluate a mother/child interaction in light of the work of Mary Ainsworth, who is best known for her research on *attachment theory*. Note that there is something wrong with the relationship in that the child seems conflicted about receiving the mother's comfort. *Predict the Answer:* You can easily eliminate (A) because the attachment does not seem *secure*. Choice (B) states that the mother has *never* tried to comfort her child before; this is a very extreme statement that is impossible to support based only on the information provided. Choice (D) can similarly be eliminated; we have no information about Tonya's attachment to her father. With our choices narrowed down to (C) and (E), the word "ambivalent" strongly suggests that (C) is the answer; Tonya seemed to want comfort yet would not receive it. Children with an *avoidant* attachment are more indifferent than ambivalent.

84. **B** *Understand the Question/Key Words:* The word *primarily* is important here. You're being asked what the officer is mainly looking for when she instructs the driver to touch his finger to his nose with his eyes closed. *Predict the Answer:* The cop is primarily testing proprioception here, the ability to sense the position and movement of our body parts, which can be impaired by alcohol ((B) is correct). The officer might also notice impairment in short-term memory, (A), attention span, (C), and reaction time, (D), but these observations are incidental. The officer is not testing visual acuity, (E), because the driver's eyes are closed.

85. **E** *Understand the Question/Key Words:* Here you're being asked to identify a factor that would support the idea that antisocial behavior is genetic (as opposed to being the result of environmental factors). *Predict the Answer:* Monozygotic (one egg) twins are identical; they share 100% of their DNA. Dizygotic (two egg) twins are fraternal and just like any other siblings; they share only 50% of their DNA. Look for the situation in which identical twins are reared apart, but still share antisocial traits! Choice (A) has fraternal twins reared together and both are antisocial; this could easily be due to environmental influences ((A) is out). Choice (B) has identical twins reared apart (so far, so good)—but neither twin is antisocial (in which case the scenario is irrelevant; eliminate (B)). Choice (C) deals with identical twins who are both antisocial, but they were reared *together*; if they grew up in the same environment, their antisocial traits could be due to environmental factors ((C) is out). Choice (D) can be eliminated: here we have fraternal twins reared apart and only one is antisocial (no evidence of a genetic link there)! Choice (E) is exactly what we're looking for: the twins are both antisocial, despite having grown up in different environments.

86. **D** *Understand the Question/Key Words:* This question involves assessing whether various survey results are truly measuring what they purport to measure. *Predict the Answer:* When reading each answer choice, ask yourself "is there any reason why this sample is not *representative* of the larger population?" For (A), the sample isn't representative of the statewide population because Jeffrey is only surveying people who shop at one expensive store. Most of these folks will be from the same geographical area and have similar socioeconomic statuses. For (B), the problem is that college students are typically more affluent, academically oriented, and politically homogenous than are "young people in America" in general. Choice (C) is problematic because the 100 people (out of 500) who took the time to complete the survey and mail it back probably care more about environmental issues than those who didn't bother. Choice (E) is wrong because Jeffrey spoiled

his own sample by showing a film about the evils of poverty before asking them to assess how important a political issue it is. Choice (D) is the best choice here. The population to which the sample generalizes is only sixth-graders at that particular school and Jeffrey surveyed 3 of the 4 classes randomly.

87. **D** *Understand the Question/Key Words:* Here you're being asked to characterize two contrasting personality profiles in terms of the theories of Alfred Adler. Note that Elsie and Edward are described as having had highly critical parents. *Predict the Answer:* You should be thinking in terms of inferiority complex and compensation! According to Adler, two types of negative compensation are overcompensation (striving for power, dominance, etc.) and undercompensation (becoming overly dependent and insecure); Elsie fits the former profile while Edward fits the latter ((D) is correct). If you didn't remember that, you could eliminate (E) based on common sense: Elsie doesn't seem to be compensating in a positive way (she obviously has some personality problems). Similarly, (A) and (B) are unlikely in that both siblings seem to be struggling with feelings of inferiority (albeit in very different ways).

88. **A** *Understand the Question/Key Words:* This question is testing your knowledge of the structure and function of the ear. *Predict the Answer:* The tympanic membrane (eardrum) is a membrane that divides the outer ear from the middle ear ((A) is correct). The cochlea, (B), is a spiral-shaped cavity that divides the inner ear and contains the nerves that are required for hearing. The semicircular canals, (C), are curved tubular canals that contain receptors required for balance. The incus, (D), and the malleus, (E), are small bones that transmit sound waves to the inner ear.

89. **C** *Understand the Question/Key Words:* Note that this is a "NOT" question: all the wrong answers will be symptoms of fetal alcohol syndrome. *Predict the Answer:* Fetal alcohol syndrome is often associated with a small head, not a large one ((C) is the answer). All the remaining choices are symptoms of FAS.

90. **C** *Understand the Question/Key Words:* This question tests your knowledge of *efferent* neurons, asking you to evaluate the truth of the answer choices. *Predict the Answer*: Ideally you'll remember that efferent neurons are motor neurons that carry neural impulses away from the central nervous system to the muscles ((C) is correct). You can use POE here if you know other terms: *afferent* neurons are sensory neurons that carry impulses from sensory stimuli to the central nervous system ((A) and (D) are wrong). *Interneurons* transmit impulses between other neurons and enable communication ((B) and (E) are wrong).

91. **E** *Understand the Question/Key Words:* You'll need to be familiar with Eysenck's three personality scales in order to assess Brad. *Predict the Answer:* Brad's aggressiveness and antisocial behavior put him high on the psychoticism scale (eliminate (B)). Further, his instability puts him towards the "neurotic" end of the stability/neuroticism continuum (eliminate (A)). Finally, his sociable nature puts him on the "extravert" end of the introversion/extraversion continuum (eliminate (D)). Eysenck's theory is biologically based, with people like Brad being predisposed to seek out arousal and stimulation (eliminate (C)). Choice (E) is correct.

92. **E** *Understand the Question/Key Words:* Here you're being asked to identify an example of *top-down processing.* *Predict the Answer:* Look for the situation wherein somebody first recognizes a pattern, then perceives incoming stimuli in that context. Choice (E) exemplifies this process: Ned only saw the letters "b" and "u," but, in the context of a cookie recipe, he knew the word must be "butter" ((E) is correct). Choice (C) exemplifies the opposite: bottom-up processing, in which the incoming stimuli are perceived and *then* the pattern is recognized. Ned perceives the woman, the uniform, and the plate of food—then realizes that she's an employee of the store offering samples. Choice (A) simply involves mistaking one object for another because they feel similar when touched. Choice (B) simply involves Ned being unable to recognize an object by sight until he is closer to it. Choice (D) simply involves a color-blind person using other properties of objects in order to identify them.

93. **B** *Understand the Question/Key Words:* This scenario involves a store owner who won't hire an otherwise qualified young woman as a manager because he believes pretty young blondes are flighty, flirtatious, etc. Keep in mind that this is a NOT question, so the correct answer will be inapplicable here. *Predict the Answer:* Your brain should be screaming words like prejudice, discrimination, etc. Prejudice refers to an attitude (usually negative) towards a group of people based on preconceived notions, (A), and discrimination refers to action taken either for or against someone based on membership in a group, as opposed to individual merit (eliminate (A) and (D)). Out-group homogeneity refers to the tendency to view members of an out-group as more similar than members of an in-group (e.g., an older man believing that attractive young blond women are more apt to resemble one another in terms of personality and behavior; (C) can be eliminated as well). Out-group bias can lead to the development of a stereotype, or standardized image of a group (e.g., young pretty blondes are flighty and flirtatious; (E) is wrong too). Self-serving bias refers to the tendency to take credit for one's own successes and is inapplicable here ((B) is correct).

94. **A** *Understand the Question/Key Words:* This question is asking you to evaluate the ethics of various hypothetical research experiments. Remember that this is a LEAST question, so the "best" scenario (ethically speaking) will be correct. *Predict the Answer:* Eliminate scenarios that seriously violate any of the basic ethical requirements: confidentiality, informed consent, protection from harm, etc. Use your common sense here too! Ethical guidelines are basically reasonable, so lean towards the scenario that doesn't seem all that bad from a layperson's perspective. As for (A)—is it unethical to lie to subjects about the purpose of the study? This one is a bit tricky. Deception is discouraged but allowed when necessary to carry out the experiment. Also, this study seems pretty benign in general. Keep (A) for now. Is it unethical to essentially force prisoners to participate in a drug study—or else lose important privileges? Absolutely! Participation must be voluntary (eliminate (B)). Is it unethical to publish the names of subjects in a study about mental illness? Yes! Findings must be kept confidential (eliminate (C)). Is it unethical to study the extent to which subjects are willing to murder one another with electric shocks? It certainly is, according to modern ethical standards and guidelines (we're looking at you, Stanley Milgram)! Such a study would likely cause subjects extreme psychological distress (eliminate (D)). Is it unethical to give kids vitamins without their parents' knowledge? Undoubtedly! Researchers must obtain informed consent (and giving children any kind of pills without parental permission obviously just won't fly)! Choice (A) is the answer.

95. **B** *Understand the Question/Key Words:* Allie seems not to notice that her perfume is strong, and you're asked which condition or phenomenon is the most likely explanation. *Predict the Answer:* Allie most likely doesn't notice that her perfume is intense due to olfactory fatigue; she's simply become accustomed to the smell. Choice (A), anosmia, involves a loss of the ability to smell and is obviously much more serious. While anosmia *could* explain the fact that Allie is unaware of her perfume's strength, simple olfactory fatigue is much more likely. Ageusia, (D), involves a loss of taste, cocktail party syndrome, (C), is an auditory phenomenon, and aphasia, (E), involves loss of speech. Choice (B) is correct.

96. **C** *Understand the Question/Key Words:* Here you're being asked to choose a pair of symptoms that would warrant a diagnosis of schizophrenia, as opposed to schizotypal personality disorder. *Predict the Answer:* Schizophrenia is a psychosis and can be distinguished on that basis. Choose the symptoms that are hallmarks of psychosis: delusions and hallucinations ((C) is correct). All the other symptoms listed are commonly seen in both disorders.

97. **A** *Understand the Question/Key Words:* You're being asked to identify an example of the *availability heuristic*. *Predict the Answer:* Choose the scenario in which somebody miscalculates the likelihood that something will occur based on how many similar instances come to mind. In (A), Greg overestimates the number of good-looking murderers out there because the media chooses to focus on these cases (presumably to increase ratings). Choice (A) fits perfectly and is the correct answer. Choice (B) is an example of the *Gambler's fallacy*: Greg falsely believes that the fact that his last five kids were boys affects the likelihood that his next child will be a girl (the odds are still about 50/50). Choices (C) and (D) aren't the best examples because Greg seems to be dealing with all the relevant data in each case. Choice (E) doesn't exemplify any heuristic; Greg merely adopts a dog that is *available* (making (E) a bit of an attractive wrong answer).

98. **C** *Understand the Question/Key Words:* It appears that Fluffy has been classically conditioned to meow at the sound of the tuna can, and then this stimulus generalized to the corn, but not to the mushrooms. Further, this *conditioned response* is probably not extinguished yet, since the can has only been presented twice without Fluffy getting any tuna. *Predict the Answer:* The can of corn probably sounds more like the can of tuna than the mushroom can does; that would explain why Fluffy *discriminated* between the mushrooms and the tuna—but *not* between the corn and the tuna ((A) and (B) are the opposite of what we need; (C) looks pretty good). Choices (D) and (E) are wrong because the conditioned response to the tuna can has not yet been extinguished ((C) is correct).

99. **C** *Understand the Question/Key Words:* The phrase "*reduces* prison violence" is critical here! The question is asking you to decide which of the answer choices (if true) should prevent you from inferring *causality* from this experiment. Keep in mind that this is a "NOT" question, so all the *wrong* answer choices will be potential problems with the study. *Predict the Answer:* Right now your brain should be screaming "confounding variable"! Anything other than anger management that could possibly account for the reduction in reported violence on Block A, compared to the rest of the prison, is potentially a confounding variable here. If only Block A prisoners were served a special diet, could that account for the reduction in violence? Absolutely! Behavioral improvement could

be caused by something prisoners are (or are not) eating, so (A) is out. If security is much stricter on Block A, could that account for the reduction in violence? This one might require a bit of thought. If security is very tight, prisoners may simply lack the opportunity to be violent (having an armed guard right beside you or security cameras everywhere might keep you on your best behavior!); (B) is out. Could the fact that only highly violent inmates were studied account for the results? No, not really. The study's findings concern *violent* inmates. The fact that the subjects were very violent individuals would not make it more likely that something other than anger-management caused the results ((C) looks good). Could the fact that Block A staff wants the anger-management program to succeed account for the results? Definitely! Staff members are the ones documenting the violence and, if biased, they may (perhaps unknowingly) underreport violent incidents in order to validate their own work ((D) is out). Choice (E) is basically another way of stating that this study lacks a control group—which makes it vulnerable to confounding variables. The researcher should have given only *some* Block A inmates anger management. Then if those inmates were less violent than the others on Block A, we would know that this difference wasn't due to some other variable unique to the Block A area or program ((C) is correct).

100. **E**   *Understand the Question/Key Words:* "Factitious disorder" means faking symptoms in order to gain attention from friends, family, and/or the medical community. *Predict the Answer:* Look for the situation that, based on your knowledge of psychology, seems somehow sketchy or unlikely. Is there anything suspicious about a woman with bipolar disorder who's suicidal, (A)? No! Bipolar individuals have a mood disorder; they can get very depressed and sometimes contemplate suicide. Is there anything suspicious about a schizophrenic man hearing voices, (B)? Nope—that makes perfect sense. How about a sixteen-year-old anorexic girl having thoughts of hurting herself? No. Self-injury does occur among teenagers, and anorexia isn't inconsistent with such behavior. A seventy-year-old woman with Parkinson's may have trouble breathing for several reasons, including restrictive lung disease and sleep apnea. Choice (D) is wrong. While it is not unusual for a twenty-five-year-old woman to present with abdominal pain, it is not very likely to be related to her complaint of vision loss. Signs of factitious disorder include strange sets of symptoms, and it is more common in women. Choice (E) is correct.

Section II: Free Response

1. This question is worth seven points. Points are given based on a student's ability to explain behavior and apply theories and perspectives in authentic contexts. Each essay is unique, but here is our run-down of what a student should definitely address in order to earn these points:

    - ADHD is attention-deficit hyperactivity disorder, a neurodevelopmental disorder, and Simon is displaying several of the key symptoms, including hyperactivity (fidgeting), difficulty staying on task, and problems with executive function (see below). This would likely be Simon's diagnosis if his parents were amenable.

    - Executive function involves planning ahead and staying organized. Problems in this area are often a component of ADHD. These issues are evident in the condition of Simon's notebook and the fact that he has been missing class deadlines.

    - In Erik Erikson's theory, Simon would be at the stage of "Industry versus Inferiority." As such, it would be very important to his development that he be recognized for his efforts and his display of competence in given areas. Based on his reaction to a lack of praise, it seems that Simon is sensitive to this dynamic. So, it will be important for the teacher to recognize times when Simon is producing good work.

    - Behaviorism prioritizes the study and manipulation of observable, measurable behaviors. Here, behaviorism is in practice when the teacher and the parents set up a behavior modification program using rewards and punishments to alter Simon's behavior.

    - A fixed-interval schedule is a schedule of reinforcement whereby reinforcement arrives at set time periods. When Simon is rewarded at the conclusion of every 15-minute period of on-task behavior, this is an example of fixed-interval reinforcement.

    - Negative punishment has the intent of reducing a behavior by taking something away. Here, when "time out" is applied it functions as negative punishment because the intent is to reduce Simon's problematic behavior and the means to do this is to take away his opportunity to participate in the classroom environment.

    - Shaping involves rewarding successive approximations of a goal. The goal here is to get Simon to stay on task for a full class period, but that may be too ambitious to start. So, a shorter period of 15 minutes is sufficient for him to earn a reward initially, and then that time period is gradually lengthened until it reaches the ultimate goal.

2.	This free response question is worth seven points, one for each bullet point. Points are given based on students' ability to analyze psychological research studies, including analyzing and interpreting quantitative data. Different suitable responses are possible; the following response would earn all of the points:

Sample Essay

This study is not an experiment for several reasons: those conducting the study are not manipulating a variable, they have not created experimental and control groups, and they have not controlled for numerous, and possibly confounding, variables. For example, subjects may come from a variety of backgrounds and may have a variety of reasons, beyond their individual personalities, for having an overwhelmingly positive or negative reaction to starting college or being away from home.

It is unclear from the limited data presented whether or not the results of this study are statistically significant. It needs to be determined what the likelihood is that the commonality of "high emotionality" between the "moving-in" episode and the "relationship" rating could occur at this rate as a matter of random coincidence. Only if this possibility were less than five percent (.05) would it be legitimate to claim that the results are statistically significant.

It is a good thing that this article is being presented to a professional journal because it will give the authors' peers two opportunities to challenge the validity of their procedures and their findings. The editorial board of the journal, consisting of scientific peers, will first make a decision about whether the study is worthy of publication and, if the article is published, a wider group of peers will be able to offer opinions and counter-arguments.

Subject selection and exclusion criteria can have unintended consequences for the study findings. For example, by seeking out students with vivid memories of their first day, as opposed to all students, researchers might be allowing subjects to self-select based on how much emotion they were experiencing; emotion and memory are often linked. By excluding students with less-than-vivid memories for this event, they may be excluding students who did not have a very emotional reaction. Having more "highly emotional" subjects and fewer "low-to-moderate emotion" subjects at the outset could have affected the data produced.

Subjects are relying upon episodic memory in recalling that first day of college and also, probably, when assessing their feelings about their relationships. Those feelings probably involve specific events in the past.

Trait theory assumes that people have relatively stable patterns of behavior that underlie their personalities. This study, and the theory it seeks to support, hypothesize a personality trait of "emotionality" that will not be a one-time event; rather it would be expected to show up as a regular part of the individuals' personalities.

Confirmation bias is a tendency to only look for evidence that supports a pre-existing notion, or to interpret ambiguous evidence as supportive of that notion. Here, researchers went into the study with an idea of what they were hoping to find. Therefore, they need to be particularly careful that they did not exhibit this bias. For example, they may want to look carefully at individuals who displayed "high emotionality" about moving-in day but not about other significant events. Perhaps some qualities of moving-in day are unique and it should not be used to generalize.

HOW TO SCORE PRACTICE TEST 1

Section I: Multiple Choice

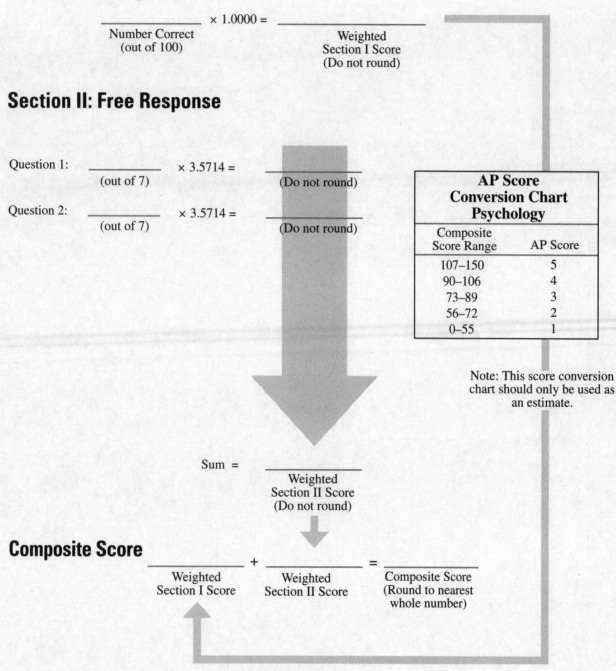

_____ × 1.0000 = _____
Number Correct   Weighted
(out of 100)   Section I Score
                                (Do not round)

Section II: Free Response

Question 1:   _____ × 3.5714 =   _____
              (out of 7)   (Do not round)

Question 2:   _____ × 3.5714 =   _____
              (out of 7)   (Do not round)

AP Score Conversion Chart Psychology	
Composite Score Range	AP Score
107–150	5
90–106	4
73–89	3
56–72	2
0–55	1

Note: This score conversion chart should only be used as an estimate.

Sum =   _____
        Weighted
        Section II Score
        (Do not round)

Composite Score

_____ + _____ = _____
Weighted   Weighted   Composite Score
Section I Score   Section II Score   (Round to nearest
                                    whole number)

Part III
About the
AP Psychology
Exam

- The Structure of the AP Psychology Exam
- How the AP Psychology Exam Is Scored
- Overview of Content Topics
- How AP Exams Are Used
- Other Resources
- Designing Your Study Plan

THE STRUCTURE OF THE AP PSYCHOLOGY EXAM

The AP Psychology Exam is divided into two sections with the following time allotments:

→   Section I—Multiple Choice

100 questions . . . . 70 minutes

→   Section II—Free Response

2 essay questions . . . . 50 minutes

Section I

Section I of the AP Psychology Exam contains 100 multiple-choice questions. You have 70 minutes to complete the section, and your Section I score counts for two-thirds of your overall AP Psychology grade.

If you did a double-take when you saw that you are given only 70 minutes to do 100 questions, take a deep breath. Although having less than a minute per question poses a definite challenge, knowing certain techniques, which we will discuss in more detail in Part IV, will make this severe time constraint seem much less daunting.

Section II

Section II of the AP Psychology Exam consists of two free-response questions (aka essays). They each count for the same percentage of your grade, and you must answer both. Section II counts for one-third of your AP Psychology grade. You have 50 minutes to complete BOTH essays—again, take a deep breath. Part IV will teach you strategies so that you can be a smart essay-writer. Plus, you will have several opportunities to practice writing essays before exam day. Use your tools and your practice tests to master this portion of the exam. When the time comes, you will have all the tools you need to create high-scoring essays in a limited period of time.

HOW THE AP PSYCHOLOGY EXAM IS SCORED

Your Section I score counts for 66 2/3 percent (two thirds) of your overall AP Psychology Exam grade. Why the unusual division? Only the College Board knows, and it's not saying. Regardless, you can score well on this section with the techniques covered in this book. Similarly, Section II accounts for 33 1/3 percent (one third) of your total score. With this breakdown, you can think of the exam as totaling 150 points, with Section I accounting for 100 points and Section II accounting for the remaining 50 points.

How Much Is Each Section Worth?

Each of the two essays in Section II is worth 25 of the total 150 points, and based on data most recently released by the College Board, most essays ask for 7 pieces of information. On average, each piece of information is usually worth a little bit more than 3 points.

Score	2022 Percentage	Credit Recommendation	College Grade Equivalent
5	17.0	Extremely Well Qualified	A
4	22.2	Well Qualified	A−, B+, B
3	19.1	Qualified	B−, C+, C
2	13.1	Possibly Qualified	−
1	28.5	No Recommendation	−

Scores from May 2022 AP administration. Data taken from the College Board website.

OVERVIEW OF CONTENT TOPICS

The multiple-choice questions in Section I cover the 9 units of the AP Psychology course, as outlined by the College Board. The College Board gives a range for the number of questions devoted to each topic. For example, 8–10 percent of Section I will be devoted to social psychology.

Which Topics Are Tested the Most?

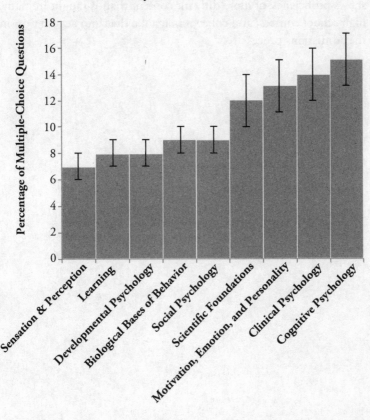

Looking for More Help with Your APs?

We now offer specialized AP tutoring and course packages that guarantee a 4 or 5 on the AP. To see which courses are offered and available, and to learn more about the guarantee, visit PrincetonReview.com/college/ap-test-prep.

The overall units for the AP Psychology course, and how they correspond with this book:

Unit 1: Scientific Foundations of Psychology (Chapters 5 and 6)

Unit 2: Biological Bases of Behavior (Chapters 7 and 8)

Unit 3: Sensation and Perception (Chapter 9)

Unit 4: Learning (Chapter 10)

Unit 5: Cognitive Psychology (Chapters 11 and 12)

Unit 6: Developmental Psychology (Chapter 13)

Unit 7: Motivation, Emotion, and Personality (Chapters 14 and 15)

Unit 8: Clinical Psychology (Chapters 16 and 17)

Unit 9: Social Psychology (Chapter 18)

Notice that we have divided the review portion of this book (Part V) into chapters based on those units for your convenience. Again, by focusing strictly on psychology as it's tested by the AP Exam, we'll teach you what you need to know to make the grade.

HOW AP EXAMS ARE USED

Different colleges use AP Exam scores in different ways, so it is important that you go to a particular college's website to determine how it uses those scores. The following three items represent the main ways in which AP Exam scores can be used.

- **College Credit**. Some colleges will give you college credit if you score well on an AP Exam. These credits count toward your graduation requirements, meaning that you can take fewer courses while in college. Given the cost of college, this could be quite a benefit, indeed.

- **Satisfy Requirements**. Some colleges will allow you to "place out" of certain requirements if you do well on an AP Exam, even if they do not give you actual college credits. For example, you might not need to take an introductory-level course, or perhaps you might not need to take a class in a certain discipline at all.

- **Admissions Plus.** Even if your AP Exam will not result in college credit or even allow you to place out of certain courses, most colleges will respect your decision to push yourself by taking an AP course or even an AP Exam outside of a course. A high score on an AP Exam shows proficiency of more difficult content than is taught in many high school courses, and colleges may take that into account during the admissions process.

OTHER RESOURCES

There are many resources available to help you improve your score on the AP Psychology Exam, not the least of which are your **teachers**. If you are taking an AP class, you may be able to get extra attention from your teacher, such as obtaining feedback on your essays.

Another wonderful resource is **AP Students**, the official site of the AP Exams. The scope of the information at this site is quite broad and includes:

- the course description, which provides details on what content is covered (and a handful of sample questions)

- the scoring guidelines

- access to AP Classroom if you are enrolled in a course (teacher assistance required)

- free-response prompts from previous years and exam tips

The AP Students home page address is <u>apstudents.collegeboard.org/home</u>.

For up-to-date information about any potential changes to the AP Psychology Exam, please visit <u>apstudents.collegeboard.org/courses/ap-psychology</u>.

Finally, The Princeton Review offers tutoring for the AP Psychology Exam. Our expert instructors can help you refine your strategic approach and add to your content knowledge. For more information, call 1-800-2REVIEW.

Stay Up to Date!

For late-breaking information about test dates, exam formats, and any other changes pertaining to AP Psychology, make sure to check the College Board's website at <u>apstudents.collegeboard.org/courses/ap-psychology</u>.

DESIGNING YOUR STUDY PLAN

In Part I you identified some areas of potential improvement. Let's now delve further into your performance on Practice Test 1, with the goal of developing a study plan appropriate to your needs and time commitment.

Read the answers and explanations associated with the multiple-choice questions (starting at page 33). After you have done so, respond to the following questions:

- How many days/weeks/months away is your AP Psychology Exam?

- What time of day is your best, most focused study time?

- How much time per day/week/month will you devote to preparing for your AP Psychology Exam?

- When will you do this preparation? (Be as specific as possible: Mondays and Wednesdays from 3:00 to 4:00 p.m., for example.)

- Based on the answers above, will you focus on strategy (Part IV), content (Part V), or both?

- What are your overall goals in using this book?

Based on your answers to these questions, you should now have a better understanding of how to study for the exam. Use your answers to build a study plan that meets your specific needs based on the amount of time you have until test day. It is important to tailor your study plan to your schedule and topics you need to further review.

Part IV
Test-Taking Strategies for the AP Psychology Exam

PREVIEW

Review your responses to the questions on page 4 of Part I and then respond to the following questions:

- How many multiple-choice questions did you miss even though you knew the answer?

- On how many multiple-choice questions did you guess randomly?

- How many multiple-choice questions did you miss after eliminating some answers and guessing based on the remaining answers?

- Did you create an outline before you wrote each essay?

- Did you find either of the essays easier/harder than the other—and, if so, why?

HOW TO USE THE CHAPTERS IN THIS PART

Before you read the following chapters, think about what you are doing now. As you read and engage in the directed practice, be sure to consider the ways you can change your approach. At the end of Part IV, you will have the opportunity to reflect on how you will change your approach.

Chapter 1
How to Approach
Multiple-Choice
Questions

OVERVIEW OF THE MULTIPLE-CHOICE SECTION

As we discussed in Part III, Section I of the AP Psychology Exam contains 100 multiple-choice questions that cover the 9 units of the AP Psychology course. You have 70 minutes to complete this section, and it counts for two-thirds of your overall score. This time limit gives you less than one minute to answer each question. You might ask: "How can I possibly do well on this test when I have only about 42 seconds to answer each question?"

The answer: You do *not* need to work through all of the questions to do well on Section I of the AP Psychology Exam. In fact, smart testers often do not try to attempt every question and risk careless errors. Instead, smart testers choose which questions to tackle and which questions to simply guess on. "How do I choose?" you ask. To answer that question, let's take a closer look at the way the test is set up.

Order of Difficulty

If you have taken tests like the SAT, you may have noticed that each time you begin a multiple-choice section, you find the questions manageable or even easy. But after a while, the test seems to become more difficult. Finally, near the end of the test, you may feel overwhelmed, as though you don't know any of the answers. Lots of students attribute this phenomenon to time pressure or exhaustion. But there's something else going on.

Many multiple-choice tests, including the AP Psychology Exam, have test questions arranged in a rough order of difficulty. In other words, the first part of the test contains mostly easy questions, the middle of the test contains questions of medium difficulty, and the last third of the exam contains primarily difficult questions. Now, why would a testing company set up a test in order of difficulty? Think about it: the company is trying to assess the psychology knowledge of thousands of students. If they placed all the hard questions at the beginning of the test or stuck them in intermittently, lots of students with pretty good, but not great, psychology knowledge would get stuck on the early questions and never get to the questions they could answer. They would lose time, have trouble building momentum, and generally get bogged down. The results would show two groups—a high-scoring group (the students who know almost all of the material and can answer almost all of the questions) and a low-scoring group (everyone else)—as opposed to a nice bell curve (where most students score somewhere around the middle).

Easy Ones First, Please

When a test is arranged in order of difficulty, everyone starts out answering easy questions. As students work through the test, they will hit a point at which they begin to have trouble. Companies that write standardized tests assert that this stumbling point shows where a student's knowledge of a subject pretty much ends. Although this is open to debate, arranging a test in order of difficulty does create a more nearly fair test for everyone.

So What?

How does all this information help you? If the easiest questions are at the beginning of the exam, followed by questions of medium difficulty, and then the tough stuff, what is the point of rushing through the first questions to get to the questions you can't answer? Easy questions are worth just as much as difficult questions. Therefore, to score well on Section I, you need to slow down and get as many of the easy and medium questions right as you can.

How to Score Your Personal Best on Section I

- Get all easy questions right

- Get most medium questions right

- Do the right thing on hard questions*

*See "Do The Right Thing" later in this chapter.

In Chapter 3, we'll discuss in more depth how to pace yourself to maximize your score. Now, we'll introduce you to some specific multiple-choice strategies.

SMART-TESTER STRATEGIES

Your own knowledge of psychology will be the key to doing well, but certain strategies will help you stretch your psych knowledge and crack the trickier questions. Once you've mastered some of the smart-tester strategies, we'll talk about how you can develop your personal approach to Section I.

Smart-Tester Strategy #1:
Understand the Question/Key Words

How often have you zipped through a question and picked the obvious answer, only to find that you misread the question? The most important thing you can do to increase your score on Section I is to make sure you understand what you are being asked.

After you read a question, take a second to make sure you understand it. Put the question in your own words, or circle the key words in the question. Taking this first step will eliminate the possibility of your answering the wrong thing. Try the following example:

1. A person's refusal to accept an accurate diagnosis of a spouse's mental illness demonstrates the use of which of the following defense mechanisms?

How would you ask this question in your own words?

When someone doesn't want to accept really bad news, they are in…

No One Will Ever Know
Raw scores are not reported to you, your school, or your colleges. Only the final score, ranging from 1 to 5, is reported. In other words, no one will ever know that you got an AP Psych Grade of 5 (extremely well qualified), but got only 75 percent of Section I questions correct and rocked the essays. It's the final grade that matters here, so take the test the smart way.

Now the answer should be obvious: *denial*. By stating this question in everyday language, the answer pops out at you. Try another example:

> 19. The failure of bystanders to respond to a stranger's cries for help is sometimes explained as an instance of

How would you ask the question?

> *Why don't people do anything when someone is yelling "help"?*

In the case of question 19, you may not know the answer off the top of your head, but clarifying the question makes you better prepared to deal with the answer choices.

Let's look at one more:

> 22. The dependent variable in the experiment above is

In this case, you don't need to put the question into your own words. However, you want to make sure you look for the right thing when you hit the answer choices. Therefore, circle the key words *dependent variable* before you head to the answer choices.

Understand the Question/Key Words

For each of the following questions, circle the key words in the question. Then, if appropriate, jot down in your own words exactly what is being asked. Answers are on page 312.

> 3. Angie is a scientist who is interested in the physical basis of psychological phenomena such as motivation, emotion, and stress. She is called a(n)

> 10. One of the primary tools of the school of structuralism was

> 18. Binocular cues provide important cues for depth perception because

> 35. Constance is presented with a list of words. When asked to recall the words, she remembers only the words from the beginning and the end of the list. This phenomenon demonstrates which of the following types of effect?

> 47. The recognition-by-components theory asserts that we categorize objects by breaking them down into their component parts and then

> 56. Veronica is competing in a regional gymnastics competition. As she waits for her turn on the mat, she ignores the sounds of the crowd and instead mentally reviews her routine. Veronica is managing an anxiety-producing situation by employing

Question Numbering
Whenever you start a question, check out the question number. It will tell you approximately how hard the question is (easy: 1–33ish; medium: 34ish–66ish; difficult: 67ish–100). We've numbered all the questions in this book to reflect their approximate difficulty.

70. Which of the following was true of Stanley Milgram's studies of obedience?

88. In their discussions of the process of development, the advocates of the importance of nurture in the nature-nurture controversy emphasize which of the following?

Smart-Tester Strategy #2: Predict the Answer

Once you've translated the question, you go to the answer choices, right? *Stop right there....*Do you really think it's that easy? Of course not, or everyone would get all the questions right. You need to do a little work before you get mired down in the answer choices.

Beware of the Answer Choices

Answer choices are not our friends. In fact, think about what it takes for a test-writer to develop five answer choices for each question. First, she needs to write the correct answer, making sure it is accurate but not too obvious. Then, she has to put in at least one or two close second choices. Finally, she needs to fill in the remaining choices and move on to the next question.

When taking a standardized test, most students read the question and then read each answer choice. What they fail to realize is that the answer choices are riddled with tricks, traps, and distractors designed to bump them off course.

Enter: The Smart Tester

Unlike your less-savvy compatriots, you are a smart tester. You know that if you have an idea of the answer before you read the answer choices, you won't be tempted to pick something that is way off base. You also know that, because four of the five choices you read are wrong, it's best to assume that an answer is wrong until proven right.

After you translate the question into your own words, answer it *in your own words*. Now, that may mean actually knowing the exact answer (as in the case of *denial*), or it may mean putting yourself in the right ballpark before looking at the answer choices. Sometimes, it's actually helpful to cover the answer choices to make your best prediction of what the answer should be. Then look at the choices and see which comes closest to your original thought. Let's look at one of the questions from your last drill:

3. Angie is a scientist who is interested in the physical basis of psychological phenomena such as motivation, emotion, and stress. She is called a(n)

Question Types
Although many of the questions on Section I ask you for factual information, about 30 percent of the questions are application questions—questions that ask you to use your knowledge of psychology to address a given situation. Application questions are no problem as long as you understand the question first. Just be sure to *Understand the Question/ Key Words!*

First, how would you ask this question in your own words? Okay, now maybe you know the answer to this question, and maybe you don't. No problem. You can still answer the question before you look at the answer choices. If you can't spit out Angie's correct title immediately, answer the question by saying:

Angie is called a person who is into the physical basis of psychology.

With your answer in mind, look at each answer choice.

> (A) psychologist
> (B) anthropologist
> (C) physical therapist
> (D) paleontologist
> (E) biopsychologist

Now, use your answer to find the credited response:

(A) Is a *psychologist* a person who's into the physical basis of psychology? No, this person is into more than just the physical basis.

(B) Is an *anthropologist* a person who's into the physical basis of psychology? No, an anthropologist is into cultures.

(C) Is a *physical therapist* a person who's into the physical basis of psychology? No, this person is not into the psychology part.

(D) Is a *paleontologist* a person who's into the physical basis of psychology? No idea what this person is.

(E) Is a *biopsychologist* a person who's into the physical basis of psychology? Yes.

Your answer? Choice (E), *biopsychologist*. By predicting the answer to the question before reading the answer choices, you were able to avoid getting tripped up in the first three answer choices. Plus, you realized the answer had to be (E), *biopsychologist*, without necessarily knowing anything about (D), *paleontologist* (a paleontologist studies fossils, by the way).

Smart-Tester Strategy #3: Process of Elimination (POE)

You have just learned your next big strategy: Process of Elimination (POE for short). Every time you answer a question, you will use POE, which means eliminating wrong answer choices and then choosing from what you have left. Why does it make sense to always answer questions this way? Because four of the five answer choices you read for each question are wrong. In other words, most of the answers you read on the test are wrong. Sometimes, it is much easier to identify two or three wrong answers on each question than it is to concentrate on finding the one right answer each time. By getting rid of two or three wrong answer choices on each question, you have substantially increased your accuracy and your guessing power.

Let's try another example:

> 97. Which of the following is an example of metacognition?

Understand the Question/Key Words: Circle *metacognition*, and then define it:

Understanding cognitive (thought) processes

Predict the Answer:

Find an example of people understanding how they think and learn.

Now, use POE to get rid of wrong answers:

> (A) Recognizing the faces of new in-laws after seeing them only in pictures
> (B) Memorizing 100 words from the dictionary
> (C) Understanding the role of various parts of the brain in perception
> (D) Accurately completing the logic in a deductive-reasoning problem
> (E) Knowing the effectiveness of different strategies for learning statistical formulas

(A) Is *recognizing the faces* of people the same as understanding how one thinks and learns? No. Cross off this answer choice. Every time you decide an answer is not the one you want, cross it off.

(B) Is *memorizing* something the same as understanding how one thinks and learns? No. Cross it off.

(C) Is *understanding the role of various parts of the brain in perception* the same as understanding how one thinks and learns? Not sure? Keep it and read the rest.

(D) Is *accurately completing* a logic problem the same as understanding how one thinks and learns? No. Cross it off.

(E) Is *knowing the effectiveness of different strategies for learning* the same as understanding how one thinks and learns? Sounds pretty close.

By using POE, you were able to easily narrow your choices down to (C) and (E). Once you have it down to two, compare your choices. Which one is closer to the answer you came up with? In this case, the answer is (E). *Understanding the role of various parts of the brain in perception* is still only knowledge of fact, not of mental processes. Notice the word *understanding* was used in (C), and not by coincidence. By using POE, you were able to escape the trap and answer the question correctly. Did you notice that this was question number 97? (Remember, questions are arranged from least to most difficult, making the highest-numbered questions the hardest.) Only about 20 percent of test-takers would answer this question correctly.

Meta What?

Okay, so POE is a great strategy, but what if you don't know what the key term in a question actually means? You have two choices: If this is a very hard question, which it was, you can simply skip it and come back to it if you have time. However, don't underestimate your knowledge. You may not be able to cough up the dictionary definition of *metacognition*, but you can pull the word apart. If you have spent more than a week in AP Psych class, you know that cognition has something to do with thinking. Then recall how you have heard the prefix *meta* used. How about metaphysics? So there's physics and metaphysics, and there's thinking (cognition) and meta-thinking (metacognition). It's probably some higher level of thinking. Although this rough definition may not get you to the exact answer, it will help you cross off some answer choices and help you make an educated guess.

Smart-Tester Strategy Review

Strategy #1: Understand the Question/Key Words: Read the question, and put it into your own words. Circle any key words or phrases that might point you in the right direction.

Strategy #2: Predict the Answer: Come up with your own answer to the question (exact or ballpark).

Strategy #3: Process of Elimination (POE): Cross off each answer that is not close to yours. Pick the best match.

More on POE

Now let's say you read a question and don't know the answer. All is not lost. You can use your brain, the information in the question, and POE to get to the answer (or at least to a fifty-fifty chance of guessing the right answer). Look at the following example:

74. Which of the following best supports the assertion that intelligence is at least in part inherited?

  (A) Pairs of fraternal twins have a greater correlation of IQ score than do other pairs of siblings.

  (B) Pairs of twins reared together have a greater correlation of IQ score than do pairs of twins reared apart.

  (C) Pairs of identical twins have a greater correlation of IQ score than do pairs of fraternal twins.

  (D) Adopted children and their adoptive parents have a correlation of IQ score that is greater than zero.

  (E) Adopted children and their adoptive parents have a greater correlation of IQ score than do the same children and their biological parents.

Did you read the answer choices for question 74 before you answered on your own? Don't forget, wrong answers are designed to confuse, not to assist. Be sure to follow your smart strategy and *not* look at the answer choices too soon. First, let's do smart strategies for question 74.

Understand the Question/Key Words: Circle the words *intelligence* and *inherited*. Then restate the question:

Which of the answers says genetics affects smarts?

Predict the Answer: If you answered, I don't know, no problem. Simply use what you do know and POE.

Use POE for each answer choice:

(A) Does the fact that *pairs of fraternal twins have a greater correlation of IQ score than do other pairs of siblings* indicate that genetics affects smarts? Careful—are fraternal twins any different genetically from other sibling pairs? If you are unsure, leave this choice and go on.

(B) Does the fact that *pairs of twins reared together have a greater correlation of IQ score than do pairs of twins reared apart* indicate that genetics affects smarts? No, it indicates the opposite because it implies that the nongenetic factors are more significant. Cross it off.

(C) Does the fact that *pairs of identical twins have a greater correlation of IQ score than do pairs of fraternal twins* indicate that genetics affects smarts? Yes. Identical twins come from one egg, while fraternal twins come from two, making fraternal twins genetically less similar. Keep this answer choice and read on.

(D) Does the fact that *adopted children and their adoptive parents have a correlation of IQ score that is greater than zero* indicate that genetics affects smarts? No, it indicates the opposite—nurture over nature. Cross this choice off.

(E) Does the fact that *adopted children and their adoptive parents have a greater correlation of IQ score than do the same children and their biological parents* indicate that genetics affects smarts? No, it also indicates nurture over nature. Cross it off.

You've at least narrowed it down to two choices without even really knowing the answer—that's pretty cool. Now look at the two choices you have not crossed off. Choice (C) very clearly shows genetics affects smarts, while (A) may or may not. What's your best guess? You got it: (C).

Even if you're left with two very hard answer choices to choose between, just choose one and move on. Don't sweat it; **there's no penalty for guessing**. And you can't score another point without moving on to another question!

There's no penalty for guessing, so don't leave anything blank! Maybe you don't spend time on every question, but take an educated guess on those you work on, and choose the same letter for all those you have no idea on or don't have time for. By using the same letter when guessing randomly (what we call your Letter of the Day, or LOTD), you will most likely guarantee yourself a couple extra points!

Your Personal Pace

It is imperative that you choose a pace that is efficient and effective for *you*. It doesn't matter if your best friend can complete the entire section in 30 minutes. You need to work at a pace that will allow you to do as many questions as you can while maintaining accuracy. Set your own personal pace and you will do your personal best.

HOW LONG IS 70 MINUTES?

Right about now you are probably thinking, "Nice idea, and I'll probably finish about 10 questions in 70 minutes following this strategy." Even though you don't need to work through every question on the test to do well, you do need to work efficiently and effectively.

As you know, rushing through the test and getting easy questions wrong is a bad idea. But how slow is too slow? After all, this is a timed test, and you do need to complete a significant number of the questions to do well.

Work Efficiently and Effectively

The best way for you to determine your own personal pace is to work efficiently (don't dawdle) and effectively (get right what you do answer). In other words, although you don't want to rush through and make careless errors, you don't want to spend all day on one question. Work at a pace that allows you to get questions right without dragging your heels. If you find yourself lingering for too long over a question, make a decision and move on. However, if you are doing some good, effective work on a question and have narrowed it down to two choices, don't lose the point because you "need to get to the next question."

Let's take a closer look at the order of difficulty to help you with this idea of working efficiently and effectively.

Question Difficulty, Redux

> **Easy Questions**
>
> - Tend to come early in the test
> - *Always* ask about something you know

Even if you're on Question 3, if you don't know anything about the subject of the question, it won't be easy for you. Conversely, a question on the last third of the test may be tricky, but if you know the topic well, it won't be that hard for you.

How can you score your personal best? Use your smart strategies efficiently and effectively.

Easy Questions Drill

On easy questions, you will be able to accomplish these steps rapidly. Most short, easy questions will take very little time from start to finish. Try this drill, working quickly but carefully. Before you begin, jot down your start time. Once you have finished, note your end time and check your answers for accuracy. Remember, the goal is to be efficient (work rapidly) and effective (work accurately). Let's dive in and test drive those smart-tester strategies.

Start Time: _____

1. Sigmund Freud is thought of as the originator of which of the following perspectives of psychology?

    (A) Biological
    (B) Psychoanalytic
    (C) Behavioral
    (D) Humanistic
    (E) Cognitive

2. A person who is attempting to overcome a heroin addiction is experiencing hallucinations, tremors, and other side effects. These painful experiences associated with the termination of an addiction are known as

    (A) denial
    (B) transduction
    (C) withdrawal
    (D) transference
    (E) psychosis

3. After several trials during which a dog is given a specific type of food each time a light is lit, there is evidence of conditioning if the dog salivates when

    (A) the food is presented and the light is not lit
    (B) the light is lit and the food is not present
    (C) the food and the light occur simultaneously
    (D) a different kind of food is presented
    (E) a tone is sounded when the food is presented

4. The basic unit of the nervous system is called the

    (A) soma
    (B) axon
    (C) cell
    (D) neuron
    (E) synapse

5. Which of the following methods of research is central to the behaviorist perspective?

    (A) Inferential statistics
    (B) Naturalistic observation
    (C) Surveying
    (D) Case study
    (E) Experimentation

End Time: _____

Right: _____

Turn to page 312–313 to check your answers. How did you do? Remember, if you finished in two minutes but missed even one question, you were working too fast. Don't throw away points on the easy questions.

By the Way...

The more psychology you have under your belt, the easier this test will be. The strategies you are learning here are designed to make the most of the psychology knowledge you possess—to keep you from missing answers to questions that you should be getting right. The strategies will also help you stretch your knowledge so you can answer questions about topics you only sort-of know. However, although they will help you make smart guesses, the strategies won't make a question on a completely unfamiliar topic easy.

Medium Questions Drill

You will spend most of your test time on the medium questions. These are the questions that you will know, or sort-of know, but will need to answer very carefully so you don't lose points to tricks and traps. Try the next five questions as you did on the previous drill, working more slowly but still efficiently and effectively: that is, using the strategies that we've been discussing throughout this chapter.

Start Time: _____

33. The primary drives of hunger and thirst are, for the most part, regulated by which of the following?

    (A) The medulla oblongata
    (B) The thalamus
    (C) The hypothalamus
    (D) The kidneys
    (E) The adrenal glands

34. Imposing order on individual details in order to view them as part of a whole is a basic principle of which of the following types of psychologists?

    (A) Behaviorist
    (B) Psychodynamic
    (C) Humanistic
    (D) Gestalt
    (E) Cognitive socialist

35. To determine the number of students in the school who own personal computers, a school bookstore decides to survey the members of the introductory computer science class. A problem with this study is that

   (A) the survey may not elicit the information the store is looking for
   (B) the store is not surveying a representative sample of students
   (C) the survey is being constructed without a hypothesis
   (D) it is unclear as to whether the bookstore will be able to establish causation
   (E) the survey is being given during school hours

36. When an individual looks through a window in the morning, the two regions of the cortex that are stimulated are

   (A) the temporal lobes and the occipital lobes
   (B) the parietal lobes and the frontal lobes
   (C) the frontal lobes and the temporal lobes
   (D) the temporal lobes and the parietal lobes
   (E) the occipital lobes and the parietal lobes

37. Which of the following statements is true of behaviorism?

   (A) It holds that most behaviors are the result of unconscious motives that come into conflict.
   (B) It focuses on the development of the cognitive self in regard to behavior.
   (C) It holds that development is largely a product of learning.
   (D) It emphasizes the role of nature over the impact of nurture.
   (E) It was developed to replace the cognitive and humanistic perspectives.

End Time: _____

Right: _____

Turn to page 313 to check how you did this time. If you missed a question, no big deal. (All the questions in the above two drills are about topics covered in the first five psych-review chapters of this book, so you'll have a chance to review them if you had trouble.) If you missed more than one question and were finished in less than five minutes, you were working too fast. Slow your pace, and pick up your accuracy.

Long Questions

You may have noticed on the medium drill that some questions have much longer answer choices than others. In the earlier sections of the test, you will have a *long-answer* question about every seven or so questions. Near the later part of the test, long-answer questions will occur more frequently. Throwing in questions with long answer choices is one of the ways a test-writer can make a question more difficult and more time-consuming.

To Skip or Not to Skip

Should You Ever Leave a Question Blank?

Maybe you skip it for later, but make sure to bubble in a response through POE and common sense, or your Letter of the Day if you are completely lost.

Imagine yourself taking Section I. You're cruising along through the easy section, feelin' fine. Suddenly, you hit a speed bump. Question 10, a question that should be easy, seems much harder than you would expect. Keep in mind that no order of difficulty is perfect for each individual, especially on an exam that is testing each individual's knowledge of a particular subject. Chances are this particular question is either a misplaced difficult question, or it's about a topic you don't happen to know very well. In any case, does it make sense for you to spend several minutes on question 10 when there are 90 questions to go, many of which will be easier for you than this one? Of course not. Remember, this is your test—you should take it in the order that is best for you. If you have time, circle it and come back. If you have no idea, bubble in your Letter of the Day and move on!

Are We There Yet?—The Toughest Third

How about those tough questions? Should you just skip all of them? Of course not. You should work efficiently and effectively through the easy and medium portions of the test, making sure that you've gotten as many points as you can from those sections. With your remaining time, you should work your way smartly through the most challenging questions.

Once you pass question 70, you can be pretty sure that you have entered the most difficult third of the test. Even without looking at the question number, you can often tell when you've hit the difficult third because, suddenly, every question requires a lot more brainpower than before. How can you get the most points out of this portion of the test?

Do the Right Thing. As we've mentioned, a question is difficult not only if it appears in the tough section of the test, but also if it is about a topic with which you are unfamiliar. Conversely, if you know a particular topic well, a question about it that happens to appear in the difficult portion of the test need not be difficult. Therefore, once you pass question 70, *Do the Right Thing!* This means, you should read each question first to see whether you are familiar with the topic. If you are, go for it. If it sounds like Greek, skip it (draw a box around it so you can come back to it). If you are familiar with the topic of a question, proceed as usual but with caution. Remember, this question was placed late in the test because it is somehow more difficult than the rest. Be sure to use your smart-tester strategies: Understand the Question/Key Words, Predict the Answer, and POE. If you get it down to two choices and don't know which one is correct, make a smart guess and move on. You have a fifty-fifty chance of guessing correctly, so you are a lot better off than when you started.

Smart Guessing = Common Sense. Sometimes you will be familiar with the topic of a question, but not enough to answer the question. In addition to using your usual strategy, you can also use your common sense, and the information you do have, to use POE and then take a smart guess. Look at the following example:

87. Which of the following most accurately lists the stages of Hans Selye's general adaptation syndrome?
     (A) Shock, anger, self-control
     (B) Appraisal, stress response, coping
     (C) Alarm, resistance, exhaustion
     (D) Anxiety, fighting, adapting
     (E) Attack, flight, defense

Now, let's assume you have no idea what Hans Selye's general adaptation syndrome is. You can still follow the smart strategy, and use your common sense to get close to the answer.

Understand the Question/Key Words: Circle *general adaptation syndrome.* Think about what that term might mean:

It has something to do with adapting, and it's a syndrome, which often means something negative.

Predict the Answer: Stages of adaptation that seem to characterize a kind of syndrome.

Use POE:

(A) Are *shock, anger,* and *self-control* stages of adaptation that characterize a kind of syndrome? No, a syndrome would not end up in self-control. Cross it off.

(B) Are *appraisal, stress response,* and *coping* stages of adaptation that characterize a kind of syndrome? No, they seem much more normal and positive. Cross it off.

(C) Are *alarm, resistance,* and *exhaustion* stages of adaptation that characterize a kind of syndrome? This is the most feasible choice so far. Keep it and read on.

(D) Are *anxiety, fighting,* and *adapting* stages of adaptation that characterize a kind of syndrome? Again, a syndrome would not have a last stage of adapting. Cross it off. Don't let the word *adapting* in this choice throw you off.

(E) Are *attack, flight,* and *defense* stages of adaptation that characterize a kind of syndrome? This one also has negative attributes that could constitute a syndrome.

Bonus Tips and Tricks...

Check us out on YouTube for additional test-taking tips and must-know strategies at www.youtube.com/ThePrincetonReview.

Keeping It Clean
Of course, the more psychology you know, the easier all the questions will be. Using common sense and POE will help you out not only when you are unsure of the material, but also when you know the material and want to avoid careless errors and trap answers.

You are left with (C) and (E). Take a guess, and remember that you have narrowed your choices down to a fifty-fifty shot on a question about which you had no clue. The correct answer, by the way, is (C). Given that the name of the syndrome is the "general adaptation syndrome" and not the "best way to cause a fight" syndrome, (C) is your smarter guess.

Here's another example of how your common sense can help you eliminate wrong answers:

(A) Personal conscience is innate, and all human beings develop it at the same rate.
(B) By adulthood, all people judge moral issues in terms of self-chosen principles.

Hey, wait a minute. Where's the question? We've given you these two answer choices to demonstrate how common sense can play an important role in getting rid of wrong answer choices. Let's evaluate these two answer choices. Choice (A) says that *personal conscience is innate, and all human beings develop it at the same rate.* Does that sound accurate? Even without knowing the question, it is hard to imagine that any psychologist would suggest that all human beings develop personal conscience at the same rate. You know this answer cannot be the answer to the question simply by using common sense. Cross it off.

How about (B): *By adulthood, all people judge moral issues in terms of self-chosen principles.* Again, is this statement true? Even if a lot of people judge moral issues in terms of self-chosen principles, it is rare that all people ever do anything the same way. The extreme language of this answer choice can help you determine that it is wrong. Without even knowing the question, you are able to eliminate two answer choices by using your common sense.

Be Selective. In dealing with hard questions, remember that you don't need to work through them all. You choose the difficult questions you want to do and in what order you want to do them. For example, after question 70, you may wish to concentrate on all the short-answer questions because the long-answer questions are more time-consuming and difficult. Place a box around each question you skip so that you can go back to them, and make sure to be careful when bubbling in your answer sheet. If there are particular questions you want to attempt, mark them with a star.

CREATE YOUR PERSONAL PACING STRATEGY

Finally, you will score your best on Section I of the AP Psychology Exam by developing your own optimal strategy. Use the tools we have given you; practice them to make them second nature (the strategy drills in Chapter 4 will help you fine-tune your skills). Once you are comfortable with your question strategy, do some timed work to help determine your personal pacing strategy. As you strengthen your test-taking skills, try to finish more and more of Section I. Determine what working *efficiently and effectively* means for you. And remember, you have an essay portion that will contribute to your final grade, as well. Emphasize your strengths to get the best grade you can. Oh yeah, and you'd better review some psychology, too!

Chapter 2
How to Approach
Free-Response
Questions

OVERVIEW OF THE FREE-RESPONSE SECTION

Section II: Free Response. It has a nice ring to it, doesn't it? That word *free* gives it a melodic sound. Well, don't be fooled. On the AP Psychology Exam, "free response" is simply a euphemism for *timed essays*. Let's review the facts about Section II.

How Do They Score Them?

Before the graders begin reading essays, they are given a "checklist" of points they should look for. The AP Psych bigwigs determine exactly how many points each essay is worth by doing a count. Keep in mind that the readers are locked into that scale—they will not give you an extra point for unrelated information or anything else.

- You are required to answer two essays. The first is Concept Application: you must apply psychological theories to a given fact pattern. The second is Research Design: you must analyze a research study and interpret quantitative data.

- There is no choice—two essays are presented, and you must do both.

- Each essay is worth $16\frac{2}{3}$ percent of your score, or 25 out of the 150 points on the exam.

- Each essay has a specified number of pieces of information you need to provide, usually 7.

Sound Familiar?

Often, when a student realizes he needs to write an essay under timed conditions, panic sets in. As he begins to read the question, his heart races, and he has difficulty concentrating on what the question is asking. He knows he should outline something, but he is afraid he will run out of time, so he just jumps in and starts writing. Midway through paragraph one, feeling a little light-headed, he realizes that he doesn't really understand the question. He glances back at the question but, worried that he's losing precious minutes, decides he needs to forge ahead.

Partway through paragraph two (yes, he did remember to use paragraphs), he realizes that he has skipped a big point he needs to make. Should he cross off what he has written, or do the verbal backpedal until he can work it in? "How much time is left, anyway?" he asks himself. And on it goes.

Relax: All of us at one time or another have felt our sympathetic nervous system kick into gear at the mention of a timed essay. How can you effectively write not one but two essays in a limited period of time? By being a smart tester, of course.

SMART-TESTER ESSAY WRITING

Compare the smart tester's approach to our panicked tester from above. The smart tester knows that she can't write an effective essay without understanding the question. She spends her first 1–2 minutes "working the question over," pulling it apart to make sure she knows exactly what she is being asked to do. Next, she sets up a chart and spends 3–5 minutes outlining the points she will make. She then counts up her points and sketches out the layout of the essay.

In that first 7–10 minutes, the smart tester has done the bulk of the work for her essay without actually writing a word of it. She can then spend the next 15 minutes writing the essay, whose framework she has already created; no skipped points, no major cross-outs. She may even be able to put in some impressive vocabulary. Spending time planning the essay actually gives you more time for writing the essay.

Be the Smart Tester

Because you have read this far in the book, you must be a smart tester. We're now going to teach you all the secrets of writing a great essay (or two, for that matter) without activating your adrenal glands. To become the smart essay-writer, you first need to know what the readers—the people who will grade your essays—are looking for.

What's in an Essay

There are lots of different ways to write a quality essay. However, you have a more specific goal in mind when it comes to the AP Psychology essays—you want to get points. Therefore, you need to know what the graders want so that you can write an essay that will earn a good score. Let's start by taking a peek at what they say they want from a good essay.

According to the College Board's published materials on the AP Psychology free-response questions, you may be asked to do one of the following:

- **Construct/Draw:** Create a graph that illustrates or explains relationships or phenomena.

- **Define:** Provide a specific meaning for a word or concept.

- **Describe:** Provide the relevant characteristics of a specified topic.

- **Draw a conclusion:** Use available information to formulate an accurate statement that demonstrates understanding based on evidence. This is sometimes phrased as, "What is the most appropriate conclusion?"

- **Explain:** Provide information about how or why a relationship, situation, or outcome occurs, using evidence and/or reasoning to support or qualify a claim. **Explain how** typically requires analyzing the relationship, situation, or outcome. **Explain why** typically requires analysis of motivations or reasons for the relationship, situation, or outcome.

- **Identify/State:** Indicate or provide information about a specified topic, without elaboration or explanation.

"Huh?" you ask. Let's simplify. To get a good score on an AP Psych essay, you should do the following in order to make it easy for the grader to award points to you:

- Get right to the point.

- Use psychology terms and proper names of theories, theorists, and so on.

- Define all terms.

Need More Help on Essays?

We've got just the book for that! *How to Write Essays for Standardized Tests* contains advice and examples of best practices on an assortment of AP exams, plus the ACT, and others!

- Support everything with an example or study, preferably from your course work (*not* an example from your own personal life).

- Clearly state the purpose of the example or study (support or contrast).

- Be clear, concise, and direct.

- Underline all key terms.

What Not to Do

In addition, there are a few no-nos that the College Board implies or states outright.

- Do *not* restate the question in your essay.

- Do *not* suggest anything that can be misconstrued as unethical.

- Do *not* write everything you know on the topic; stay focused on the question.

- Do *not* begin writing until you have a clue about what you are going to write.

Beginning to get the picture? Although this may seem like a tall order, let us ease your mind a bit: each of your essays will receive approximately five minutes of the reader's time. What? All that work for a lousy five minutes? Yup. Check out how AP essays are scored.

The Reading

After the AP Exams are given, the College Board and ETS get together a slew of high school teachers and college professors and stick them in a room for six days to do nothing but read essays. ETS and the Board fondly refer to this process as the Reading (always capitalized). During the Reading, the readers are typically required to read hundreds of essays.

The readers first create a rubric by which to grade the essays. Most essays require around 7 pieces of information. Each essay is then read, and a point is given for each required component covered accurately and completely. The points are then added together; most recently, each essay was worth 7 points. Here's an example: A particular essay question has 7 required pieces of information, of which you wrote accurately and completely about 5. 3.5714 is the multiplier because there were 7 points available ($7 \times 3.5714 \approx 25$). Because you supplied 5 pieces of information correctly and accurately, 5 is multiplied by 3.5714, giving you 17.857 out of a possible 25. Note that there are no deductions—just points given for discussing the information correctly and completely. Your essay may be read and scored by a number of readers. For the most recent essay questions, you can read the individual rubrics and required information at https://apstudents.collegeboard.org/courses/ap-psychology/assessment.

Talkin' About Good News

This is all good news for you because it means that you can put together a high-scoring essay without panicking about time constraints and exact wording. Let's work through the smart-tester strategies for writing a high-scoring essay, and then finish up with some pointers for adding polish.

Smart-Tester Strategy #1: Work It

Imagine you are in the boxing ring of the AP Psychology Championship. You have already sustained 70 minutes of multiple-choice sparring, and now you have to take on two more big questions in 50 minutes to come out the winner. When the proctor says "go," you come out of your corner ready to take on that essay question. You're not hanging back, passively reading the question, hoping to understand it. If you took that approach, you'd get pummeled, and so would your score. Instead, you get in there and work it over; you pull it apart, examine each piece, and determine what the important stuff is.

Work It

The first step is reading the entire question. Then, start taking it apart piece by piece.

1. Katya, a computer programmer, is being recruited to join a start-up computer gaming company. She has heard good things about the company and is excited by this opportunity. On the other hand, the company is not conducting face-to-face meetings at the moment and Katya will be interviewed for the position online by a group of managers, which makes her a bit nervous.

Now you should "work over" the above fact pattern. Circle the trigger words—words that indicate transitions and changes in the direction of the sentence—and then underline the critical terms. Make notes as needed to ensure that you understand what is written.

Here's what we did:

1. Katya, a computer programmer, is being recruited to join a start-up computer gaming company. She has <u>heard good</u> things about the company and is <u>excited</u> by this opportunity. (On the other hand,) the company is not conducting face-to-face meetings at the moment and Katya will be interviewed for the position online by a group of managers, which makes her a bit <u>nervous</u>.

She feels conflicted about this opportunity.

Smart-Tester Strategy #2: Chart It

Most first essays start with a fact pattern like this and then go on to ask you about the application of various concepts and theories to these facts. Often the essays have two parts (A and B) that you have to write about. Look at one part at a time:

Part A
Explain how each of the following could apply to Katya's interview experience.

- Sympathetic nervous system
- Approach-avoidance conflict
- Self-efficacy
- Central route of persuasion
- Schachter-Singer two-factor theory

Let's work Part A together. We're being asked to *explain* and *apply* these theories and concepts to Katya's situation. You need to know what the graders are told about this: **definitions alone do NOT score points!** So, no matter how well you might know some of these concepts and how expertly you may define them, without application to these facts you will get no credit for your response. From our breakdown of the introduction, we know that Katya has both positive and negative feelings about her interview. Let's chart accordingly to keep our thinking straight:

Next, look at each topic to make sure that you can 1) define it and 2) apply it. Before you assign a topic to the "positive" or "negative" column, you need to define what it is and apply it to Katya's interview. You will only need an entry in one of these columns, not both. Remember, you're trying to do only enough to earn the point and then move on so that you can hit all of the topics in the 25 minutes you have. So now, your chart might look like this:

	define/apply	positive	negative
• Sympathetic nervous system			
• Approach-avoidance conflict			
• Self-efficacy			
• Central route of persuasion			
• Schachter-Singer two-factor theory			

So far, so good. Now, let's look at Part B:

Part B
Explain how each of the following could apply to the decision-making of the managers.

- Groupthink
- Gender typing

Once again, mark the critical stuff: you must explain and apply, but this time in regard to the managers' hiring decision. Perhaps each topic could tilt the managers' decision in a positive or a negative direction, but remember that you should just cover one or the other. How do you know which one to choose? Choose the one for which you can most easily explain the connection to the topic. Here's how your chart might look:

	define/apply	positive	negative
• Groupthink			
• Gender typing			

But Wait, There's More

You're well on your way to a great essay, but first you need to complete your charts. And don't worry about this taking a long time; it won't after a little practice. Just jot a few notes under the define/apply column and EITHER the "positive" or the "negative" column once you're decided which is the clearer connection for you to explain. Let's do the first part of A together:

For the "Sympathetic Nervous System" part of A, write the following in your define/apply column:

Fight-or-flight; heart rate and respirations increase; maybe "adrenaline rush"

So, you'll begin your response with a brief explanation of what happens when the sympathetic nervous system is activated. Now, you have a decision to make: do you think that this would positively or negatively affect her interview experience? Your "positive" column might have a note like this:

Katya is competent and she knows the company wants her, so activation of the SNS causes her to "get up for the big game" and she will nail the interview.

Or, your "negative" column might look like this:

Activation of the SNS might intensify the nervousness that Katya already feels from having an online interview and might therefore cause her to fumble the interview.

Obviously, if you're not into sports, you'll use some other analogies, but you get the idea. Remember, only do one or the other, not both! Either one of these responses would earn you the point, and then you can move on to the next concept. Avoid the tendency to try to download everything you know about the concepts in your responses. Save time and avoid overkill!

Smart-Tester Strategies #1 and #2

Let's review. Smart-Tester Strategy #1: Work It—work the question over so that you know exactly what you are being asked. While you are working over the question, you will also begin to do Smart-Tester Strategy #2: Chart It—draw your charts and, if you feel comfortable, fill them in at the same time (why add another step?). You may wish to give the question a quick read-through before you begin, but you don't need to artificially separate working the question from writing your outline. This entire process should take you between five and seven minutes.

Smart-Tester Strategy #3: Count It

Most recently, the College Board Readers score your essay on a 0–7 scale. In the case of this question, that means they would assign one point per topic if you did the two things required of you: explain *and* apply. So, now is a good time to go back over what you've charted out and make sure that you have all of the points covered.

Do not despair if there are one or two concepts that you do not know or are unclear about. Students have achieved overall scores of 5 in such situations. The important thing is that if you are hung up on a concept or two, and racking your brain for information that you vaguely remember from a class or from your textbook, you do NOT get bogged down by every individual part of the question and you do NOT ruin your pacing! If necessary, leave a blank for now and move on. Perhaps, during the writing process, when you look at the question with fresh eyes, it will shake something loose from your memory. If not, so be it. You can miss some things here and there and still achieve an excellent score.

One thing that you never want to do is go past 25 minutes for the first essay, "borrowing" time from the second essay. The proctors will not tell you when you have reached the halfway point of your 50 minutes and need to move on to the second question. You need to keep track of that. If you "borrow" time from the second essay, you can wind up in a situation in which you have insufficient time to generate a quality response. Don't do that!

Smart-Tester Strategy #4: Sketch It

Sketch out your essay in the one minute or so before you begin to write. Often, these questions do not require either an introduction or a conclusion. Sometimes, an opening statement can be beneficial.

You are going to define and apply five concepts in part A, so you are going to have five separate paragraphs, which you will indicate by drawing a box around what will be in each paragraph. After that, you will have two paragraphs for Part B. But in which order should you address the five points in Part A? If you feel relatively confident about the five concepts, address them in the order in which they are presented. This makes things easier for the grader and, if there is a paragraph whose subject you haven't been clear about, the grader is instructed to give you credit for the concept that fits in the sequence. If, however, your confidence level varies greatly among the concepts, start with the ones you feel best about and leave any that you feel shaky about to the end. This way, the grader gets a sense of your overall understanding of the material and may give you the benefit of the doubt later on. If you take this "out-of-order" approach, however, you MUST indicate clearly within each paragraph which concept you are addressing. So, it might look like this:

Opening sentence

1   Define and apply sympathetic nervous system

2   Define and apply approach-avoidance conflict

3   Define and apply self-efficacy

4   Define and apply central route of persuasion

5   Define and apply Schachter-Singer two-factor theory

6   Define and apply groupthink

7   Define and apply gender typing

Smart-Tester Strategy #5: Write It

Now that you have a sketch, your essay will practically write itself. You just need to piece it together in a clear, concise manner. As you write, check off each point on your sketch as you complete it. That way you'll be sure not to skip anything. Keep in mind that the readers will not grade your charts or outlines. The essay must be written in paragraph form. Be sure to write in complete sentences. Don't use symbols or bulleted lists to define or give examples. If you are running out of time, continue writing pertinent information. Your essay should take about 10 to 15 minutes to write. Then it's on to the second essay!

The Opening

Did you think we'd desert you without first guiding you through the actual writing? Never! Let's review how to get a good score according to the College Board.

Essay-Writing Guidelines

- If you wish to write an introductory sentence, make sure that it is not a repeat of the question.

- Use psychology terms and proper names of theories, theorists, and other important concepts.

- Define and underline all key terms.

- Support each part with an example or study, preferably from your course work (*not* an example from your own personal life).

- Clearly state the purpose of the example or study (support or contrast).

- Be clear, concise, and direct.

You could simply jump into your discussion of the effect of the sympathetic nervous system (or another concept you felt more confident about if you were going out of order). On the other hand, an acceptable opening sentence might be:

> Katya felt competing emotions when it came to this interview opportunity and each of the following concepts could play into one or the other of these emotions.

Note that this sentence is not going to earn you any points on its own, which is why it is optional. However, it does indicate to the grader that you carefully read the question and that your discussion of each concept might go in a different direction than the one before or after it.

Choose Your Words Wisely

The more appropriate psychological terms you use, the better the point-value of your essay. For example, in your discussion of the sympathetic nervous system, if you use terms like *fight-or-flight* or *adrenaline*, all the better. If your pacing is going along well, you might consider ending this section with the following line:

> Once her interview is over, Katya's parasympathetic nervous system will calm her and bring her back to homeostasis.

While this sentence isn't going to earn you additional points, it may solidify in the grader's mind that you know your stuff and resolve any benefit of the doubt in your favor. But remember that it's only going to help if you have related this new PNS concept to the fact pattern of the interview.

Examples, Examples, Examples

All the College Board literature clearly states that the graders like, and often expect, to see students' points supported by appropriate examples. When inserting examples, remember the following:

1. Don't use examples from your personal life.

2. Make sure they are relevant to your point and make a clear reference to the question being asked.

3. Flag your examples with the words "for example."

A good example is something that you learned in your course, from your own reading, or from this book. A bad example is, "I always feel my heart speed up when I talk online." Enough said.

Before you give the example, make it clear whether it is supporting your point or contesting your point. This procedure ties in perfectly with the third point about examples: always flag your examples with an introductory phrase. Again, the readers are reading your essay quickly. They will pause if they see an example and will be impressed by examples that are clearly delineated. If your example supports a point you just made, flag it with "for example." If it contrasts the point, insert a sentence that introduces it:

> Gender typing may cause these managers to view Katya's candidacy negatively due to their own experiences. For example, due to diversity issues in technology, they may not have encountered many female candidates for these jobs and so be predisposed to view them as unsuitable. As this situation changes, we would hope that there would be accommodation; that is, the managers would change their schemas so as to be more receptive.

Note that the phrase "as this situation changes" introduces a change in direction of the paragraph and further indicates to the grader your understanding of the concept.

Closing

As with the opening, a closing statement is not necessary and is not likely to earn you any specific points. However, if you have time and wish to sum up, make sure that your statement is consistent with the points you have already made.

Plain, Good Writing

Finally, don't add in a lot of fluff. The AP Psych essay questions are pretty meaty. Your job is to write an essay that has no additives or fillers. At the same time, it's important that your essay be complete. Don't skip over points. Your reader is counting up the 7 points you are supposed to make. If you miss one, you lose a point. That also goes for running out of time. There is no reason to run out of time on an essay, and if you do, it will hurt your score. To avoid this problem, use the plan below.

Essay Smart-Tester Strategies	Total Time 7–10 minutes
#1 Work It	1–2 minutes
#2 Chart It	3–5 minutes
#3 Count It	1 minute
#4 Sketch It	1–2 minutes

Essay Smart-Tester Strategies	Total Time 10–15 minutes
#5 Write It	Keep track of your own time. Finish the essay before time is called.

Follow this same timetable for both essays. When you hit the 25-minute mark, you better hustle on to the second essay. If you are still working on essay number one, finish up as quickly as possible and move on.

Finishing Touches

There are just a few more things to make sure you get all the points you can. First, when you've finished an essay, double-check that you have addressed all the points you originally counted. Second, as you move from one thought to another, use trigger words and transitional phrases. For example:

> Just as Katya's high self-efficacy, her belief in her skills as a programmer, could lead to a good performance in the interview, so too might her confidence in knowing that the company is recruiting her lead her to employ the central route of persuasion.

As compared with:

> Katya would use the central route of persuasion because she knows that the managers are recruiting her and will be deeply engaged in the interview.

Although there's nothing wrong with the second sentence, the first sentence creates better flow and more cohesion in the essay.

Also, use the highest level of vocabulary that is comfortable for you. In other words, don't use too much slang, but don't write in a way that will sound awkward or forced. Do your best to use the most concise terminology possible. Misused words stick out like sore thumbs. Err on the side of caution.

Lookin' Good

Lastly, remember that first impressions count. In the case of your essays, the better they look, the more positive a reader is likely to regard them at the outset. Readers can't help but feel better about an essay that is legible and long enough to appear complete. Make sure you indent the paragraphs and neatly cross out mistakes (if you need to).

TIME!
Don't rely on your proctor to keep the time accurately or to remember to give you the 25-minute warning. If, for some reason, your proctor is a flake, you won't be able to use that excuse to explain why your essay is only half done. Wear a watch, and keep your own time.

Put It All Together

Now that you have the knowledge to be a smart essay-writer, put your skills to the test on the following question. (It's a question #2, so "Research Design.") When you are finished, check your work against ours (page 314). You can find many more sample prompts from real tests to practice on at the College Board's AP Students website: apstudents.collegeboard.org/courses/ap-psychology/free-response-questions-by-year. Good luck and good writing!

2. Researchers believe that students' exposure to negative life events is a significant cause of poor school performance. To test their idea, they first analyzed the sorts of events they had in mind and assigned them point values indicating how serious an adverse effect they might have.

   For example, "witnessing a violent crime" was assigned 70 points; experiencing the death of a close family member, 100 points; breaking up with a boyfriend or girlfriend, 30 points; being diagnosed with a sexually transmitted disease, 85 points; and so on.

   Researchers then got permission from the school system to administer a questionnaire to students who gave, or whose parents gave (if they were minors), an informed consent to participate. As part of the questionnaire, students listed the negative life events that they had experienced in the preceding two years. Researchers added the points for each student and found that the totals fell into three clear categories that they labeled "low stress," "medium stress," and "high stress." They then looked at the students' grade point averages and found that these varied inversely with the stress groups (i.e., high stress was correlated with low GPA, etc.), thereby validating their hypothesis. The students and parents involved first found out about these findings when the researchers published them in a professional journal.

Part A

   1. Identify the type of research design used in this study.

   2. State the operational definition of the variable "stress."

   3. Explain how statistical significance would apply to an analysis of this study.

   4. Identify a possible ethical concern about how this research was conducted.

Part B

Explain how the following concepts apply to the study described above.

   5. Hans Selye's general adaptation syndrome

   6. Learned helplessness

   7. Maslow's Hierarchy of Needs

Chapter 3
Using Time
Effectively to
Maximize Points

BECOMING A BETTER TEST-TAKER

Very few students stop to think about how to improve their test-taking skills. Most assume that if they study hard, they will test well, and if they do not study, they will do poorly. Most students continue to believe this even after experience teaches them otherwise. Have you ever studied really hard for an exam and then blown it on test day? Have you ever aced an exam for which you thought you weren't well prepared? Most students have had one, if not both, of these experiences. The lesson should be clear: factors other than your level of preparation influence your final test score. This chapter will provide you with some insights that will help you perform better on the AP Psychology Exam and on other exams, as well.

PACING AND TIMING

A big part of scoring well on an exam is working at a consistent pace. The worst mistake made by inexperienced or unsavvy test-takers is that they come to a question that stumps them, and rather than just skip it, they panic and stall. Time stands still when you're working on a question you cannot answer, and it is not unusual for students to waste five minutes on a single question (especially a question involving a graph or the word EXCEPT) because they are too stubborn to cut their losses. It is important to be aware of how much time you have spent on a given question and on the section you are working. There are several ways to improve your pacing and timing for the test.

Remember, when guessing randomly, choose a letter that you will use consistently, your Letter of the Day (LOTD). If you choose the same letter, odds are that one in five random guesses will be correct. There's a statistical advantage to guessing this way over random guessing.

- **Know your average pace.** While you prepare for your test, try to gauge how long you take on 5, 10, or 20 questions. Knowing how long you spend, on average, per question will help you identify the number of questions you can answer effectively and how best to pace yourself for the test.

- **Have a watch or clock nearby.** You are permitted to have a watch or clock nearby to help you keep track of time. It is important to remember, however, that constantly checking the clock is in itself a waste of time and can be distracting. Devise a plan. Try checking the clock after every 15 or 30 questions to see whether you are keeping the correct pace or whether you need to speed up. This will ensure that you're cognizant of the time but will not permit you to fall into the trap of dwelling on it.

- **Know when to move on.** Because all questions are scored equally, investing appreciable amounts of time on a single question is inefficient and can potentially deprive you of the chance to answer easier questions later on. If you are able to eliminate answer choices, do so, but don't worry about picking a random answer (try picking your Letter of the Day!) and moving on if you cannot find the correct answer. Remember, tests are like marathons; you do best when you work through them at a steady pace. You can always come back to a question you don't know the answer to. When you do, very often you will find that your previous mental block is gone, and you will wonder why the question perplexed you the first time around (as you gleefully move on to the next question). Even if you still don't know the answer, you will not have wasted valuable time you could have spent on easier questions.

- **Be selective.** You don't have to do any of the questions in a given section in order. If you are stumped by an essay or multiple-choice question, skip it or choose a different one. In the section below, you will see that you may not have to answer every question correctly to achieve your desired score. Select the questions or essays that you can answer, and work on them first. This will make you more efficient and give you the greatest chance of getting the most questions correct.

- **Use Process of Elimination on multiple-choice questions.** Many times, one or more answer choices can be eliminated. Every answer choice that can be eliminated increases the odds that you will answer the question correctly. Review the strategies in Chapter 1 to find these incorrect answer choices and increase your odds of getting the question correct.

Remember, when all the questions on a test are of equal value, no one question is that important, and your overall goal for pacing is to get the most questions correct. Finally, you should set a realistic goal for your final score. In the next section, we will break down how to achieve your desired score and ways of pacing yourself to do so.

GETTING THE SCORE YOU WANT

Depending on the score you need, it may be in your best interest not to try to work through every question. Check with the schools to which you are applying. Do you need a 3 to earn credit for the test? If you get a raw score of 68 (out of 100) on the multiple-choice section and do as well on the essays, you will get a 3.

AP Exams in all subjects no longer include a "guessing penalty" of a quarter of a point for every incorrect answer. Instead, students are assessed only on the total number of correct answers. A lot of AP materials, even those you receive in your AP class, may not include this information. It is really important to remember that if you are running out of time, you should fill in all the bubbles before the time for the multiple-choice section is up, using your LOTD. Even if you don't plan to spend a lot of time on every question and even if you have no idea what the correct answer is, it is to your advantage to fill something in.

TEST ANXIETY

Everybody experiences anxiety before and during an exam. To a certain extent, test anxiety can be helpful. Some people find that they perform more quickly and efficiently under stress. If you have ever pulled an all-nighter to write a paper and ended up doing good work, you know the feeling.

However, *too much* stress is definitely a bad thing. Hyperventilating during the test, for example, almost always leads to a lower score. If you find that you stress out during exams, here are a few preemptive actions you can take.

- **Take a reality check.** Evaluate your situation before the test begins. If you have studied hard, remind yourself that you are well prepared. Remember that many others taking the test are not as well prepared, and (in your classes, at least) you are being graded against them, so you have an advantage. If you didn't study, accept the fact that you will probably not ace the test. Make sure you get to every question you know something about. Don't stress out or fixate on how much you don't know. Your job is to score as high as you can by maximizing the benefits of what you do know. In either scenario, it is best to think of a test as if it were a game. How can you get the most points in the time allotted to you? Always answer questions you can answer easily and quickly before you answer those that will take more time.

- **Try to relax.** Slow, deep breathing works for almost everyone. Close your eyes, take a few slow, deep breaths, and concentrate on nothing but your inhalation and exhalation for a few seconds. This is a basic form of meditation, and it should help you to clear your mind of stress and, as a result, concentrate better on the test. If you have ever taken yoga classes, you probably know some other good relaxation techniques. Use them when you can (obviously, anything that requires leaving your seat and, say, assuming a handstand position won't be allowed by any but the most free-spirited proctors). Additionally, chewing gum may help relax you, and studies have suggested that chewing gum before (but not during) an exam may increase your score.

- **Eliminate as many surprises as you can.** Make sure you know where the test will be given, when it starts, what type of questions are going to be asked, and how long the test will take. You don't want to be worrying about any of these things on test day or, even worse, after the test has already begun.

The best way to avoid stress is to study both the test material and the test itself. Congratulations! By reading this book, you are taking a major step toward a stress-free AP Psychology Exam.

Chapter 4
Strategy Drills

USING THE DRILLS IN THIS CHAPTER

The drills in this chapter are designed to help you hone your test-taking skills before you begin your psychology review. Use these drills to practice the various smart-tester strategies you have learned.

DRILL 1: UNDERSTAND THE QUESTION/KEY WORDS

Before you can answer a question, you need to know what it is asking. To avoid careless errors, put the question into your own words before you try to answer it. On some questions, you may find it useful to circle the key word(s) in the question. Use the following drill questions to practice Smart-Tester Strategy #1: Understand the Question/Key Words. The answers are on page 315.

7. Which of the following best summarizes the differences between the psychoanalytic and the behaviorist perspectives?

22. Louis is suffering from severe headaches and occasional moments of disorientation or even mental paralysis. His doctors are interested in examining his brain for lesions. Which of the following technologies would prove most useful in examining various regions of Louis's brain?

39. The somatosensory cortex is the primary area of the

58. In the processing of visual information, a fully integrated image does not appear until the information has reached which of the following regions of the brain?

78. If a participant does not report a stimulus when no stimulus is present in a signal-detection experimental trial, it is known as a

89. The lower the p-value of a study, the

DRILL 2: PREDICT THE ANSWER

Before you even think about looking at the answer choices, you need to have an idea of what the answer to the question might be; otherwise, you will be adrift in a sea of confusion, tricks, and traps. Use the following questions to practice both Understand the Question/Key Words and Predict the Answer. Speaking of answers, see page 315 to check your work on these questions.

5. Thomas knows how to roast meat, cook vegetables, and prepare salad. In order for him to learn to prepare a meal for 20 people, Thomas will most likely employ which of the following learning techniques?

What does the question ask?

What's your answer?

22. The endocrine system is a collection of glands that

What does the question ask?

What's your answer?

35. What was Wilhelm Wundt's contribution to the field of psychology?

What does the question ask?

What's your answer?

45. Which of the following best explains why regeneration is essential for taste receptors?

What does the question ask?

What's your answer?

72. Which of the following technologies is most useful in the study of brain waves?

What does the question ask?

What's your answer?

DRILL 3: USING ALL THREE

Now, practice the first two smart-tester strategies (Understand the Question/Key Words and Predict the Answer) and then find the "credited response" from the choices given. If you're having trouble, use POE to get your answers into the right ballpark. Once you've crossed off what you can, take a smart guess! Answers are on pages 316–317.

15. Of the following variables, which typically requires a measurement that is more complex?

Understand the Question/Key Words.

Predict the Answer.

 (A) Categorical
 (B) Continuous
 (C) Extraneous
 (D) Independent
 (E) Dependent

35. Which of the following most accurately states the role of the iris?

Understand the Question/Key Words.

Predict the Answer.

(A) To provide adaptive trait distinctions (eye color) within a species
(B) To dilate or constrict the pupil in order to regulate the amount of light that enters the eye
(C) To refract light that enters the eye, projecting it onto the retina
(D) To house the aqueous humor and supply the eye with oxygen and nutrients
(E) To transduce visual sensations into visual perceptions of color

42. The nature-nurture controversy concerns

Understand the Question/Key Words.

Predict the Answer.

(A) the question of determinism versus free will
(B) the degree to which the kinesthetic prowess of an individual overrides other aspects of intelligence
(C) the degree to which inborn processes versus environmental factors determine behavior
(D) the natural tendency of humans to nurture their young
(E) the role of unconscious processes as a determinant of behavior

66. Prior to the fall of the Berlin wall, East Berlin schools de-emphasized the individuality of the student. As a result, many of the children from those schools tend to have a(n)

Understand the Question/Key Words.

Predict the Answer.

(A) optimistic explanatory style
(B) pessimistic explanatory style
(C) internal locus of control
(D) external locus of control
(E) indiscriminate set of expectancies

85. A prototypic example of a category is called a(n)

Understand the Question/Key Words.

Predict the Answer.

    (A) expectancy
    (B) defining feature
    (C) concept
    (D) phenotype
    (E) exemplar

DRILL 4: ESSAY DRILL

Before you can write a smart essay, you need to Work Over the Question, then Chart It, Count It, and Sketch It. Practice your smart essay steps on the following essay question. You don't need to write the full essay now, but if you feel like taking it all the way, go "write" ahead! Before you do, be sure to compare your smart steps with ours on pages 317–318.

1. One of the major approaches to learning is classical conditioning.

    A. Explain the process of classical conditioning, defining and illustrating all necessary terms. Show how classical conditioning could be used to

        (1) Condition a monkey to "appreciate" the works of only certain artists

        (2) Teach a group of students a mathematical concept

    B. Explain how both extinction and spontaneous recovery transpire. Use one of the above examples to illustrate.

DRILL 5: POE

You are going to read an awful lot of wrong answer choices while working on Section I of the AP Psychology Exam. And, believe it or not, a lot of those choices are not only wrong, but also just plain silly. Using your knowledge of psychology, plus the information in the question itself, examine each of the following sets of answer choices to determine which is the best answer to the question. Remember, if it's silly, extreme, or fallacious, it cannot be the answer to any question. Check your POE smarts on page 318 when you're finished.

    4. Blah, Blah, Blah?
        (A) Obese people have fewer but larger fat cells than average-weight people.
        (B) Obese people have many more fat cells than average-weight people.

27. Connectionist approaches blah, blah

   (A) are carried out by individual segments of the brain
   (B) occur simultaneously through the action of multiple networks

47. Blah, blah, chunking?

   (A) Christina remembers two new phone numbers by recognizing that each has a familiar exchange and that the second half of each represents a familiar date in history.
   (B) Chelsea learns her times tables by methodically practicing one set each night and then reviewing with flashcards.

85. Blah, blah, person-centered psychotherapy blah

   (A) suppresses negative feelings that arise within the client
   (B) uses a didactic approach to teach the client to correct maladaptive behavior
   (C) accepts the client unconditionally so that their desire for healing will grow

92. Blah, blah, blah, blah, blah

   (A) repressing the client's deviant feelings
   (B) slowly altering the contingencies of reinforcement for the client
   (C) removing the underlying causes of a client's problems for the client

REFLECT

Think about what you've learned in Part IV, and respond to the following questions:

- How will you change your approach to multiple-choice questions?

- What is your multiple-choice guessing strategy? On which part of the test should you be most willing to guess?

- What will you do before you begin writing an essay?

- How will you change your approach to the essays, now that you know that graders are usually looking for 7 pieces of information on which to judge your essay?

- Will you seek further help, outside of this book (such as from a teacher, Princeton Review tutor, or AP Students), on how to approach multiple-choice questions, the essay, or a pacing strategy?

Part V
Content Review for the AP Psychology Exam

HOW TO USE THE CHAPTERS IN THIS PART

You may need to come back to the following content chapters more than once. Your goal is to obtain proficiency of the content you are missing, and a single read of a chapter may not be sufficient. At the end of each chapter, you will have an opportunity to reflect on whether you truly have mastered the content of that chapter. In addition to our review, we strongly urge you to study your textbook and class notes. If there is a topic that you don't fully understand or that is not covered here, be sure to go through your textbook and ask your teacher about it well before test day.

Chapter 5
Foundations: History

PRE-HISTORY AND HISTORY OF PSYCHOLOGY

Psychology is the study of behavior and the mind. **Behavior**, a natural process subject to natural laws, refers to the observable actions of a person or an animal. The **mind** refers to the sensations, memories, motives, emotions, thoughts, and other subjective phenomena particular to an individual or animal that are not readily observed.

Psychology today is a science because it uses systematic observation and the collection of data to try to answer questions about the mind, behavior, and their interactions. Psychology seeks to describe, predict, and explain behavior and the mental processes underlying behavior. In psychology, as in science in general, people tend to accept one theory and proceed under the assumptions of that theory until sufficient data inconsistent with the theory is collected. At this point, the prevailing theory is replaced by another theory. Many theories are simply elaborations or revisions of previous ones. As you read over the history of psychology, pay attention to how theories relate to and influence one another.

The ancient Greeks' speculations on the nature of the mind heavily influenced the pre-history of psychology as a science. Socrates and his student, Plato, argued that humans possess innate knowledge that is not obtainable simply by observing the physical world. Aristotle, by contrast, believed that we derive truth from the physical world. Aristotle's application of logic and systematic observation of the world laid the basis for an empirical, scientific method.

The questions raised by the early Greeks pertain to the concept of **dualism**. Dualism divides the world and all things in it into two parts: body and spirit. Dualism is a theme that recurs often in early psychology, but the distinction between body and spirit prefigures current debates around the difference between the **brain** (that is, the command center of the central nervous system) and the mind (that is, the sensations, memories, emotions, thoughts, and other subjective experiences of a particular individual).

After the heyday of the Greek philosophers, there was a long period of time during which relatively little systematic investigation of psychological issues was conducted. This dearth of investigation was due, in part, to religious beliefs that said that the "spirit" portion of human nature could not be studied scientifically. These same prevailing theological views indicated that studying the natural world was only useful for what it demonstrated about God. These views changed with the advent of the scientific revolution (c. 1600–1700) when great discoveries were being made in biology, astronomy, and other sciences. These discoveries, along with corresponding movements in philosophy and art, made it clear that human nature was indeed subject to scientific inquiry.

René Descartes (1596–1650), an early modern philosopher, continued the dualist view of the human being. He believed that the physical world and all of the creatures in it are like machines, in that they behave in observable, predictable ways. However, Descartes believed that humans were the exception to this rule because they possess minds. The mind, according to Descartes, is not observable and is not subject to natural laws. Descartes hypothesized that the mind and body interact, and the mind controls the body while the body provides the mind with sensory input for it to decipher.

John Locke (1632–1704), another philosopher, extended Descartes's application of natural laws to all things, believing that even the mind is under the control of such laws. Locke's school of thought is known as **empiricism**—the acquisition of truth through observations and experiences. In his book, *Essay Concerning Human Understanding,* Locke proposed that humans are born knowing nothing; Locke used the term **tabula rasa** (Latin for "blank slate") to describe the mind of an infant. Almost all knowledge we have must be learned; almost nothing is innate. Locke felt that all knowledge must derive from experience. Like the future psychologist, B.F. Skinner, Locke emphasized nurture over nature as the greater influence on development.

Thomas Hobbes (1588–1679) believed that the idea of a soul or spirit, or even of a mind, is meaningless. Hobbes's philosophy is known as **materialism**, which is the belief that the only things that exist are matter and energy. What we experience as consciousness is simply a by-product of the machinery of the brain. In addition to Locke, Hobbes greatly influenced behaviorism, which will be discussed later.

The 19th century was a time of great discovery in biology and medicine. One new theory in particular revolutionized science—the theory of natural selection. In *On the Origin of Species* (1859), **Charles Darwin** (1809–1882) proposed a theory of **natural selection**, according to which all creatures have evolved into their present states over long periods of time. This evolution occurs because there exists naturally occurring variation among individuals in a species, and the individuals that are best adapted to the environment are more likely to survive and then reproduce—and are likely to produce more successful offspring. Their offspring, in turn, will probably have some of the traits that made their predecessors more likely to survive. Over time, this process 'selects' physical and behavioral characteristics that promote survival in a particular environment. **Evolutionary theory** affected psychology by providing a way to explain differences between species and justifying the use of animals as a means to study the roots of human behavior.

Many credit **Wilhelm Wundt** (1832–1920) as the founder of the science of psychology. In 1879 in Leipzig, Germany, Wundt opened a laboratory to study consciousness. Wundt was trained in physiology and hoped to apply the methods that he used to study the body to the study of the mind. **Edward Titchener** (1867–1927) was a student in Wundt's laboratory and was one of the first to bring the science of psychology to the United States. Titchener sought to identify the smallest possible elements of the mind, theorizing that understanding all of the parts would lead to the understanding of the greater structure of the mind. This theory, known as **structuralism**, entails looking for patterns in thought, which are illuminated through interviews with a subject describing their conscious experience. This interview process is known as **introspection**. For example, the experimenter could present stimuli to subjects, ask them to describe their conscious experience, and then work to identify commonalities among various participants' conscious descriptions.

William James (1842–1910), an American psychologist, opposed the structuralist approach. Instead, he argued that what is important is the function of the mind, such as how it solves a complex problem. James, heavily influenced by Darwin, believed that the important thing to understand is how the mind fulfills its purpose. This function-oriented approach is appropriately called **functionalism**.

Darwin in a Nutshell

Behavior evolves just like physiology: both function to help individuals survive.

A number of major historical figures in psychology are discussed in the following chapters, as their work informs the units of study in AP Psychology. But other figures also play an important role in the history of psychology, due to both their individual accomplishments as well as the light they shed on the gender biases that affected their careers in particular and the field as a whole.

Dorothea Dix was crucial in advocating for the rights of mentally ill poor people, and she was instrumental in founding the first public mental hospital in the United States. **Mary Whiton Calkins** was the first female graduate student in psychology, although she was denied a PhD because of her gender. (She outscored all of the male students in her qualifying exams.) **Margaret Floy Washburn** was not only the first female PhD in psychology, she also served as the second female president of the American Psychological Association (APA), an organization formed in 1892. (**G. Stanley Hall** was its first president.) Although Washburn's thesis was the first foreign study published by Wilhelm Wundt, she was not allowed to join the official organization of experimental psychologists because of her gender.

Today, about two-thirds of doctorates in psychology are held by women, and about half of the presidents of the Association for Psychological Science have been women.

APPROACHES

The theories discussed above laid the groundwork for modern psychology as a science. This next section will deal with nine of the most prominent approaches to modern psychology. The roots of these approaches are in the theoretical perspectives we discussed above.

Approach 1: Biological

Biological psychology is the field of psychology that seeks to understand the interactions between anatomy and physiology (particularly, the physiology of the nervous system) and behavior. This approach is practiced by directly applying biological experimentation to psychological problems: for example, in determining which portion of the brain is involved in a particular behavioral process. To accomplish this, researchers might use CAT scans, MRIs, EEGs, or PET scans.

Approach 2: Behavioral Genetics

Behavioral genetics is the field of psychology that explores how particular behaviors may be attributed to specific, genetically based psychological characteristics. This perspective takes into account biological predispositions as well as the extent of influence that the environment had on the manifestation of that trait. For example, a person studying behavioral genetics might investigate to what extent risk-taking behavior in adolescents is attributable to genetics.

Approach 3: Behavioralist

Behaviorism posits that psychology is the study of observable behavior. The mind or mental events are unimportant, as they cannot be observed. **Classical conditioning**, first identified by Ivan Pavlov (1849–1936), was one of the behaviorists' most important early findings. Classical conditioning is defined as a basic form of learning in which a behavior comes to be elicited by a formerly neutral stimulus. **John Watson** (1878–1958) and his assistant Rosalie Rayner applied classical conditioning to humans in the famed Little Albert experiment: they made loud sounds behind a 9-month-old whenever he would touch something white and furry, and voila: he was afraid of everything white and furry afterwards. **B.F. Skinner** (1904–1990), through the development of his Skinner Box, described **operant conditioning**, in which a subject learns to associate a behavior with an environmental outcome. Although behaviorism is no longer the prevailing approach in psychology, many behavioral principles are still used in **behavior modification**—a set of techniques in which psychological problems are considered to be the product of learned habits, which can be unlearned by the application of behavioral methods.

Approach 4: Cognitive

Cognitive psychology is an approach rooted in the idea that to understand people's behavior, we must first understand how they construe their environment—in other words, how they think. This approach combines both the structuralist approach of looking at the subcomponents of thought and the functionalist approach of understanding the purpose of thought. The cognitive approach, sometimes called the cognitive-behavioral approach, largely replaced the purely behavioral approach as the predominant psychological method used in the United States.

Approach 5: Humanistic

The **humanistic approach** is rooted in the philosophical tradition of studying the roles of consciousness, free will, and awareness of the human condition. This is a holistic study of personality that developed in response to a general dissatisfaction with behaviorism's inattention to the mind and its function. Humanistic psychologists emphasize personal values and goals and how they influence behavior, rather than attempting to divide personality into smaller components. **Abraham Maslow** (1908–1970) proposed the idea of self-actualization, the need for individuals to reach their full potential in a creative way. Attaining **self-actualization** means accepting yourself and your nature, while knowing your limits and strengths. **Carl Rogers** (1902–1987) stressed the role of **unconditional positive regard** in interactions and the need for a positive self-concept as critical factors in attaining self-actualization.

Are You a Visual Learner?

If you're getting overwhelmed by all of the concepts for an AP course, consider looking at our *Fast Track* or *ASAP* books, available for some AP subjects. These handy guides focus on the most-tested content or present it in a friendly, illustrated fashion.

Approach 6: Psychoanalytic/Psychodynamic

While laboratory psychology was passing through its various theories, **Sigmund Freud** (1856–1939) developed a theory of human behavior known as **psychoanalytic theory**. Freud was concerned with individuals and their mental problems. Freud drew a distinction between the **conscious mind**—a mental state of awareness that we have ready access to—and the **unconscious mind**—those mental processes that we do not normally have access to but that still influence our behaviors, thoughts, and feelings. Psychoanalytic theory stresses the importance of early childhood experiences and a child's relationship with their parents to the development of personality. The psychoanalytic approach to therapy focuses on the resolution of unconscious conflicts through uncovering information that has been **repressed**, or buried in the unconscious.

Approach 7: Sociocultural

Those subscribing to the **sociocultural approach** believe that the environment a person lives in has a great deal to do with how the person behaves and how others perceive that behavior. According to this approach, cultural values vary from society to society and must be taken into account if one wishes to understand, predict, or control behavior.

Approach 8: Evolutionary

The **evolutionary approach** draws upon the theories of Darwin. Behavior can best be explained in terms of how adaptive that behavior is to our survival. For example, fear is an adaptive evolutionary response; without fear, our survival would be jeopardized.

Approach 9: Biopsychosocial

As the name implies, the **biopsychosocial approach** emphasizes the need to investigate the interaction of biological, psychological, and social factors as contributing to a behavior or a mental process.

Study Tip

The distinctions among the different approaches in psychology are absolutely some of the most essential ideas for you to understand for the AP Psychology Exam. Let's use the common example of risk-taking in adolescence and explore that using each of the nine different approaches. Often, the questions on the exam that explore these distinctions will have five different approaches in the answer choices. Think about what words you might look for in the question stem that will guide you to one rather than the others.

Approach	Question	Cause of Behavior	Methods
Biological	How is the physiology of high risk-takers different from that of non-risk-takers?	Physiology	Brain scans
Behavioral genetics	Which genes contribute to the development of risk-taking?	Genes	Genetic analysis
Behavioral	How does rewarding or punishing a risk-taker affect their behavior?	Learning and reflexes	Behavior modification
Cognitive	How do risk-takers think and solve problems?	Thoughts	Computer models of memory networks
Humanistic	How does the adolescent's self-esteem encourage or discourage risk-taking behavior?	Self-concept	Talk therapy
Psychoanalytic/ Psychodynamic	How might a child's early experiences affect risk-taking in adolescence?	Unconscious mind	Dream analysis, talk therapy
Sociocultural	How might an adolescent's culture lead to risk-taking?	Cultural environment	Cross-cultural studies
Evolutionary	Is risk-taking an evolutionarily adaptive trait?	Natural selection	Species comparison
Biopsychosocial	What factors predict risk-taking?	Interaction of biology with individual psychological and social factors	Combination of the above

DOMAINS

Broad areas of psychological research are also known as domains. A question that concerns the effect of drugs on behavior refers to the **biological** domain. But a question that deals with relationships between drug users and their families refers to the **social** domain. And a question that considers treatment options for someone addicted to drugs deals with the **clinical** domain.

Other domains include: **cognitive** (What thoughts might someone entertain to justify their drug use?), **counseling** (How might a school counselor talk to a student about drugs?), **developmental** (At what ages might someone be more susceptible to peer pressure?), and **educational** (How effective are school-based programs?).

Yet other domains include: **experimental** (dealing with experiments, as discussed in the next chapter), **industrial-organizational** (dealing with workplaces), **personality** (dealing with—you guessed it!—personality), **psychometric** (dealing with how to measure things in psychology), and the **positive domain** (which focuses on positive aspects and strengths of human behavior).

KEY TERMS

History
psychology
behavior
mind and brain
René Descartes and dualism
John Locke and empiricism
tabula rasa
Thomas Hobbes and materialism
Charles Darwin and evolutionary
    theory
natural selection
Wilhelm Wundt and structuralism
Edward Titchener and introspection
William James and functionalism
Dorothea Dix
Mary Whiton Calkins
Margaret Floy Washburn
G. Stanley Hall

Approaches
biological psychology
behavioral genetics
behaviorism
    John Watson and classical
        conditioning
    B.F. Skinner and operant
        conditioning
    behavior modification
cognitive psychology

humanistic approach
    Abraham Maslow and self-
        actualization
    Carl Rogers and unconditional
        positive regard
psychodynamic/psychoanalytic
    approach
    Sigmund Freud and
        psychoanalytic theory
    conscious mind vs. unconscious
        mind
    repressed
sociocultural approach
evolutionary approach
biopsychosocial approach

Domains
biological
social
clinical
cognitive
counseling
developmental
educational
experimental
industrial-organizational
personality
psychometric
positive

Chapter 5 Drill

See Chapter 19 for answers and explanations.

1. A cognitive psychologist would likely be most interested in

   (A) concentration of neural transmitters in the spinal cord
   (B) unconditional positive regard in the therapeutic setting
   (C) token economies in prisons
   (D) perceptual speed on word-association tests
   (E) development of fine motor skills in toddlers

2. The concept of *tabula rasa*, or "blank slate" (the idea that human beings come into the world knowing nothing, and thereafter acquire all of their knowledge through experience) is most closely associated with

   (A) David Hume
   (B) Charles Darwin
   (C) John Locke
   (D) Sigmund Freud
   (E) Erich Fromm

3. The concept of dualism refers to the division of all things in the world into

   (A) thought and action
   (B) body and spirit
   (C) structural and functional
   (D) theoretical and practical
   (E) dependent and independent

4. The humanistic approach to psychology emphasizes the importance of

   (A) childhood experiences
   (B) biological predispositions
   (C) maladaptive thoughts
   (D) free will and conscious awareness
   (E) cultural experiences

5. Psychologists who emphasize the importance of repressed memories and childhood experiences subscribe to which of the following perspectives?

   (A) Cognitive
   (B) Behavioral
   (C) Psychodynamic
   (D) Sociocultural
   (E) Medical/biological

6. Psychologists who believe behaviors are learned most likely ascribe to the philosophy of

   (A) Abraham Maslow
   (B) B.F. Skinner
   (C) Carl Rogers
   (D) Sigmund Freud
   (E) Wilhelm Wundt

7. According to the psychoanalytic perspective, a person who does not remember a painful event experiences which defense mechanism?

   (A) Denial
   (B) Self-actualization
   (C) Projection
   (D) Consciousness
   (E) Repression

8. Carl Rogers is most closely associated with which psychological approach?

   (A) Unconditional positive regard
   (B) Cognitive psychology
   (C) Humanistic
   (D) Sociocultural
   (E) Behaviorism

9. According to Abraham Maslow's hierarchy of needs, the most basic of human needs is

   (A) self-actualization
   (B) esteem
   (C) belonging
   (D) safety
   (E) physiological

10. Which approach would most likely involve the study of identical twins separated at birth?

    (A) Biological
    (B) Behavioral genetics
    (C) Humanistic
    (D) Sociocultural
    (E) Biopsychosocial

REFLECT

Respond to the following questions:

- Which topics in this chapter do you hope to see on the multiple-choice section or essay?

- Which topics in this chapter do you hope not to see on the multiple-choice section or essay?

- Regarding any psychologists mentioned, can you pair the psychologists with their contributions to the field? Did they contribute significant experiments, theories, or both?

- Regarding any theories mentioned, can you distinguish between differing theories well enough to recognize them on the multiple-choice section? Can you distinguish them well enough to write a fluent essay on them?

- Can you define the key terms at the end of the chapter?

- Which parts of the chapter will you review?

- Will you seek further help, outside of this book (such as from a teacher, Princeton Review tutor, or AP Students), on any of the content in this chapter—and, if so, on what content?

Chapter 6
Foundations:
Methods and
Approaches

EXPERIMENTAL, CORRELATIONAL, AND CLINICAL RESEARCH

Three major types of research in psychology include: experimental, correlational, and clinical. An **experiment** is an investigation seeking to understand relations of cause and effect. The experimenter changes a variable (cause) and measures how it, in turn, changes another variable (effect). At the same time, the investigator tries to hold all other variables constant so she can attribute any changes to the manipulation. The manipulated variable is called the **independent variable**. The **dependent variable** is what is measured. For example, an experiment is designed to determine whether watching violence on television causes aggression in its viewers. Two groups of children are randomly placed in front of either violent or nonviolent television programs for one hour. The program type is the independent variable because it can be manipulated by the experimenter. Afterward, a large doll may be placed in front of each child for one hour while the experimenter records the number of times that child hits, kicks, or punches the doll. This behavior is the dependent variable because it is the variable that is measured. The presence of the doll in both groups is the **control variable**, because it is constant in both groups.

Also Remember...

Other terms to remember include the following: the group receiving or reacting to the independent variable is the **experimental group;** the **control group** does not receive the independent variable but should be kept identical in all other respects. Using two groups allows for a comparison to be made and causation to be determined.

In order to draw conclusions about the result of the controlled experiment, it is important that certain other conditions are met. The researcher identifies a specific **population,** or group of interest, to be studied. Because the population may be too large to study effectively, a **representative sample** of the population may be drawn. **Representativeness** is the degree to which a sample reflects the diverse characteristics of the population that is being studied.

Random sampling is a way of ensuring maximum representativeness. Once sampling has been addressed, subjects are **randomly assigned** into both the experimental and control groups. Random assignment is done to ensure that each group has minimal differences.

Sampling Bias

A classic example of unintentional sampling bias occurred during the 1948 U.S. Presidential Election: a survey was conducted by randomly calling households and asking them whom they intended to vote for, Harry Truman or Thomas Dewey. Based on this phone survey, Dewey was projected to win. The results of the election proved otherwise, as Truman was re-elected. What could have possibly gone wrong? In 1948, having a telephone was not such a common thing, and households that had them were generally wealthier. As a result, the "random" selection of telephone numbers was not a representative sample because many people (a large proportion of whom voted for Truman) did not have telephone numbers. A more recent example occurred in the 1990's and early 2000's when telephone polls were found to have undercounted young voters because all of the calls were being made over landlines, while younger people were relying exclusively on cell phones. For the purposes of the test, you should be able to identify the following types of sampling **biases**:

- The **bias of selection** from a specific real area occurs when people are selected in a physical space. For example, if you wanted to survey college students on whether or not they like their football team, you could stand on the quad and survey the first 100 people that walk by. However, this would not be completely random because people who don't have an upcoming class at that time are unlikely to be represented.

- **Self-selection bias** occurs when the people being studied have some control over whether or not to participate. A participant's decision to participate may affect the results. For example, an Internet survey might elicit responses only from people who are highly opinionated and motivated to complete the survey.

- **Pre-screening** or **advertising bias** occurs often in medical research; how volunteers are screened or where advertising is placed might skew the sample. For example, if a researcher wanted to prove that a certain treatment helps people to stop smoking, the mere act of advertising for people who "want to quit smoking" might provide only a sample of people who are already highly motivated to quit and might have done so without the treatment.

- **Healthy user bias** occurs when the study population tends to be in better shape than the general population. As with the bias of selection from a specific real area, this is an instance in which those subjects might not, in turn, accurately represent the true diversity of the target population.

To avoid inadvertently influencing the results, as in the previous examples, researchers use a **single-** or **double-blind design**. Single-blind design means that the subjects do not know whether they are in the control or experimental group. In a double-blind design, neither the subjects nor the researcher knows who is in the two groups. Double-blind studies are designed so that the experimenter does not inadvertently change the responses of the subject, such as by using a different tone of voice with members of the control group than with the experimental group. Obviously, a third party has the appropriate records so that the data can be analyzed later. In some double-blind experiments, the control group is given a **placebo**, a seemingly therapeutic object or procedure, which causes the control group to believe they could be in the experimental group but actually contains none of the tested material.

Correlational research involves assessing the degree of association between two or more variables or characteristics of interest that occur naturally. It is important to note that, in this type of design, researchers do not directly manipulate variables but rather observe naturally occurring differences. If the characteristics under consideration are related, they are correlated. It is important to note that *correlation does not prove causation;* correlation simply shows the strength of the relationship among variables. For example, poor school performance may be correlated with lack of sleep. However, we do not know whether lack of sleep caused the poor performance, or whether the poor school performance caused the lack of sleep, or whether some other unidentified factor influenced them both. If an unknown factor is playing a role, it is known as a **confounding variable**, a **third variable**, or an **extraneous variable**. One way to gather information for correlational studies is through **surveys**. Using either questionnaires or interviews, one can accumulate a tremendous amount of data and study relationships among variables. Such techniques are often used to assess voter characteristics, teen alcohol and drug use, and criminal behavior. For example, survey studies might examine the relationship between socioeconomic status and educational levels.

Types of Research

Two specific types of research that can be set up as correlational or experimental designs are **longitudinal studies** and **cross-sectional studies**. Longitudinal studies happen over long periods of time with the same subjects (e.g., studying the long-term effects of diet and exercise on heart disease), and cross-sectional studies are designed to test a wide array of subjects from different backgrounds to increase generalizability.

Correlational studies can be preferred to experiments because they are less expensive, not as time consuming, and easier to conduct. In addition, some relationships cannot be ethically studied in experiments. For example, you may want to study how child abuse affects self-efficacy in adulthood, but no one will allow you to randomly assign half of your baby participants to the child-abuse condition. One danger in surveys that researchers need to take into account is that some responders may not be completely honest in their answers, especially when asked about controversial subjects. They may respond with what they think is socially correct or what the questioner wants to hear. This is referred to as social desirability bias, or courtesy bias.

Clinical research often takes the form of case studies. **Case studies** are intensive psychological studies of single individuals. These studies are conducted under the assumption that an in-depth understanding of single cases will allow for general conclusions about other similar cases. Case studies have also been used to investigate the circumstances of the lives of notable figures in history. Frequently, multiple case studies on similar cases are combined to draw inferences about issues. Researchers must be careful, though, because case studies, like correlational ones, cannot lead to conclusions regarding causality. Sigmund Freud and Carl Rogers used numerous case studies to draw their conclusions about psychology. The danger of generalizing from the outcomes of case studies is that the individuals studied may be atypical of the larger population. This is why researchers try to ensure that their studies are **generalizable**—that is, applicable to similar circumstances because of the predictable outcomes of repeated tests.

Experimental Design

Two important features of studies are the **conceptual definition** and the **operational definition**. Whereas the conceptual definition is the theory or issue being studied, the operational definition refers to the way in which that theory or issue will be directly observed or measured in the study. For example, in a study on the effects of adolescent substance abuse, the way in which taking drugs affects adolescent behavior is the conceptual definition, while the number of recorded days the student is absent from school due to excessive use of substances is the operational definition.

Operational definitions have to be internally and externally valid. **Internal validity** is the certainty with which the results of an experiment can be attributed to the manipulation of the independent variable rather than to some other, confounding variable. **External validity** is the extent to which the findings of a study can be generalized to other contexts in the "real world." The principal threats to internal validity are confounding variables, variables that haven't been adequately controlled by the experimenter. The principal threat to the external validity of an experiment is the often artificial nature of the experimental environment. A laboratory may not resemble the real world very much, making it difficult to generalize results to the real world. It is also important that the study have **reliability**, which is whether or not the same results appear if the experiment is repeated under similar conditions. A related concept is **inter-rater reliability**, the degree to which different raters agree on their observations of the same data.

Study Tip

Think about creating a simple chart for the key types of research: experiment, correlational study (e.g. a survey), naturalistic observation, case study. Have a column marked "advantages" and one marked "disadvantages." Each has its strengths and weaknesses. Your ability to complete the chart will go a long way to helping answer this type of question.

OTHER TYPES OF RESEARCH

In addition to organizing experiments inside of a lab, researchers can observe behavior outside of the lab; such naturalistic observation has enriched our knowledge of psychology. The advantage of **naturalistic observation** is that it allows the study of authentic real-world behaviors; however, its disadvantage is the difficulty of controlling for the numerous extraneous variables present in real-world environments, which can limit the reliability of findings.

STATISTICS

Psychologists and other scientists collect data. This data is then subjected to statistical analysis. Statistical methods can be divided into descriptive and inferential statistics. **Descriptive statistics** summarize data, whereas **inferential statistics** allow researchers to test hypotheses about data and determine how confident they can be in their inferences about the data.

Descriptive Statistics

Descriptive statistics do just what their name implies—they describe data. They do not allow for conclusions to be made about anything other than the particular set of numbers they describe. Commonly used descriptive statistics are the mean, the mode, and the median. These descriptive statistics are measures of **central tendency**—that is, they characterize the typical value in a set of data.

MMM MM!

The Mean, Mode, and Median Measure the Middle!

The **mean** is the arithmetic average of a set of numbers. The **mode** is the most frequently occurring value in the data set. (If two numbers both appear with the greatest frequency, the distribution is called **bimodal**.) The **median** is the number that falls exactly in the middle of a distribution of numbers. These statistics can be represented by a **normal curve.** In a perfectly normal distribution, the mean, median, and mode are identical. The **range** is simply the largest number minus the smallest number.

Although the mean, the mode, and the median give approximations of the central tendency of a group of numbers, they do not tell us much about the variability in that set of numbers. **Variability** refers to how much the numbers in the set differ from one another. The **standard deviation** measures a function of the average dispersion of numbers around the mean and is a commonly used measure of variability. For example, say you have a set of numbers that has a mean of 100. If most of those numbers are close to 100, say, ranging from 95 to 105, then the standard deviation will be small. However, if the mean of 100 comes from a set of numbers ranging from 50 to 150, then the standard deviation will be large.

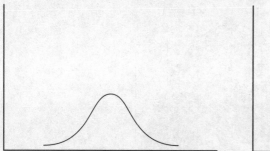 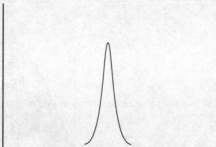

The curve on the left is shorter and wider than the curve on the right, because the curve on the left has a bigger standard deviation.

The graph of the normal distribution depends on two factors—the mean and the standard deviation. The mean of the distribution determines the location of the center of the graph, and the standard deviation determines the height and width of the graph. When the standard deviation is large, the curve is short and wide; when the standard deviation is small, the curve is tall and narrow. All normal distributions look like a symmetric, bell-shaped curve, as shown below.

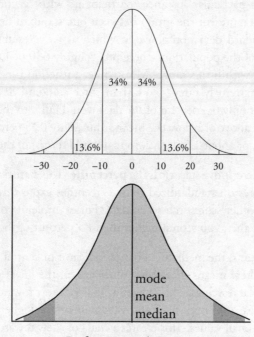

Perfect Normal Curve

In a typical distribution of numbers, about 68 percent of all scores are within one standard deviation above or below the mean, and about 95 percent of all scores are within two standard deviations above or below the mean. So, for example, IQ is typically said to have a mean of 100 and a standard deviation of 15, so a person with a score of 115 is one standard deviation above the mean.

Q: What is standard deviation?

Answer on page 130.

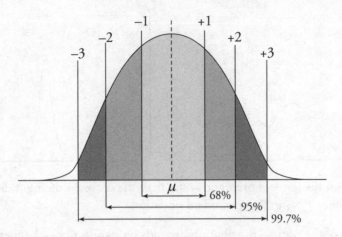

It's unlikely that there will be any questions that actually exercise your math skills, but you should be able to read and interpret a graph and understand what the standard deviation represents in a study. For example, suppose that 1,000 subjects participate in a study on reaction time and that the reaction times of the subjects are normally distributed with a mean of 1.3 seconds and a standard deviation of 0.2 second. In this particular instance, participants with reaction times between 1.1 and 1.5 seconds represent the group between one standard deviation below the mean and one standard deviation above it, which as we've established is generally around 68 percent of the population. Therefore, roughly 680 of 1,000 people would have reaction times within this range. Meanwhile, a reaction time of more than 1.9 seconds would be extremely rare—more than three standard deviations above the mean. It's likely that only 0.3 percent of the data would fall into the category of three standard deviations above or below the mean. Thus, only 0.15 percent would be that far above the mean, or about 1.5 (1 or 2, in real-world terms) of the 1,000 subjects.

A: Standard deviation measures the average distribution of numbers around the mean.

Another common descriptive statistic is the **percentile**. This statistic is used frequently when reporting scores on standardized tests. Percentiles express the standing of one score relative to all other scores in a set of data. For example, if your SAT score is in the 85th percentile, then you scored higher than 85 percent of the other test-takers.

In skewed distributions, the median is a better indicator of central tendency than the mean. A **positive skew** means that most values are on the lower end, but there are some exceptionally large values. This creates a "tail" or skew toward the positive end. A **negative skew** means the opposite: most values are on the higher end, but there are some exceptionally small values. This creates a "tail" or skew toward the negative end.

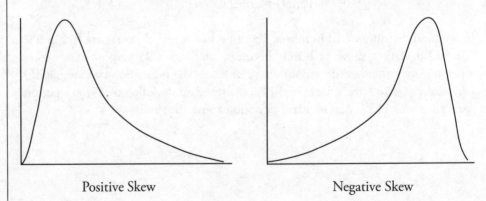

Positive Skew   Negative Skew

Be aware that math questions about normal distributions can appear on the test. Because skewed distributions do not all share the same mathematical properties, questions about percentages and these distributions are often trick questions.

When looking at correlational data, as described above, we need statistical techniques to describe how the attributes we are studying relate to one another. The **correlation coefficient** is a statistic that will give us such information. The correlation coefficient is a numerical value that indicates the degree and direction of the relationship between two variables. Correlation coefficients range from +1.00 to –1.00. The sign (+ or –) indicates the direction of the correlation, and the number (0 to 1.00) indicates the strength of the relationship. The **Pearson correlation coefficient** is a specific type of correlation coefficient that describes how close to linear the relationship between two attributes is. Pearson correlations are typically measured on a scale ranging from 1 to 0 to –1. A correlation of 1 indicates a perfect positive correlation. This means that as attribute X increases, attribute Y always increases proportionally. A correlation of –1 is a perfect negative correlation: as the value of attribute X increases, the value of attribute Y always decreases proportionally. A correlation of 0 indicates that the attributes are not related.

Positive Correlation (As years of education increase, income increases.)

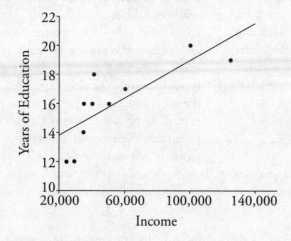

Negative Correlation (As absences for math lessons increase, math score decreases.)

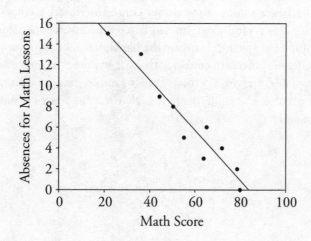

To use another example, take the following study, which assessed 200 male children from ages 1 to 12. A standardized questionnaire was given to the parents of the children and used to check the children's "agreeableness" on a scale from 0 to 5. Additionally, psychologists took standard measures of the behavioral problems exhibited by the children. After the incidents were totaled for each subject, the psychologists found a correlation between child agreeableness and later behavioral problems of –0.6.

Correlation and Causation

A famous example of the tricky relationship between correlation and causation can be taken from an observation once made about New York City: that the murder rate is directly correlated to the sale of ice cream (as ice-cream sales increase, so do the number of murders). Does this mean that buying ice cream is definitively the cause of the increase in murders? Of course not! When two variables are correlated (especially two variables that are as complex as the measures of human behavior studied in the example above), there are always a number of other factors that could be influencing either correlated variable. In the ice cream/murder example, one such potential confounding variable might be temperature; as the temperature rises, more crimes are committed, but people also tend to eat more cold foods, such as ice cream.

You don't need any math here either, but you do have to understand that this is an inverse correlation between the scores: as the child's agreeableness increases, behavioral problems decrease. Don't forget, however, what we stressed earlier in this chapter: *correlation does not imply causation.*

Inferential Statistics

Inferential statistics are used to determine our level of confidence in claiming that a given set of results would be extremely unlikely to occur if the result were only up to chance. When experiments are conducted, they are typically conducted using small groups of people. However, psychologists typically want to be able to generalize the results of the experiments to larger groups of people, perhaps even to all people. The small group of people in an experiment constitutes the sample, and the large group to whom the psychologist is trying to generalize is called the population. It is important that the sample reflects the characteristics of the population as a whole. If it does, then the sample is referred to as being representative.

Sample size refers to the number of observations or individuals measured. The sample size is typically denoted by N (the total number of subjects in the sample being studied) or n (the total number of subjects in a subgroup of the sample being studied). While larger sample sizes always confer increased accuracy, the sample size used in a study is typically determined based on convenience, expense, and the need to have sufficient statistical power (the likelihood that your sample includes a sufficient number of subjects to conclude that the hypothesis being evaluated is true within an acceptable margin of error). Larger sample sizes are always better—the larger the sample size, the more likely it is that the inferences about the broader population are correct.

Inferential statistics are tools for hypothesis testing. The **null hypothesis** states that a treatment had no effect in an experiment. The **alternative hypothesis** is that the treatment did have an effect. Inferential statistics allow us the possibility of rejecting the null hypothesis with a known level of confidence—that is, of saying that our data would be extremely unlikely to have occurred were the null hypothesis true. Tests such as these are statistically significant because they enable us to examine whether effects are likely to be a result of treatment or are likely to be simply the normal variations that occur among samples from the same population. If a result is found to be statistically significant, then that result may be generalized with some level of confidence to the population.

Alpha is the accepted probability that the result of an experiment can be attributed to chance rather than the manipulation of the independent variable. Given that there is always the possibility that an experiment's outcome can happen by chance, no matter how improbable, psychologists usually set alpha at 0.05, which means that an experiment's results will be considered statistically significant if the probability of the results happening by chance is less than 5 percent.

Two primary types of errors can occur when testing a hypothesis. A **Type I error** refers to the conclusion that a difference exists when, in fact, this difference does not exist. A **Type II error** refers to the conclusion that there is no difference when, in fact, there is a difference. Psychologists pay particularly close attention to Type I errors because they want to be conservative in their inferences: they do not want to conclude that a difference exists if, in fact, it does not. A good analogy for Type I and Type II errors is that a Type I error is a "false positive," and a Type II error is a "false negative." The probability of making a Type I error is called the **p-value**. A p-value indicates that the results are statistically significant (not due only to chance). If $p = 0.05$, we have only a 5 percent chance of making a Type I error. In other words, a difference as extreme as what was obtained would be found only 5 percent of the time if the null hypothesis were correct.

		Reality	
		The null is True	The null is False
Your Statistical Decision	Fail to reject the null	Correct decision	**Type II error**
	Reject the null	**Type I error**	Correct decision

Statistical Decision-Making: The Four Possible Outcomes

ETHICS IN RESEARCH

Occasionally, psychological experiments involve **deception**, which may be used if informing participants of the nature of the experiment might bias results. This deception is typically small, but in rare instances it can be extreme. For example, in the 1970s, **Stanley Milgram** conducted obedience experiments in which he convinced participants that they were administering painful electric shocks to other participants, when, in fact, no shocks were given. The shocked "participants" were in fact **confederates**; that is, they were aware of the true nature of the experiment but pretended to be participants. Those giving the shocks were the real participants. Many people felt that this study was unethical because the participants were not aware of the nature of the study and could have believed that they had done serious harm to other people. Since this time, ethical standards have been set forth by the American Psychological Association (APA) to ensure the proper treatment of animal and human subjects. **Institutional Review Boards (IRBs)** assess research plans before the research is approved to ensure that it meets all ethical standards. Additionally, participants must give **informed consent**; in other words, they agree to participate in the study only after they have been told what their participation entails. Participants are also allowed to leave the experimental situation if they become uncomfortable about their participation. After the experiment is concluded, participants must receive a **debriefing,** in which they are told the exact purpose of their participation in the research and of any deception that may have been used in the process of experimentation.

Confidentiality is another area of concern for psychology. Many experiments involve collecting sensitive information about participants that the participants might not want to be revealed. For this reason, most psychological data is collected anonymously, with the participants' names not attached to the collected data. If such anonymity is not possible, it is the researcher's ethical obligation to ensure that names and sensitive information about participants are not revealed.

The use of animals in psychological experiments is a topic of controversy. According to animal-rights activists, animals often endure both physiological and psychological stress in experiments. Often, the animals are euthanized at the end of the research. Psychologists counter that many lifesaving drugs could not be tested were it not for tests with animals. Moreover, animal models afford a level of experimental control that is not attainable with human participants. Of course, no ethical researcher wants to cause unnecessary pain or discomfort to any subject—animal or human.

Painless Experiments

Pain, both physiological and psychological, is also an issue in experiments. In the past, shock was an acceptable technique with human participants. However, physical pain is infrequently used in experiments today. Psychological stress is also minimized.

KEY TERMS

Experimental, Correlational, and Clinical Research

experiment
independent variable
dependent variable
control variable
population
representative sample
representativeness
experimental group
control group
random sampling
randomly assigned
biases
    bias of selection
    self-selection bias
    pre-screening/advertising bias
    healthy user bias
single-/double-blind design
placebo
correlational research
confounding/third/extraneous
  variable
surveys
longitudinal studies
cross-sectional studies
clinical research
case studies
generalizable
conceptual definition
operational definition
internal validity
external validity
reliability
inter-rater reliability
naturalistic observation

Statistics

descriptive statistics
inferential statistics
central tendency
mean
mode
bimodal
median
normal curve
range
variability
standard deviation
percentile
positive skew
negative skew
correlation coefficient
Pearson correlation coefficient
positive correlation
negative correlation
sample size
null hypothesis
alternative hypothesis
alpha
Type I error
Type II error
p-value

Ethics in Research

deception
Stanley Milgram
confederates
Institutional Review Boards (IRBs)
informed consent
debriefing
confidentiality

Chapter 6 Drill

See Chapter 19 for answers and explanations.

1. In a double-blind experimental design, which of the following would be true?

    (A) The experimental subjects know whether they are in an experimental group or in a control group, but the researchers do not.

    (B) The researchers know whether particular subjects have been assigned to an experimental group or a control group, but the experimental subjects do not.

    (C) Both the researchers and the experimental subjects know whether the latter have been assigned to an experimental group or a control group.

    (D) Neither the researchers nor the experimental subjects know whether the latter have been assigned to an experimental group or a control group.

    (E) The observers are unable to see the responses or behaviors of the experimental group during the course of the experimental manipulation.

2. In a normal distribution of scores, approximately what percentage of all scores will occur within one standard deviation from the mean?

    (A) 34
    (B) 68
    (C) 95
    (D) 97.5
    (E) 100

3. A Type II error involves

    (A) concluding a difference between groups exists after the experimental manipulation when, in fact, a difference does not exist

    (B) concluding a difference between groups does not exist after the experimental manipulation when, in fact, a difference does exist

    (C) concluding a score is two standard deviations above the mean when, in fact, it is two standard deviations below the mean

    (D) concluding a score is two standard deviations below the mean when, in fact, it is two standard deviations above the mean

    (E) rejecting the null hypothesis when, in fact, it should have been accepted

4. Which of the following would NOT be considered essential for a proposed research design to meet the requirements for ethicality?

    (A) Research subjects must consent to participate in the project, and a full description of what their participation consists of must be spelled out before they are asked to give consent.

    (B) Participants must be allowed to withdraw from the project at any time.

    (C) Both the subjects and the researchers must know which of the subjects will be part of the experimental group.

    (D) If deception is involved, a full debriefing of the subjects must occur soon after the completion of the project.

    (E) In keeping with protecting the privacy and confidentiality of the subjects, data should be obtained as anonymously as possible.

5. The correlation between two observed variables is −0.84. From this, it can be concluded that

    (A) as one variable increases, the other is likely to increase, showing a direct relationship

    (B) as one variable increases, the other is likely to decrease, showing an inverse relationship

    (C) the two variables are unrelated

    (D) one variable causes the other variable to occur

    (E) one variable causes the other variable not to occur

6. A study seeks to find the effects of video games on violent behavior. The researcher creates an experimental design in which 100 random participants play violent video games and another 100 play non-violent video games for one hour. The researcher then records and observes the behavior of the subjects. The behavior of the subjects is known as the

    (A) control variable
    (B) independent variable
    (C) dependent variable
    (D) confounding variable
    (E) categorical variable

7. Which of the following is concerned with the real-life applicability of a study?

   (A) Test-retest reliability
   (B) Inter-rater reliability
   (C) Construct validity
   (D) External validity
   (E) Internal validity

8. A study that analyzes the effects of heart disease in different regions of the country and socioeconomic statuses is called a

   (A) longitudinal study
   (B) experimental design
   (C) double-blind study
   (D) cross-sectional design
   (E) case study

9. A researcher seeks to study the effects of a weight-loss supplement and decides to place an advertisement on buses and subways in New York City to attract subjects. All could happen with this type of subject selection EXCEPT

   (A) pre-screening bias
   (B) self-selection bias
   (C) selection bias
   (D) healthy user bias
   (E) courtesy bias

10. When graphing the distribution of a study, a researcher notices that a disproportionate number of subjects scored low on their test, shifting the peak of the bell curve she was expecting. This is called a

   (A) positive skew
   (B) negative skew
   (C) normal curve
   (D) positive correlation
   (E) negative correlation

REFLECT

Respond to the following questions:

- Which topics in this chapter do you hope to see on the multiple-choice section or essay?

- Which topics in this chapter do you hope not to see on the multiple-choice section or essay?

- Regarding any figures given, if you were given a labeled figure from within this chapter, would you be able to give the significance of each part of the figure?

- Can you define the key terms at the end of the chapter?

- Which parts of the chapter will you review?

- Will you seek further help, outside of this book (such as from a teacher, Princeton Review tutor, or AP Students), on any of the content in this chapter—and, if so, on what content?

Chapter 7
Biological Bases:
The Brain and
Nervous System

INTRODUCTION TO BIOLOGY AND BEHAVIOR

Physiological psychology is the study of behavior as influenced by biology. It draws its techniques and research methods from biology and medicine to examine psychological phenomena.

IMAGING TECHNIQUES

Many different techniques are used to examine the interrelationship between the brain and behavior. **Imaging techniques** allow researchers to map the structure and/or activity of the brain and correlate this data with behavior. An **EEG (electroencephalogram)** measures subtle changes in brain electrical activity through electrodes placed on the head. This data can be filtered mathematically to yield evoked potentials, which allow psychologists to get an electrical picture of brain activity during various cognitive states or tasks. EEG is especially useful in sleep studies, since different brain wave patterns are indicative of different stages of sleep.

Computerized axial tomography scans, better known as **CAT scans**, generate cross-sectional images of the brain using a series of X-ray pictures taken from different angles. **MRI (magnetic resonance imaging)** uses extremely powerful electromagnets and radio waves to get 3-D structural information from the brain. These techniques capture only "snapshots" of the brain. They do not allow observation of the brain in action over time. **Functional MRI (fMRI)** and **PET scans (positron emission tomography)** do allow scientists to view the brain as it is working. Functional MRI provides such viewing by rapid sequencing of MRI images; PET scans provide images via diffusion of radioactive glucose in the brain. Glucose is the primary "fuel" of brain cells; the more glucose being used in a given brain area, the more that area is in active use. This procedure allows psychologists to observe what brain areas are at work during various tasks and psychological events.

FUNCTIONAL ORGANIZATION OF THE NERVOUS SYSTEM

The **nervous system** can be divided into two distinct subsystems: the **central nervous system (CNS)**—comprising the brain and the spinal cord—and the **peripheral nervous system (PNS)**—comprising all other nerves in the body.

The brain is located in the skull and is the central processing center for thoughts, motivations, and emotions. The brain, as well as the rest of the nervous system, is made up of **neurons**, or nerve cells. The neurons form a network that extends to the spinal cord, which is encased in the protective bones of the spine, or the vertebrae. Both the brain and the spinal cord are bathed in a protective liquid called cerebrospinal fluid. In the spinal cord, the neurons are bundled into strands of interconnected neurons known as nerves. The nerves of the spine are responsible for conveying information to and from the brain and the PNS. Nerves sending information to the brain are sensory (or **afferent**) neurons; those

Test Tip

A memory tip for *afferent* and *efferent* is that **a**fferent connections are **a**rriving to the brain and **e**fferent are **e**xiting the brain.

conveying information from the brain are motor (or **efferent**) neurons. Although most movements are controlled by the brain, a certain small subset of movements are controlled by direct transmission from afferent to efferent cells at the level of the spinal cord. These responses, known as **reflexes**, are quick and involuntary responses to environmental stimuli. The path of a reflex arc goes from sensory neurons to motor neurons.

The PNS comprises all of the nerve cells in the body with the exception of those in the CNS (the brain and spinal cord). The PNS can be subdivided into the **somatic nervous system** and the **autonomic nervous system**. The somatic nervous system is responsible for voluntary movement of large skeletal muscles. The autonomic nervous system controls the nonskeletal or smooth muscles, such as those of the heart and digestive tract. These muscles are typically not under voluntary control. (Think *autonomic = automatic*.) The autonomic nervous system can be further divided into the sympathetic and parasympathetic nervous systems.

The **sympathetic nervous system** is associated with processes that burn energy. This is the system responsible for the heightened state of physiological arousal known as the **fight-or-flight reaction**—an increase in heart rate and respiration, accompanied by a decrease in digestion and salivation. The **parasympathetic nervous system** is the complementary system responsible for conserving energy. When the sympathetic system is aroused in a fight, for example, digestion ceases, blood transfers to skeletal muscle, and heart rate increases. When the fight ends, however, the parasympathetic system becomes active, sending blood to the stomach for digestion, slowing the heart rate, and conserving energy. This returns the body to homeostasis.

> **Mnemonic Tip!**
>
> The *sympathetic* system is *sympathetic* to you while you deal with a problem. The *parasympathetic* system helps you come down afterwards, like a *parachute*.

NEUROANATOMY

The brain is divided into three distinct regions that have evolved over time. These are the **hindbrain**, the **midbrain**, and the **forebrain** (limbic system and cerebral cortex).

The Hindbrain

- The oldest part of the brain to develop, in evolutionary terms

- Composed of the cerebellum, medulla oblongata, reticular activating system (RAS), and pons

- **Cerebellum**—controls muscle tone and balance

- **Medulla oblongata**—controls involuntary actions, such as breathing, digestion, heart rate, and swallowing (basic life functions)

- **Reticular activating system (RAS)**—controls arousal (wakefulness and alertness). This is also known as the reticular formation.

- **Pons**—Latin for "bridge," the pons is a way station, passing neural information from one brain region to another. The pons is also implicated in REM sleep.

The Midbrain

- Major components of the midbrain are the **tectum** and the **tegmentum**

- These two act as the brain's roof (tectum) and floor (tegmentum).

- The tectum and tegmentum govern visual and auditory reflexes, such as orienting to a sight or sound.

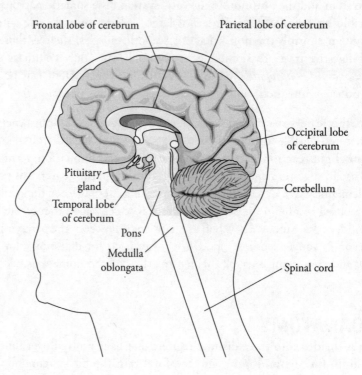

Frontal lobe of cerebrum

Parietal lobe of cerebrum

Occipital lobe of cerebrum

Pituitary gland

Temporal lobe of cerebrum

Cerebellum

Pons

Medulla oblongata

Spinal cord

The Forebrain

- Contains the **limbic system**, or emotional center of the brain

  - The limbic system is composed of the thalamus, hippocampus, amygdala, and hypothalamus

  - **Thalamus**—relays sensory information; receives and directs sensory information from visual and auditory systems

  - **Hippocampus**—involved in processing and integrating memories. Damage to the hippocampus does not eliminate existing memories, because memories are stored in the neocortex, but rather it prevents the formation of new memories. This condition is known as **anterograde amnesia.**

  - **Amygdala**—implicated in the expression of anger, frustration, and fear

Q: What parts of the brain make up the limbic system?

Answer on page 144.

- **Hypothalamus**—controls the temperature and water balance of the body; controls hunger and sex drives; orchestrates the activation of the sympathetic nervous system and the endocrine system; and it can be divided into the **lateral hypothalamus** and **ventromedial hypothalamus**, the combination of which regulates eating behaviors and body weight. The lateral hypothalamus is the "on switch" for eating, while the ventromedial hypothalamus is the "off switch." A lesion to the ventromedial part would cause obesity and even death from overeating, while a lesion to the lateral part would lead to a decreased hunger drive and even self-starvation.

- Also contains the **cerebral cortex**, or the wrinkled outer layer of the brain

  - The cortex is involved in higher cognitive functions such as thinking, planning, language use, and fine motor control.

  - This area receives sensory input (**sensory cortex**) and sends out motor information (**motor cortex**).

  - The cortex covers two symmetrical-looking sides of the brain known as the **left and right cerebral hemispheres**. These hemispheres are joined together by a band of connective nerve fibers called the **corpus callosum**.

  - The left hemisphere is typically specialized for language processing, as first noticed by **Paul Broca**, who observed that brain damage to the left hemisphere in stroke patients resulted in **expressive aphasia**, or loss of the ability to speak. This area of the brain is known as **Broca's area**. Another researcher, **Carl Wernicke**, discovered an area in the left temporal lobe that, when damaged in stroke patients, resulted in **receptive aphasia**, or the inability to comprehend speech. This is called **Wernicke's area**.

  - Others have noted that the right hemisphere processes certain kinds of visual and spatial information. **Roger Sperry** demonstrated that the two hemispheres of the brain can operate independently of each other. He did this by performing experiments on **split-brain patients** who had their corpora callosa severed to control their epileptic seizures. Split-brain patients can describe objects without deficit if presented in the right visual field (processed on the left, more verbal side of the brain), but they have great difficulty drawing the image; whereas, if the image is presented in the left visual field (and processed in the more visual right side of the brain), the person can draw or choose the object but cannot explain it verbally. Thus, split-brain patients demonstrate a lack of **contralateral processing**—the ability of (non-split) brains to use both hemispheres and integrate information between them via the corpus callosum.

Mnemonic Tip!
Ventromedial lesion ⇒
Give me **V**ery much food!

Lateral lesion ⇒
Give me **L**ess food!.

Cortex Components

- The cortex can be divided into four distinct lobes: the frontal, the parietal, the temporal, and the occipital.

  o The **frontal lobe** is responsible for higher-level thought and reasoning. That includes accessing working memory, paying attention, solving problems, making plans, forming judgments, and performing movements.

  o The **parietal lobe** handles somatosensory information and is the home of the primary somatosensory cortex. This area receives information about temperature, pressure, texture, and pain.

  o The **temporal lobe** handles auditory input and is critical for processing speech and appreciating music.

  o Finally, the **occipital lobe** processes visual input. This information crosses the **optic chiasm**.

- Much of the cerebral cortex is composed of **association areas**, which are responsible for associating information in the sensory and motor cortices (this is the plural of *cortex*!). Damage to these association areas can lead to a variety of dysfunctions, including **apraxia**, the inability to organize movement; **agnosia**, a difficulty processing sensory input; **alexia**, the inability to read; and **agraphia**, the inability to write.

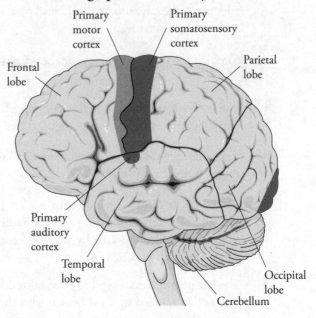

A: The limbic system is home to the hippocampus, amygdala, and hypothalamus.

NEURAL TRANSMISSION

Much of our discussion has involved the idea of information or stimulation being passed along nerves. **Nerves** are bundles of **neurons**, the basic unit of the nervous system. Neurons are cells with a clearly defined, nucleated cell body, or **soma**. Branching out from the soma are **dendrites**, which receive input from other neurons through receptors on their surface. The **axon** is a long, tubelike structure that responds to input from the dendrites and soma. The axon transmits a neural message down its length and then passes its information on to other cells. Some neurons have a fatty coating known as a **myelin sheath** surrounding the axon. Myelin serves as insulation for axons and also speeds up the rate at which electrical information travels down them. The better insulated the myelin sheath, the faster and more efficient the sending of action potentials. The myelin looks like beads on a string; the small gaps between the "beads" are known as the **nodes of Ranvier**. These nodes help speed up neural transmission. The axon ends in **terminal buttons**, knobs on the branched end of the axon. The terminal buttons come very close to the cell bodies and dendrites of other neurons, but they do not touch. The gap between them is known as a **synapse**. A terminal button releases **neurotransmitters**, chemical messengers, across the synapse, where they bind with receptors on subsequent dendrites.

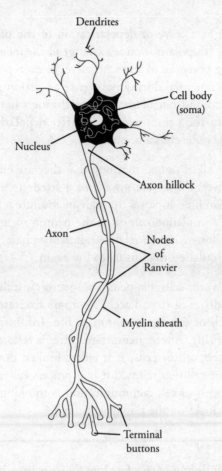

Dendrites

Cell body
(soma)

Nucleus

Axon hillock

Axon

Nodes
of
Ranvier

Myelin sheath

Terminal
buttons

Neuronal communication occurs both within and between cells. Communication within cells is electrochemical. An electric potential across the plasma membrane of approximately –70 millivolts (mV), known as the **resting membrane potential**, exists, in which the interior of the cell is negatively charged with respect to the exterior of the cell. Two primary membrane proteins are required to establish the resting membrane potential: the Na^+/K^+ ATPase and the potassium leak channels. The Na^+/K^+ ATPase pumps three sodium ions out of the cell and two potassium ions into the cell. The result is a sodium gradient with high sodium concentration outside of the cell and a potassium gradient with high potassium concentration inside the cell. **Leak channels** are channels that are open all the time and that simply allow ions to "leak" across the membrane according to their gradient. Potassium leak channels allow potassium, but no other ions, to flow down its gradient out of the cell. The combined loss of many positive ions through Na^+/K^+ ATPases and the potassium leak channels leaves the interior of the cell with a net negative charge, approximately 70 mV more negative than the exterior of the cell; this difference is the resting membrane potential. Note that there are very few sodium leak channels in the membrane (the ratio of K^+ leak channels to Na^+ leak channels is about 100:1), so the cell membrane is virtually impermeable to sodium.

The resting membrane potential establishes a negative charge along the interior of axons (along with the rest of the neuronal interior). Thus, the cells can be described as polarized: negative on the inside and positive on the outside. An **action potential**, also referred to as a **nerve impulse**, is a disturbance in this membrane potential.

This Won't Be Tested, But...

With each administration of the test, the specific topics covered change, and good news if you're feeling overwhelmed: this level of specificity will almost certainly not be required. Skip it if you're pressed for time! However, this is good information to learn, and mastering a complex topic in context can help you get an even firmer grasp on everything else that will be tested.

It can be thought of as a wave of depolarization of the plasma membrane that travels along an axon. (Depolarization is a change in the membrane potential from the resting membrane potential to a less negative, or even positive, potential.) The change in membrane potential during passage of an action potential is caused by movement of ions into and out of the neuron through ion channels, leading to the eventual release of the neurotransmitter. After depolarization, repolarization returns the membrane potential to normal.

Action potentials are "all or none," meaning that they are either generated or not, with nothing in between. They are always of a fixed strength, never weaker or stronger. After a neuron fires, it passes through an absolute refractory phase, during which no amount of stimulation can cause the neuron to fire again. The absolute refractory phase is followed by the relative refractory phase, in which the neuron needs much more stimulation than usual to fire again.

Communication between cells happens via neurotransmitters, which bind to receptors on the dendrites of the adjacent neurons. **Excitatory** neurotransmitters serve to excite the cell or cause the neuron to fire. **Inhibitory** neurotransmitters inhibit (or stop) cell firing. After a neurotransmitter is released and has conducted the impulse to the next cell or cells, it is either broken down by **enzymes** or is absorbed back into the cell that released it in a process called **reuptake**. A helpful metaphor for the process of cell communication is thinking of neurotransmitters as keys that open the locks on the postsynaptic cell.

The following are a few key neurotransmitters:

- **Acetylcholine**, which affects memory function, as well as muscle contraction, particularly in the heart

- **Serotonin**, which is related to arousal, sleep, pain sensitivity, and mood and hunger regulation

- **Dopamine**, which is associated with movement, attention, and reward; dopamine imbalances may play a role in Parkinson's disease and in schizophrenia

- **GABA**, or *gamma*-Aminobutyric acid, which is an inhibitory neurotransmitter

- **Glutamate**, which is an excitatory neurotransmitter and the all-purpose counterpart to GABA

- **Norepinephrine**, which affects levels of alertness; a lack of norepinephrine is implicated in depression

- **Endorphins**, which are the body's natural painkillers

Study Tip

Some textbooks and test questions have used the category of antidepressants known as SSRI's (e.g. Prozac, Paxil, Zoloft) as a way to illustrate neuron transmission. See whether you can explain why these drugs are "selective serotonin reuptake inhibitors" and why the effects of these medications might help someone with depression.

It is important to note that the brain can reorganize itself by forming or severing neural connections throughout one's life. This important ability, called **neuroplasticity**, allows the brain to compensate for injury or disease, in order to continue responding adaptably to the environment. **Michael Gazzaniga** has not only done pioneering research in this area, focusing on split-brain patients, but also published works in cognitive neuroscience for the general reader.

ENDOCRINE SYSTEM

The **endocrine system** provides another way by which various parts of our bodies relay information to one another. This system works through groups of cells known as glands, which release substances called **hormones.** Hormones affect cell growth and proliferation. The primary gland is the **pituitary gland**, which is also known as the master gland. The pituitary releases hormones that in turn control hormonal release by many other glands. Hormones are different from neurotransmitters in many ways. Neurotransmitters are released locally in the synapses of neurons, while hormones are released into the bloodstream and travel throughout the body. Hormones coordinate a wide range of responses, while neurotransmitters trigger highly localized and specific reactions. Hormones also affect the body for long periods of time compared with neurotransmitters.

The pituitary is located just under the part of the brain that controls it—the hypothalamus. Stressful situations cause the pituitary to release **adrenocorticotropic hormone (ACTH)**, which stimulates the **adrenal glands**, resulting in fight-or-flight reactions. The adrenal glands secrete **epinephrine** (adrenaline) and **norepinephrine** (noradrenaline). The **thyroid gland**, located at the front of the neck, produces **thyroxine**, which is important for regulating cellular metabolism.

HEREDITY AND ENVIRONMENT: BEHAVIORAL GENETICS

Behavioral genetics is the application of the principles of evolutionary theory to the study of behavior. **Traits** are distinctive characteristics or behavior patterns that are determined by genetics. Genes are the basic biological elements responsible for carrying information about traits between successive generations. A **dominant trait** is more likely to be expressed in offspring than is a **recessive trait**. A **genotype** is the genetic makeup of a cell or of an organism. The genotype is distinct from the expressed features, or **phenotype,** of the cell or organism. Whenever a dominant gene is paired with a recessive gene, the dominant one typically will be shown in the phenotype, the observable result. The phenotype tends to show the recessive trait only when two recessive genes are paired together. Genes reside on rod-shaped chromosomes. Humans have 46 chromosomes, with one set of 23 inherited from each parent, so that half of our genetic makeup comes from each parent.

Some disorders are the result of genetic abnormalities. **Down syndrome** occurs when there are three copies of the 21st chromosome, which generally causes some degree of intellectual disability. **Huntington's chorea** is a genetic disorder that results in muscle impairment that does not typically occur until after age 40. It is caused by the degeneration of the structure of the brain known as the basal ganglia, and it is fatal. Because of the late onset of the disease, it is frequently passed down to the next generation before its symptoms are manifested. New genetic mapping techniques are revealing other relationships between specific genes and disorders, and scientists are trying to address ways to correct genetic flaws and provide genetic counseling.

Nature versus Nurture

As mentioned earlier, the behavioral-genetics approach examines the ways in which we are different from one another. The term **heritability** is used here to discuss the degree of variance among individuals that can be attributed to genetic variations. Many physical and psychological characteristics are inherited. However, genes do not determine everything about us. **Environmentality** is the degree to which a trait's expression is caused by the environment in which an organism lives. Psychology has long been concerned with the relative influences of genetics and environment. This controversy is known as the **nature versus nurture debate**. Today, the common view is that nature and nurture work together; our psychological makeup is largely the result of the interaction of these two forces.

KEY TERMS

physiological psychology

Imaging Techniques

EEG (electroencephalogram)

CAT scans (computerized axial tomography scans)

MRI (magnetic resonance imaging)

Functional MRI (fMRI)

PET scans (positron emission tomography)

Functional Organization of the Nervous System

nervous system

    central nervous system (CNS)

    peripheral nervous system (PNS)

neurons

afferent

efferent

reflexes

somatic nervous system

autonomic nervous system

sympathetic nervous system

fight-or-flight reaction

parasympathetic nervous system

Neuroanatomy

hindbrain

    cerebellum

    medulla oblongata

    reticular activating system (RAS)

    pons

midbrain

    tectum

    tegmentum

forebrain

    limbic system

        thalamus

        hippocampus

        anterograde amnesia

        amygdala

        hypothalamus

        lateral hypothalamus

        ventromedial hypothalamus

cerebral cortex

    sensory cortex

    motor cortex

    left and right cerebral hemispheres

    corpus callosum

Paul Broca

    Broca's area and expressive aphasia

Carl Wernicke

    Wernicke's area and receptive aphasia

Roger Sperry

split-brain patients

contralateral processing

association areas

apraxia

agnosia

alexia

agraphia

frontal lobe

parietal lobe

temporal lobe

occipital lobe

optic chiasm

Neural Transmission

nerves

neurons

soma

dendrites

axon

myelin sheath

nodes of Ranvier

terminal buttons

synapse

neurotransmitters

resting membrane potential

leak channels

nerve impulse (action potential)

excitatory

inhibitory

enzymes

reuptake

acetylcholine

serotonin

dopamine

GABA

glutamate

norepinephrine

endorphins

neuroplasticity

Michael Gazzaniga

Endocrine System

hormones

pituitary gland

adrenocorticotropic hormone (ACTH)

adrenal glands

epinephrine

norepinephrine

thyroid gland

thyroxine

Heredity and Environment: Behavioral Genetics

traits

dominant trait

recessive trait

genotype

phenotype

heritability

environmentality

nature versus nurture debate

Down syndrome

Huntington's chorea

Chapter 7 Drill

See Chapter 19 for answers and explanations.

1. Damage to Broca's area in the left cerebral hemisphere of the brain would likely result in which of the following?

    (A) A repetition of the speech of others
    (B) A loss of the ability to speak
    (C) A loss of the ability to visually integrate information
    (D) A loss of the ability to comprehend speech
    (E) An inability to solve verbal problems

2. In the neuron, the main function of the dendrites is to

    (A) release neurotransmitters to signal subsequent neurons
    (B) preserve the speed and integrity of the neural signal as it propagates down the axon
    (C) perform the metabolic reactions necessary to nourish and maintain the nerve cell
    (D) receive input from other neurons
    (E) connect the cell body to the axon

3. Veronica is having trouble balancing as she walks, and her muscles seem to have lost strength and tone. A neuroanatomist looking into her condition would most likely suspect a problem with Veronica's

    (A) medulla oblongata
    (B) right cerebral hemisphere
    (C) cerebellum
    (D) occipital lobes
    (E) thalamus

4. Which of the following neurotransmitters is generally associated with the inhibition of continued neural signaling?

    (A) Dopamine
    (B) Adrenaline
    (C) GABA
    (D) Serotonin
    (E) Acetylcholine

5. A phenotype is best defined as

    (A) an observable trait or behavior that results from a particular genetic combination
    (B) the underlying genetic composition of a species
    (C) a biological unit within which genetic information is encoded
    (D) a recessive genetic combination that remains physically unexpressed
    (E) the genetic combination given by a parent to their offspring

6. John is constantly overeating and can't seem to control his appetite, no matter how hard he tries. It is possible that John may have damage in which of the following brain structures?

    (A) Thalamus
    (B) Pons
    (C) Hypothalamus
    (D) Amygdala
    (E) Association areas

7. A demyelinating disorder, such as multiple sclerosis, would cause all of the following symptoms EXCEPT

    (A) a reduction of white matter in the central nervous system
    (B) an increased rate of neuronal conduction
    (C) a slower propagation of signals along the axon
    (D) a deficiency of sensation
    (E) a decreased neuronal insulation

8. Which area of the brain is responsible for coordinating complex motor functions?

    (A) Frontal lobe
    (B) Occipital lobe
    (C) Reticular activating system
    (D) Cerebellum
    (E) Temporal lobe

9. All of the following brain areas are associated with the experience of emotion EXCEPT the

    (A) temporal lobe
    (B) amygdala
    (C) hypothalamus
    (D) pons
    (E) frontal lobe

REFLECT

Respond to the following questions:

- Which topics in this chapter do you hope to see on the multiple-choice section or essay?

- Which topics in this chapter do you hope not to see on the multiple-choice section or essay?

- Regarding any psychologists mentioned, can you pair the psychologists with their contributions to the field? Did they contribute significant experiments, theories, or both?

- Regarding any figures given, if you were given a labeled figure from within this chapter, would you be able to give the significance of each part of the figure?

- Can you define the key terms at the end of the chapter?

- Which parts of the chapter will you review?

- Will you seek further help, outside of this book (such as from a teacher, Princeton Review tutor, or AP Students), on any of the content in this chapter—and, if so, on what content?

Chapter 8
Biological Bases:
Consciousness

CONSCIOUSNESS

Consciousness is defined as the awareness that we have of ourselves, our internal states, and the environment. A **state of consciousness** enables us to evaluate the environment and to filter information from the environment through the mind, while being aware of the occurrence of this complex process. One state of consciousness is that of being alert. **Alertness** and the associated state of **arousal** involve the ability to remain attentive to our surroundings. It is something that we often take for granted; however, many patients who arrive in an emergency room are not alert for various reasons, arriving in a so-called **altered state of consciousness**. This can be due to head injuries, toxins, or other medical conditions. The ability to be alert is impaired in a variety of disorders, including narcolepsy, attention-deficit disorder, depression, and chronic fatigue syndrome. Even without these disorders, it is not possible to maintain a heightened state of alertness indefinitely, and alertness varies over a 24-hour cycle. Alertness and arousal are controlled by structures within the brainstem. These structures are known as the reticular formation (also known as the reticular activating system, or RAS).

Philosophers and psychologists have debated the nature of consciousness for centuries. **William James** spoke of a **stream of consciousness**. The cognitive psychologist **Robert Sternberg** refers to consciousness as a **mental reality** that we create in order to adapt to the world. The **unconscious** level commonly refers to automatic processes, such as breathing or the beating of the heart. These occur because the brain tells them to occur, but they do not happen as a result of conscious intervention. Sigmund Freud referred to the unconscious as an area of mental life that has a huge impact on our thoughts, feelings, and behaviors, but which is only indirectly accessible, through symptoms, slips of the tongue or physical accidents, and dreams, for example.

Consciousness serves two important functions. First, consciousness is responsible for keeping track of ourselves, our environment, and our relationship with the environment. Additionally, consciousness serves a controlling role, planning our responses to the information gathered by this monitoring. We typically think of ourselves as fully conscious, but there are lower levels of consciousness, specifically the preconscious and unconscious levels.

The **preconscious level** contains information that is available to consciousness but is not always in consciousness. It can be retrieved when needed. This is where directions to frequently visited places might be stored. The preconscious is also where many automatic behaviors are stored. You use these behaviors in tasks that you can do nearly without thought, such as riding a bicycle.

Consciousness exists on a continuum—starting from **controlled processing**, in which we are very aware of what we are doing, and moving on to **automatic processing**, in which we perform tasks mechanically, such as brushing our teeth. The continuum proceeds through daydreaming, a state in which we can regain consciousness in a moment, and meditation. Next comes sleep and dreaming and, at the far end of the spectrum, coma and unconsciousness.

SLEEP AND DREAMING

Sleep is an altered state of consciousness. Interestingly, scientists still do not precisely understand the function of sleep. One theory holds that sleep is necessary for restorative processes. If this theory is correct, then some chemical in the body should be associated with sleep. Researchers have discovered some neurochemicals, notably **melatonin**, that play a role in sleep, yet a definitive cause-and-effect relationship between a brain chemical and the control of sleep has not been demonstrated.

In addition to conducting chemical investigations of sleep, psychologists investigate the functions of sleep by depriving animals or humans of it. It is difficult to deprive organisms of sleep, as the need for sleep is very strong. One 24-hour cycle without sleep is tolerable, but the second such cycle is considerably more difficult. By the third 24-hour cycle, **hallucinations** can begin, as well as **delusions.** Four 24-hour cycles of sleep deprivation can lead to paranoia and other psychological disturbances. All of the symptoms of sleep deprivation disappear when the deprived person is allowed to sleep again.

Another approach to the study of sleep is to investigate the pattern of sleeping. Sleeping generally occurs in humans during the time their area of the world is in darkness—that is, at night. People who live in extreme northern or southern exposures, where it may be light for close to 24 hours, generally try to create conditions of darkness in order to sleep. Our body temperature and other physiological markers follow a day-to-night pattern, known as a **circadian rhythm.** Body temperature rises as the morning approaches, peaks during the day, dips in early afternoon, and then begins to drop again before sleep at night. Although this is a general description of the flow of alertness throughout the day, the pattern varies by individual, and circadian rhythms also vary with age. Newborns can spend two-thirds of a day asleep. Older adults tend to peak in the morning and decline as the day progresses, while adolescents and young adults tend to be more energetic in the mid- to late evening.

Light, both natural and artificial, also influences the biological clock by activating light-sensitive photoreceptors in the retina. Photoreceptors send signals to the brain's **pineal gland**, which is the region responsible for the production of melatonin. Because of the nature of the relationship of the Earth and the Sun, this natural day-night rhythm is a 24-hour one. Our circadian rhythms generally match this pattern. However, if all time cues (such as sunlight, clocks, and television) are removed, then we tend to follow roughly a 25-hour rhythm, called free-running rhythm.

External stimuli are important to setting our circadian rhythms. Rapidly changing these stimuli, such as in the case of traveling across time zones, can disturb circadian rhythms. In this example, the result can be the unpleasant feelings associated with jet lag.

Sleep itself is not a uniform process. Rather, sleep can be divided into stages based on brain-wave patterns. Brain waves are usually measured with **electroencephalograms (EEGs)**, which provide a picture of the electrical activity of the brain. When we are awake and focused, **beta wave** activity is happening. While still awake but more relaxed, we drift into **alpha waves**. Then, when we drift off to sleep, **theta wave**

circa = around

dia = day

circadian = around the day

activity takes over. In stage 2 sleep, a pattern of waves known as **sleep spindles** appears. These spindles are occasionally broken up by **K complexes**, which are large, slow waves. The skeletal muscles relax during this portion of sleep. In stages 3 and 4, **delta waves** are most common, with a larger proportion of delta waves occurring during stage 4 sleep. The last stage of sleep is called **REM (rapid eye movement)** sleep. In all other stages of sleep, which often are referred to collectively as NREM or non-REM sleep, the eyes are relatively still. Researchers **Eugene Aserinsky** and **Nathaniel Kleitman** discovered that the eyes move vigorously during the REM stage. This stage of sleep is typically associated with dreaming, although it is not the only stage of sleep in which dreaming occurs. In REM sleep, our brain waves are mostly theta and beta. The fact that this is a very deep stage of sleep, characterized by suppressed skeletal muscle tone, but in which our brain waves resemble those observed when we are nearly awake, has led investigators to refer to REM sleep as **paradoxical sleep**.

> ## Study Tip
> Questions about the paradoxical nature of REM sleep are common, so make sure that you can describe brain activity, the status of the autonomic nervous system, and muscle tone during REM.

Each sleep cycle is approximately 90 minutes long; therefore, if we sleep seven and one-half hours we will experience 5 cycles. We drift through the stages of sleep as follows:

- Stage 1: for up to 5 minutes

- Stage 2: for about 20 minutes

- Stage 3: for another 10 minutes

- Stage 4: for about 30 minutes

- Then back up through stage 3 for 10 minutes

- Stage 2: for 10 minutes

- Stage 1: for 1 or 2 minutes

- Then into REM sleep for 10 minutes

As the period of sleep progresses, stages 3 and 4 diminish and eventually disappear. Meanwhile, the REM or dream sleep gets longer until near morning when the dreams are approximately one hour long. Because of their proximity to an awakened state and their length, dreams occurring toward the end of sleep are more easily remembered. Psychologists note that the big difference in sleep is between REM and non-REM.

Sleep researcher **William Dement** studied the effects of the deprivation of REM sleep. When participants were deprived of REM sleep (waking them every time they entered a REM period) and then allowed to sleep normally after the experimental period, participants' REM periods increased from the normal 90 minutes of REM per night to 120 minutes of REM sleep in the period immediately following the deprivation. This is known as **REM rebound**, and it helps reinforce the idea that we need to sleep.

Dreams, like sleep itself, are mysterious. We all dream every night, yet we do not always remember our dreams, and the function of dreams remains unknown. Freud hypothesized that dreams are the expression of unconscious wishes or desires. In psychoanalytic theory, the **manifest content**, or storyline and imagery of the dream, offers insight into and important symbols relating to unconscious processes. The **latent content** is the emotional significance and underlying meaning of the dream. The **activation-synthesis hypothesis of dreaming** postulates that dreams are the product of our awareness of neural activity due to sensory input while we are sleeping. Thus, if it starts raining while you are sleeping, you may dream of a waterfall. The **problem-solving theory of dreaming** holds that dreams provide a chance for the mind to work out issues that occupy its attention during waking hours. Neural repair, consolidation of memories, and protein synthesis seem to occur during dreams. A **nightmare** is an elaborate dream sequence that produces a high level of anxiety or fear for the dreamer. The dreamer may experience a sense of physical danger to himself or his loved ones or a strong sense of embarrassment about doing something unacceptable. These dreams are vivid and can often be elaborately described by the dreamer upon awakening; they generally occur during REM sleep.

Given that sleep is such an important factor in our lives, it is not surprising that psychologists are interested in disorders of sleep. **Dyssomnias** are abnormalities in the amount, quality, or timing of sleep, and they include insomnia, narcolepsy, and sleep apnea. **Insomnia** is the most common of the sleep disorders and represents the inability to fall asleep or to maintain sleep. Chronic stress can cause temporary insomnia, as can the use of alcohol or stimulants such as caffeine.

Narcolepsy is the inability to stay awake. A narcoleptic has irresistible and persistent urges to sleep throughout the day and at inappropriate times, such as when driving. Interestingly, when narcoleptics fall asleep, it is typically only for a few minutes, and the sleep is almost all REM sleep. Although narcolepsy can be treated, the cause of the disorder is unknown. However, recent research suggests that the cause of narcolepsy is a dysfunction in the region of the hypothalamus that produces the neurotransmitter hypocretin (also called orexin).

Sleep apnea is a disorder in which a person repeatedly stops breathing while sleeping, which results in awakening after a minute or so without air. This disorder can occur hundreds of times in a night, leaving the sufferer exhausted during the day. Sleep apnea is associated with obesity and also may be linked to alcohol consumption. **Sudden infant death syndrome (SIDS)** may also be linked to sleep apnea.

Parasomnias involve abnormalities of movement during deep sleep; they include sleepwalking (or **somnambulism**) and **night terrors.** Sleepwalking occurs when an individual walks around, and sometimes even talks, while sleeping. Scientists have shown that sleepwalking is not simply acting out dreams, as it occurs during stage 3 and 4 sleep, rather than during REM. Night terrors involve actual behaviors such as screaming, crying, and jerking/lunging movements while asleep. A person suffering a night terror may also be quite mobile, going through all the motions of being attacked by some horror, and yet be fully asleep. Nevertheless, there is usually no memory of these actions later on.

HYPNOSIS

Hypnosis is an altered state of consciousness in which the hypnotized person is very relaxed and open to suggestion. Hypnotized people can be convinced that they see things that are not there or that they are having experiences that are not really taking place. Hypnotized individuals can sometimes also recall things that they could not recall when they were in a normal state of consciousness. Typically, a person who is hypnotized has no recollection of the hypnosis upon returning to normal consciousness. Some theories hold that hypnosis is a state of deep relaxation, whereas other theories hold that hypnosis is not a real effect at all, but is rather a form of the participant's living up to the expectations of the hypnotist or experimenter. Another theory of hypnosis is the **neodissociative theory**. According to **Hilgard's theory of the hidden observer**, hypnosis somehow divides or dissociates the mind into two parts. One part obeys the hypnotist, while the other part, referred to as the hidden observer, silently observes everything. While this theory may explain the phenomenology of hypnotism, the physiology of hypnotism remains unexplained. Explaining hypnosis is made more difficult by the finding that hypnotic suggestibility varies on a normally distributed curve—in other words, some people are more susceptible to hypnosis than others.

The Clinical Uses of Hypnosis

Hypnosis has some clinical applications. In some types of psychotherapy, hypnotism is used to extract memories so terrible that they were repressed from the conscious into the unconscious mind. It is controversial whether such repressed memories are valid. Such reports of repressed memories may be dubious in a legal setting and have been used to falsely accuse people of crimes they did not commit. People who are hypnotized may also be susceptible to **posthypnotic suggestion**. Posthypnotic suggestions are instructions given to people when they are hypnotized that are to be implemented after they wake. Such suggestions have had limited success in treating chronic pain, reducing blood pressure, and even in helping people quit smoking.

MEDITATION

Meditation refers to a variety of techniques, many of which have been practiced for thousands of years, and which usually involve learning to train one's attention. Meditators may focus intensely on a single thing, such as their breathing, or they may broaden their attention and be aware of multiple stimuli, such as anything in their auditory field. Meditation has been utilized successfully to manage pain, stress, and anxiety disorders. Mindfulness-based stress reduction (MBSR) is a protocol commonly used in the medical setting to help alleviate stress; it incorporates meditation along with several other techniques. Meditators have increased alpha and theta waves while they are meditating (and to some extent sustain these increases above their baseline after stopping), with more experienced meditators showing greater improvements.

PSYCHOACTIVE DRUG EFFECTS

Drug	Effect on CNS	Effects on the Brain and Body	Effects on Behavior
Alcohol	Depressant	Decreases dopamine levels	Dizziness, slurred speech, impaired judgment High doses can result in respiratory depression and death.
Barbiturates Examples: Seconal, Nebutal	Depressant	Inhibit neural arousal centers	Decrease anxiety; increase relaxation High doses can result in respiratory depression and death. Can be very addictive and dangerous when mixed with other depressants or alcohol
Tranquilizers Examples: Xanax, Valium, Librium	Depressant	Inhibit neural arousal centers	Reduce anxiety without inducing sleep
Caffeine	Stimulant	Accelerates heart rate; constricts blood vessels Reduces levels of adenosine, a neurochemical regulator of norepinephrine release	Can lead to irritability, anxiety, insomnia
Amphetamines Examples: diet pills, Ritalin	Stimulant	Increase body temperature and heart rate Increase production of dopamine and norepinephrine	Can be addictive Produce feelings of euphoria High doses can lead to motor dysfunction.

Q: Why are narcotics effective?

Answer on page 161.

Drug	Effect on CNS	Effects on the Brain and Body	Effects on Behavior
Cocaine	Stimulant	Stimulates heart rate and blood pressure Increases dopamine, serotonin, and norepinephrine release	Users feel as though they have increased mental abilities and social ability. Can be highly addictive
Nicotine	Stimulant	Stimulates acetylcholine transmission Increases heart rate	Has depressant behavioral effects such as decreasing appetite while increasing heart rate and respiration Can sometimes cause euphoria and dizziness Highly addictive
Narcotics Example: Oxycodone, Heroin	Depressant	Activate receptors for endogenous endorphins	Induce relaxation and euphoria; can relieve pain May cause impaired cognitive ability, sweating, nausea, and respiratory depression Highly addictive and available only by prescription or through illicit means
Hallucinogens Examples: LSD and marijuana	Distort sensory perceptions	May increase serotonin levels	May induce sensory synesthesia, in which stimuli from one sense, such as hearing, produce sensory effects in other modalities, such as vision Occasionally, the perceptual alterations are extremely unpleasant and terrifying. This state may also be accompanied by paranoia.

In discussing psychoactive drugs, it is important to distinguish among dependence, tolerance, and withdrawal. **Dependence** occurs when an individual continues using a drug despite overarching negative consequences in order to avoid unpleasant physical and/or psychological feelings associated with not taking it. (This term has generally replaced the term *addiction* in psychological and health circles.) Like physical dependence, psychological dependence is biologically based. Enjoyable behaviors produce activity in dopamine circuits in the brainstem, most notably in the nucleus accumbens, the "pleasure center" of the brain. This dopaminergic pathway naturally leads to feelings of reward and pleasure. Many addictive drugs share the characteristic of stimulating the release of dopamine in the nucleus accumbens.

A person has developed **tolerance** to a drug when increasingly larger doses are needed in order for the same effect to occur. It is possible to develop tolerance without being dependent. **Withdrawal** refers to the process of weaning off a drug one has become dependent upon; this often involves physical and psychological symptoms of a highly unpleasant nature.

A: They are effective because they bear a striking resemblance to the endogenous endorphins, neurochemicals responsible for pain relief and implicated in pleasant feelings and euphoria.

KEY TERMS

Consciousness
state of consciousness
alertness
arousal
altered state of consciousness
William James and stream of consciousness
Robert Sternberg and mental reality
unconscious
preconscious level
controlled processing
automatic processing

Sleep and Dreaming
melatonin
hallucinations
delusions
circadian rhythm
pineal gland
electroencephalograms (EEGs)
beta wave
alpha waves
theta wave
sleep spindles
K complexes
delta waves
rapid eye movement (REM) (paradoxical sleep)
Eugene Aserinsky
Nathaniel Kleitman
William Dement
REM rebound
manifest content
latent content

activation-synthesis hypothesis of dreaming
problem-solving theory of dreaming
nightmare
dyssomnias
    insomnia
    narcolepsy
    sleep apnea
    sudden infant death syndrome (SIDS)
parasomnias
    somnambulism
    night terrors

Hypnosis
neodissociative theory
Hilgard's theory of the hidden observer
posthypnotic suggestion

Psychoactive Drug Effects
drugs
    alcohol
    barbiturates
    tranquilizers
    caffeine
    amphetamines
    cocaine
    nicotine
    narcotics
    hallucinogens
effects
    dependence
    tolerance
    withdrawal

Chapter 8 Drill

See Chapter 19 for answers and explanations.

1. The brain wave patterns known as "sleep spindles" are most characteristic of which stage of sleep?

   (A) Stage 1 sleep
   (B) Stage 2 sleep
   (C) Stage 3 sleep
   (D) Stage 4 sleep
   (E) REM sleep

2. If all external time cues are removed or blocked, the human circadian "free-running" rhythm tends to cycle every

   (A) 20 hours
   (B) 24 hours
   (C) 25 hours
   (D) 27 hours
   (E) 36 hours

3. All of the following are differences between nightmares and night terrors EXCEPT

   (A) nightmares typically occur during REM sleep, while night terrors typically occur during other sleep stages
   (B) nightmares are often recalled vividly and in detail upon waking, whereas night terrors are not
   (C) people are usually relatively still during nightmares, while they may move around quite a lot, even sleepwalk, during night terrors
   (D) while people may vocalize during nightmares, night terrors are more likely to involve screaming, crying, or shouting
   (E) nightmares are generally expressions of the dreamer's conscious issues, while night terrors reflect unconscious concerns

4. Which of the following is NOT a member of the class of psychoactive drugs collectively known as narcotics?

   (A) Codeine
   (B) Morphine
   (C) Heroin
   (D) Opium
   (E) Cocaine

5. Alcohol withdrawal syndrome occurs when an individual with a dependence on alcohol suddenly limits or stops their consumption of alcohol. Nervous symptoms of withdrawal include seizures and uncontrollable shaking of the extremities. What is the most plausible mechanism of action for these physical symptoms?

   (A) Chronic alcohol consumption causes down-regulation of GABA receptors, leading to a reduction in CNS inhibition, and excito-neurotoxicity.
   (B) Long-term alcohol abuse stimulates the autonomic nervous system, causing tremors.
   (C) Cessation of alcohol consumption leads to a reduction in dopamine production in the nucleus accumbens.
   (D) Alcohol is a hallucinogenic, and withdrawal causes the body to respond by relaxing, disinhibiting, and amplifying sensory information.
   (E) Alcohol is a depressant, decreasing inhibitory GABA-binding activity in the central nervous system.

6. A patient goes to the doctor's office citing symptoms of wakefulness in the night and tiredness during the day. Given these symptoms, which of the following might be a correct diagnosis?

   (A) Narcolepsy
   (B) Sleep apnea
   (C) Somnambulism
   (D) Paradoxical sleep
   (E) Night terrors

7. A 62-year-old female is on hypertension medication. Over the past three years, her dosage has increased twice. If she forgets to take her medication, her blood pressure increases dramatically. This increase in her blood pressure is an example of

(A) addiction
(B) psychological dependence
(C) physical dependence
(D) tolerance
(E) stimulants

8. Paradoxical sleep occurs during

(A) stage 1 sleep
(B) stage 2 sleep
(C) stage 3 sleep
(D) stage 4 sleep
(E) REM sleep

9. Over the course of the night, which is true about the sleep cycles?

(A) Stages 3 and 4 eventually disappear while REM cycles lengthen to approximately one hour long.
(B) Stages 2 and 3 eventually disappear while REM cycles lengthen to approximately 30 minutes long.
(C) Stages 3 and 4 eventually disappear while stages 1 and 2 lengthen to approximately 20 minutes each.
(D) REM cycles eventually disappear while stages 3 and 4 lengthen to approximately one hour long.
(E) Stages 1 and 2 eventually disappear while stages 3 and 4 lengthen to approximately 20 minutes each.

REFLECT

Respond to the following questions:

- Which topics in this chapter do you hope to see on the multiple-choice section or essay?

- Which topics in this chapter do you hope not to see on the multiple-choice section or essay?

- Regarding any psychologists mentioned, can you pair the psychologists with their contributions to the field? Did they contribute significant experiments, theories, or both?

- Regarding any theories mentioned, can you distinguish between differing theories well enough to recognize them on the multiple-choice section? Can you distinguish them well enough to write a fluent essay on them?

- Can you define the key terms at the end of the chapter?

- Which parts of the chapter will you review?

- Will you seek further help, outside of this book (such as from a teacher, Princeton Review tutor, or AP Students), on any of the content in this chapter—and, if so, on what content?

Chapter 9
Sensation and Perception

Sensation **EN**codes information.

Perception **DE**codes information.

INTRODUCTION TO SENSATION AND PERCEPTION

To study **sensation** is to study the relationship between physical stimulation and its psychological effects. Sensation is the process of taking in information from the environment. **Perception** refers to the way in which we recognize, interpret, and organize our sensations.

THRESHOLDS

In **psychophysics**, the branch of psychology that deals with the effects of physical stimuli on sensory response, researchers determine the smallest amount of sound, pressure, taste, or other stimuli that an individual can detect. Psychologists conducting this type of experiment are attempting to determine the **absolute threshold**—the minimum amount of stimulation needed to detect a stimulus. "Detection" means that the stimulus is correctly identified as either present or absent at least 50% of the time. This number is important, because it is the point at which you are no longer guessing. Imagine you are looking five miles down the road at someone with a flashlight; you are likely not detecting whether it is in one of two states: on or off. If asked to report on the flashlight's status, you'll only be right about 50% of the time. But as you get closer to that person, at some point, you will start answering more accurately. That point, where your eyes can begin to detect the light, exceeds the absolute threshold.

Gustav Fechner (1801–1887), the founder of psychophysics, determined that the perceived brightness of a visual sensation and the perceived loudness of an auditory sensation are both proportional to the logarithm of their actual intensity. (See Weber's law on the next page.)

In a typical absolute-threshold experiment, an experimenter plays a series of tones of varying volume to determine at exactly what volume the participant first reports that she can hear the tone. Another approach to measuring **detection thresholds** involves **signal detection theory (SDT)**. This theory takes into consideration that there are four possible outcomes for each trial in a detection experiment: the signal (stimulus) is either present or it is not, and the participants respond that they can detect a signal or they cannot. Therefore, we have the following four possibilities:

- **Hit**—the signal was present, and the participant reported sensing it.

- **Miss**—the signal was present, but the participant did not sense it.

- **False alarm**—the signal was absent, but the participant reported sensing it.

- **Correct rejection**—the signal was absent, and the participant did not report sensing it.

For example, if you are sick and the doctor confirms this, that's a hit. If you are sick and the doctor says "You're fine! Go take that vacation," then unfortunately, that's a miss. If you are healthy, but the doctor says "you are sick," you will definitely be alarmed for a reason that was false. And if you're healthy, and the doctor says "you're fine!," then this is a correct rejection. SDT takes into account response bias, moods, feelings, and decision-making strategies that affect our likelihood of having a given response.

Another type of threshold is the **discrimination threshold**, which is the point at which one can first distinguish the difference between two stimuli. The minimum amount of distance between two stimuli that can be detected as distinct is called the **just noticeable difference (JND)** or **difference threshold**.

In this case, the experiment might involve playing pairs of tones of varying volumes. The participants would try to determine whether the volumes of those tones were the same or different.

> ## Weber's Law
> **Ernst Weber** (1795–1878) noticed that at low weights, say one ounce, it was easy to notice half-ounce increases or decreases in weight; however, at high weights, say 32 ounces, participants were not well able to judge half-ounce differences. The observation that the JND is a proportion of stimulus intensity is called **Weber's law**. Simply put, this law states that the greater the magnitude of the stimulus, the larger the differences must be to be noticed.

Subliminal perception is a form of preconscious processing that occurs when we are presented with stimuli so rapidly that we are not consciously aware of them. When later presented with the same stimuli for a longer period of time, we recognize them more quickly than stimuli we were not subliminally exposed to. Clearly, there was some processing occurring, even if we were not aware of it. This preconscious processing is known as **priming**. Another example of preconscious information processing can be seen in the **tip-of-the-tongue phenomenon**, in which we try to recall something, but find that it is not easily available for conscious awareness. Think of the last time you said something like this: "Hey, can you hand me the...um,...the...um, um, um... the remote?" This phenomenon demonstrates that certain preconscious information may be available to the conscious mind but quite difficult to access.

That moment at the optometrist's when they ask "Which is better—lens 1 or lens 2? Lens 1 or lens 2?" and you freak out because they seem the same? Don't worry! You're right at the JND!

RECEPTOR PROCESSES

Sensory organs have specialized cells, known as **receptor cells**, which are designed to detect specific types of energy. For example, the visual system has specialized receptor cells for detecting light waves. The area from which our receptor cells receive input is the **receptive field**. Incoming forms of energy to which our receptors are sensitive include mechanical (such as in touch), electromagnetic (such as in vision), and chemical (such as in taste and smell). No matter what the form of the input at the level of the receptor, it must first be converted into the electrochemical form of communication used by the nervous system. Through a process called **transduction**, the receptors convert the input, or stimulus, into neural impulses, which are sent to the brain. For example, in order for us to hear something, tiny receptor cells in the inner ear convert vibrations coming from the outer and then middle ear into electrochemical signals. These signals are then carried by neurons to the brain. Transduction takes place at the level of the receptor cells, and then the neural message is passed to the nervous system. The incoming information from all of our senses (except for that of smell) travels to the sensory neurons of the thalamus. The thalamus, as you may recall from the neuroanatomy section, redirects this information to various sensory cortices in the cerebral cortex, where it is processed.

The thalamus may also filter out some sensory inputs; this is an adaptive mechanism for humans because it means that they will not be overwhelmed by incoming sensory information. It is at the level of the thalamus that the **contralateral shift** occurs, in which much of the sensory input from one side of the body travels to the opposite side of the brain. Olfaction, or the sense of smell, travels in a more direct path to the cerebral cortex, without stopping at or being relayed by the thalamus.

SENSORY MECHANISMS

Sensory receptors deal with a wide range of stimuli, and we experience a wide variety of input within each given sensory dimension. Imagine, for example, the gamut of colors and intensities that the eye can sense and relate to the brain. **Sensory coding** is the process by which receptors convey such a range of information to the brain. Every stimulus has two dimensions: what it is (its **qualitative dimension**) and how much of it there is (its **quantitative dimension**). The qualitative dimension is coded and expressed by which neurons are firing. For example, neurons firing in the occipital lobe would indicate that the sensory information is light, and neurons firing in the temporal lobe might indicate that the sensory stimulus is sound. In contrast, the quantitative information is coded by the number of cells firing. Bright lights and loud noises involve the excitation of more neurons than those brought on by dim lights and quiet noises. The wavelengths of light and frequency of sound are perceived as hue and pitch, respectively. The physical characteristic of amplitude is perceived as brightness for light and loudness for sound. The complexity of light is called saturation, and the complexity of sound is called timbre. Sensory neurons respond to differing environmental stimuli by altering their firing rate and the regularity of their firing pattern. **Single-cell recording** is a technique by which the firing rate and pattern of a single receptor cell can be measured in response to varying sensory input.

Talk about a complex sound: "timbre" is pronounced "tamber," not "timber"!

Visual Mechanisms

Visual sensation occurs when the eye receives light input from the outside world. Note that the object as it exists in the environment is known as the **distal stimulus**, whereas the image of that object on the retina is called the **proximal stimulus**. Because of the shape of the retina and the positions of the cornea and the lens, the proximal stimulus is inverted. The brain, through perceptual processes, is then capable of interpreting this image correctly.

Visual sensation is a complex process. First, light passes through the **cornea**, a protective layer on the outside of the eye. Just under the cornea is the **lens**. The curvature of the lens changes to accommodate for distance. These changes are called, logically, **accommodations**. The **retina** is at the back of the eye and serves as the screen onto which the proximal stimulus is projected. The retina is covered with receptors known as **rods** and **cones**. Rods, located on the periphery of the retina, are sensitive to low light. Cones, concentrated in the center of the retina, or **fovea**, are sensitive to bright light and color vision. After light stimulates the receptors, this information passes through horizontal cells to **bipolar** and **amacrine cells**. Some low-level information processing may occur here. The stimulation then travels to the ganglion cells of the **optic nerves.** Where the optic nerve exits the retina, humans have a **blind spot** because

Tip!

Think C for cones and C for color.

there are no photoreceptors there. We rarely notice the blind spot for two reasons: First, our two eyes are set a few inches apart, so they individually have different blind spots. Second, due to Gestalt principles (see pages 176–179), our brains "fill in" the gaps in the visual field without us even recognizing that this is happening. The optic nerves cross at the **optic chiasm**, sending half of the information from each visual field to the opposite side of the brain. Each visual field includes information from both the left and the right eye. From here, information travels to the primary visual cortex areas for processing. The brain processes the information received from vision—color, movement, depth, and form—in parallel, not serial, fashion. **Serial processing** occurs when the brain computes information step-by-step in a methodical and linear matter, while **parallel processing** happens when the brain computes multiple pieces of information simultaneously. In other words, the brain is simultaneously identifying the patterns of what is seen. Over time and through practice, serial processes can turn into parallel processes, just as riding a bike initially requires a person to consider each decision, but later is done seemingly automatically. **Feature detector** neurons "see" different parts of the pattern, such as a line set at a specific angle to the background. Like pieces of a jigsaw puzzle, these parts are amalgamated to produce a perception of the pattern in the environment. This process starts at the back of the occipital lobe and moves forward. As the information moves forward, it becomes more complex and integrated. This process, by which information becomes more complex as it travels through the sensory system, is known as **convergence** and occurs across all sensory systems. Once lines and colors have been sensed, the information travels through two pathways: the dorsal stream and the ventral stream. The ventral stream is the "what" pathway that connects to the prefrontal cortex, allowing a person to recognize an object. The dorsal stream is the "where" pathway that integrates visual information with the other senses through a connection to the somatosensory cortex at the top of the brain. **David Hubel** (1926–2013) and **Torsten Wiesel** (1924–), through experiments with cats, determined that mammals, including humans, will develop normal vision along these lines so long as any impairments are corrected during the **critical period,** the first months after birth.

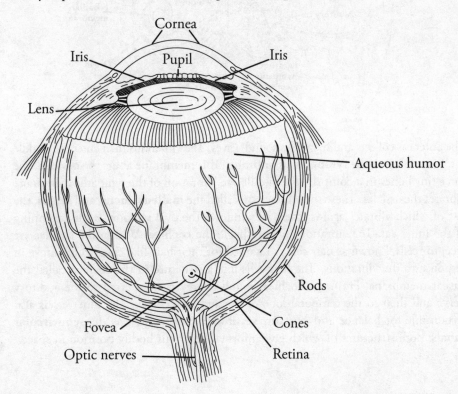

Two different processes contribute to our ability to see in color. The first is based on the **Young-Helmholtz** or **trichromatic theory**. According to this theory, the cones in the retina of the eye are activated by light waves associated with blue, red, and green. We see all colors by mixing these three, much as a television does. However, this does not tell the whole story. Another theory, known as **opponent process theory**, contends that cells within the thalamus respond to opponent pairs of receptor sets—namely, black/white, red/green, and blue/yellow. If one color of the set is activated, the other is essentially turned off. For example, when you stare at a red dot on a page and then you turn away to a blank piece of white paper, you will see a green dot on the blank piece of paper because the red receptors have become fatigued and, in comparison, the green receptors are now more active. This is known as an **afterimage**. **Color blindness** responds to this theory, as well. Most color blindness occurs in males, which provides strong evidence that this is a sex-linked genetic condition. **Dichromats** are people who cannot distinguish along the red/green or blue/yellow continuums. **Monochromats** see only in shades of black and white (this is much more rare). Most color blindness is genetic.

Auditory Mechanisms

Auditory input, in the form of sound waves, enters the ear by passing through the outer ear, the part of the ear that is on the outside of your head, and into the ear canal.

Q: What are the ossicles?

Answer on page 172.

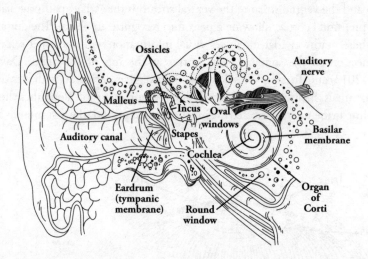

The outer ear collects and magnifies sound waves. The vibrations then enter the middle ear, first vibrating the **tympanic membrane**. This membrane abuts the **ossicles**, the three tiny bones that comprise the middle ear. Vibration of the tympanic membrane vibrates the ossicles. These three bones are called the **malleus**, **incus**, and **stapes**, the last of which vibrates against the oval window. The oval window is the beginning of the inner ear. The vibrations further jiggle the **cochlea**. Within the cochlea are receptor cells, known as hair cells, so named for their hair-like cilia, which move in response to the vibrations. The hair cells line a structure in the cochlea called the basilar membrane. From the cochlea, sound energy is transferred to the auditory nerve and then to the temporal lobe of the auditory cortex. The inner ear is also responsible for balance and contains **vestibular sacs**, as well as the **semicircular canals**: both structures of which give information about bodily position in space.

Various theories have been suggested for how hearing occurs. Current thinking relies on the work of Georg von Békésy, which asserts that a traveling wave energizes the basilar membrane. As frequencies get higher, so do the peaks of the traveling wave, increasing the stimulation of the receptors for hearing. This accounts for recognition of sound above 150 Hz. However, humans can hear from 20 to 20,000 Hz. The volley principle—which states that receptor cells fire alternatively, increasing their firing capacity—appears to account for the reception of sound in the lower ranges. **Place theory** asserts that sound waves generate activity at different places along the basilar membrane. **Frequency theory** in hearing states that we sense pitch because the rate of neural impulses is equal to the frequency of a particular sound. **Deafness** can occur from damage to the ear structure or the neural pathway. **Conductive deafness** refers to injury to the outer or middle ear structures, such as the eardrum. Impairment of some structure or structures from the cochlea to the auditory cortex results in **sensorineural**, or nerve, **deafness.** Conductive deafness and milder forms of sensorineural deafness may be addressed successfully with hearing aids. However, profound sensorineural hearing loss may require a cochlear implant, which stimulates the auditory nerve directly.

Study Tip

Of all the individual parts of the visual and auditory system, the most likely to show up on exam questions are the retina and the cochlea. This is because that is where transduction takes place. So, make sure that you understand this process and how it takes place in each.

Other Sensory Mechanisms

Olfaction (smell) is a chemical sense. Scent molecules reach the olfactory epithelium, deep in the nasal cavity. The scent molecules contact receptor cells at this location. Axons from these receptors project directly to the olfactory bulbs of the brain. From there, information travels to the olfactory cortex and the limbic system. Because the amygdala and hippocampus connect to olfactory nerves, it is easy to understand why certain smells trigger memories.

Gustation (taste) is also a chemical sense. The tongue is coated with small protrusions known as papillae. Located on the papillae are the taste buds, the receptors for gustatory information. There are five basic tastes: sweet, salty, bitter, sour, and umami (savory). These five tastes may have evolved for specific reasons. For example, sweetness, which we tend to like, is often accompanied by calories. Most poisonous plants, in contrast, taste bitter, a taste we generally do not like. Information from the taste buds travels to the medulla oblongata and then to the pons and the thalamus. This information is then relayed to the gustatory areas of the cerebral cortex, as well as the hypothalamus and limbic system.

The skin has **cutaneous** and **tactile receptors** that provide information about pressure, pain, and temperature. The receptor cells sensitive to pressure and movement are fast-conducting myelinated neurons, which send information to the spinal cord. From here, the information goes to the medulla oblongata, the thalamus, and finally, to the somatosensory cortex. Pain information is sent via two types of neurons; C fibers are unmyelinated and responsible for the throbbing sense of chronic pain, while myelinated A-delta fibers send information about acute pain. The pain signal first reaches the spinal cord and triggers the release of "substance P" (a neuropeptide, or chemical signal similar to a neurotransmitter, that alerts the spinal cord to the presence of a painful stimulus). The signal then travels to the thalamus and to the cingulate cortex, which is responsible for attention. Once pain is perceived, the brain begins to reduce the intensity of the signal through a process known as "pain-gating." As described by the **gate theory of pain**, a signal is sent from the brain to opiate receptors in the spinal cord, which reduces the sensation of pain. This information projects to the limbic system and then to the somatosensory cortex. The receptor cells for temperature can be divided into **cold fibers**, which fire in response to cold stimuli, and **warm fibers**, which are sensitive to warm stimuli.

Other senses include the **vestibular sense**, which involves the sensation of balance. This sense is located in the semicircular canals of the inner ear. **Kinesthesis** refers to one's sense of the body's location and motion; this sense is supported by sensors in the joints and ligaments.

Use this table to compare and contrast different sensory systems.

Sensory System	Receptor Cells Location	Type of Energy	Transduction	Processing Center Location
Visual	Eye	Light	Rods and cones in the retina	Occipital lobe
Auditory	Ear	Sound	Cochlea	Temporal lobe
Tactile	Tactile and cutaneous cells on the skin	Pressure	Tactile cells	Somatosensory cortex
Olfaction (smell)	Nose	Chemical	Olfactory receptor cells	Olfactory bulb
Gustation (taste)	Tongue	Chemical	Taste buds	Cerebral cortex

Synesthesia is a neurological condition in which stimulation of one sense leads to automatic activation of another sense; for example, one might "hear" colors.

A: The ossicles are three tiny bones in the middle ear, called the malleus, incus, and stapes, that connect the eardrum to the oval window.

SENSORY ADAPTATION

Our sensory systems need to do more than simply detect the presence and absence of stimulation. They also need to do more than detect the intensity or quality of stimuli. A key feature of our sensory systems is that they are dynamic: that is, they detect changes in stimulus intensity and quality. Two processes are used in responding to changing stimuli: adaptation and habituation.

Adaptation is an unconscious, temporary change in response to environmental stimuli. An example of this process is our adaptation to being in darkness. At first, it is difficult to see, but our visual system soon adapts to the lack of light. Sensory adaptation to differing stimuli leaves our sensory systems at various adaptation levels. The adaptation level is the new reference standard of stimulation against which new stimuli are judged. A familiar example is that of the swimming pool. If you enter a 75-degree swimming pool directly from an air-conditioned room, it will feel warm, as your adaptation level is set for the cold room. If, however, you are on a hot beach and then enter the same pool, it will feel cold, as your adaptation level is set for the heat of the beach.

Habituation is the process by which we become accustomed to a stimulus, and notice it less and less over time. **Dishabituation** occurs when a change in the stimulus, even a small change, causes us to notice it again. Dishabituation also occurs when a stimulus is removed and then re-presented. A good example of this pair of processes is in the noise from an air conditioner. We may notice a noisy air conditioner when we first enter a room, but after a few minutes, we stop noticing it; we have habituated to the noise. However, when the air conditioner's compressor turns on, slightly altering the sound being generated, we once again notice the noise. This noticing is dishabituation. Although habituation is not typically a conscious process, we can control it under certain circumstances. If, in the examples above, we are unaware of the air-conditioner noise, but then someone asks us whether the noise of the air conditioner sounds like something else, we can force ourselves to dishabituate, and again notice the noise. This control over our information processing is the key to distinguishing habituation from sensory adaptation: you cannot control sensory adaptation; for example, you cannot force your eyes to adapt to darkness by mere force of will. You can, however, force yourself to pay attention to things to which you have habituated.

ATTENTION

The term **attention** refers to the processing through cognition of a select portion of the massive amount of information incoming from the senses and contained in memory. In common terms, attention is what allows us to focus on one small aspect of our perceptual world, such as a conversation, while constantly being assailed by massive input to all of our sensory systems. Attention serves as a bottleneck, or funnel, that channels out some information in order to focus on other information. This process is essential because the brain is not equipped to process and pay attention to all of the information it is presented with at a particular moment. The fact that the brain must take shortcuts and focus on particular information is a key issue in perception, which explains why the brain can be tricked through illusions.

Selective attention, or focusing on one thing (like a movie) while ignoring another (like a loud talker), is a good example of this type of focus. So is the **cocktail party phenomenon**, wherein a person can carry on and follow a single conversation in a room full of them but also still have their attention quickly drawn to another conversation by a key stimulus, such as someone saying their name. The ability to switch from an active conversation to one that you had not previously been focused on proves that a part of your brain was subconsciously attending to that information. When it attended to that key stimulus, it sent a signal to the frontal lobe to make you fully aware of it.

Differentiating Messages

It is easiest for people to tell the difference between messages when they are physically different, such as when one message is spoken by a woman and the other by a man.

This phenomenon has been studied in the laboratory with headphones, by playing a different message in each of a participant's ears. The participant is instructed to repeat only one of the conversations. This repetition is referred to as **shadowing**. The message played into the nonshadowed ear is largely ignored; however, changes in that message or key words, like names, can draw attention to that message. There are two main types of theories explaining selective attention: filter theories and attentional resource theories. **Filter theories** propose that stimuli must pass through some form of screen or filter to enter into attention. Donald Broadbent proposed a filter at the receptor level. However, the notion of a filter at this level has generally been discarded, based on findings showing that meaningful stimuli, such as our own names, can catch our attention. Therefore, the filter must be at a higher processing level than that of the receptors because meaning has already been processed.

Attentional resource theories, in contrast, posit that we have only a fixed amount of attention, and this resource can be divided up as is required in a given situation. So, if you are deeply engrossed in this book, you are giving it nearly all of your attentional resources. Only strong stimulation could capture your attention. This theory is also inadequate, however, because all attention is not equal. For example, a conversation occurring near you is more likely to interfere with your reading than is some other nonverbal noise.

Divided attention, trying to focus on more than one task at a time, is most difficult when attending to two or more stimuli that activate the same sense, as in watching TV and reading. The ability to successfully divide attention declines with age. **Inattentional blindness,** also known as change blindness, demonstrates a potential weakness of selective attention. Sometimes, when people focus too intently on specific stimuli, they can miss the bigger picture going on around them. There are many entertaining videos available online that display this phenomenon.

> A classic video asks the viewer to pay attention to the number of times a basketball is passed. Most people who watch for this tend not to notice that someone in a gorilla costume walks right through the game.

PERCEPTUAL PROCESSES

When we were describing sensory mechanisms, we talked about how environmental stimuli affect the receptor systems. This section deals with **perceptual processes**—how our mind interprets these stimuli. There are two main theories of perception: bottom-up and top-down.

> **Remember This!**
> Sensation =
> bottom-up process
> Perception =
> top-down process

Bottom-up processing achieves recognition of an object by breaking it down into its component parts. It relies heavily on the sensory receptors. Bottom-up processing is the brain's analysis and acknowledgment of the raw data. **Top-down processing**, by contrast, occurs when the brain labels a particular stimulus or experience. For example, let's think about the first time a person tastes the sourness of a lemon. In this example, the neurons firing to alert the brain of the presence of some taste in the mouth is a bottom-up process, whereas labeling it "sour" is the top-down process. However, the next time the person sees a lemon, they might salivate or wince before ever tasting the lemon. This is top-down processing because the expectation based on experience influences the perception of the lemon. Top-down processing can be a factor in optical illusions when people see what they expect to see rather than what is actually in front of them.

Visual perception is quite complex. We need to perceive depth, size, shape, and motion. Depth perception is facilitated by various perceptual cues. Because of the limited ability of the brain to process information, it must take certain shortcuts and educated guesses based on how the world is normally structured. As such, the brain uses these cues but can also fall victim to illusions.

Visual perception cues can be divided into monocular and binocular cues. **Monocular depth cues** refer to the qualities of a visual scene that let you know how close or how far things are from you, using just one eye. **Relative size** refers to the fact that images that are farther from us project a smaller image on the retina than do those that are closer to us. Therefore, we expect an object that appears much larger than another to be closer to us. Related to this idea is the idea of **texture gradient**. Textures, or the patterns of distribution of objects, appear to grow more dense as distance increases. If we are looking at pebbles in the distance, they appear smooth and uniform, but close up may appear jagged and rough. Another monocular depth cue is **interposition**, also known as occlusion, which occurs when a near object partially blocks the view of an object behind it. **Linear perspective** is a monocular cue based on the perception that parallel lines seem to draw closer together as the lines recede into the distance. Picture yourself standing on a train track, looking at the two rails. As the rails move away from you, they appear to draw closer together. The place where the rails seem to join is called the **vanishing point**. This is the point at which the two lines become indistinguishable from a single line and then disappear. Objects present near the vanishing point are assumed to be farther away than those along the tracks at a point where they diverge greatly. **Aerial perspective**, another perceptual cue, is based on the observation that atmospheric moisture and dust tend to obscure objects in the distance more than they do nearby objects. An example of this notion occurs when one is driving in the fog; a far-off building looks more distant than it really is through the fog, but its image quickly becomes clearer and clearer as you approach. **Relative clarity** is a perceptual clue that explains why less distinct, fuzzy images appear to be more distant. **Motion parallax** is the difference in the apparent movement of objects at different distances, when the observer is in motion. For example, when riding on a train, a person sees distant objects out of a window as seeming to move fairly slowly; they may appear to move in the same direction as the train. Nearer objects seem to move more quickly and in the opposite direction to the movement of the train.

Binocular depth cues rely on both eyes viewing an image. They result from the fact that each eye sees a given image from a slightly different angle: this difference is called **retinal disparity**. When the brain fuses the images produced on the two separate retinas, it creates a three-dimensional or **stereoptic** image. **Retinal convergence** is a depth cue that results from the fact that your eyes must turn inward slightly to focus on near objects. The

Nature, Nurture, and the Visual Cliff

Together, the binocular cues for vision enable us to have depth perception. To test whether depth perception was innate (nature) or learned (nurture), researchers **Eleanor Gibson** and **Richard Walk** developed the **visual cliff** to test depth perception. The visual cliff was a glass tabletop that appeared to be clear on one side and had a checkerboard design visible on the other side. Infants were placed on the checkerboard side of the "cliff," and researchers tracked whether they would crawl onto the clear side, thus going "over the cliff." Most infants refused to do so, which implies that depth perception is at least partially innate. Because the infants had to be a few months old, it was unclear how much learning had influenced depth perception. With other animals tested (chicks, pigs, kittens, turtles), it was concluded that the animal's visual skills depended on the importance of vision to the organism's survival.

closer the object, the more the eyes must turn inward. The complement to stereopsis is **binocular disparity**, which results from the fact that the closer an object is, the less similar the information arriving at each eye will be. This process can be demonstrated by covering one eye, then the other, while looking at something directly in front of you. This procedure reveals two very different views of the object. Repeat this procedure with an object across the room, however, and the two views appear more similar.

As previously stated, the visual system also needs to perceive and recognize form: that is, size and shape. The **Gestalt approach** to form perception is based on a top-down theory. This view holds that most perceptions involve figure-ground relationships. Figures are those things that stand out, whereas the ground is the field against which the figures stand out. The famous vase-face example shows us that figure and ground are often reversible.

Some basic Gestalt principles of figure detection include the following:

- **Proximity**—the tendency to see objects near each other as forming groups

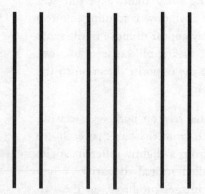

The Gestalt Principle of Proximity: We tend to see these
as three pairs of lines, rather than as six individual lines.

- **Similarity**—the tendency to prefer grouping like objects together

The Gestalt Principle of Similarity: We tend to see these as rows of circles and rows of squares, rather than as columns of circles and squares.

- **Symmetry**—the tendency to perceive forms that make up mirror images

The Gestalt Principle of Symmetry: We tend to see the top figures as a single circle, and the lower figures as forming a single triangle.

- **Continuity**—the tendency to perceive fluid or continuous forms, rather than jagged or irregular ones

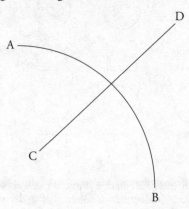

The Gestalt Principle of Continuity: We tend to see this as a curve from point A to point B and a line from C to D, rather than seeing angular paths from A to D and C to B.

- **Closure**—the tendency to see closed objects rather than those that are incomplete

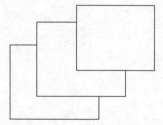

The Gestalt Principle of Closure: We tend to see this as three rectangles, even though there is actually only one rectangle that is completely visible.

These Gestalt principles represent the **Law of Prägnanz**, which suggests that we tend to see objects in their simplest forms.

A different theory of form recognition is based on a **feature detector approach**. This approach differs from the Law of Prägnanz, which reduces an image to its simplest form, by positing that organisms respond to specific aspects of a particular stimulus. For example, when driving a car, we use feature detection to anticipate the movement of other cars and pedestrians that demand our immediate attention, helping us to be more aware of the environment.

Constancy is another important perceptual process. Constancy means that we know that a stimulus remains the same size, shape, brightness, weight, and/or volume even though it does not appear to. People who have never seen airplanes on the ground will have trouble perceiving the actual size of a plane because of their experience with the size of the object when airborne. The *ability* to achieve constancy, which is innate, and the *experience*, which is learned, both contribute to our development of the various types of constancy.

One of the most complex abilities we have is **motion detection**. We perceive motion through two processes. One records the changing position of an object as it moves across the retina. The other tracks how we move our heads to follow the stimulus. In both cases, the brain interprets the information with special motion detectors. A related issue is the perception of **apparent motion**. Examples of apparent movement include blinking lights on a roadside arrow, which give the appearance of movement (**phi phenomenon**); a motion picture, wherein still pictures move at a fast enough pace to imply movement (**stroboscopic effect**); and still light that appears to twinkle in darkness (**autokinetic effect**).

KEY TERMS

Introduction to Sensation and Perception
sensation
perception

Thresholds
psychophysics
absolute threshold
Gustav Fechner
detection thresholds
signal detection theory (SDT)
hit
miss
false alarm
correct rejection
discrimination threshold
just noticeable difference
  (JND) (difference threshold)
Ernst Weber
Weber's law
subliminal perception
priming
tip-of-the-tongue phenomenon

Receptor Processes
receptor cells
receptive field
transduction
contralateral shift

Sensory Mechanisms
sensory coding
qualitative dimension
quantitative dimension
single-cell recording
visual sensation
distal stimulus
proximal stimulus
cornea
lens
accommodations
retina
rods
cones
fovea
bipolar cells
amacrine cells
optic nerves

blind spot
optic chiasm
serial processing
parallel processing
feature detector
convergence
David Hubel
Torsten Wiesel
critical period
Young-Helmholtz theory
  (trichromatic theory)
opponent process theory
afterimage
color blindness
dichromats
monochromats
auditory input
tympanic membrane
ossicles
  malleus
  incus
  stapes
cochlea
vestibular sacs
semicircular canals
place theory
frequency theory
deafness
conductive deafness
sensorineural deafness
olfaction
gustation
cutaneous receptors
tactile receptors
gate theory of pain
cold fibers
warm fibers
vestibular sense
kinesthesis
synesthesia

Sensory Adaptation
adaptation
habituation
dishabituation

Attention
selective attention
cocktail party phenomenon
shadowing
filter theories
attentional resource theories
divided attention
inattentional blindness

Perceptual Processes
bottom-up processing
top-down processing
visual perception
monocular depth cues
  relative size
  texture gradient
  interposition
  linear perspective
  vanishing point
  aerial perspective
  relative clarity
  motion parallax
Eleanor Gibson and Richard
  Walk
visual cliff
binocular depth cues
  retinal disparity
  stereoptic
  retinal convergence
  binocular disparity
Gestalt approach
  proximity
  similarity
  symmetry
  continuity
  closure
Law of Prägnanz
feature detector approach
constancy
motion detection
apparent motion
  phi phenomenon
  stroboscopic effect
  autokinetic effect

Chapter 9 Drill

See Chapter 19 for answers and explanations.

1. If a person is supposed to press a button when he sees a red triangle but instead presses the button when he sees a green triangle, what is this called?

   (A) Opponent process
   (B) Hit
   (C) False alarm
   (D) Miss
   (E) Correct rejection

2. The five basic gustatory sensations that most animals possess are

   (A) bitter, salty, sweet, tangy, sour
   (B) salty, sweet, bitter, sour, umami
   (C) smooth, grainy, cold, hot, prickly
   (D) grain, fruit, meat, vegetable, dairy
   (E) salty, sharp, umami, sour, bitter

3. Cats tend to notice slight movements under low lighting conditions with greater ease than do humans; they do not, however, find it easy to distinguish colors. This is primarily due to their retinas containing, in comparison to humans,

   (A) relatively fewer amacrine cells and relatively more bipolar cells
   (B) relatively fewer ganglion cells and relatively more osmoreceptors
   (C) relatively fewer cilia and relatively more optic nerve cells
   (D) relatively fewer cones and relatively more rods
   (E) relatively fewer mechanoreceptors and relatively more ossicles

4. The Gestalt concept of perceptual continuity refers to

   (A) our tendency to see objects near to each other as belonging to the same group
   (B) our tendency to see objects that are closer to us as larger than objects that are farther away
   (C) our tendency to see fluid or complete forms rather than irregular or incomplete ones
   (D) our tendency to see similar-looking objects as part of the same group
   (E) our tendency to see two slightly different images from each of our eyes

5. Which of the following would be the best illustration of Weber's law?

   (A) Most people can recognize the difference between a 40- and 42-decibel sound, but not an 80- and 82-decibel sound.
   (B) A person can recognize an imperceptible amount of perfume in a ten-foot-by-ten-foot room.
   (C) People cannot attend to more than one stimulus at a time.
   (D) A person has the ability to tell the difference between a 20-watt bulb and a 100-watt bulb 50 percent of the time.
   (E) All auditory stimuli above a certain frequency "sound" as if their frequencies are the same.

6. What structure in the middle ear generates vibrations that match the sound waves striking it?

   (A) Basilar membrane
   (B) Tympanic membrane
   (C) Cochlea
   (D) Malleus
   (E) Stapes

7. In the human visual pathway, what cell type comprises the bundle of fibers called the optic nerve?

   (A) Rods
   (B) Bipolar cells
   (C) Ganglion cells
   (D) Fovea cells
   (E) Cones

8. In a given drawing, instead of perceiving a series of lines, humans perceive two shapes: a circle and a rectangle. What best accounts for this phenomenon?

   (A) The principles of Gestalt psychology
   (B) Bottom-up processing
   (C) Parallel processing
   (D) Weber's law
   (E) Summation

9. Claire views the figure above and reports seeing a triangle in the center supported by some concentric discs. Which Gestalt principle does Claire rely on most heavily to render this description?

    (A) Proximity
    (B) Symmetry
    (C) Similarity
    (D) Closure
    (E) Continuity

10. Laretta walks into a classroom and notices a strange odor. She sits down for class and, over time, forgets about the smell. When she returns to class the next day, she notices the odor again. This phenomenon is known as

    (A) habituation
    (B) dishabituation
    (C) adaptation
    (D) sensitization
    (E) desensitization

11. Subliminal perception is a form of preconscious processing that occurs when stimuli are presented too rapidly for us to be consciously aware of them. The fact that these stimuli were perceived and processed on some level can be demonstrated by

    (A) immediate recognition of these stimuli
    (B) subtle influence to do or say something that has been presented subliminally
    (C) inability of the stimuli to be subject to the tip-of-the-tongue phenomenon
    (D) greater tendency of these stimuli to be subject to proactive interference
    (E) slower recall of these stimuli in a matched-pairs trial

REFLECT

Respond to the following questions:

- Which topics in this chapter do you hope to see on the multiple-choice section or essay?

- Which topics in this chapter do you hope not to see on the multiple-choice section or essay?

- Regarding any psychologists mentioned, can you pair the psychologists with their contributions to the field? Did they contribute significant experiments, theories, or both?

- Regarding any theories mentioned, can you distinguish between differing theories well enough to recognize them on the multiple-choice section? Can you distinguish them well enough to write a fluent essay on them?

- Regarding any figures given, if you were given a labeled figure from within this chapter, would you be able to give the significance of each part of the figure?

- Can you define the key terms at the end of the chapter?

- Which parts of the chapter will you review?

- Will you seek further help, outside of this book (such as from a teacher, Princeton Review tutor, or AP Students), on any of the content in this chapter—and, if so, on what content?

Chapter 10
Learning

LEARNING: AN OVERVIEW

Learning is a relatively permanent or stable change in behavior as a result of experience. Such changes may be associated with certain changes in the connections within the nervous system. Learning occurs by various methods, including classical conditioning, operant conditioning, and social learning. Cognitive factors are also implicated in learning, particularly in humans.

NONASSOCIATIVE LEARNING

Nonassociative learning occurs when an organism is repeatedly exposed to one type of stimulus. Two important types of nonassociative learning are habituation and **sensitization**. We discussed habituation in Chapter 9, so let's look at sensitization!

Sensitization is, in many ways, the opposite of habituation. During sensitization, there is an increase in responsiveness due to either a repeated application of a stimulus or a particularly aversive or noxious stimulus. Instead of being able to "tune out" or ignore the stimulus so as to avoid reacting at all (as in habituation), the stimulus actually produces a more exaggerated response. Imagine that you attend a rock concert and sit near the stage. The feedback noise from the amplifier may at first be merely irritating, but as the aversive noise continues, instead of getting used to it, it actually becomes much more painful, to the point at which you have to cover your ears and perhaps even move. Sensitization may also cause you to respond more vigorously to similar stimuli. For example, as you leave the rock concert, an ambulance passes. The siren, which usually doesn't bother you, seems particularly loud and abrasive, as you've been sensitized to the noise of the rock concert. Thankfully, sensitization is usually temporary and unlikely to result in any long-term behavior change. **Desensitization** refers to a decreased responsiveness to an aversive stimulus after repeated exposure. This phenomenon may occur on its own or in the context of **desensitization therapy**. For example, if you have a phobia of snakes, you might engage in **systematic desensitization**: you look at a picture of a snake until your reaction is normal; then you come into a room with a snake until your reaction is normal. In various therapy sessions, you get closer and closer to the snake, eventually even handling it. By being exposed to the stimulus but having no bad outcomes, you can become desensitized to the stimulus and thus overcome your phobia.

CLASSICAL CONDITIONING

Classical conditioning was first described by **Ivan Pavlov** and is sometimes called **Pavlovian conditioning**. Classical conditioning occurs when a neutral stimulus, paired with a previously meaningful stimulus, eventually takes on some meaning itself. For example, if you shine a light in your fish tank, the fish will ignore it. If you put food in the tank, they will all typically swim to the top to get the food. If, however, each time you feed the fish, you shine the light in the tank before putting in the food, the fish will begin to learn about the light. Eventually, the light alone will cause the fish to swim to the top, as if food had been placed in the tank. The previously neutral light has now taken on some meaning.

Psychologists use specific terms for the various stimuli in classical conditioning. The **conditioned stimulus (CS)** is the initially neutral stimulus—in our example, the light. The **unconditioned stimulus (US)** is the initially meaningful stimulus. In our example, the US is food. The response to the US does not have to be learned; this naturally occurring response is the **unconditioned response (UR)**. In our example, the UR is swimming to the top of the tank. The **conditioned response (CR)** is the response to the CS after conditioning. Again, in our example, the CR is swimming to the top. If you are having a difficult time understanding the different parts of classical conditioning, note that *conditioning* is another word for *learning*. For instance, *unconditioned response* is just another way of saying *unlearned response*.

What has just been presented is the simplest case of classical conditioning. The CS and the US can be paired into classical conditioning in a number of ways. **Forward conditioning**, in which the CS is presented before the US, can be further divided into **delay conditioning**, in which the CS is present until the US begins, and **trace conditioning**, in which the CS is removed some time before the US is presented. For the most part, the CS, or neutral stimulus, should come before the US. In the fish example above, this point is true because if the US (the food) was present first, the fish could be distracted from noticing the presence of the CS (the light) and would therefore not learn the association. Forward conditioning has been found to be the most effective at modifying behavior.

John Watson and his assistant Rosalie Rayner demonstrated classical conditioning with a child known now as Little Albert. Albert was first tested and found to have no fear of small animals, though he did show fear whenever a steel bar was banged loudly with a hammer. Watson then presented Albert repeatedly with a small, harmless white rat, and at the same time, banged the steel bar, making the child cry. (Today, this procedure would not be considered ethical.) Afterward, Albert cringed and cried any time he was presented with the rat—even if the noise wasn't made. Furthermore, Albert showed that he was afraid of other white fluffy objects; the closer they resembled the white rat, the more he cried and cringed. This is known as **generalization**. If Albert could distinguish among similar but distinct stimuli, he would be exhibiting **discrimination**. We can use this example to demonstrate other terms related to classical conditioning. **Acquisition** takes place when the pairing of the natural and neutral stimuli (the loud noise and the rat) have occurred with enough frequency that the neutral stimulus alone will elicit the conditional response (cringing and crying). **Extinction**, or the elimination of the conditioned response, can be achieved by presenting the CS without the US repeatedly (in other words, the white rat without the loud noise). Eventually, the white rat will not produce the unpleasant response. However, **spontaneous recovery**, in which the original response disappears on its own, but then is elicited again by the previous CS at a later time, is also possible under certain circumstances. Returning to the fish: if after having taught them to associate a light with feeding, you shine a light and give no food a number of times, the fish will initially swim to the top looking for food, but will eventually ignore the light. However, after a period of time of not shining the light, if you shine the light again, the fish will again swim to the top. Notice that they do so spontaneously, without having been taught again. Of course, if there is no food, then the fish will even more quickly stop responding to the light. Spontaneous recovery demonstrates that even though the learning is not evident during the extinction period, the association between the CS and CR is still stored in the brain.

In **second-order conditioning**, a previous CS is used as the US. In our example, the fish would now be trained with a new CS, such as a tone, which would be paired with the light, which would now serve as the US. If the conditioning were successful, the fish would learn to swim to the top in response to the tone. Second-order conditioning is a special case of higher-order conditioning, which, in theory, can go up to any order as new CSs are linked to old ones. In practice, higher-order conditioning is rarely effective beyond the second order.

There are two distinct theories as to why classical conditioning works. Pavlov and Watson believed that the pairing of the neutral (eventual CS) and the natural (US) stimuli occurred because they were paired in time. This is the **contiguity approach**. Robert Rescorla believes that the CS and US get paired because the CS comes to predict the US. The fish from the initial example come to expect food upon seeing the light. This is known as the **contingency approach**.

OPERANT CONDITIONING

Operant conditioning (also called **instrumental conditioning**) involves an organism's learning to engage in an action in order to obtain a reward or avoid punishment. **B.F. Skinner** pioneered the study of operant conditioning, although the phenomenon first was discovered by **Edward L. Thorndike**, who proposed the **law of effect**, which states that a behavior is more likely to recur if reinforced. Skinner ran many operant conditioning experiments. He often used a specially designed testing apparatus known as an operant conditioning chamber, or a Skinner box.

This box typically was empty except for a lever and a hole through which food pellets could be delivered. Skinner trained rats to press the lever (not a typical behavior for rats) in order to get food. To get the rats to learn to press a lever, the experimenter would use a procedure called **shaping**, in which a rat first receives a food reward for being near the lever, then for touching the lever, and finally for pressing the lever. In the end, the rat is rewarded only for pressing the lever. This process is also referred to as **differential reinforcement of successive approximations**.

In a typical operant conditioning experiment, pressing the bar is the operant behavior, and food is the reinforcer. Food is a form of **natural reinforcement**; you don't have to learn to like it. These types of natural reinforcers, such as food, water, and sex, provide **primary reinforcement**. **Secondary reinforcement** is provided by learned reinforcers. Money is a good example of a secondary reinforcer. In nature, money is just paper or metal; it has no intrinsic value. We have learned, however, that money can be exchanged for primary reinforcers.

Reinforcement can be divided into positive and negative reinforcement. **Positive reinforcement** is a reward or event that increases the likelihood that a particular type of behavior will be repeated. For example, in the experiment in which a rat is given a food pellet every time it presses a lever, the food provides positive reinforcement, increasing the likelihood that the rat will press the lever again. **Negative reinforcement** is the removal of an aversive event in order to encourage the behavior. An example of negative reinforcement occurs in an experiment in which a rat is sitting on a mildly electrified cage floor. Pressing a bar in the cage turns off the electrical current. The removal of the negative experience (shock) is rewarding. **Omission training**, in contrast, seeks to decrease the frequency of behavior by withholding the reward until the desired behavior is demonstrated.

	reinforcement (think **re**ward)	punishment
positive (think addition!)	giving food, giving praise, giving money, giving a good grade, giving gold stars	giving pain, giving a chore, giving extra homework, giving a bad grade
negative (think subtraction!)	taking away a chore, ending a punishment, removing pain, canceling homework	taking away food, taking away money (a fine), taking away freedom (being grounded, getting a time-out)

Behaviorists use various schedules of reinforcement in their experiments. A **schedule of reinforcement** refers to the frequency with which an organism receives reinforcement for a given type of response. In a **continuous reinforcement schedule**, every correct response that is emitted results in a reward. This produces rapid learning, but it also results in rapid extinction, where extinction is a decrease and eventual disappearance of a response once the behavior is no longer reinforced.

Schedules of reinforcement in which not all behaviors are reinforced are called **partial** (or **intermittent**) **reinforcement schedules**. A **fixed-ratio schedule** is one in which the reward always occurs after a fixed number of behaviors. For example, a rat might have to press a lever 10 times in order to receive a food pellet. This schedule is called a 10:1 ratio schedule. Fixed-ratio schedules produce strong learning, but the learning extinguishes relatively quickly, as the rat quickly detects that the reinforcement schedule no longer is operative. A **variable-ratio schedule** is one in which the ratio of operant behaviors to reinforcement is variable and unpredictable. A good example of this is slot machines. The operant behavior, putting in money and pulling the lever, is reinforced with a payoff in a seemingly random manner. Reinforcement can come at any time. This type of schedule takes

Variable-Interval in the Classroom

This schedule of reinforcement is illustrated by a teacher who gives pop quizzes. The time at which the quiz will be given is always changing.

longer to condition a behavior; however, the learning that occurs is resistant to extinction, which helps explain why people can become addicted to gambling. A **fixed-interval schedule** is one in which reinforcement is presented as a function of fixed periods of time, as long as there is at least one operant behavior. This schedule is similar to being a salaried employee. Every two weeks, the paycheck arrives regardless of your work performance (as long as you show up at all). Finally, in the **variable-interval schedule**, reinforcement is presented at differing time intervals, as long as there is at least one operant behavior. Variable-interval, like variable-ratio, is more difficult to extinguish than fixed schedules.

Study Tip

Make sure that you can explain why the different partial reinforcement schedules produce different behaviors in people being reinforced. See whether you can apply it to your own life and how you are reinforced for various behaviors. For variable-ratio reinforcement, focus on the gambling example presented and try to imagine why this schedule can prove so addictive.

Like reinforcement, **punishment** is also an important element of operant conditioning, but the effect is the opposite: reinforcement increases behavior, while punishment decreases it. Punishment is an event that decreases the likelihood that the behavior will be repeated. Like reinforcement, punishment can be both positive AND negative. Positive punishment involves the application, or pairing, of an unpleasant stimulus with the behavior. For example, if cadets speak out of turn in military boot camp, the drill sergeant makes them do 20 push-ups. In contrast, negative punishment involves the removal of a reinforcing (desirable) stimulus after the behavior has occurred. For example, a child who breaks a window loses TV privileges for a week. Positive punishment adds and negative punishment subtracts. Commonly, both reinforcement and punishment are used in conjunction when shaping behaviors; however, it is uncommon for punishment to have as much of a lasting effect as reinforcement. Once the punishment has been removed, it is no longer effective. Furthermore, punishment instructs only what not to do, whereas reinforcement instructs what to do. Reinforcement is therefore a better choice to encourage behavioral changes and learning. Additionally, the processes described for classical conditioning (acquisition, extinction, spontaneous recovery, generalization, and discrimination) occur in operant conditioning, as well.

Let's further examine two specific types of operant learning: **escape** and **avoidance**. In escape, an individual learns how to get away from an aversive stimulus by engaging in a particular behavior. This helps reinforce the behavior so they will be willing to engage in it again. For example, a child does not want to eat her vegetables (aversive stimulus), so she throws a temper tantrum. If the parents respond by not making the child eat the vegetables, then she will learn that behaving in that specific way will help her escape that particular aversive stimulus. On the other hand, avoidance occurs when a person performs a behavior to ensure an aversive stimulus is not presented. For example, a child notices Mom cooking vegetables for dinner and fakes an illness so Mom will send him to bed with ginger ale and crackers. The child has effectively avoided confronting the aversive stimulus (the offensive vegetables) altogether. As long as either of these techniques work (meaning the parents do not force the child to eat the vegetables), the child is reinforced to perform the escape and/or avoidance behaviors.

A combination of reinforcers and punishers designed to alter behavior is referred to as **behavior modification.** Operant conditioning techniques are used quite frequently in places that have controlled populations, such as prisons and mental institutions. Such an institution might set up a **token economy**—an artificial economy based on tokens (such as points or gold stars). These tokens act as secondary reinforcers, in that the tokens can be used for purchasing primary reinforcers, such as food. The participants in a token economy are reinforced for desired behaviors (responses) with tokens; this reinforcement is designed to increase the number of positive behaviors that occur.

Learned helplessness occurs when efforts consistently fail to bring rewards. If this situation persists, the subject will stop trying. Psychologist Martin Seligman's original experiment placed dogs in a room with an electrified floor. At first, the dogs would try to escape the room or avoid the floor, but they ultimately learned that there was nothing they could do to prevent being shocked. Eventually, when the dogs' leashes were removed, they still stayed on the electrified floor, even though they could have escaped. This fact shows that they had learned to be helpless. Seligman sees this condition as possibly precipitating depression in humans. If people try repeatedly to succeed at work, school, and/or relationships, and find their efforts are in vain no matter how hard they try, depression may result.

Reinforcement can also lead to the development of superstitions. People can make specious connections between their behaviors and positive outcomes, leading to perpetuation of the "lucky" behaviors.

BIOLOGICAL FACTORS

The biological basis of learning is of great interest to psychologists. Neuroscientists have tried to identify the neural correlates of learning. In other words, what physiological changes are brought about when we learn?

In the 1960s, psychologists noticed that neurons themselves could be affected by environmental stimulation. Experiments were conducted in which some rats were raised in an enriched environment, while others were raised in a deprived environment. The enriched environment included things to explore and lots of room in which to move, whereas the deprived environment was just a small, empty cage. At the end of the experiment, the rats were sacrificed, and their brains were examined. The experimenters found that the rats from the enriched environment had thicker cortices, higher brain weight, and greater neural connectivity in their brains. This pattern of results suggests that neurons can change in response to environmental stimuli.

Donald Hebb proposed that human learning takes place by neurons forming new connections with one another or by the strengthening of connections that already exist. To study how learning affects specific neurons, scientists study the sea slug *Aplysia*. This is a good animal to study because it has only about 20,000 neurons, whereas humans have millions. *Aplysia* can be classically conditioned to withdraw its gill, a protective response. **Eric Kandel**, a neuroscientist, examined classical conditioning in *Aplysia*. Kandel paired a light touch (CS) with a shock (US). This pairing causes the *Aplysia* to withdraw its gill (UR). After training, the light touch alone can elicit the gill withdrawal (now a CR). Kandel found that when a strong stimulus, such as a shock, happens repeatedly, special neurons called modulatory neurons release neuromodulators. **Neuromodulators** strengthen the synapses between the sensory neurons (the ones that sense the touch) and the motor neurons (the ones that withdraw the gill) involved. Additionally, new synapses were created. In other words, the neurons sensing shock and those that withdrew the gill became more connected than they were before. This experiment illustrated a neural basis for learning: namely, a physiological change that correlates with a relatively stable change in behavior as a result of experience. This increased synaptic connection is known as **long-term potentiation** (LTP). The same basic process has been shown to be the neural basis of learning in mammals. An easy way to remember this information is that "neurons that fire together, wire together."

At a given synapse, long-term potentiation involves both presynaptic and postsynaptic neurons. For example, dopamine is one of the neurotransmitters involved in pleasurable or rewarding actions. In operant conditioning, reinforcement activates the limbic circuits that involve memory, learning, and emotions. Because reinforcement of a good behavior is generally intrinsically pleasurable (like food or praise), the circuits are strengthened as dopamine floods the system, making it more likely the behavior will be repeated.

After long-term potentiation has occurred, passing an electrical current through the brain doesn't disrupt the memory associations between the neurons involved, although other memories will be wiped out. For example, when people receive a blow to the head resulting in a concussion, they lose their memory for events shortly preceding the concussion. This is due to the fact that long-term potentiation has not had a chance to occur (and leave traces of memory connections), while old memories, which were already potentiated, remain.

Long-term memory storage involves more permanent changes to the brain, including structural and functional connections between neurons. For example, long-term memory storage includes new synaptic connections between neurons, permanent changes in pre- and postsynaptic membranes, and a permanent increase or decrease in neurotransmitter synthesis. Furthermore, visual imaging studies suggest that there is greater branching of dendrites in regions of the brain thought to be involved with memory storage. Other studies suggest that protein synthesis somehow influences memory formation; drugs that prevent protein synthesis appear to block long-term memory formation.

The neural processes described above occur when animals or people learn new behaviors or change their behaviors based on experience (that is, environmental feedback). However, not all behaviors are learned: some are innate. These are the things we know how to do instinctively (or our body just does without us consciously thinking about it), not because someone taught us to do them (for example, breathing or pulling away from a hot stove). Further, innate behaviors are always the same between members of the species, even for those performing them for the first time.

SOCIAL LEARNING

Classical and operant conditioning obviously do not account for all forms of learning. A third kind of learning is **social learning** (also called **observational learning**), which is learning based on observing the behavior of others as well as the consequences of that behavior. Because this learning takes place through observing others, it is also referred to as **vicarious learning**.

Albert Bandura conducted some of the most important research on social learning. In a classic study, Bandura had children in a waiting room with an adult **confederate** (someone who was "in" on the experiment). For one group of children, the adult would simply wait. For another group of children, the adult would punch and kick an inflatable doll (thus the experiment is now nicknamed the **Bobo Doll Experiment**). In both groups, the children were then brought into another room to play with interesting toys, but after a short time, the experimenters told the children they had to stop playing with the interesting toys, and were brought back to the initial waiting room. The idea was to frustrate the children, and then see how they managed their frustration. Many of the children who had witnessed an adult abusing the doll proceeded to abuse the doll themselves. But most of the children who had witnessed an adult quietly waiting proceeded to quietly wait themselves. This experiment illustrated the power of **modeling** in affecting changes in behavior. This finding calls into question the behaviorist assertion that learning must occur through direct experience.

> Bandura concluded that four conditions must be met for observational learning to occur. First, the learner must pay attention to the behavior in question. Second, there must be retention of the observed behavior, meaning that it must be remembered. Third, there must be a motivation for the learner to produce the behavior at a later time. Finally, the potential for reproduction must exist: that is, the learner must be able to reproduce the learned behavior.

Observational learning is a phenomenon frequently discussed in the debate over violence in the media. This issue is a particularly relevant one for television programs designed for children, as studies have shown that young children are particularly likely to engage in observational learning. However, even toddlers have shown unsolicited helping behaviors in experimental settings, suggesting that observational learning occurs in both desirable and undesirable directions.

Building on recent views that there are multiple types of intelligence, including emotional intelligence, a number of schools have developed programs in **social and emotional learning**. These programs are designed to help develop empathy and conflict resolution in students.

COGNITIVE PROCESSES IN LEARNING

The behaviorist view, championed by Skinner, is that behavior is a series of behavior-reward pairings, and cognition is not as important to the learning process. In more recent years, many psychologists have abandoned this view. One more recent view of learning posits that organisms start the learning process by observing a stimulus; then they continue the process by evaluating that stimulus; then they move on to a consideration of possible responses; and finally, they make a response. Various lines of evidence indicate that cognitive factors play a role in both animal and human learning. For example, if humans could be conditioned to salivate to the word *style*, they also would be likely to salivate to the word *fashion*. These words are not acoustically similar, but rather semantically similar, meaning they have a related meaning instead of sounding alike, so this pattern of behavior results from **cognitive** evaluation.

Perhaps a more profound demonstration of a similar phenomenon comes from work with pigeons. Pigeons were shown pictures containing either trees or no trees. They were trained to peck a key for food, but only when a picture of a tree was shown. As you might expect, they would peck the key only when tree pictures were shown, even after reinforcement stopped. They even pecked at pictures of trees that they had never seen before. Therefore, the birds must have formed a concept of trees (a concept being defined as a cognitive rule for categorizing stimuli into groups). Any new stimuli were categorized according to the concept.

An example of classical conditioning worthy of special mention is **conditioned taste aversion (CTA)**, also known as the **Garcia effect**, after the psychologist who discovered it. John Garcia demonstrated that animals that eat a food and then experience nausea induced by a drug or radiation will not eat that food if they ever encounter it again. This effect is profound and can be demonstrated with forward or backward conditioning. It is also highly resistant to extinction. A notable feature of this phenomenon is that it works best with food. It is hard to condition an aversion to a light paired with illness, for example. Psychologists have used this finding as evidence that animals are biologically predisposed to associate illness with food, as opposed to, say, light. This predisposition is a useful feature for a creature that samples many types of food, such as a rat. Humans also experience CTA. If you have ever eaten a food and vomited afterward, you may never want to eat that food again, even if you know that the food itself did not cause you to be ill.

CTA demonstrates another learning phenomenon: **stimulus generalization**. Let's say that you eat a peach and get sick. You may never want to eat a peach again, but you may also develop an aversion to other similar fruits, such as nectarines. The two fruits are similar, so you generalize from one stimulus (the peach) to the other (the nectarine).

Garcia's research is profound for two reasons: (1) it shows that certain species are built to learn certain associations more easily than others; (2) it shows that classical conditioning might be occurring through the access of some concept. The fact that someone might get sick from eating a peach, and then refuses to eat all fruit, suggests that this person has attached that negative feeling to the concept of fruit. If it were simple classical conditioning, this effect would not occur, because the person did not have a direct experience of getting sick while eating other types of fruit. There must be some concept at work, which discredits the "black box" theory of the brain held by behaviorists. It also calls into question the assertion that direct experience is necessary to learn and associate. Looking at this learning as cognitive provides an explanation for why someone would develop a food aversion even though that person doesn't become sick until hours after she has eaten the food. That person must access the concept of what she ate earlier and attach the association with getting sick. A final way to tell that this is a cognitive issue is that sometimes people develop food aversions to food items they think made them ill, such as sushi, even though it could have been something else that brought upon the illness, such as bacteria in the water at the sushi restaurant.

Other evidence for a cognitive component to learning derives from the work of **Edward Tolman**. Rats permitted to explore a maze without being reinforced would find the exit after following an indirect path; the time it took them to exit the maze without reinforcement decreased quite slowly. However, when reinforcers were applied after several trials without reinforcement, the rats' time to exit the maze decreased dramatically, indicating that the rats knew how to navigate to a specific location within the maze and so had formed a **cognitive map**, or mental representation of the maze. This demonstrates **latent learning**, or learning that is not outwardly expressed until the situation calls for it.

Biofeedback refers to people learning to alter their physiological processes by various cognitive control techniques. They receive feedback about their physiological signals, which allows them to see whether these techniques are working and to refine them.

Another form of learning is **insight learning**. This occurs when we puzzle over a solution to a problem, unsuccessfully, and then suddenly the complete solution appears to us. As discussed in the next chapter, this can be quite useful for solving problems.

KEY TERMS

Learning: An Overview
learning

Nonassociative Learning
sensitization
desensitization
desensitization therapy
systematic desensitization

Classical Conditioning
classical conditioning (Pavlovian conditioning)
Ivan Pavlov
conditioned stimulus (CS)
unconditioned stimulus (US)
unconditioned response (UR)
conditioned response (CR)
forward conditioning
delay conditioning
trace conditioning
generalization
discrimination
acquisition
extinction
spontaneous recovery
second-order conditioning
contiguity approach
contingency approach

Operant Conditioning
operant conditioning (instrumental conditioning)
B.F. Skinner
Edward L. Thorndike
law of effect
shaping (differential reinforcement of successive approximations)
natural reinforcement
primary reinforcement
secondary reinforcement
positive reinforcement
negative reinforcement

omission training
schedule of reinforcement
continuous reinforcement schedule
partial (intermittent) reinforcement schedule
fixed-ratio schedule
variable-ratio schedule
fixed-interval schedule
variable-interval schedule
punishment
escape
avoidance
behavior modification
token economy
learned helplessness

Biological Factors
Donald Hebb
Eric Kandel
neuromodulators
long-term potentiation

Social Learning
social learning (observational learning/vicarious learning)
Albert Bandura
confederate
Bobo Doll Experiment
modeling
social and emotional learning

Cognitive Processes in Learning
cognitive
conditioned taste aversion (CTA) (Garcia effect)
stimulus generalization
Edward Tolman
cognitive map
latent learning
biofeedback
insight learning

Chapter 10 Drill

See Chapter 19 for answers and explanations.

1. After having been struck by a car, a dog now exhibits fear responses every time a car approaches. The dog also exhibits a fear response to the approach of a bus, a truck, a bicycle, and even a child's wagon. The dog has undergone a process of

   (A) stimulus discrimination
   (B) stimulus generalization
   (C) spontaneous recovery
   (D) backward conditioning
   (E) differential reinforcement

2. Which of the following would be an example of second-order conditioning?

   (A) A cat tastes a sour plant that makes it feel nauseated and will not approach that plant again.
   (B) A horse that is fed sugar cubes by a particular person salivates every time that person walks by.
   (C) A pigeon that has received food every time a red light is presented exhibits food-seeking behavior when a yellow light is presented.
   (D) A rabbit that has repeatedly seen a picture of a feared predator paired with a musical tone exhibits a fear response to the musical tone as well as to a flashed light alone that had been repeatedly paired with the tone.
   (E) Wild rats instinctively avoid canine predators, but domesticated rats show little fear of the domesticated dogs they encounter, and may even join them in exploration or play.

3. The reinforcement schedule that generally provides the most resistance to response extinction is

   (A) fixed-ratio
   (B) fixed-interval
   (C) variable-ratio
   (D) variable-interval
   (E) continuous

4. The importance of enrichment and stimulation of the brain during critical periods in development can be seen in all of the following EXCEPT

   (A) an increase in the number of neurons
   (B) an increase in the number of connections between neurons
   (C) strengthening of already existing connections between neurons
   (D) an increase in the size of neurons
   (E) higher levels of neurotransmitters

5. According to Albert Bandura, observational learning can occur even in the absence of

   (A) observed consequences of behavior
   (B) direct attention to the behavior
   (C) retention of the observed behavior over time
   (D) ability to reproduce the behavior
   (E) motivation to reproduce the behavior at a later time

6. Jay joins a social media website to lose weight. He receives points based on the intensity of his daily exercise and praise from fellow users for each workout he logs on the website. This increases his exercise frequency and intensity. Eventually he stops logging onto the website, but continues to exercise with increased frequency. This is an example of

   (A) vicarious reinforcement
   (B) operant conditioning
   (C) innate behavior
   (D) classical conditioning
   (E) observational learning

7. Which of the following scenarios is an example of negative reinforcement?

   (A) After staying out past her curfew, Stephanie is grounded the next weekend.
   (B) When Toni finishes her homework, she does not have to take out the trash.
   (C) When Ben received an A for his research project, his family treated him to dinner at his favorite restaurant.
   (D) When Lola the dog jumps on her owner, the owner takes a step away from her.
   (E) When the rat in a Skinner box presses the lever, the box delivers an electric shock.

8. Chemotherapy is well known to cause nausea and vomiting. A chemotherapy patient's care team cautions the patient to eat only "novel" or new foods before treatment as opposed to food staples, like chicken, rice, or pasta. This is most likely due to

(A) operant conditioning
(B) taste aversion
(C) Yerkes-Dodson Law
(D) observational learning
(E) stimulus generalization

9. Leigha, who is expecting college acceptance letters, knows the mail carrier comes every day around 1:30 P.M. Hoping that the mail arrives early, she checks the mailbox at 12:45, 1:15, and 1:40. She does not check again until the next day around the same time. This is an example of which reinforcement schedule?

(A) Fixed-interval
(B) Variable-interval
(C) Fixed-ratio
(D) Variable-ratio
(E) Continuous

10. Kevin tries to teach his dog Muka to roll over. First, he teaches her to lie down. Then, he teaches her to lie on her side. Eventually, Kevin gets Muka to roll onto her back and, finally, all the way around. He gives her a treat with every step. This process is known as

(A) habituation
(B) discrimination
(C) generalization
(D) shaping
(E) sensitization

REFLECT

Respond to the following questions:

- Which topics in this chapter do you hope to see on the multiple-choice section or essay?

- Which topics in this chapter do you hope not to see on the multiple-choice section or essay?

- Regarding any psychologists mentioned, can you pair the psychologists with their contributions to the field? Did they contribute significant experiments, theories, or both?

- Regarding any theories mentioned, can you distinguish between differing theories well enough to recognize them on the multiple-choice section? Can you distinguish them well enough to write a fluent essay on them?

- Can you define the key terms at the end of the chapter?

- Which parts of the chapter will you review?

- Will you seek further help, outside of this book (such as from a teacher, Princeton Review tutor, or AP Students), on any of the content in this chapter—and, if so, on what content?

Chapter 11
Cognitive Psychology: Memory, Language, and Problem-Solving

MEMORY

According to the **modal model**, memory is divided into three separate storage areas: **sensory**, **short-term**, and **long-term**. Each type of memory has four components: storage capacity, duration of code, nature of code, and a way by which information is lost. Consider each type of memory in turn.

Sensory Memory

Sensory memory is the gateway between perception and memory. This store is quite limited. Information in sensory memory is referred to as **iconic** if it is visual and **echoic** if it is auditory. The iconic store lasts for only a few tenths of a second while the echoic store lasts for three or four seconds. The items in sensory memory are constantly being replaced by new input, with only certain items entering into short-term memory.

The nature of sensory memory is clarified by certain types of events. If you have ever watched someone jump rope quickly, you may have noticed the perception of the rope being at many points in its rotation at once. A quickly moving fan also may generate such a perception. This phenomenon is called **visual persistence**. Sensory information in sensory memory remains in attention briefly; the speed of the rope or fan causes the sensory information to run together.

In 1960, researcher **George Sperling** experimented on memory and **partial report**. He first presented participants with a matrix of three rows of four letters each for just milliseconds.

G Z E P
R K O D
B T X F

Next, he asked participants to either recite the entire matrix or to recollect just one of the rows. He found that while participants were not able to recall all twelve letters presented due to the rapid decay of iconic memory, they were generally able to accurately recall the cued row, meaning they had an image of the entire matrix stored in memory. Sperling called this ability to recall these lines of letters **iconic memory** or **short-term visual memory**. This suggests that the capacity for iconic memory is quite large, but the duration is incredibly short, and the information is not easily manipulable. Additionally, further studies emphasized the brief window for retention—the longer the amount of time between seeing the matrix and being cued to recall the row, the worse the participants performed.

Short-Term Memory (STM)

Short-term memory holds information from a few seconds up to about a minute. Psychologist **George Miller** found that the information stored in this portion of memory is primarily acoustically coded, regardless of the nature of the original source. Short-term memory can hold about seven items, plus or minus two (convenient for telephone numbers, which can still be useful to memorize in the event of an emergency). Items in the short-term store are maintained there by rehearsal.

Rehearsal can be divided into two types: **maintenance rehearsal** and **elaborative rehearsal**. Maintenance rehearsal is simple repetition to keep an item in short-term memory until it can be used (as when you say a phone number to yourself over and over again until you can add it to your contacts). Elaborative rehearsal involves organization and understanding of the information that has been encoded in order to transfer the information to long-term memory (as when you try to remember the name of someone you have just met at a party). Elaborative rehearsal is more effective than maintenance rehearsal for ensuring short-term memory information is sent to long-term memory; therefore, it is a preferred way to study. Both types of rehearsal are forms of **effortful processing,** when we make a conscious effort to retain information. This is distinguished from the **automatic processing** that can occur unconsciously when we are engaged with well-practiced skills, like riding a bicycle.

There is some evidence that the depth of processing is important for encoding memories. Information that is thought about at a deeper level is better remembered. For example, it is easier to remember the general plot of a book than the exact words, meaning that semantic information (meaning) is more easily remembered than grammatical information (form) when the goal is to learn a concept. On the other hand, rhyme can be useful in aiding phonological processing. Another useful **mnemonic device** is to use short words or phrases that represent longer strings of information. For example, ROYGBIV is an acronym that is helpful in memorizing the colors of the rainbow (red, orange, yellow, green, blue, indigo, violet). A mnemonic device is any technique that makes it easier to learn and remember something.

The **dual-coding hypothesis** indicates that it is easier to remember words with associated images than either words or images alone. By encoding both a visual mental representation and an associated word, there are more connections made to the memory and there is more of an opportunity to process the information at a deeper level. For this reason, imagery is a useful mnemonic device. One aid for memory is to use the **method of loci**. This involves imagining moving through a familiar place, such as your home, and in each place, leaving a visual representation of a topic to be remembered. For recall, then, the images of the places could be called upon to bring into awareness the associated topics.

It is also easier to remember things that are personally relevant, known as the **self-reference effect**. We have excellent recall for information that we can personally relate to because it interacts with our own views or can be linked to existing memories. Another useful tool for memory, then, is to relate new information to existing knowledge by making it personally relevant.

Items in short-term memory may be forgotten or they may be **encoded** (stored and able to be recalled later) into long-term memory. Items that are forgotten exit short-term memory either by **decay**—that is, the passage of time—or by **interference**—that is, they are displaced by new information. One type of interference is **retroactive interference**, in which new information pushes old information out of short-term memory. The opposite of retroactive interference is **proactive interference**, in which old information makes it more difficult to learn new information.

An additional feature of short-term memory is that it seems to store items from a list sequentially. This sequential storage leads to our tendency to remember the first few and last few items in a list better than the ones in the middle. These effects are called the **primacy** (remembering the first items) and **recency** (remembering the last items) **effects**. The recency effect tends to fade in about a day; the primacy effect tends to persist longer. The overall effect is called the **serial position effect**.

The Serial Position Effect

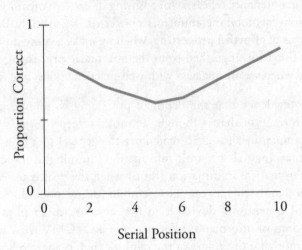

An interesting feature of short-term memory is that its limit of about seven items is not as limiting as it would seem. The reason is that what constitutes an item need not be something as simple as a single digit. In fact, it can be a fairly large block of information. George Miller defined grouping items of information into units as **chunking**. For example, when learning a friend's phone number (typically seven digits), you probably chunk the information into a 3-digit and a 4-digit number in order to better retain the information.

Long-Term Memory (LTM)

Long-term memory is the repository for all of our lasting memories and knowledge, and it is organized as a gigantic network of interrelated information. It is capable of permanent retention for the duration of our lives. Evidence suggests that information in this store is primarily **semantically encoded**—that is, encoded in the form of word meanings. However, certain types of information in this store can be either **visually encoded** or **acoustically encoded**.

Everyday Example
Remembering song lyrics is an example of acoustic encoding.

Information in the long-term store can be stored in different ways, depending on the type of information it is. One kind of storage is through **episodic memory**, or memory for events that we ourselves have experienced. Another kind is through **semantic memory**, also known as declarative memory, which comprises facts, figures, and general world knowledge. A third type is **procedural memory**—that is, memory consisting of skills and habits. Because these memories are stored in the striatum, they are frequently not subject to damage and injury. A final way to classify memory is into categories based on whether or not it can be accessed consciously or not. **Declarative** (or **explicit**) **memory** is a memory a person can consciously consider and retrieve, such as episodic and semantic memory. In contrast, **nondeclarative (or implicit) memory** is beyond conscious consideration and would include procedural memory, priming, and classical conditioning.

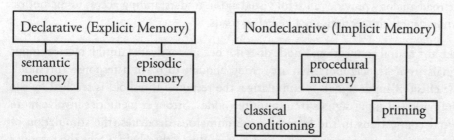

Recalling items in long-term memory is subject to **context-dependent memory**. This principle states that information is more likely to be recalled if the attempt to retrieve it occurs in a situation similar to the situation in which it was encoded. For example, if you memorize information about psychology while in a classroom, you should remember it better in that same classroom than if the information was memorized at home. **State-dependent memory** also applies to states of mind, meaning that information memorized when under the influence of a drug is easier to access when in a similar state than when not on that drug.

The process of retrieval is thought to involve the activation of semantic networks. If our long-term memories contained isolated pockets of information without any organization, they might be more difficult to access. A person might have numerous memories for directions, people's faces, the definitions of tens of thousands of words, and other such content; with that much information, it could be nearly impossible to find anything. Just as hierarchies are useful for handling information during the encoding process, it is believed that information is stored in long-term memory as an organized network. In this network exist individual ideas called nodes, which can be thought of as cities on a map. Connecting these nodes are associations, which are like roads connecting the cities. Not all roads are created equal; some are superhighways while others are dirt roads. For example, for a person living in a city, there may be a stronger association between the nodes "bird" and "pigeon" than between "bird" and "penguin." According to this model, the strength of an association in the network is related to how frequently and how deeply the connection is made. Processing material in different ways leads to the establishment of multiple connections. In this model, searching through memory is the process of starting at one node and traveling the connected roads until one arrives at the idea one is looking

Working Memory

Some psychologists believe there is an additional type of memory called **working memory**. Within the modal model, it is argued that working memory would fall between the sensory registry and short-term memory, and it can last up to about 30 seconds before decaying or being transferred into either short- or long-term memory. It is believed that the information stored in working memory can be manipulated in a way that iconic or echoic memory could not be, which helps distinguish working memory from other more evanescent forms of memory. For example, iconic memory would allow a person to remember five letters presented visually, whereas working memory would allow a person to remember those five letters and rearrange them in alphabetical order. While some psychologists are certain that working memory is a distinct part of the memory system, other psychologists believe that working memory is simply a part of short-term memory.

for. Retrieval of information can be improved by building more and stronger connections to an idea. Because all memories are, in essence, neural connections, the road analogy provides a useful visual aid in understanding access to memories: strong neural connections are like better roads.

Like any neural connection, a node does not become activated until it receives input signals from its neighbors that are strong enough to reach a response threshold. The effect of input signals is cumulative: the response threshold is reached by the summation of input signals from multiple nodes. Stronger memories involve more neural connections in the form of more numerous dendrites, the stimulation of which can summate more quickly and powerfully to threshold. Once the response threshold is reached, the node "fires" and sends a stimulus to all of its neighbors, contributing to their activation. In this way, the activation of a few nodes can lead to a pattern of activation within the network that spreads onward. This process is known as **spreading activation**. It suggests that when trying to retrieve information, we start the search from one node. We do not then "choose" where to go next; rather, that activated node spreads its activation to other nodes around it to an extent related to the strength of association between that node and each other. This pattern continues, with well-established links carrying activation more efficiently than more obscure ones. The network approach helps explain why hints may be helpful. They serve to activate nodes that are closely connected to the node being sought after, which may therefore contribute to that node's activation. It also explains the relevance of contextual cues in state-dependent memory.

A phenomenon that many psychologists believe occurs in the long-term store is the **flashbulb memory**, which is a very deep, vivid memory in the form of a visual image associated with a particular emotionally arousing event. For example, many people remember exactly what they were doing when they heard that planes had crashed into the World Trade Center on September 11, 2001. However, some psychologists believe that recall of such events is no more accurate than recall of other memories.

Sometimes what we remember happened only in part or even not at all. Memory **reconstruction** occurs when we fit together pieces of an event that seem likely. **Source confusion** is one likely cause of memory reconstruction. In this case, we attribute the event to a different source than it actually came from. For example, if children read and reread a story, they may come to think the events of the story happened to them rather than to the character. Similarly, childhood memories of both trivial and serious events can be reconstructed (falsified) by repeated suggestion. **Elizabeth Loftus** and other psychologists are studying the existence of false or implanted memories. They have demonstrated that repeated suggestions and misleading questions can create false memories. This is called **framing**. Similarly, eyewitness accounts, thought to be very strong evidence in courts of law, are accurate only about half the time. This is particularly true when dealing with children as eyewitnesses. The degree of confidence in the testimony of the witness does not necessarily correlate to accuracy of the account.

Long-term memory, like short-term memory, is subject to interference. To review what we discussed briefly in the short-term memory section: Retroactive interference occurs when newly memorized information interferes with the ability to remember previously memorized information. To give an example, when you learn a new language (such as Spanish), it can interfere with your memory of a language that you learned previously (for example, Italian). Proactive interference occurs when previously memorized information interferes with the ability to learn and memorize new information.

Hermann Ebbinghaus (1850–1909) studied the phenomenon of forgetting. His "forgetting curve" showed that most forgetting occurs immediately after learning, and he then showed that this could best be addressed by spaced review of materials. This has important implications for effective studying.

LANGUAGE

Language is the arrangement of sounds, written symbols, or gestures to communicate ideas. Language has several key features.

- First, language is arbitrary—that is, words rarely sound like the ideas that they convey.

- Second, language has a structure that is additive in a certain sense. For example, words are added together to form sentences, sentences to form paragraphs, and so on.

- Third, language has multiplicity of structure, meaning that it can be analyzed and understood in a number of different ways.

- Fourth, language is productive, meaning that there are nearly endless meaningful combinations of words.

- Finally, language is dynamic, meaning that it is constantly changing and evolving.

Language can be broken down into subcomponents. **Phonemes** are the smallest units of speech sounds in a given language that are still distinct in sound from each other. Phonemes combine to form **morphemes**, the smallest semantically meaningful parts of language. **Grammar**, the set of rules by which language is constructed, is governed by syntax and semantics. **Syntax** is the set of rules used in the arrangement of morphemes into meaningful sentences; this can also be thought of as word order. **Semantics** refers to word meaning or word choice. **Prosody** is the rhythm, stress, and intonation of speech.

Children acquire language in stages. Infants make cooing noises, which consist of the utterance of phonemes that do not correspond to actual words, until roughly 4 months of age. The next stage after cooing is babbling, which is the production of phonemes only within the infants' own to-be-learned language. Sounds not relevant to this language drop out at this stage, which usually lasts until the first year of life.

Soon the infant uses single words to convey demands and desires. These single words filled with meaning are called **holophrases**. Holophrases are single terms that are applied by the infant to broad categories of things. For example, any infant calling any passing woman "mama." This type of error is known as an **overextension**, and it results from the infant not knowing enough words to express something fully. **Underextension** is when a child thinks that their "mama" is the only "mama." Infants develop vocabulary as time goes on and tend to have up to 100 words in their vocabulary by 18 months.

At about two years of age, infants start combining words. Two- or three-word groups are termed **telegraphic speech**. This speech lacks many parts of speech. For example, a two-year-old would say, "mommy food," which means "mommy, give me food." This is called "telegraphic speech" because people used to remove what they deemed unnecessary words when sending telegrams, in order to save money.

Vocabulary is increasing rapidly at this point. By age 3, children know more than 1,000 words, but they frequently make **overgeneralization** errors. These are errors in which the rules of language are overextended, such as in saying, "I goed to the store." *Go* is an irregular verb, but the child applies the standard rules of grammar to it. By age 5, most grammatical mistakes in the child's speech have disappeared, and the child's vocabulary has expanded dramatically. At 10 years old, a child's language is essentially the same as an adult's.

Noam Chomsky postulated a system for the organization of language based on the concept of what he referred to as **transformational grammar**. Transformational grammar differentiates between the **surface structure of language**—the superficial way in which the words are arranged in a text or in speech—and the **deep structure of language**—the underlying meaning of the words. Chomsky was struck by the similarities between the grammar of different languages, as well as by the similarities of language acquisition in children, regardless of the language they were learning. Based on this similarity, he proposed an innate **language acquisition device**, which facilitates the acquisition of language in children, and a **critical period** for the learning of language. **B.F. Skinner**, a noted behaviorist, countered Chomsky's argument for language acquisition. Skinner explored the idea of the "language acquisition support system," which is the language-rich or language-poor environment the child is exposed to while growing up. Chomsky's language acquisition device (LAD) provides the foundational structure of language, while the language acquisition support system (LASS) provides the scaffolding to help young children learn language.

Language and thought are interactive processes. Language can influence thought, and cognition can influence language. **Benjamin Lee Whorf**, in collaboration with **Edward Sapir**, proposed a **theory of linguistic relativity**, according to which speakers of different languages develop different cognitive systems as a result of their differences in language. An example of this idea is illustrated by the research of M. Keith Chen, who found in 2013 that speakers of "futureless" languages—that is, languages that grammatically associate the future and the present—tend to be healthier and wealthier.

Deaf and hard of hearing children, when exposed to sign language, acquire language in slightly different but parallel stages.

CONCEPTS

We are constantly being inundated with information about our surroundings. In order to organize all of this information, we devise concepts. A **concept** is a way of grouping or classifying the world around us. For example, chairs come in a large variety of sizes and shapes, yet we can identify them as chairs. The concept of chairs allows us to identify them without learning every possible trait of all chairs. **Typicality** is the degree to which an object fits the average. What are the average characteristics of a chair? When we picture "chair," an image emerges in our brain. This typical picture that we envision is referred to as a **prototype**. But we can imagine other images of a chair that are distant from the prototype to varying degrees.

Concepts can be small or large, more or less inclusive. A **superordinate concept** is very broad and encompasses a large group of items, such as the concept of "food." A **basic concept** is smaller and more specific—for example, "bread." A **subordinate concept** is even smaller and more specific, such as "rye bread." Concepts are essential for thinking and reasoning. Without such categorization, we would be so overwhelmed by our surroundings that we would be incapable of any deeper thought.

COGNITION

Cognition encompasses the mental processes involved in acquiring, organizing, remembering, using, and constructing knowledge.

Reasoning, the drawing of conclusions from evidence, can be further divided into deductive and inductive reasoning. **Deductive reasoning** is the process of drawing logical conclusions from general statements. **Syllogisms** are deductive conclusions drawn from two premises. For example, consider the following argument:

> All politicians are trustworthy.
>
> Janet is a politician.
>
> Therefore, Janet is trustworthy.

The logical conclusion is that *Janet is trustworthy*. This is drawn from the general statements that *all politicians are trustworthy* and that *Janet is a politician*. In general, statements can be sound (the conclusion follows the premises) or unsound, and valid (the conclusion is true—Janet *is* trustworthy) or invalid.

Inductive reasoning is the process of drawing general inferences from specific observations. For example, you might notice that everybody on the football team seems to be a good student. You could infer that all people who play football are good students. However, this is not necessarily true. You are drawing an inference based on a common occurrence. Inductive reasoning, while useful, is not as airtight as deductive reasoning.

PROBLEM-SOLVING AND CREATIVITY

Problem-solving involves the removal of one or more impediments to the finding of a solution in a situation. The problems to be solved can be either well-structured, with paths to solution (for example, "What is the square footage of my room?"), or ill-structured, with no single, clear path to solution (for example, "How can I succeed in school?"). In order to solve problems, we must decide whether the problem has one or more solutions. If many correct answers are possible, we use a process known as **divergent thinking**. Brainstorming is an example of divergent thinking. If the problem can be solved only by one answer, **convergent thinking** must be used. Convergent thinking, then, requires narrowing of the many choices available.

Study Tip

The two problematic types of heuristic, availability and representativeness, are often asked about. To make sure that you understand them, see whether you can come up with an example of each, other than the one mentioned below.

When solving well-structured problems, we often rely on **heuristics**, or intuitive rules that may or may not be useful in a given situation. There are a number of types of heuristics and all may lead to incorrect conclusions. The **availability heuristic** means that the conclusion is drawn from what events come readily to mind. For example, many people mistakenly believe that air travel is more dangerous than car travel because airplane crashes are so vividly and repeatedly reported. The **representativeness heuristic** also can lead to incorrect conclusions. In this case, we judge objects and events in terms of how closely they match the prototype of that object or event. For example, many people view high school athletes as less intelligent. However, most high school athletes must meet certain academic standards in order to participate in sports. A person's particular view of the athlete will determine whether the representativeness heuristic is leading to a correct or incorrect conclusion. Unfortunately, such erroneous conclusions are how racism, sexism, and ageism persist. Heuristics contrast with **algorithms**, which are systematic, mechanical approaches that guarantee an eventual answer to a problem.

Insight and Köhler's Chimps

A famous example of insight is the example of Köhler's chimps. **Wolfgang Köhler** had a chimp in a cage with two sticks. Outside of the cage were some bananas. The chimp wanted the bananas but could not reach them with either stick. After struggling for a while, the chimp took the two sticks, and put the thinner end of one into the hollow end of the other, making one long stick of sufficient length to reach the bananas. The novel approach of combining the sticks was presumably the result of an insight.

Ill-structured problems often require insight to be solved. **Insight** is the sudden understanding of a problem or a potential strategy for solving a problem that usually involves conceptualizing the problem in a new way. Recent studies have demonstrated that insight is more likely to occur when the problem-solvers are able to create some mental and/or physical space between themselves and the problem.

Problems requiring insight are often difficult to solve because we have a **mental set**, or fixed frame of mind, that we use when approaching the problems. An example of a mental set is **functional fixedness**, which is the tendency to assume that a given item is useful only for the task for which it was designed. For example, many people might see this AP Psychology book as only a source of information for the AP Exam, but it can also serve as a bed support, a writing surface, a source of kindling, or much more!

Other obstacles to problem-solving include confirmation bias, hindsight bias, belief perseverance, and framing. **Confirmation bias**, the search for information that supports a particular view, hinders problem-solving by distorting objectivity. The **hindsight bias**, or the tendency after the fact to think you knew what the outcome would be, also distorts our ability to view situations objectively. Similarly, **belief perseverance** affects problem-solving. In this mental error, a person sees only the evidence that supports a particular position, despite evidence presented to the contrary. **Framing**, or the way a question is phrased, can alter the objective outcome of problem-solving or decision-making.

Creativity can be defined as the process of producing something novel yet worthwhile. The elusive nature of creativity makes it a difficult topic to study. For example, what is truly novel, and who is the judge of what is or is not worthwhile? Briefly, creative people tend to be motivated to create primarily for the sheer joy of creation, rather than for financial or material gain. Creative people also seem to exhibit care and consideration when choosing a specific area of interest to pursue. Once they have chosen that area, they tend to immerse themselves in it and to develop extensive knowledge of all aspects of the topic. Creativity seems to correlate with nonconformity to the rules governing the area of creativity. For example, Copernicus had to disregard the common belief that the Earth was the center of the solar system to make his discoveries about planetary motion.

KEY TERMS

Memory

modal model
sensory memory
short-term memory
long-term memory
iconic
echoic
visual persistence
George Sperling
partial report
short-term visual memory
    (iconic memory)
George Miller
maintenance rehearsal
elaborative rehearsal
effortful processing
automatic processing
mnemonic device
dual-coding hypothesis
method of loci
self-reference effect
encoded
decay
interference
retroactive interference
proactive interference
primacy effect
recency effect
serial position effect
chunking
semantically encoded
visually encoded
acoustically encoded
episodic memory
semantic memory
procedural memory

declarative (explicit) memory
nondeclarative (implicit)
    memory
context-dependent memory
state-dependent memory
working memory
spreading activation
flashbulb memory
reconstruction
source confusion
Elizabeth Loftus
framing
Hermann Ebbinghaus

Language

phonemes
morphemes
grammar
syntax
semantics
prosody
holophrases
overextension
underextension
telegraphic speech
overgeneralization
Noam Chomsky
transformational grammar
surface structure of language
deep structure of language
language acquisition device
critical period
B.F. Skinner
Benjamin Lee Whorf
Edward Sapir
theory of linguistic relativity

Concepts

typicality
prototype
superordinate concept
basic concept
subordinate concept

Cognition

reasoning
deductive reasoning
syllogisms
inductive reasoning

Problem-Solving and Creativity

divergent thinking
convergent thinking
heuristics
availability heuristic
representativeness heuristic
algorithms
insight
Wolfgang Köhler
mental set
functional fixedness
confirmation bias
hindsight bias
belief perseverance
framing
creativity

Chapter 11 Drill

See Chapter 19 for answers and explanations.

1. The main difference between auditory and visual sensory memory is that

   (A) visual memory dominates auditory memory
   (B) visual sensory memory lasts for a shorter period of time than auditory sensory memory
   (C) visual sensory memory has a higher storage capacity than auditory sensory memory
   (D) a phone number read to an individual will be lost before a phone number that was glanced at for 15 seconds
   (E) if both visual and auditory stimuli are presented at the same time, the visual stimulus is more likely to be transferred to the long-term memory than is the auditory stimulus

2. The greater likelihood of recalling information from memory while in the same or similar environment in which the memory was originally encoded is an example of

   (A) retroactive interference
   (B) chunking
   (C) elaborative rehearsal
   (D) context-dependent memory
   (E) procedural memory

3. The term given to that part of language composed of tones and inflections that add or change meaning without alterations in word usage is

   (A) syntax
   (B) grammar
   (C) phonemics
   (D) semantics
   (E) prosody

4. Which of the following would NOT be an example of a two-year-old's usage of telegraphic speech?

   (A) "Where ball?"
   (B) "Boy hurt."
   (C) "Milk."
   (D) "Mommy give hug."
   (E) "Go play group."

5. Students are given a reasoning task in which they are asked, in 60 seconds, to come up with as many ways as possible to use a spoon that do not involve eating or preparing food. The number and diversity of responses could most accurately reflect the students'

   (A) divergent thinking abilities
   (B) convergent thinking abilities
   (C) intelligence quotients
   (D) working memories
   (E) subordinate concepts

6. Recalling the fact that Abraham Lincoln was the president of the United States during the Civil War is an example of

   (A) procedural memory
   (B) implicit memory
   (C) semantic memory
   (D) episodic memory
   (E) nondeclarative memory

7. Stefano tries his hardest to learn German, but he continues to replace words with Spanish words by accident. This is most likely a result of

   (A) proactive interference
   (B) retroactive interference
   (C) telegraphic speech
   (D) surface structure of language
   (E) semantic encoding

8. Ben continues to get stuck on a physics problem, approaching it the same way every time. This is an example of

   (A) functional fixedness
   (B) a mental set
   (C) a representativeness heuristic
   (D) insight learning
   (E) framing

9. Which of the following is an example of a representativeness heuristic?

(A) Kelly creates a perfect mental image of a rose in her mind and uses it to judge the roses she encounters.

(B) Malik thinks that cancer is more deadly than heart disease because he sees advertisements for cancer research frequently.

(C) Priscilla uses a box as a stepstool to reach the highest shelf.

(D) In an effort to prove her theory true, Jennifer interprets the otherwise objective facts as supporting evidence for her claims.

(E) Looking back, Justino feels he should have been able to predict the ending of the horror movie all along.

10. Sheldon memorizes organic chemistry functional groups by relating them to his passion and understanding of landscaping. This memorization technique is known as

(A) functional fixedness
(B) chunking
(C) maintenance rehearsal
(D) state-dependent memory
(E) self-referential effect

REFLECT

Respond to the following questions:

- Which topics in this chapter do you hope to see on the multiple-choice section or essay?

- Which topics in this chapter do you hope not to see on the multiple-choice section or essay?

- Regarding any psychologists mentioned, can you pair the psychologists with their contributions to the field? Did they contribute significant experiments, theories, or both?

- Regarding any theories mentioned, can you distinguish between differing theories well enough to recognize them on the multiple-choice section? Can you distinguish them well enough to write a fluent essay on them?

- Regarding any figures given, if you were given a labeled figure from within this chapter, would you be able to give the significance of each part of the figure?

- Can you define the key terms at the end of the chapter?

- Which parts of the chapter will you review?

- Will you seek further help, outside of this book (such as from a teacher, Princeton Review tutor, or AP Students), on any of the content in this chapter—and, if so, on what content?

Chapter 12
Cognitive Psychology: Intelligence and Testing

STANDARDIZATION AND NORMS

When we use tests designed to measure psychological characteristics, we need to know what the scores mean. For example, if a test measures your IQ, and you score a 125 on this IQ test, how do you know what your IQ is relative to the rest of the world? To determine such relative standing, tests are standardized. Standardization is accomplished by administering the test to a **standardization sample,** a group of people who represent the entire population. The data collected from the standardization sample is compared against **norms**, which are standards of performance against which anyone who takes a given test can be compared. Tests need to be restandardized when a new, different population takes the test. The **Flynn effect** supports the need to restandardize because the data indicates that the population has become smarter over the past 50 years. Thus, an IQ of 100 may mean different things in different years, depending on the standardization sample.

RELIABILITY AND VALIDITY

Tests used to measure any psychological trait or ability must be both reliable and valid. **Reliability** is a measure of how consistent a test is in the measurements it provides. In other words, reliability refers to the likelihood that the same individual would get a similar score if tested with the same test on separate occasions (disallowing for practice effects or effects due to familiarity with the test items from the first testing). In fact, reliability is often assessed by giving participants a test and later—preferably after they have forgotten the specific items—administering the same test again. The two sets of scores are compared and a correlation coefficient is computed between them. This is called the **test-retest method**. Tests that are perfectly reliable have a reliability coefficient of one. Reliabilities apply only to groups, however, so that even though a given test is highly reliable, a given individual may show substantial fluctuations in scores.

Validity refers to the extent to which a test measures what it intends to measure. (This instance is known as construct validity.) Validity is calculated by comparing how well the results from a test correlate with other measures that assess what the test is supposed to predict. So, for example, if you just developed a new IQ test, and you wanted to know whether it was valid, you might compare your results to those that the same participants had achieved on other IQ measures. Even better, you might correlate the IQ test scores with school grades, on the notion that IQ test scores should predict school grades. It is possible to have a test that is reliable but not valid. Such a test consistently measures something, but not what it is intended to measure. However, it is impossible to have a test that is valid but not reliable. If individuals' scores fluctuate wildly, then they cannot consistently correlate with others' scores, whatever these other scores may be. **Internal validity** is the degree to which the subject's results are due to the questions being asked and not another variable. **External validity** is true validity—that is, the degree to which results from the test can be generalized to the "real world." An IQ test would be externally valid if the findings applied in other settings. If it does, in fact, measure intelligence, rather than another construct like level of education, the IQ test is also high in construct validity.

More Reliability Methods

Other methods of testing reliability include **split-half**, in which two halves of the same test are given to the same subjects, and the results are correlated, and **equivalent form**, in which different but similar tests covering the same concepts are given to the same group of subjects and the results are correlated.

TYPES OF TESTS

Tests used in psychology can be **projective tests**, in which ambiguous stimuli, open to interpretation, are presented; or **inventory-type tests**, in which participants answer a standard series of questions.

Two popular projective tests are the **Rorschach Inkblot Test** and the **Thematic Apperception Test (TAT)**. The Rorschach is a sequence of 10 inkblots, each of which the participant is asked to observe and then characterize. For example, a participant might see one inkblot as a bat or another as two people staring at each other. Sometimes, people see multiple images in a single inkblot. Different aspects of the participant's descriptions, such as form and movement of objects, are scored to yield an evaluation of the individual's personality.

The TAT is a series of pictures of people in ambiguous relationships with other people. The participant's task is to generate a story to accompany each picture. The story includes both what led up to the scene in the picture and what will occur next. Again, participants' responses are used to make judgments about their personalities. Both of these tests are used by followers of the psychoanalytic view of personality. The major criticism of projective personality tests is that the assessment of the responses can be too subjective.

Inventory-type tests contain fixed answers to questions. They typically do not allow free responses. A classic example is the MMPI-2-RF mentioned in Chapter 15. This test presents the participant with a variety of statements. The participant's task is to answer "true," "false," or "can't say." This test, too, yields a characterization of personality. It is often used to diagnose abnormalities.

Other Test Types

There are many other types of tests. **Power tests** gauge abilities in certain areas. These are usually extremely difficult tests in which it is unlikely that a person could answer all the questions correctly. At the other end of the spectrum are **speed tests**. These have very easy items, but the test is timed, making completion difficult. **Achievement tests** assess knowledge gained; the Advanced Placement exams are of this type. In contrast to these are **aptitude tests**, which evaluate a person's abilities. A road test before getting a driver's license is an example of an aptitude test.

INTELLIGENCE

Intelligence can be defined as goal-directed adaptive thinking. Such thinking is difficult to measure on a standardized test. In fact, the nature of intelligence itself is an issue of contention among psychologists. Before the advent of IQ tests, the anthropologist **Francis Galton** had attempted to measure intelligence by means of reaction time tests. This reflects the notion that **speed of processing** is an essential component of intelligence. Few psychologists would claim that the popular "intelligence" tests measure all aspects of intelligence. **Alfred Binet** was a French psychologist who first began to measure children's intelligence for the French government. Binet's test measured the "mental ages" of school-age children so that children needing extra help could be placed in special classrooms. An American psychologist and Stanford University professor named **Lewis Terman** modified Binet's test to create a test commonly referred to as the **Stanford-Binet Test**. The Stanford-Binet became the first widely administered intelligence test during World War I, when the United States Army used it to rank recruits. Most modern psychologists measure an aspect of intelligence, called the **IQ** or **intelligence quotient**. This quotient originally was

Measuring IQs Today
Today, IQs are rarely computed as quotients, but rather are computed on the basis of the extent to which a person's score is above or below the average.

conceived of as a ratio of mental age over chronological (physical) age, multiplied by 100. Mental age is a measure of performance based on comparing the participant's performance to that of an "average" person of a given age. Therefore, if you take a test and your score is comparable to that of an average 10-year-old, then your mental age is 10. IQ scores are normally distributed, with a mean, median, and mode of about 100, and a standard deviation of 15 or 16 points.

The most common intelligence tests given to children today are the **Stanford-Binet Intelligence Scale** and the **Wechsler Intelligence Scale for Children** (WISC-IV). There is also a version of the Wechsler specifically geared toward adults, the **Wechsler Adult Intelligence Scale** (WAIS). The WISC-IV and WAIS generally have six types of questions: information (how many wings does a bird have?), comprehension (what is the advantage of keeping money in a bank?), arithmetic (if 3 pencils cost $1, what will be the cost of 15 pencils?), similarities (in what ways are seals and sea lions alike?), vocabulary (what does *retain* mean?), and digit span questions in which subjects are asked to hold information in short-term memory. This reflects the idea that IQ tests tend to have a combination of **abstract and verbal measures.**

There has been an ongoing debate as to whether intelligence is one specific set of abilities or many different sets of abilities. In the early part of the 20th century, **Charles Spearman** proposed that there was a general intelligence (or *g* **factor**) that was the basis of all other intelligence. The *g* factor is the intelligence applied across mental activities, which is close to the standard definition for "intelligence." The *s* factor is the breakdown of this intelligence into a specific component, such as one's ability to process math equations or linguistic puns. Spearman used **factor analysis**, a statistical measure for analyzing test data. **Robert Sternberg** proposed that intelligence could be more broadly defined as having three major components: **analytical, practical,** and **creative intelligence**. **Louis Thurstone**, a researcher in the field of intelligence, posited that we need to think of intelligence more broadly because intelligence can come in many different forms. The most famous proponent of the idea of multiple intelligences is **Howard Gardner** of Harvard University. Gardner has identified the following types of intelligence: **verbal** and **mathematical** (these are the two traditionally measured by IQ tests) as well as **musical, spatial, kinesthetic, environmental, interpersonal** (people perceptive), and **intrapersonal** (insightful, self-awareness). **Daniel Goleman**, a psychologist at Rutgers, has done recent work on the importance of **emotional intelligence** (being able to recognize people's intents and motivations) and has created programs for enhancing one's emotional intelligence.

One distinction often made is between **fluid intelligence** and **crystallized intelligence.** Crystallized intelligence is accumulated knowledge. Fluid intelligence is the ability to process information quickly and to solve new problems. Fluid intelligence is likely to have earlier and more pronounced decay with aging than crystallized intelligence.

Heredity/Environment and Intelligence

Nature and nurture interact in the formation of human intelligence. One way to measure the influence of inheritance on IQ is through a **heritability coefficient**. This coefficient, which ranges from 0 to 1, is a rough measure of the proportion of variation among individuals that can be attributed to genetic effects. Heritability is sometimes computed by comparing the IQs of identical twins who were raised separately. The assumption is that because the identical twins have identical genes, all variation in identical twins reared apart must be due to environment. Of course, the assumption is rarely completely met because identical twins are usually not separated at birth and even if they are, they still have shared the intrauterine environment of the mother. This type of analysis typically yields heritability quotients of about 0.6–0.8 (on a scale of 0–1.0). The percentage not due to heritability can be contributed to the environmentality of a particular trait. When psychologists compare the IQs of identical twins raised together to those of fraternal twins raised together, the resulting heritability quotient is about 0.75. This analysis assumes that families and people outside families treat identical and fraternal twins in the same way, an assumption that seems questionable. Many psychologists believe that the true heritability quotient for IQ is about 0.5. Thus, half of the variation among people is due to heredity, half to environment. It is important to realize that the heritability of a trait has nothing to do with its modifiability. For example, height is highly heritable, but heights have been increasing over the past several generations, especially in certain Asian countries such as Japan, as a result of changing diet. Here's a helpful analogy to illustrate modifiability of intelligence and the interplay of nature and nurture: think of nature as the soil in which intelligence can grow and nurture as the degree of care for the crop.

Study Tip

Intelligence is probably the most controversial domain for the nature versus nurture debate in psychology. Don't expect it to be treated as a settled issue on the exam, but do understand what a heritability quotient means. For testing in general, make sure to understand the difference between reliability and validity of a test.

HUMAN DIVERSITY

As previously stated, IQs are roughly normally distributed. As a result, a large majority of people will have an IQ near 100. However, in a normal distribution, there will also be a small number of people at the high and low ends of the IQ range.

Very high IQs are one basis for considering people to be intellectually gifted. Sometimes, an IQ in the 99th percentile (higher than about 135) is considered "gifted," although there is no set standard. Moreover, other measures besides IQ should be used in assigning a label of "gifted." Lewis Terman conducted a study of gifted children, following them into adulthood. Many of the participants went on to be very successful; however, part of their success may have been due to the socioeconomic

Between the *DSM-IV* and *DSM-5*, the term "mental retardation" became "intellectual disability." It's unlikely that you'll see the outdated former term on the AP Psychology Exam, but better safe than sorry!

status of their parents. Other factors unrelated to IQ may also have influenced the ability of the participants to succeed.

Intellectual disability refers to low levels of intelligence and adaptive behavior. Low IQ alone does not signify this. To be classified as intellectually disabled, a person must also demonstrate a low level of adaptive competence, or the ability to get along in the world. Intellectual disability can be categorized by severity ranging from mild, with an IQ range of 50–70, to profound, characterized by an IQ lower than 25.

Savant syndrome is a rare phenomenon in which individuals with low IQ scores display certain specific skills at a very high aptitude. Many of these skills tend to involve memory; for example, they may be able to quickly memorize extensive written materials. Other examples include very rapid mathematical calculations and the ability to play a piece of music having just heard it once. This phenomenon was the subject of the movie "Rain Man."

ETHICS IN TESTING

Those who are involved in **psychometrics**, or psychological testing, must be sure that they follow certain guidelines. Confidentiality must be protected. The purposes of the test must be clear to those administering and those taking the test. A group of individuals at each research institution sits on the Institutional Review Board, which combs through the proposed methodology of a study to determine whether there may be any unethical behavior in or adverse consequences of a scientist's research before granting them permission to perform any experiments. Questions should be asked and answered concerning who will see the results of the test and how the scores will be used. Furthermore, the impact of the scores should be ascertained before the test is given.

An issue that has received a great deal of attention in recent years is **stereotype threat**. This occurs when a message is sent, intentionally or unintentionally, to a group of people that their group tends to perform below average on a given measure. This often becomes a self-fulfilling prophecy, resulting in poorer performance than expected for members of that group. (There can also be stereotype boost if a group is told that its members tend to perform above average on a certain measure.)

KEY TERMS

Standardization and Norms

standardization sample

norms

Flynn effect

Reliability and Validity

reliability

test-retest method

split-half reliability

equivalent-form reliability

validity

internal validity

external validity

Types of Tests

projective tests

inventory-type tests

Rorschach Inkblot Test

Thematic Apperception Test (TAT)

power tests

speed tests

achievement tests

aptitude tests

Intelligence

Francis Galton

speed of processing

Alfred Binet

Lewis Terman

Stanford-Binet Test

intelligence quotient (IQ)

Stanford-Binet Intelligence Scale

Wechsler Intelligence Scale for
    Children

Wechsler Adult Intelligence Scale

abstract and verbal measures

Charles Spearman

g factor

factor analysis

Robert Sternberg

analytical intelligence

practical intelligence

creative intelligence

Louis Thurstone

Howard Gardner

verbal intelligence

mathematical intelligence

musical intelligence

spatial intelligence

kinesthetic intelligence

environmental intelligence

interpersonal intelligence

intrapersonal intelligence

Daniel Goleman

emotional intelligence

fluid intelligence

crystallized intelligence

heritability coefficient

Human Diversity

savant syndrome

Ethics in Testing

psychometrics

stereotype threat

Chapter 12 Drill

See Chapter 19 for answers and explanations.

1. In the context of psychometric testing, content validity is defined as

   (A) the extent to which the test actually measures what it is purported to measure
   (B) the degree to which there is a correlation between results on the test and future performance on another measure
   (C) the degree to which the test will yield similar results across administrations
   (D) the extent to which scores on two versions of the test are highly correlated
   (E) the degree to which scores on two sections of the same test are consistent with each other

2. Which of the following is an example of a projective test?

   (A) The Stanford-Binet Intelligence Scale
   (B) The Thematic Apperception Test (TAT)
   (C) The Minnesota Multiphasic Personality Inventory (MMPI)
   (D) The Strong Vocational Interest Blank
   (E) The F-scale

3. On a normal score distribution, an IQ score of 85 would be located

   (A) approximately one standard deviation above the mean
   (B) approximately one standard deviation below the mean
   (C) approximately two standard deviations above the mean
   (D) approximately two standard deviations below the mean
   (E) in a variable position—it would depend on the age of the respondent

4. Test standardization is accomplished by

   (A) administering the test to a sample chosen to reflect the characteristics of the population in question
   (B) administering different parts of the test to different samples meant to reflect different populations
   (C) correlating the results on the test with results on other tests that claim to measure the same dimension
   (D) correlating the consistency of scores given by different sets of graders
   (E) equilibrating the number of times each answer choice appears

5. Which of the following is NOT a dimension of intelligence in Howard Gardner's theory of multiple intelligences?

   (A) Environmental
   (B) Mathematical
   (C) Spatial
   (D) Musical
   (E) Emotional

6. Reliability measures

   (A) how consistently the test holds up over time
   (B) how well the test measures what it means to test
   (C) a way in which you can be sure that an experiment tests only one variable at a time
   (D) how consistently an individual will score on the same test on subsequent occasions
   (E) to what extent the findings of a study can be generalized to the whole population

7. A multiple-choice or a true/false question test is an example of a(n)

   (A) projective test
   (B) inventory-type test
   (C) intelligence test
   (D) hereditary test
   (E) environment test

8. Which of the following is necessary for a test to be ethical?

   (A) Confidentiality
   (B) Full disclosure of deception
   (C) Double-blind design
   (D) Internal validity
   (E) Generalization

REFLECT

Respond to the following questions:

- Which topics in this chapter do you hope to see on the multiple-choice section or essay?

- Which topics in this chapter do you hope not to see on the multiple-choice section or essay?

- Regarding any psychologists mentioned, can you pair the psychologists with their contributions to the field? Did they contribute significant experiments, theories, or both?

- Regarding any theories mentioned, can you distinguish between differing theories well enough to recognize them on the multiple-choice section? Can you distinguish them well enough to write a fluent essay on them?

- Can you define the key terms at the end of the chapter?

- Which parts of the chapter will you review?

- Will you seek further help, outside of this book (such as from a teacher, Princeton Review tutor, or AP Students), on any of the content in this chapter—and, if so, on what content?

Chapter 13
Developmental
Psychology

LIFE-SPAN APPROACH

The life-span approach to **developmental psychology** takes the view that development is not a process with a clear ending. For decades, development was thought to end with the onset of adolescence. Rather, it is now viewed as a process that continues from birth to death. From this perspective, developmental psychology can be defined as the study of the changes that occur in people's abilities and behaviors as they age. It is important to differentiate between **life-span psychologists** and **child psychologists**. Although both study development, the child psychologist has decided to focus on a particular earlier portion of the typical life span. **Erik Erikson** was the first to successfully champion the view that development occurs across an entire lifetime.

Research Methods

Research methods in developmental psychology vary according to the questions being asked by the researcher. Some developmental psychologists are interested in studying **normative development**, which is the typical sequence of developmental changes for a group of people. For example, some developmental psychologists talk about development occurring in a series of stages, universal to human development. Other developmental psychologists are more interested in individual development, or the individual pattern of development, including differences among individuals during development. Often, the techniques and research methods useful for studying one type of development are not useful for studying other types of development.

Normative development is often studied using the **cross-sectional method**. The cross-sectional method seeks to compare groups of people of various ages on similar tasks. So, for example, a cross-sectional study might involve administering cognitive tests to a group of two-year-olds, a group of four-year-olds, and a group of six-year-olds, and then comparing the means of the groups. This approach can reveal the average ages at which certain skills or abilities appear. However, the data collected in cross-sectional studies tells us little about the actual development of any single individual.

To research the developmental process, many developmental psychologists use the **longitudinal method**. The longitudinal method involves following a small group of people over a long portion of their lives, assessing change at set intervals. As you might imagine, longitudinal research is more difficult and more expensive to conduct and, therefore, is conducted less frequently than cross-sectional research. However, the longitudinal method does have some benefits because the study of individuals over time rules out the differences between subjects that other studies include. It also allows for the study of the temporal order of events.

DEVELOPMENTAL ISSUES

Developmental psychology, like most aspects of psychology, must deal with the so-called **nature-nurture debate**. **Maturationists** emphasize the role of genetically programmed growth and development on the body, particularly on the nervous system. **Maturation** can best be defined as biological readiness. From their point of view, greater preprogrammed physiological development of the brain allows for more complex conceptualization and reasoning.

The opposing position is the learning perspective, and adherents to this position are sometimes referred to as **environmentalists**. The extreme form can be found in Locke's idea, which states that almost all development is the direct result of learning—infants are born as blank slates onto which experience etches its lessons. The organism develops more complex behaviors and cognition because it acquires more associations through learning.

There are other issues to be considered when studying development. One is whether development is **continuous** or **discontinuous**—gradual or stage-oriented. Evidence of growth spurts and leaps of cognition support the discontinuous approach, but other studies show gradual development, particularly in social skill building. A **critical period** refers to a time during which a skill or ability must develop; if the ability does not develop during that time, it probably will never develop or may not develop as well. An example of a skill with a critical period is language. Scientists believe that, if a person is not exposed to language by roughly age 12, the ability to learn language significantly diminishes or disappears.

Culture also impacts development in important ways. A **collectivist culture** is one in which the needs of society are placed before the needs of the individual. Conversely, **individualist cultures** promote personal needs above the needs of society. It is important to realize that a developing child's relationship with her environment and culture is bidirectional, meaning that just as a child's social environment plays a role in how she develops, she also contributes to the society in which she is born.

The Feral Child
One famous example in favor of the critical period is Genie, the "feral child" who was isolated from other humans from infancy until age 13, preventing her from learning spoken language.

DEVELOPMENTAL THEORIES

Developmental theories can be divided into two broad classes: those that conceptualize development as a single, continuous, unitary process and those that view it as occurring in discrete stages. **Stages** are patterns of behavior that occur in a fixed sequence. Each stage has a unique set of cognitive structures, or sets of mental abilities, that build on the cognitive structures established in the previous stage. Quite likely, some aspects of development may occur in stages at the same time that others occur along a continuum. Psychologists typically agree that the edges of stages are blurred and may overlap for various domains within a stage.

The four stage theories that follow Physical Development (Piaget, Freud, Erikson, and Kohlberg) are frequently tested: make sure that you know them!

> ## Dimensions of Development
> Development typically occurs within three realms: physical, cognitive, and social.

Physical Development

Physical development starts at conception. The **zygote**, or fertilized egg, goes through three distinct phases of gestation prior to birth. The first stage is the **germinal stage**, in which the zygote undergoes cell division, expanding to 64 cells and implanting itself in the uterine wall. This stage lasts about two weeks. The **embryonic stage** consists of organ formation and lasts until the beginning of the third month. In the **fetal stage**, sexual differentiation occurs and movement begins to develop. Growth is rapid in this stage. Various harmful environmental agents, known as **teratogens**, may affect fetal development. One such agent is alcohol. Some fetuses exposed to alcohol develop **fetal alcohol syndrome (FAS)**, resulting in physical abnormalities and cognitive deficiencies.

Rudimentary movements are the first voluntary movements performed by a child. They occur in very predictable stages from birth to age 2, and they include rolling, sitting, crawling, standing, and walking. These form the foundation on which the fundamental movements are built and are primarily dictated by genetics (that is, these movements are more or less "pre-programmed").

The **fundamental movement** stage occurs from age 2 to age 7; during this time, the child is learning to manipulate their body through actions such as running, jumping, throwing, and catching. This stage is highly influenced by environment, much more so than the rudimentary movement stage that precedes it. Children are typically in school at this stage, and physical activity and games are necessary for proper motor development. Movements initially start out uncoordinated and poorly controlled, but as the child advances in age, movements become more refined, coordinated, and efficient.

During the stage of **specialized movement**, children learn to combine the fundamental movements and apply them to specific tasks. This stage can be subdivided into two shorter stages: a **transitional substage** and an **application substage**. During the transitional substage, a combination of movements occurs; for example, grasping, jumping, and throwing are combined to take a shot in basketball. The application substage is defined more by conscious decisions to apply these skills to specific types of activity; for example, one child might choose to play basketball, whereas another might use the same set of skills and abilities to play baseball. Additionally, the application of strategy to movement is now possible; for example, a child choosing to delay shooting the basketball until she has a clear shot at the basket.

Ultimately, children progress to a lifelong application stage, typically beginning in adolescence and progressing through adulthood. During this time, movements are continually refined and applied to normal daily activities as well as recreational and competitive activities.

Both of these processes are dependent on neural development. There is evidence that the brain is still organizing itself in the months after birth. In fact, nervous system development continues into early adulthood. It is important to note that although perceptual and motor development depend on the development of the nervous system, the development of the nervous system depends on **environmental interaction** on the part of the child. It has been demonstrated that children raised in situations in which their ability to crawl or walk is restricted have impaired motor skills. This occurs, for example, in some institutions in countries without regulation of childcare facilities. Additionally, perceptual development can be delayed by lack of stimulation. An important theme in developmental psychology is that of the critical period—that for some parts of the brain, the phrase "use it or lose it" holds true.

Experiments with animals (see Hubel and Wiesel on page 169) have shown that depriving an eye of stimuli by covering it at the very beginning of life will lead to the underdevelopment of the part of the occipital lobe responsible for vision in that eye. As a result, that section of the brain will be allocated to another function. This plasticity, or changeability, of the brain is illustrated in an experiment in which a third eye was added to a frog. The occipital lobe flexibly responded by dividing the processing power of the occipital lobe among three eyes rather than two. This experiment worked only if the eye was introduced very close to birth, demonstrating the limited critical period during which some experience must occur for the brain to develop in a particular way.

Puberty is another landmark of physical development. It is characterized by growth spurts, the development of secondary sex characteristics, and other physical developments. There are also social and cognitive changes that are discussed later in this section.

Nature, Nurture, and the Critical Period

This phenomenon is informative with regard to the nature-nurture issue. The child is not born as a blank slate: it has some innate reflexes. However, the physiological development of the child depends on its interactions with the environment. Nature and nurture play complementary roles in development.

Most people peak physically in early adulthood. One just needs to look at professional athletes to recognize this fact. Adulthood is marked by gradual decrease of physical abilities, although a healthy lifestyle will slow this process. At approximately 50 years old, women experience menopause, a change in estrogen production causing menstruation to cease.

In the elderly population, the gradual diminution of adulthood reaches noticeable proportions. The senses lose much of their efficacy. For example, half of those over age 80 have lost their sense of smell. Diseases such as Alzheimer's can affect memory, cognition, and personality.

Cognitive Development

Cognitive development refers to the development of learning, memory, reasoning, problem-solving, and related skills.

Piaget

Jean Piaget proposed an influential theory of the cognitive development of children. Piaget's developmental theory is based on the concept of **equilibration**. Equilibration is a child's attempt to reach a balance between what the child encounters in the environment and what cognitive structures the child brings to the situation. Children try to reach equilibration through **assimilation**, incorporating new ideas into existing schemas. For example, a child may develop a **schema**, or mental representational model, for animals after encountering dogs and cats. When he goes to the zoo and sees more exotic four-legged animals like elephants or giraffes, he must assimilate this new information into his existing category of animals. However, when facing information that does not easily fit into an existing schema, the child must modify the schema to include the new information. This process is called **accommodation**. For example, this child's schema of animal might go through a process of accommodation if he encounters a kangaroo that hops on two legs.

According to Piaget, children go through a series of developmental stages. Piaget believed that these stages occur in a fixed order, and a child can be in only one stage at any given time. The following are the four stages Piaget proposed, first presented as a chart and then in more detail.

Each stage can be categorized by the presence/absence of schemas, the types of mental operations the child can perform, and the presence or absence of theoretical thought.

Q: What are the typical age ranges for Piaget's stages of development?

Answer on page 234.

Criticism of Piaget

Piaget's theory is not universally accepted. Other researchers have found flaws in his research methods and his underestimation of children's abilities, especially at ages four to five. Critics attest that some children that age can take another's perspective and are not so egocentric. Other criticisms include the failure of Piaget to recognize the environmental factors pushing child development.

Stage	Explanation	Schemas	Mental Operations	Theoretical Thinking
Sensorimotor	Act on objects that are present and begin to develop schemas but incapable of operations			
Preoperational	Able to use schemas not present (symbolic thought) but lacks ability to perform mental operations	X		
Concrete Operational	Able to access schemas and perform mental operations but still limited to experiences	X	X	
Formal Operational	Able to use schemas, understand operations, and apply both to theoretical questions not based on experiences	X	X	X

- **Sensorimotor Stage.** This stage usually occurs during the first two years of life and is typified by reflexive reactions and then circular reactions, which are repeated behaviors by which the infant manipulates the environment. For example, if an infant kicks its legs and hits the mobile on its crib with its foot, stimulating movement, the infant is likely to repeat the action in the future. **Object permanence**, which develops during this stage, is the knowledge that objects continue to exist when they are outside the field of view. For example, if a ball rolls under a chair, the child will continue to look for it. At this age, the child lacks the ability to access mental schemas or solve problems through performing a mental operation, which is the ability to represent and manipulate information in a person's mind. Schemas are acquired in the preoperational stage, while mental operations become accessible during the concrete operational stage. Another hallmark of the sensorimotor stage is the development of goal-oriented behavior. For example, a very young child who is able to roll over at will, but not yet able to crawl, may consciously roll over multiple times to reach a favorite toy.

- **Preoperational Stage.** The preoperational stage typically occurs from ages two to seven. Children generally begin this stage with the development of language. Language represents a shift to **symbolic thinking**, or the ability to use words to substitute for objects. Other characteristics of the stage are **egocentrism**, seeing the world only from one's own point of view, **artificialism**, believing that all things are human-made, and **animism**, believing that all things are living.

- **Concrete Operational Stage.** Typically occur-ring from ages seven to eleven, this is the stage when children develop the ability to perform a mental operation and then reverse their thinking back to a starting point, a concept called **reversibility**. Another important concept is **conservation**—the idea that the amount of a substance does not change just because it is arranged differently. For example, conservation of mass might be demonstrated by taking a large ball of clay and using it to create several smaller balls of clay. A child in the concrete operational stage will understand that the total amount of clay has not changed, while a child in the preoperational stage might think that there is more clay because there are more balls.

- **Formal Operational Stage.** This stage begins at about age 12. At this level, children are fully capable of understanding abstractions and symbolic relationships. They are also capable of **metacognition**, or the ability to recognize one's cognitive processes and adapt those processes if they aren't successful. The formal operational stage is also the point at which a child acquires hypothetical reasoning, which is the ability to figure out answers to problems with which a person does not have direct experience. For example, a child in the concrete operational stage would have great difficulty imagining how the world might change as a result of an alien invasion, while a 12-year-old could posit numerous theories on the issue.

Theory of Mind (TOM) and the False Belief Task

A: Sensorimotor: 0–2 years old Preoperational: 2–7 years old Concrete Operational: 7–11 years old Formal Operational: 12 years +

A key cognitive ability that develops in childhood around the age of four is theory of mind. TOM allows children to understand that other people see the world differently than they do. It is the opposite of egocentrism. Psychologists test theory of mind through the "false belief task." For example, in this test, a child under the age of four opens a container that is labeled "pencils" and finds gumballs instead. The child is asked what another child, who is not present, would think is in the container. The correct answer is "pencils," but because a child under the age of four does not have TOM, that child will answer "gumballs." Psychologists now believe that the absence of theory of mind helps to explain the actions of people with autism, which is discussed in Chapter 16.

Vygotsky

Another influential theory of cognitive development was proposed by **Lev Vygotsky**. Piaget believed that biological maturation is the driving force in development. Vygotsky, on the other hand, stressed social factors as critical to the developmental process. Vygotsky believed that much of development occurs by **internalization**, the absorption of knowledge into the self from environmental and social contexts. Vygotsky also proposed the concept of a **zone of proximal development**, which is the range between the developed level of ability that a child displays and the potential level of ability of which the child is actually capable. These two levels are often referred to as the **actual development level** and the **potential development level**, respectively. Actual development rarely lives up to its potential because ability depends on input from the environment, and environmental input is rarely truly optimal. According to Vygotsky, the way in which a child realizes his potential is through the process of scaffolding. Scaffolding is the support system that allows a person to move across the zone of proximal development incrementally, with environmental supports, such as teachers and parents. If a person fails to advance, it might mean that the scaffolding steps are too high above the person's current abilities.

Life-span psychologists have realized that cognitive development continues into adulthood. Childhood and early adulthood are times marked by relatively rapid neural growth. However, we lose a small percentage of brain weight between our early 20s and our 80s. In the later years, many adults show a decrease in **fluid intelligence**—that is, the ability to think in terms of abstract concepts and symbolic relationships. This decrease, however, is accompanied by increased **crystallized intelligence**, or specific knowledge of facts and information.

Older but Wiser

A related feature of adult cognitive development is **wisdom**. It is assumed in many cultures that older members of a society have a perspective or level of accumulated knowledge that gives them wisdom. Wisdom is a form of insight into life situations and conditions that results in good judgments about difficult life problems.

Psychosexual Development

Psychosexual development is the development of an awareness of one's own sexuality, including the identification of the self with a particular gender. Attempting to understand the **fixations** of his patients, **Sigmund Freud** elaborated a theory of psychosexual development. This is a stage theory in which attention was given to parts of the body that were especially significant for the developing person. During the **oral stage**, from birth to about two, the primary source of pleasure for the infant comes from sucking, as well as using the voice to cry out for caretakers. People who develop fixations during this stage may become addicted to gum, cigarettes, or alcohol, or may become verbally abusive. During the **anal stage**, from about two to three, toddlers learn that they are praised when they do well with toilet training, and are not praised (or even scolded) when they do not. People who develop fixations during this stage may have issues with control, either being overcontrolling (he's so anal!) or being willfully messy (she throws her crap everywhere!). During the **phallic stage**, from about three to six, children connect their sex to their gender, and begin to puzzle out what that means. Although Freud wrote later (non-judgmentally) about bisexuality and homosexuality, this early theory focused on heterosexual development. Accordingly, the opposite-sex parent is taken as an ideal for future partner choices. People who develop fixations during this stage may be extremely picky about their partner choices, only selecting people who are similar to their parent. During the **latency stage**, from about six to twelve, there is no one particular part of the body that has the most importance for the developing mind. Children in this stage are partly focused on gender identification, which is why many boys associate primarily with other boys, and many girls associate primarily with other girls, and the two groups regard each other with a mixture of interest and suspicion. This is the age of "cooties." People who develop fixations in this stage primarily socialize with their own gender as adults, even when they are heterosexual. During the **genital stage**, from about twelve until death, the genital region becomes the primary source of sensual/sexual pleasure, unless traumas in prior stages have resulted in fixations.

Sex Roles, Sex Differences

Though there are many criticisms of Freud's stage theory, it's certainly true that human psychological development includes aspects of sex and gender. There are differences between the sexes at birth, and, although most observable sexual development occurs during adolescence, psychosexual development starts at a much younger age.

Children develop **gender identity**, the awareness that they are boys or girls, by age two or three. The acquisition of sex-related roles, called **gender typing**, also occurs very early, from the ages of two to seven. This age range is also when children come to understand that there is **gender constancy**—that is, that gender is a fixed, unchangeable characteristic. At this age, children begin to understand that gender is a characteristic of the individual and that items such as clothes or even behavior do not define the sex of the individual. **Androgyny** may develop as children begin to blur the lines between stereotypical male and female roles in society. These individuals may adopt behaviors from both types of roles.

Another theory of how sex roles develop has been proposed by **Albert Bandura**. Bandura felt that, like violent behavior, sexual roles could be acquired through social or vicarious learning. Young boys see older boys being rewarded for being masculine and punished for being feminine. This pattern creates a self-perpetuating cycle, according to Bandura, with each successive generation providing the model for the following generation. This view has been supported by research showing that parents reward independence and competition in boys, while they reward nurturing and caring behaviors in girls.

It is important to consider that biological, social, and cognitive factors all play a role in sexual development. Additionally, we must consider that, when discussing sexual development, there is much disagreement on what is "normal." Theories of sexual development are often products of the culture and time in which they were developed and do not always reflect what is considered normal in modern society.

In the 1950's, **Alfred Kinsey** did extensive, and very widely-read, work on the attitudes and behaviors of American adults pertaining to sexuality. He did this by conducting numerous subjective interviews. Among his important contributions

Though the language around this topic is changing on a social level, this book intends to prepare you for the uses most commonly seen from the AP Psychology exam. We will update your free student tools accordingly should any new context for this subject be introduced to the test.

was the **Kinsey Scale,** which posited that sexuality is not binary, either exclusively heterosexual or homosexual; rather, it exists along a continuum of attractions and practices. Kinsey's books played a role in liberalizing Americans' attitudes toward sexuality in the following decades.

Social Development

Social development involves the ability to interact with others and with the social structures in which we live. Erik Erikson tried to capture the complexities of social development in his psychosocial theory. This theory is important not only for its description of the developmental process as a series of stages marked by the resolution of specific developmental "tasks," but also because it was the first theory to assert that development is a life-span process. Erikson's stages of **psychosocial development** include the following.

Trust versus Mistrust

This stage occurs during the first year of life. Infants decide whether the world is friendly or hostile, depending on whether or not they can trust that their basic needs will be met. Trust and hopefulness are the outcomes of positive resolutions of this stage.

Autonomy versus Shame and Doubt

Between the ages of one and three, the child must develop a sense of control over bodily functions as well as over the environment. Successful resolution of this stage involves learning how to use the toilet, to walk, and to perform other skills related to control of the self.

Initiative versus Guilt

This is the stage that occurs at about three to six years of age and often corresponds with a child's entry into a broader social world outside the home. Children at this stage must take initiative and learn to assert themselves socially, without overstepping their bounds. The successful resolution of this stage results in the development of a sense of purpose.

Industry versus Inferiority

Children from ages six to twelve are in this stage. They are now in school and are becoming accustomed to receiving feedback for their work. Thus, they must gain a sense of accomplishment and pride in their work. They begin to understand what they are capable of doing. The successful resolution of this stage produces a sense of competence.

Identity versus Role Confusion

This stage involves the adolescent search for identity. Adolescents question what type of people they are and begin to develop their own values at this stage. The resolution of this stage is **fidelity**, or truthfulness to one's self.

Intimacy versus Isolation

This is the stage of early adulthood when we attempt to form loving, lasting relationships. The successful resolution of this stage results in one's learning how to love in a mature, giving way. If this stage is not successfully resolved, feelings of isolation or a lack of intimacy may result.

Generativity versus Stagnation

This stage occurs during middle adulthood and brings with it the struggle to be productive in both career and home, and to contribute to the next generation with ideas and possibly with children. Being productive in these ways is called **generativity**. This is the stage where we try to leave our "mark" on the world. Failure to resolve this stage can result in feelings of **stagnation** or isolation.

Integrity versus Despair

This stage occurs during old age and brings with it the struggle to come to terms with one's life, which involves accepting both successes and failures. The positive outcome of this stage is wisdom, whereas the failure to resolve this stage can lead to bitterness and despair.

Study Tip

It may be helpful to study Freud's theory of psychosexual development and Erikson's theory of psychosocial development side-by-side. Comparisons of the first five stages of each may help you remember them. Since Freud's theory ends at puberty, there will be no comparisons for the last three of Erikson's stages. Similarly, you may want to look at Piaget's theory of cognitive development and Kohlberg's theory of moral development side-by-side. Do Kohlberg's earliest stages reflect egocentrism? Do the later stages reflect complex reasoning ability?

Erikson's is not the only social development theory. Some theories have been based on a child's **temperament,** the notion that some childhood behavior is biologically based rather than learned (see p. 269). Beginning in the 1930's, **Konrad Lorenz** posited that much child attachment behavior is innate. Lorenz was an ethologist: he studied animal behavior and he based his ideas about attachment on his observations of imprinting in animals. In the 1950s, **Harry and Margaret Harlow** demonstrated that rhesus monkey infants need comfort and security as much as food. Through the use of artificial, inanimate surrogate mothers, Harlow ascertained that these infants become more attached to soft "mothers" without food than to wire ones with food. **Attachment** is defined as the tendency to prefer specific familiar individuals to others. **John Bowlby** is considered the father of attachment theory. He devoted extensive research to the concept of attachment and pioneered the psychoanalytic view that early experiences in childhood have an important influence on development and behavior later in life. Bowlby believed that a close and loving relationship between a child and a caregiver is critical to the infant's healthy development and provides a model that the growing child will use to build mutually beneficial relationships in their life. In contrast, a lack of responsiveness and physical support on the part of the parent will hurt the child in the short-term and the child's relationships in the long-term. In the 1970s, **Mary Ainsworth** studied human infant attachment. Using the **strange situation,** in which a parent or primary guardian leaves a child with a stranger and then returns, Ainsworth recognized four attachment patterns.

- **Secure**—The child is generally happy in the presence of the primary caretaker, is distressed when the caretaker leaves, and can be consoled again quickly after the caregiver returns.

- **Avoidant**—The child may be inhibited in the presence of the primary caretaker, and may pretend to not be distressed when the caretaker leaves. (Blood pressure and cortisol analyses show that the child is in fact quite stressed out.)

- **Ambivalent**—The child may have a "stormy" relationship with the primary caretaker, is distressed when the caretaker leaves, and has difficulty being consoled after the caretaker's return.

- **Disorganized**—The child has an erratic relationship with the primary caretaker and with other adults. This attachment style is more common in cases of severe neglect and/or abuse.

Diana Baumrind has identified the following three types of parenting styles.

- **Authoritarian**—Parents have high expectations for their child to comply with rules without debate or explanation. This style is the most likely to use corporal punishment (like spanking) for disobedience. Children of these parents are socially withdrawn, lack decision-making capabilities, and lack curiosity. Authoritarian parents will exert a high level of control and low level of warmth.

- **Authoritative**—Parents also expect compliance to rules but explain rules and encourage independence. Parents set limits, give out punishments, and forgive. Children of these parents have high self-esteem, are independent, and are articulate. Authoritative parents will exert a high level of control and high level of warmth.

- **Permissive**—Parents have few expectations and are warm and non-demanding. Children are rarely punished, and parents consider themselves friends of the child. Children of these parents are not good at accepting responsibility, controlling their impulses, or being generous in social relationships. Permissive parents will exert a low level of control and high level of warmth.

Another theory of social development concerns the stages of death and dying developed by **Elisabeth Kubler-Ross**. She identified the following ways people tend to come to terms with terminal illnesses—denial, anger, bargaining, depression, and acceptance. Later psychologists have acknowledged that these as well as other emotions are involved in grieving and have shown that the stages are not necessarily ordered.

Moral Development

The most influential theory of **moral development** was advanced by **Lawrence Kohlberg**, who expanded on an early theory proposed by Piaget. Kohlberg's theory can be divided into levels, each of which has two distinct stages.

Kohlberg's Level I

Level I encompasses ages seven to ten and is the level of preconventional morality. **Preconventional morality** is a two-stage system of moral judgment. In the first stage, it is based on avoiding punishment and receiving rewards. In this stage, children often will mention a fear of being punished as a reason why rules should not be broken. As children age, preconventional morality changes slightly. The second stage of preconventional morality is characterized by a focus on individualism and exchange. Children work for their own interest at this stage, and while they will strike deals with others to satisfy the other person, their primary interest is a selfish one. In summary, in stage 1 of preconventional morality, children make judgments motivated by fear; in stage 2, they make judgments by evaluating the benefit for themselves.

Kohlberg's Level II

Level II typically occurs from about ages 10 to 16 and sometimes beyond. This is the stage of **conventional morality**. Conventional morality is the internalizing of society's rules and morals. The motivation to follow these rules is generated by the child's knowing that it is "right" to do so. The first stage of this level (stage 3) is typified by the child's effort to live up to the expectations of others, especially those of authority figures. The child understands that the rules set forth by society are important, and the child tries to conform to these rules. The second stage of conventional morality (stage 4) involves the development of conscience. Young teens at this stage obey rules and feel moral, societal obligations.

Criticism of Kohlberg

Although Kohlberg's theory is an important and influential one, it has been challenged as being inadequate for describing the moral development of people who live in non-Western culture and of women. **Carol Gilligan** has developed a revised version of Kohlberg's theory. Rather than focusing on the awareness and development of the concept of justice, as Kohlberg did, Gilligan's theory places the development of caring relationships as central to moral progress.

Kohlberg's Level III

Level III occurs from age 16 and onward. This is the level of **postconventional morality**. At this level, societal rules are still important, but an internal set of values has developed that may generate occasional conflict with societal values. The first stage of this level (stage 5) is characterized by a belief in individual rights and social contracts. Individual rights, such as those of life and liberty, may outweigh social contracts. In general, however, a balance must be maintained between individual interests and societal rules. The second stage of postconventional morality (stage 6) represents the highest stage of moral development in Kohlberg's model. This stage involves the belief in universal principles of justice. Universal principles of justice are universal rules of morality that typically do, but occasionally do not, agree with the rules of society. An individual at stage 6 believes that the universal principles of justice outweigh societal rules and acts accordingly. Few people reach this level, according to Kohlberg.

KEY TERMS

Life-Span Approach
- developmental psychology
- life-span psychologists
- child psychologists
- Erik Erikson
- normative development
- cross-sectional method
- longitudinal method

Developmental Issues
- nature-nurture debate
- maturationists
- maturation
- environmentalists
- continuous
- discontinuous
- critical period
- culture
- collectivist culture
- individualist cultures

Developmental Theories
- stages
- physical development
- zygote
- germinal stage
- embryonic stage
- fetal stage
- teratogens
- fetal alcohol syndrome (FAS)
- rudimentary movements
- fundamental movement
- specialized movement
- transitional substage
- application substage
- environmental interaction
- cognitive development

- Jean Piaget
- equilibration
- assimilation
- schema
- accommodation
- sensorimotor stage
- object permanence
- preoperational stage
- symbolic thinking
- egocentrism
- artificialism
- animism
- concrete operational stage
- reversibility
- conservation
- formal operational stage
- metacognition
- Lev Vygotsky
- internalization
- zone of proximal development
- actual development level
- potential development level
- wisdom
- fluid intelligence
- crystallized intelligence
- psychosexual development
- fixations
- Sigmund Freud
- stages of psychosexual development: oral, anal, phallic, latency, genital
- gender identity
- gender typing
- gender constancy
- androgyny

- Albert Bandura
- Alfred Kinsey
- Kinsey Scale
- social development
- psychosocial development
- fidelity
- generativity
- stagnation
- temperament
- Konrad Lorenz
- Harry and Margaret Harlow
- attachment
- John Bowlby
- Mary Ainsworth
- strange situation
- child attachment patterns: secure, avoidant, ambivalent, disorganized
- Diana Baumrind
- parenting styles: authoritarian, authoritative, permissive
- Elizabeth Kubler-Ross
- moral development
- Lawrence Kohlberg
- preconventional morality
- conventional morality
- postconventional morality
- Carol Gilligan

Chapter 13 Drill

See Chapter 19 for answers and explanations.

1. In neonates, the response to a feeling of lost bodily support (like falling) that involves a splaying out of the limbs is called the

   (A) palmar reflex
   (B) Babinski reflex
   (C) orienting reflex
   (D) Moro reflex
   (E) rooting reflex

2. The belief that there is often a discrepancy between children's outward cognitive abilities and their true cognitive abilities is most closely associated with which of the following theorists?

   (A) Jean Piaget
   (B) Lev Vygotsky
   (C) Leon Festinger
   (D) Sigmund Freud
   (E) Julian Rotter

3. According to Erik Erikson, the major developmental task of school-age children before puberty is to develop

   (A) a sense of competence in their efforts
   (B) the ability to form stable intimate relationships
   (C) a feeling of trust that their basic needs will be met
   (D) control over basic bodily functions
   (E) a consistent self-view of identity and roles

4. Shyera, approaching the age of five, believes that all things, from people to animals to plants to objects, are alive, but she has trouble understanding circumstances from these other "living" things' points of view. Piaget's theory would place Shyera

   (A) at the sensorimotor stage
   (B) at the preoperational stage
   (C) at the concrete operational stage
   (D) at the formal operational stage
   (E) at the latency stage

5. Lawrence Kohlberg's theory of moral development posits that a child at the first stage of preconventional morality

   (A) is motivated primarily by the evaluation of self-benefit
   (B) is motivated primarily by the desire to live up to expectations
   (C) is motivated primarily by a belief in balancing individual rights with social contracts
   (D) is motivated primarily by the desire to maintain a "just world"
   (E) is motivated primarily by the desire to receive reward and avoid punishment

6. An infant cries when his mother leaves the room but is quickly consoled when she returns. The infant feels comfortable to explore and wander around when the mother is in the room. Mary Ainsworth would describe this infant as having

   (A) insecure attachment
   (B) avoidant attachment
   (C) secure attachment
   (D) disorganized attachment
   (E) generalized attachment

7. A school-age student is able to recognize that the water she poured from a short wide cup is still the same amount of water in a tall, skinny vase. This concept is known as

   (A) conservation
   (B) object permanence
   (C) conditioning
   (D) crystallized intelligence
   (E) egocentrism

8. Trivial Pursuit, a board game that asks for answers to questions about random facts, relies most heavily on which form of knowledge?

   (A) Assimilation
   (B) Crystallized intelligence
   (C) Internalization
   (D) Wisdom
   (E) Fluid intelligence

9. In a modern art museum, Mira comes across an abstract furniture exhibit. She sees one particular piece that looks like a desk, but is later told it is actually a bookshelf. After looking at the furniture piece a little longer, she then sees it can be a book-shelf. This concept of learning is called

    (A) functional fixedness
    (B) object permanence
    (C) a mental set
    (D) accommodation
    (E) assimilation

10. Bandura believed which of the following statements about gender development?

    (A) Gender is a learned behavior that has a critical period right before puberty.
    (B) Gender is genetically based and does not have to do with socialization.
    (C) Gender is a result of hormonal fluctuations that happen during puberty.
    (D) Gender roles are a result of cognitive development only.
    (E) Gender roles are at least in part observed and rewarded through socialization.

REFLECT

Respond to the following questions:

- Which topics in this chapter do you hope to see on the multiple-choice section or essay?

- Which topics in this chapter do you hope not to see on the multiple-choice section or essay?

- Regarding any psychologists mentioned, can you pair the psychologists with their contributions to the field? Did they contribute significant experiments, theories, or both?

- Regarding any theories mentioned, can you distinguish between differing theories well enough to recognize them on the multiple-choice section? Can you distinguish them well enough to write a fluent essay on them?

- Can you define the key terms at the end of the chapter?

- Which parts of the chapter will you review?

- Will you seek further help, outside of this book (such as from a teacher, Princeton Review tutor, or AP Students), on any of the content in this chapter—and, if so, on what content?

Chapter 14
Motivation and Emotion

BIOLOGICAL BASES

Motivation is defined as a need or desire that serves to energize or direct behavior.

Learning is motivated by biological and physiological factors. Without motivation, action and learning do not occur. **Evolutionary theory** states that animals are motivated to act by basic needs critical to the survival of the organism. For a given organism to survive, it needs food, water, and sleep. For the genes of the organism to replicate, reproductive behavior is needed to produce offspring and to foster their survival. Hunger, thirst, sleep, and reproduction needs are **primary drives**. The desire to obtain learned reinforcers, such as money or social acceptance, is a **secondary drive**.

The interaction between the brain and motivation was noticed when **Olds and Milner** discovered that rats would press a bar in order to send a small electrical pulse into certain areas of their brains. This phenomenon is known as intracranial self-stimulation. Further research demonstrated that if the electrode was implanted into certain parts of the limbic system, the rat would self-stimulate nearly constantly. The rats were motivated to stimulate themselves. This finding also suggests that the limbic system, particularly the nucleus accumbens, must play a pivotal role in motivated behavior, and that dopamine, which is the prominent neurotransmitter in this region, must be associated with reward-seeking behavior.

> Four primary theories attempt to explain the link between neurophysiology and motivated behavior: instinct theory, arousal theory, opponent process theory, and drive-reduction theory.

Instinct theory, supported by evolutionary psychology, posits that the learning of species-specific behavior motivates organisms to do what is necessary to ensure their survival. For example, cats and other predatory animals have an instinctive motivation to react to movement in their environment to protect themselves and their offspring.

Arousal theory states that the main reason people are motivated to perform any action is to maintain an ideal level of physiological arousal. Arousal is a direct correlate of nervous system activity. A moderate arousal level seems optimal for most tasks, but keep in mind that what is optimal varies by person as well as task. The **Yerkes-Dodson law** states that tasks of moderate difficulty, neither too easy nor too hard, elicit the highest level of performance. The Yerkes-Dodson law also posits that high levels of arousal for difficult tasks and low levels of arousal for easy tasks are detrimental, while high levels of arousal for easy tasks and low levels of arousal for difficult tasks are preferred.

The **opponent process theory** is a theory of motivation that is clearly relevant to the concept of addiction. It posits that we start off at a motivational baseline, at which we are not motivated to act. Then we encounter a stimulus that feels good, such as a drug or even a positive social interaction. The pleasurable feelings we experience are the result of neuronal activity in the pleasure centers of the brain (the nucleus accumbens). We now have acquired a motivation to seek out the stimulus that made us feel good. Our brains, however, tend to revert back to a state of emotional neutrality over time. This reversion is a result of an opponent process, which works in opposition to the initial motivation toward seeking the stimulus. In other words, we are motivated to seek stimuli that make us feel emotion, after which an opposing motivational force brings us back in the direction of a baseline. After repeated exposure to a stimulus, its emotional effects begin to wear off; that is, we begin to habituate to the stimulus. The opponent process, however, does not habituate as quickly, so what used to cause a very positive response now barely produces one at all. Additionally, the opponent process overcompensates, producing withdrawal. As with drugs, we now need larger amounts of the formerly positive stimuli just to maintain a baseline state. In other words, we are addicted.

The **drive-reduction theory** of motivation posits that psychological needs put stress on the body and that we are motivated to reduce this negative experience. Another way to view motivation is using the homeostatic regulation theory, or homeostasis. **Homeostasis** is a state of regulatory equilibrium. When the balance of that equilibrium shifts, we are motivated to try to right the balance. A key concept in the operation of homeostasis is the negative feedback loop. When we are running out of something, like fuel, a metabolic signal is generated that tells us to eat food. When our nutrient supply is replenished, a signal is issued to stop eating. The common analogy for this process is a home thermostat in a heating-cooling system. It has a target temperature, called the **set point**. The job of the thermostat is to maintain the set point.

Homeostasis in Action
In the example to the left, hunger is the result of homeostasis. If you go without eating for too long you will become increasingly famished and very motivated to eat.

HUNGER, THIRST, AND SEX

The homeostatic regulation model provides a biological explanation for the efficacy of primary reinforcers such as hunger and sex. The brain provides a large amount of the control over feeding behavior. Specifically, the **hypothalamus** has been identified as an area controlling feeding. If body weight rises above the set point, the action of the **ventromedial hypothalamus** will send messages to the brain to eat less and to exercise more. Conversely, when body weight falls below the set point, the brain sends messages to eat more and exercise less through the **lateral hypothalamus**. This control can be demonstrated by lesion studies in animals. If the ventromedial hypothalamus (VMH) is lesioned, the animal eats constantly. The negative feedback loop that should turn off eating has been disrupted. If we damage a neighboring portion of the hypothalamus, the lateral hypothalamus (LH), then the animal stops eating, often starving to death. In more normal circumstances, **leptin** plays a role in the feedback loop between signals from the hypothalamus and those from the stomach. Leptin is released in response to a buildup of fat cells when enough energy has been consumed. This signal is then interpreted by the satiety center in the hypothalamus, working as a safety valve to decrease the feeling of hunger.

The Long and the Short of It

In reality, both glucose and body fat are probably monitored, with glucostatic homeostasis responsible for the starting and stopping of individual meals and lipostatic homeostasis responsible for larger long-term patterns of eating behavior.

The feedback loop that controls eating can be broken by damaging the hypothalamus, but the operation of this mechanism raises the question of what is actually monitored and regulated in normal feeding behavior. Two prime candidates exist. The first candidate hypothesis is **blood glucose**. This idea forms the basis for the **glucostatic hypothesis**. Glucose is the primary fuel of the brain and most other organs. When **insulin** (a hormone produced by the pancreas to regulate glucose) rises, glucose decreases. To restore glucostatic balance, a person needs to eat something. If cellular fuel gets low, then it needs to be replenished. The glucostatic theory of energy regulation gains support from the finding that the hypothalamus has cells that detect glucose.

The glucostatic theory is not without flaws, however. Blood glucose levels are very transient, rising and falling quite dramatically for a variety of reasons. How could it be, then, that such a variable measure could control body weight, which remains relatively stable from early adulthood onward? Another phenomenon inconsistent with a glucostatic hypothesis is diabetes, a disorder of insulin production. Diabetics have greatly elevated blood glucose, but they are no less hungry than everyone else.

A second candidate hypothesis is called the **lipostatic hypothesis**. As you might have guessed, this theory states that fat is the measured and controlled substance in the body that regulates hunger. Fat provides the long-term energy store for our bodies. The fat stores in our bodies are fairly fixed, and any significant decrease in fat is a result of starvation. The lipostatic hypothesis gained support from the discovery of leptin, which is a hormone secreted by fat cells. Leptin may be the substance used by the brain to monitor the amount of fat in the body.

There are several disorders related to eating habits, body weight, and body image that have their roots in psychological causes. **Anorexia nervosa**, which is more prevalent in females, is an eating disorder characterized by an intense fear of gaining weight or becoming fat despite having a significantly low body weight for one's age, sex, developmental trajectory, and physical health. **Body dysmorphia**, or a distorted body image, is key to understanding this disorder. Another related eating disorder is **bulimia nervosa,** which is characterized by alternating periods of binging and purging. If there is no purging or over-exercising, it is likely to be a **binge-eating disorder**.

The Great Motivator: Thirst

Another great motivator of action in humans and animals is thirst. A human can live for weeks without food, but only for a few days without water. Water leaves the body constantly through sweat, urine, and exhalation. This water needs to be replaced, and the body regulates our patterns of intake so that water is consumed before we are severely water depleted. The lateral hypothalamus is implicated in drinking. Lesions of this area greatly reduce drinking behavior. Another part of the hypothalamus, the preoptic area, is also involved. Lesions of the preoptic area result in excessive drinking.

As mentioned earlier, biological drives are those that ensure the survival not only of the individual, but also the survival of the individual's genes. Like the motivations to eat and drink, the motivation to reproduce relies on the hypothalamus, which stimulates the **pituitary gland** and ultimately the production of androgens and estrogens. **Androgens** and **estrogens** are the primary sexual hormones in males and females, respectively. Without these hormones, sexual desire is eliminated in animals and is greatly reduced in humans.

THEORIES OF MOTIVATION

Biological Theory

As discussed in the "biological bases" of motivation, early theories on motivation relied on purely biological explanations of motivated behavior. Animals, especially less complex animals, are thought to be motivated by **instinct**, genetically programmed patterns of behavior. These early theories, along with arousal theory and drive-reduction theory, have given us an understanding of nature's role in motivating behavior.

Humanistic Theory

Abraham Maslow proposed a hierarchical system for organizing needs. This hierarchy can be divided into five levels. Each lower-level need must be met in order for an attempt to be made to fill the next category of needs in the hierarchy, which is illustrated in the diagram below.

Needs arise both from unsatisfied physiological drives as well as higher-level psychological needs, such as the needs for safety, belonging and love, and achievement. Along with instincts, drives, and arousal, needs provide an additional explanation for motivation. Maslow's hierarchy is somewhat arbitrary—it comes from a Western emphasis on individuality, and some individuals have shown the ability to reorganize these motives (as, for example, in hunger strikes or eating disorders). Nevertheless, it has been generally accepted that we are only motivated to satisfy higher-level needs once certain lower-level needs have been met. The inclusion of higher-level needs, such as self-actualization and the need for recognition and respect from others, also explains behaviors that the previous theories do not.

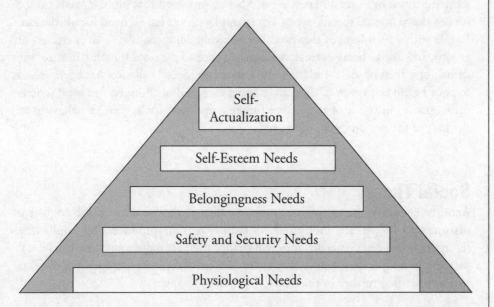

Self-actualization occurs when people creatively and meaningfully fulfill their own potential. This is the ultimate goal of human beings according to Maslow's theory.

Cognitive Theories

Cognitive psychologists divide the factors that motivate behavior into **intrinsic** and **extrinsic factors**: that is, factors originating from within ourselves and factors coming from the outside world, respectively. A single type of behavior can be motivated by either intrinsic or extrinsic factors. Extrinsic motivators are often associated with the pressures of society, such as getting an education, having a job, and being sociable. Intrinsic motivators, in contrast, are associated with creativity and enjoyment. Over time, our intrinsic motivation may decrease if we receive extrinsic rewards for the same behavior. This phenomenon is called the **overjustification effect**. For example, a person may love to play the violin for fun but when he is a paid concert performer, he will play less for fun and view playing the violin as part of his job.

An important intrinsic motivator is the need for **self-determination**, or the need to feel competent and in control. This need frequently conflicts with the pressures brought to bear by extrinsic motivators. The goal is to seek a balance between the fulfillment of the two categories of need. Related to the concept of self-determination is **self-efficacy**, or the belief that we can or cannot attain a particular goal. In general, the higher the level of self-efficacy, the more we believe that we can attain a particular goal and the more likely we are to achieve it, as well. Also closely related to this is **achievement motivation,** the need to reach realistic goals that we set for ourselves.

Although physiological needs form the basis for motivation, humans are not automatons, simply responding to biological pressures. Various theories have attempted to describe the interactions among motivation, personality, and cognition. **Henry Murray** believed that, although motivation is rooted in biology, individual differences and varying environments can cause motivations and needs to be expressed in many different ways. Murray proposed that human needs can be broken down into 20 specific types. For example, people have a **need for affiliation**. People with a high level of this need like to avoid conflicts, like to be members of groups, and dislike being evaluated. Closely linked to the need for affiliation are the damaging effects of social isolation and **ostracism**. Social isolation has been linked to poor health outcomes. Deliberately being excluded or shunned can have serious consequences in terms of reduced self-esteem and perhaps aggressive behavior on the part of the person being ostracized.

Social Theory

Another cognitive theory of motivation concerns the need to avoid **cognitive dissonance**. People are motivated to reduce tension produced by conflicting thoughts or choices. Generally, they will change their attitudes to fit their behavioral patterns, as long as they believe they are in control of their choices and actions. This will be discussed further in the Social Psychology chapter.

Sometimes, motives are in conflict. **Kurt Lewin** classified conflicts into four types. In an **approach-approach** conflict, one has to decide between two desirable options, such as having to choose between two colleges of similar characteristics. **Avoidance-**

Intrinsic or Extrinsic?

We may read because we enjoy it. In this case, reading is a behavior motivated by an intrinsic need. However, we may read because we need to know some information that will be on a test. Here, reading is driven by extrinsic motivation.

avoidance is a similar dilemma. Here, one has to choose between two unpleasant alternatives. In **approach-avoidance** conflicts, only one choice is presented, but it carries both pluses and minuses. For example, imagine that only one college has the major the student wants but that college is also prohibitively expensive. The last set of conflicts is **multiple approach-avoidance**. In this scenario, many options are available, but each has positives and negatives. Choosing one college out of many that are suitable, but not ideal, represents a multiple approach-avoidance conflict.

THEORIES OF EMOTION

Emotions are experiential and subjective responses to certain internal and external stimuli. These experiential responses have both physical and behavioral components. Various theories have arisen to explain emotion.

Emotion consists of three components: a physiological (body) component, a behavioral (action) component, and a cognitive (mind) component. The physical aspect of emotion is one of physiological arousal, or an excitation of the body's internal state. For example, when being startled at a surprise party, you may feel your heart pounding, your breathing becoming shallow and rapid, and your palms becoming sweaty. These are the sensations that accompany emotion (in this instance, surprise). The behavioral aspect of emotion includes some kind of expressive behavior: for example, spontaneously screaming and bringing your hands over your mouth. The cognitive aspect of emotion involves an appraisal or interpretation of the situation. Upon first being startled, the thought "dangerous situation" or "fear" may arise, only to be reassessed as "surprise" and "excitement" after recognizing the circumstances as a surprise party. This describes how the situation is interpreted or labeled. Interestingly, many emotions share the same or very similar physiological and behavioral responses; it is the mind that interprets one situation that evokes a quickened heart rate and tears as "joyful" and another with the same responses as "fearful."

One class of theories relies on physiological explanations of emotion. The **James-Lange theory** posits that environmental stimuli cause physiological changes and responses. The experience of emotion, according to this theory, is a result of a physiological change. In other words, if an argument makes you angry, it is the physiological response (increased heart rate, increased respiratory rate) that prompts the experience of emotion.

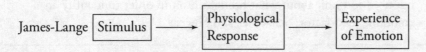

There are many reasons why we now know that this theory is incorrect. We know that a given state of physiological arousal is common to many emotions. For example, people might feel tenseness in their bodies as a result of being nervous, scared, or even excited. How, then, is it possible that the identical physiological state could lead to the rich variety of emotions that we experience? Another common experience that conflicts with the logic of the James-Lange theory is cutting onions. The physiological response to cutting onions is watering eyes; however, this physiological response does not make us sad.

The **Cannon-Bard theory** arose as a response to the James-Lange theory. The Cannon-Bard theory asserts that the physiological response to an emotion and the experience of emotion occur simultaneously in response to an emotion-provoking stimulus. For example, the sight of a tarantula, which acts as an emotion-provoking stimulus, would stimulate the thalamus. The thalamus would send simultaneous messages to both the autonomic nervous system and the cerebral cortex. Messages to the cortex produce the experience of emotion (fear), and messages to the autonomic nervous system produce physiological arousal (running, heart palpitations).

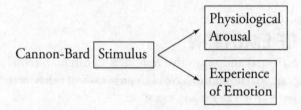

The **two-factor theory,** proposed by **Schachter and Singer,** adds a cognitive twist to the James-Lange theory. The first factor is physiological arousal; the second factor is the way in which we cognitively label the experience of arousal. Central to this theory is the understanding that many emotional responses involve very similar physiological properties. The emotion that we experience, according to this theory, is the result of the label that we apply. For example, if we cry at a wedding, we interpret our emotion as happiness, but if we cry at a funeral, we interpret our emotion as sadness.

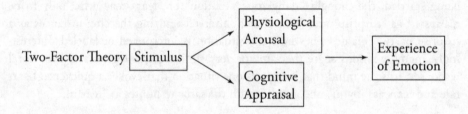

> ## Study Tip
> The three theories of emotion are often tested, so make sure that you understand them. When can your physiological arousal directly drive an emotional state? (James-Lange) When do the arousal and the emotion occur simultaneously? (Cannon-Bard) When do you experience arousal, but need to think about what brought it on in order to identify an emotion? (two-factor; Schachter and Singer)

Processing Emotions
Different sides of the brain also seem to be responsible for different emotional states. That is, the right brain is dominant in processing negative emotions, while the left brain seems to be more involved in processing positive emotions.

According to more recent studies by Zajonc, Le Doux, and Armony, some emotions are felt before being cognitively appraised. A scary sight travels through the eye to the thalamus, where it is then relayed to the amygdala before being labeled and evaluated by the cortex. According to these studies, the amygdala's position relative to the thalamus may account for the quick emotional response. There are several parts of the brain implicated in emotional processing. The main area of the brain responsible for emotions is the limbic system, which includes the amygdala. The amygdala is most active when processing negative emotions, particularly fear.

Although theorists have disagreed over time about how emotions are processed, there has been a great deal of agreement about the universality of certain emotions. Darwin assumed that emotions had a strong biological basis. If this is true, then emotions should be experienced and expressed in similar ways across cultures, and in fact, this has been found to be the case. A scientist and pioneer in the study of emotions, **Paul Ekman**, observed facial expressions from a variety of cultures and pointed out that, regardless of where two people were from, their expressions of certain emotions were almost identical. In particular, Ekman identified six basic emotions that appeared across cultures: anger, fear, disgust, surprise, happiness, and sadness. These findings suggest that emotions and how they are expressed are innate parts of the human experience. Darwin's ideas also led to the **facial feedback hypothesis,** the idea that a person's facial expression can influence the actual emotion being experienced. These observations about facial expressions can also apply to other examples of body language.

The evolutionary basis for emotion is thought to be related to its adaptive roles. It enhances survival by serving as a useful guide for quick decisions. A feeling of fear one experiences when walking alone down a dark alley while a shadowy figure approaches can be a valuable tool to indicate that the situation may be dangerous. A feeling of anger may enhance survival by encouraging one to fight back against an intruder. Other emotions may have a role in influencing individual behaviors within a social context. For example, embarrassment may encourage social conformity. Additionally, in social contexts, emotions provide a means for nonverbal communication and empathy, allowing for cooperative interactions.

On a more subtle level, emotions are a large influence on our everyday lives. Our choices often require consideration of our emotions. A person with a brain injury to their prefrontal cortex (which plays a role in processing emotion) has trouble imagining their own emotional responses to the possible outcomes of decisions. This can lead to making inappropriate decisions that can cost someone a job, a marriage, or a life's savings. Imagine how difficult it could be to refrain from risky behaviors, such as gambling or spending huge sums of money, without the ability to imagine your emotional response to the possible outcomes.

THE ROLE OF THE LIMBIC SYSTEM IN EMOTION

The limbic system is a collection of brain structures that lie on both sides of the thalamus; together, these structures appear to be primarily responsible for emotional experiences. The main structure involved in emotion in the limbic system is the amygdala, an almond-shaped structure deep within the brain. The amygdala serves as the conductor of the orchestra of our emotional experiences. It can communicate with the hypothalamus, a brain structure that controls the physiological aspects of emotion (largely through its modulating of the endocrine system), such as sweating and a racing heart. It also communicates with the prefrontal cortex, located at the front of the brain, which controls approach and avoidance behaviors—the behavioral aspects of emotion. The amygdala plays an especially key role in the identification and expression of fear and aggression.

Emotion, Memory, Decision-Making, and the Autonomic Nervous System

Emotional experiences can be stored as memories that can be recalled by similar circumstances. The limbic system also includes the hippocampus, a brain structure that plays a key role in forming memories.

When memories are formed, the emotions associated with these memories are often also encoded. Take a second to close your eyes and imagine someone whom you love very much. Notice the emotional state that arises with your memory of that person. Recalling an event can bring about the emotions associated with it. Note that this isn't always a pleasant experience. It has an important role in the suffering of patients who have experienced traumatic events. Similar circumstances to a traumatic event can lead to recall of the memory of the experience, referred to as a **flashback.** Sometimes this recall isn't even conscious; for example, for someone involved in a traumatic car accident, driving past the intersection where the incident occurred might cause an increase in muscle tension, heart rate, and respiratory rate.

The **prefrontal cortex** is critical for emotional experience, and it is also important in temperament and decision-making. It is associated with a reduction in emotional feelings, especially fear and anxiety, and is often activated by methods of emotion regulation and stress relief. The prefrontal cortex is like a soft voice, calming down the amygdala when it is overly aroused. The prefrontal cortex also plays a role in executive functions—higher-order thinking processes such as planning, organizing, inhibiting behavior, and decision-making. Damage to this area may lead to inappropriateness, impulsivity, and trouble with initiation. This area is not fully developed in humans until they reach their mid-twenties, explaining the sometimes erratic and emotionally charged behavior of teenagers. The most famous case of damage to the prefrontal cortex occurred to a man in the 1800s named Phineas Gage. Gage was a railroad worker who, at age 25, suffered an accident in which a railroad tie blasted through his head, entering under his cheekbone and exiting through the top of his skull. After the accident, Gage was described as "no longer himself," prone to impulsivity, unable to stick to plans, and unable to demonstrate empathy. The accident severely damaged his prefrontal cortex, and while the reports about the change to his personality and behavior have been debated, this case led to the discovery of the role of the prefrontal cortex in personality.

The **autonomic nervous system** (ANS) is responsible for controlling the activities of most of the organs and glands, and it controls arousal. As mentioned earlier, it answers primarily to the hypothalamus. The **sympathetic nervous system** (SNS) provides the body with brief, intense, vigorous responses. It is often referred to as the fight-or-flight system because it prepares an individual for action. It increases heart rate, blood pressure, and blood sugar levels in preparation for action. It also directs the adrenal glands to release the stress hormones epinephrine and norepinephrine. The **parasympathetic nervous system** (PNS) provides signals to the internal organs during a calm resting state when no crisis is present. When activated, it leads to changes that allow for recovery and the conservation of energy, including an increase in digestion and the repair of body tissues.

Many physiological states associated with emotion have been discussed. These include heart rate, blood pressure, respiratory rate, sweating, and the release of stress hormones. An increase in these physiological functions is associated with the sympathetic response, or **fight-or-flight response**. In order to measure autonomic function, clinicians can measure heart rate, finger temperature, skin conductance (sweating), and muscle activity. Keep in mind that different patterns tend to exist during different emotional states, but states such as fear and sexual arousal may display very similar patterns.

STRESS

A concept related to emotion is the feeling of stress. **Stress** causes a person to feel challenged or endangered. Although this definition may make you think of experiences such as being attacked, in reality, most **stressors** (events that cause stress) are everyday events or situations that challenge us in more subtle ways. Stressors can be significant life-changing events, such as the death of a loved one, a divorce, a wedding, or the birth of a child. There are also many smaller, more manageable stressors, such as holidays, traffic jams, and other nuisances. Although these situations are varied, they share a common factor: they are all challenging for the person experiencing them.

As you may have inferred, the same situation may have different value as a stressor for different people. The perception of a stimulus as stressful may be more consequential than the actual nature of the stimulus itself. For example, some people find putting together children's toys or electronic items quite stressful, yet other people find relaxation in similar tasks, such as building models.

What is most important for determining the stressful nature of an event is its appraisal, or how the individual interprets it. When stressors are appraised as being challenges, as one may perceive the AP Psychology Exam, they can actually be motivating. On the other hand, when they are perceived as threatening aspects of our identity, well-being, or safety, they may cause severe stress. Additionally, events that are considered negative and uncontrollable produce a greater stress response than those that are perceived as negative but controllable.

Some stressors are **transient**, meaning that they are temporary challenges. Others, such as those that lead to job-related stress, are **chronic** and can have a negative impact on one's health. The physiological response to stress is related to the fight-or-flight response, a concept developed by **Walter Cannon** and enhanced by **Hans Selye** into the **general adaptation syndrome**. The three stages of this response to prolonged stress are alarm, resistance, and exhaustion. **Alarm** refers to the arousal of the sympathetic nervous system, resulting in the release of various stimulatory hormones, including **corticosterone,** which is used as a physiological index of stress. In the alarm phase, the body is energized for immediate action, which is adaptive for transient, but not chronic, stressors. **Resistance** is the result of parasympathetic rebound. The body cannot be aroused forever, and the parasympathetic system starts to reduce the arousal state. If the stressor does not relent, however, the body does not reduce its arousal state to baseline. If the stressor persists for long periods of time, the stress response continues into the **exhaustion** phase. In this phase, the body's resources are exhausted, and tissue cannot be repaired. The immune system becomes impaired in its functioning, which is why we are more susceptible to illness during prolonged stress.

Richard Lazarus developed a cognitive theory of how we respond to stress. In this approach, the individual evaluates whether the event appears to be stressful. This is called primary appraisal. If the event is seen to be a threat, a secondary appraisal takes place, assessing whether the individual can handle the stress. Stress is minimized or maximized by the individual's ability to respond to the stressor.

Research into stress has revealed that people generally show one of two different types of behavior patterns based on their responses to stress. The **Type-A pattern** of behavior is typified by competitiveness, a sense of time urgency, and elevated feelings of anger and hostility. The **Type-B pattern** of behavior is characterized by a low level of competitiveness, low preoccupation with time issues, and a generally easygoing attitude. People with Type-A patterns of behavior respond to stress quickly and aggressively. Type-A people also act in ways that tend to increase the likelihood that they will have stressful experiences. They seek jobs or tasks that put great demands on them. People with a Type-B pattern of behavior get stressed more slowly, and their stress levels do not seem to reach those heights seen in people with the Type-A pattern of behavior. There is some evidence that people with Type-A behavior patterns are more susceptible to stress-related diseases, including heart attacks, but may survive them more frequently than Type-Bs.

KEY TERMS

Biological Bases

motivation
evolutionary theory
primary drives
secondary drive
Olds and Milner
instinct theory
arousal theory
Yerkes-Dodson law
opponent process theory
drive-reduction theory
homeostasis
set point

Hunger, Thirst, and Sex

hypothalamus
ventromedial hypothalamus
lateral hypothalamus
leptin
blood glucose
glucostatic hypothesis
insulin
lipostatic hypothesis
anorexia nervosa
body dysmorphia
bulimia nervosa
binge-eating disorder
pituitary gland
androgens
estrogens

Theories of Motivation

instinct
Abraham Maslow
self-actualization
intrinsic factors
extrinsic factors
overjustification effect
self-determination
self-efficacy
achievement motivation

Henry Murray
need for affiliation
ostracism
cognitive dissonance
Kurt Lewin
approach-approach
avoidance-avoidance
approach-avoidance
multiple approach-avoidance

Theories of Emotion

James-Lange theory
Cannon-Bard theory
Schachter-Singer two-factor theory
Paul Ekman
facial feedback hypothesis

The Role of the Limbic System in Emotion

flashback
prefrontal cortex
autonomic nervous system
sympathetic nervous system
parasympathetic nervous system
fight-or-flight response

Stress

stressors
transient
chronic
Walter Cannon
Hans Selye
general adaptation syndrome
alarm
corticosterone
resistance
exhaustion
Richard Lazarus
Type-A pattern
Type-B pattern

Chapter 14 Drill

See Chapter 19 for answers and explanations.

1. An example of a secondary drive is

   (A) the satisfying of a basic need critical to one's survival
   (B) an attempt to get food to maintain homeostatic equilibrium related to hunger
   (C) an attempt to act only on instinct
   (D) an effort to obtain something that has been shown to have reinforcing properties
   (E) an effort to continue an optimal state of arousal

2. An example of the Yerkes-Dodson law is

   (A) the need to remain calm and relaxed while taking the SAT while letting adrenaline give a little boost
   (B) performing at the highest level of arousal in order to obtain a primary reinforcer
   (C) a task designed to restore the body to homeostasis
   (D) the need to remain calm and peaceful while addressing envelopes for a charity event
   (E) working at maximum arousal on a challenging project

3. A substance that can act directly on brain receptors to stimulate thirst is

   (A) angiotensin
   (B) endorphin
   (C) thyroxin
   (D) lipoprotein
   (E) acetylcholine

4. Rhoni is a driven woman who feels the need to constantly excel in her career in order to help maintain the lifestyle her family has become accustomed to and in order to be seen as successful in her parents' eyes. The factors that motivate Rhoni's career behavior can be described as primarily

   (A) intrinsic
   (B) extrinsic
   (C) hierarchical
   (D) self-determined
   (E) instinctual

5. Which of the following is less likely to be characteristic of a Type-A personality than of a Type-B personality?

   (A) A constant sense of time urgency
   (B) A tendency toward easier arousability
   (C) A greater likelihood to anger slowly
   (D) A higher rate of stress-related physical complaints
   (E) A need to see situations as competitive

6. Sanju is hungry and buys a donut at the nearby donut shop. According to drive-reduction theory, she

   (A) has returned her body to homeostasis
   (B) will need to eat something else, since a donut is rich in nutrients
   (C) will continue to feel hungry
   (D) will have created another imbalance and feel thirsty
   (E) has raised her glucose levels to an unhealthy level

7. Jorge walks into a dark room, turns on the light, and his friends yell "Surprise!" Jorge's racing heartbeat is interpreted as surprise and joy instead of fear. This supports which theory of emotion?

   (A) The opponent-process theory
   (B) The James-Lange theory
   (C) The Cannon-Bard theory
   (D) The Schachter-Singer theory
   (E) The Yerkes-Dodson law

8. A person addicted to prescription drugs started by taking the prescribed amount, but then increased the dosage more and more to feel the same effect as when she first started. This progression is consistent with the

   (A) instinct theory
   (B) arousal theory
   (C) two-factor theory
   (D) drive-reduction theory
   (E) opponent-process theory

9. All of the following are symptoms of chronic stress EXCEPT

   (A) hypertension
   (B) immunosuppression
   (C) chronic fatigue
   (D) tissue damage
   (E) suppressed appetite

10. The hypothalamus does which of the following?

   (A) Serves as a relay center
   (B) Regulates homeostasis
   (C) Aids in encoding memory
   (D) Regulates most hormones to be secreted
   (E) Regulates fear and aggression

REFLECT
Respond to the following questions:

- Which topics in this chapter do you hope to see on the multiple-choice section or essay?

- Which topics in this chapter do you hope not to see on the multiple-choice section or essay?

- Regarding any psychologists mentioned, can you pair the psychologists with their contributions to the field? Did they contribute significant experiments, theories, or both?

- Regarding any theories mentioned, can you distinguish between differing theories well enough to recognize them on the multiple-choice section? Can you distinguish them well enough to write a fluent essay on them?

- Regarding any figures given, if you were given a labeled figure from within this chapter, would you be able to give the significance of each part of the figure?

- Can you define the key terms at the end of the chapter?

- Which parts of the chapter will you review?

- Will you seek further help, outside of this book (such as from a teacher, Princeton Review tutor, or AP Students), on any of the content in this chapter—and, if so, on what content?

Chapter 15
Personality

PERSONALITY THEORIES AND APPROACHES

Personality can be defined as a person's enduring general style of dealing with others and with the world around them. Personality theories can be divided into four broad categories: psychoanalytic, humanistic, social-cognitive, and trait theories.

Psychoanalytic Theories

Sigmund Freud and those who followed his basic beliefs and practices typify **psychoanalytic** theories of personality. The term **psychodynamic** means a psychological approach based on a marriage of Freudian concepts, such as the unconscious, with more modern ideas. Freud, the first and most influential personality psychologist, believed that the mind can be divided broadly into the conscious and the unconscious. The unconscious, according to Freud, plays a major role in behavior; however, the contents of the unconscious mind are not readily accessible. People's motivations and the sources of their problems lie within the unconscious. A popular metaphor of the mind is to imagine it as an iceberg with the "conscious" brain sitting above the water and the dark recesses of the "unconscious" lying below. Although the unconscious is typically not open to scrutiny, certain events, according to Freud, allow for glimpses into the unconscious mind. When people make slips of the tongue or reveal the latent content of dreams, they provide brief looks into their unconscious minds. Freud also discovered that free association is a way to get a glimpse of the unconscious mind. In **free association**, a therapist actively listens, while the patient relaxes and reports anything that comes into his mind, no matter how absurd it might seem. The therapist then analyzes this seemingly random jumble of thoughts, looking for themes that may demonstrate some of what lies in the unconscious.

Freud was also a pioneer in the analysis of dreams, which he viewed as windows into the unconscious mind. Freud believed that the remembered parts of a dream, or the manifest content, amounted to a coded version of the real conflict, or the latent content. For example, knives and stabbing might symbolize male genitalia and intercourse, while boxes, ships, or other containers might symbolize the female uterus. Freud further described the mind as consisting of three distinct components: the id, the superego, and the ego. (Freud actually used regular German words to describe these mental structures; his English translators came up with these Latin terms. Since AP will test you on the Latin terms, we'll retain them.)

Q: According to Freud, what are the three components of the mind?

Answer on page 266.

The **id** is the source of mental energy and drive. It encompasses all of the basic human needs and desires, including those for food and sex. The id operates on the **pleasure principle**, which is the desire to maximize pleasure while minimizing pain.

The **superego** is the internal representation of all of society's rules, morals, and obligations. The superego represents the polar opposite of the id.

The **ego**, according to Freud, is the part of the mind that allows a person to function in the environment and to be logical. It operates on the **reality principle**, which is that set of desires that can be satisfied only if the means to satisfy them exists and is available. The ego works as an intermediary between the id and the superego.

Freud hypothesized that the ego deals with the anxiety produced by the id-superego conflict using various defense mechanisms. Defense mechanisms often serve a useful purpose in helping the individual reduce tension and maintain a healthy outlook, even if they mean using self-deception. Repression is one of these defense mechanisms. **Repression** is the process by which memories or desires that provoke too much anxiety to deal with are pushed into the unconscious. For example, some people involved in terrible accidents have no memory of the accidents at all. The memory, according to Freudian theory, has been repressed.

Displacement is a defense mechanism that directs anger away from the source of the anger to a less threatening person or object. A boy who is angry with his father may not want to show hostility directly to his father; instead, he may yell at a friend or stuffed animal, thereby displaying his rage, but in a way that does not make his situation worse.

Reaction formation is another defense mechanism by which the ego reverses the direction of a disturbing desire to make that desire safer or more socially acceptable. For example, a person who unconsciously hates the poor might consciously experience this feeling as a strong desire to help the homeless. Or a lawmaker who is gay but closeted may speak and vote against gay rights. Other defense mechanisms include the following:

- **Compensation**—making up for failures in one area through success in others

- **Rationalization**—creating logical excuses for emotional or irrational behavior

- **Regression**—reverting to childish behaviors

- **Denial**—the refusal to acknowledge or accept unwanted beliefs or actions

- **Sublimation**—the channeling or redirecting of sexual or aggressive feelings into a more socially acceptable outlet

Freud's theory paved the way for a variety of psychodynamic theories, many of which were developed in direct response to Freud's own. **Karen Horney**, for example, pointed out the inherent male bias in Freud's work. She developed a theory of personality based on the need for security. According to Horney's theory, **basic anxiety**, or the feeling of being alone in an unfamiliar or hostile world, is a central theme in childhood. The interactions between the child and the parent, as the child deals with this anxiety, form the basis for adult personality. Children who find security in their relationships with their parents will find security in other adult relationships. Children who lack security in their relationships with their parents and their surroundings will grow up insecure and distrusting, and they are likely to end up with various unhealthy personality styles.

Carl Jung formulated another theory of personality that was, in part, a response to Freud's theory. Jung believed that the mind comprises pairs of opposing forces. For example, each person has a **persona,** the mask the person presents to the outside world, and a **shadow**, the deep, passionate, inner person (including the person's "dark side"). Jung also proposed that we each have an **anima** and an **animus**, a female and a

The ego is most involved in conscious thought and attempts to balance the interaction with the environment along with the opposing forces of the id and superego.

male side to our personality. Jung believed that all of the opposing forces and desires of the mind were balanced by a force called the **Self**. Jung also divided the unconscious differently than Freud. Jung proposed that each of us has a **personal unconscious** comprised of repressed memories and clusters of thought and a **collective unconscious** of behavior and memory common to all humans and passed down from our ancient and common ancestors. **Archetypes** are the behaviors and memories in the collective unconscious. Reverence for motherhood is an example of an archetype.

Alfred Adler, like other psychoanalytic psychologists, believed that childhood is the crucial formative period. He also thought, however, that all children develop feelings of inferiority because of their size and level of competence. He speculated that people spend the rest of their lives trying to overcome this inferiority and develop lifestyles suited to this purpose. Adler thought the best way to overcome inferiority is to develop a lifestyle of social interest; that is, one of contribution to society. Failure to make these accommodations may result in the development of an **inferiority complex**. Adler also saw personality as a product of birth order.

Humanistic Theories

Humanistic theories of personality emphasize the uniqueness and richness of being human. These theories arose partially in response to behaviorism (see Chapters 5 and 10). As a result, they focus on subjective reality and subjective mental events. In contrast to behaviorism's attempts to reduce behavior to its smallest components, humanistic theories take a holistic view. They view people as unitary, not separable into learned reactions, and certainly not divisible into compartments such as the ego and superego. The final and most important concept in humanistic theories is the concept of self-actualization. **Self-actualization** is becoming, in a creative way, the person you are capable of being. According to humanistic theories, self-actualization is the ultimate purpose for existence.

Two humanistic theorists whose work typifies this school of thought are **Abraham Maslow** (discussed in Chapter 14) and **Carl Rogers**.

A: The id, the ego, and the superego

Rogers believed that the self constitutes the most important aspect of personality. Our **self-concept** is our mental representation of who we feel we truly are. Internal conflicts arise when we experience **incongruence**, or discrepancies between our self-concept and our actual thoughts and behavior, as well as feedback from our surroundings. Rogers believed that **conditions of worth**, or other people's evaluations of our worth, distort our self-concept. Parents and teachers play a critical role in child development, Rogers hypothesized, and should not impose conditions of worth on children. Instead, people should be treated with **unconditional positive regard**. This means that people, particularly children, should be loved despite failures. Saying, for example, "I love you only when you're good," creates poor self-concept.

Humanistic theories also address the distinction between **collectivistic** and **individualistic cultures.** A collectivistic culture stresses the importance of community, while an individualistic culture prioritizes personal independence and autonomy. The United States is considered a very individualistic culture. Many cultures in Asia, Africa, and Central and South America are considered primarily collectivist. The nature of the culture can have a profound effect on individual personalities and behaviors.

Social-Cognitive Theories

Social-cognitive theories of personality are based on the assumption that cognitive constructs are the basis for personality. We bring constructs, such as expectations, to every social situation. These constructs are developed and modified through learning in social environments.

A representative example of a social-cognitive theory of personality was developed by **Albert Bandura**. Bandura focuses on the concept of self-efficacy as central to personality. **Self-efficacy** refers to a person's beliefs about their own abilities in a given situation. Basically, the belief that you can do a particular task greatly increases the chances that you actually can do it. People have different **explanatory styles,** or ways in which people explain themselves or react in different situations. Explanatory styles can be either positive or negative.

Another important social-cognitive theory is the **locus of control theory**. **Julian Rotter** proposed that the extent to which people believe that their successes or failures are due to their own efforts plays a major role in personality. People who have an **internal locus of control** believe that successes or failures are a direct result of their efforts, whereas people with an **external locus of control** are more likely to attribute success or failure to luck or chance.

Self-Efficacy and Success

Bandura has proposed that this theory has implications for education. Emphasizing accomplishments rather than failures should, according to self-efficacy theory, increase the likelihood of future successes.

Trait Theories

Trait theories of personality provide quantitative systems for describing and comparing traits, or stable predispositions to behave in a certain way. A particular trait theory stipulates that certain traits are part of the person and are not typically environmentally dependent. Additionally, we each have traits in some degree or another. Trait theorists generally believe that traits are largely inherited, rather than acquired through experience. Trait theorists are divided over how to categorize traits. A relatively recent and influential theory focuses on the **Big Five** personality traits, which are introversion-extroversion, neuroticism-stability, agreeableness-antagonism, conscientiousness-undirectedness, and openness-nonopenness.

Two ways of researching traits are by **nomothetic** and **idiographic analysis**. Nomothetic traits such as the Big Five are thought to be universal. Idiographic traits are those that are unique to the individual, such as openness or curiosity. **Gordon Allport**, a trait theorist, identified three types of traits: **cardinal** (traits that override a person's whole being), **central** (the primary characteristics of the person), and **secondary** (traits that constitute interests). **Raymond Cattell** saw traits differently, because he believed that 16 **source traits** were the basis of personality. Source traits are the person's underlying characteristics. They give rise to clusters of **surface traits**, those readily seen in the individual. **Walter Mischel** recognized that traits are not necessarily consistent across various situations but often vary depending upon the circumstances.

Evaluation of the Various Personality Theories

Each of the personality theories provides some insight into the formation of personality, but each also has its flaws. The main problem with the psychoanalytic theory is that it was not developed through empirical testing, although recent psychologists have subjected Freud's theories to the scientific method. Testing supports some of his theories but not others. The humanistic theories also suffer from lack of empirical evidence in addition to what some believe is an overly optimistic outlook on life. Nevertheless, they are frequently the basis of counseling today. Cognitive theories, also popular in today's world, describe personality as a function of environmental perception and rational thought. However, critics suggest that this approach does not take into account the breadth of humanness. Trait theories face criticism that they are unable to explain the origin of personality.

Other Theories

There are other theories of which you should be aware. Behavioralist theory, which you already know from the Foundations and Learning chapters, explains personality in much the way you would expect: personality characteristics that have proved successful are repeated, while those that have not been successful wither away. This is sometimes referenced within the Social-Cognitive Theories described above. Biological theories, noted in Chapters 5 and 7, suggest that personality is based on brain structure and chemistry (we are who we are due to balances or imbalances of neurotransmitters and/or hormones). Another explanation comes from Evolutionary Theory: our personalities are shaped by our genes and contain characteristics that enhanced our ancestors' chances of survival.

ASSESSMENT TECHNIQUES

Techniques used for assessing personality vary. The psychoanalytic approach has traditionally involved the classic one-on-one therapist and patient relationship. In this situation, the therapist's role is to use various techniques, such as free association and dream recall, to gain access to the unconscious.

The humanistic theorists fall short in the area of assessment. Maslow described the characteristics of self-actualizing people, but the characteristics were chosen by Maslow himself, and are not necessarily quantifiable or useful for assessment. The very personal nature of the self makes it nearly impossible for a test or assessment tool to measure the levels at which people are true to themselves. Rogers and others relied primarily on interviews.

Study Tip

Other than the trait theories, the theories noted here all suggest different types of therapy for mental or personality disorders. Make sure that you can establish linkages between these understandings of human personality and the therapies discussed in Chapter 17.

Social-cognitive theorists have the benefit of questionnaire-type assessment tools. Rotter developed a locus-of-control questionnaire, versions of which are still used in psychological assessment today. There are also a number of scales or questionnaires designed to evaluate people's levels of self-efficacy. These measures have been used to look at the validity of Maslow's hypothesis by computing correlations between people's levels of self-efficacy and their actual performance levels.

Trait Theory Assessments

If there were a competition among the various kinds of theorists as to who had the most complete tools for assessment, the trait theorists would win hands down. **Hans Eysenck** developed the **Eysenck Personality Inventory**, a questionnaire designed to examine people's personalities based on their traits. Raymond Cattell also developed a questionnaire to quantify traits. Cattell named his assessment tool the **16 PF (Personality Factor) Questionnaire**, signifying the 16 traits or personality factors it measures. These are just two of a number of questionnaires designed to evaluate personality traits.

Perhaps the most widely used assessment tool that measures traits is the **MMPI-2-RF** (Minnesota Multiphasic Personality Inventory-2, Restructured Form). This test is frequently used as a prepackaged assessment tool, measuring everything from traits to mental disorders.

Our previous discussion of projective tests, inventory-type tests, reliability, and validity in the context of intelligence and testing (pages 218–219) applies here as well.

SELF-CONCEPT, SELF-ESTEEM

Self-concept refers to how we view ourselves, whereas **self-esteem** refers to how much we value ourselves. Self-understanding can be divided into two parts: the *me* and the *I*. The *me* is comprised of the following:

- The **physical self**—our bodies, names, and the like

- The **active self**—how we behave

- The **social self**—how we interact with others

- The **psychological self**—our feelings and personalities

The self-knower, the *I*, is responsible for the coordination and interpretation of the four parts of the *me*. The *I* is responsible for how we perceive ourselves as consistent over time, as individuals, and as having free will. The *I* allows us to reflect on ourselves and to have a self-concept.

Self-esteem develops and differentiates as we age. As children, we are able only to make judgments about ourselves in the general domains of cognitive, physical, social, and behavioral competence. Young children also make errors of self-evaluation due to the **halo effect**, which refers to the error by which we generalize a high self-evaluation from one domain to another. (It also applies to evaluations of others, such as when one assumes a successful athlete would also be articulate.) Domains continue to emerge as we age and are faced with increasingly differentiated areas in which to test ourselves. Low self-esteem can result in reluctance to try new tasks and to persist at tasks already started. Self-esteem is also related to whom we compare ourselves to, which is posited by Leon Festinger in his **social comparison theory**. People can also inflate their self-esteem by basking in reflective glory, which is when someone takes pride in the accomplishments of an individual or group that the person strongly affiliates with in their life.

11 Domains of Competency

By the time we reach adulthood, self-esteem can be broken into 11 domains of competency within which we evaluate ourselves. These domains are morality, sociability, intimacy, athleticism, intelligence, sense of humor, nurturance, job competence, adequacy as a provider, physical appearance, and household management.

TEMPERAMENT

Temperament is the early appearing set of individual differences in reaction and regulation that form the nucleus of personality. For a trait to be considered part of temperament, it must be early appearing, stable, and constitutionally based, meaning that it is rooted in the physiology of the child. According to developmental psychologist **Mary Rothbart**, temperament is generally assessed on three scales: **surgency** (amount of positive affect and activity level), **negative affect** (amount of frustration and sadness), and **effortful control** (ability of a child to self-regulate moods and behavior). **Jerome Kagan**'s work on the physiology of young children showed that children classified as low in effortful control were more likely to have higher baseline heart rates, more muscle tension, and greater pupil dilation. The stability of temperament is also quite remarkable, with surgency at 21 months correlating with the person's behavior at 18 years old.

KEY TERMS

Personality Theories and Approaches

- personality
- Sigmund Freud
- psychoanalytic
- psychodynamic
- free association
- id
- pleasure principle
- superego
- ego
- reality principle
- repression
- displacement
- reaction formation
- compensation
- rationalization
- regression
- denial
- sublimation
- Karen Horney
- basic anxiety
- Carl Jung
- persona
- shadow
- anima
- animus
- Self
- personal unconscious
- collective unconscious
- archetypes
- Alfred Adler
- inferiority complex
- humanistic
- self-actualization
- Abraham Maslow
- Carl Rogers
- self-concept
- incongruence
- conditions of worth
- unconditional positive regard
- collectivistic cultures
- individualistic cultures
- social-cognitive theories
- Albert Bandura
- self-efficacy
- explanatory styles
- locus of control theory
- Julian Rotter
- internal locus of control
- external locus of control
- Big Five
- nomothetic analysis
- idiographic analysis
- Gordon Allport
- cardinal traits
- central traits
- secondary traits
- Raymond Cattell
- source traits
- surface traits
- Walter Mischel

Assessment Techniques

- Hans Eysenck
- Eysenck Personality Inventory
- 16 PF (Personality Factor) Questionnaire
- MMPI-2-RF

Self-concept, Self-esteem

- self-concept
- self-esteem
- physical self
- active self
- social self
- psychological self
- halo effect
- social comparison theory

Temperament

- Mary Rothbart
- surgency
- negative affect
- effortful control
- Jerome Kagan

Chapter 15 Drill

See Chapter 19 for answers and explanations.

1. According to Freudian theory, which part of the mind operates according to the reality principle?

   (A) The superego
   (B) The ego
   (C) The id
   (D) The archetype
   (E) The shadow

2. The defense mechanism reaction formation is defined as

   (A) directing angry feelings away from the source of the anger to a less threatening object
   (B) reverting to behaviors more characteristic of childhood
   (C) attempting to make up for failures in certain areas by overcompensating efforts in other areas
   (D) creating excuses for irrational feelings or behaviors that sound logical
   (E) reversing the direction of a disturbing feeling or desire to make it safer or more socially acceptable

3. All of the following personality theorists can be considered psychodynamic in approach EXCEPT

   (A) Karen Horney
   (B) Carl Jung
   (C) Alfred Adler
   (D) Albert Bandura
   (E) Erik Erikson

4. According to Maslow and Rogers, the process by which human beings attain their full creativity and potential is termed

   (A) self-esteem
   (B) self-amplification
   (C) self-efficacy
   (D) self-actualization
   (E) self-reflection

5. A psychologist interested in demarcating and measuring traits would most likely use which of the following?

   (A) The 16 PF Questionnaire
   (B) The WAIS
   (C) The *DSM-5*
   (D) The ANOVA
   (E) The WISC

6. Anne is terrible at riding a bike, but she knows that she has the ability to get better if she practices more often. This is an example of

   (A) high self-efficacy and an external locus of control
   (B) low self-efficacy and an internal locus of control
   (C) high self-efficacy and an internal locus of control
   (D) low self-efficacy and an external locus of control
   (E) low self-efficacy and learned helplessness

7. Lukas is a handsome guy who gets great grades and is the star of the football team. Ian assumes he is trustworthy, as well. This is most likely an example of

   (A) gender bias
   (B) an archetype
   (C) an inferiority complex
   (D) self-actualization
   (E) the halo effect

8. Tanya is a competitive figure skater trying to land her quadruple salchow. She gets frustrated with her coach and herself for not landing it and kicks the ice. This is an example of

   (A) displacement
   (B) sublimation
   (C) denial
   (D) regression
   (E) compensation

9. Carl Jung's theory of the anima and animus posits that

   (A) the self is a collection of archetypes from the collective unconscious
   (B) a person must first learn to trust their caregiver as an infant to thrive
   (C) there is both a male and female side to each personality
   (D) a positive self-worth comes from a balanced Self
   (E) individuals should not overcompensate for their weaknesses, but rather embrace them

10. Cara feels good about herself because she is going to become a doctor. This is an example of

    (A) self-efficacy
    (B) self-esteem
    (C) self-concept
    (D) rationalization
    (E) reaction formation

REFLECT

Respond to the following questions:

- Which topics in this chapter do you hope to see on the multiple-choice section or essay?

- Which topics in this chapter do you hope not to see on the multiple-choice section or essay?

- Regarding any psychologists mentioned, can you pair the psychologists with their contributions to the field? Did they contribute significant experiments, theories, or both?

- Regarding any theories mentioned, can you distinguish between differing theories well enough to recognize them on the multiple-choice section? Can you distinguish them well enough to write a fluent essay on them?

- Can you define the key terms at the end of the chapter?

- Which parts of the chapter will you review?

- Will you seek further help, outside of this book (such as from a teacher, Princeton Review tutor, or AP Students), on any of the content in this chapter—and, if so, on what content?

Chapter 16
Clinical Psychology: Disorders

DEFINITIONS OF DISORDER

When is behavior disordered? The definition of **disordered behavior** has four components. First, disordered behavior is unusual—it deviates statistically from typical behavior. Second, disordered behavior is maladaptive: that is, it interferes with a person's ability to function in a particular situation. Third, disordered behavior is labeled as abnormal by the society in which it occurs. Finally, disordered behavior is characterized by perceptual or cognitive dysfunction. In order for behavior to be disordered, it should meet all of these criteria. Behavior must be compared with the behavior of the society in which it occurs. So, for example, self-mutilation in this country is behavior that stands apart from what society considers normal. In other parts of the world, however, scarring is an important part of certain rituals.

THEORIES OF PSYCHOPATHOLOGY

Different schools of psychology have attempted to understand the causes of disordered behavior in different ways. Sigmund Freud engaged in careful observation and analysis of people with varying degrees of behavioral abnormalities. Freud and the **psychoanalytic school** hypothesized that the interactions among conscious and especially unconscious parts of the mind were responsible for a great deal of disordered behavior. The power of unconscious motives drives behavior. To protect the ego, painful or threatening impulses are repressed into the unconscious. This repression stems from issues that arose during childhood. Generally speaking, if intrapsychic conflicts are not resolved, they may lead us to act abnormally. Much of Freud's writing described his analyses of maladaptive behavior.

The **humanistic school** of psychology suggests that disordered behavior is, in part, a result of people being too sensitive to the criticisms and judgments of others. This tendency is related to people being unable to accept their own nature and having low self-esteem. This lack of acceptance may result, according to the humanistic view, from feelings of isolation due to a lack of unconditional positive regard received as a child.

The **cognitive perspective** views disordered behavior as the result of faulty or illogical thoughts. Distortions in the cognitive process, according to this point of view, lead to misperceptions and misinterpretations of the world, which in turn lead to disordered behavior. The cognitive approach to treatment involves changing the contents of thought or changing the ways in which those contents are processed.

The **behavioral approach** to disordered behavior is based on the notion that all behavior, including disordered behavior, is learned. Disordered behavior has, at some point, been rewarded or reinforced, and has now been established as a pattern of behavior. Treatment involves the unlearning of the maladaptive behavior, or the modification of the learned responses to certain stimuli.

The **biological view** of disordered behavior, which is a popular one in the United States at the present time, views disordered behavior as a manifestation of abnormal brain function, due to either structural or chemical abnormalities in the brain. This point of view supports medication as providing appropriate treatment for various types of disordered behavior.

The **sociocultural approach** holds that society and culture help define what is acceptable behavior.

There are commonalities among theories on psychopathology, though. Psychologists of all perspectives realize that disorders have multiple causes. One part of explaining a disorder is to look at the predisposing causes, which are the environmental or genetic influences that exist before the disorder begins and make people vulnerable to the disorder. The next factors to consider are the precipitating causes, which are the triggering events that bring about the disorder. Lastly, psychologists consider the maintaining causes, which are the factors that make the disorder more likely to continue.

Causes of Disorder	
Psychoanalytic	Negative early childhood experiences or a conflict between the superego and id
Humanistic	Low self-esteem or negative self-regard
Cognitive	Maladaptive thought processes
Behavioral	Reinforcement of depressive behavior
Biological	Neurons or neurotransmitters
Sociocultural	Cultural and environmental influences

DIAGNOSIS OF PSYCHOPATHOLOGY

The ***Diagnostic and Statistical Manual of Mental Disorders (DSM-5)*** is the American Psychiatric Association's handbook for the identification and classification of behavioral disorders. The *DSM-5* calls for the separate notation of important social factors and physical disabilities, in addition to the diagnosis of mental disorders. There are overarching categories in which specific disorders are classified. Below are some of the major categories, though be sure to do some extra research, as this list does not cover all of them.

NEURODEVELOPMENTAL DISORDERS

The term *neurodevelopmental* refers to the developing brain. Related disorders manifest early in development, and may be due to genetic issues, trauma in the womb, or brain damage acquired at birth or in the first years of life. These disorders can range from very specific learning deficits to very global impairments to social skills or intelligence.

Intellectual disability (formerly known as mental retardation) is characterized by delayed development in general mental abilities (reasoning, problem-solving, judgment, academic learning, etc.). These delays translate into an impairment of adaptive functioning in aspects of daily life such as self-care, communication, or occupation. The severity can range from mild to moderate to severe to profound.

The *DSM-5-TR* is a text revision to the *DSM-5* that was published in 2022. A full list of the disorders that were updated, including information on the newly added Prolonged Grief Disorder, can be found on the American Psychiatric Association's site (www.psychiatry.org/psychiatrists/practice/dsm/educational-resources/dsm-5-tr-fact-sheets).

Autism spectrum disorder is a neurodevelopmental disorder that often manifests early on in childhood development. This may manifest itself in social communication deficits, both verbal and nonverbal, in which the individual has difficulty noticing social cues and has difficulty engaging others. ASD can also manifest itself in the form of restrictive or repetitive behaviors, difficulty coping with change, or difficulty with accepting change in activity. The spectrum varies widely from person to person, ranging from mild to severe. The term *Asperger's disorder* is no longer used.

Attention-deficit hyperactivity disorder (ADHD) is described as patterned inattention and/or hyperactivity-impulsivity. While everyone experiences spurts of inattention or impulsivity, ADHD interferes with an individual's ability to function at home, at work, at school, during activities, etc. It may sometimes interfere with friendships and relationships, and at least some symptoms must have been present before the age of 12 for diagnosis.

Other neurodevelopmental disorders include **communication disorders** such as language disorder, speech sound disorder, and fluency disorder (stuttering); **motor disorders** such as developmental coordination disorder, stereotypic movement disorder, and tics; and **specific learning disorders**.

SCHIZOPHRENIA SPECTRUM AND OTHER PSYCHOTIC DISORDERS

Although the term **schizophrenia** literally means "split brain," these disorders have nothing to do with what used to be called Multiple Personality Disorder. Rather, these disorders are marked by disturbances in thought, perception, and speech, as well as motor behavior and emotional experience.

It is important to distinguish between delusions and hallucinations. **Delusions** are beliefs that are not based in reality, such as believing that one can fly, that one is the president of a country, or that one is being pursued by the CIA (assuming that these things are not true). **Hallucinations** are perceptions that are not based in reality, such as seeing things or hearing voices that are not there, or feeling spiders on one's skin (assuming they are not really there).

Disorganized thinking and **disorganized speech** are typical. A person with such a disorder may switch from one topic to another in illogical fashion, may respond to questions with irrelevant answers, and may produce streams of speech that have little or no coherence ("word salad").

It is important to distinguish between **positive symptoms** and **negative symptoms**. Just as with Skinner's learning theory, the terms *positive* and *negative* here have nothing to do with good or bad, but rather refer to adding and subtracting. A positive symptom of schizophrenic disorders refers to something that a person has that typical people do not. Thus, delusions and hallucinations are positive symptoms. A negative symptom refers to something that typical people do have, but that one does not have. In schizophrenic disorders, a limited range of emotion and the lack of desire to initiate activities are both particularly noticeable. A number of antipsychotic medications can alleviate the positive symptoms of schizophrenia spectrum disorders.

Brain Changes

While less likely to be tested, cognitive symptoms represent the degenerative nature of this disease. There are structural and functional changes in the brain of a patient with schizophrenia that affect cognition, memory, attention, and inhibition. The structural include an enlargement of the ventricles in the brain and the functional are detected on PET or fMRI as low frontal-lobe activity.

BIPOLAR AND RELATED DISORDERS

Bipolar disorders, as the name suggests, involves movement between two poles: depressive states on the one hand, and manic states on the other hand. Because manic states often have psychotic features, the *DSM-5* now regards bipolar disorders as a bridge between the psychoses and the major depressive disorders.

DEPRESSIVE DISORDERS

Unlike the everyday-language use of the term ("I'm so depressed about that test"), **depressive disorders** involve the presence of a sad, empty, or irritable mood, combined with changes in thinking and bodily functioning that significantly impair one's ability to function. These disorders go far beyond normal sadness or grief, and last longer than usual periods of sadness. Separate or combined treatments such as psychotherapy (in particular cognitive-behavioral therapy) and antidepressant medications may assist in recovery.

ANXIETY DISORDERS

Fear is an emotional response to something present; anxiety is a related emotional response, but to a future threat or a possibility of danger. In a state of anxiety, the nervous system wants to get into fight-or-flight mode, but there is nothing there to fight and nothing to flee from. Physical effects of anxiety may include but are not limited to muscle tension, hyperalertness for danger signs, and avoidance behaviors. Sleep disturbances, irritability, and inability to concentrate are common related symptoms.

Treatments vary from behavioral modification in the case of specific phobias to cognitive-behavioral therapy to psychotherapy to medical treatment through **anxiolytics**, anti-anxiety medications.

Panic disorder is an anxiety disorder characterized by recurring **panic attacks**, as well as the constant worry of another panic attack occurring. While panic attacks last only a few minutes, they are debilitating. They are accompanied by sweating, increased heart rate, and a general feeling of being paralyzed with fright.

Generalized anxiety disorder (GAD) is an anxiety disorder characterized by an almost constant state of autonomic nervous system arousal and feelings of dread and worry.

Phobias, or persistent, irrational fears of common events or objects, are also anxiety disorders. Phobias include fear of objects, such as snakes, and fear of situations. **Agoraphobia**, for example, is the fear of being in open spaces, public places, or other places from which escape is perceived to be difficult.

OBSESSIVE-COMPULSIVE AND RELATED DISORDERS

As the name suggests, these disorders involve **obsessions** and/or **compulsions**. Be clear on the difference between these terms: obsessions are thoughts; compulsions are actions. Specifically, obsessions are intrusive (unwanted) thoughts, urges, or images that plague the individual. Compulsions are repetitive behaviors (or mental acts) that one feels compelled to perform, often in relation to an obsession. For example, intrusive thoughts about germs could lead to repeated hand-washing. This is the textbook example for **obsessive-compulsive disorder (OCD)**. OCD is characterized by involuntary, persistent thoughts or obsessions, as well as compulsions, or repetitive behaviors that are time consuming and maladaptive, that an individual believes will prevent a particular (usually unrelated) outcome. Related disorders include **body dysmorphic disorder** and **hoarding disorder**, which involve obsessive thoughts about bodily defects or the need to save possessions. Some other specific related disorders involve hair-pulling and skin-picking.

TRAUMA- AND STRESSOR-RELATED DISORDERS

By definition, these disorders follow a particularly disturbing event or set of events (the trauma or the stressor), like war or violence. Although it is completely normal for people to respond to a stressful event with stress symptoms, some people recover naturally, whereas others develop symptoms. The best-known such disorder is **post-traumatic stress disorder (PTSD)**, which can involve intrusive thoughts or dreams related to the trauma, irritability, avoidance of situations that might recall the traumatic event, sleep disturbances, diminished interest in formerly pleasurable activities, and social withdrawal. These PTSD symptoms, in turn, lead to a decreased ability to function as well as to a general detachment from reality. Other disorders include **reactive attachment disorder**, which can occur in seriously neglected children who are unable to form attachments to their adult caregivers, and **adjustment disorders**, or maladaptive responses to particular stressors.

DISSOCIATIVE DISORDERS

What gets dissociated in dissociative disorders is primarily consciousness or identity. In many cases, these disorders appear following a trauma, and may be seen as the mind's attempt to protect itself by splitting itself into parts. Thus, one might experience **derealization**, the sense that "this is not really happening," or **depersonalization**, the sense that "this is not happening to me." Significant gaps in memory may be related to **dissociative amnesia**, an inability to recall life events that goes far beyond normal forgetting. Perhaps the most extreme of these disorders is **dissociative identity disorder** (formerly known as multiple personality disorder), in which one may not only "lose time," but also manifest a separate personality during that lost time. This disorder is most often associated with significant trauma or abuse in childhood.

SOMATIC SYMPTOM AND RELATED DISORDERS

Soma means "body." **Somatic symptom disorder** involves, as one might expect, bodily symptoms combined with disordered thoughts, feelings, and/or behaviors connected to these symptoms. It is not the symptoms themselves, but how the individual experiences them, that is striking and seems maladaptive. That is, the level of worry seems out of proportion to the symptom itself. Related worries appear in **illness anxiety disorder**, in which one worries excessively about the possibility of falling ill. **Conversion disorder** (formerly known as hysteria) involves bodily symptoms like changed motor function or changed sensory function that are incompatible with neurological explanations. There may be a suspicion that the symptoms are **psychogenic**, meaning created by the mind. This may prompt some people to say, "It's all in your mind." However, a symptom can originate from the mind but actually end up in the body. According to an old joke, the difference between Americans and Russians is that if an American doesn't want to go to a dinner, they will pretend to have a headache; the Russian has to actually have the headache. In conversion disorder, the individual may be completely unaware of the mental origin of the physical symptoms. Finally, there is also **factitious disorder**, in which an individual knowingly falsifies symptoms in order to get medical care, or sympathy or aid from others. This disorder differs from simple lying (malingering) in that the deception occurs even when there are no obvious rewards.

FEEDING AND EATING DISORDERS

Anorexia nervosa (commonly called anorexia) involves not only restriction of food intake, but also intense fear of gaining weight and disturbances in self-perception, such as thinking one looks fat, when one does not. The self-starvation behavior associated with this disorder can lead to life-threatening medical conditions. **Bulimia nervosa** (commonly called bulimia) involves recurrent episodes of **binge-eating**: eating large amounts of food in short amounts of time, followed by inappropriate behaviors to prevent weight gain, such as self-induced vomiting (**purging**), using laxatives, or intense exercising. There is usually a heightened sense of shame in connection with both binging and purging. Self-image is also unduly affected by body shape and weight. **Binge-eating disorder** might be thought of as bulimia without purging. But this occurs in both normal-weight and overweight/obese people. There is a loss of control associated with the binge-eating in this disorder. Finally, **pica** refers to regular consumption of non-nutritive substances (plastic, paper, dirt, string, chalk, etc.). This occurs more often in children, but can occur in adults. Pica is occasionally seen in pregnant women and individuals with iron deficiency. While it is not clear why this occurs, it is most likely a result of biochemical, physiological, and cultural factors.

PERSONALITY DISORDERS

Consider data that suggests that 15% of U.S. adults have at least one personality disorder. This is roughly one in seven people. While we do not encourage you to start diagnosing people without training, you might think about the people you have met as you study personality disorders.

A personality disorder refers to a stable (and inflexible) way of experiencing and acting in the world, one that is at variance with the person's culture, that starts in adolescence or adulthood, and leads to either personal distress or impairment of social functioning. (It is important to note that, by definition, children cannot have personality disorders. Think of it this way: children are still developing their personalities.) Ten personality disorders are organized into three clusters. You might think of them as the three Ws: the weird, the wild, and the worried.

Cluster A includes paranoid, schizoid, and schizotypal personality disorders. These individuals appear to be markedly odd or eccentric. With **paranoid personality disorder**, there may be a pattern of general distrust of others that is not justified by real circumstances. **Schizoid personality disorder** is marked by disturbances in feeling (detachment from social relationships, flat affect, does not enjoy close relationships with people), whereas **schizotypal personality disorder** is marked by disturbances in thought (odd beliefs that do not quite qualify as delusions, such as superstitions, belief in a "sixth sense," etc.; odd speech; eccentric behavior or appearance).

Cluster B includes antisocial, borderline, histrionic, and narcissistic personality disorders. These individuals appear to be dramatic, emotional, or erratic. Terms like *psychopath* or *sociopath* have been used to describe people with **antisocial personality disorder**, which is characterized by a persistent pattern of disregard for, and violation of, the rights of others. Lying, cheating, stealing, and having no remorse are common. **Borderline personality disorder** involves a very stormy relationship with the world, with others, and with one's own feelings. People with this disorder have a regular pattern of instability in relationships, often involving frantic efforts to avoid abandonment (imagined or real), alternating between extremes of idealization and devaluation ("You're the best ever!" → "I hate you!") with the same person, identity disturbance, impulsivity, chronic feelings of emptiness, and anger control issues. **Histrionic personality disorder** involves a pattern of excessive emotionality and attention-seeking, beyond what might be considered normal (even in a "culture of selfies"). **Narcissistic personality disorder** involves an overinflated sense of self-importance, fantasies of success, beliefs that one is special, a sense of entitlement, a lack of empathy for others, and a display of arrogant behaviors or attitudes.

Cluster C includes avoidant, dependent, and obsessive-compulsive personality disorders. These individuals appear to be anxious or fearful. **Avoidant personality disorder** involves an enduring pattern of social inhibition, feelings of inadequacy, and hypersensitivity to real or perceived criticism, which lead to avoidance behavior in relation to social, personal, and intimate relationships. **Dependent personality disorder** is marked by an excessive need to be cared for, leading to clingy and submissive behavior and fears of separation. People with this disorder may feel unable to make everyday decisions without constantly consulting others and getting their advice and approval. Finally, **obsessive-compulsive person-ality disorder (OCPD)** is marked by a rigid concern with order, perfectionism, control, and work, at the expense of flexibility, spontaneity, openness, and play. These people may be described using Freud's term "anal." In distinction to OCD, which involves unwanted or intrusive thoughts along with unwanted or intrusive compulsions, OCPD can involve similar thoughts and compulsions, but they are not seen by the person as intrusive. Rather, the person with OCPD may think that the problem lies with other people, who do not see the need for things to be ordered in a certain way.

In many cases, people do not seek treatment for their personality disorders. But if their disorder leads them to become depressed or anxious, due to social or occupa-tional impairments, they may seek help for depression or anxiety, and may become diagnosed in that way.

Study Tip

It can seem quite daunting to know all of the disorders listed in the *DSM-5*. Focus on the ones highlighted in this chapter. More and more in modern times, famous people have been open about their diagnoses and their struggles with some of these conditions. If you are aware of such individuals, it may be helpful to link these disorders with real-world people as a way to remember the associated symptoms.

IN ADDITION

We have only given an overview and selection of the disorders listed in the *DSM-5*. Other disorders include the following: elimination disorders; sleep-wake disorders; sexual dysfunctions; gender dysphoria; disruptive, impulse-control and conduct disorders; substance-related and addictive disorders; neurocognitive disorders; paraphilic disorders; and others.

KEY TERMS

Definitions of Disorder
disordered behavior

Theories of Psychopathology
psychoanalytic school
humanistic school
cognitive perspective
behavioral approach
biological view
sociocultural approach

Diagnosis of Psychopathology
*Diagnostic and Statistical
Manual of Mental Disorders
(DSM-5)*

Neurodevelopmental Disorders
intellectual disability
autism spectrum disorder
attention-deficit hyperactivity
disorder (ADHD)
communication disorders
motor disorders
specific learning disorders

**Schizophrenia Spectrum and
Other Psychotic Disorders**
schizophrenia
delusions
hallucinations
disorganized thinking
disorganized speech
positive symptoms
negative symptoms

Bipolar and Related Disorders
bipolar disorders

Depressive Disorders
depressive disorders

Anxiety Disorders
anxiolytics
panic disorder
panic attacks
generalized anxiety disorder
(GAD)
phobias
agoraphobia

**Obsessive-Compulsive and
Related Disorders**
obsessions
compulsions
obsessive-compulsive disorder
(OCD)
body dysmorphic disorder
hoarding disorder

**Trauma- and Stressor-Related
Disorders**
post-traumatic stress disorder
(PTSD)
reactive attachment disorder
adjustment disorders

Dissociative Disorders
derealization
depersonalization
dissociative amnesia
dissociative identity disorder

**Somatic Symptom and Related
Disorders**
somatic symptom disorder
illness anxiety disorder
conversion disorder
psychogenic
factitious disorder

Feeding and Eating Disorders
anorexia nervosa
bulimia nervosa
binge eating
purging
binge-eating disorder
pica

Personality Disorders
Cluster A
paranoid personality
disorder
schizoid personality
disorder
schizotypal personality
disorder
Cluster B
antisocial personality
disorder
borderline personality
disorder
histrionic personality
disorder
narcissistic personality
disorder
Cluster C
avoidant personality
disorder
dependent personality
disorder
obsessive-compulsive
personality disorder
(OCPD)

Chapter 16 Drill

See Chapter 19 for answers and explanations.

1. A man claims to hear voices telling him to run for president. He is most likely experiencing

   (A) delusions
   (B) obsessions
   (C) hallucinations
   (D) compulsions
   (E) inceptions

2. The disorder characterized by psychological difficulties that manifest themselves as physical symptoms is

   (A) bipolar disorder
   (B) conversion disorder
   (C) organic disorder
   (D) undifferentiated disorder
   (E) paranoid disorder

3. Which of the following are most characteristic of a dissociative disorder?

   (A) A persistent, irrational fear of objects or situations
   (B) Difficulties in forming lasting personal relationships
   (C) Involuntary and persistent thoughts that interfere with daily activity
   (D) Auditory and tactile hallucinations
   (E) Memory dysfunction and/or altered perceptions of identity

4. Depression has been associated with low levels of the neurotransmitter

   (A) acetylcholine
   (B) GABA
   (C) serotonin
   (D) chlorpromazine
   (E) dopamine

5. Which of the following is NOT characterized by the *DSM-5* as an anxiety disorder?

   (A) Phobia
   (B) Social phobia
   (C) Anxious personality disorder
   (D) Panic disorder
   (E) Generalized anxiety disorder

6. A high-school girl goes missing, and when she is found in a town 100 miles away a week later, she has assumed a new personality and has no apparent recollection of her life at home. Which category of disorder is she most likely suffering from?

   (A) Somatoform disorder
   (B) Delusional disorder
   (C) Personality disorder
   (D) Dissociative disorder
   (E) Schizophrenia

7. Conversion disorder is best characterized by

   (A) a constant fear of being ill
   (B) panic attacks and severe anxiety
   (C) frequent vague complaints about physical symptoms
   (D) functional impairment of a limb or sensory ability with no apparent physical cause
   (E) religious obsessions

8. All of the following are Cluster B personality disorders EXCEPT

   (A) borderline personality disorder
   (B) schizoid personality disorder
   (C) histrionic behavior disorder
   (D) narcissistic personality disorder
   (E) antisocial personality disorder

9. A child shows difficulty engaging with other children and needs to follow a very strict routine every day to function properly. If the routine is broken, he cries and has a very difficult time adjusting. These symptoms may satisfy which of the following diagnoses?

   (A) Attention-deficit hyperactivity disorder
   (B) Reactive attachment disorder
   (C) Obsessive-compulsive disorder
   (D) Adjustment disorder
   (E) Autism spectrum disorder

REFLECT
Respond to the following questions:

- Which topics in this chapter do you hope to see on the multiple-choice section or essay?

- Which topics in this chapter do you hope not to see on the multiple-choice section or essay?

- Regarding any psychologists mentioned, can you pair the psychologists with their contributions to the field? Did they contribute significant experiments, theories, or both?

- Regarding any theories mentioned, can you distinguish between differing theories well enough to recognize them on the multiple-choice section? Can you distinguish them well enough to write a fluent essay on them?

- Can you define the key terms at the end of the chapter?

- Which parts of the chapter will you review?

- Will you seek further help, outside of this book (such as from a teacher, Princeton Review tutor, or AP Students), on any of the content in this chapter—and, if so, on what content?

Chapter 17
Clinical Psychology:
Treatment

TREATMENT APPROACHES

The various disordered behaviors described in the previous chapter can be viewed from varying perspectives. Often, insight into the true nature of a disorder can be derived from examining the strategy that is most effective in treating the disorder.

Insight Therapies: Psychoanalytic and Humanistic Approaches

The psychoanalytic approach to the treatment of disordered behavior is rooted in the concept of **insight**. Insight into the cause of the problem, according to this theory, is the primary key to eliminating the problem.

Psychoanalysis

Psychoanalysis, or psychoanalytic therapy, as it is sometimes called, was first developed by Freud and focuses on probing past defense mechanisms of repression and rationalization to understand the unconscious cause of a problem. A primary tool for revealing the contents of the unconscious is **free association**, in which the patient reports any and all conscious thoughts and ideas. Within the pattern of free associations are hints to the nature of the unconscious conflict. The insight process does not occur quickly, however, as patients exhibit resistance to the uncovering of repressed thoughts and feelings.

In psychoanalytic therapy, the therapist strives to remain detached from the patient, resisting emotional or personal involvement. This detachment is intended to encourage **transference**, which occurs when the patient shifts thoughts and feelings about certain people or events onto the therapist. This process is thought to help reveal the nature of the patient's conflicts. **Countertransference** may occur if the therapist transfers their own feelings onto the patient. In order to avoid countertransference, psychotherapists have typically undergone analysis themselves and many continue to do so while practicing therapy.

Freud and Dreams

According to psychoanalytic theory, another window into the unconscious is provided by dreams. Freud believed that the images and occurrences in dreams—the **manifest content** of dreams—are actually symbols representing the **latent**, or truly meaningful, **content** of dreams.

Humanistic Therapy

The humanistic school of psychology takes a related, yet different approach to the treatment of disordered behavior. Rather than treating the person seeking help as a patient, the humanistic approach treats the individual as a client. **Client-centered therapy** was invented by **Carl Rogers** and involves the assumption that clients can be understood only in terms of their own realities. This approach differs from the Freudian approach in its focus on the client's present perception of reality, rather than the past and its analysis of conscious, instead of unconscious, motives. The goal of the therapy is to help the client realize full potential through self-actualization. In order to accomplish this, the client-centered therapist takes a somewhat different approach from that of the Freudian. Rather than remaining detached, the therapist is open, honest, and expressive of feelings with the client (an active listener). Rogers referred to this way of relating to the client as **genuineness**.

The next key for successful client-centered therapy, according to Rogers, is **unconditional positive regard**. You may recall from previous chapters that Rogers believed that unconditional positive regard for the child by the parent was critical for healthy development. The therapist provides this unconditional positive regard to help the client reach a state of unconditional self-worth.

The final key to successful therapy is **accurate empathic understanding**. Rogers used this term to describe the therapist's ability to view the world from the eyes of the client. This empathy is critical to successful communication between the therapist and client.

A different type of approach toward treatment is **Gestalt therapy**, which combines both physical and mental therapies. **Fritz Perls** developed this approach to blend an awareness of unconscious tensions with the belief that one must become aware of and deal with those tensions by taking personal responsibility. Clients may be asked to physically "act out" psychological conflicts in order to make them aware of the interaction between mind and body.

Behavioral Therapy

Behavioral therapy stands in dramatic contrast to the insight therapies. First, behavioral therapy is a short-term process, whereas the insight approaches are extended over long periods of time, often spanning years. Secondly, behavior therapy treats symptoms because, in this school of thought, there is no deep underlying cause of the problem. The disordered behavior itself is both the problem and symptom. To change behavior, behavioral therapists use specific techniques with clearly defined methods of application and clear ways to evaluate their efficacy.

Counterconditioning is a technique in which a response to a given stimulus is replaced by a different response. For example, if a patient seeks behavioral therapy to stop drinking alcohol, the therapist must take the learned responses, the positive feelings generated by drinking alcohol, and replace them with a new reaction, namely, negative feelings concerning alcohol.

Counterconditioning can be accomplished in a few ways. One is to use **aversion therapy**, in which an aversive stimulus is repeatedly paired with the behavior that the client wishes to stop. So, to use our alcohol example, the therapist might administer a punishment to the patient each time the patient drinks alcohol.

Another method used for counterconditioning is **systematic desensitization**. This technique involves replacing one response, such as anxiety, with another response, such as relaxation. In order to achieve this goal, a therapist constructs, with the help of the client, a hierarchical set of mental images related to the stressful stimulus. These mental images are laid out in an order such that each one is slightly more anxiety-inducing than the previous one. The patient then learns a deep-relaxation technique. Next, the therapist asks the patient to bring to mind the least stressful of the mental images. As the client imagines the scene, they may become anxious.

Alcoholics and Aversion Therapy

This approach is sometimes used in treating alcoholism. Patients are administered a drug called Antabuse, which makes them violently ill if they consume alcohol.

Changing It Up
A variation of systematic desensitization can occur when a therapist introduces the client to increasingly more anxiety-inducing stimuli instead of relying solely on imagination.

The client is instructed to practice the relaxation technique the moment the feelings of anxiety begin and to continue using the relaxation technique until they feel fully relaxed while imagining the scene. The therapist, over time, systematically helps the client work up the hierarchy until they are able to imagine the most stressful scene in the hierarchy without experiencing anxiety. This technique relies on learning mechanisms to associate the formerly anxiety-provoking stimuli with relaxation.

Other forms of behavioral therapy involve **extinction procedures**, which are designed to weaken maladaptive responses. One way of trying to extinguish a behavior is called **flooding**. Flooding involves exposing a client to the stimulus that causes the undesirable response. If, for example, a client has come to a therapist to try to overcome a fear of spiders, the therapist will actually expose the client to spiders. Of course, the client will have a high anxiety level, but after a few minutes of being near the spider without any negative consequences, the client will presumably realize that the situation is not dangerous. **Implosion** is a similar technique, in which the client imagines the disruptive stimuli rather than actually confronting them.

Operant conditioning is a behavior-control technique that we discussed in the chapter on learning. A related approach is **behavioral contracting**, in which the therapist and the client draw up a contract by which they both agree to abide. The client must, according to the contract, act in certain ways, such as not exhibiting undesirable behaviors; meanwhile, the therapist must provide stated rewards if the client holds up their end of the bargain.

Modeling is a therapeutic approach based on Bandura's social learning theory. This technique is based on the principle of vicarious learning. Clients watch someone act in a certain way and then receive a reward. Presumably, the client will then be disposed to imitate that behavior.

Cognitive Therapy

Cognitive approaches to the treatment of disordered behavior rely on changing cognitions, or the ways people think about situations, in order to change behavior. One such approach is **rational-emotive behavior therapy (REBT)** (sometimes called simply **RET**, for **rational-emotive therapy**), formulated by **Albert Ellis**. REBT is based on the idea that when confronted with situations, people recite statements to themselves that express maladaptive thoughts. The maladaptive thoughts result in maladaptive emotional responses. The goal of REBT is to change the maladaptive thoughts and emotional responses by confronting the irrational thoughts directly. Incorrect thoughts are changed in a simple way: the patient is told that they are incorrect and why. Some examples of maladaptive thoughts are, "I always have to be perfect in everything I do" and "Other people's opinions are crucial to my happiness."

Another cognitive approach is **cognitive therapy,** formulated by **Aaron Beck**, in which the focus is on maladaptive schemas. These schemas cause clients to experience cognitive distortions, which in turn lead them to feel worthless or incompetent. Beck asserted that there is a **negative triad** of depression that involves a negative view of self, of the world, and of the future. This view is learned through experiences and then becomes a cycle of response that needs to be addressed through cognitive therapy. Maladaptive schemas include **arbitrary inference**, in which a person draws conclusions without evidence, and **dichotomous thinking**, which involves all-or-nothing conceptions of situations. An example might be that of a person, faced with the stress of a job interview, who thinks, "If I don't get this job, I'll be a complete failure." The goal of cognitive therapy is to eliminate or modify the individual's maladaptive schemas.

Study Tip

As mentioned previously, these different treatment approaches are linked to the different theories of personality development described in Chapter 15. See whether you can identify how the therapy has a logical connection to the underlying theory. For example, in psychoanalysis, techniques like free association and dream analysis are designed to afford access to the patient's unconscious mind. This makes sense, since the unconscious mind is a central aspect of Freud's theory.

Biological Therapies

Biological therapies are medical approaches to behavioral problems. Biological therapies are typically used in conjunction with one of the previously mentioned forms of treatment.

Electroconvulsive therapy (ECT) is a form of treatment in which fairly high voltages of electricity are passed across a patient's head. This treatment causes temporary amnesia and can result in seizures. It has been successful in the treatment of major depression, but today it is used only when all other means of treating depression have failed because of the risks involved with memory loss.

Another form of biological treatment is **psychosurgery**. Perhaps the most well-known form of psychosurgery is the **prefrontal lobotomy**, in which parts of the frontal lobes are cut off from the rest of the brain. This surgery was a popular treatment for violent patients from the 1930s to the 1950s. It frequently left patients in a zombie-like or catatonic state. Its use marked a controversial chapter in the history of psychotherapy.

Psychopharmacology is the treatment of psychological and behavioral maladaptations with drugs. There are four broad classes of **psychotropic**, or psychologically active **drugs:** antipsychotics, antidepressants, anxiolytics, and lithium salts.

Antipsychotics like Clozapine, Thorazine, and Haldol reduce the symptoms of schizophrenia by blocking the neural receptors for dopamine. You may recall that dopamine is implicated in schizophrenia and in movement disorders. Unfortunately, jerky movements, tremors, and muscle stiffness are among the side effects of these drugs. The clinician must decide which is worse—the psychological disorder being treated or the side effects of the drugs.

Antidepressants can be grouped into three types: monoamine oxidase (MAO) inhibitors, tricyclics, and selective reuptake inhibitors. **MAO inhibitors,** like Eutron,

Alternative Therapies

Did you know that biofeedback is often used to treat disorders like anxiety, chronic pain, and ADHD? It is a non-invasive technique that may reduce or eliminate the need for medications and it enables patients to feel in control of their health. Other alternative therapies include therapeutic touch, eye movement desensitization and reprocessing (EMDR), and light therapy.

work by increasing the amount of serotonin and norepinephrine in the synaptic cleft. They produce this increase by blocking monoamine oxidase, which is responsible for the breakdown of many neurotransmitters. These drugs are effective but toxic and require special dietary modifications. **Tricyclics,** like Norpramin, Amitriptyline, and Imipramine increase the amount of serotonin and norepinephrine.

The third class of antidepressants, **selective reuptake inhibitors** (often called the selective serotonin reuptake inhibitors, or **SSRIs**, for the neurotransmitter most affected by them) also work by increasing the amount of neurotransmitter at the synaptic cleft, in this case by blocking the reuptake mechanism of the cell that released the neurotransmitters. Prozac (Fluoxetine) is one example of such a drug. The indirect mechanism of action of these drugs means that they have fewer side effects. They are the most frequently prescribed class of antidepressant drugs in the United States.

Anxiolytics depress the central nervous system and reduce anxiety while increasing feelings of well-being and reducing insomnia. A commonly prescribed anti-anxiety medication is Xanax. Anxiolytics also include barbiturates, which are rarely used because of their potential for addiction and their danger when mixed with other drugs. **Benzodiazepines**, which also include Valium (Diazepam) and Librium (Chlordiazepoxide), cause muscle relaxation and a feeling of tranquility.

Lithium carbonate, a salt, is effective in the treatment of bipolar disorder. The mechanism of action is not known, however.

MODES OF THERAPY

Not all forms of therapy involve an individual client seeing a therapist. **Group therapy**, in which clients meet together with a therapist as an interactive group, has some advantages over individual therapy. It is less expensive, and the group dynamic may be therapeutic in and of itself. Of course, the psychological effect of the therapist also may be diluted across the members of the group because attention is focused on the group rather than on a specific individual. One area in which group therapy has gained popularity is in the treatment of substance abuse. **Twelve-step programs** are one form of group therapy, although they are usually not moderated by professional psychotherapists. These programs, modeled after Alcoholics Anonymous, are a combination of spirituality and group therapy. The twelve-step programs focus on a strong social support system of people who are experiencing or who have experienced addictions or other types of maladaptive adjustments to life.

Another form of therapy in which there is more than a single client is **couples** or **family therapy**. This type of treatment arose out of the simple observation that some dysfunctional behavior affects the afflicted person's loved ones. Couples therapy approaches the couple dyad as a system that involves complex interactions. Family therapy has distinct advantages in that it allows family members to express their feelings to one another and to the therapist simultaneously. This behavior, in turn, encourages family members to listen to one another in a way that might not occur in other settings.

KEY TERMS

Treatment Approaches

insight

psychoanalysis

free association

transference

countertransference

manifest content

latent content

client-centered therapy

Carl Rogers

genuineness

unconditional positive regard

accurate empathic understanding

Gestalt therapy

Fritz Perls

behavioral therapy

counterconditioning

aversion therapy

systematic desensitization

extinction procedures

flooding

implosion

operant conditioning

behavioral contracting

modeling

rational-emotive behavior therapy (REBT) / rational-emotive therapy (RET)

Albert Ellis

cognitive therapy

Aaron Beck

negative triad

arbitrary inference

dichotomous thinking

electroconvulsive therapy (ECT)

psychosurgery

prefrontal lobotomy

psychopharmacology

psychotropic drugs

antipsychotics

antidepressants

MAO inhibitors

tricyclics

selective reuptake inhibitors (SSRIs)

anxiolytics

benzodiazepines

lithium carbonate

Modes of Therapy

group therapy

twelve-step programs

couples therapy

family therapy

Chapter 17 Drill

See Chapter 19 for answers and explanations.

1. The concept of *accurate empathic understanding* is most closely associated with which of the following therapeutic approaches?

   (A) Psychoanalytic therapy
   (B) Inductive therapy
   (C) Client-centered therapy
   (D) Implosion therapy
   (E) Reductionist therapy

2. Behavioral therapeutic approaches, such as systematic desensitization, have been most often used with those experiencing or diagnosed with

   (A) fugue
   (B) dementia
   (C) dissociative disorder
   (D) schizophrenia
   (E) phobia

3. A psychoanalytically oriented therapist would most likely be in accord with which of the following criticisms regarding behaviorally oriented therapies?

   (A) Behaviorally oriented therapies often take years to complete and create an onerous financial burden for the patient.
   (B) Behaviorally oriented therapies are concerned solely with the modification of troubling behavioral symptoms and do not address the underlying problems which may have produced those symptoms.
   (C) Behaviorally oriented therapies can be performed only by therapists who have had the longest and most rigorous training and, as a result, can never impact as many people as can other treatment approaches.
   (D) Behaviorally oriented therapies are relatively uninterested in the development of an egalitarian client-therapist relationship and miss opportunities to promote emotional growth and empowerment.
   (E) Behaviorally oriented therapies avoid the technique of role-playing and may not be suitable for group or family therapy situations.

4. The cognitively oriented therapeutic approach known as rational-emotive behavior therapy is most closely associated with

   (A) Julian Rotter
   (B) Albert Ellis
   (C) Abraham Maslow
   (D) Raymond Cattell
   (E) Rollo May

5. Which of the following is NOT a major class of drugs used for psychotherapeutic effect?

   (A) Anticoagulants
   (B) Anxiolytics
   (C) Monoamine oxidase inhibitors
   (D) Lithium salts
   (E) Selective reuptake inhibitors

6. Judy has acrophobia, a fear of heights. A behavioral therapist creates a treatment plan to take her to the top of the Empire State Building on the first session, where she will remain until her reaction to the stimulus subsides. This technique is known as

   (A) systematic desensitization
   (B) aversion therapy
   (C) flooding
   (D) implosion
   (E) behavior contracting

7. A behavioral therapist uses which of the following techniques?

   (A) Free association
   (B) Dream analysis
   (C) Hypnosis
   (D) Extinction procedures
   (E) Unconditional positive regard

8. Selective serotonin reuptake inhibitors, more commonly known as SSRIs, are generally effective in treating which of the following?

   (A) Depressive disorders
   (B) Anxiety disorders
   (C) Bipolar disorder
   (D) Feeding and eating disorders
   (E) Schizophrenic disorders

9. A psychotherapist would most likely use which of the following therapies?

    (A) Implosion
    (B) Systematic desensitization
    (C) Free association
    (D) Flooding
    (E) Positive self-talk

10. Carl Rogers is most closely identified with which of the following therapy perspectives?

    (A) Humanistic therapy
    (B) Psychoanalytic therapy
    (C) Behavioral therapy
    (D) Cognitive behavioral therapy
    (E) Biological therapy

REFLECT

Respond to the following questions:

- Which topics in this chapter do you hope to see on the multiple-choice section or essay?

- Which topics in this chapter do you hope not to see on the multiple-choice section or essay?

- Regarding any psychologists mentioned, can you pair the psychologists with their contributions to the field? Did they contribute significant experiments, theories, or both?

- Regarding any theories mentioned, can you distinguish between differing theories well enough to recognize them on the multiple-choice section? Can you distinguish them well enough to write a fluent essay on them?

- Can you define the key terms at the end of the chapter?

- Which parts of the chapter will you review?

- Will you seek further help, outside of this book (such as from a teacher, Princeton Review tutor, or AP Students), on any of the content in this chapter—and, if so, on what content?

Chapter 18
Social
Psychology

Social psychology refers to the study of psychology within the context of social or interpersonal interactions. Sociology is the study of cultures and societies, and these have a large effect on an individual's environment, which can influence cognition and behavior. Here are a few theories and important concepts of sociology and how they relate to the intersecting discipline of social psychology.

IDENTITIES AND GROUPS

Societies, organizations of individuals, each have a shared **culture**, a common set of beliefs, behaviors, values, and material symbols. Therefore, identities begin to form as collective **social identities** that are placed upon individuals by others, and individuals form their own **personal identities** about themselves. Personal identities are generally words that describe personality, such as *kind, generous, thoughtful, insightful*, etc., while social identities are how individuals are seen in the context of their society. Social identities can be related to religion, work, appearance, disability, gender, sexual orientation, immigration status, or any other label that societies have come to understand through their shared culture. For instance, someone's social identities might be lawyer, young adult, Muslim, and female. These traits do not have anything to do with personality traits, yet they are factors that influence how individuals are seen by others in society, which may color social interactions. These identities can give some individuals an inherent advantage in some societies while other identities can be a disadvantage. For instance, those who have citizenship in a certain country have more power and rights than those who are considered immigrants, noncitizens, or undocumented. Similarly, in the United States, adults tend to hold more power in society than children or the very elderly. Individuals hold multiple social identities, and the effects and nature of these overlapping identities is referred to as **intersectionality**. Someone who identifies as female, Latina, and bisexual can provide a window into each of these social identities and how they intersect and create complexity when combined.

The closest group that individuals create with one another is called the **primary group**, which usually consists of family and close friends. These relationships are generally long-lasting and emotionally deep. Individuals spend time with others in their primary groups for the sake of spending quality time with them, not for any other gain. Most others fall into a **secondary group**, a group of friends and acquaintances who perhaps have shared interests or values. For instance, a person may take classes at school with classmates who have a shared interest in the material or take part in a running group with others who share a passion for running. Within societies, these identities underpin ideas of sameness and difference, which generate **in-groups** and **out-groups**. In-groups refer to groups of individuals with a shared identity. For example, teachers share an in-group with other teachers, while, to them, accountants would be considered an out-group.

While this example is harmless, in- and out-groups can create harmful situations when one group believes it is superior to another. **Ethnocentrism** refers to holding the values or beliefs of one's own in-group as better than those of another's, which can lead to conflict, prejudice, and more. On the other hand, **cultural relativism** is the idea that the beliefs and values of one's in-group may be different than those of another, but that they are not necessarily better or worse: just different. Sometimes, individuals try to enter a new in-group through **assimilation**, a process of taking on another's culture in order to fit in to a new society. Assimilation is common amongst immigrants and individuals settling into a new culture. Individuals who do not shed their former identities, but rather keep elements of their own culture and take on elements of their new culture show **multiculturalism**.

As individuals immigrate or emigrate, study abroad, or even visit other societies and cultures, they may experience **culture shock** or **cultural lag**. Culture shock refers to the way in which behaviors and values can be seen differently across cultures. Language barriers are common examples of culture shock, as are small social faux pas that get lost in translation or contain different meanings across cultures. Cultural lag refers to the time it takes for cultures to catch up to technological innovations or practices.

Individuals play **roles** within groups and societies, some of which may change or conflict with each other over the course of a lifetime. Someone could have the roles father, husband, son, and teacher simultaneously. **Role conflict** occurs when two or more of these roles are at odds with each other: imagine the man described receives a phone call at work to say that his child went home from school sick. Does he stay at work and fulfill his role as a teacher or does he leave work early to tend to his child? Similarly, **role strain** can occur within the same role: college students are in college to study, but are also at school to meet friends from around the world and learn to take care of themselves on their own. The balance of study and experience can create strain within that role. **Role exit** occurs when a person leaves behind a role to take on another: graduating from college and starting off in the workforce means the person leaves the role of student and takes on the role of employee.

SOCIAL INSTITUTIONS

In societies, there are a variety of **social institutions** designed to promote and transmit social norms to members through a variety of constructs.

Family, religion, government, economy, politics, health, medicine, and education are all social institutions and have an impact on the way individuals interact with each other and within their respective societies. Family is an important institution that provides kinship and belonging within a society, while religion provides belonging as well as a sense of purpose and connection to the supernatural. Governments create laws to maintain order in societies, and various structures of governments can directly affect individuals' quality of life. Economies manage transactions between individuals, organizations, and groups. Health and medicine are interesting institutions that can change dramatically from culture to culture, especially with regard to mental health. Some cultures may treat a condition as a sickness, while other cultures may not recognize that same condition as abnormal. Finally, education is an institution that transmits knowledge from generation to generation and teaches individuals about the values of their societies.

Even where education is free for all, not everyone has the same opportunities, depending on where individuals live. **Institutionalized discrimination** is a particular type of discrimination that refers to unfair treatment of certain groups by organizations. Zoning laws, government, and other organizations can create rules that, unintentionally or intentionally, put certain groups at a social disadvantage. Institutionalized discrimination can lead to unequal opportunities for access to quality education and healthcare, as well as suppressed attainment of wealth.

Closely related to institutionalized discrimination are the concepts of **availability** and **accessibility**. Availability refers to whether something even exists for a person to use. If, for example, a low-income housing complex does not have any grocery stores within 5 miles, this would be an issue of availability: it might be more difficult for people who live there to be able to get to grocery stores. This particular scenario of not having available grocery stores (except maybe convenience stores that sell chips and candy) is called a **food desert**. Because people may not have cars or ways of reaching farther-away grocery stores, healthy food is not available to them, and this can have resounding health consequences. Accessibility refers to whether a person can actually use the tools and resources that are available to them. For instance, a class uses a particular textbook for readings, but one student is visually impaired. Even though that book is available to the student for purchase, it is not usable to the student as is. The book would have to be made accessible, either through braille or voice-over computer programs, for it to be usable for that student.

The Power of Groupthink

Another interesting phenomenon that may occur when people are in groups is what **Irving Janis** has referred to as "groupthink." **Groupthink** occurs when members of a group are so driven to reach unanimous decisions that they no longer truly evaluate the repercussions or implications of their decisions. Groupthink may be observed when the groups making decisions are isolated and homogeneous, when there is a lack of impartial leadership inside or outside the group, and when there is a high level of pressure for a decision to be made. Often, groups experiencing groupthink start to acquire feelings of invulnerability and omnipotence. They do not believe they can make a mistake and as a result, often do. A **mindguard** in the group may take on the responsibility of criticizing or even ostracizing members of the group who do not agree with the rest. The groupthink hypothesis has been applied to understand political situations, such as how political leaders can make decisions that seem, in retrospect, so obviously bad to people outside of the group.

GROUP DYNAMICS

Group dynamics is a general term for some of the phenomena we observe when people interact. For example, **social facilitation** is an increase in performance on a task that occurs when that task is performed in the presence of others. You may have experienced this effect if you play sports. The opposite effect is called **social inhibition**, which occurs when the presence of others makes performance worse. Many people experience social inhibition when they give speeches. People experience social facilitation when they find a task to be easy or well-practiced, and they suffer from social inhibition when a task is overly difficult or novel.

Another effect that occurs when people interact in groups is **social loafing**, or the reduced effort group members put into a shared task as a result of the size of the group. For example, when you are assigned a group project, you may put in less effort than you would if it were an individual project, hoping that the other group members will pick up some of your slack. People are prone to social loafing when they believe their performance is not being assessed or monitored.

Another interesting effect of being in groups is the exaggeration of our initial attitudes. This effect is known as **group polarization**. Group polarization occurs when a judgment or decision of a group is more extreme than what individual members of the group would have reached on their own. For example, if people with negative racial attitudes are placed into a group and told to discuss racial issues, those who started off the experiment with high prejudice often end up with an even higher prejudice after the discussion. **Peer pressure** occurs when an individual feels unduly influenced by their peers to engage in behaviors they otherwise would not. One example of peer pressure is someone encouraging a friend to try smoking. But peer pressure has a flip side: A friend can also inspire another to participate in positive activities. Motivating a friend to lose weight by becoming work-out partners is an example. While more common in adolescence, peer pressure is also common in adulthood.

Research has been conducted on the resolution of conflicts within groups. The most effective method to resolve a conflict between two groups is to have them cooperate toward a superordinate goal. For example, in the Robbers Cave experiment, campers who had been feuding for weeks were able to overcome their differences when they cooperated to solve problems, such as a water leak that threatened the whole camp. Another effective technique is **GRIT (Graduated and Reciprocated Initiatives in Tension-Reduction)**. This approach encourages groups to announce intent to reduce tensions and show small, conciliatory behaviors, as long as these reduced tensions and behaviors are reciprocated.

ATTRIBUTION

Attribution refers to the way in which people assign responsibility for certain outcomes. Typically, attribution falls into two categories—dispositional (or individual) and situational. **Dispositional attribution** assumes that the cause of a behavior or outcome is internal. **Situational attribution** assigns the cause to the environment or external conditions. When students fail a test, they might attribute that failure to their own poor work habits or lack of intellectual abilities (a dispositional attribute), or they could attribute their failure to some external factor such as bad instruction (a situational attribute).

A **self-serving bias** sees the cause of actions as internal (or dispositional) when the outcomes are positive and external (or situational) when the results are negative. When a teacher's class fails a test, that teacher blames the students for their lack of initiative and motivation. However, when the class does very well, the teacher attributes the students' success to their own superior teaching and motivational ability. When your class gets back a paper, think about how often you've heard fellow students say things like, "I got an A" but "He gave me a C." A related concept is the **fundamental attribution error**. In this process of judging the behavior of others, people are more likely to overestimate the role of dispositional attributes and to underestimate the role of the situation. For example, if you are waiting for your friend to meet you at the movies and she is so late that the movie has already started, you would be more likely to blame your friend's lateness on her laziness or procrastination than on a traffic jam or car accident. Your judgment exemplifies a fundamental attribution error.

The Mob Mentality

The phenomenon of **deindividuation** is a common occurrence at riots and protests that have gotten angry. Even at a protest that started peaceably enough, when the crowd's emotions are running high in arousal, individuals tend to engage in behaviors they ordinarily would not when alone. These behaviors are often aggressive, and members of the crowd feel a low sense of personal responsibility. They also feel little risk of getting into trouble. ("They can't possibly arrest all of us. Give me a brick, I want to throw it!")

Some attributions actually affect the outcome of the behavior, as in the case of the **self-fulfilling prophecy**. Because Person A expects Person B to achieve or fail, Person B is likely to do just that. This is especially true in education and is known as the **Rosenthal Effect**. When teachers are told that certain children are expected to achieve in the following year, those children tend to do better than others, even when there is actually no difference in ability levels.

INTERPERSONAL PERCEPTION

Psychologists have studied **interpersonal attraction**, the tendency to positively evaluate a person and then to gravitate toward that person. Interpersonal attraction is obviously based on characteristics of the person to whom we are attracted, but it may be subject to environmental and social influences, as well. Factors leading to interpersonal attraction include positive evaluation, shared opinions, good physical appearance, familiarity, and proximity of the individuals to each other. **Positive evaluation** refers to the fact that we all like to be positively evaluated, and therefore, we tend to prefer the company of people who think highly of us. **Shared opinions** as a basis for interpersonal attraction are typically thought of as a form of social reinforcement. If we are praised and rewarded by a person for our opinions, then we tend to prefer their company. It is important to note that similarity across other factors, such as age and race, also tends to be a good predictor of interpersonal attraction. The variable of proximity is an interesting factor. It has been shown that people are more likely to be attracted to those in close physical proximity to them. Studies have shown that apartment building residents are much more likely to have friends who live on their floor than they are to have friends who live on other floors. This is an example of the **mere exposure effect**, which states that people tend to prefer people and experiences that are familiar.

Q: What factors may lend themselves to interpersonal attraction?

See answer on page 302.

CONFORMITY, COMPLIANCE, OBEDIENCE

Conformity is the modification of behavior to make it agree with that of a group. **Solomon Asch** performed studies on the nature of conformity. In these studies, participants thought that they were being evaluated on their perceptual judgments. Small groups of people sitting together were shown stimuli, such as lines of differing lengths. Each member of the group was to report which of several comparison lines matched a standard line in length. Each individual in the group was asked to respond orally in turn. The participants did not know that the other members of a given group were not naïve participants, but rather were confederates of the experimenter. The correct answers in the experiment were obvious. However, the confederates, pretending to be naïve participants, would purposely respond incorrectly. Asch found that, in general, the naïve participants agreed with the other members of the group, even though the answer they gave was obviously incorrect. Furthermore, Asch demonstrated that the participants knew that the answers they gave were wrong, but said them anyway.

Conformity Factors
Factors influencing conformity include group size, the cohesiveness of the group opinion, gender, social status, culture, and the appearance of unanimity.

Generally speaking, three or more members of a group are sufficient for conformity effects to occur. The desire to conform seems higher if the participants see themselves as members of a cohesive group. In general, women are more likely to conform than are men. People who view themselves as being of medium or low social status are more likely to conform than are those who perceive themselves as being of high social status. The cultural influence on conformity is also marked: people in more collective societies tend to conform more than do those in individualistic societies. Finally, unanimity is important. A participant is much less likely to conform if even one other person in the group did not conform.

Compliance is the propensity to accede to the requests of others, even at the expense of your own interests. One method of eliciting compliance is justification, in which you present reasons why a person should comply. Another method is **reciprocity**, which involves creating the appearance that you are giving someone something in order to induce that individual to comply with your wishes. Salespeople have perfected the **foot-in-the-door phenomenon**, which involves making requests in small steps at first (to gain compliance), in order to work up to big requests. The opposite of this phenomenon is called the **door-in-the-face phenomenon**, in which a large request is made first, making subsequent smaller requests more appealing. The likelihood of compliance to a particular request also depends on our regard for the person making the request. Generally speaking, the more highly we regard the person making the request, the more likely we are to comply with the person's request. In general, there are two reasons why people will resist compliance. One reason is that people have been exposed to a weak version of an argument and are, therefore, inoculated to further attempts to get them to comply. This theory is known as the **inoculation hypothesis**. Another reason people resist is that they feel that they are being forced against their will to comply, which is known as **psychological reactance**.

Obedience was studied by **Stanley Milgram** in a series of famous experiments. The basic paradigm was as follows: participants were led to believe that their job was to administer shocks of increasing intensity to another participant if that participant performed poorly on a given learning task. The other participant was actually a confederate, intentionally performing badly, so that the real participant would be obliged to administer shock. The confederate also acted as if the shocks were painful, pleading with the participant to stop. (In fact, no shocks were given.) The participant was instructed by the experimenter to continue the shocks, despite the obvious pain the "other participant" was enduring. You might think that you would not administer painful shocks in this paradigm, but a very high percentage of people did just that. Through additional studies, Milgram found that several factors were critical to whether or not the person would obey. The first was the perceived authority of the test administrator. For example, when the person overseeing the experiment introduced himself as a graduate student instead of as a scientist, the subject was much less likely to comply. Another factor was physical distance. If the subject was forced to sit in the room with the person receiving the shocks, his level of obedience dropped; the subject was also less likely to obey if the experimenter communicated the commands by phone instead of in person. Obedience also tended to go down if the subject was told that he was responsible for the outcome, if the subject witnessed someone else disobeying the experimenter, and if the experimenter instructed the subject to immediately apply a high level of voltage to the "learner." The major conclusion from this study was that people tended to be obedient to a figure of authority, but only if certain criteria were met. It also demonstrated that people are much less likely to obey when they feel that they have an ally in standing up to the pressure.

ATTITUDES AND ATTITUDE CHANGE

Attitudes are combinations of affective (emotional) and cognitive (perceptual) reactions to different stimuli. The affective component is the emotional response an item or issue arouses, whereas the cognitive component is what we think about the item or issue. Attitudes are acquired, in part, by vicarious conditioning. If, for example, we observe a person being bitten by a dog, we form an attitude about that dog. In this case, the affective component might be fear, and the cognitive component might be the understanding that this particular dog bites.

Cognitive dissonance occurs when attitudes and behaviors contradict each other. Generally, such tension is not pleasant, and people tend to change in order to achieve cognitive consistency. **Leon Festinger** studied this phenomenon and came to the conclusion that people are likely to alter their attitudes to fit their behavior. For example, law-abiding citizens speed frequently. A cognitive conflict exists. Which is going to change—their attitude toward the law or their over-the-limit driving? Generally, people adjust their attitudes and continue their behavior. Cognitive dissonance tends to occur only when the person feels that he has a choice in the matter. If someone feels that he is being forced to speed, his attitude will remain intact.

Persuasion is the process by which a person or group can influence the attitudes of others. The efficacy of persuasion derives in part from the characteristics of the persuader. People who have positions of authority or who appear to be experts on a given topic are more likely to be viewed as persuasive. The motive of the persuader is also critical. If an author tries to convince you that authors are poor, and that you should donate five dollars to the poor authors' fund, you probably would not believe the author. Your disbelief would stem from your confidence that the author's motive is selfish. However, if an author asks for five dollars for disaster relief, you might be more likely to be persuaded because the motive seems more altruistic.

An additional factor affecting persuasive ability is interpersonal attractiveness. More attractive, likable, trustworthy, and knowledgeable people are viewed as more persuasive. Most people are also swayed by the presentation of facts. Another factor influencing the persuasion process is the nature of the message. Repetition is an effective technique for achieving persuasion, which is why the same advertisements run so frequently. Fear is another motivator of attitudinal change. A prime example of the use of fear in persuasive attempts is the practice of putting cars wrecked in DWI (driving-while-intoxicated) accidents on display. The idea is that seeing the result of such an accident will induce an attitudinal change about drunk driving. The **elaboration likelihood model** explains when people will be persuaded by the content of a message (or the logic of its arguments), and when people will be influenced by other, more superficial characteristics like the length of the message, or the appearance of the person delivering it. Because persuasion can be such a

A: Interpersonal attraction may occur as a result of positive evaluation, shared opinions, good physical appearance, familiarity, or proximity.

Marketing and Persuasion
Market researchers refer to the use of facts as the central route to persuasion.

powerful means for influencing what people think and do, much research has gone into studying the various elements of a message that might have an impact on its persuasiveness.

The three key elements are message characteristics, source characteristics, and target characteristics.

1. The message characteristics are the features of the message itself, such as its logic and the number of key points in the argument. This category also includes more superficial things, such as the length and grammatical complexity.

2. The source characteristics of the person or group delivering the message, such as expertise, knowledge, and trustworthiness, are also of importance. People are much more likely to be persuaded by a major study described in the *New England Journal of Medicine* than by something in the pages of the local supermarket tabloid.

3. Finally, the target characteristics of the person receiving the message (such as self-esteem, intelligence, and mood) have an important influence on whether a message will be perceived as persuasive. For instance, some studies have suggested that those with higher intelligence are less easily persuaded by one-sided messages.

The two cognitive routes that persuasion follows under this model are the **central route** and the **peripheral route**. Under the central route, people are persuaded by the content of the argument. They ruminate over the key features of the argument and allow those features to influence their decision to change their point of view. The peripheral route functions when people focus on superficial or secondary characteristics of the speech or the orator. Under these circumstances, people are persuaded by the attractiveness of the orator, the length of the speech, whether the orator is considered an expert in his field, and other features. The elaboration likelihood model argues that people will choose the central route only when they are both motivated to listen to the logic of the argument (they are interested in the topic) and not distracted, thus focusing their attention on the argument. If those conditions are not met, individuals will choose the peripheral route, and they will be persuaded by more superficial factors. Messages processed via the central route are more likely to have longer-lasting persuasive outcomes than messages processed via the peripheral route.

Finally, some people can be influenced to change their attitudes more easily than others. In general, people with high self-esteem are less easily persuaded than are those with low self-esteem. Thus, many hate groups recruit people who are considered outsiders or who have few friends. These people with low self-esteem are susceptible to being persuaded to change their attitudes on issues such as race to match those of the hate group.

Q: What is the bystander effect?

See answer on page 306.

ALTRUISM AND HELPING BEHAVIOR

Some psychologists are interested in **altruism** and **helping behavior**. Research into these topics emerged in part as a result of the case of Kitty Genovese, a woman who was murdered outside of her apartment complex. According to media reports, between 15 and 41 neighbors saw or heard part of the attack, but many did not intervene or contact the police. Psychologists refer to this failure to act as the **bystander effect**. It occurs as a result of **diffusion of responsibility**. Simply put, each person assumes that someone else will (or should) help or call the police.

Altruism can help reduce the tendency toward the bystander effect. Altruism is selfless sacrifice, and it occurs more frequently than it might appear to. Altruism has been explained in terms of an empathic response to the plight of others. People place themselves in the positions of others in distress, and they act toward others as they would like others to act toward them.

ORGANIZATIONAL PSYCHOLOGY

This area of social psychology deals primarily with the workplace. The **equity theory** proposes a view whereby workers evaluate their efforts versus their rewards. Job satisfaction is often based on this concept. **Human factors research** deals with the interaction of person and machine. Many job-related accidents are caused by design flaws in equipment related to the expectancy of the worker. The **Hawthorne effect** indicates that workers being monitored for any reason work more efficiently and productively. This was demonstrated in an experiment that took place in a Western Electric plant. The study was intended to test whether levels of light increased or decreased worker productivity. The outcome, however, showed that worker productivity increased at all levels of light simply because of the presence of the monitors.

AGGRESSION/ANTISOCIAL BEHAVIOR

Antisocial behavior, behavior that is harmful to society or others, can be divided roughly into two kinds: **prejudice** and **aggression**.

Prejudice is a negative attitude toward members of a particular group without evidentiary backing. Quite literally, prejudice is the result of prejudging members of a group. Note that bias and prejudice are not the same. Bias simply refers to a tendency or preference, and biases are not necessarily negative. Whereas prejudice refers to a belief, **discrimination** refers to an action. That is, discrimination involves treating members of a group differently from members of another group.

People tend to categorize things into groups based on common attributes. One theory of this phenomenon is that classification occurs when people compare new stimuli or people to preexisting prototypes in order to determine the group to which the novel stimuli belong. **Stereotypes** are prototypes of people. Although stereotypes can be useful for categorization, they can be harmful by leading us from incorrect assumptions to incorrect conclusions. One assumption we tend to make is **outgroup homogeneity:** that is, that every member of a group other than our own is similar. Another false conclusion is **illusory correlation**, in which we tend to see relationships where they don't actually exist. An example of illusory correlation is noticing that people of a certain ethnic group are apprehended for crimes while ignoring that people of the same ethnic group also do positive things for the society.

Aggression is behavior directed toward another with the intention of causing harm. Aggression occurs for multiple reasons. **Hostile aggression** is emotional and impulsive, and it is typically induced by pain or stress. **Instrumental aggression**, in contrast, is aggression committed to gain something of value. For example, a child pushing another child on a playground to get a prized toy is an example of instrumental aggression.

Biological factors play a role in aggression in all species, including humans. Aggression is sensitive to hormonal fluctuations, particularly fluctuations of the androgen testosterone, which increases aggressive tendencies. Steroid abusers, who use large quantities of synthetic hormones, may experience uncontrollable aggression.

The Contact Hypothesis

Attempts to understand how to reduce prejudice and stereotyping have included the **contact hypothesis**, which posits that groups with stereotypes about each other would lose these stereotypes if the groups were exposed to each other. This hypothesis has not been supported by data, because contact can also serve merely to reinforce existing stereotypes. Factors such as the different social status of the two groups or a lack of common interests may stand in the way of groups reducing stereotypes through contact. These factors are also illustrated in the Robbers Cave experiment, discussed previously.

As **Albert Bandura'**s work has demonstrated, aggression has a strong learned component. If children see adults rewarded for aggression, it is likely that they will learn that aggression is an effective strategy for coping with problems. Additionally, pornography frequently depicts violence toward women. Again, vicarious learning theory tells us that watching such pornographic films can lead to learning that might result in violence at a later time.

Environmental factors also can lead to aggression. Experiencing pain, being surrounded by aggressive behavior, discomfort, and frustration have all been shown to be possible causes of aggressive behavior. Additionally, we have the ability to view the victims of violence as somehow less than human, a process called **dehumanization**. This phenomenon was demonstrated in the famous Stanford Prison Experiment by **Philip Zimbardo,** which tested the effect of **role-playing** in the subject of obedience and conformity. In the experiment, he randomly selected participants to play "jailed" roles while others were randomly selected to act as guards. The prisoners had numbers, not names. The guards wore uniforms and mirrored glasses. Within a short period of time, the participants in each group began to act as though they hated the participants in the other group. The two groups, when stripped of their individual identities, turned to mob identity and violence. In effect, what started out as role-playing became serious identification with the roles. The experiment got out of hand and had to be stopped prematurely to preserve the participants' well-being.

A: The bystander effect asserts that the more people there are witnessing a crime, the less likely any one of them is to help the victim.

Research on reducing aggression has identified some successful techniques. Punishment, which is frequently used as a treatment for aggression, is not particularly effective in reducing aggression. Rather, the observation of nonaggressive models of conflict resolution or the diffusion of aggression with humor or empathy are more effective at disrupting violent behavior.

Study Tip

As you can see in this chapter, Social Psychology is a very broad area of study. It may be fruitful to focus on a few famous experiments that get tested frequently, such as those demonstrating the bystander effect, conformity (Asch), obedience (Milgram), and the effect of role-playing on attitude (Zimbardo).

KEY TERMS

social psychology

Identities and Groups

societies
culture
social identities
personal identities
intersectionality
primary group
secondary group
in-groups
out-groups
ethnocentrism
cultural relativism
assimilation
multiculturalism
culture shock
cultural lag
roles
role conflict
role strain
role exit

Social Institutions

institutionalized discrimination
availability
accessibility
food desert

Group Dynamics

social facilitation
social inhibition
social loafing
group polarization
peer pressure
deindividuation
GRIT (Graduated and
    Reciprocated Initiatives in
    Tension-Reduction)
Irving Janis
groupthink
mindguard

Attribution

dispositional attribution
situational attribution
self-serving bias
fundamental attribution error
self-fulfilling prophecy
Rosenthal Effect

Interpersonal Perception

interpersonal attraction
positive evaluation
shared opinions
mere exposure effect

Conformity, Compliance, Obedience

conformity
Solomon Asch
compliance
reciprocity
foot-in-the-door phenomenon
door-in-the-face phenomenon
inoculation hypothesis
psychological reactance
obedience
Stanley Milgram

Attitudes and Attitude Change

attitudes
cognitive dissonance
Leon Festinger
persuasion
elaboration likelihood model
central route
peripheral route

Altruism and Helping Behavior

altruism
helping behavior
bystander effect
diffusion of responsibility

Organizational Psychology

equity theory
human factors research
Hawthorne effect

Aggression/Antisocial Behavior

antisocial behavior
prejudice
aggression
discrimination
stereotypes
outgroup homogeneity
illusory correlation
hostile aggression
instrumental aggression
contact hypothesis
Albert Bandura
dehumanization
Philip Zimbardo
role-playing

Chapter 18 Drill

See Chapter 19 for answers and explanations.

1. The "fundamental attribution error" phenomenon can best be seen in which of the following examples?

   (A) John blames his failure to get a job on his lack of appropriate skills and ill-preparedness.
   (B) Phyllis doesn't get the lead in the school play and blames her drama teacher for this failure.
   (C) Jane blames herself for forgetting that she has a term paper due in two days.
   (D) Bill doesn't hire John because he believes that John's lateness is a result of John's laziness and lack of respect for the job. In reality, John was late because he got a flat tire on the way to the interview.
   (E) Karen understands that her friend is late because she was caught in rush-hour traffic.

2. In the Asch conformity experiments, which of these was NOT a consistent factor influencing the degree to which conformity to the group answer would be shown by the experimental subject?

   (A) Unanimity of group opinion
   (B) Size of the group
   (C) The subjects' perceptions of their social status compared with that of group members
   (D) Age of the subject
   (E) Gender of the subject

3. Students are randomly designated by experimenters as likely to experience significant jumps in academic test scores in the coming semester, and this designation is communicated to their teachers. When actual test scores are examined at the end of the semester, it is found that these randomly designated students did indeed tend to experience jumps in performance. This phenomenon is known as

   (A) the Hawthorne effect
   (B) the Kandel effect
   (C) cognitive dissonance
   (D) self-fulfilling prophecy
   (E) the Ainsworth effect

4. An old woman carrying a number of packages trips and falls on a busy urban sidewalk and is having trouble getting back up. The fact that few people are likely to stop and offer her help is referred to by social psychologists as an example of

   (A) illusory correlation
   (B) diffusion of responsibility
   (C) cognitive dissonance
   (D) altruistic orientation
   (E) just-world hypothesis

5. Which of the following would illustrate the "foot-in-the-door" technique of facilitating compliance with a request?

   (A) A professional fundraiser, needing to get $10,000 from a foundation, first requests four times that amount, expecting to be turned down so that she can then ask for the lesser amount.
   (B) A teenager, wanting to extend his curfew from 10:00 P.M. to midnight, first asks whether it can be extended to 11:00 P.M. for a specific "special" occasion; he plans to ask for the further extension at a later date after pointing out to his parents that he was able to handle the 11:00 P.M. curfew.
   (C) A mother wishing to get her twins to do their homework each day upon coming home from school and before other activities tells each of them separately that the other twin has agreed to do just that.
   (D) An interviewee desperately needing to get a new job researches the mode of dress in each company he lands an interview with and always shows up at the meeting in that exact mode of dress.
   (E) A teacher wishing all her students to get their assignments in on time promises her class extra grading points for turning them in early.

6. According to Attribution Theory, which of the following is an example of the self-serving bias?

 (A) A man does not have health insurance, but is not worried because he is young and healthy.
 (B) A woman knows a man who does not have insurance. That man gets into a car accident, and medical expenses cause him to lose his home. She wonders why he didn't have insurance.
 (C) A toddler builds a tall tower with blocks and says "Me good!" when she completes the tower. However, she bumps it and it falls down. She frowns and says, "Bad blocks!"
 (D) Yuan's teacher believes he is well prepared for his history exam and offers encouragement to him as he approaches the final. Yuan continues to study hard for the exam and gets an A on the final.
 (E) A hurricane devastates an area of Mississippi and many residents seek grief counseling.

7. A group of five students and a group of three students, all roughly the same size and strength, engage in a game of tug of war. The game is equal for a long while, neither side immediately gaining an advantage. This is most likely an example of

 (A) social loafing
 (B) dehumanization
 (C) conformity
 (D) group polarization
 (E) social facilitation

8. A child tries to get a raise on his weekly allowance. When he first approaches his parents, he asks for $100 per week. His parents scoff and tell him this is out of the question. Then, he asks for $50 per week, and receives the same reply. Finally, he asks for $10 per week and his parents agree. This is an example of

 (A) foot-in-the-door phenomenon
 (B) central route of persuasion
 (C) peripheral route of persuasion
 (D) door-in-the-face phenomenon
 (E) elaboration likelihood model

9. Stanley Milgram's study involving the "teacher," "learner," and "experimenter" tested which of the following principles?

 (A) Conformity
 (B) Dehumanization
 (C) Groupthink
 (D) Role-playing
 (E) Obedience

10. Albert Bandura's famous Bobo Doll experiment shows the power of

 (A) observation
 (B) conformity
 (C) hostile aggression
 (D) dehumanization
 (E) instrumental aggression

REFLECT

Respond to the following questions:

- Which topics in this chapter do you hope to see on the multiple-choice section or essay?

- Which topics in this chapter do you hope not to see on the multiple-choice section or essay?

- Regarding any psychologists mentioned, can you pair the psychologists with their contributions to the field? Did they contribute significant experiments, theories, or both?

- Regarding any theories mentioned, can you distinguish between differing theories well enough to recognize them on the multiple-choice section? Can you distinguish them well enough to write a fluent essay on them?

- Can you define the key terms at the end of the chapter?

- Which parts of the chapter will you review?

- Will you seek further help, outside of this book (such as from a teacher, Princeton Review tutor, or AP Students), on any of the content in this chapter—and, if so, on what content?

Chapter 19
Chapter Drills:
Answers and
Explanations

CHAPTER 1

Understand the Question/Key Words Drill

3. What's a scientist who's into the physical basis of psychological phenomena called?

10. One of the primary tools of the school of structuralism was

18. Binocular cues help you see depth because

35. What type of effect is this: person only remembers words from the beginning and end of a list?

47. The recognition-by-components theory asserts that we categorize objects by breaking them down into their component parts and then

    We break stuff down and then do what?

56. The fact that V. can ignore the crowd is called what?

70. Which of the following was true of Stanley Milgram's studies of obedience?

88. In their discussions of the process of development, the advocates of the importance of nurture in the nature-nurture controversy emphasize which of the following?

    Nurture emphasizes what?

Easy Questions Drill

1. Understand the Question/Key Words: Freud = which perspective?
   Predict the Answer: Psychoanalytic
   Answer: **(B)** Easy enough.

2. Understand the Question/Key Words: When you stop using a drug, you go through what?
   Predict the Answer: Withdrawal
   Answer: **(C)** Be careful not to rush through and accidentally pick another answer.

3. Understand the Question/Key Words: Conditioning: when the dog salivates at what?
   Predict the Answer: The light without the food
   Answer: **(B)** Watch for (A) and (C). Both are wrong, but close enough to trip up someone who is rushing. If you picked (D) or (E), better hit the books.

4. Understand the Question/Key Words: Circle *basic unit* and *nervous system.*

    Predict the Answer: Neuron

    Answer: **(D)** Watch out for the others—(A), (B), and (E) are all parts of the neuron, while (C) is too general—a neuron is a type of cell.

5. Understand the Question/Key Words: Circle *methods of research* and *central to the behaviorist.*

    Predict the Answer: Experimenting

    Answer: **(E)** Again, if you don't know, start reviewing. POE should easily get rid of (B), (C), and (D).

Medium Questions Drill

33. Understand the Question/Key Words: What regulates hunger and thirst?

    Predict the Answer: I'm not sure, but I know what it's not (use POE).

    Answer: **(C)** Using POE, you should have been able to get rid of at least (D) and (E), and most likely (A) (review Chapter 7).

34. Understand the Question/Key Words: Which psychologists were into viewing things as part of a whole?

    Predict the Answer: Don't remember, but I know all the main perspectives well (use POE).

    Answer: **(D)** If you know your perspectives well, you could easily have gotten rid of at least (A), (B), and (C). Cognitive socialist doesn't make sense, so the answer must be (D).

35. Understand the Question/Key Words: What's wrong with the study: Survey comp sci class to find out who in the school has computers.

    Predict the Answer: The sample is biased.

    Answer: **(B)** It's the closest answer to yours. Use POE for the rest.

36. Understand the Question/Key Words: Looking out the window stimulates which two parts of the brain?

    Predict the Answer: Occipital and another (use POE)

    Answer: **(E)** Knowing occipital gets it down to two answer choices. If you don't know it from there, guess and move on (review Chapter 7).

37. Understand the Question/Key Words: Circle *behaviorism* and *true of.*

    Predict the Answer: Experimenting, everything is learned, consequences

    Answer: **(C)** It's the closest answer to yours. Choice (A) is psychodynamic, (B) is a sort of cognitive behaviorism, (D) is wrong, and (E) is silly.

CHAPTER 2

Put It All Together

Our Sample Essay

This is a correlational study because the researchers are trying to see whether or not there is a relationship between two variables: stress and grade-point average. It isn't an experiment because the researchers haven't controlled the students' lives to any degree; for example, regulating how much time they spend studying. Also, there are no experimental or control groups.

An operational definition makes a subjective variable measurable. Here, the operational definition of "stress" is the point value assigned to each student based on the negative life experiences they've had over the preceding two years.

We have been told that the researchers found an inverse relationship between the variables, but we do not know the strength of this relationship. A measure of statistical significance, like a p-value, would give us this information. To have statistical significance in a psychological study, we would want to know that there is less than a five percent chance that the results were due to randomness rather than an actual relationship between the variables.

The failure of the researchers to debrief the students and their parents, as well as the school system, about the outcome of the study prior to its publication is definitely an ethical problem here. Knowing the results of the study could have been extremely valuable to all of the participants and the students, in particular, might have a limited amount of time in which to make the best use of their educational opportunities. If students had known about the potentially adverse effects of these life events on their school performance, they might have been more motivated to seek out counseling or other forms of treatment. They might have sought accommodations from their teachers and schools to account for the negative impact of their experiences. Their parents and other family members and friends might have been made more alert to their problems and assisted them in seeking help. If the school system had known about this connection earlier, it might have offered more services to these students and it might have advised teachers about possible accommodations to implement for students with these issues.

In Selye's general adaptation syndrome, people react to stress in three phases: they respond to the stress with alarm; then they resist its effects; but then, if it goes on for a long time, they can become exhausted. This exhaustion can then lead to physical illness. Here, if the stress these students are experiencing, especially from an accumulation of negative life events, extends over a significant period of time, it could lead to exhaustion and illness. This is another possible explanation for their reduced school performance.

Learned helplessness can occur when someone's efforts to avoid negative outcomes don't work time after time. When that happens, people can learn to be helpless and stop trying to change their situations. Here, students might have been making some effort to avoid bad grades, either by working on their emotions regarding the negative life events or by paying more attention to school work, or both. However, if these efforts keep failing, students might eventually give up.

Maslow's Hierarchy of Needs says that people have priorities in what they are motivated to do. Their key priorities are basic needs and they only turn their attention to higher-level needs once the more basic needs are satisfied. Here, students who have had a number of negative life experiences might make "safety needs," like getting psychological and emotional help, a priority ahead of their educational needs. Education might relate more to "self-esteem" and "self-actualization," which are higher up on Maslow's hierarchy.

CHAPTER 4

Drill 1: Understand the Question/Key Words

7. Psychoanalytic vs. behaviorist: How are they different?

22. What technology should you use to look at different regions of the brain?

39. The somatosensory cortex is the primary area of the

   The circled words mean what?

58. To know what a picture is, the info has to get to which part of the brain?

78. What's it called when someone doesn't give false positives—if there is no sound, there is no report?

89. The lower the p-value of a study, the

   Lower p-value means what?

Drill 2: Predict the Answer

5. How will Thomas learn to make a big meal using the stuff he knows?

   He can link together what he knows (called *chaining*, if you remember that).

22. What does the endocrine system do?

   It secretes hormones into the body.

35. What big thing did Wilhelm Wundt do for psychology?

   He created the first psychology lab in 1879, and he is considered the father of experimental psychology.

45. Why do taste buds need to be able to replace themselves?

   Otherwise, if you burned your mouth, you would lose your sense of taste forever.

72. What technology should you use to study brain waves?

   Electrosomething…(Electroencephalogram or EEG, if you remember)

Drill 3: Using All Three

15. Of the following (variables,) which typically requires a measurement that is more complex?

Understand the Question/Key Words:	Which variable requires more complex measurement?
Predict the Answer:	The complex one—not categorical.
Answer:	**(B) It's continuous.** Choice (A) is out, (C) doesn't make sense, and (D) and (E) aren't those kinds of variables.

35. Which of the following most accurately states the role of the (iris)?

Understand the Question/Key Words:	What does the iris do?
Predict the Answer:	It opens and closes the pupil (controls amount of light, if you remember).
Answer:	**(B) It says to open and close the pupil and regulate the entrance of light.** Choice (A) is way off. Choice (C) describes the lens, (D) is basically just the inside of the eyeball, and (E) is the optic nerve.

42. The nature-nurture controversy concerns

Understand the Question/Key Words:	What is the nature-nurture debate about?
Predict the Answer:	It's about which is more important: genes or environment. Inborn and external processes determine behavior.
Answer:	**(C) It's the closest to yours: "inborn processes" (genes) and "environmental factors" (environment).** Be careful of (A): it is a similar idea, but not the same. Choice (B) is way off base, (D) is a silly trap answer (using the words *natural* and *nurture* to lure you), and (E) doesn't answer the question at all.

66. Prior to the fall of the Berlin wall, East Berlin schools de-emphasized the (individuality) of the student. As a result, many of the children from those schools tend to have a(n)

Understand the Question/Key Words:	What happens if kids are taught to not be individuals?
Predict the Answer:	They depend on others for their self-identity and self-esteem.
Answer:	**(D) They have an external locus of control—looking to others for their self-esteem and self-identity.** Choices (A) and (B) are not close to yours (no optimism, pessimism). Choice (C) is the opposite of what you want, and (E) is just filler.

85. A prototypic example of a category is called a(n)

Understand the Question/Key Words:	A major example of something is called what?
Predict the Answer:	I don't know—a major example.
Answer:	**(E) Exemplar—a major example.** Choice (A) does not mean a major example. Choice (B) is only a feature, not an example of the whole category. Choice (C) is weak. Don't pick (D)! It's a verbal trap.

Drill 4: Essay Drill

Here is our Work It, Chart It, Count It, and Sketch It:

1. One of the major approaches to learning is classical conditioning.

    A. Explain the process of classical conditioning, defining and illustrating all necessary terms. Show how classical conditioning could be used to

    (1) Condition a monkey to "appreciate" only the works of certain artists

    (2) Teach a group of students a mathematical concept

D and I	Do It
UCS, CS, UCR, CR, and so on. Use Pavlov ex. and create another.	Reward for id-ing Monet, none for Munch. Teach writing out proofs by rewarding through examples.

    B. Explain how both extinction and spontaneous recovery transpire. Use one of the above examples to illustrate.

Define	Illustrate How
extinction—loss of learning because of no reinforcement	Substitute teacher so no reward for detailed proofs. Students stop.
Spon rec.—comes back instantly with reward	Return of teacher, spontaneous rec.

```
Opening
4 points
1.            CS                    Pavlov example
2.            UCS
3.            CR
4.            UCR
```

```
2 points:     Monkeys
5.            Use the right terms
6.            Set up the conditioning
```

```
2 points:     Math class
7.            Use the right terms
8.            Set up the conditioning
```

```
2 points:
9.            Define Extinction and Spontaneous recovery
10.           Use class example with substitute teacher
Closing
```

Drill 5: POE

4. **B**   Can obese people have *fewer* fat cells than average-weight people?

27. **B**   Your key word from the question is "connectionist approaches." Would connectionists think things occurred in individual segments or in a bunch of networks simultaneously?

47. **A**   Your key word is "chunking." Even if you don't remember this memory technique, (A) sounds more like chunking than (B).

85. **C**   Your key word is "person-centered psychotherapy." Even without that clue, suppressing negative feelings of a client or using a didactic approach are not typically the chosen methods of most psychotherapists.

92. **B**   Even without a clue, it's understood in the field of psychology that counselors do not do either (A) or (C) for clients.

CHAPTER 5 DRILL

1. **D** A cognitive psychologist is primarily interested in thought processes and products, and (D), involving word association, is most directly connected to such processes and products. Choice (A) is more the province of biological psychologists, (B) that of humanistic psychotherapists, (C) that of clinical psychotherapists or behaviorists, and (E) that of developmental psychologists.

2. **C** The idea of *tabula rasa* is most closely associated with the philosopher John Locke. Choice (A), David Hume, was a philosopher who speculated on the nature of knowledge and perception; (B), Charles Darwin, is more closely identified with the theory of natural selection and evolution of species; (D), Sigmund Freud, was the founder of psychoanalytic theory; and (E), Erich Fromm, was one of the theorists influenced by Freud.

3. **B** The concept of dualism refers to the division of the world and all things in it into two parts: body and spirit. Choice (C) refers to two ways of conceptualizing the structure and function of the mind and (E) to two different types of experimental variables.

4. **D** Humanistic psychologists are primarily concerned with the impact of free will on behavior. Choice (A), childhood experiences, are emphasized in the psychoanalytic approach. Choice (B), biological predispositions, refers to either the biological/medical model or the behavioral-genetics approach. The cognitive approach focuses on how maladaptive thoughts, (C), can influence behavior, and the social-cognitive approach centers on the interaction of cultural experiences, (E), and behavior.

5. **C** Proponents of the psychoanalytic or psychodynamic approach believe that the source of all current trauma can be traced back to childhood through repressed memories. Choice (A), the cognitive approach, stresses the importance of thought processes and schemas in evaluating behaviors. Choice (B), behaviorists, believe in the power of learning and other environmental influences on behavior. Choice (D), the sociocultural perspective, focuses instead on individuals' cultures and how those shape them into who they are; (E), the medical/biological approach, seeks physiological answers in brain and body chemistry to explain behavior.

6. **B** Circle the key words *behavior* and *learned*. These words indicate that the answer is associated with behaviorism. The person synonymous with behaviorism is B.F. Skinner, (B).

7. **E** First, eliminate anything that is not a defense mechanism: self-actualization, (B), and consciousness, (D). Because denial is a state that dismisses an event as unimportant or trivial, but does not involve the individual not remembering what happened, you can eliminate (A). Projection is placing one's problems onto someone else's actions or emotions. This is not the case in this situation, so cross out (C). The answer choice left is repression, (E), the correct answer; repression is a defense mechanism in which the subconscious keeps painful memories from surfacing.

8. **C** Carl Rogers is one of the major players in the humanistic approach to psychology, so the correct answer is (C). He coined the term *unconditional positive regard*, (A), meaning a therapist's proper regard toward his patients, always viewing them in a positive light. However, this is not a psychological approach. Cognitive psychology is focused on cognition and thought processes. While maladaptive thoughts are part of treating the whole person, that is not the only component of what makes up a person, so eliminate (B). The sociocultural components of a person, (D), are

also another aspect of an individual's experience, but Carl Rogers sought to treat the individual rather than systemic problems. Behaviorism, (E), is associated with B.F. Skinner.

9. **E** According to Maslow's hierarchy of needs, the physiological needs of a person, such as the needs for food and water, are at the base of the pyramid. Maslow suggested that if a person cannot have these basic needs satisfied, it is much more difficult to accomplish a sense of belonging, esteem, and potentially self-actualization.

10. **B** Behavioral genetics often involves the study of identical twins separated at birth. This allows researchers to examine the contributions of genetics versus those of environment in the development of various traits.

CHAPTER 6 DRILL

1. **D** By definition, a double-blind experimental design is one in which neither the researchers nor the experimental subjects know whether the subjects have been assigned to an experimental group or a control group; this is done to minimize the chance that either the researchers will influence the results through their own expectations or the subjects will influence the results by trying to act in accordance with what is thought to be desired. Choice (B) describes a single-blind experimental design; (E) is completely nonsensical.

2. **B** In a normal statistical curve, about 68 percent of all scores will fall within one standard deviation of the mean; this includes scores both above and below the mean. Choice (A) is the percentage that would occur between the mean and one standard deviation above or below it only; (C) is the percentage that would occur within two standard deviations of the mean.

3. **B** This is the definition of a Type II error—concluding there is no difference when in fact there is a difference. Choice (A) is the definition of a Type I error. Choice (E) is an erroneous conclusion drawn when, in fact, a Type I error has been made.

4. **C** All of the other answers are standard tenets for designing and carrying out ethically acceptable research. Choice (C) has nothing to do with ethics, though it would not be very good for the research design in another way—if both the subjects and the researchers knew which of the former would be part of the experimental group, there would be a great likelihood of expectancy effects confounding the study.

5. **B** A correlation of -0.84 implies that as one variable increases, the other is likely to decrease—positive correlations indicate that two variables vary directly, while negative correlations indicate that two variables vary inversely. Remember the famous research statement, "correlation does not imply causation," and you'll know that neither (D) nor (E) is correct.

6. **C** The behavior of the subjects is measured here as the outcome of the study. The control and independent variables in this study are the violent and nonviolent video games and the behavior supposedly "depends" on which games were played. Therefore, the behavior of the subjects is the dependent variable, (C). Of course, there are most likely some confounding variables and

possibly some sampling bias in this study, but the behavior [...] [...] variable.

7. **D**   External validity measures the real-life applicability of an [...] validity measure how well the experiment itself is designed [...] outside of the experiment. Reliability measures whether [...] among raters.

8. **D**   Circle the key words here: *different regions* and *socioec[...]* [...] at different backgrounds and regions of the country, resea[...] are [...] cross-sectional population. Longitudinal studies measure the same sub[...] over a long period of time, and there is no lapse in time here, so eliminate (A). There is not enoug[...] [...] about the design of this study to know whether it is experimental or not (though it's most likely correlational), so eliminate (B) and (C), as well. Choice (E), a case study, studies only one subject or a few subjects at a time. This is not true of this study, so the correct answer is (D).

9. **E**   As you most likely noticed, there are many things wrong with this method of procuring subjects for a study. Eliminate (A) because there is a pre-screening bias with weight-loss studies. People who respond to this ad most likely already want to or are trying to lose weight. The answer cannot be (B) because the people inquiring about the ad have control over whether they participate in the study, so they are self-selecting. The selection bias is also present here because these ads are only in New York City buses and subways. Many people visit New York City, but this area is not representative of the entire country. Therefore, eliminate (C). The healthy user bias may or may not be as large of a factor here. However, potential subjects who already engage in a healthy lifestyle or are in the process of losing weight can make this supplement look more effective than unhealthy subjects can. Eliminate (D). Courtesy bias applies to people answering surveys who respond in ways that they think are more socially or politically correct than their true responses. Since this is a study and does not involve a survey, the correct answer is (E).

10. **A**   A normal bell curve has most of the data around the middle of the graph, creating a symmetrical bell shape. Since this is not the case, eliminate (C). If the peak of a bell curve is not centered but rather in the lower end of the chart, it is called a positive skew. If the curve sits to the right of the graph's center, it is a negative skew. The curve described here is a positive skew, since many subjects scored low totals. The correct answer is (A).

CHAPTER 7 DRILL

1. **B**   Broca's area, which is on the left side of the frontal lobe of the cortex, controls the muscles of speech. Choice (A), repetition of the speech of others, is often referred to as echolalia. Choice (C), the loss of the ability to visually integrate information, or prosopagnosia, is often the result of damage to the occipital lobe. Choice (D), the loss of the ability to comprehend speech, refers to damage in the Wernicke's area of the temporal lobe, and (E), the inability to solve verbal problems, stems from some kind of damage to the left hemisphere.

drites are attached to the cell body, and their purpose is to receive signals and information other neurons, usually by receiving neurotransmitters; these signals will determine whether not the neuron will "fire." Choice (A) is the function of the terminal buttons, (B) is that of the myelin sheaths, (C) is that of the cell body, and (E) is that of the axon hillock.

The cerebellum is the part of the brain most involved with maintaining balance and muscular strength and tone. Choice (A) is the part of the brain that controls heart rate, swallowing, breathing, and digestion; (B) is the part, in most people, that is specialized for spatial and intuitive processing; (D) is involved in processing visual input; and (E) is the brain's primary relay station for sensory information.

4. **C** GABA is the neurotransmitter most associated with inhibitory neural processes; the others generally act to excite neurons further.

5. **A** The phenotype is the actual observable trait or behavior that results from a specific genetic combination. Due to dominant and recessive trait expressions, the phenotype can represent more than one specific possible genotype, or genetic contribution, which (E) is talking about. Choice (C) is the definition of a gene itself.

6. **C** The hypothalamus, part of the limbic system, controls motivated behaviors such as hunger, thirst, and sex. Choice (A), the thalamus, routes sensory information to the sensory areas of the brain; (B), the pons, connects the lower brain regions with the higher functioning areas of the brain. Choice (D), the amygdala, controls fear and aggression via the limbic system, and (E), the association areas of the brain, match existing information with incoming information already stored in the brain.

7. **B** Myelin is an insulating sheath wrapped around the axons of neurons. White matter in the central nervous system is composed of myelinated axons; thus, a reduction in myelination would result in a decrease in white matter and neuronal insulation—(A) and (E), as symptoms, can be eliminated. Gaps in the myelin sheath (called nodes of Ranvier) allow depolarization of the axon and conduction of neuronal signals along the length of the axon. Myelination speeds the movement of the action potential along the length of the axon in a process called saltatory conduction. Choice (C) would be a symptom and can be eliminated; a reduction in myelination would decrease (not increase) saltatory conduction (which makes (B) the correct answer choice). This would decrease sensation, as sensory information from the peripheral nervous system would be hindered from reaching the central nervous system. Choice (D) is a symptom and can be eliminated.

8. **D** The cerebellum, located behind the pons and below the cerebrum, receives input from the primary motor cortex in the forebrain and coordinates complex motor function, making (D) correct. The frontal lobes contain the primary motor cortices, which are responsible for initiating movement, but do not coordinate complex motor functions, so (A) is wrong. The occipital lobes are responsible for vision, ruling out (B), and the reticular activating system is responsible for arousal and wakefulness, which eliminates (C). The temporal lobes are involved in processing sensory input related to visual memories, language comprehension, and emotion, so it's not (E).

9. **D** The pons is located below the midbrain and above the medulla oblongata, and it connects the brain stem and the cerebellum. Along with the medulla, the pons controls some autonomic functions and plays a role in equilibrium and posture, but it is not associated with the experience of emotion, so (D) is correct. The amygdala, located in the temporal lobe, is part of the limbic system, and it is responsible for processing information about emotion, which means that (A) and (B), which are associated with emotion, can be eliminated. The amygdala and temporal lobe both send projections associated with the experience and regulation of emotional expression to the prefrontal cortices of the frontal lobe, and so (E) can be ruled out. The hypothalamus links the nervous system to the endocrine system, and it also plays a role in emotion, which allows (C) to be cut.

CHAPTER 8 DRILL

1. **B** The specific pattern of brain waves known as sleep spindles is characteristic of stage 2 sleep, and it is associated with a relaxation of the skeletal musculature. Stage 1 sleep and REM sleep characteristically show the smaller, less regular theta waves, and stages 3 and 4 sleep are both more likely to show the longer, slower delta waves.

2. **C** Though the natural day/night cycle of humans and most other organisms matches the 24-hour cycle of the Earth and the Sun, if all cues (such as sunshine) are removed, humans and many other organisms tend to follow a free-running rhythm that cycles approximately every 25 hours, which can be demonstrated through varying body temperature and hormonal levels.

3. **E** There is no evidence that there is any distinction between what kinds of concerns give rise to nightmares versus night terrors. The hypothesis that one of the functions of dreams is to express conscious or unconscious concerns has its roots in Freudian or psychoanalytic theory, and it is only one of a number of competing theories of dream function, none of which has yet proven conclusive. Choices (A), (B), (C), and (D) all represent characteristic differences between nightmares and night terrors.

4. **E** Cocaine is a strong stimulant, not a narcotic. Narcotics, such as those mentioned in (A), (B), (C), and (D), are derived originally from the opium poppy and tend to have analgesic and relaxation effects that depress the central nervous system.

5. **A** Alcohol is a depressant that inhibits neural activity, so eliminate (D). GABA receptors in the central nervous system respond to GABA, an inhibitory neurotransmitter. Alcohol acts on GABA receptors, inhibiting neuronal signaling. Chronic alcohol consumption causes a down-regulation of GABA receptors; therefore, once the artificial depressant (alcohol) is removed from the system, the CNS no longer has an inhibitory influence and excito-neurotoxicity occurs, which can result in seizures and tremors, so (A) is the answer. Alcohol is a depressant and does not stimulate the autonomic nervous system, so (B) cannot be correct. While alcohol consumption does promote dopamine release in the nucleus accumbens (which stimulates the reward pathway in the brain and helps to explain why alcohol is addictive), and cessation of alcohol consumption would surely lead to a decrease in dopamine, this does not explain the physical symptoms of withdrawal described in

the question stem, ruling out (C). While alcohol is a depressant, decreasing GABA activity would be excitatory, not inhibitory. Furthermore, this explanation would not account for the symptoms seen in alcohol withdrawal, and so (E) can be eliminated.

6. **B**   The doctor needs to ask more questions before diagnosing the patient, but their first thought should be insomnia or sleep apnea. None of the other terms listed in the answer choices constitutes periods of wakefulness during the night. Narcolepsy is overwhelming periods of sleep needed during the day, so eliminate (A). Somnambulism and night terrors happen during sleep, so even though the person seems to be active, they would not report being awake, eliminating (C) and (E). Paradoxical sleep occurs during dreaming, so eliminate (D). The correct answer is (B), sleep apnea.

7. **C**   The question does not mention that the woman is in any state of psychological dependence or addiction, so eliminate (A) and (B). Her body has grown tolerant to the drug, as shown by her dosage being increased twice, but that is not the reason for this increase in her blood pressure. Blood pressure medications are different from stimulants. You can cross out (D) and (E). The clear reason for this increase is that she forgets to take her medication, and the physical symptom that results is an example of physical dependence, (C).

8. **E**   Paradoxical sleep occurs during dreaming. The mind is active, but the paradox is that the body remains almost still. REM sleep represents this sleep state.

9. **A**   Stages 3 and 4 are the deepest stages of sleep and, over the course of the night, the cycles contain less and less of them until the cycles contain mostly REM. The REM period can last up to approximately an hour toward the morning hours. The correct answer is (A).

CHAPTER 9 DRILL

1. **C**   If the individual hits the button to indicate that he has seen a particular stimulus when it was not present, this is called a false alarm.

2. **B**   Choice (B) is the only one that contains the five basic taste sensations—bitter, salty, sweet, sour, and umami; relative combinations of these result in the full range of taste sensations. Choice (C) refers to types of touch sensations and (D) to the five basic food groups!

3. **D**   Know your retinal receptor cells; the rods are sensitive to low light conditions and to movement, while the cones are responsible for color vision and work best at higher illumination levels. Choice (A) contains two other types of cells found in the retina, but not the ones that make the distinction noted here. The same is true of the ganglion cells, (B), and osmoreceptors sense thirst, anyway. In (E), mechanoreceptors sense physical touch and ossicles are bones of the middle ear.

4. **C**   Among the Gestalt principles of perception, continuity refers to our tendency to perceive fluid or continuous forms preferentially, rather than jagged or irregular ones—we would tend to see an image as two lines that cross at a point, rather than as two angles sharing a vertex. Choices (A) and

(D) are two other Gestalt perceptual principles—proximity and similarity, respectively, and (E) refers to binocular disparity, a depth perception cue.

5. **A** Weber's law relates to the issue of thresholds in sensation and perception. The law states that the greater the magnitude of the stimuli, the larger the differences must be if we are to distinguish among the stimuli. Recognition of an imperceptible amount of perfume, (B), relates to the issue of absolute threshold. People not attending to more than one stimulus at a time, (C), focuses on selective attention. The ability to tell the difference between 20- and 100-watt bulbs 50 percent of the time, (D), refers again to the absolute threshold. All auditory stimuli sounding the same above a certain frequency, (E), negates frequency theory in audition.

6. **B** The tympanic membrane (also known as the eardrum), located in the middle ear, generates vibrations that match the sound waves striking it, so (B) is correct. Vibrations generated in the tympanic membrane pass through three small bones—the malleus (hammer), the incus (anvil), and the stapes (stirrup); these bones magnify the incoming vibrations by focusing them onto a structure known as the oval window, which means that (D) and (E) are wrong. Once the vibrations pass through the oval window, they enter the cochlea, a fluid-filled spiral structure in the inner ear, so (C) can be eliminated. The base of the cochlea is lined with a long, fluid-filled duct known as the basilar membrane, which rules out (A).

7. **C** The axons of ganglion cells in the retina make up the optic nerve, which carries visual information to the brain, so (C) is correct. Photoreceptors such as rods and cones are specialized cells in the retina that transduce light energy into nerve cell activity and synapse with bipolar cells, but none of those are a part of the optic nerve, which rules out (A), (B), and (E). The fovea is the area of highest visual acuity and contains a high concentration of cones, which are a type of photoreceptor and do not comprise the optic nerve, thereby eliminating (D).

8. **A** Gestalt psychology proposes that humans tend to see objects in their entirety, and our visual processing systems and brain will superimpose a larger organization or structure that makes holistic sense. The "shapes" are technically composed of a series of unconnected lines, but according to Gestalt psychologists, humans are more likely to use both top-down and bottom-up processing to perceive them as a complete circle or a complete rectangle, so (A) is the answer. Bottom-up processing begins with the sensory receptors and works up to the complex integration of information occurring in the brain; while bottom-up processing is a requirement of perceiving the lines in the figure, it does not explain why we see two shapes instead of perceiving many unconnected lines, which makes (B) incorrect. Parallel processing refers to the brain's capability to process multiple sensory inputs simultaneously, and Weber's law explains that the greater the magnitude of the stimuli, the larger the difference must be for their difference to be perceptible; neither accounts for the phenomenon described in the question stem, and so (C) and (D) are both wrong. Summation, also referred to as frequency summation, is related to neuronal signal conduction, when the combined polysynaptic potential of multiple excitatory and inhibitory neurotransmitters determines whether or not an action potential is generated, thereby eliminating (E).

9. **D**   Oddly enough, there is not a triangle drawn, but Claire reports seeing a triangle because people have a natural tendency to want to see closed figures as opposed to incomplete figures. This supports the law of closure. She could have said she sees three incomplete concentric discs, but her mind configured it in a way that organizes the information as closed, complete figures.

10. **B**   When Laretta sits down in class and eventually forgets about the odor, this is known as habituation. However, when the stimulus is removed and then re-presented (e.g., when she leaves the class and returns to notice the smell again), this is known as dishabituation. The correct answer is (B).

11. **B**   Subliminal information is presented just below the threshold. This information is often referred to as imperceptible, yet it is believed to influence behavior. Choice (A), immediate recognition of the stimuli, refers to the absolute threshold. Choice (C) mentions the tip-of-the-tongue phenomenon, which is another kind of preconscious processing, but the inability of a stimulus to be on the tip of the tongue would not be an indication of its presence. There is no evidence that there is proactive interference or that recall of these stimuli is slower in a matched-pairs trial, so eliminate (D) and (E).

CHAPTER 10 DRILL

1. **B**   The fact that the dog is now exhibiting a fear response to any moving, wheeled vehicle represents a stimulus generalization. Choice (A) is the opposite process—if the dog was originally struck by a blue van of a certain make, for example, and did not show a fear response to any vehicle but that type of blue van. Choice (C) refers to the process whereby a conditioned response was made extinct by removing a conditioned stimulus, but might be elicited by a presentation of that stimulus at a later time. Choice (D), backward conditioning, occurs when an unconditioned stimulus is presented before a conditioned one and has nothing to do with this situation.

2. **D**   Second-order conditioning occurs when a previously conditioned stimulus—originally neutral, but now response-eliciting—acts as an unconditioned stimulus and is paired with a new neutral stimulus to be conditioned; eventually, this second stimulus is successful at eliciting a conditioned response. In (D), the rabbit was conditioned to fear the musical tone; then the musical tone was paired with a flashed light; and eventually the flashed light elicited fear even in the absence of the tone. Choice (A) is an example of conditioned taste aversion; (B) is a simple classic conditioning paradigm; (C) is stimulus generalization; and (E), which may be a result of social learning, does not apply to this situation.

3. **C**   A variable-ratio reinforcement schedule is one in which the ratio of responses to reward is variable and therefore unpredictable. Although the original conditioning may take longer, the response is quite resistant to extinction. In a fixed-ratio schedule (A), rewards always come after a certain number of correct responses; learning is quick but so is extinction, as it is easy to determine when the reinforcement schedule is no longer operative. This can also be said for (E), a continuous schedule. Choice (B), fixed-interval schedules, with rewards presented after a set time period, have a

similar learning/extinction profile to fixed-ratio schedules. Choice (D), variable-interval schedules, with rewards presented at variable time periods, are more resistant to extinction than fixed-interval schedules but not as resistant as variable-ratio schedules.

4. **A** The number of neurons does not increase with learning; in fact, the number of neurons is at its highest for most animals at birth—neurons do not reproduce under normal circumstances. However, they do grow in size and number of connections, alter the strength of already existing connections, and produce higher levels of neurotransmitters in response to learning. Neurons that wire together, fire together.

5. **A** Though there are many social or observational learning situations that involve rewards or punishments, Bandura's experiments showed that such learning can occur even if there were no rewards or punishments—that is, consequences—to the observed behaviors. According to Bandura, attention to the behavior, retention of it, the ability to reproduce it, and the motivation to reproduce it at some point are what is necessary for observational learning.

6. **B** Operant conditioning, (B), is accomplished when someone receives a reward after performing a task; after the person has performed the task and received the reward enough times, they will perform the task without the reward, as occurs here. Choice (A), vicarious reinforcement, involves watching another person receive a reward for their behavior; there is no mention of Jay being motived by other people getting rewarded. Choice (C), an innate behavior, is one that does not need to be conditioned and therefore not what is being described in the question stem. Choice (D), classical conditioning, is accomplished by pairing two stimuli, one that is neutral with another that is unconditioned. Over time, the neutral stimulus becomes the conditioned stimulus. Because the question is not describing the pairing of two stimuli, nor is a stimulus presented before the behavior, classical conditioning does not explain the behavior described in the question stem. Choice (E), observational learning, involves the observation of a behavior or set of behaviors and a subsequent modification of behavior on the part of the observer in modeling what they've seen.

7. **B** Negative reinforcement occurs when an unpleasant stimulus is removed. Remember, negative is equivalent to taking something away from a situation and positive is equivalent to adding something in reinforcement terms. Choice (A) describes negative punishment, since Stephanie's weekend privileges are revoked for the next weekend. Choice (B) works because the negative stimulus, taking out the trash, is removed in order to reinforce a behavior. In (C), Ben receives positive reinforcement, because he is rewarded with a pleasant stimulus for having done good work on his project. Choice (D) is another example of negative punishment because the dog does an undesirable behavior and the owner removes himself from contact. Choice (E) introduces something unpleasant to the situation, an example of positive punishment. The correct answer is (B).

8. **B** The care team does not want the patient to develop a taste aversion to food staples or favorite foods. The unconditioned stimulus in this case would be the chemotherapy, but the patient would likely associate the foods (a neutral stimulus) with the nausea. While stimulus generalization is part of the concept of taste aversion, the care team is trying to keep the association from occurring in the first place, not to keep it from becoming generalized before the connection is in place.

9. **A** When dealing with periods of time, always think of "interval" to decipher reinforcement schedules. For number of instances, think "ratio." In this scenario, the mail comes consistently at the same time every day, so it must be an interval schedule, eliminating (C) and (D). Choice (E) is incorrect because continual reinforcement is a reward for every single instance, and she doesn't receive mail every time she goes to the mailbox. Since the time interval between mail deliveries is consistent, this is a fixed-interval schedule. The correct answer is (A).

10. **D** The process of teaching a skill through gradually molding specific behavior is called shaping, (D). Kevin rewards the dog for accomplishing intermediate steps along the way, which shapes Muka's behavior to learn a new trick.

CHAPTER 11 DRILL

1. **B** Visual sensory memory is referred to as *iconic*, and auditory sensory memory is called *echoic*. Iconic memory has a shorter duration than echoic memory, making (A) inaccurate. Visual and auditory memory have approximately the same capacity before encoding, so eliminate (C). The phone number read out loud (echoic) should have a longer duration than visually presented information, so eliminate (D). Choice (E) is wrong because if both auditory and visual information are presented at the same time, auditory information is more likely to be transferred to long-term memory.

2. **D** The principle of context-dependent memory states that information is more likely to be recalled if the attempt to retrieve it occurs in a situation similar to the situation in which it was first encoded. Choice (A) refers to the process of new information pushing old information out of short-term memory; (B) to the grouping of items of information in order to better hold them in short-term memory; (C) to organizing short-term memory items in order to transfer them to long-term memory; and (E) to the memory for motor skills and habits.

3. **E** Prosody is the term given to the tones and inflections added to language that elaborate meaning with no word alterations. Choice (A), syntax, refers to the set of rules in a language for arranging words into sentences; (B), grammar, is the set of rules by which language is constructed, which includes syntax and semantics; (C) indicates the study of the smallest units of speech sounds in a language that are still distinct from one another; and (D) refers to the meanings of chosen words, not their expressed tone.

4. **C** Telegraphic speech is a common occurrence in toddlers who are combining words for the first time; it consists of two- or three-word utterances that are composed mostly of salient nouns, verbs, and adjectives with an absence of articles, conjunctions, and prepositions, and a limited use of pronouns. All of the answers except (C) involve two- or three-word utterances that fit that definition; (C) is an example of a holophrase—a single-word utterance of younger children that has a broad meaning.

5. **A** Divergent thinking is the name we give to the problem-solving process used when there are many possible solutions. In contrast, (B) is the process used when the problem has only one solution, such as is the case with most math problems. The intelligence quotient, (C), was originally conceived of as

a ratio of mental age over chronological age, multiplied by 100; this was determined by comparing performance to that of others over a range of problem-solving tasks, which might involve both divergent and convergent abilities.

6. **C**   This type of knowledge is a fact to be recalled, so it must be part of the explicit memory. Eliminate (A), (B), and (E). Episodic memory refers to memories the person has experienced, and semantic memory is the memory of facts and figures (remember, semantic is meaning-making). No one living today was around to experience Abraham Lincoln's presidency, so it cannot be episodic. The fact is, instead, semantic. The correct answer is (C).

7. **A**   Stefano's knowledge of Spanish is interfering with his effort to speak German. In other words, his prior knowledge is hindering his ability to retain new knowledge, so this is an example of proactive interference.

8. **B**   Ben cannot get past this physics problem because he is approaching it the same way instead of thinking outside the box. This is known as a mental set, (B). Functional fixedness is a type of mental set; however, it is specifically concerning an object's intended use versus its other creative uses, so eliminate (A). A representativeness heuristic is using a prototypical representation of an image or concept to judge a particular case, so eliminate (C), and insight learning refers to having a sudden understanding of a problem or a potential strategy for solving a problem. The question does not state that Ben has solved the problem, so eliminate (D). Framing involves either false memories or leading questions, so eliminate (E), as well. The correct answer is (B).

9. **A**   A representativeness heuristic is using a prototypical representation to judge a particular case. The mental image of a rose is an example of this, so (A) is the correct answer. Choice (B) is an example of an availability heuristic, which pulls upon readily available images or memories, such as seeing advertisements recently. Choice (C) shows someone who is not limited by functional fixedness and thus is able to solve her dilemma. Choice (D) describes a confirmation bias, and (E) describes hindsight bias.

10. **E**   Sheldon is relating new knowledge to something he already understands. Functional fixedness refers to only using an object for its intended use, so (A) cannot be the answer. Choice (B) is more related to grouping pieces of information, and there is no evidence of this in the question. Maintenance rehearsal is related to short-term memory only and state-dependent memory depends on the mental state a person is in when learning the information. Choices (C) and (D) can be eliminated. The self-referential effect works here because Sheldon is relating the new information to something he is familiar with. This is (E).

CHAPTER 12 DRILL

1. **A**   Content validity is a measure of the degree to which material on the test is balanced and is measuring what it is said to measure. Choice (B) refers to another type of validity—predictive validity. Choices (C), (D), and (E) refer not to measures of test validity, but to measures of test reliability.

2. **B**   A projective test is one in which ambiguous stimuli, which are open to various kinds of interpretation, are presented, in contrast to the more common inventory-type tests in which participants answer a standard series of questions. The Thematic Apperception Test (TAT) is a well-known projective test; it involves a series of pictures of people in ambiguous relationships with other people, and the respondent's task is to generate a story for each picture, including what led up to the scene in the picture, what is happening now, and what might occur next. All of the other choices are inventory-style tests in which participants are faced with standardized answer choices.

3. **B**   IQ scores over a population are distributed along a normal curve, with the mean, median, and modal scores at 100 and a standard deviation of roughly 15 to 16 points; therefore, a score of 85 would be located approximately one standard deviation below the mean. Choice (E) is deceptive, as the original definition of IQ as mental age divided by physical age multiplied by 100 makes it attractive, but physical age would have no effect on where an IQ score is located relative to established means, medians, modes, or standard deviations.

4. **A**   Test standardization is used to set the norms for a given population of subjects; these norms can then be used to compare the test results of groups or individuals with specific characteristics to the whole population. In order to set these norms, the test is administered to a (usually fairly large) standardization sample which, as much as is feasible, possesses characteristics reflective of the entire population. Choice (C) actually refers to the measurement of validity, (D) is more of a way of ensuring reliability on tests where scoring is not computerized, and (E) has more to do with the format of the test than the population.

5. **E**   Howard Gardner's theory of multiple intelligences—not just verbal and mathematical, the dimensions measured by most intelligence tests—posits that there are measurable intelligences in all of the dimensions listed except for (E), which is a dimension added by two other theorists, Peter Salovey and John Mayer.

6. **D**   Reliability measures how consistent the results will be if the same subject takes the test multiple times. Choice (A) calls into question current versus noncurrent practices, while (B) describes validity instead. Choice (C) should be true of any experiment. Choice (E) describes generalizability. The correct answer is (D).

7. **B**   A true/false or other type of multiple-choice test is one that does not allow for much creativity, so you can eliminate (A). Since there is a very clear-cut answer to each question through multiple-choice responses, the correct answer is (B), inventory-type test. The test could be about intelligence, environment, or hereditary information, but none of these are the name for a multiple-choice test, eliminating (C), (D) and (E).

8. **A**   There are several components to making sure the administration of a test is done ethically, but the key component is that the subjects must be protected under confidentiality no matter what, (A). Choice (B) refers to a concern of studies, not tests; usually tests don't involve deception unless it has to do with how they are used within a study. Double-blind design is a characteristic of experiments, not tests, and it does not guarantee an ethical study (perhaps it is testing a drug that is not yet safe for human consumption), so eliminate (C). Validity and generalization have nothing to do with ethics, but rather effectiveness in what a test intends to measure internally and in a general population. Methodology is not included in these two terms, so eliminate (D) and (E). The correct answer is (A).

CHAPTER 13 DRILL

1. **D**   The Moro reflex in newborns is the startle response that involves the splaying of limbs in response to a falling sensation. Choice (A) is the neonatal reflex of grabbing anything placed in the hand; (B), the Babinski reflex, is produced when stroking the bottom of the neonate's foot results in a splaying out of the toes; and (E) is the reflex that causes a newborn to turn in the direction of a touch on the cheek. While the orienting reflex, (C), may be elicited by a loud noise, it occurs whenever there is any other sudden change in the environment, as well.

2. **B**   The cognitive theory of Vygotsky stresses social and environmental, not just biological/maturational, factors as critical to development; he proposed the concept of a zone of proximal development, which is the range between the developed level of ability a child displays and the potential, or latent, level of ability a child is actually capable of. He further theorized that this latent level is hard to elicit due to a lack of optimal environmental circumstances. Choices (A), Jean Piaget, and (D), Sigmund Freud, created alternate theories of development; (C), Leon Festinger, is most closely identified with the theory of cognitive dissonance (see Chapter 18) and (E), Julian Rotter, with the concept of locus of control (Chapter 15).

3. **A**   Erik Erikson's psychosocial theory of development describes a series of "conflicts" or "tasks" at each stage of life, from infancy to old age. In his theory, the successful resolution of each developmental task results in the development of a certain ability or belief, which serves as the foundation for the resolution of the next "task." The developmental task for school-age children is termed "industry vs. inferiority," and the resolution of this stage produces a sense of competence in one's own efforts and work. Choice (B) is the resolution of the task of early adulthood—"intimacy vs. isolation"; (C) is the resolution of the task of infancy—"trust vs. mistrust"; (D) is the resolution of the task of toddlerhood—"autonomy vs. shame/doubt"; and (E) is the resolution of the task of adolescence— "identity vs. role confusion."

4. **B**   According to the developmental theory of Jean Piaget, a child of about five would generally be at the preoperational stage, characterized by both animism—the belief that all things are alive—and egocentrism—the ability to see the world only from one's own point of view. Choices (A), (C), and (D) are other stages of Piaget's developmental model. Choice (E) is a developmental stage in Sigmund Freud's theory.

5. **E** The theory of moral development, elaborated by Lawrence Kohlberg, divides such development into three levels—preconventional, conventional, and postconventional—each subdivided into two stages. At the first stage of preconventional morality, generally the first stage young children progress through, moral concerns are primarily motivated by the need to avoid punishment and to receive rewards. Choice (A) characterizes the next stage of the preconventional level; (B) is the first stage of the conventional level; and (C) is the first stage of the postconventional level. Choice (D) refers to the belief that everybody gets what they deserve, which is not one of Kohlberg's levels.

6. **C** An infant who is securely attached will feel secure when he is around his mother, as evidenced by his comfort when his mother is in the room. When she leaves the room, the infant cries, but is easily consoled upon her return. If the child were insecurely attached, his reaction would differ. In the "strange situation" experiment, the insecurely attached children had varied reactions. Some children did not react as much when the mother left the room, and other children did a combination of both behaviors (disorganized behavior). The correct answer is (C).

7. **A** Conservation is the concept that the amount of a material is still the same in different forms. In this case, it is the same amount of water in both the cup and the vase, though the water level may change.

8. **B** Knowledge of certain facts and figures is crystallized intelligence. Perhaps you reasoned your way to a good guess and chose fluid intelligence, but remember, fluid intelligence is mental agility, problem-solving ability, and other qualities that are not necessarily parroting back facts. Assimilation is a type of learning, incorporating information into mental schemas. Wisdom is knowledge that comes from life experiences.

9. **D** Since Mira learns to understand that the object is in fact a bookshelf instead of a desk, she is accommodating this information, making adjustments to her already preexisting schema. If it were, in fact, a desk, as she originally thought, this would have been assimilation. But it wasn't, so you can cross out (E). Functional fixedness is a type of mental set, but there is no problem-solving in this question, so eliminate (A) and (C). Choice (B) is a milestone from Jean Piaget's preoperational stage. The correct answer is (D).

10. **E** Bandura's name is synonymous with observational learning. Through this perspective, Bandura posited that gender roles are at least partially observed by the individual. Choice (A) alludes to a behavioral perspective since it involves learning, so eliminate (A). Choice (B) is also incorrect because Bandura was not concerned with genetics. Choice (C) is also an incomplete explanation for the complex subject of gender, aside from it not relating to Bandura's theories. Choice (D) is too extreme because of the word *only,* and does not address the observational nature of Bandura's work. Only (E) is consistent with Bandura's research.

CHAPTER 14 DRILL

1. **D** Secondary drives, like secondary reinforcers, are learned by association with primary drives and primary reinforcers. Satisfying basic needs, as in (A), is a primary drive, as is the attempt to maintain homeostatic equilibrium, as in (B). Choice (C), instinct, refers to unlearned behaviors and (E), optimal arousal, refers to biological theory.

2. **A** The Yerkes-Dodson law relates levels of arousal and task difficulty. Here, a high-difficulty task (SAT) requires low levels of arousal (calm and relaxed). Arousal and obtaining a primary reinforcer, as in (B), is an inaccurate comparison for this theory. Tasks related to homeostasis, as in (C), involve drive-reduction theory. Choices (D) and (E) give scenarios opposite to what the law dictates: low arousal and low difficulty in (D) and high arousal and high difficulty in (E).

3. **A** Angiotensin is a chemical messenger released when the volumetric receptors that monitor extracellular body levels, particularly in the circulatory system, sense low fluid levels, and it acts directly on brain receptors to stimulate thirst. Choice (B) is an opiate-like brain chemical that binds to neural receptor sites, but it has nothing to do with thirst; neither does the neurotransmitter acetylcholine, (E); and (C) is a thyroid, not thirst, hormone.

4. **B** An extrinsic factor is one that motivates behavior but does not originate within the individual performing the behavior; it instead originates from the outside world. In Rhoni's case, feeling the need to excel at her career in order to keep up her family's lifestyle and her parents' opinion of her qualifies as being primarily from outside of her (though she may enjoy the lifestyle herself). Choice (A) would be a factor that originated within the individual displaying the behavior; (D) and (E) would also describe such internal factors.

5. **C** As compared to Type-B personalities, Type-As have a greater arousal response overall to stress and a greater tendency to seek it out, as in (B); they also tend to be more competitive, as in (E), more prone to stress-related physical conditions, as in (D), and to feel a greater sense of being pressed for time, as in (A). Type-As also tend to anger more quickly (part of being easier to arouse), so they would be less likely to anger slowly.

6. **A** According to drive-reduction theory, the drive is hunger in this case, so to reduce the need, Sanju needs to eat something. Since she does this, theoretically, she will return to homeostasis, as in (A). Yes, she may be thirsty as well, but that is not stated in the question, nor will a donut necessarily cause thirst. The donut may increase insulin levels in the body, but it is not certain that they will be raised to unhealthy levels, so (A) is the only provable response.

7. **D** The Yerkes-Dodson law and the opponent process theory are not theories of emotion, so eliminate (A) and (E). Jorge is able to cognitively appraise the situation to know he is not in danger. He is experiencing a physiological response to a stimulus, but the cognitive interpretation of that physiological response is the two-factor theory that Schachter and Singer posited. The James-Lange theory would not work here because the physiological response would lead to only one emotional output, most likely fear. Eliminate (B). The Cannon-Bard theory does not connect the cognitive interpretation of the physiological response either, so eliminate (C). The correct answer is (D).

8. **E** The opponent-process theory explains how addiction can create this vicious cycle, in which the user takes increasingly more and more of a drug to achieve the original effect, while the opposite "lows" get lower and lower. Drug use is not an instinct, so eliminate (A). Similarly, you can eliminate (B) because there is nothing in the question concerning arousal. Choice (C) cannot be correct because the two-factor theory is one of emotion, and you can also cross out (D) because this exacerbated cycle would not exist in the drive-reduction theory. This leaves (E), the correct answer.

9. **E** Suppressed appetite is not a symptom of chronic stress, though it may be one of acute stress, which lasts for only a short amount of time. Remember that chronic stress is defined as lasting for weeks, months, or even years.

10. **B** The hypothalamus is mostly in charge of maintaining homeostasis in the body, (B). Choice (A) describes the thalamus, (C) the hippocampus, (D) the pituitary gland, and (E) the amygdala. The correct answer is (B).

CHAPTER 15 DRILL

1. **B** In Freudian theory, the ego is the part of the mind that mediates between the wants/demands of the part of the mind known as the id, (C); the internal representation of rules, morals, and social obligations known as the superego, (A); and the realities of the outside world. The ego involves conscious thought and choice, and attempts to find acceptable ways to satisfy desires. Choices (D) and (E) are not parts of the mind in Freudian theory; they are concepts from Jungian theory.

2. **E** Reaction formation is the psychodynamic defense mechanism that involves the ego reversing the direction of a disturbing or unacceptable desire to make that desire safer and more acceptable, as when a person who unconsciously hates children might feel the need to volunteer at a day-care center. The other answers are all definitions of other defense mechanisms: (A) is displacement, (B) is regression, (C) is compensation, and (D) is rationalization.

3. **D** Albert Bandura is identified with a social-cognitive, rather than psychodynamic, theory of personality; his theory does not concern itself very much with unconscious desires and mechanisms, as psychodynamic theories do, but rather focuses on an individual's concepts and beliefs. Horney, Jung, Adler, and Erikson are all psychodynamic theorists who expanded on or modified Freud's original conception of personality.

4. **D** In the personality and therapeutic theories of Carl Rogers, self-actualization refers to the process by which individuals learn and grow over time in ways that allow them to reach their full potential and ability. To humanistic theorists, such as Rogers, self-actualization is the ultimate purpose of human existence. Choice (A) refers to the value we place on ourselves—often a product of self-actualization, but not the actual process. Choice (C), self-efficacy, refers to a person's belief in their own competence in a given situation.

5. **A** The 16 PF (Personality Factor) Questionnaire, designed by Raymond Cattell, is designed specifically for investigating the traits, or primarily inherited, enduring, and situationally stable tendencies, that govern individual personality. (Cattell theorized there were 16 basic traits, which his instrument purported to measure.) Choices (B) and (E) are intelligence tests—the Weschler Adult Intelligence Scale and the Weschler Intelligence Scale for Children, respectively. Choice (C) is the *Diagnostic and Statistical Manual, Version Five,* currently in use for identification and classification of mental/behavioral disorders, and (D) is analysis of variance, a statistical technique.

6. **B** Anne is not very competent at riding a bike, which shows she has a low self-efficacy, so eliminate (A) and (C). However, she knows she is in control of getting better at riding a bike if she practices. This means that she has an internal locus of control; she has control over her improvements. The correct answer is (B).

7. **E** The concept of the halo effect is that multiple positive attributes will surround a person who already possesses some. Since Lukas has good looks, grades, and athleticism, the halo effect suggests that he has other positive attributes as well, such as being trustworthy. The correct answer is (E).

8. **A** When Tanya kicks the ice instead of her coach or herself, she is showing displacement, since she directs her anger toward the ice. The correct answer is (A).

9. **C** In Jung's theory, the anima and animus are the male and female qualities that lie in each personality. This supports (C). Beware of the recycled Jungian language in (A) and (D). Neither addresses the subject of this question, but test-makers hope that those key words might be enticing. Choice (B) describes Erikson's trust versus mistrust, and (E) is more of a humanistic viewpoint.

10. **B** Cara feels good about herself, showing that she is exhibiting positive self-esteem, (B). The question does not show whether she is proficient at a task or not, so eliminate self-efficacy, (A). The self-concept is a larger umbrella including self-esteem, efficacy, schemata, etc., so eliminate (C) as well. Choices (D) and (E) are incorrect because those are defense mechanisms of psychoanalysis. The correct answer is (B).

CHAPTER 16 DRILL

1. **C** This person is most likely experiencing a psychotic episode. Choices (B) and (D), obsessions and compulsions, refer to a different disorder. Choice (A), delusions, are relevant to psychosis, but they are beliefs not based in reality, and the question stem explicitly says he hears voices, not that he believes anything in particular. Choice (E), inceptions, is not a psychological concept. Only (C), hallucinations, fits the question stem.

2. **B**   Conversion disorder occurs when a psychological difficulty manifests itself as a deficit in physiological function for which there is no actual discernible physical cause. Choice (A), bipolar disorder, is characterized by alternating periods of depression and mania, and (E), paranoid disorder, by extreme mistrust and suspicion, often with feelings of persecution. Choice (C), an organic disorder, would be linked to an actual physical deficit, usually of the brain or nervous system.

3. **E**   Dissociative disorders, such as amnesia, fugue, or dissociative identity disorder, are characterized by dysfunction of memory and disruption in the sense of identity. Choice (A) is more characteristic of phobias, (C) of obsessive disorders, and (D) of certain types of schizophrenia. Choice (B) might be descriptive of some individuals with dissociative disorders, but it is not a diagnostic criterion or a widely seen characteristic of the disorder (many with such disorders have quite extensive social networks).

4. **C**   Serotonin is a neurotransmitter that influences mood and seems to be present at lower-than-usual levels in many of those diagnosed with depression (at least, unipolar depression). Choice (A), acetylcholine, has, at least in some studies, been associated with the expression of bipolar behavior when present in greater-than-average amounts. Dopamine deficits have been implicated in Parkinson's disease, and may be implicated in certain instances of schizophrenia, but not depression, so eliminate (E).

5. **C**   By *DSM-5* definition, anxiety disorders are characterized by feelings of tension, nervousness, fear, and sometimes panic. All of the choices here qualify except for anxious personality disorder, which is made up.

6. **D**   The girl is most likely suffering from dissociative fugue (a type of dissociative disorder, (D)), which causes her to experience personal amnesia. Sufferers of dissociative fugue tend to wander or travel and often establish new identities based on who they believe they are. Choice (A), somatoform disorder, involves physical illness or injury. Choice (B), delusional disorder, is a psychotic illness that is characterized by non-bizarre delusions, with no accompanying hallucinations, mood disturbances, or flattening of affect; furthermore, amnesia is not a symptom of a delusional disorder. Choice (C), personality disorder, is characterized by a set of personality traits that deviates from cultural norms, impairs functioning, and causes distress; there are three major clusters of personality disorders, none of which accurately explain the girl described in the question stem. Although it is possible that the girl's symptoms are feigned in an attempt to seek attention, a possible symptom of histrionic personality disorder, the question stem would need to provide concrete information to draw this conclusion, which it does not. Also, there is no direct evidence of schizophrenia demonstrated in the question stem, so eliminate (E).

7. **D**   Conversion disorder is a somatoform disorder in which a person displays blindness, deafness, or other symptoms of sensory or motor failure without a physical cause, as best expressed by (D). Choice (A), a constant fear of illness, refers to hypochondriasis, not conversion disorder. Choice (B), panic attacks and severe anxiety, are symptoms of anxiety disorders, while conversion disorder is a type of somatoform disorder. Frequent vague complaints about physical symptoms, (C), is characteristic of somatization disorder and (E), religious obsessions, may remind you of religious conversion, but that is not the meaning of *conversion* in this question.

8. **B** Schizoid personality disorder, (B), is classified under Cluster A personality disorders. This person will likely be markedly detached from friends and family members and have a flat affect, whereas Cluster B disorders are more emotional and dramatic.

9. **E** Many diagnoses, such as obsessive-compulsive disorder, are diagnosed only in adulthood. This is a child, so this must be a neurodevelopmental disorder, narrowing options to (A) and (E). The child is not exhibiting impulsivity/hyperactivity or inattention, but rather restrictive behavior and difficulty in social situations, since he is having difficulty engaging with peers. This is descriptive of ASD. The correct answer is (E).

CHAPTER 17 DRILL

1. **C** Client-centered therapy, as an outgrowth of the humanistic school of psychology, is very concerned with trying to understand the client's view of the world and how it affects them, in order to facilitate the client's own tendencies toward growth and fulfillment. Therapists utilizing this approach see accurate empathic understanding—the therapist's ability to view the world through the eyes of the client—as critical to successful communication between client and therapist. While (A), psychoanalytic therapy, also considers communication and understanding the client's view of the world important, it tends to discourage emotional or personal involvement with the patient through such empathy. Psychoanalytic therapists believe a stance of detachment is best for the encouragement of transference, which helps to reveal the nature of the patient's conflicts. Choice (D), implosion therapy, is a behavioral approach with little emphasis on the kind of client–therapist relationship considered essential to client-centered therapy.

2. **E** Behavioral approaches to therapy are concerned with treating maladaptive or troubling symptoms, rather than underlying causes, and in this school of thought, there are no hidden, "deep" underlying causes—the disordered behavior itself is the problem. As such, behavioral therapies have been most often used with those who seek to change specific behaviors, such as those who suffer from phobias. While behavioral approaches might be tried for individuals with some of the other conditions listed, the more symptom-oriented behavioral techniques are usually not the treatment of choice with conditions that involve more than just a specific maladaptive behavior and/or altered mental states.

3. **B** Psychoanalytic therapy focuses on probing past defense mechanisms to understand the unconscious roots of problems; indeed, its practitioners believe that troubling behaviors or symptoms cannot possibly cease until a patient gains insight into such unconscious roots. In this approach, treating just symptoms through behavioral methods without addressing the underlying hidden causes will not result in a lasting "cure" and may instead result in symptoms returning or new ones manifesting. Choices (A) and (C) are not generally criticisms leveled at behavioral therapy by psychoanalysts; indeed, for those it's the other way around—these are criticisms of psychoanalytic approaches often made by behaviorists. The criticism in (D) would more likely be made by humanistic or client-centered therapists.

4. **B**   Rational-emotive behavioral therapy, or simply rational-emotive therapy, is primarily associated with Albert Ellis, who formulated this cognitive approach, which concentrates on modifying incorrect thoughts or cognitions that lead to maladaptive emotional and behavioral responses. Choice (A), Julian Rotter, is associated with the concept of locus of control; (C), Abraham Maslow, with the concepts of hierarchy of needs and self-actualization; (D), Raymond Cattell, with a trait theory of personality and the 16 PF Questionnaire; and (E), Rollo May, with the existential approach to psychotherapy.

5. **A**   Anticoagulants are not drugs used for psychotherapeutic purposes; they are, instead, used to modulate the ability of the blood to clot and form vessel blockages. Both (C) and (E) are classes of drugs that belong to the larger family of antidepressants; (B), anxiolytics, as the name implies, are used primarily for the reduction of anxiety; and (D), lithium salts, are useful in the treatment of some cases of bipolar disorder.

6. **C**   There is nothing systematic or progressive about going to the top of the Empire State Building on a first therapy session for acrophobia. Instead, the therapist is choosing a situation in which Judy will most likely have a very strong reaction at first, but will hopefully have less of a reaction the longer she realizes she will not fall off the ledge. This is a technique called flooding, (C). Choice (B) is not the answer because the therapist is not trying to condition Judy not to like something. Choice (D), implosion, is similar to flooding, but it uses visualization techniques instead of physically going to a location or confronting a stimulus. There is not a contract in the question stem either, eliminating (E).

7. **D**   A behavioral therapist will seek to modify behavior by extinguishing maladaptive behaviors and conditioning more adaptive ones. Therefore, extinction procedures will be used to modify behaviors. Choices (A), (B), and (C) are specific to psychoanalysis, while (E) is most closely associated with humanistic therapy. The correct answer is (D).

8. **A**   SSRIs are most commonly used as antidepressants. Therefore, they would most likely be used for depressive disorders.

9. **C**   A psychotherapist would most likely use free association, (C). Choices (A), (B), and (D) are techniques used in behavioral therapy, and (E) is used in humanistic therapy.

10. **A**   Carl Rogers is synonymous with humanistic therapy. If you were unsure, remember that he coined the phrase *unconditional positive regard*, so he was most concerned with treating other humans with the utmost respect and compassion. Hence, the term humanism came forth.

CHAPTER 18 DRILL

1. **D** The fundamental attribution error is defined as the tendency of people to overestimate a person's disposition and to underestimate the situational circumstances when evaluating another person's behavior. Both (A) and (C) are examples of an internal locus of control. Choice (B), blaming a teacher for one's failures, is an example of an external attribution. In evaluating her friend's behavior, Karen is balancing personal and situational attributes, so eliminate (E) as well.

2. **D** In the Asch conformity experiments, many factors influenced the degree to which an experimental subject would show conformity to the obviously wrong group opinion, but the subject's age did not show a consistent effect in this regard. Choice (A) certainly did—unanimity was very important; only one dissenting opinion drastically reduced the tendency of the subject to go along with the rest of the group; (B), size of the group, had an influence in that it seemed to take a group of at least three members for such conformity to be shown consistently; (C), the subjects' perceptions of their own social status versus that of the group, was important—subjects who perceived themselves as of low/medium status were much more likely to conform than those who perceived themselves as of high status; and (E), gender of the subject, was an influencing factor, with females more likely to conform than males.

3. **D** The self-fulfilling prophecy refers to the scenario in the question—students randomly labeled as likely to experience significant jumps in academic test scores in the coming semester did indeed seem to perform to those expectations on those tests at the end of the semester. Choice (A), the Hawthorne effect, refers to the observation that students or workers who know they are being monitored tend to perform better, even if they do not know why they are being monitored. Choice (B), the Kandel effect, is associated with research into learning and neurophysiology in sea slugs; (C), cognitive dissonance, refers to the discomfort that comes from conflicting behavior and beliefs; and (E), the Ainsworth effect, comes from studies of attachment in human infants.

4. **B** Diffusion of responsibility, also sometimes referred to as the bystander effect, occurs when every person in a crowded social situation defers to another to make the effort to mount a response to the situation. It can also occur when members of a group perform negative behaviors that no specific individual or individuals will take responsibility for. Choice (D), an altruistic orientation, usually refers to the decision-making paradigm in which individuals wish to maximize the outcome for others, but it could also be applied to this situation as a countervailing force to the diffusion of responsibility. Choice (A), illusory correlation, refers to the false presumption that certain groups are associated with certain stereotypes or behaviors, and (E), the just-world hypothesis, is the belief that because the world is basically fair, people deserve whatever befalls them, positive or negative. Choice (C), cognitive dissonance, deals with conflicting beliefs and behaviors, not responsibility.

5. **B** The "foot-in-the-door" technique involves making requests in small increments that people are more likely to initially comply with, and then working from those up to bigger requests; the incremental approach seems to work better than "going for the whole ball of wax all at once." This is what the teenager is trying to do in getting his curfew extended in small increments until he gets the curfew he actually wants. Choice (A) is an example of the "door-in-the-face" technique, in which one asks for much more than what one actually wants, expecting to be turned down; one

can then ask for the smaller, "more reasonable" request, which is more likely to be granted. People also tend to be more likely to comply with or be persuaded by those they feel they are similar to, as in (D), or by those they will receive a desired reward from (hardly a surprise), as in (E).

6. **C** The man who does not have health insurance in (A) thinks nothing bad will happen to him, which is known as an optimism bias. The woman observing the man who loses his house in (B) most likely feels for the man, but exhibits the just-world bias since she most likely thinks the man failed to act on obtaining health insurance. Choice (C) is the clearest example of the self-serving bias, since the toddler attributes building the block tower to herself, but blames the blocks instead of herself when they tumble to the ground. Remember, the self-serving bias is when a person takes credit for positive achievements and attributes something or someone else as the cause of negative ones. Choice (D) most clearly shows a self-fulfilling prophecy and the Rosenthal Effect, in which the teacher believes in Yuan, and he then goes and studies for his exam. Finally, (E) is an example of a situational attribution, in which the environment causes conditions that affect a large number of the residents described in the answer choice. The correct answer is (C).

7. **A** Since both groups remained equal for a while, the group that had five members shows evidence of social loafing. The more people assigned to that side of the rope, the less force they thought they needed to exert individually. The three students on the other side of the rope felt more individually responsible and had an increased need to contribute.

8. **D** The child in this question uses the door-in-the-face technique to get what he wants from his parents. This technique is named for his parents metaphorically "slamming the door in his face" at his outrageous request of $100 per week. However, when he asks for less money, he is met with less resistance.

9. **E** Stanley Milgram's study involved a significant amount of deception, tricking the subjects into thinking they were participating in a study on learning. They played roles within the experiment, though this was not the point of the experiment, so eliminate (D). There is not a group in the experiment, so conformity, dehumanization, and groupthink are not factors here either, eliminating (A), (B), and (C). The point of the experiment was to test obedience to the "experimenter" when he told the subject (the "teacher") to administer what the subject believed to be an electric shock to the "learner" (a confederate to the experimenter in another room). A large percentage of subjects obeyed the experimenter and administered the highest level of electric shock. The correct answer is (E).

10. **A** Though Bandura was measuring aggressive behavior in the children, the crucial part of the experiment was the children's observation of the adults. If the children observed the adults behaving aggressively toward the bobo doll, they were more apt to act aggressively themselves. If they observed the adults behaving nonaggressively, they were also less likely to act aggressively.

Part VI
Practice Test 2

- Practice Test 2
- Practice Test 2: Answers and Explanations

Practice Test 2

AP® Psychology Exam

SECTION I: Multiple-Choice Questions

DO NOT OPEN THIS BOOKLET UNTIL YOU ARE TOLD TO DO SO.

Instructions

Section I of this exam contains 100 multiple-choice questions. Fill in only the ovals for numbers 1 through 100 on your answer sheet.

Indicate all of your answers to the multiple-choice questions on the answer sheet. No credit will be given for anything written in this exam booklet, but you may use the booklet for notes or scratch work. After you have decided which of the suggested answers is best, completely fill in the corresponding oval on the answer sheet. Give only one answer to each question. If you change an answer, be sure that the previous mark is erased completely. Here is a sample question and answer.

Sample Question   Sample Answer

Omaha is a

(A) state
(B) city
(C) country
(D) continent
(E) village

Use your time effectively, working as quickly as you can without losing accuracy. Do not spend too much time on any one question. Go on to other questions and come back to the ones you have not answered if you have time. It is not expected that everyone will know the answers to all of the multiple-choice questions.

About Guessing

Many candidates wonder whether or not to guess the answers to questions about which they are not certain. Multiple-choice scores are based on the number of questions answered correctly. Points are not deducted for incorrect answers and no points are awarded for unanswered questions. Because points are not deducted for incorrect answers, you are encouraged to answer all multiple-choice questions. On any questions you do not know the answer to, you should eliminate as many choices as you can and then select the best answer among the remaining choices.

GO ON TO THE NEXT PAGE.

At a Glance

Total Time
1 hour and 10 minutes
Number of Questions
100
Percent of Total Grade
66.6%
Writing Instrument
Pencil required

This page intentionally left blank.

GO ON TO THE NEXT PAGE.

PSYCHOLOGY
Section I
Time—1 hour and 10 minutes
100 Questions

Directions: Each of the questions or incomplete statements below is followed by five answer choices. Select the one that is best in each case and then completely fill in the corresponding oval on the answer sheet.

1. Solomon Asch conducted a study in which individuals tried to match lines of the same length being displayed on cards. They performed this activity either by themselves or in a room with confederates who sometimes gave deliberately incorrect responses. Asch was studying

   (A) social loafing
   (B) conformity
   (C) groupthink
   (D) social facilitation
   (E) deindividuation

2. Scientists found a young woman who had memorized a dictionary and displayed other attributes of a "super memory." They were interested in what factors may have contributed to her amazing abilities. So, they obtained permission to follow her around for a week; during that time, they looked at her daily activities: her diet, her exercise, her sleep habits, her reading habits, her hobbies, and her social and family relationships. These scientists were engaged in what form of research?

   (A) Single-blind experiment
   (B) Correlational study
   (C) Double-blind experiment
   (D) Case study
   (E) Longitudinal study

3. Neurotransmitters pass from neuron to neuron across a gap known as the

   (A) axon terminal
   (B) dendrite
   (C) node of Ranvier
   (D) myelin sheath
   (E) synapse

4. Suddenly and involuntarily falling asleep during daytime hours is referred to as

   (A) non-REM sleep
   (B) circadian dysfunction
   (C) narcolepsy
   (D) sleep apnea
   (E) somnambulism

5. Which psychological approach provides many of the organizing principles of visual perception?

   (A) Gestalt
   (B) Psychoanalytic
   (C) Cognitive
   (D) Humanistic
   (E) Evolutionary

6. Learned helplessness is a result of what combination of factors?

   (A) Internal locus of control and high degree of self-efficacy
   (B) Internal locus of control and low degree of self-efficacy
   (C) External locus of control and low degree of self-efficacy
   (D) External locus of control and high degree of self-efficacy
   (E) Differentiated sense of self and unconditional positive regard

7. In drive reduction theory, an individual's behavior is supposed to bring about

   (A) maximum relaxation
   (B) self-actualization
   (C) a sense of achievement
   (D) positive relationships with others
   (E) homeostasis

8. The method of loci, the peg-word system, and chunking are all examples of

   (A) artificial intelligence
   (B) syntax errors
   (C) displacement errors
   (D) mnemonic devices
   (E) problem-solving strategies

GO ON TO THE NEXT PAGE.

9. It has been many years since Cassie first rode on a roller coaster, yet she continues to have vivid memories of that experience. This might be explained by the proximity of which two parts of the brain?

    (A) Frontal lobes; occipital lobes
    (B) Amygdala; hippocampus
    (C) Broca's area; Wernicke's area
    (D) Brain stem; cerebellum
    (E) Thalamus; hypothalamus

10. Marty referees high school basketball games. He knows that it is a difficult job and that players, coaches, and spectators are often unfairly critical of the referees. Nevertheless, when he attends his daughter's games, he often yells at the referees. During one such hostile confrontation the referee tells Marty that his behavior is strange in light of the fact that Marty is a referee himself. Marty looks uncomfortable and then says: "If people pay their money for a ticket, they have a right to say whatever they want." Marty's response exemplifies

    (A) projection
    (B) denial
    (C) groupthink
    (D) cognitive dissonance
    (E) social facilitation

11. Assume that researchers have found that there is a strong inverse relationship between the amount of alcohol that college freshmen consume and their grade point averages. Which of the following is the likeliest correlation coefficient produced by this research?

    (A) +1.0
    (B) +0.2
    (C) −0.1
    (D) −0.75
    (E) −10

12. Someone who is lacking empathy and, as a result, finds it easy to exploit others would be diagnosed with which personality disorder?

    (A) Borderline
    (B) Dependent
    (C) Antisocial
    (D) Histrionic
    (E) Schizotypal

13. Martin is cleaning out a closet. There was something he wanted to reach on a top shelf, but he could not reach it and he finally gave up. It never occurred to him to use the hook end of the umbrella in the closet to reach this item. He only considered the umbrella useful for keeping rain off one's head. Martin's problem was

    (A) functional fixedness
    (B) confirmation bias
    (C) the trial-and-error approach
    (D) algorithmic thinking
    (E) the availability heuristic

14. The center of emotion in the brain is the

    (A) autonomic nervous system
    (B) limbic system
    (C) vestibular system
    (D) dopamine reward system
    (E) parasympathetic nervous system

15. Events that are very important and that create intense emotions, such as the Kennedy assassination in the 1960's, the space shuttle Challenger explosion in the 1980's, or 9/11 in 2001, often produce

    (A) reconstructive memories
    (B) retroactive interference
    (C) flashbulb memories
    (D) proactive interference
    (E) eidetic memories

16. For the *Diagnostic and Statistical Manual of Mental Disorders,* commonly abbreviated as *DSM-5,* the "5" refers to

    (A) five classifications of mental disorders: anxiety disorders, mood disorders, psychotic disorders, eating disorders, and sleep disorders
    (B) consideration of the five major psychological approaches: psychoanalytic, behavioral, humanistic, cognitive, and neurobiological
    (C) the fifth version of the manual
    (D) bringing disorders into focus with the five stages of Freud's developmental theory: oral, anal, phallic, latency, genital
    (E) the five domains in which the manual may be used: psychiatric hospital, general hospital, psychiatric clinic, sole practitioner, professional education

GO ON TO THE NEXT PAGE.

17. Mason has sustained a stroke affecting the left side of his brain. While he can understand what is being said to him, he is unable to produce intelligible speech. Mason probably sustained damage to his

    (A) Wernicke's area
    (B) Broca's area
    (C) auditory nerve
    (D) optic chiasm
    (E) parietal lobe

18. Wanda is in line at the post office. She observes another customer become angry with the postal worker at the window, yelling at him and accusing him of poor service. Wanda assumes that this is because the customer is a jerk. Wanda's thinking is characteristic of

    (A) self-serving bias
    (B) just world belief
    (C) fundamental attribution error
    (D) optimism bias
    (E) stereotype boost

19. Some individuals come to believe that they have a physical characteristic that is grotesque or offensive to others, even when they are reassured by family and friends that this is not the case. Some of them have repeated plastic surgeries to address this perceived deformity and have been described as having an "addiction" to plastic surgery. There is no such "addiction" listed in *DSM-5*. In *DSM-5,* these individuals would probably be diagnosed with

    (A) panic disorder
    (B) histrionic personality disorder
    (C) obsessive compulsive disorder
    (D) narcissistic personality disorder
    (E) body dysmorphic disorder

20. Hans Selye studied animals' responses to short-term and long-term stressors and he developed the general adaptation syndrome (GAS). The three phases of GAS are

    (A) denial, anger, acceptance
    (B) alarm, resistance, exhaustion
    (C) appraisal, reaction, rebound
    (D) agitation, acceptance, relaxation
    (E) procrastination, response, resolution

21. Both the Big Five and Minnesota Multiphasic Personality Inventory (MMPI-2-RF) rely on

    (A) trait theory
    (B) Freudian theory
    (C) humanistic theory
    (D) social learning theory
    (E) behaviorism

22. Which of the following is NOT a symptom of a major depressive disorder?

    (A) Not getting enjoyment from activities that used to bring enjoyment
    (B) Feelings of worthlessness
    (C) A feeling of great energy and an ability to go without sleep for long periods
    (D) An inability to concentrate on tasks
    (E) Alterations in eating habits

23. The rules for how words are ordered in order to create meaningful sentences are called

    (A) syntax
    (B) morphemes
    (C) phonemes
    (D) holographic speech
    (E) semantics

24. According to Erik Erikson, the primary developmental task for young adults is to

    (A) develop integrity about their life experiences
    (B) develop competence in basic skills
    (C) develop meaningful lives and avoid stagnation
    (D) develop trust in having their needs met by others
    (E) develop intimate relationships with others

25. In *DSM-5,* the term for what used to be called "Multiple Personality Disorder," wherein individuals have two or more distinct personalities, often accompanied by amnesia regarding these transformations, is

    (A) schizophrenia
    (B) borderline personality disorder
    (C) conversion disorder
    (D) dissociative identity disorder
    (E) depersonalization

GO ON TO THE NEXT PAGE.

Questions 26–28 refer to the situation described below.

Subjects previously diagnosed with age-related cognitive impairment are being brought into the lab for a one-month drug study during which they will be given either an experimental medication or a placebo. Subjects will be tested at the outset and then at the end of the trial to see whether or not the medication reduced the severity of their symptoms.

26. Which of the following is NOT an ethical consideration for the experimenters at the outset?

    (A) The need to obtain informed consent
    (B) The need to minimize possible harm to the subjects
    (C) The need to maintain confidentiality about the subjects
    (D) The need to control potentially confounding variables
    (E) The need to arrange debriefing for the subjects at the conclusion of the trial

27. Which piece of data compiled on the subjects is NOT a categorical variable?

    (A) Ethnicity
    (B) IQ score
    (C) Race
    (D) Nationality
    (E) Immigration status

28. If the subjects do not know whether they are part of the experimental group (receiving the medication) or the control group (receiving the placebo), we can say that this study is

    (A) double-blind
    (B) single-blind
    (C) reliable
    (D) valid
    (E) statistically significant

29. Sheila is a track coach, working with an athlete who has a personal best time of 5:20 in the mile. Sheila wants to get this time down to 5:00. She knows that this runner really enjoys massages provided by the training staff, but these can only occur with the coach's authorization. She thought about offering this runner a week's worth of massages when the time got down to the goal. Instead, she has decided to authorize a massage each time the runner reduces her personal best by at least four seconds. What strategy is Sheila employing?

    (A) Fixed-interval reinforcement
    (B) Variable-interval reinforcement
    (C) Discrimination
    (D) Fixed-ratio reinforcement
    (E) Generalization

30. A student is very good at knowing which studying techniques work well for him and which do not. This is a result of his

    (A) metacognition
    (B) interpersonal intelligence
    (C) state-dependent memory
    (D) crystallized intelligence
    (E) insight learning

31. A method of operant conditioning that encourages positive behaviors and that has proven successful, particularly in institutional settings, is known as a

    (A) fixed-interval schedule of reinforcement
    (B) shaping experience
    (C) discriminatory task
    (D) signaling stimulus
    (E) token economy

32. When a neuron is excited by a chemical messenger, the change in electrical charge that must be reached in order to trigger an action potential is referred to as the

    (A) dendrite
    (B) axon terminal
    (C) permeable membrane
    (D) inhibitory effect
    (E) threshold

GO ON TO THE NEXT PAGE.

33. Francois needed to get a dozen items from the supermarket. However, when he got there, he discovered that he had left his list at home. In trying to shop from memory, he found that he remembered the items at the beginning of his list and those at the end of the list, but he had made errors on several of the items in the middle. What is the phenomenon that expresses the likelihood of this outcome?

(A) Motivated forgetting
(B) Repression
(C) Anterograde amnesia
(D) Serial position effect
(E) Flashbulb memory

34. Shoshanna has scored 115 on an IQ test with a normal distribution, a mean score of 100, and a standard deviation of 15 points. At approximately what percentile of test-takers does she fall?

(A) 98
(B) 84
(C) 65
(D) 50
(E) 34

35. Harry and Margaret Harlow's work with orphaned baby monkeys suggested that

(A) monkeys always use insight as opposed to problem-solving processes
(B) mother-infant bonding during breastfeeding is largely based on contact comfort
(C) intelligence remained intact because it was based on genetic inheritance
(D) mother-infant bonding during breastfeeding was based almost exclusively on the nutrient value of the activity
(E) intelligence was compromised due to the lack of parent-led enrichment activities

36. Which of the following is NOT a recognized basic taste?

(A) Spicy
(B) Salty
(C) Sweet
(D) Bitter
(E) Sour

37. After our "fight-or-flight" system arouses our physiology to meet an external threat, which system returns us to homeostasis?

(A) Sympathetic
(B) Parasympathetic
(C) Vestibular
(D) Dopamine reward
(E) Limbic

38. What accounts for the fact that most people will eat dessert at the end of an enormous Thanksgiving meal?

(A) Drive reduction theory
(B) Sociocultural factors
(C) Glucose levels in the bloodstream
(D) The ventromedial hypothalamus
(E) Liver enzymes

39. An accepted explanation of the bystander effect is that

(A) people are generally motivated to be good Samaritans when someone else is in trouble
(B) people feel empathy for others in difficult circumstances
(C) people feel less responsibility for the welfare of others when more people are aware that help is needed
(D) people are generally insensitive to the needs of their fellow human beings
(E) people are frightened when they see that others are vulnerable, and this causes them to withdraw

40. When Marco seems sad and unmotivated, his parents take him to see a therapist. The therapist concludes that Marco is depressed because he has set unrealistically high expectations for himself. This therapist probably subscribes to the

(A) psychoanalytical approach
(B) behaviorist approach
(C) cognitive approach
(D) evolutionary approach
(E) biological approach

GO ON TO THE NEXT PAGE.

41. Margery, Olu, and Fred are each seeking a college scholarship based on foreign language proficiency. They must pass an oral exam in order to qualify. Fred did not take this opportunity very seriously and showed up groggy for the exam after a late-night movie. Margery thought that this scholarship was crucial to her college plans, had been nervous about it for days, and drank an energy drink just before going in. Olu took the exam seriously, but did not feel stressed about the outcome; he believed that he had other available routes to college. When Olu had the best performance on the exam, this would most likely be explained by which of the following?

    (A) Yerkes-Dodson Law
    (B) Availability heuristic
    (C) Erikson's "identity versus role confusion" stage
    (D) Schachter-Singer theory of emotion
    (E) Whorf's linguistic relativity

42. REM sleep is often referred to as *paradoxical* because

    (A) it is a light-sleep phenomenon, but the restorative properties of sleep are restricted to deep sleep
    (B) it is a deep-sleep phenomenon, but most dreaming takes place during light sleep
    (C) it involves arousal of both physiology and brain activity while muscular activity is minimized
    (D) dreaming is paradoxical in that it is a fictional recap of our daily lives
    (E) our eyes must be still in order for us to dream

43. The semicircular canals in the inner ear are essential for

    (A) accurate processing of loudness
    (B) accurate processing of pitch
    (C) the ability to swallow
    (D) proper functioning of the vestibular sense
    (E) lubricating the tympanic membrane (eardrum)

44. The most durable human behaviors are produced by which schedule of reinforcement?

    (A) Continuous
    (B) Fixed-interval
    (C) Variable-interval
    (D) Fixed-ratio
    (E) Variable-ratio

45. A mouse in a Skinner box is receiving periodic electric shocks. If the mouse learns to press a lever to stop the shocks whenever they begin, what process is responsible for the increased lever pressing?

    (A) Positive punishment
    (B) Negative punishment
    (C) Negative reinforcement
    (D) Positive reinforcement
    (E) Shaping

46. Hypnosis has proven most effective for what purpose?

    (A) Treatment of drug addiction
    (B) Reduction of chronic pain
    (C) Reducing symptoms of ADHD
    (D) Restoring memories of those suffering from retrograde amnesia
    (E) Helping individuals accurately recall their dreams

47. In his stage theory of moral development, Kohlberg proposes three levels that correspond to which sorts of considerations as the individual matures?

    (A) From amorality to immorality to religious morality
    (B) From individual morality to government morality to the morality of a divine being
    (C) From punishment/reward to rule following to individual morality
    (D) From unwritten law to written law to universally understood law
    (E) From seeking guidance from authority figures, to seeking guidance from peers, to seeking guidance from laws

48. When entering a crowded room with many conversations going on at roughly the same loudness level, individuals are often able to focus in on one conversation that interests them, to the exclusion of the others. What is the name of this phenomenon?

    (A) Motivated multitasking
    (B) Dichotic listening
    (C) Auditory discrimination
    (D) Spatial reasoning
    (E) The cocktail party effect

49. Which of the following was NOT a finding of Stanley Milgram's Yale electric shock experiment?

    (A) Obedience to an authority figure was a powerful motivator of behavior.
    (B) Nearly two-thirds of participants would go to the top of the shock board even if they believed that they might be causing pain.
    (C) Putting confederates who took issue with the morality of administering shock in the room with the experimental subject would reduce compliance.
    (D) Subjects would frequently question the authority figure about the advisability of going forward with the shocks.
    (E) Women were more likely than men to refuse to go on with the shocks.

GO ON TO THE NEXT PAGE.

50. Piaget theorized that children develop *schemas*, concepts about objects and ideas in the world around them. They then evaluate those *schemas* based on information from their daily experiences. When children found that this new information could fit into the *schemas* they had already developed, Piaget referred to this process as

    (A) assimilation
    (B) accommodation
    (C) object permanence
    (D) cognitive congruence
    (E) conservation

51. Suchi is playing a video game in which visual and auditory inputs from space aliens flash onto the screen very quickly; the player must absorb this information and make immediate strategic decisions. This game primarily tests her

    (A) sensory adaptation
    (B) habituation
    (C) crystallized intelligence
    (D) fluid intelligence
    (E) episodic memory

52. Researchers located at the campus of a major technology company in Silicon Valley wanted to assess employees' attitudes toward the idea of increasing diversity among the company's work force. So, one day they stationed themselves at the entrance of the building that houses the web design department and they selected every fifth person entering the building. The selected people were led down the hall to a private room where they could complete a survey. These subjects were assigned code numbers so that their responses would not be personally identifiable. The researchers are now using their findings to make recommendations to the company's board of directors. What is a possible flaw in this research methodology?

    (A) Non-random sampling
    (B) Non-representative sampling
    (C) Lack of confidentiality
    (D) Observer bias
    (E) Observer effect

53. Ron was the track coach at a very diverse high school. Early on in the team's practices, Ron mentioned that, in his experience, students of Scandinavian heritage did much better in sprints than in distance events. He had students run a variety of races for time. He found that the Scandinavian students were the only group that had worse times for distance events now than they had achieved during tryouts. Ron may have contributed to this outcome by way of

    (A) institutional discrimination
    (B) stereotype threat
    (C) self-serving bias
    (D) representativeness heuristic
    (E) availability heuristic

54. When Penelope is sitting on the bench watching her softball team play and one of her teammates hits a long fly ball into the outfield, it often seems as if the ball is the size of a pea as it heads to the fence. However, Penelope never loses her understanding of the true size of the softball. This is due to

    (A) size constancy
    (B) feature detectors
    (C) perceptual shift
    (D) bipolar cells
    (E) the optic chiasm

55. Students were working in their AP Psychology textbooks. They were looking at a picture of a green, yellow, and black flag that looked oddly familiar. They were instructed to stare intently at a black dot in the middle of the flag and then immediately transfer their gaze to a white surface. When they did this, they were shocked to see a red, white, and blue American flag. This exercise was conducted to demonstrate the phenomenon of

    (A) afterimages
    (B) color blindness
    (C) selective attention
    (D) visual acuity for color
    (E) the trichromatic theory of color vision

56. Jackson has been traveling a great deal for business and suffering the effects of jet lag. He goes to the pharmacy and asks whether there is an over-the-counter medication that can help reset his body clock and get his sleep schedule back on track. When the pharmacist recommends such a product, it will probably contain which chemical?

    (A) Acetylcholine
    (B) Melatonin
    (C) Adrenaline
    (D) Human growth hormone
    (E) Cortisol

57. Scientists wish to determine which part of the brain becomes most active when people are confronted with a moral dilemma. After exposing a person to such a dilemma, which type of scanning technology should be used to investigate brain activity?

    (A) EEG
    (B) MRI
    (C) CAT
    (D) EKG
    (E) PET

GO ON TO THE NEXT PAGE.

58. Braxton has great difficulty leaving his house. He can make it to his car in the driveway, but then he feels he needs to return to the house to check whether or not he locked the door, set the burglar alarm, closed all the windows, etc. Sometimes he will make as many as a dozen return trips and delay his departure by up to a half hour. What would Braxton's disorder probably be classified as, and what would his "checking behaviors" be defined as?

    (A) OCD; compulsions
    (B) PTSD; flashbacks
    (C) OCD; obsessions
    (D) Tourette's Syndrome; tics
    (E) PTSD; stress reactions

59. Jamie was headed to the mall to do some last-minute holiday shopping. When she got to the parking lot, she saw a large group of motorcyclists assembled and she decided to immediately return home to avoid any possible trouble. When she got home, she turned on the TV news and saw a story about these very same motorcyclists raising money for the "Toys for Tots" campaign. The fact that her less-than-positive image of motorcyclists caused her to make a bad decision was an example of

    (A) negative priming
    (B) stereotype threat
    (C) stereotype boost
    (D) representativeness heuristic
    (E) availability heuristic

60. Schachter and Singer's two-factor theory states that the emotions we experience

    (A) are directly caused by our physiological arousal in response to a stimulus
    (B) occur simultaneously with our physiological arousal, and neither one causes the other
    (C) are expected to be expressed with the same intensity in every culture
    (D) produce similar facial expression in all cultures
    (E) are the result of cognitive labels that we attach to the physiological arousal that we experience

61. Erin has always been told that she is a right-brain-dominant person and she accepts that assessment. As a result, she is actively exploring careers that emphasize

    (A) mathematics
    (B) public speaking
    (C) spatial design
    (D) laboratory science
    (E) data analysis

62. An automobile company buys advertising during football games on television. Its research indicates that most viewers are uninterested and even, sometimes, annoyed because their game is being interrupted. According to the elaboration likelihood model, what is the company's best course of action if it wants to persuade these viewers to buy its cars?

    (A) It should provide a wealth of statistics about gas mileage, crash test ratings, and reliability.
    (B) It should emphasize comparative prices with its competitors' models.
    (C) It should show its cars being driven by average people in typical, everyday situations.
    (D) It should explain that viewers must pay close attention because a car purchase may be an individual's next most expensive purchase after their home.
    (E) It should use an attractive spokesperson, have the vehicle in an exotic location, like a beach, and play popular music in the background.

63. Psychology students have a hypothesis that female performers are more sensitive to comments made on social media than are male performers. They decide to study performers in the college's drama department. After performances, they plant comments, favorable or unfavorable, about the individual performances on social media sites that they know the performers follow. They periodically administer a reliable, well-regarded mood inventory to the performers and they track to see how the performers' moods track with the comments. In this study, gender is

    (A) an extraneous variable
    (B) a dependent variable
    (C) an independent variable
    (D) an operational definition
    (E) a *p*-value

64. College students started a chapter of PETA, People for the Ethical Treatment of Animals, on their campus. At the first meeting, they gave out a questionnaire, which indicated, not surprisingly, that the students in attendance strongly favored animal rights. After the group had been meeting for several months, the questionnaire was re-administered to the same students. The results indicated that the membership had become even more strongly in favor of animal rights. This illustrates which phenomenon?

    (A) Social facilitation
    (B) Groupthink
    (C) Group polarization
    (D) Deindividuation
    (E) Peer pressure

GO ON TO THE NEXT PAGE.

65. "Miller's magic number" (seven items, plus or minus two) refers to

    (A) how many items can be stored in short-term, or working, memory
    (B) how many items on a given topic can be stored in long-term memory in one study session
    (C) how many items on a given topic can be retrieved from long-term memory at any one time
    (D) how many details can be attended to in sensory memory
    (E) how many items can be recalled by setting them to music

66. Which of the following would be most important to the way that Carl Rogers would approach talk therapy?

    (A) Unconditional positive regard
    (B) Free association
    (C) Changing the individual's dysfunctional thought patterns
    (D) Providing reinforcement opportunities for individuals who are making positive strides
    (E) Transference

67. Based on her research, Diana Baumrind identified which three types of parenting styles?

    (A) Absolutist, negotiating, and laissez-faire
    (B) Stable, sporadic, and unstable
    (C) Disciplinarian, mentor, and friend
    (D) Authoritarian, authoritative, and permissive
    (E) Married, divorced, and single

68. The Rorschach inkblots are an example of which type of personality test?

    (A) Projective
    (B) Objective
    (C) Trait-based
    (D) Right brain-based
    (E) Left brain-based

69. The most likely effect of chronic, long-term stress, like job-related stress, is to cause a person to

    (A) experience flashbacks and nightmares
    (B) develop phobias related to the stressor
    (C) experience violent mood swings
    (D) develop multiple personalities
    (E) experience greater risk of physical illness

70. Which of the following is NOT a symptom of attention-deficit hyperactivity disorder (ADHD)?

    (A) Difficulty communicating with others
    (B) Difficulty staying on task
    (C) Impulsive behaviors
    (D) Fidgeting
    (E) Difficulty with planning, organization, and executive function

71. Astronauts are using weighted vests to simulate the different levels of gravity that they will experience during their space flight. If they are trying to distinguish small differences in weight, Weber's law would dictate that they would perform this task better if

    (A) their eyes are closed during this assessment
    (B) the vests they are using are very heavy
    (C) the vests they are using are close to their own body weights
    (D) the vests they are using are relatively lightweight
    (E) they are making this assessment in a sound-proof room

72. There is a scuba diving class being taught at the local YMCA. Students are taught about the equipment they will be using while they are in the swimming pool. They are taught about water pressure and medical issues while in a classroom. When they are tested at the end of the course, it is more likely that students will remember information about the scuba diving equipment if

    (A) they are eagerly anticipating a class trip and dive at a nearby lake the next day
    (B) they are played "island music" that reminds them of a trip they plan to take to a tropical location
    (C) it is combined with information about water pressure and medical issues
    (D) they are tested on this information while in the swimming pool
    (E) they know that they will have more chances to pass the test

73. At age 7, Kai had two passions: skateboarding and origami. He is now 15. He has continued to pursue skateboarding and his skills are now quite good. He gave up origami around age 9. When he recently tried to make a folded paper animal for his niece, he found that he could remember the necessary steps, but his skills had deteriorated badly. This discovery reveals

    (A) proactive interference
    (B) retroactive interference
    (C) positive cues
    (D) negative cues
    (E) pruning of neural networks

74. Chemicals that produce similar effects to those produced by opiates are called

    (A) antagonists
    (B) barbiturates
    (C) amphetamines
    (D) beta blockers
    (E) endorphins

GO ON TO THE NEXT PAGE.

75. A study was done concerning emotional expression among individuals who had been paralyzed from the neck down due to serious accidents, comparing them to individuals whose neuromuscular systems were intact. Which finding would most cast doubt on the James-Lange Theory of emotion?

    (A) The individuals who were paralyzed displayed less intense emotions than individuals whose neuromuscular systems were fully intact.
    (B) The individuals who were paralyzed displayed the same intensity of emotions as did individuals whose neuromuscular systems were intact.
    (C) The individuals who were paralyzed had less inclination to cognitively assess the arousal brought on by emotional events, as compared to individuals whose neuromuscular systems were intact.
    (D) The individuals who were paralyzed had greater inclination to cognitively assess the arousal brought on by emotional events, as compared to individuals whose neuromuscular systems were intact.
    (E) The facial expressions accompanying various emotions were common to all of the participants in the study.

76. Felipe intends to study the behavior of apes in their native African highlands. Rather than be near the apes himself, Felipe plans to use drones, which will be undetectable by the apes, to track the apes' movements and living arrangements. Based on prior research, Felipe expects to find that the apes will organize themselves according to kinship roles rather than territorial disputes, food sources, terrain, or other factors. Which of the following poses the greatest threat to the validity of Felipe's research?

    (A) Observer bias
    (B) Observer effect
    (C) The artificiality of the research environment
    (D) Lack of informed consent
    (E) Non-representative sample

77. Teresa has been diagnosed with nerve deafness. Which of the following medical procedures is most likely to restore Teresa's functional hearing?

    (A) Ablation of the temporal lobes
    (B) Repair of her perforated eardrum (tympanic membrane)
    (C) Cochlear implant
    (D) Prescription hearing aids for amplification
    (E) Removal of ear wax

78. Which of the following is NOT a significant factor in one's progression through the stages of psychosexual development, according to Sigmund Freud?

    (A) Breastfeeding
    (B) Toilet training
    (C) Starting school
    (D) Relationships with one's parents
    (E) Puberty

79. When a young child is asked what he did the previous day and his response is "I goed to the store with mommy," this displays

    (A) overgeneralization of grammar
    (B) intellectual disability
    (C) reconstructive memory
    (D) insight learning
    (E) linguistic relativity

80. Aaron Beck, the father of cognitive therapy, did his research on patients with depression. He found commonalities in that these individuals focused on

    (A) difficult events from their childhoods, usually related to sex and/or aggression
    (B) medications that could affect imbalances of neurotransmitters that they were experiencing
    (C) catastrophic assessments of life events and selective perceptions
    (D) obstacles that they had encountered to reaching their potentials
    (E) getting increased attention from family and friends when they had mood swings

81. Many members of Benjamin's family have had sleeping problems over the years and he has heard many discussions about these issues. He has watched these family members try a number of different remedies. When he was studying psychological disorders in his AP Psychology class, Benjamin found he did particularly well remembering information about sleep disorders. This was probably due to

    (A) procedural memory
    (B) state-dependent memory
    (C) context-dependent memory
    (D) self-reference effect
    (E) sensory memory

GO ON TO THE NEXT PAGE.

82. Schizophrenia has both positive and negative symptoms. Which is an example of a positive symptom, and which is an example of a negative symptom, respectively?

    (A) Amnesia; multiple personalities
    (B) Hallucinations; flat affect
    (C) Bursts of creativity; delusions
    (D) No speech; phobias
    (E) Focused attention; social isolation

83. Marta is enrolled in her first martial arts class. She would like to learn black belt skills immediately, but her instructor tells her that she needs to work her way up gradually. As a beginning white belt, she needs to work on the skills necessary to achieve a yellow belt. The instructor's guidance would most likely be based on

    (A) Piaget's concrete operations stage
    (B) Vygotsky's zone of proximal development
    (C) Bowlby's attachment theories
    (D) Kohlberg's conventional morality
    (E) Freud's latency stage

84. Which of the following is NOT a characteristic of, or an anticipated result of, Freudian psychoanalysis?

    (A) Transference
    (B) Exploration of childhood conflicts
    (C) Free association
    (D) Resistance
    (E) Unconditional positive regard

85. In order to facilitate healthy eating habits, a law was passed requiring restaurants to post the calorie counts of their menu offerings. Public health researchers wanted to know whether implementation of this law was changing the way that consumers made their dining decisions. So, every weekend they set up tables at the community hiking/biking trail and randomly stopped people going by to have them answer questionnaires about their dining practices. After several months, they compiled the results and reported that over eighty percent of respondents were making food ordering decisions in restaurants based on the posted calorie counts. They concluded that the law was having the desired effect. Which of the following is the most significant flaw in this research methodology?

    (A) They did not take into account the meals that people ate in their homes.
    (B) They did not make sure that the respondents were gender-balanced.
    (C) Their subjects were likely more health conscious than the overall population.
    (D) They did not account for the cost of the food being ordered.
    (E) People who go to restaurants are wealthier than the overall average of the population.

86. Robert has a debilitating fear of snakes that prevents him from participating in outdoor activities, such as picnicking or golfing, even when no snakes are anywhere near the area. His psychologist initially had Robert simply look at photos of garden snakes, then encouraged him to watch a series of videos featuring increasingly threatening-looking snakes, then ultimately brought him to the local zoo to handle nonvenomous snakes under supervision, all while encouraging Robert to remain relaxed. The psychologist is employing what therapeutic technique?

    (A) Systematic desensitization
    (B) Flooding
    (C) Cognitive Behavioral Therapy
    (D) Client-centered therapy
    (E) Aversive stimulation

87. Philip Zimbardo explained the results of his Stanford Prison Experiment by attributing the bad behavior exhibited by some individuals toward other participants in the study to

    (A) the roles that they were called on to play in the simulation
    (B) the prejudiced views they had toward the other participants before the simulation began
    (C) the explicit instructions given to them by those who designed the experiment
    (D) the physical characteristics of the mock prison that they had constructed
    (E) the deindividuation that participants experienced during the simulation

88. Mary Ainsworth, in her *strange situation* experiments, differentiated between children who are securely attached and those who are insecurely attached. She attributed the level and type of attachment each child had to the

    (A) number and gender of siblings the child had
    (B) birth experiences the child had
    (C) breastfeeding experiences the child had
    (D) quality of parenting the child had experienced
    (E) score on an IQ test the child had taken

GO ON TO THE NEXT PAGE.

89. Psychologists at State University conducted a study of children who had been given up for adoption at birth and did not meet their biological parents. They restricted the subjects to those who remained with the same adoptive family from that point until age 18. When they looked at personality traits, they found, to their surprise, that their subjects displayed more in common with their biological parents than with their adoptive parents. This provided powerful evidence for

    (A) trait theory over behaviorism
    (B) empiricism over genetics
    (C) Freud over Erikson
    (D) maturation over temperament
    (E) heritability over environmental influence

90. Rodrigo watches as his friend Phil goes through the cafeteria line every day at lunch. Phil is very nice to the workers on the lunch line and they often reward him with extra servings of food. Rodrigo is planning to emulate Phil's behavior in the future. Rodrigo is experiencing

    (A) indirect reward
    (B) latent learning
    (C) fluid intelligence
    (D) fixed-ratio reinforcement
    (E) vicarious learning

91. When Congress considers movie ratings or warning labels on music lyrics, reference is often made to Albert Bandura's *Bobo doll* experiments. That is because these experiments stand for the proposition that

    (A) children often prefer watching movies or listening to music to doing their homework
    (B) children often follow the examples of their peers rather than those of their parents
    (C) children engage in pretend play well into their teens
    (D) children often imitate what they see or hear adults doing
    (E) children usually respond to audio and visual stimuli more forcefully when they are presented together as opposed to just one modality on its own

92. Many psychological disorders tend to occur together ("comorbidity"). People who suffer from panic disorder are often unaware of what brought about their attacks; therefore, they do not know what "triggers" to avoid. This may result in comorbidity with what disorder that causes people to stay at home for fear that they will create a scene in public?

    (A) Schizotypal disorder
    (B) Dependent personality disorder
    (C) Generalized anxiety disorder
    (D) Agoraphobia
    (E) Histrionic personality disorder

93. Assume that Pavlov had many bells, each with a different pitch, available to use in his Classical Conditioning experiments. However, he only brought food to his dogs after a certain pitch bell was rung and, as a result, he trained the dogs to salivate only after that particular bell was rung. He would have been most clearly demonstrating what principle?

    (A) Shaping
    (B) Generalization
    (C) Discrimination
    (D) Fixed-ratio reinforcement
    (E) Acquisition

94. Which of the following is NOT one of the levels of Abraham Maslow's hierarchy of needs?

    (A) Love and belonging needs
    (B) Physiological needs
    (C) Self-actualization
    (D) Safety needs
    (E) Self-acceptance needs

95. Often, in fictional works, when a main character is faced with a difficult decision, the following occurs: a devil pops up on one shoulder and encourages this individual to engage in a risky, if pleasurable, activity. An angel pops up on the other shoulder and tells him all of the moral reasons why he should not engage in this behavior. Then the character needs to decide on a course of action based on the real risks and benefits. Freud referred to these three components of the psyche (the "devil," the "angel," and the "decider," respectively) as the

    (A) ego, id, and superego
    (B) oral, anal, and phallic expressions
    (C) superego, ego, and id
    (D) Thanatos, Eros, and libido
    (E) id, superego, and ego

96. Sigmund Freud identified several of his patients as suffering from anxiety or other problems that had led to physical symptoms, such as loss of use of a limb (in his terms, "hysterical paralysis") or loss of use of a sense (in his terms, "hysterical blindness"). Today, under the *DSM-5*, we would likely refer to the condition of such patients as

    (A) dissociative disorder
    (B) panic disorder
    (C) compulsive disorder
    (D) conversion disorder
    (E) fugue

GO ON TO THE NEXT PAGE.

97. Anthropologists discover that inhabitants of a remote Pacific island have relatively few words in their language describing color. If they also find that these islanders do not spend very much time thinking about or assessing color in their environment, this would support which idea?

    (A) Chomsky's innate language acquisition device
    (B) The Sapir-Whorf theory of linguistic relativity
    (C) The behaviorist theory of language development
    (D) Piaget's theory of cognitive development
    (E) The self-reference effect

98. Descriptive statistics, such as mean, median, and mode, summarize data and tell us how it is distributed. Inferential statistics

    (A) provide only the raw data, without any analysis
    (B) provide estimates of how data might change if researchers changed certain experimental conditions
    (C) allow us to see what data would look like if confounding variables were controlled
    (D) are the basis for a meta-analysis that compares results of different studies
    (E) provide a level of confidence that researchers can reject the null hypothesis

99. A factory called in efficiency experts to assess how the assembly line could work better. The efficiency experts spent time at the factory, observed workers on the job, and then made recommendations. Sure enough, productivity increased. Once the efficiency experts left, however, productivity declined. The experts returned and made more recommendations. Productivity again increased, but also decreased again once the experts left. This process kept repeating itself. Ultimately, it was concluded that what caused the productivity increases was not the experts' recommendations, but rather their presence on-site observing the workers. This is referred to as

    (A) the Hawthorne effect
    (B) a self-fulfilling prophecy
    (C) vicarious reinforcement
    (D) shaping
    (E) social facilitation

100. A good example of negative punishment would be

    (A) providing a youngster with more video game time in order to get him to do his homework
    (B) grounding a teenager because he has been persistently violating his curfew
    (C) administering a mild electric shock to an animal in a Skinner box in order to get it to stop gnawing at the wire mesh cage
    (D) giving a teenager additional chores to do when he has refused to do the ones originally assigned
    (E) putting a foul-tasting chemical on a child's fingers to get him to stop chewing his fingernails

END OF SECTION I

IF YOU FINISH BEFORE TIME IS CALLED, YOU MAY CHECK YOUR WORK ON THIS SECTION. DO NOT GO ON TO SECTION II UNTIL YOU ARE TOLD TO DO SO.

PSYCHOLOGY
Section II
Time—50 minutes

Percent of total grade—33$\frac{1}{3}$

Directions: You have 50 minutes to answer BOTH of the following questions. It is not enough to answer a question by merely listing facts. You should present a cogent argument based on your critical analysis of the question posed, using appropriate psychological terminology.

1. From the beginning, Mercedes found the college admissions process quite daunting: so many schools, so many choices! It helped that she knew, unlike many of her friends, that she wanted a small, liberal arts college. However, there were still many choices. Then, she discovered materials in her high school's guidance office about Provincial College. She also found out that she had a cousin who had attended Provincial, so she got information from him. He told her many good things about the school that mirrored what she had read in the brochures. She did not ask him many questions. She knew relatively little about the other small colleges to which she thought she could apply successfully. She convened the "family council": her parents, grandparents, aunts, and uncles who lived nearby and would meet to help solve family problems. Initially, they had many different points of view about the right school for Mercedes. However, they quickly decided to reach consensus about her preliminary selection of Provincial, they stopped looking at the other possibilities, and Mercedes accepted their decision.

Mercedes had assumed that a small, private school like Provincial would have a close-knit, though geographically diverse, student body and many opportunities for student-faculty contact. When she arrived, however, she discovered that neither of these was true: the students were primarily from the area where the school was located and were not very welcoming; faculty members were hard to find outside class. Far from her family and friends, Mercedes became depressed.

Define the following terms and explain how each might have affected Mercedes' situation.
(Just a definition will not suffice to earn full credit for the question.)

- Availability heuristic
- Representativeness heuristic
- Individualism
- Groupthink
- Social support
- Confirmation bias
- Mental set

GO ON TO THE NEXT PAGE.

2. A researcher had a hypothesis that playing classical music during breastfeeding would enhance mother-infant bonding. So, she contacted *Modern Mother* magazine, obtained a list of its subscriber base, and contacted one hundred women to see whether or not they would be interested in participating in an experiment. The first fifty women who responded positively were selected to come into the lab with their infants. Once there, they were randomly selected to be part of the group that had classical music playing in their breastfeeding room or the group that had no music playing. The breastfeeding rooms were designed to be as home-like as possible. During breastfeeding, the mothers and their infants were videotaped; later, graduate students studied the tapes and calculated how much eye contact the mothers and their infants maintained for each ten minutes of breastfeeding. They found a significant increase in eye contact for the group that had the classical music, as opposed to the other group, and the researcher concluded that her hypothesis was supported.

Part A

Identify each of the following in this study.

- The operational definition of the dependent variable.
- One possible ethical problem and how it might be corrected.
- One possible confounding variable and how it could be avoided.

Part B

- Explain why this study is not a naturalistic observation.
- Explain what it means to "double blind" an experiment and why that might have been necessary based on measurement of the dependent variable in this situation.
- Explain why the researcher cannot generalize her findings to all children and mothers.

STOP

END OF EXAM

Practice Test 2:
Answers and
Explanations

PRACTICE TEST 2: ANSWER KEY

1.	B	26.	D	51.	D	76.	A
2.	D	27.	B	52.	B	77.	C
3.	E	28.	B	53.	B	78.	C
4.	C	29.	D	54.	A	79.	A
5.	A	30.	A	55.	A	80.	C
6.	C	31.	E	56.	B	81.	D
7.	E	32.	E	57.	E	82.	B
8.	D	33.	D	58.	A	83.	B
9.	B	34.	B	59.	D	84.	E
10.	D	35.	B	60.	E	85.	C
11.	D	36.	A	61.	C	86.	A
12.	C	37.	B	62.	E	87.	A
13.	A	38.	B	63.	C	88.	D
14.	B	39.	C	64.	C	89.	E
15.	C	40.	C	65.	A	90.	E
16.	C	41.	A	66.	A	91.	D
17.	B	42.	C	67.	D	92.	D
18.	C	43.	D	68.	A	93.	C
19.	E	44.	E	69.	E	94.	E
20.	B	45.	C	70.	A	95.	E
21.	A	46.	B	71.	D	96.	D
22.	C	47.	C	72.	D	97.	B
23.	A	48.	E	73.	E	98.	E
24.	E	49.	E	74.	E	99.	A
25.	D	50.	A	75.	B	100.	B

PRACTICE TEST 2: ANSWERS AND EXPLANATIONS

Section I: Multiple Choice

1. **B** *Understand the Question/Key Words*: The key words are *Asch* and *confederates who sometimes gave deliberately incorrect responses*. *Predict the Answer*: Asch was testing to see whether the subjects would stick with their own perceptions or make the same response as the confederates. Conformity means aligning one's behavior with the behavior of others, so (B) is correct.

2. **D** *Understand the Question/Key Words*: The key language is that indicating that the researchers were taking an in-depth look at one unusual subject. Use POE to eliminate (A) and (C) because this is not an experiment. Eliminate (B) because a correlational study would require many more subjects in order to establish a relationship between variables. Eliminate (E) because this study was not conducted at multiple points in time. Choice (D) is correct because a case study takes a detailed look at an unusual subject or situation.

3. **E** *Understand the Question/Key Words:* The key words are *neurotransmitters pass…across a gap*. *Predict the Answer:* This gap is the synapse, so (E) is the correct answer.

4. **C** *Understand the Question/Key Words:* The key words are *suddenly and involuntarily falling asleep during daytime hours*. Use POE to find the answer. Eliminate (A) because it refers to a particular state of sleep during the night. Eliminate (B) because it refers to a problem with bodily rhythms during a typical 24-hour period. Eliminate (D) because it refers to a dysfunction occurring during nighttime sleep. Eliminate (E) because sleep-walking is an abnormal behavior occurring during nighttime sleep. Choice (C) is correct because narcolepsy is just what the key words describe.

5. **A** *Understand the Question/Key Words*: The key words are *visual perception*. *Predict the Answer:* Gestalt, meaning "pattern" and having as its guiding principle the idea that "the whole is greater than the sum of its parts," is the only approach focused primarily on perception. Choice (A) is correct.

6. **C** *Understand the Question/Key Words*: The key concept is *learned helplessness*. *Predict the Answer:* Learned helplessness may befall individuals who have experienced futility in improving their situations and who therefore feel a lack of control over their environments. The correct answer choice has the right combination of locus of control and self-efficacy to describe this situation, and that correct answer choice is (C).

7. **E** *Understand the Question/Key Words*: The key words are *drive reduction theory*. *Predict the Answer:* Drive reduction theory applies to physiological drives like hunger and thirst; hence, the correct response involves the physiological state of homeostasis, (E). At that point, the individual's "drive" is satisfied. You can also use POE here. Individuals would not attain a steady state of relaxation, (A); self-actualization, (B); achievement, (C); or positive relationships, (D) just from reducing drives, so eliminate these choices. Choice (E) is correct.

8. **D** *Understand the Question/Key Words:* The key words are *the method of loci, the peg-word system, and chunking*. *Predict the Answer:* Choice (D), mnemonic devices. These are strategies designed to improve memory for information.

9. **B** *Understand the Question/Key Words*: The key words here are *roller coaster, vivid memories, proximity,* and *brain*. The question is seeking what it is about brain structure that would make recall of an arousing event more likely. *Predict the Answer:* Anytime that you see "memory" and "brain" together you should be thinking about the hippocampus, which is only found in (B). If you didn't remember that, you can also use POE. Eliminate (C) because these areas deal with language. Eliminate (D) because the cerebellum relates to procedural memory and the question is about episodic memory. Eliminate (E): though the hypothalamus is part of the limbic system, it is not related to memory. Eliminate (A): though the lobes contain parts of the association cortex, and thus are related to memory, the frontal lobes are not specifically related to arousal. It is significant that the amygdala is the "fear center" of the brain.

10. **D** *Understand the Question/Key Words*: The key language here indicates that Marty's beliefs and actions are not in sync and that this makes him *uncomfortable*. Try using POE. Marty is not projecting either his thoughts or his actions onto others, so (A) should be eliminated. Neither is he denying the existence of a problem; the problem is why he is uncomfortable. Eliminate (B). There is no group decision-making, so eliminate (C). The quality of Marty's performance is not affected by whether or not others are around, so eliminate (E). Choice (D) is correct because Marty's discomfort when providing an excuse for his behavior is evidence of the tension predicted by cognitive dissonance.

11. **D** *Understand the Question/Key Words*: The key is *correlation coefficient*. *Predict the Answer:* Correlation coefficients range from –1.0 to 1.0, with a negative sign indicating an inverse relationship, such as the one described here. Use POE to eliminate (A) and (B) because this is not a direct relationship and eliminate (E) because it is not a legitimate correlation coefficient. Choice (C) would reflect a weak inverse relationship. Choice (D) is the correct answer.

12. **C** *Understand the Question/Key Words*: The key words are *lacking empathy, exploit others,* and *personality disorder. Predict the Answer:* Look for the disorder that is characterized by a lack of empathy and a tendency to manipulate others; that is antisocial personality disorder (contrary to the often-used definition of "antisocial," here it does not refer to someone who wants to be apart from others).

13. **A** *Understand the Question/Key Words*: The key language is that indicating that Martin was unable to view the umbrella as useful for anything other than its traditional use. *Predict the Answer:* You are looking for a barrier to effective problem-solving that involves objects. Use POE. Choices (B), (C), (D), and (E) refer to other problem-solving strategies or issues. Only (A) refers to the barrier to effective problem-solving that involves the inability to see any but the most common possible uses for an object.

14. **B** *Understand the Question/Key Words*: The key words are *center of emotion in the brain*. Try using POE to find the answer. Eliminate (A) because this is the part of the nervous system that controls bodily functions not consciously directed, like breathing. Eliminate (C) because this is the system responsible for balance. Eliminate (D) because this involves the brain's response to reinforcing stimuli. Eliminate (E) because this system calms us down after a fight-or-flight response. The correct answer is (B), the limbic system.

15. **C** *Understand the Question/Key Words*: The key words are *Events…that create intense emotions. Predict the Answer*: Events like these often produce powerful memories for people about where they were

and how they learned about the event. Use POE. Eliminate (A) because it involves people changing their memories in response to later events, expectations, and other factors. Eliminate (B) because this involves new information interfering with one's recollection of previously learned information. Eliminate (D) because it involves previously learned information interfering with retention of more recently learned information. Eliminate (E) because it involves the ability to recall an image from memory after seeing it only once. Only (C) refers specifically to events involving high levels of arousal and emotion.

16. **C** *Understand the Question/Key Words:* The key word is *DSM-5*. *Predict the Answer:* The *DSM-5* is the fifth edition of this important reference book, so (C) is the correct answer.

17. **B** *Understand the Question/Key Words:* The key words are *stroke affecting the left side* and *unable to produce intelligible speech*. *Predict the Answer*: Choice (B), Broca's area, is responsible for the production of intelligible speech. If this were not immediately known, consider your options and use POE. Eliminate (A) because it involves comprehension of speech. Eliminate (C) because it involves hearing. Eliminate (D) because it involves vision. Eliminate (E) because it involves the touch sensation.

18. **C** *Understand the Question/Key Words:* The key language is that which describes the customer's bad behavior and Wanda's assessment of the customer as *a jerk*. *Predict the Answer:* This involves attribution theory and Wanda is making a dispositional attribution about the customer's behavior. The correct answer is (C), fundamental attribution error.

19. **E** *Understand the Question/Key Words:* The key language is that which describes people who are distressed by a physical characteristic that they have to the point that they would have surgery to "correct" it. The question seeks the *DSM-5* designation for such a condition. Go ahead and use POE. Eliminate (A), (B), and (C) because they do not involve physical characteristics. Individuals with narcissistic personality disorder are greatly concerned with their physical appearances, but they would tend to overvalue their own beauty, not think that they were grotesque to others. Choice (E) is correct because body dysmorphic disorder refers to overwhelming concern about a perceived physical defect.

20. **B** *Understand the Question/Key Words:* The key term is *general adaptation syndrome (GAS)*. *Predict the Answer:* Selye's finding was that animals under long-term stress become more and more susceptible to physical illness over time. You can use POE here. Neither "acceptance," nor "rebound," nor "relaxation," nor "resolution" would tend to produce illness; eliminate (A), (C), (D), and (E). Choice (B) is correct.

21. **A** *Understand the Question/Key Words:* The key words are *Big Five* and *MMPI-2-RF*. *Predict the Answer:* These are both trait inventories: they are trying to categorize personality characteristics, not explain how they came to be. Choice (A), trait theory, is correct.

22. **C** *Understand the Question/Key Words*: The key words are *NOT a symptom of a major depressive disorder*. *Predict the Answer:* The symptoms in (C) relate to mania, which is not a component of a major depressive disorder, so (C) is your answer. Through POE, you can eliminate (A), (B), (D), and (E) because they are symptoms of depression.

23. **A** *Understand the Question/Key Words:* The question is seeking the term for these rules. *Predict the* Answer: We're looking at sentence creation here, so (A), syntax, is what you want. If you don't know or remember the definition of *syntax*, use POE. Eliminate (B) because these are the smallest meaningful units in language. Eliminate (C) because these are the basic sounds in a language. Eliminate (D) because this involves a young child producing a single word to try to convey the meaning of an entire sentence. Eliminate (E) because this involves the meanings of words, not their correct ordering.

24. **E** *Understand the Question/Key Words:* The key words are *Erik Erikson* and *primary developmental task for young adults. Predict the Answer:* The stage for young adults is "intimacy versus isolation," so it is about developing meaningful relationships.

25. **D** *Understand the Question/Key Words:* The key words are *DSM-5*, *Multiple Personality Disorder*, and *two or more distinct personalities, often accompanied by amnesia. Predict the Answer:* Though schizophrenia is often mistakenly thought to have these characteristics, only (D), dissociative identity disorder, actually does. Choice (D) is correct.

26. **D** *Understand the Question/Key Words:* The key words are *NOT an ethical consideration.* Use POE. The concerns addressed in (A), (B), (C), and (E) are legitimate ethical concerns for this research, so eliminate them. While controlling potentially confounding variables might be an important concern for these experimenters, it is not an issue of ethics. Choice (D) is the correct answer.

27. **B** *Understand the Question/Key Words:* The key words are *NOT a categorical variable. Predict the Answer:* Essentially, you are looking for a variable that is not a check-off box on a census form. An IQ score is continuous: it exists over a range of values. Choice (B) is correct!

28. **B** *Understand the Question/Key Words:* The key words are those indicating that the subjects do not know to which group they were assigned. Use POE. To double-blind an experiment means that the experimenters as well as the subjects do not know to which groups subjects were assigned. Eliminate (A). Reliability involves whether a test will produce similar results when re-administered. Eliminate (C). Validity involves whether a test actually measures what it intends to measure. Eliminate (D). Statistical significance indicates to what extent researchers can have confidence in the fact that their data support their conclusions. Eliminate (E). Choice (B) is correct because the single-blind precaution prevents subjects from knowing whether they are in the experimental group or the control group.

29. **D** *Understand the Question/Key Words:* The question is asking *what strategy* the coach is using when she rewards the runner *each time (she) reduces her personal best by at least four seconds. Predict the Answer:* Choice (D), fixed-ratio reinforcement, is defined as providing a reward every time a certain behavior (in this case, reducing the time by four seconds) is performed. That looks like the correct answer, but you can use POE to be sure. This is not about an interval-based schedule of reinforcement (eliminate (A) and (B)); neither is it about either restricting the sorts of behaviors that will bring about a reward or expanding the sorts of behaviors that could be reinforced (eliminate (C) and (E)). Choice (D) is correct because the coach is using a fixed ratio to reinforce the runner's behavior.

30. **A** *Understand the Question/Key Words:* The key words are *knowing which studying techniques work well for him. Predict the Answer*: Choice (A). The subject matter is clearly cognition but use POE to check out your options. Eliminate (B) because knowing yourself is intrapersonal, not interpersonal,

intelligence. Eliminate (C) because state-dependent memory involves one's mood when learning and remembering information. Eliminate (D) because it refers to knowledge of facts, not studying techniques. Eliminate (E) because it involves solving problems via a "Eureka!" moment rather than through a learning process.

31. **E** *Understand the Question/Key Words*: The key words are *operant conditioning*, *positive behaviors*, and *institutional settings*. *Predict the Answer:* Operant conditioning is all about reinforcement, in this case by rewarding good behavior with tokens that can be redeemed for primary reinforcers. Looks like (E), token economy, is the correct answer, but you can use POE to be sure. The other answer choices contain language that is relevant to conditioning, but it is not specific to either positive behaviors or to institutional settings. Eliminate them.

32. **E** *Understand the Question/Key Words*: The key language is *change in electrical charge* and *trigger an action potential*. Go ahead and use POE! If the correct term is not immediately apparent, consider your options. Eliminate (A) because this is the receiving end of the neuron for incoming chemical messages. Eliminate (B) because this is the part of the neuron that sends such messages. Eliminate (C) because this describes the nature of the axon. Eliminate (D) because this effect would move the neuron away from triggering an action potential. Choice (E) is correct because reaching the threshold change in electrical charge is what triggers an action potential.

33. **D** *Understand the Question/Key Words*: The key words are *from memory* and *errors…in the middle* of a list. *Predict the Answer*: This phenomenon, with better memory for beginnings and endings of lists, is (D), serial position effect. If you didn't remember that, you could've used POE. Eliminate (A) because Francois did not want to forget this information. Eliminate (B) because it involves unconsciously burying a memory because it is distressing and that is not the issue here. Eliminate (C) because it involves an inability to create new memories and does not involve placement within a list. Eliminate (E) because this involves particularly memorable events.

34. **B** *Understand the Question/Key Words*: The key terms are *normal distribution*, *standard deviation*, and *mean*. *Predict the Answer:* Shoshanna has scored exactly one standard deviation above the mean. Your knowledge of a normal distribution would tell you that 34% of test-takers score between the mean and one standard deviation above it. Shoshanna has outscored 50% of the students, plus an additional 34%. The correct answer is (B). You can also use POE. Eliminate (D) and (E) because Shoshanna clearly scored above half of the test-takers. Eliminate (A) because, in order to achieve the 98th percentile, Shoshanna would have needed to score two standard deviations above the mean, or 130.

35. **B** *Understand the Question/Key Words*: The key words here are *Harlow* and *monkeys*, and these should be circled. *Predict the Answer:* Choice (B) looks right if you remember this famous research led to a prediction about mother-infant bonding. You can use POE to check out the other answer choices. Eliminate (A), (C), and (E) as not related to bonding. Eliminate (D) because, though this was the Harlows' hypothesis, it is not what they found.

36. **A** *Understand the Question/Key Words*: Circle *NOT* and *recognized*. Use a "true/false" method for evaluating the answer choices in a "NOT" question. Eliminate (B), (C), (D), and (E) because they should be marked "True" as recognized basic tastes. The correct answer is (A), spicy.

37. **B** *Understand the Question/Key Words*: The key concepts are *fight-or-flight* and *homeostasis*. Go ahead and use POE. Choice (A) is synonymous with the "fight-or-flight" arousal response and thus incorrect. Choices (C), (D), and (E) involve balance, reward, and emotion, respectively, and do not involve achieving homeostasis. Choice (B) is correct because, after sympathetic activation, it is the parasympathetic system that brings us back to homeostasis.

38. **B** *Understand the Question/Key Words*: The question asks for a reason for behavior that wouldn't be explained by any commonly accepted definition of "hunger." *Predict the Answer*: You want an answer that deals with why this behavior is expected, as opposed to any sense of "need." Choice (B) looks correct, but you can use POE to be sure. Choices (A), (C), (D), and (E) all deal with physiological indicators of hunger and do not address why this behavior might be expected of us. Yep, (B) is the right answer.

39. **C** *Understand the Question/Key Words*: Here, circle *bystander effect* as the key concept. *Predict the Answer*: As you think about this concept, remember that it relates to our willingness to help other people, and specifically it relates to the number of other people who are aware that this individual needs help. Sounds like (C), and you can use POE to eliminate (A), (B), (D), and (E), as they relate to motivations and emotions, not the number of others aware of the person needing help.

40. **C** *Understand the Question/Key Words*: As you read the question, note that the reason for the depression will need to match the "approach." So, circle *unrealistically high expectations*. *Predict the Answer*: You are looking for an approach that focuses on how people view their situations. That'll be (C), the cognitive approach. You can also use POE to find the answer. Eliminate (A) because this approach focuses on the unconscious and repressed memories of childhood conflict. Eliminate (B) because this approach focuses on reinforcement from one's environment. Eliminate (D) because this approach focuses on behaviors that are adaptive for survival. Eliminate (E) because this approach focuses on genetics and brain chemistry.

41. **A** *Understand the Question/Key Words*: Performance seems to be based on one's state of mind going into the exam, so focus on words like *not...very seriously*, *groggy* versus *nervous*, *energy drink* versus *seriously*, and *not feel stressed*. Use POE. Once it's apparent that the issue is about level of arousal, you can eliminate answers that deal with problem-solving, (B), adolescent development, (C), emotion sequencing, (D), or language, (E). Choice (A) is correct because the Yerkes-Dodson Law is about the optimal level of arousal for a given task.

42. **C** *Understand the Question/Key Words*: Since the question is about the paradoxical nature of *REM sleep*, circle that; it is important to know that REM stands for "rapid eye movement" and a paradox is an apparent contradiction. *Predict the Answer*: The contradiction should involve our near paralysis during REM while other aspects of our physiology are quite active, so (C) looks correct. Use POE to be sure. Choices (A), (B), (D), and (E) can be eliminated as they deal with restorative properties and dreaming, they contain incorrect information, and, to the extent that they present paradoxes, they are unrelated to muscular activity.

43. **D** *Understand the Question/Key Words*: The function of the *semicircular canals* is the issue; circle it. *Predict the Answer*: The semicircular canals are related to balance, not hearing. Use POE. Choices (A), (B), and (E) are related to hearing. Choice (C) is unrelated to hearing, but also to balance. Choice (D) is correct.

44. **E** *Understand the Question/Key Words*: The key language is *most durable*, equivalent to "long-lasting." Use POE. Choice (A) produces very fast extinction of behavior in the absence of reinforcement; eliminate it. Choice (D) also produces fast extinction, and (B) and (C) produce extinction, in the absence of prompt reinforcement, faster than the correct response. Eliminate them as well. Choice (E), variable-ratio reinforcement, is usually illustrated with examples from the world of gambling (e.g., slot machines, lotteries); think about the tendency of die-hard gamblers to continue gambling, even in the absence of reinforcement. Choice (E) is correct.

45. **C** *Understand the Question/Key Words*: The key language is *learns to press a lever to stop the shocks. Predict the Answer*: Choice (C), negative reinforcement. You can use POE. Punishment involves producing less of a behavior; here, more of a behavior (lever pressing) is being produced, so eliminate (A) and (B). While this is reinforcement, nothing is being added for the mouse's benefit; rather, an aversive stimulus (the shock) is being removed. So, eliminate (D). Shaping involves rewarding successive approximations of a goal. Here, there is no specific goal established for the mouse's behavior, so eliminate (E). Choice (C) is the correct answer.

46. **B** *Understand the Question/Key Words*: The key here is *hypnosis. Predict the Answer:* Hypnosis can produce an altered state of consciousness with heightened suggestibility. So, think about a "mind over matter" scenario. Use POE. Hypnosis has not been proven to have much value in treating addiction, ADHD, or memory issues, eliminating (A), (C), (D), and (E). Choice (B) is correct because hypnosis has proven successful in providing pain relief in cases of pain that have required pain relieving drugs or mild sedation.

47. **C** *Understand the Question/Key Words*: The key idea is *Kohlberg's stage theory of moral development.* Circle this. *Predict the Answer:* Following the decision-making rationales at the pre-conventional, conventional, and post-conventional levels of Kohlberg's theory, one sees a progression from "what's in it for me?" to "what will others think of me?" to "what are my ideas about right and wrong?" Choice (C) looks like a pretty good option, but consider the others through POE. Eliminate (A) and (B) because Kohlberg makes no reference to religion as the basis for decision-making. Eliminate (D) because Kohlberg does not distinguish rules that are written down from those that are not. Eliminate (E) because Kohlberg does not emphasize the source of guidance and because laws, for example, can be important at all of the levels, but for different reasons.

48. **E** *Understand the Question/Key Words*: The key phrase is *focus in on one conversation. Predict the Answer:* What is being described is a process of "selective attention" and the answer should be related to that. *POE:* Eliminate (A) because multitasking is a form of divided attention. Eliminate (B) because this involves hearing different things in each ear. Eliminate (C) because this involves distinguishing sound qualities, not tuning out conversations. Choice (E) is correct because the cocktail party effect allows the listener to tune out, or at least "turn down the volume" for competing conversations, making this an example of selective attention.

49. **E** *Understand the Question/Key Words*: The key words are *NOT* and *Stanley Milgram's Yale electric shock experiment. Predict the Answer:* Milgram was looking into obedience, specifically whether or not having an authority figure present might cause individuals to engage in behaviors that they would otherwise consider morally questionable. Use POE. Eliminate (A), (B), (C), and (D) because these were findings of the Milgram study. With regard to (E), Milgram used only male subjects in

the original experiment. Moreover, when he later replicated the study using female subjects, women demonstrated very similar rates of obedience (so female reluctance to shock was NOT a finding and (E) is correct).

50. **A** *Understand the Question/Key Words*: The key language here is the definition of *schema* and the fact that *new information could fit*. *Predict the Answer*: Assimilation and accommodation are the relevant processes and the issue is whether or not children had to change the existing schema. Here, they did not. The correct answer is (A). Accommodation is the process that would require alteration of the existing schema.

51. **D** *Understand the Question/Key Words*: The key language is *visual and auditory inputs*, *very quickly*, and *immediate strategic decisions*. *Predict the Answer*: Focusing on the speed of responsiveness should lead to the correct answer. Use POE to go through your options. Choice (A) involves a sense organ sending fewer messages to the brain when there has been a constant stimulus over time. Eliminate it. Choice (B) also involves a constant stimulus; in this case, there is a cognitive process that allows an individual to get used to the stimulus, so eliminate it. Choice (C) involves knowledge of facts. Eliminate it. Choice (E) involves recollection of events in one's life. Eliminate it. Only (D) involves processing of sensory inputs at speed.

52. **B** *Understand the Question/Key Words*: The key words are *the building that houses the web design department* and *flaw*. *Predict the Answer*: Choice (B), non-representative sampling. Researchers are not sampling from the entire company. Web designers could have different attitudes than other employees. They may, for example, present a different gender mix than other departments. You can also use POE to find the right answer. If the flaw is not immediately apparent, consider your options. Eliminate (A) because the sampling was done randomly ("every fifth person"). Eliminate (C) because subjects were able to take the survey in a confidential manner. Eliminate (D) because this is not an observation study and the researchers are interpreting the subjects' responses. Eliminate (E) because the subjects are not being observed as they respond to the survey.

53. **B** *Understand the Question/Key Words:* The key language is what the coach said to students *of Scandinavian heritage* and what their results were. *Predict the Answer:* Generalizations about anticipated performance based on gender, race, ethnicity, etc. can have the effect of creating a self-fulfilling prophecy. That idea is what (B) is all about.

54. **A** *Understand the Question/Key Words:* The key words are *never loses her understanding of the true size*. *Predict the Answer:* The correct response should involve an unchanging perception despite external cues, which means you're looking at (A). You can use POE to eliminate answer choices that simply name elements of the visual system ((B), (D), and (E)) or that indicate a change in perception, (C).

55. **A** *Understand the Question/Key Words:* The question is asking for an explanation of why, after students *stare intently* at a colorful image, different colors may emerge. *Predict the Answer:* Since the image has changed from what was evident at the stage of sensation, this is a matter of perception, specifically the appearance of opponent colors as predicted by opponent process theory. Use POE. Choice (B) involves an inability to distinguish certain colors. Eliminate it. Choice (C) is not specific to color. Eliminate it. Choice (D) involves clarity of color vision. Eliminate it. Choice (E) names the other major theory, besides opponent process, about how we process color; it posits that there are different types of cones responsible for processing particular colors. Eliminate it. Choice (A) is

correct because, according to opponent process theory, when we saturate on a particular color, our brains bring out the opponent color.

56. **B** *Understand the Question/Key Words:* The key words are *jet lag*, *reset his body clock*, and *get his sleep schedule back on track*. The question is seeking the name of a chemical relevant to these concepts. *Predict the Answer:* Melatonin, but if you don't remember that, go ahead and use POE. Eliminate (A) because it is a neurotransmitter primarily involved with physical movement. Eliminate (C) because it is a hormone related to arousal. Eliminate (D) because it is a hormone that accelerates growth. Eliminate (E) because it is a hormone related to stress.

57. **E** *Understand the Question/Key Words:* The key words are *part of the brain that becomes most active*, *scanning technology*, and *investigate brain activity*. Use POE. Eliminate (A) because, while EEG does record brain wave activity, it is not effective in identifying specific parts of the brain. Eliminate (B) and (C) because these are most useful in investigating brain structure. Eliminate (D) because it is a test of heart function. Choice (E) is correct because a PET scan measures glucose consumption in the brain in real time, making it possible to see which part of the brain "lights up" to perform a particular function.

58. **A** *Understand the Question/Key Words:* The key language is describing Braxton's dysfunctional *checking behaviors*. *Predict the Answer:* This sort of repetitive behavior is typical of OCD. It is important to differentiate the "O" from the "C" in OCD. The "O" is the obsession, the intrusive thoughts that cause the person anxiety. The "C" is the compulsion, the ritualistic behavior that the person engages in in order to reduce this anxiety. While (A) and (C) both correctly identify OCD, only (A) correctly classifies the behaviors.

59. **D** *Understand the Question/Key Words:* The key words are *less-than-positive image of motorcyclists caused her to make a bad decision*. *Predict the Answer:* The correct response will involve a barrier to effective problem-solving. Go ahead and use POE. Eliminate (A) because it is a memory concept. While this fact pattern does seem to involve stereotyping, neither (B) nor (C) involves problem-solving, so eliminate them. While (E) is a barrier to effective problem-solving, it involves the amount of information available to the solver and the fact pattern does not address this; rather, the facts suggest that the solver used an inaccurate prototype, which is a description of the representativeness heuristic: hence, (D).

60. **E** *Understand the Question/Key Words:* The key words are *Schachter and Singer's two-factor theory*. *Predict the Answer:* This theory is also sometimes known as the cognitive theory. Choice (E) looks correct, but use POE to be sure. Choice (A) describes the James-Lange theory; eliminate it. Choice (B) describes the Cannon-Bard theory; eliminate it. These theories of emotion are about sequencing. Choices (C) and (D) do not address this; eliminate them. Choice (E) is correct because this theory states that, after experiencing physiological arousal, the individual must make a cognitive assessment of the context of the arousal in order to identify the emotion.

61. **C** *Understand the Question/Key Words:* The key words are *right brain dominant*. *Predict the Answer:* Choice (C), spatial design. In brain lateralization, the left brain is primarily engaged in analytical thinking, breaking things down into their component parts and being highly mathematical. It is also where speech functions are usually located. The right brain tends to be more holistic in orientation, seeing the big picture and discerning patterns.

62. **E** *Understand the Question/Key Words:* The key words are *most viewers are uninterested* and *elaboration likelihood model. Predict the Answer*: The elaboration likelihood model suggests that, if the target audience is not engaged in the subject matter, persuasion should be pursued via the peripheral route (emphasizing superficial qualities) rather than the central route (emphasizing facts and logic). Use POE. Eliminate (A), (B), (C), and (D) because they follow the central route approach. Choice (E) contains the sort of superficial elements that are characteristic of the peripheral route.

63. **C** *Understand the Question/Key Words:* The key word is *gender.* The question seeks to know what role gender plays in this study. *Predict the Answer:* Though not technically a "manipulation" by the experimenter in this instance, gender is an independent variable here because it is the factor that separates the experimental group from the control group. Choice (C) is the correct answer.

64. **C** *Understand the Question/Key Words:* The key words are *strongly favored animal rights* and *even more strongly in favor of animal rights. Predict the Answer:* You are looking for a concept in social psychology that explains how like-minded people, when they have been meeting over a period of time, tend to become even more intensely aligned with their original points of view. That is (C), group polarization.

65. **A** *Understand the Question/Key Words:* The key words are *Miller's magic number* and *seven plus or minus two. Predict the Answer:* This is about the capacity of short-term, or working, memory. Choice (A) is what you want.

66. **A** *Understand the Question/Key Words:* The key words are *Carl Rogers* and *talk therapy. Predict the Answer:* Carl Rogers was a humanist, so the correct response should be part of the humanist approach. Use POE. Eliminate (B) and (E) because they are part of psychoanalytical, or Freudian, therapy. Eliminate (C) because it is part of cognitive therapy. Eliminate (D) because it is part of behavioral therapy. Choice (A) is correct because this is an essential component of humanistic, or client-centered, therapy.

67. **D** *Understand the Question/Key Words:* The key words are *Baumrind* and *parenting styles. Predict the Answer:* Baumrind differentiated among parents who enforced strict, unquestioned discipline (authoritarian), those who enforced firm discipline while discussing the reasons for it with their children (authoritative), and those who enforced insufficient discipline (permissive). Choice (D) is the correct answer.

68. **A** *Understand the Question/Key Words:* The key words are *Rorschach inkblots* and *personality test. Predict the Answer:* The inkblots do not have "correct" or "graded" responses. They are supposed to provide the therapist with insight into the patient's unconscious mind. This aligns with the psychoanalytic approach. Projective tests present ambiguous stimuli and a person's responses allow the therapist to detect hidden feelings and urges. So, (A) is correct.

69. **E** *Understand the Question/Key Words:* The key words are *most likely effect of chronic, long-term stress. Predict the Answer:* Selye's general adaptation syndrome would predict exhaustion that would lead to physical illness. Choice (E) looks correct, but use POE to consider the other options. Eliminate (A) because these symptoms of PTSD would likely follow a deeply traumatic event. Eliminate (B) and (C) because phobias and violent mood swings are also not likely outcomes of prolonged, low-level stress. Eliminate (D) because multiple personalities (at least in theory) emerge in response to extremely traumatic and abusive events in childhood.

70. **A** *Understand the Question/Key Words*: The key words are *NOT a symptom* and *ADHD*. *Predict the Answer*: Symptoms of ADHD include difficulties in staying on task, (B); difficulties in executive function, (E); hyperactivity, (D); and impulsivity, (C). Choice (A), difficulty communicating with others, is not a symptom, thus making it correct.

71. **D** *Understand the Question/Key Words*: The key idea here is *Weber's law* and how it relates to an assessment of weight. *Predict the Answer*: Since Weber's law is about just noticeable differences and their proportionality with the original stimulus strength, you will be looking for an answer that relates to the JND for weight. Use POE. Eliminate (A) and (E) because they relate to other senses, not weight. Applying the idea of proportionality, we would be more sensitive to small differences at a smaller overall weight, eliminating (B) and (C).

72. **D** *Understand the Question/Key Words*: This question asks when students will best *remember information*, thus involving retrieval of information from memory. The fact pattern distinguishes between *classroom* and *swimming pool*. Circle these ideas. *Predict the Answer*: Many factors could influence retrieval: positive or negative cues, a person's emotional state at the time of learning and retrieval, etc. The language in this question suggests that the location of learning and retrieval is key. Use POE. Eliminate (A) and (B) as they have to do with mood and are quite similar. Choice (E) also relates to mood and should be eliminated. Choice (C) may relate to cues or interference, but not to location. Choice (D) is correct because, according to context-dependent memory, individuals will remember information better in the location where they learned it.

73. **E** *Understand the Question/Key Words*: This question involves strengthening versus deterioration of skills. Use POE. Choices (A) and (B) involve the relationship between newly learned and older information. Since that distinction is not made here, eliminate these. Cues for remembering information are not mentioned here, so eliminate (C) and (D). Choice (E) is correct because, especially during the teenage years, unused neural pathways will atrophy or be pruned away.

74. **E** *Understand the Question/Key Words*: The key word is *opiates*. Opiates are a class of drugs used to treat pain and, in some cases, produce sleep. *Predict the Answer*: Endorphins. A hint here is that *endorphins* contains the same root as *morphine*, a prominent opiate. However, if you don't remember or know that, you can use POE. Choices (A), (C), and (D) are chemicals that produce different effects and should be eliminated. While barbiturates are sleeping pills, they do not provide pain relief, so you can also eliminate (B). You're left with (E), the correct answer.

75. **B** *Understand the Question/Key Words*: This question is about the James-Lange theory of emotion and the other key words are *paralyzed from the neck down* and *cast doubt on*. *Predict the Answer*: The James-Lange theory states that emotions are caused by physiological arousal. Anything that weakens this linkage would cast doubt on the validity of the theory. Use POE. Choice (A) supports this linkage and is what the James-Lange theory tells us to expect if an individual has less capacity for physical expression of arousal; eliminate it. Choices (C) and (D), in referencing a cognitive assessment of the arousal, are about the Schachter-Singer theory; eliminate them. Choice (E) can be eliminated because it does not indicate that the facial expressions cause the emotions, only that they accompany them. Choice (B) is correct because, if the impaired physiology has no impact on the intensity of emotional expression, this calls the James-Lange theory into question.

76. **A**   *Understand the Question/Key Words*: The key language is *Felipe expects* and *greatest threat to the validity* of the research. *Predict the Answer*: You should recognize this research as a naturalistic observation. Two potential threats would be observer bias and observer effect. You can use POE to consider the answer choices. Eliminate (C), (D), and (E) because artificiality, informed consent, and sampling are not issues in a naturalistic observation. Eliminate (B) because the observer effect occurs when the subjects know that they are being watched; the fact pattern indicates that the apes will not be aware of the drones. Observer bias, (A), is correct because Felipe has certain expectations going into the research and this creates concern that he may "see what he hopes to see."

77. **C**   *Understand the Question/Key Words*: The key words are *nerve deafness*. *Predict the Answer*: Choice (C), cochlear implant. Nerve deafness is caused by damage to the stereocilia in the cochlea, or to the auditory nerve itself. Restoring hearing would need to address one of these issues. If you didn't immediately remember that, you could also use POE. Eliminate (B), (D), and (E) because these interventions are intended to improve conduction of sound waves in Teresa's ears and that is not her problem. Eliminate (A) because removal of brain tissue will also not address Teresa's problem.

78. **C**   *Understand the Question/Key Words*: The key words are *NOT* and Freud's *stage theory of psychosexual development*. *Predict the Answer*: Freud's theory involves which erogenous zones might be important in a child's development and what sorts of traumatic experiences the child may have. If you don't remember that (C), starting school, isn't a significant factor, you can use POE. Eliminate (A) because breastfeeding is key in the oral stage. Eliminate (B) because toilet training is key to the anal stage. Eliminate (D) because relationships with parents are key to the phallic stage. Eliminate (E) because puberty denotes the onset of the genital stage.

79. **A**   *Understand the Question/Key Words*: The key here is what the child said: *I goed to the store with mommy*. *Predict the Answer*: This child is overusing the rule in English that we often add "-ed" to the ends of words to make them past tense and he has not learned exceptions to this rule. This involves grammar, so the correct answer is (A).

80. **C**   *Understand the Question/Key Words*: The key words are *Aaron Beck*, *cognitive therapy*, and *depression*. *Predict the Answer*: In the cognitive approach, problems would be caused by dysfunctional thinking patterns. Choice (C) looks pretty good, but you can use POE to be sure. If the correct match is not immediately apparent, consider your options. Eliminate (A) because it references Freudian, or psychoanalytical, factors. Eliminate (B) because the emphasis is on biology. Eliminate (D) because reaching one's potential is central to the humanistic approach. Eliminate (E) because getting attention is reinforcing and that indicates a behavioristic approach. Choice (C) is correct because these "assessments" and "perceptions" are cognitive processes.

81. **D**   *Understand the Question/Key Words*: The key language is that which indicates that Benjamin did particularly well studying information with which he had personal connection. *Predict the Answer*: Choice (D), self-reference effect. Benjamin's memory was better for information that was personally relevant to him. You can also use POE. Eliminate (A) because it involves memory for physical activities, or "muscle memory." Eliminate (B) because it involves remembering information better when you are in the same frame of mind as you were when you learned it. Eliminate (C) because it involves remembering information better when you are in the same place that you were when you learned it. Eliminate (E) because the question involves long-term memories and sensory memory only lasts for a second or two.

82. **B** *Understand the Question/Key Words*: The key words are *schizophrenia*, *positive symptoms*, and *negative symptoms*. *Predict the Answer*: Positive symptoms are those that are not usually present, but that the disease introduces into the individual's reality. Negative symptoms are behaviors that are normally present, but the mental disorder takes them away. Use POE. Eliminate (A) because amnesia is a negative symptom and multiple personalities is a positive symptom. Eliminate (C) because delusions are a positive symptom. Eliminate (D) because no speech is a negative symptom and phobias are a positive symptom. Eliminate (E) because focused attention is not a symptom of schizophrenia. Choice (B) is correct: hallucinations are a positive symptom, produced by the illness, whereas under normal circumstances someone would have a full range of emotional expression and "flat affect" indicates that the illness has taken that away.

83. **B** *Understand the Question/Key Words*: The key words are *needs to work her way up gradually*. *Predict the Answer:* The correct response will be a learning theory that supports step-by-step improvement. Eliminate (C), (D), and (E) because they are not theories about how learning takes place. Eliminate (A) because, while it is a stage in a theory of cognitive development, it does not specify the sort of sequential learning suggested by the question. Choice (B) is correct because Vygotsky's idea is that it is only possible to scaffold an individual to a higher level of skill development once that individual is reasonably close to that level.

84. **E** *Understand the Question/Key Words*: The key words are *NOT* and *Freudian psychoanalysis*. *Predict the Answer*: Choice (E), unconditional positive regard, is characteristic of humanistic therapy. You can use POE to eliminate (A), (B), (C), and (D), which are characteristic of psychoanalysis.

85. **C** *Understand the Question/Key Words*: The key words are *the most significant flaw in this research*. *Predict the Answer:* There are several potential flaws in this research. However, because they are assessing health-related attitudes and behaviors, the most significant is sampling error: people at the hiking/biking trail are likely to be more health-conscious than the average. The correct answer is (C).

86. **A** *Understand the Question/Key Words*: The key words are *debilitating fear of snakes*, followed by descriptions of increasing exposure to snakes, all while being *relaxed*. *Predict the Answer:* Having a phobia described, and then seeing a hierarchy of increasing exposure used by the therapist is an example of (A), systematic desensitization.

87. **A** *Understand the Question/Key Words*: The key words are *Stanford Prison Experiment* and *bad behavior*. *Predict the Answer*: Role-play, (A). Zimbardo believed that subjects' attitudes toward other subjects changed based upon whether they were playing the roles of prison guards or prisoners in the simulation.

88. **D** *Understand the Question/Key Words*: The key words are *Ainsworth, strange situation, securely attached*, and *insecurely attached*. *Predict the Answer:* Ainsworth believed that whether children were securely or insecurely attached as toddlers was based on whether they had sensitive and understanding parents. The answer you want is (D).

89. **E** *Understand the Question/Key Words*: The key phrase is *more in common with their biological parents than with their adoptive parents*. *Predict the Answer:* These facts seem to prioritize genetics over life experiences. This sounds like (E), but use POE to consider the other choices. Eliminate (A)

because trait theory is about categorizing behavior, but not about explaining its origin. Eliminate (B) because it is a reversal of the correct response. Eliminate (C) because Freud did not explain behavior as genetically determined. Eliminate (D) because it is also a reversal of the correct response: temperament is one's innate personality. Choice (E) is correct because "genetics over life experiences" translates to heritability (the extent to which a trait is determined by genetic factors) over environmental influence.

90.   **E**   *Understand the Question/Key Words:* The key language is that which indicates that Rodrigo has observed nice behavior being rewarded and has learned from it. *Predict the Answer:* Vicarious learning is a type of learning that comes from watching others go through a situation and seeing whether the result is reward or punishment. This is what you want, so (E) is the correct answer.

91.   **D**   *Understand the Question/Key Words:* The key language is *Bandura's* Bobo doll *experiments. Predict the Answer:* Choice (D) is correct. These experiments focused on the tendency of children to imitate adults' behavior.

92.   **D**   *Understand the Question/Key Words:* This question is seeking the name of a "disorder" that is described in the language leading up to the question mark. *Predict the Answer:* Phobias are irrational or exaggerated fears. The "agora" was the marketplace in ancient Greece; hence, agoraphobia is a fear of being in public. Choice (D) is correct.

93.   **C**   *Understand the Question/Key Words:* The key language is *he only brought food to his dogs after a certain pitch bell was rung* and *he trained them to salivate only after that particular bell was rung. Predict the Answer:* The correct response will involve specificity in the stimulus that accompanies the food and then elicits the behavior. Use POE. Eliminate (A) because it involves specific behavior, not a specific stimulus. Eliminate (B) because it is the opposite of what you are looking for. Eliminate (D) because it is an operant conditioning schedule, and this is about classical conditioning. Eliminate (E) because it describes the process of conditioning the behavior through pairing, not restricting the behavior to a specific stimulus. Choice (C) is correct because it refers to only a particular stimulus producing the desired behavior.

94.   **E**   *Understand the Question/Key Words:* The key words are *NOT one of the levels of…Maslow's hierarchy of needs.* Use POE. Eliminate (B) because it is the lowest level of the pyramid, (D) because it is the next level up, (A) because it is another level up, and (C) because it is the top level. The level below self-actualization is self-esteem, not self-acceptance. Choice (E) is the correct answer.

95.   **E**   *Understand the Question/Key Words:* The key words are *Freud* and *components of the psyche. Predict the Answer:* Choice (E). Freud proposed three components of the psyche: the id (animalistic, childlike urges for pleasure), the superego (our conscience and concern for parental expectations), and the ego (which must decide on a course of action based on the reality principle). Remember that the question asks for the respective order, so (E) is correct.

96.   **D**   *Understand the Question/Key Words:* The key language is that which indicates that psychological problems are being manifested as physical problems. The question wants to know the *DSM-5* designation for this category of disorder. Use POE. Eliminate (A) because dissociative disorders involve a lack of continuity between thoughts, memories, behaviors, and identity, but do not manifest as physical problems. Eliminate (B) because, while panic disorder is an anxiety disorder

and has physical symptoms associated with it (e.g. rapid heartbeat, sweating) these are temporary, not longstanding, conditions. Eliminate (C) because compulsions do not typically involve physical limitations. Eliminate (E) because fugue is a dissociative disorder involving amnesia, not physical disability. Choice (D) is correct because this is a somatic disorder that involves converting a psychological problem into a physical one.

97. **B** *Understand the Question/Key Words:* The key language is *have relatively few words in their language describing color* and *spend very little time thinking about or assessing color. Predict the Answer*: Choice (B), the Sapir-Whorf theory, is correct because it says that the language one uses affects the way one thinks. You can also use POE. Eliminate (A) and (C) because these are theories about how children develop language. Eliminate (D) because it is about cognitive development generally, not specifically about language. Eliminate (E) because it is a memory concept.

98. **E** *Understand the Question/Key Words:* The key term is *inferential statistics. Predict the Answer:* These are statistics that let researchers know to what extent they can feel comfortable making inferences based on the data they generate. Examples include normal distributions, z-scores, and confidence intervals. Choice (E) is correct.

99. **A** *Understand the Question/Key Words:* The key words are those in the next-to-last sentence indicating that the productivity increase was found to be due to workers being observed rather than to the experts' recommendations. *Predict the Answer*: This sounds like (A), the Hawthorne effect, but use POE to consider the other options. Eliminate (B) because the experts did not predict that productivity would decline. Eliminate (C) and (D) because they are forms of reinforcement and reinforcement is not an issue in this fact pattern. Social facilitation in this context involves whether workers' productivity improves or declines when other workers are around. Here, there is no evidence that productivity changed in response to the number of workers around; it was the observation that was key. Eliminate (E).

100. **B** *Understand the Question/Key Words:* The key term is *negative punishment. Predict the Answer:* "Punishment" means that the intention of the measure is to reduce a behavior. "Negative" means that the behavior reduction is being achieved by removing something from the individual, as opposed to applying something new. Use POE. Choice (A) describes a reward scenario; eliminate it. Choices (C), (D), and (E) are all positive punishments ((C) and (E) are aversive stimuli) in that they add something to the individual's environment. Choice (B) is "negative" in that it removes the individual's usual social activities.

Section II: Free Response

1. Essay number one is worth seven points, one for each of the concepts and its application. Points are given based on a student's ability to explain behavior and apply theories and perspectives in authentic contexts. Each essay is unique, but here is our run-down of what a student should definitely cover in their Free Response Essay for this question:

- The availability heuristic is a mental shortcut that evaluates the likelihood of an outcome based on how easily information about that outcome comes to mind. Mercedes may have overestimated the likelihood that Provincial College would be a suitable destination for her based on the ease with which information about Provincial came to her from her guidance office and her cousin.

- The representativeness heuristic is a mental shortcut that evaluates the similarity of things based on a category prototype. Here, Mercedes had a prototypical small, liberal arts college in mind and she assigned characteristics to Provincial that may not, in fact, have applied had she done further investigation.

- Individualism involves taking care of one's own needs. Mercedes is making a college choice based upon her individual preferences.

- Groupthink occurs when a group prioritizes consensus above the continued exploration of divergent opinions. Mercedes' "family council" had differing points of view about her college selection, but, at a certain point, prioritized unanimity and harmony over continued discussion. Groupthink often results in poor decision-making.

- Social support is the network of family, friends, neighbors, etc. whose support helps cushion the negative effects of stressful events. When she left for school, Mercedes left behind her usual networks and she was vulnerable to the stresses bound to come with a new school and new living arrangements.

- Confirmation bias is the tendency to seek out evidence to support one's preexisting views, or to interpret ambiguous evidence as supportive of one's views. Mercedes easily accepted the information about Provincial that she obtained from her guidance office and her cousin and she did not seek out additional, and possibly contrary, evidence.

- Mental set is a tendency to think about solutions to a problem in a predetermined way. Mercedes adopted a certain point of view about her college selection early on and never diverged from that. She might have benefited from a broader exploration of possibilities.

2.   Essay number two is worth seven points, one each for the three sections of Part A and the first and last explanations in Part B, plus two points for the second explanation in Part B (one for defining "double blind" and one for applying it here). Points are given based on students' ability to analyze psychological research studies, including analyzing and interpreting quantitative data.

This is what our "student" chose to do for his essay. Use this as an example of a high-scoring essay.

Sample Essay

The dependent variable is mother-infant bonding, a subjective concept. An operational definition makes a subjective concept measurable, in this case calculating mother-infant eye contact over ten-minute periods.

One possible ethical problem involves confidentiality. These mothers had not given permission for their subscriber information to be shared with the researchers. That permission should have been obtained.

This is not a naturalistic observation because the experimenters are manipulating a variable in the subjects' environment: whether or not they are exposed to the music.

One reason to be skeptical about whether these findings can be generalized is that the subscriber base of this magazine may not be representative of the population as a whole. For example, these subscribers may, on the whole, be much wealthier than the population and this might have affected the results.

To "double blind" the experiment would mean that the experimenters would not know which subjects were part of the experimental group and which were part of the control group. With this experiment specifically, it would be best if the graduate students who were evaluating "eye contact" from the tapes were unaware of whether or not music had been playing in the room at the time; otherwise, this knowledge might affect their judgment.

A possible confounding variable would be what music, if any, was played in subjects' homes prior to their involvement in this experiment. Unless the experimenters account for this by inquiring about it, and possibly excluding those who routinely played classical music, they may wind up only assessing whether music with which mothers and infants were already familiar was helpful in bonding as opposed to any special benefits of classical music.

HOW TO SCORE PRACTICE TEST 2

Section I: Multiple Choice

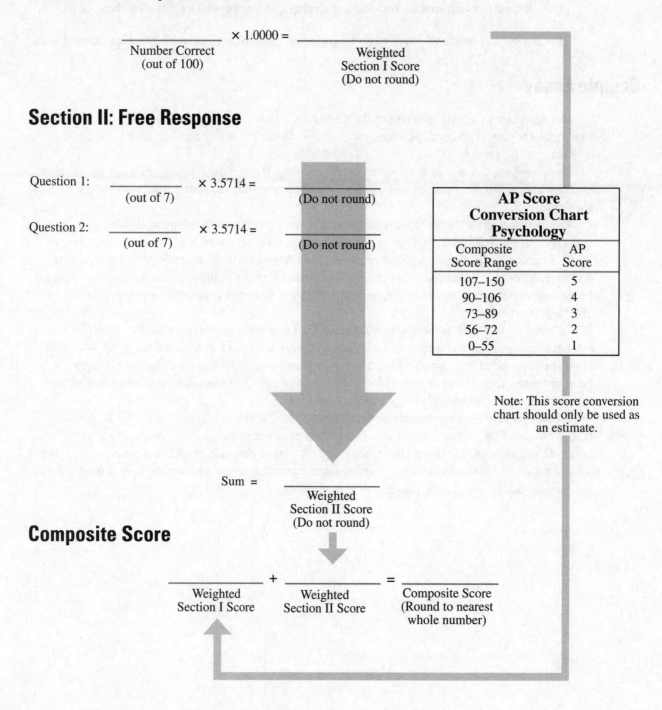

$$\underline{\hspace{3cm}} \times 1.0000 = \underline{\hspace{4cm}}$$

Number Correct
(out of 100)

Weighted
Section I Score
(Do not round)

Section II: Free Response

Question 1: $\underline{\hspace{2cm}} \times 3.5714 = \underline{\hspace{3cm}}$
(out of 7)   (Do not round)

Question 2: $\underline{\hspace{2cm}} \times 3.5714 = \underline{\hspace{3cm}}$
(out of 7)   (Do not round)

AP Score Conversion Chart Psychology

Composite Score Range	AP Score
107–150	5
90–106	4
73–89	3
56–72	2
0–55	1

Note: This score conversion chart should only be used as an estimate.

Sum = $\underline{\hspace{3cm}}$

Weighted
Section II Score
(Do not round)

Composite Score

$$\underline{\hspace{3cm}} + \underline{\hspace{3cm}} = \underline{\hspace{3cm}}$$

Weighted
Section I Score

Weighted
Section II Score

Composite Score
(Round to nearest
whole number)

Part VII
Additional
Practice Tests

Practice Test 3

AP® Psychology Exam

SECTION I: Multiple-Choice Questions

DO NOT OPEN THIS BOOKLET UNTIL YOU ARE TOLD TO DO SO.

At a Glance

Total Time
1 hour and 10 minutes
Number of Questions
100
Percent of Total Grade
66.6%
Writing Instrument
Pencil required

Instructions

Section I of this exam contains 100 multiple-choice questions. Fill in only the ovals for numbers 1 through 100 on your answer sheet.

Indicate all of your answers to the multiple-choice questions on the answer sheet. No credit will be given for anything written in this exam booklet, but you may use the booklet for notes or scratch work. After you have decided which of the suggested answers is best, completely fill in the corresponding oval on the answer sheet. Give only one answer to each question. If you change an answer, be sure that the previous mark is erased completely. Here is a sample question and answer.

Sample Question   Sample Answer

Omaha is a

(A) state
(B) city
(C) country
(D) continent
(E) village

Use your time effectively, working as quickly as you can without losing accuracy. Do not spend too much time on any one question. Go on to other questions and come back to the ones you have not answered if you have time. It is not expected that everyone will know the answers to all of the multiple-choice questions.

About Guessing

Many candidates wonder whether or not to guess the answers to questions about which they are not certain. Multiple-choice scores are based on the number of questions answered correctly. Points are not deducted for incorrect answers and no points are awarded for unanswered questions. Because points are not deducted for incorrect answers, you are encouraged to answer all multiple-choice questions. On any questions you do not know the answer to, you should eliminate as many choices as you can and then select the best answer among the remaining choices.

GO ON TO THE NEXT PAGE.

This page intentionally left blank.

GO ON TO THE NEXT PAGE.

PSYCHOLOGY
Section I
Time—1 hour and 10 minutes
100 Questions

Directions: Each of the questions or incomplete statements below is followed by five answer choices. Select the one that is best in each case and then completely fill in the corresponding oval on the answer sheet.

1. The relationship between heritability and environment is referred to as

(A) the nature versus nurture debate
(B) the mind-body problem
(C) *tabula rasa*
(D) efferent versus afferent
(E) reaction formation

2. The sympathetic nervous system is most associated with which of the following?

(A) Chronic stress
(B) Fight or flight
(C) Resistance
(D) Exhaustion
(E) Impaired immune systems

3. Which of the following tests is designed to measure intelligence?

(A) Rorschach Inkblot Test
(B) Thematic Apperception Test
(C) Achievement tests
(D) External validity test
(E) Stanford-Binet Test

4. Which of the following people is often thought of as the founder of psychology as a science?

(A) William Wundt
(B) Edward Titchener
(C) Sigmund Freud
(D) B.F. Skinner
(E) René Descartes

5. Ever since sophomore year, Brianna has felt it very comforting to come home and fix 10 pieces of cinnamon toast. She eats them in her bedroom, and later vomits all of them up so she doesn't gain weight. Brianna likely has what?

(A) Pica
(B) Anorexia nervosa
(C) Binge-eating disorder
(D) Bulimia nervosa
(E) Borderline personality disorder

6. Relatively more of which cell type enables humans to see in color, while sloths see in black and white?

(A) Rods
(B) Amacrine
(C) Ganglion
(D) Cones
(E) Bipolar

7. Leon Festinger proposed the idea that we are uncomfortable when our ideas, beliefs, and behaviors conflict with how we really act. Which of the following terms refers to this discomfort?

(A) General adaptation syndrome
(B) Learned helplessness
(C) Cognitive dissonance
(D) Fluid intelligence
(E) Mere exposure effect

8. A newborn baby grabs a pacifier placed in her hands. This is an example of which of the following?

(A) The Moro reflex
(B) The palmar reflex
(C) The head-turning reflex
(D) The sucking reflex
(E) The Babinski reflex

9. A behaviorist is most likely to consider

(A) a person's response to reward and punishment
(B) a person's response to unconditional positive regard
(C) a person's recounting of their dreams
(D) a person's thoughts regarding things that cause them anxiety
(E) a person's heredity versus their response to environment

GO ON TO THE NEXT PAGE.

10. Five students who wrote excellent individual essays were then chosen to do a group written project. Although each of them believes that they worked hard on it, the end result is generally weaker than expected. This outcome can be best explained by what phenomenon?

    (A) Social inhibition
    (B) Mindguard
    (C) Role exit
    (D) Social loafing
    (E) Role conflict

11. Which of the following people was involved in founding the first U.S. hospital for the mentally ill?

    (A) Mary Rothbart
    (B) Mary Whiton Calkins
    (C) Margaret Floy Washburn
    (D) Edward Titchener
    (E) Dorothea Dix

12. In the endocrine system, which of the following is known as the master gland?

    (A) Pituitary
    (B) Thyroid
    (C) Hypothalamus
    (D) Acetylcholine
    (E) Pineal

13. Howard Gardner believed that all of the following were types of intelligence EXCEPT

    (A) spatial
    (B) musical
    (C) creative
    (D) environmental
    (E) intrapersonal

14. Which of the following was a finding of the Milgram obedience experiments?

    (A) Moving the "learner" closer to the "teacher" increased obedience rates.
    (B) Having the experimenter issue his instructions remotely decreased obedience rates.
    (C) Including other "teachers" in the room who were noncompliant had no significant effect on obedience rates.
    (D) Varying the physical attractiveness of the "learner" significantly affected obedience rates.
    (E) Moving the experiment to a less prestigious area increased obedience rates.

15. Which of the following concepts is NOT part of psychoanalytic theory?

    (A) Id
    (B) Ego
    (C) Repression
    (D) Incongruence
    (E) Reaction formation

16. Pavlov is best-known for which discovery?

    (A) Finding that rats can learn to navigate a maze to find food
    (B) Finding that dogs will salivate when seeing the attendant who brought them food, even before receiving the food
    (C) Finding that rats will learn to avoid negative experiences such as electric shocks
    (D) Finding that pigeons can be trained to associate food with pecking at a particular key
    (E) Finding that people will continue to do activities for which they are praised, even when the praise stops

17. Ayesha's new job requires employees to punch in a numeric code to enter certain rooms. She repeats the code over and over to herself to remember it. Ayesha is using which of the following?

    (A) Elaborative rehearsal
    (B) Maintenance rehearsal
    (C) Semantic memory
    (D) Chunking
    (E) Echoic memory

18. Hanna goes to Bread and Cheese, a sandwich shop, on the way home from school about twice a week. She likes it partly because she gets a card that is punched every time she purchases a sandwich. When she buys a dozen, she gets the 13th free. Bread and Cheese is encouraging Hanna's business using which of the following reinforcement schedules?

    (A) Continuous
    (B) Variable-ratio
    (C) Fixed-interval
    (D) Variable-interval
    (E) Fixed-ratio

GO ON TO THE NEXT PAGE.

19. Kohlberg's second (conventional) level of moral development is characterized by

    (A) following rules in order to avoid punishment
    (B) following rules in order to obtain reward
    (C) maintaining order above all
    (D) defining morality for oneself
    (E) determining what is right by reference to what others say, especially those in authority

20. According to Richard Lazarus, which of the following is the first stage of response to stress?

    (A) Primary appraisal
    (B) Exhaustion
    (C) Corticosterone
    (D) Alarm
    (E) Resistance

21. All of the following are characteristics of psychologically disordered behavior EXCEPT

    (A) cognitive or perceptual dysfunction
    (B) unusual deviation from typical behavior
    (C) labeled as abnormal by society
    (D) patient's history of trauma
    (E) maladaptive adjustment

22. Addison was in a car accident and sustained a brain injury. Since then, he can't feel much difference between hot and cold temperatures. His neuroanatomist suspects that the head injury caused damage to which of the following?

    (A) Occipital lobe
    (B) Temporal lobe
    (C) Parietal lobe
    (D) Frontal lobe
    (E) Cerebellum

23. Sean is preparing to study for an AP Psychology exam, and is attempting to learn all ten personality disorders. His friend Teresa suggests that he draw a comic strip with ten characters who represent each of the personality disorders. Her suggestion involves which of the following?

    (A) Iconic memory
    (B) Sensory memory
    (C) Maintenance rehearsal
    (D) Mnemonic device
    (E) Flashbulb memory

24. Which of the following is true of anorexia nervosa?

    (A) Contrary to popular stereotypes, males are as likely to develop anorexia as are females.
    (B) A diagnostic requirement for anorexia is a body weight that is at least 15% below ideal.
    (C) One's age and sex are relevant to whether or not one can be properly labeled anorexic.
    (D) An extremely low body weight will allow for the diagnosis even if the individual wants to gain weight.
    (E) The individual must have engaged in binging and purging behavior (e.g., eating a large amount of food and then inducing vomiting) for at least three months for the diagnosis to apply.

25. According to Freud, what happens from roughly the ages of 6 to 12, during the latency stage?

    (A) Children repress traumatic memories.
    (B) Children dream vividly.
    (C) Children focus on oral gratification.
    (D) Children's egos become fragile.
    (E) Children focus on gender identification.

26. Ellyn feels hungry four hours after she's eaten breakfast, and goes to get lunch. What's regulating her motivation to eat?

    (A) Hypothalamus
    (B) Amygdala
    (C) Somatosensory cortex
    (D) Medulla oblongata
    (E) Hippocampus

27. Remembering that Queen Elizabeth I ruled England during the Renaissance is an example of what type of memory?

    (A) Procedural memory
    (B) Semantic memory
    (C) Implicit memory
    (D) Episodic memory
    (E) Chunking

28. The concept of unconditional positive regard is most closely associated with which therapist?

    (A) Abraham Maslow
    (B) Fritz Perls
    (C) Carl Rogers
    (D) Aaron Beck
    (E) Carl Jung

GO ON TO THE NEXT PAGE.

29. Jordan keeps her grades very high to please her parents and keep her scholarship. Her motivations can be described as

    (A) hierarchical
    (B) self-determined
    (C) extrinsic
    (D) instinctual
    (E) intrinsic

30. To which perspective are issues of repression, the conscious and unconscious mind, and unresolved conflicts in childhood most central?

    (A) Psychoanalytic
    (B) Cognitive
    (C) Behaviorist
    (D) Humanistic
    (E) Biological

31. Which of the following is NOT a requirement for ethical conduct of a research experiment with human subjects?

    (A) Obtaining informed consent
    (B) Debriefing after an experiment if deception has been used
    (C) Maintaining confidentiality and anonymity
    (D) Double-blinding in the research design
    (E) Allowing subjects to leave the experiment if they become uncomfortable with what they are required to do

32. According to social psychological theory, which factor does NOT lead to interpersonal attraction?

    (A) Physical proximity
    (B) Good physical appearance
    (C) Shared opinions
    (D) Positive evaluation
    (E) Personal wealth

33. Caleb is taking part in a psychology experiment. He is to stare at a green dot on a page for 30 seconds. Then he is shown a blank white page and asked what he sees. He tells the researcher he sees a red dot. Which of the following best explains Caleb's perception?

    (A) Color blindness
    (B) Trichromatic theory
    (C) Optic chiasm
    (D) Serial processing
    (E) Opponent process theory

34. According to the modal model, memory is stored in which of these areas?

    (A) Echoic, iconic, auditory
    (B) Encoding, decay, interference
    (C) Semantic, visual, acoustic
    (D) Hippocampus, prefrontal cortex, amygdala
    (E) Sensory, short-term, long-term

35. Which of the following is NOT a condition for observational learning, according to Albert Bandura?

    (A) Reward
    (B) Attention
    (C) Reproduction
    (D) Retention
    (E) Motivation

36. A group of developmental psychologists plans to compare similar cognitive tasks for a group of 3-year-olds, a group of 6-year-olds, and a group of 9-year-olds. What research method are they using?

    (A) Cross-sectional
    (B) Longitudinal
    (C) Statistical
    (D) Correlational
    (E) Case studies

37. Internal validity refers to which of the following?

    (A) The extent to which a study's findings can be generalized to the real world
    (B) The certainty with which an experiment's results can be attributed to the independent variable rather than some other variable
    (C) The replicability of the standard deviations
    (D) The absence of Type I or Type II error
    (E) Eliminating the null hypothesis

38. Which of the following is NOT involved in neural firing in the brain?

    (A) Axons
    (B) Dendrites
    (C) Myelin sheath
    (D) Moro reflex
    (E) Nodes of Ranvier

GO ON TO THE NEXT PAGE.

39. Christa's therapist has diagnosed her with a negative triad. What class of medication is she most likely to be prescribed?

    (A) Lithium salts
    (B) Antidepressants
    (C) Antipsychotics
    (D) Anticholinergics
    (E) Anxiolytics

40. Andre works for a large multinational corporation. He is always on time to meetings, wants to be the best salesperson in his company, and is sometimes irritated by colleagues who aren't as punctual or as driven to succeed as he is. Which of the following might explain his behavior?

    (A) Type-B pattern behavior
    (B) Chronic stress
    (C) Type-A pattern behavior
    (D) Negative triad
    (E) Overactive pituitary gland

41. Weber's law best describes which of the following?

    (A) A person's ability to notice that a 30-pound dumbbell is much heavier than a 25-pound dumbbell, but not notice that a 55-pound dumbbell is heavier than a 50-pound dumbbell
    (B) The ability of people to recognize stimuli at a point of difference
    (C) A person quickly recognizing a piece of classical music at a concert that has been playing very softly as background in their language lab all term
    (D) A person recognizing shapes more readily in a dark movie theater after they have been there 10 minutes than when they first walked in
    (E) A person having no trouble conversing with other people at a large party in which everyone is talking

42. Solomon Asch's study involving perceptual stimuli tested which of the following?

    (A) Schizophrenia
    (B) Outgroups
    (C) Occipital lobe processing
    (D) Role-playing
    (E) Conformity

43. If a Type I error involving a hypothesis is made, which of the following has occurred?

    (A) The experimenter concluded that a difference did not exist after the experiment, when in fact it did.
    (B) The standard deviations were not read correctly.
    (C) Confounding variables were not accounted for.
    (D) The sample size was too low to be valid.
    (E) The experimenter concluded that a difference existed after the experiment, when in fact it didn't.

44. Drew's sleep is being monitored by an electroencephalogram. Which of the following are researchers most likely to see during the rapid eye movement (REM) stage, when he dreams?

    (A) Theta and beta waves
    (B) Spindles
    (C) Beta and alpha waves
    (D) K complexes
    (E) Delta waves

45. Harriet is on the soccer team. The coach requires daily workouts, which she praises each student for. Harriet likes the praise, and shows up for each workout, doing more than asked. Eventually, Harriet does the workout every day even in the off-season, when the coach isn't around. This is an example of

    (A) operant conditioning
    (B) vicarious reinforcement
    (C) classical conditioning
    (D) Yerkes-Dodson law
    (E) negative reinforcement

46. Leticia has developed a fear of heights. But her environmental science class is going on a field trip, hiking in the Rocky Mountains, and she hates to miss it. She starts therapy to get over her fear. First, the therapist tells Leticia to visualize standing on a mountain path. Second, she'll start hiking on gradual inclines. Finally, Leticia will go with a guide up a steep mountain for a short while, and then gradually lengthen the hikes. Which technique is her therapist using?

    (A) Systematic desensitization
    (B) Flooding
    (C) Psychopharmacology
    (D) Implosion
    (E) Extinction procedures

GO ON TO THE NEXT PAGE.

47. When his mother takes Frank to preschool, he crows "I go school!" This is an example of

    (A) language acquisition
    (B) a holophrase
    (C) overextension
    (D) underextension
    (E) telegraphic speech

48. Which of the following statements best reflects a behaviorist's view?

    (A) Behavior is influenced by both nature and nurture.
    (B) Behavior is influenced by individuals wanting self-actualization.
    (C) Behavior is influenced by unconscious desires within the person.
    (D) Behavior is influenced by reward and punishment from the outside.
    (E) Behavior is influenced by thoughts and actions.

49. Ken is in training for the state wrestling finals. It's been challenging to remain in the range for his weight class. Two days from his weigh-in, he throws a party for his eighteenth birthday, which includes his favorite type of cake. Of course he wants to eat the cake—it's his birthday!—but he's also worried about the effect on the weigh-in 48 hours away. This is an example of which of the following?

    (A) Approach-approach conflict
    (B) Approach-avoidance conflict
    (C) Avoidance-avoidance conflict
    (D) Multiple approach-avoidance
    (E) Two-factor theory

50. Jeremiah doesn't study if he doesn't feel like it, but he also doesn't take responsibility for getting low scores on his high school tests. His parents don't care about his grades, viewing themselves as his friends. Which of the following likely describes their parenting style?

    (A) Authoritative
    (B) Authoritarian
    (C) Permissive
    (D) Disorganized
    (E) Ambivalent

51. Which of the following best summarizes a view of the contact hypothesis?

    (A) Contact with someone every day for more than two weeks increases the chances of your feeling interpersonal attraction.
    (B) Contact with someone of a different social group tends to reinforce your own biases.
    (C) Conflict resolution requires frequent contact and cooperation.
    (D) Contact with a different group may reduce prejudice against members of the group, but it could also increase prejudice or leave it unchanged.
    (E) Contact is a diffuse form of altruism.

52. The Eysenck Personality Inventory measures people based on their

    (A) genetic composition
    (B) self-efficacy
    (C) sensory perception
    (D) cognitive responses
    (E) traits

53. A psychoanalytic therapist would be most likely to use which of the following to treat depression?

    (A) Free association
    (B) Prescribing selective serotonin reuptake inhibitors
    (C) Hypnosis
    (D) Flooding
    (E) Empathic understanding

54. Ivan's aunt had a stroke last week. Ivan's family has been told the Broca's area in her brain is affected. What symptoms is she likely to have?

    (A) Loss of ability to see
    (B) Loss of ability to hear
    (C) Loss of ability to understand what she hears
    (D) Frequent repetition of what is said to her
    (E) Loss of ability to speak

55. Aidan has the highest grades in class, plays the cello in the city orchestra, and is popular among his classmates. When he shows up to help build apartments for the homeless, the group leader is startled to find him clumsy and unable to hammer a nail without hitting his own thumb. The leader's surprise likely results from which of the following?

    (A) Intersectionality
    (B) Behavioral dissonance
    (C) Gender attribution
    (D) Confirmation bias
    (E) Halo effect

GO ON TO THE NEXT PAGE.

56. Karen tumbled down the steps of the library, spraining her ankle. She began to cry, as her ankle hurt and she couldn't walk without limping. She was terribly embarrassed, as at least 15 people were hanging out in front of the library and saw her fall. No one moved to help or comfort Karen. What accounts for the fact that none of these people offered her any assistance?

(A) Outgroup homogeneity
(B) Social inhibition
(C) Bystander effect
(D) Dehumanization
(E) Rosenthal effect

57. Peter is studying for a biology test. He remembers the information much better when he actually goes into the biology classroom, rather than staying in the library. This is most likely an example of

(A) proactive interference
(B) chunking
(C) procedural memory
(D) maintenance rehearsal
(E) context-dependent memory

58. Kristin and Dave are driving to a restaurant in the fog. They see the restaurant's neon sign in the distance, which they think is about 1 mile down the road. It turns out to be just half a mile. What explains the difference between their perception and reality?

(A) Vanishing point
(B) Motion parallax
(C) Aerial perspective
(D) Stereopsis
(E) Retinal convergence

59. If you design a single-blind experiment, which of the following is true?

(A) The experiment's subjects know whether they are in an experimental group or in a control group, but the researchers do not.
(B) The experiment's subjects do not know whether they are in an experimental group or in a control group, but the researchers do.
(C) Both the researchers and the experimental subjects know which group the subjects have been assigned to.
(D) Neither the researchers nor the experimental subjects know whether the latter have been assigned to an experimental group or a control group.
(E) The observers are unable to see the responses or behaviors of the experimental group during the course of the experimental manipulation.

60. Despite problems with addiction, which of the following explains why narcotics like oxycodone relieve pain?

(A) They work very similarly to endogenous serotonin.
(B) They work very similarly to endogenous acetylcholine.
(C) They work very similarly to endogenous endorphins.
(D) They work very similarly to endogenous adenosine.
(E) They work very similarly to endogenous norepinephrine.

61. Paula is a gymnast who's been practicing hard for the state finals. When the judges give her an average score of 9, she attributes the high score to her hard work, thinking "All my practice paid off!" But in one trial, her average falls to 5. She fumes, "They shortchanged me on the balance beam." Which of the following theories explains her reasoning?

(A) Situational attribution
(B) Fundamental attribution error
(C) Dispositional attribution
(D) Self-fulfilling prophecy
(E) Self-serving bias

62. What demonstrates causation in an experiment?

(A) A hypothesis that successfully predicts the outcome
(B) Operationalization of independent and dependent variables
(C) A manipulation of one variable that always leads to predicted changes in another
(D) A positive correlation between the variables
(E) Successful manipulation of the way a subject responds to some aspect of the experiment

63. Julio is an A student who received early admission to the college of his choice. He still thinks he needs to be perfect in everything he does in class this spring, even though his GPA has already secured him a place in higher education. He has such extreme anxiety that a therapist suggests he replace every thought of "I've got to nail this assignment" with "It needs to just be good enough to graduate." The therapist is using which of the following approaches?

(A) Humanistic psychology
(B) Behaviorist techniques
(C) Psychoanalytic insight
(D) Rational-emotive behavior therapy
(E) Anxiolytics

GO ON TO THE NEXT PAGE.

64. Jayden is learning to sail, but he experiences nausea every time he encounters open water. He is working with a therapist on ways to manage it. The therapist mentions that he should never eat favorite foods (chocolate, pizza) while sailing. This recommendation is made to help avoid which of the following?

    (A) Aversion therapy
    (B) Hawthorne effect
    (C) Conditioned taste aversion
    (D) Desensitization
    (E) Neural network

65. Olivia's family moves to a new house very near an airport. For the first week, all the family members are distressed that the sound of planes taking off is so loud. When a friend comes to visit the third week and complains about the noise, Olivia realizes she doesn't even hear it anymore. This is likely due to which phenomenon?

    (A) Habituation
    (B) Dishabituation
    (C) Desensitization
    (D) Interval response
    (E) Shaping

66. Diya is looking at a normal distribution of scores. Roughly what percentage should she expect to occur within two standard deviations (SDs) of the mean?

    (A) 99.7
    (B) 75
    (C) 68
    (D) 95
    (E) 34

67. Thomas is a 55-year-old journalist. When he was young, he learned that all periods at the ends of sentences should be followed by two spaces. His 27-year-old editor learned that one space is correct. She gets very frustrated with Thomas, because she's told him many times to just use one. Thomas shrugs and says "I can never remember that." What best explains Thomas's response?

    (A) Decay
    (B) Retroactive interference
    (C) Self-reference effect
    (D) Encoding
    (E) Proactive interference

68. Evelyn is 6. She is pleased when the teacher puts stars for good work on her assignments. Erikson would put her in which of the following?

    (A) Concrete operational stage
    (B) Industry versus inferiority stage
    (C) Zone of proximal development
    (D) Identity versus role confusion stage
    (E) Conventional morality stage

69. Which of the following is NOT a major class of drugs traditionally employed for psychotherapeutic use?

    (A) Selective serotonin reuptake inhibitors
    (B) Antineoplastics
    (C) Lithium salts
    (D) Anxiolytics
    (E) Monoamine oxidase inhibitors

70. Which of the following is NOT an anxiety disorder?

    (A) Generalized anxiety disorder
    (B) Conversion disorder
    (C) Panic disorder
    (D) Agoraphobia
    (E) Social phobia

71. Kris was sure Alexis would win the election for student body president because her campaign speeches were so logical and persuasive. She was shocked when her best friend said she'd voted for Raj for president because he had the best outfits of anyone in the junior class. What model best explains the friend's decision?

    (A) Elaboration likelihood model
    (B) Piaget's developmental model
    (C) Modal model
    (D) Kohlberg's model of morality
    (E) Hawthorne effect

72. Which of the following are found in the forebrain?

    (A) Thalamus, hippocampus, cerebellum
    (B) Thalamus, hippocampus, amygdala
    (C) Medulla oblongata, amygdala, cerebellum
    (D) Reticular activating system, amygdala, hippocampus
    (E) Tectum, tegmentum, cerebellum

GO ON TO THE NEXT PAGE.

73. When Ashleigh was 4, she watched a movie over and over again about a little girl whose grandmother lets her wear a tiara as a reward for good behavior. Now that she's 15, she thinks her grandmother gave her a tiara for being a good girl when she was little. Which of the following best explains this?

    (A) Retrograde amnesia
    (B) Source confusion
    (C) Framing
    (D) Preconventional morality
    (E) Retroactive inference

74. Which of the following involve sensations from the skin?

    (A) Tactile and cutaneous receptors
    (B) Malleus, incus, and stapes
    (C) Cochlea and vestibular sacs
    (D) Ganglion cells
    (E) Rods and cones

75. Amita loved playing soccer in grade school. Now, she's a professional soccer player, with the entire team depending on her. She is sponsored by sports equipment manufacturers and in demand for television appearances. She still likes playing soccer, but she isn't as happy kicking a ball as when she was 10. Which of the following phenomena explain her feelings best?

    (A) Cognitive dissonance
    (B) Overjustification effect
    (C) Cannon-Bard theory
    (D) General adaptation syndrome
    (E) Extrinsic factors

76. Hal is a patient with schizophrenia. Which positive symptom could he show?

    (A) No longer thinking he's president of the United States
    (B) Flat affect
    (C) Hallucinating that he's being stalked by a giant rat
    (D) Successfully returning to school
    (E) A lack of desire to initiate activities

77. Larry and Pat are both 50. Their children are in college. They are developing a plan to sell their home and go to work with the poor in other countries. Their plan is likely explained by which of the following?

    (A) Erikson's integrity vs. despair
    (B) Kohlberg's Level II, conventional morality
    (C) Yerkes-Dodson Law
    (D) Erikson's generativity vs. stagnation
    (E) Secondary reinforcement

78. John's parents died in a war shortly after he was born. He was sent to an orphanage, but because of the war it was severely understaffed, and the staff couldn't provide the children with any emotional stimulus or interaction. He spent nearly two years there. Since being adopted, he seems nearly unable to form attachments with his new parents and siblings. John might have which of the following?

    (A) Attachment anxiety
    (B) Reactive attachment disorder
    (C) Object permanence
    (D) Separation anxiety
    (E) Detachment adaptation

79. Zoe likes to smoke cigarettes occasionally, so she won't eat as much. But she does notice that her heart beats faster when she smokes, too. The latter is most likely due to

    (A) dopamine
    (B) GABA
    (C) acetylcholine
    (D) norepinephrine
    (E) endorphins

80. Sophie always has difficulty coming up with ideas for her research papers at the end of the term. Her teacher suggests that she jot down five ideas quickly, without trying to critically assess whether they'll work or not, as a first step. Her teacher is suggesting what type of thinking?

    (A) Creative
    (B) Inductive
    (C) Convergent
    (D) Divergent
    (E) Fixed

GO ON TO THE NEXT PAGE.

81. Alexander has developed an abnormal fear of thunder and lightning. Which of the following clinicians most likely believes that his phobia has a biological basis?

    (A) Madison Brown, who encourages him to replace his thoughts of "I'm scared! The lightning is going to strike me" with "I'm perfectly safe; the lightning is actually not near"
    (B) Joshua Smith, who encourages him to remember his dreams
    (C) Kathe Reynolds, who has him listen to recordings of thunder and prescribes a regular dose of Xanax
    (D) Aurelia Smith-Zygmunt, who stresses his ability to deal with challenges
    (E) Henry Pearson, who encourages him to join group therapy with other phobic people

82. Sebastian is on his feet screaming "Go! Go! Go!" as his favorite basketball team fights against the clock to win the game. He interprets his screaming and adrenaline as enthusiasm rather than anger or aggression. Which theory of emotion best explains this?

    (A) The Schachter-Singer theory
    (B) The James-Lange theory
    (C) Gestalt theory
    (D) Negative triad theory
    (E) Weber's law

83. Complete the following using deductive reasoning. All social media managers who work for Company X use Website A. Some social media managers who use Website A also use Software B. Henry is a social media manager who works for Company X. It can therefore be determined that

    (A) Henry uses both Website A and Software B.
    (B) Henry does not use Software B.
    (C) Henry uses either Website A or Software B, but not both.
    (D) Henry uses Website A.
    (E) Henry uses Software B.

84. Amir is shopping online for textbooks. He finds out that the site won't let him shop for anything unless he rates the product he ordered three months ago first. Amir doesn't want to spend his time giving feedback, and is irritated by being forced to respond before he can even look at books for next term. As a result, he switches to a different site entirely. His anger and resistance to the rating request is an example of

    (A) aggression
    (B) door-in-the-face phenomenon
    (C) conflicting motives
    (D) psychological reactance
    (E) systematic desensitization

85. Which of the following criticisms of psychoanalytic therapy is likely to be offered by a cognitive therapist in particular?

    (A) Psychoanalytic therapy often requires years before patients make any breakthroughs that change the way they think.
    (B) Psychoanalytic therapy focuses too much on underlying issues and not enough on changing behavior.
    (C) Psychoanalytic therapy is lengthy and creates an undue financial burden on patients.
    (D) Psychoanalytic therapy does not focus enough on unconditional acceptance and self-esteem.
    (E) Psychoanalytic therapy avoids desensitization techniques and is not suitable for phobic patients.

86. Three students are taking an AP Chemistry test. Megan is very nervous about the test, as she wants to be a doctor, and a good chemistry score is essential. Zach has been talking to his parents about taking a gap year, and hasn't really paid much attention to the test. Tamika wants to do well and is slightly anxious, but knows she has done well in class and that her overall GPA and essay are more likely to affect her chances at college. Tamika gets the highest score. What explains her performance?

    (A) Type B behavior
    (B) Classical conditioning
    (C) Yerkes-Dodson law
    (D) Bandura's concept of self-efficacy
    (E) Mary Rothbart's temperament scales

87. All humans possess which of the following five gustatory sensations?

    (A) Umami, tangy, sweet, salty, sour
    (B) Sweet, salty, bitter, sour, umami
    (C) Smooth, grainy, cold, hot, warm
    (D) Vegetable/fruit, fats, meat, dairy, grain
    (E) Sweet, salty, sour, bitter, acidic

88. What is content validity in a psychometric test?

    (A) The degree to which test-takers in the same age group get similar results
    (B) The correlation between the test results and future performance on another measure
    (C) The degree to which every administration of the same test will yield similar results
    (D) How much the test actually measures what it is designed to measure
    (E) The degree of consistency across sections of the test

GO ON TO THE NEXT PAGE.

89. Sally can never recall whether July has 30 days or 31. She remembers an old rhyme to help her. "30 days has September/April, June, and November/When short February's done/All the rest have 31." Sally is using which of the following?

    (A) Modal memory
    (B) Procedural memory
    (C) Mnemonic device
    (D) Self-reference effect
    (E) Framing

90. A researcher designs a study to find the effects of picture cues on learning in young children. In the experimental design, 100 participants are randomly assigned to each group; one group learns words via software with picture cues, and the other group learns words without picture cues. The researcher records and observes the behavior in each group. The behavior of all the subjects is called the

    (A) correlation coefficient
    (B) independent variable
    (C) dependent variable
    (D) categorical variable
    (E) working hypothesis

91. The Gestalt concept of symmetry refers to

    (A) a tendency to perceive similar forms as a part of a group
    (B) a tendency to perceive forms that are mirror images
    (C) a tendency to view objects as complete rather than incomplete
    (D) a tendency to view objects in proximity to each other as part of a group
    (E) a tendency to break down the relationship between figure and ground

92. Both Abraham Maslow and Carl Rogers are associated with which of the following?

    (A) Collective unconscious
    (B) Reality principle
    (C) Inferiority complex
    (D) Self-actualization
    (E) Unconditional positive regard

93. Mariah is anxious about studying for a test in which knowing the vocabulary will play a big part. She keeps dreaming that she sees a dictionary lying on the table, but when she opens it, it *only* contains a bunch of geometric shapes, with no words or definitions. She thinks the dream reflects her anxiety about not knowing the words likely to appear on the test. If she's right, which of the following best explains this phenomenon?

    (A) REM sleep
    (B) Paradoxical sleep
    (C) Night terror
    (D) Sleep apnea
    (E) Latent content

94. Negative reinforcement is occurring in which of the following situations?

    (A) When Tom gets an A, he doesn't have to wash the dishes.
    (B) 4-year-old Lila gets a timeout when she misbehaves.
    (C) Rover's trainer speaks to Rover sternly but calmly when she chews furniture.
    (D) When Jay is accepted to college, his family buys him tickets to Europe for the summer.
    (E) A laboratory animal doesn't receive pellets when pressing a lever.

95. Tamara doesn't think she's very good at math. She fails her math test. But she knows that all she has to do is study and her grade will rise. This is an example of what?

    (A) High self-efficacy and an external locus of control
    (B) Low self-efficacy and an external locus of control
    (C) High self-efficacy and an internal locus of control
    (D) Low self-efficacy and an internal locus of control
    (E) Low self-efficacy and learned helplessness

96. Jenny's IQ score is 135. Where does this fall on a normal score distribution?

    (A) It depends on how old she is.
    (B) It depends on the sample size.
    (C) Approximately one standard deviation above the mean
    (D) Approximately one standard deviation below the mean
    (E) Approximately two standard deviations above the mean

GO ON TO THE NEXT PAGE.

97. A K–6 school keeps boxes of juice for snacks. Each contains 4 ounces of juice, but some are in long, thin juice boxes and others are in short, squat juice boxes. Some kindergarteners who get a long, thin box are upset, because they think they are getting less juice than their classmates. But all the 10-year-olds understand they have equal amounts of juice. What cognitive development theory best explains this?

    (A) Piaget's formal operational stage
    (B) Erikson's trust versus mistrust stage
    (C) Piaget's theory of conservation
    (D) Theory of Mind
    (E) Internalization

98. Carmen is 8 years old. She loves to dress up by wearing her mother's bracelets. But her mother is afraid she'll damage them, so Carmen will be grounded if she's caught playing with them. She won't be able to go to her grandmother's house, which she also loves to do. As a result, she leaves the bracelets alone. This is most likely accounted for by which of the following?

    (A) Carol Gilligan's theory of moral development
    (B) Piaget's concept of object permanence
    (C) Ainsworth's avoidant attachment pattern
    (D) Kohlberg's theory of preconventional morality
    (E) Erikson's initiative versus guilt stage

99. What does it mean to say a test is standardized?

    (A) The results are correlated with other measures of the same dimension.
    (B) The results are consistent among different graders.
    (C) The answer choices each appear an equal number of times.
    (D) The questions are quantitative rather than projective.
    (E) The test is administered to a sample thought to reflect the characteristics of the population measured.

100. Which are the three scales on which temperament can be assessed, according to Mary Rothbart?

    (A) Surgency, insurgency, acceptance
    (B) Internal locus of control, effortful control, self-actualization
    (C) Negative affect, positive affect, positive self-regard
    (D) Surgency, agency, societal engagement
    (E) Surgency, negative affect, effortful control

END OF SECTION I

IF YOU FINISH BEFORE TIME IS CALLED, YOU MAY CHECK YOUR WORK ON THIS SECTION. DO NOT GO ON TO SECTION II UNTIL YOU ARE TOLD TO DO SO.

PSYCHOLOGY
Section II
Time—50 minutes

Percent of total grade—33 $\frac{1}{3}$

Directions: You have 50 minutes to answer BOTH of the following questions. It is not enough to answer a question by merely listing facts. You should present a cogent argument based on your critical analysis of the question posed, using appropriate psychological terminology.

1. Melody developed a fear of flying after an airplane she was on made a sudden emergency landing. She has nightmares about being on a plane. She also can't stop thinking "It's going to crash! It's going to crash!" if she sees a plane. But she is a member of a choir that is singing in Washington, D.C., in three months, and wants to be able to fly there along with other members of her choir. She wants to choose a method of combating her fear that will do the most to help her be able to fly on an airplane.

   Provide an essay that describes how Melody's situation relates to the following seven terms, giving examples for each.

   - Anxiolytics
   - Systematic desensitization
   - Phobia
   - Amygdala
   - Cognitive therapy
   - Psychoanalytic
   - Yerkes-Dodson law

2. Jonas is a graduate student in psychology. He is designing an experiment to study how having older siblings with significant student loan debt affects high school students' motivation to get college degrees. His working hypothesis is that an older sibling with $15,000 in debt or more may make a younger sibling less motivated to get a degree. He has contacted a local high school to find students applying to college whose siblings have no student loan debt. He has placed an ad on an online college advice site asking students with siblings having at least $15,000 in debt to participate in the experiment.

Part A

Explain the following concepts in the context of Jonas's planned research design.

   - Correlational study
   - Approach-avoidance
   - Type I error

Part B

Jonas presents his design to a graduate seminar for feedback. Explain how each of the following could affect the seminar's discussion of his research design.

   - Self-selection bias
   - Elaboration likelihood model
   - Type II error
   - Confounding variable

STOP

END OF EXAM

Practice Test 3:
Answers and
Explanations

PRACTICE TEST 3: ANSWER KEY

1.	A	26.	A	51.	D	76.	C
2.	B	27.	B	52.	E	77.	D
3.	E	28.	C	53.	A	78.	B
4.	A	29.	C	54.	E	79.	C
5.	D	30.	A	55.	E	80.	D
6.	D	31.	D	56.	C	81.	C
7.	C	32.	E	57.	E	82.	A
8.	B	33.	E	58.	C	83.	D
9.	A	34.	E	59.	B	84.	D
10.	D	35.	A	60.	C	85.	A
11.	E	36.	A	61.	E	86.	C
12.	A	37.	B	62.	C	87.	B
13.	C	38.	D	63.	D	88.	D
14.	B	39.	B	64.	C	89.	C
15.	D	40.	C	65.	A	90.	C
16.	B	41.	A	66.	D	91.	B
17.	B	42.	E	67.	E	92.	D
18.	E	43.	E	68.	B	93.	E
19.	E	44.	A	69.	B	94.	A
20.	A	45.	A	70.	B	95.	D
21.	D	46.	A	71.	A	96.	E
22.	C	47.	E	72.	B	97.	C
23.	D	48.	D	73.	B	98.	D
24.	C	49.	B	74.	A	99.	E
25.	E	50.	C	75.	B	100.	E

PRACTICE TEST 3: ANSWERS AND EXPLANATIONS

Section I: Multiple Choice

1. **A** *Understand the Question/Key Words*: Circle *heritability* and *environment*. *Predict the Answer*: Choice (A), the nature versus nurture debate, wins the prize. Don't overcomplicate it. If you need help, turn to POE. Besides (A), only (B) is about the relationship between two things, really—and it's between consciousness (the mind) and the body, so it isn't about your key words. Choices (C), (D), and (E) aren't related to heredity or the environment either. Choice (C) is the concept that humans are born as blank slates; (D) is about neurons going to and from the brain. Choice (E) is a term from psychoanalytic psychology.

2. **B** *Understand the Question/Key Words*: Circle *sympathetic nervous system*. *Predict the answer:* What does it do for us? Primes us to fight or run away in response to perceived danger, that's what. Choice (B) is the answer. Look to POE if you can't remember. While (C) and (D) are part of Selye's general adaptation syndrome for long-term stress, and (A), chronic stress, can impair the immune system, (E), these are all secondary to the basic function of the sympathetic nervous system: fight or flight.

3. **E** *Understand the Question/Key Words*: The test that measures intelligence is…. *Predict the Answer*: The Stanford-Binet Test, so (E) is the answer. Use POE to immediately strike out (C), as achievement tests measure achievement (such as knowledge of a subject, like an AP test!). Ditto for (D), which is a method of determining validity, not a test in itself. Choices (A) and (B) are both popular tests of personality, rather than intelligence.

4. **A** *Understand the Question/Key Words*: Circle *founder* and *science of psychology*. *Predict the Answer*: Who founded psychology as a science? The answer is (A), William Wundt. The others were important to *parts* of the discipline, but not founders of it. They all fall when you use POE. Titchener, (B), brought psychology to the United States. Freud, (C), was certainly a founder of psychoanalysis, but not of the entire discipline of psychology. Skinner, (D), is well-known for his research into conditioning, another part. And (E), René Descartes, was a philosopher about body and mind interaction—important to the beginnings of psychology, but not a founder of the discipline.

5. **D** *Understand the Question/Key Words:* The words to circle are *eats* and *vomits*. *Predict the Answer*: What's going on when eating and vomiting are conjoined? Choice (D), bulimia nervosa. Choice (C), binge-eating disorder, is the only other thing that even comes close, and in it, people don't purge. Choice (B) is characterized by not eating, while (A), pica, is an eating disorder characterized by a craving for non-nutritive substances like chalk. Choice (E) is a type of disorder that is not related to eating at all.

6. **D** *Understand the Question/Key Words*: Circle *cell* and *color*. *Predict the Answer*: Cones enable color vision, so (D) is the answer. All of the others are about visual anatomy, yes, but not about color vision, so they can all be eliminated.

7. **C** *Understand the Question/Key Words*: What do we experience when we feel a conflict between inner beliefs and outer behavior? Circle *Festinger* and c*onflict*. *Predict the Answer*: Cognitive dissonance! Festinger theorized that a difference between our inner beliefs and our outer behavior caused dissonance, or conflict, within our minds. Use POE. Does (A), general adaptation syndrome, have

to do with conflict? No. Cross it off. Does (B), learned helplessness, have to do with inner conflict? Nope. Choice (D), fluid intelligence, bites the dust because it doesn't have anything to do with conflict and neither does (E), mere exposure effect. Choice (C) rings the bell!

8. **B** *Understand the Question/Key Words*: What's the reflex when a baby grabs an object placed in her hands? *Predict the Answer*: It's (B), the palmar reflex. Think *palmar = palm* and you're close. If you came up empty, eliminate what you can. You can guess it's not (C) or (D), right? These terms give away what the baby does (turns her head and sucks, respectively). Don't think it's (D) because babies suck a pacifier—that's falling for a trick. Choice (A), the Moro reflex, is splaying out limbs in response to loss of support. Choice (E), the Babinski reflex, is splaying out toes in response to strokes on the soles of the feet.

9. **A** *Understand the Question/Key Words*: Circle *behaviorist*. *Predict the Answer*: Behaviorists seek to impact behavior through conditioning, such as reward and punishment, so (A) is the answer. Choice (B) is associated with humanistic psychology, and (C) would interest a psychoanalyst. In (D), thoughts are characteristic of cognitive psychology, and (E) would be of interest to behavioral geneticists.

10. **D** *Understand the Question/Key Words*: You're looking for why students who are excellent as individuals would produce a less than excellent group project. *Predict the Answer:* Social loafing, (D), refers to the tendency of people to expend less effort if they're working together in a group. Bingo. You can eliminate (B) right off the bat because a mindguard is a person who polices group opinions in groupthink. Role exit means someone is leaving one role for another, and role conflict means that there is tension between two or more different roles; neither is relevant, so (C) and (E) can be eliminated. There is no explicit language about anyone making anyone else feel inhibited, so (A) can be eliminated.

11. **E** *Understand the Question/Key Words*: Circle *hospital* and *mentally ill*. *Predict the Answer*: Choice (E), Dorothea Dix, was instrumental in establishing a hospital for the mentally ill in the United States. Choice (D), Edward Titchener, is often credited with bringing psychology to the United States, but not specifically associated with the mentally ill. All the other choices are significant women in psychology, but have nothing to do with a focus on mental illness: (A) was a significant developmental psychologist; (B) was the first woman psychology graduate student; (C) was the first to earn a PhD.

12. **A** *Understand the Question/Key Words*: Circle *master gland*. *Predict the Answer*: It's (A), the pituitary gland. POE and keywords can slay this one if you're not sure. Only (A), (B), and (E) are glands. Are the thyroid and pineal glands as primary as the pituitary? No, so out they both go. Choice (C) is part of the brain and (D) is a neurotransmitter, so they both bite the dust too.

13. **C** *Understand the Question/Key Words*: Circle *Gardner* and *intelligence*. Plus *EXCEPT,* of course. *Predict the Answer*: Gardner is well-known for believing there were many different types of intelligence. The one he *didn't* name is (C), creative. All the others are types he did posit existed. Although some of these, like musical, are *forms* of creativity, he didn't specifically name creative as a type.

14. **B** *Understand the Question/Key Words:* Circle *finding* and *Milgram obedience experiments*. *Predict the Answer:* In the Milgram experiments, removing the experimenter from the room (which presumably diminished his authoritative presence) decreased obedience levels—(B) is correct. You can also eliminate (A), (C), and (E) as being counterintuitive. Moving the "learner" closer would presumably increase the negative emotions associated with shocking him and therefore decrease

obedience (which is in fact what happened)—(A) is wrong. Similarly, the presence of other subjects who were noncompliant would presumably increase confidence and decrease obedience (which was the case as well)—(C) is wrong. Moving the experiment to less prestigious surroundings would (and did) lessen the experimenter's authority and decrease obedience—(E) is wrong. While (D) is plausible, the physical attractiveness of the learner was never manipulated, so you might need to remember the study to correctly choose (B) over (D).

15. **D**   *Understand the Question/Key Words*: Circle *psychoanalytic theory*. Also the three-letter word *NOT*, of course! *Predict the Answer:* The only one that isn't part of psychoanalytic treatment is (D), incongruence, which is what Carl Rogers, a humanistic practitioner, posited we feel when encountering discrepancies between our self-concepts and actual thoughts and behaviors. In other words, (D) is from a different school than psychoanalytic theory, so it's the right answer.

16. **B**   *Understand the Question/Key Words*: Circle *Pavlov. Predict the Answer*: Pavlov is known for his experiments with what? Dogs! *Pavlov's dog* has entered the lexicon as a famous phrase. The discovery led him to classical conditioning, in which an initially neutral stimulus takes on meaning. Right away hone in on (B) as your answer. Everything else can immediately be eliminated.

17. **B**   *Understand the Question/Key Words*: Circle *over and over* and *remember. Predict the Answer*: Doing something over and over to remember it is a form of maintenance rehearsal, so (B) wins the prize. This is clearly a type of rehearsal, so right away POE should have led you to zoom in on (A) or (B) as the only potential answers, eliminating (C), (D), and (E). Choice (A) is not correct because that requires more, well, elaborate cognitive processes of organizing information.

18. **E**   *Understand the Question/Key Words:* Hanna is rewarded after a specific, or fixed, number of times she does something. *Predict the Answer:* Choice (E), fixed-ratio, is the answer. Use POE if you don't recall. The reward isn't (A), continuous, so that falls by the wayside. It's not variable, either, so get rid of (B) and (D). Did (C), fixed-interval, seem enticing? An interval is a time period, rather than a number of occurrences, as fixed-ratio is. Choice (E) is the answer.

19. **E**   *Understand the Question/Key Words:* Circle *conventional* and *moral development. Predict the Answer:* In the conventional stage, people follow the moral rules of society, especially those dictated by authority figures. Yep, (E) is the answer. Not sure? Look at those key words and get your POE on. Conventional often equals following what everybody else does, so neither (A) nor (B) fit, because they're about avoiding or obtaining a specific thing. (Plus, they're the preconventional stage.) Maintaining order, (C), doesn't fit either. Defining for oneself doesn't sound like conventional at all, so strike out (D). (It's postconventional.)

20. **A**   *Understand the Question/Key Words*: Circle *Lazarus, first stage*, and *stress. Predict the Answer*: Lazarus believed that the first thing we do when encountering a stressor is evaluate it. What would that be called? Yep, primary appraisal, so (A) is correct. POE on this should lead you to get rid of (B) and (E) right off the bat, because neither exhaustion nor resistance could be first-stage responses. Choice (C), corticosterone, is activated when we feel alarm, (D). Hmmm. Did either of these seem like potential answers? Think key words. Lazarus was a cognitive researcher who didn't focus on biology, so that should lead you to reject (C). Alarm is one of the stages in Selye's general adaptation syndrome, not Lazarus's theory, so (D) is out too.

21. **D** *Understand the Question/Key Words:* Circle *characteristics* and *disordered behavior. Predict the Answer:* All of the answers are components of psychologically disordered behavior except for (D), patient's history of trauma. Be sure to notice the word EXCEPT. But all these answers may seem like reasonable characteristics. Use POE to help. Remember that schizophrenics, for example, *do* show perceptual dysfunction, so it can't be (A). Do psychological disorders affect a lot of people, statistically? No. If someone has a psychological disorder, are they thought of as abnormal? Yes. You can cross off both (B) and (C). Finally, disordered patients do have difficulty adjusting to society, so it's not (E).

22. **C** *Understand the Question/Key Words:* What part of the brain receives information about temperature? *Predict the Answer:* It's (C), the parietal lobe. Use POE to eliminate the others by thinking about what they do. The occipital lobe, (A), is all about visual information. The temporal lobe, (B), is about sound. The frontal lobe, (D), is about higher level thought and reasoning, and the cerebellum, (E), is about balance and muscular strength and tone.

23. **D** *Understand the Question/Key Words:* Sean is advised to create a visual narrative to help him learn academic content. *Predict the Answer:* Choices (A), (B), and (E) refer to different sorts of memory, rather than aides to learning new information, so they can be eliminated. Choice (C) refers to a strategy of short-term memory. Choice (D) refers to an active technique used to store information in long-term memory, and that's the correct answer.

24. **C** *Understand the Question/Key Words:* Circle *true* and *anorexia nervosa. Predict the Answer:* The diagnostic criteria and general statistical information about anorexia note that it primarily affects females and involves an intense fear of getting fat despite a low body weight for one's age, sex, physical health, etc.—(A) and (D) are wrong and (C) is correct. Choice (B) states a specific weight requirement, which has been abandoned in recent years in favor of evaluating the person's weight in the context of their personal circumstances. Choice (E) is a trap answer because it describes bulimia nervosa, which is often associated with anorexia but has distinct diagnostic requirements.

25. **E** *Understand the Question/Key Words:* Circle *Freud* and *latency. Predict the Answer:* What happens during the latency period? Children move from focusing on certain parts of their bodies (oral, anal) to focusing on people who are the same gender as themselves. Boys think girls are awful, and vice versa. The answer is (E). All the others can be eliminated.

26. **A** *Understand the Question/Key Words:* Circle *regulating* and *eat. Predict the Answer:* The hypothalamus regulates eating and feeding behavior, so the answer is (A). POE is your friend if you don't remember. Choice (B), the amygdala, is related to emotions, and (C) is related to the senses—you can tell that by pulling apart the word *somatosensory*! Hunger is a primary drive, whereas taste, touch, and smell are not. Choice (D) has more to do with the functioning of organs, and (E), the hippocampus, is all about memory.

27. **B** *Understand the Question/Key Words:* Circle *memory. Predict the Answer:* What type of memory is used when we remember facts? Semantic, that's what. Choice (B) is the answer. If you don't recall, remember that *semantic* relates to words and their meanings; that's what we're recalling when we recall facts. Use POE to get rid of (A) because procedural memory recalls skills and habits, not facts. It's also not (C) because recalling facts is explicit, not implicit. Episodic memory, (D), is what

we remember from our own lives. Do you have personal memories of Queen Elizabeth I kicking it in Merrie Olde England? Probably not. Chunking is a memory device, so eliminate (E).

28. **C** *Understand the Question/Key Words:* Circle *unconditional positive regard*. *Predict the Answer*: Carl Rogers is closely associated with this concept, a humanistic approach: (C) is therefore the answer. POE should cause you to strike out (D), Beck, because he's associated with cognitive treatment and (E), Jung, because he's all about the collective unconscious. Both (A), Maslow, and (B), Perls, are also humanistic therapists, but Maslow is closely associated with the hierarchy of needs and Perls with Gestalt therapy.

29. **C** *Understand the Question/Key Words*: Circle *motivations*. *Predict the Answer*: Motivations are (C), extrinsic, when they stem from factors outside ourselves, as Jordan's do. Both (B) and (E) refer to motivations from within ourselves, so they are immediate strike-outs. Choice (D) is biologically based and (A) comes from a humanistic theory of motivations; neither is relevant here.

30. **A** *Understand the Question/Key Words:* Circle *repression, conscious,* and *unconscious*. *Predict the Answer*: Ding, ding, ding! Your brain should associate these key words with (A), the psychoanalytic perspective pioneered by Sigmund Freud. If your brain doesn't, POE is your friend. Choice (B), cognitive psychologists, believe that the cause of disorders is illogical thoughts. That doesn't jibe with the unconscious mind, or with repression. Eliminate it. Behaviorists, (C), believe the cause is reinforced behavior. That doesn't have anything to do with your key words either. Neither does (D), the humanistic perspective, because it focuses on self-esteem, positive self-regard, and sensitivity to criticism. Choice (E), the biological perspective, is an outlier because the key words are clearly not from biology. Choice (A) is the only one that fits the key words.

31. **D** *Understand the Question/Key Words*: Circle *ethical* and *NOT*. *Predict the Answer*: Only (D) fits the bill as a correct NOT answer. The answer is a choice in research design and has nothing to do with ethics. All the other choices are standard parts of ethical research.

32. **E** *Understand the Question/Key Words:* Circle *interpersonal attraction*. *Predict the Answer*: When do we feel attracted to someone? When they live, study, or work close by, are attractive, are familiar, evaluate us positively, or have shared opinions. Remember, this is a NOT question, and we are looking for an answer that is NOT a force in interpersonal attraction. Although (E), personal wealth, may seem like it could be a force in interpersonal attraction, it is not considered a factor and therefore is the correct answer.

33. **E** *Understand the Question/Key Words*: Circle *perception*. *Predict the Answer*: What is going on when we see a color that isn't there? Opponent process theory, (E), tells us that we perceive colors through opponent pairs of receptor sets. Green/red are one potential pair; so are black/white and blue/yellow. If you're using one color in the set, the other is "turned off"—but after a period of time, the receptors for the one you're using get fatigued, and you'll see the other. Hence (E) is the correct answer. Having trouble remembering? POE comes to the rescue. Choice (A) should bite the dust immediately, because Caleb can see both red and green—you have no evidence that he's color blind. So should (C), which is about optic nerve biology, and (D), which is about how the brain computes received information. Nothing in either of these is about color perception. Choice (B) is also a theory of how we perceive color, but posits that we mix the colors, not that they are in opponent pairs of receptor sets.

34. **E** *Understand the Question/Key Words*: Circle *modal model* and *memory. Predict the Answer*: The modal model says that memory is stored in sensory, short-term, and long-term areas. Once you've got this, the answer is (E). You can knock (D) out immediately with POE, because the modal model is not about brain biology. Choices (A), (B), and (C) can all be crossed out too, because they are either types of memory or models of how memory takes place—they don't represent the modal model.

35. **A** *Understand the Question/Key Words*: Circle *observational learning* and *Bandura*. Plus *NOT,* of course. *Predict the Answer*: Bandura worked with children and posited that they modeled the behavior they saw adults performing, as in the Bobo doll experiment. Choice (A) is the only condition NOT in his experiment; all the others can be eliminated, as they are the conditions Bandura deemed essential for observational learning to take place.

36. **A** *Understand the Question/Key Words*: Circle *research method* and *group*. Which method compares similar tasks, but in different age groups? *Predict the Answer*: Choice (A), cross-sectional, is correct. The rest can be eliminated by hanging tight with your key words and using POE. Choice (B), longitudinal, doesn't compare between groups, but follows the same people; (C) is a method of analysis, not a research method. Correlational, (D), has to look at two or more variables. Choice (E), case studies, follow just one person, not a group.

37. **B** *Understand the Question/Key Words:* Circle *internal validity. Predict the Answer:* Internal validity, by definition, is the certainty with which results can be attributed to the independent variable in an experiment: (B) is the correct answer. POE to the rescue if you don't recall. Choice (A) represents *external* validity, not internal. Choices (C), (D), and (E) all fall by the wayside because internal validity has to do with research design, not with standard deviations or with hypotheses and conclusions about them.

38. **D** *Understand the Question/Key Words*: Circle *neural firing* and *NOT. Predict the Answer*: You need something that has nothing to do with neural firing or the biology of the brain. Choice (D), the Moro reflex, is one of the reflexes of a newborn baby. It fits the bill to be the answer. All the other choices are involved in neural firing.

39. **B** *Understand the Question/Key Words:* Circle *negative triad* and *medication. Predict the Answer:* You'll need to recall what the negative triad is. The word *negative* is a clue if you don't remember. In depression, people think negatively, right? The triad is depression about yourself, the world, and the future. Once you've got that, (B) is pretty clearly the answer. Lithium salts are for bipolar disorder and anxiolytics treat anxiety. Antipsychotics treat major disorders such as schizophrenia. While anticholinergics work by blocking acetylcholine, they aren't used for psychological disorders.

40. **C** *Understand the Question/Key Words*: Circle *on time, best,* and *irritated*. You're being asked what these all add up to. *Predict the Answer:* This is classic type-A pattern behavior; (C) is the answer. POE should cause you to eliminate (D), because the negative triad pertains to depression. Andre wouldn't be such a go-getter if he were depressed. People with (A), Type-B pattern behavior, are relaxed, so that's incorrect. Choice (E) doesn't fit: the pituitary gland controls hormones, but it's too broad to be the answer. Choice (B), chronic stress, could be tempting only if you see his behavior as *maybe* a stress response—but stress is more directly related to anxiety-provoking situations or danger.

41. **A** *Understand the Question/Key Words*: *Weber's law* is about thresholds in sensation and perception. It holds that the greater the magnitude of the stimulus, the larger the difference needs to be to be noticed. *Predict the Answer*: In (A), the same 5-pound difference is noticeable in the lower weight range (30 versus 25 pounds) but not the higher one (55 versus 50 pounds). Choice (A) is the correct answer. Use POE if you need to! Choice (B) may seem tempting because Weber's law is part of how we ascertain differences between stimuli, but this choice is too broad. You can immediately eliminate (D) and (E) because they are not about noticing differences. Choice (D) is all about sensory adaptation and (E) is about selective attention, in which we can pay attention to one thing while ignoring others. Choice (C) is an example of priming, which is subconscious perception.

42. **E** Solomon Asch's study tested perceptions of line length in a study about conformity. It didn't have anything to do with brain physiology, so eliminate (C). Asch is a social psychologist, so strike out an individual condition like (A), schizophrenia. His purpose was to test conformity in a group. No one in Asch's study was playing roles (except perhaps the confederates, but they weren't the people being studied), so eliminate (D). Although there was a group of naïve participants, they were not an outgroup, so (B) is not part of this experiment. The correct answer is (E).

43. **E** *Understand the Question/Key Words*: Circle *Type I error*. *Predict the Answer*: A Type I error is by definition deciding that a difference exists as a result of your experiment when it fact it doesn't. And the correct answer is…(E). When in doubt, use POE. Choices (B), (C), and (D) should all fall to the strikeout of your mighty pencil, because standard deviations, confounding variables, and sample sizes, respectively, all have nothing to do with Type I errors. Choice (A) is the opposite of Type I: it's a Type II error.

44. **A** *Understand the Question/Key Words*: Circle *electroencephalogram* and *REM*. *Predict the Answer*: Which type of waves and movement occur when we dream? Choice (A), theta and beta waves, are most common in REM sleep, which is when most dreams occur. You can get rid of all the others via POE.

45. **A** *Understand the Question/Key Words*: Circle *praise* and *off-season*. *Predict the Answer*: Harriet continues doing something even after there is no specific request to do so, because she's been rewarded with praise. This is (A), operant conditioning, which tells us that a rewarded subject will continue doing the task even when the reward stops. Use POE to immediately get rid of (D) and (E); (D) isn't relevant and it's clearly not (E). Choice (B), vicarious reinforcement, means watching someone else receive a reward. Choice (C), classical conditioning, is about the pairing of two stimuli, one neutral and one unconditioned. That is not going on here.

46. **A** *Understand the Question/Key Words*: Circle *fear*. *Predict the Answer*: Fear of heights is a common phobia. The treatment being used to treat the phobia starts slow, which makes it what kind of treatment? It's (A), systematic desensitization. If you can't remember, immediately eliminate (C) because treatment with medication is irrelevant in this example. Is it (B), flooding? That's the opposite of (A), because you start with a big phobia trigger that floods you with stimuli. You might be tempted by (D), implosion. It's partly right, but it's *only* imagining without progressing into the real world. Choice (E), extinction procedures, might also be tempting, but it's too broad. Choice (A) is correct.

47. **E** *Understand the Question/Key Words*: Frank isn't saying the complete, grammatically correct sentence "I go to school." *Predict the Answer*: What's that called? Choice (E), telegraphic speech, is the correct answer. You could guess this by the abbreviated quality of the sentence if you don't remember. You should realize (A) is too broad by the time you see (E). None of the others are correct: (B) is the stage in which children communicate in sentences of just one word; (C), overextension, is when a child applies one word to a broad category ("rose" to any flower); and (D), underextension, is when a child thinks, for example, that a rose is the only type of flower.

48. **D** *Understand the Question/Key Words:* Circle *behaviorist. Predict the Answer:* What do behaviorists believe? That behavior can be changed by outside stimuli, both positive and negative. They might, for example, encourage a parent to make a misbehaving child perform an additional chore. Punishment! And the answer is…(D). POE away if you can't recall. Hmmm, (A) seems not that relevant, but is it wrong? Keep it for now. Choice (B) is what a humanistic psychologist would think, and (C) is the classic psychoanalytic view. You might be tempted by (E)…but then you see the word *thought* and eliminate it, because that's cognitive. Compared to (D), you can tell that (A) is not relevant.

49. **B** *Understand the Question/Key Words*: Ken wants two things, but they could be in conflict with each other. *Predict the Answer*: What happens when what we want is in conflict? It's (B), approach-avoidance behavior. POE can come to your aid if you're unsure. Approach-approach is two things we want, while avoidance-avoidance is two things we *don't* want. Strike out both (A) and (C). Choice (D) might seem possible, but it involves more than one positive and one negative choice. Out it goes. Choice (E) is about the interplay of body and mind in emotion, not about choosing between two motives.

50. **C** *Understand the Question/Key Words:* Circle *responsibility, parenting style, friends*. Which type of parenting style has those traits? *Predict the Answer*: A permissive parenting style, (C), will often result in the child's not taking responsibility. The parents are also likely to think of themselves as friends rather than parents. If you can't remember, common sense and POE should cause you to get rid of (A) and (B), just by looking at the meanings of the words. Both of these types of parents would be concerned about poor grades—and not be friends, in the bargain. Both (D) and (E) are children's attachment patterns, not parenting styles. Remember your key words!

51. **D** *Understand the Question/Key Words:* Circle *contact hypothesis*. If you don't remember what it is, use POE. Is it related to being attracted to a person, as (A) indicates? While proximity may increase interpersonal attraction, it's not quite the same as contact. Also, there's no "two weeks" involved. Choice (B) could be partially true. But (B) could also be untrue, because sometimes contact lessens biases or leaves them the same. Also, the contact hypothesis was designed to reduce prejudice, and biases are not necessarily negative. Choice (C), hmmm, is partially correct. Leave it, but see whether there are answers that more fully summarize the entire hypothesis. Ah, (D) is a fuller summary, because it gets at more key facts about the contact hypothesis. Choice (E) is incorrect, because contact is not a form of altruism.

52. **E** *Understand the Question/Key Words*: Circle *Eysenck Personality Inventory. Predict the Answer*: What does this tool measure? Traits, so (E) is the answer. Trait theorists are far more likely to use assessment measures like this than any other group, so you could have guessed that (A), (B), and (C) could be eliminated. Only (D) even comes close.

53. **A**   *Understand the Question/Key Words:* Circle *psychoanalytic. Predict the Answer:* When you think *psychoanalytic*, think things like free association, unconscious mind—techniques intended to spur insight. Even if you don't remember the specific terms, all their techniques are grounded in *insight*. So the answer has to be related to that. Is (B) related? No. Plus, prescribing anything would be more likely for a biological-based clinician. Choices (C) and (D) are both about changing behavior more than gaining insight. While (E) could lead to insight as well, its use is more typical of a humanistic practitioner, not a psychoanalytic one.

54. **E**   *Understand the Question/Key Words*: Circle *Broca's area. Predict the Answer:* Broca's area affects our ability to speak, so (E) is the correct answer. It's the left side of the frontal lobe of the cortex. Activate POE if you're stumped. Choice (A), loss of ability to visually integrate information, results from damage to the occipital lobe. Choice (B), loss of ability to hear, would originate in the temporal lobes, in the auditory cortex. Choice (C), loss of ability to understand what she hears, is the only other loss associated with a researcher's name; it would originate in Wernicke's area of the temporal lobes. Choice (D) is sometimes referred to as echolalia, and has nothing to do with Broca's area.

55. **E**   *Understand the Question/Key Words*: Because Aidan is very good at many things, the team leader assumes he'll be very good at house-building tasks, too. *Predict the Answer:* When being good in several areas leads people to think we'll be good at everything, it's (E), the halo effect. If you're stumped, try POE. Does (A), *intersectionality*, mean the assumption that someone will always be good at everything? No, intersectionality refers to the nature and effects of the overlapping identities individuals can have. Does (B), *behavioral dissonance*, mean the assumption that someone will always be good at everything? Nope; behavioral dissonance is not a term used in psychology. Neither does (C) or (D): *gender attribution* probably means that the group leader might make an assumption based on gender roles, while *confirmation bias* means when people actively seek out only information that confirms the views they already hold, the opposite of what is happening to the group leader here.

56. **C**   *Understand the Question/Key Words:* Circle *none of these people offered her any assistance. Predict the Answer:* A lot of people stand around when someone is hurt. That's (C), bystander effect. Use POE if you can't recall the answer. Assistance is a helping behavior and so it's linked with altruism, yes? They're not aggressive toward her; they just don't lift a finger even though she's hurt. Choice (A), outgroup homogeneity, is the assumption that every member of a group not our own is like each other. It's not that one. Choice (B), social inhibition, explains why you perform worse if people are around than when they're not. Did Karen fall due to the presence of so many people? She may be embarrassed by a large group seeing her fall, but there's no indication that she's inhibited— and their presence didn't have anything to do with causing her fall. Choice (D), dehumanization, means seeing people as less than human. No indication of that, so cross it out. Choice (E), the Rosenthal Effect, is a type of self-fulfilling prophecy, which is not relevant at all.

57. **E**   *Understand the Question/Key Words*: Peter remembers information more when he's physically in the place where he learned it. *Predict the Answer:* Context-dependent memory predicts that we are more likely to recall information when we're in a situation similar to the one where it was first encoded. The answer is (E). Don't remember? Use POE. All of the others can be crossed off because they have nothing to do with place or similar situations.

58. **C** *Understand the Question/Key Words*: Two people think something is twice as far away as it is in the fog. What's going on? *Predict the Answer*: Aerial perspective, (C), occurs when atmospheric moisture and dust obscure objects in the distance, making them seem farther away than they are. Don't be fooled by the word *aerial* into believing it has something to do with you (and your eyes) being in the air. It's *things* (fog, snow, dust) in the air. POE will tell you that none of the others are relevant to the situation, so they all can be eliminated.

59. **B** *Understand the Question/Key Words*: Circle *single-blind*. *Predict the Answer*: In a single-blind experiment, who doesn't know whether they are in a control group or an experimental group? The subjects. The correct answer is therefore (B). Use POE to eliminate the rest. Choice (D) describes a double-blind experiment, which is often done so the experiment isn't compromised in some way by either group's knowledge of who's in the control group and who's in the experimental group. In (C), the word *both* doesn't match with what you're looking for: it can be eliminated. Choice (A) is not a research design and (E) wouldn't make any sense in an experiment.

60. **C** *Understand the Question/Key Words*: Circle *narcotics* and *pain*. *Predict the Answer:* What occurs naturally in the body to relieve pain? Endorphins, that's what! Choice (C) is the answer. All the others can be eliminated with POE. Did (A) tempt you? Serotonin can make us feel good, but it doesn't relieve pain.

61. **E** *Understand the Question/Key Words*: Circle *attributes*. *Predict the Answer:* Paula attributes reasons for the score: to herself, when the score is good, and to the judges, when the score is low. This is classic self-serving bias, (E), when we attribute the cause to ourselves when outcomes are good and to outside forces when they are negative. Situational attribution, (A), happens when we believe only the environment matters and (C), dispositional attribution, happens when we think only internal factors (like hard work) matter. Get rid of both. You might be tempted by (B), fundamental attribution error, but that occurs when we are more likely to overestimate the role of internal behavior rather than the situation. There's no evidence here that Paula does that. This situation also isn't a self-fulfilling prophecy, (D), because no one has predicted success or failure for her—which would have to happen for the prophecy to fulfill itself.

62. **C** *Understand the Question/Key Words:* What shows that one element causes another? *Predict the Answer*: Only (C) is the way to show causation. While (A) might mean a successful experiment, by itself it doesn't demonstrate causation. Choice (B) doesn't show causation either. Careful with (D); that's just correlation, and remember that *correlation does not mean causation*! Choice (E) would be unethical, and doesn't clearly relate to causation.

63. **D** *Understand the Question/Key Words:* Circle *anxiety* and *replace every thought*. *Predict the Answer*: Which type of therapists counsel replacing one type of thought with another? Cognitive therapists, that's who. Choice (D), rational-emotive behavior therapy, is the only cognitive approach here. Everything else can be eliminated through your friend POE. It's definitely not (E) because anxiolytics are a biological treatment for anxiety. Yes, Julio is stressed, but his therapist isn't using any medications. A psychoanalyst, (C), would be interested in insight into the subconscious. A behaviorist, (B), would focus on behavior reinforcement or change, and (A), humanistic therapists, would focus on positive regard and self-esteem. None of those are going on here.

64. **C** *Understand the Question/Key Words*: What is the therapist likely trying to do? *Predict the Answer*: Make sure Jayden doesn't start associating feeling sick to his stomach with his favorite foods. If that happens, he may start to feel nauseous thinking about pizza and chocolate. So the answer is…(C), conditioned taste aversion. Choice (A), aversion therapy, may sound similar, but isn't—it's when something a person wants to stop is linked to an aversive stimulus, like alcoholic patients being given medication that makes them ill if they drink. Every other choice doesn't fit at all, so eliminate through POE.

65. **A** *Understand the Question/Key Words*: What happens when we tune out a frequently occurring stimulus? *Predict the Answer*: Habituation, so (A) is correct. POE should have led you to immediately eliminate (B), (D), and (E), as none of them are relevant to becoming so accustomed to something that happens all the time that you don't notice it. Choice (C) is very related and may seem tempting. But desensitization is more a process of being less and less sensitive to a stimulus through repeated exposure. You can become less and less afraid of thunder by gradually letting yourself experience loud noises. That's becoming desensitized. But you don't stop hearing the thunder.

66. **D** *Understand the Question/Key Words:* Circle *two standard deviations*. *Predict the Answer*: In a normal statistical curve, about 95 percent of all scores fall within two standard deviations of the mean, including those scores that fall above and below the mean. Choice (D) is the correct answer. Use POE and common sense to eliminate if you can't recall. Choice (A) is too high—it's the figure likely at three standard deviations, not two. All the others are too low. Choice (C), 68 percent, is the number that will fall within one standard deviation, while (E) is the percentage that would occur between the mean and one standard deviation above or below it only.

67. **E** *Understand the Question/Key Words*: Circle *remember*. Thomas is middle-aged and can't remember information more up-to-date than what he originally learned. *Predict the Answer*: What happens when older information pushes out newer information? Choice (E), proactive interference, is correct. You can immediately eliminate (B) because retroactive interference is the opposite; newer information pushes out old. You can also get rid of (C) because it means remembering something relevant to us personally. Did (A) and (D) give you pause? Decay is one of the ways we forget. Thomas hasn't forgotten completely; he just remembers the older rule rather than the newer one. Choice (D) describes how short-term memories get to be long-term ones. Yes, there's some encoding going on here, but once you read (E), you should realize (D) is too broad to be the correct answer.

68. **B** *Understand the Question/Key Words:* A 6-year-old is likely in first grade, and enjoying rewards for doing well. *Predict the Answer:* Erikson would put her in (B), the industry versus inferiority stage. Choice (A) is Piaget; (C) is Vygotsky; and (E) is Kohlberg, so you can eliminate those. Only (D) is another of Erikson's stages, but identity versus role confusion happens around the time of puberty, so eliminate it too.

69. **B** *Understand the Question/Key Words:* Circle *drugs* and *psychotherapeutic*. *Predict the Answer:* You need to find the one NOT used for psychological disorders. Note the trickiness of the question here; it's all too easy to read past that three-letter NOT. Be sure to read all of each question carefully throughout the test; traps like this are just lying in wait. Which of these have you not read about in AP Psych? That would be (B), antineoplastics, which are chemotherapy drugs. All of the others are part of psychopharmacological treatment.

70. **B** *Understand the Question/Key Words:* Circle *anxiety disorder. Predict the Answer*: Remember, this is asking which *isn't* an anxiety disorder. Choice (B), conversion disorder, is a somatic disorder, in which people have bodily symptoms for which there is no physical cause. That makes (B) very definitely *not* an anxiety disorder, and thus the answer. If you need help, go POE! Choices (D) and (E) are specific types of phobias. Phobias are triggered by things that make us stressed or fearful, so (D) and (E) both can be ruled out as potential correct answers. Generalized anxiety disorder, (A), and panic disorder, (C), are two other common types of anxiety disorders.

71. **A** *Understand the Question/Key Words:* Circle *win* and *election*. Both have to do with persuading people to vote for a specific candidate. *Predict the Answer*: The answer needs to be about how people are persuaded. The elaboration likelihood model explains when we are persuaded by content, such as the logic of the argument, and when we are swayed by more superficial factors, like appearance (those clothes!). Choice (A) is therefore the answer. If you don't remember, whip out POE. What do these models focus on? Piaget's development model, (B), is about childhood development. The modal model, (C), is about memory. Kohlberg's models, (D), are all about morality. The Hawthorne effect, (E), is about organizational psychology. None of these fit.

72. **B** *Understand the Question/Key Words*: Circle *forebrain*. *Predict the Answer*: What goes on in the forebrain? Emotions, memories, sensory relay. And those are found in (B), the thalamus, hippocampus, and amygdala. Look at the components of each answer carefully as you wield POE. Choice (A) looks good until you hit *cerebellum*. That controls muscle tone and balance, and it's hindbrain. Remember, if one component in a string is wrong, the whole answer is wrong. Choice (C) should give you pause with *medulla oblongata*. That's also part of the hindbrain, and controls functions we don't even think about, like breathing. In (D), the reticular activating system is hindbrain, controlling sleep and wakefulness. Choice (E) is mostly midbrain, with *cerebellum* making a guest appearance from hindbrain.

73. **B** *Understand the Question/Key Words*: Ashleigh is remembering scenes from a movie as if they actually happened to her. *Predict the Answer:* Hmmm, thinking material from a source (like a book or movie) is part of our own personal memory is (B), source confusion, so (B) is the correct answer. "Source" should have helped you if it wasn't clear. Wield POE to eliminate (D) immediately because it has nothing to do with remembering. Choice (A), retrograde amnesia, refers to forgetting what happened before an accident. Retroactive interference, (E), occurs when new information pushes out old. Eliminate both (A) and (E). Is it (C), framing? That's false memory too, but it occurs because of questions and suggestions, not a mistaken source. Eliminate (C).

74. **A** *Understand the Question/Key Words*: Circle *skin*. *Predict the Answer*: Choice (A) is the answer, because both tactile and cutaneous cells respond to stimuli on the skin. POE should lead to a complete elimination of all other choices, because none of them are about skin. Choices (B) and (C) are both related to the ear. Choices (D) and (E) are both related to vision.

75. **B** *Understand the Question/Key Words*: What explains why she isn't as happy now as when she was 10? *Predict the Answer*: Choice (B) occurs when something we once loved becomes more like a job. Did you choose (E)? It's part of the way there, because her motivations have shifted from intrinsic (this is fun!) to extrinsic (can't let the team/sponsors/TV announcers down). But (B) explains the shift itself. POE should have gotten rid of (A), (C), and (D).

76. **C** *Understand the Question/Key Words:* Circle *positive symptom* and *schizophrenia*. *Predict the Answer*: What are positive symptoms in schizophrenia? They're symptoms a patient has that other people typically don't. Hone in on that rat specter, because hallucinations are a schizophrenia symptom that others don't tend to experience; (C) is the answer. Choice (A) is the lack of a positive symptom; (B) and (E) are negative symptoms, and (D) isn't a symptom at all, but a "positive" step Hal has made—using a different meaning of the word "positive."

77. **D** *Understand the Question/Key Words:* Why would a couple want to go work with the poor? *Predict the Answer:* Larry and Pat are in midlife and thinking about how they can contribute. That's (D), Erikson's stage of generativity versus stagnation. If you weren't sure, use keywords and POE to immediately get rid of (C) and (E), neither of which fit the situation. Choice (A) occurs during old age, so that's not applicable to 50-year-olds. Does (B) fit the situation? Not really. It's gotta be (D).

78. **B** *Understand the Question/Key Words:* Circle *unable to form attachments*. *Predict the Answer*: Which answer is most about the key words? If you chose (B), reactive attachment disorder, you hit the nail on the head. Did it seem like (A), attachment anxiety, was possible? It's related, but (A) refers to some difficulty or inhibition in forming attachments, not something close to inability. It pays to circle those key words! Choice (C) describes the stage in developmental psychology when children realize objects don't disappear just because they can't see them anymore. Choice (D) refers to anxiety when children are separated from caregivers to whom they've formed attachments and (E), detachment adaptation, isn't a real term.

79. **C** *Understand the Question/Key Words*: Circle *cigarettes* and *heart*. *Predict the Answer*: We're talking about nicotine and why it may cause a faster heartbeat. It's the release of (C), acetylcholine, which causes faster heart contractions. Are any of the others about heart rate? You may be tempted by (D), norepinephrine, which also deals with heart rate. But it's a part of the fight-or-flight response, and not related to nicotine, so you can eliminate it. All the others can be eliminated via POE.

80. **D** *Understand the Question/Key Words*: Sophie is doing a type of brainstorming. *Predict the Answer*: What type of thinking is brainstorming? It's (D) for divergent! POE rides to the rescue if you can't remember. Choice (B), inductive, is a form of reasoning. That's not what Sophie is doing here. In (C), convergent, one tries to converge on just one answer. Fixed, (E), sounds like the opposite of the type of creative thinking the teacher suggests. Did (A) seem possible? Well, brainstorming can be creative, but that's too broad an answer; (D) is correct.

81. **C** *Understand the Question/Key Words:* Circle *phobia* and *biological basis*. *Predict the Answer*: If a clinician believes in a biological basis for disorders, what do they do? Prescribe medication. The only possible correct answer is (C). Eliminate everything else. Don't be thrown by the desensitization also present in this answer; medication is often combined with other forms of treatment.

82. **A** *Understand the Question/Key Words*: Circle *theory of emotion*. *Predict the Answer*: Only two of these are theories of emotion, so eliminate (C), (D), and (E). Sebastian is undergoing a physiological response, but cognitively interprets it, in accordance with (A), the two-factor theory advanced by Schachter and Singer. Choice (B) doesn't fit because James-Lange theory posits that the physiological response happens before emotional experience (and we don't cognitively label it).

83. **D**   *Understand the Question/Key Words*: Circle *deductive reasoning. Predict the Answer*: Henry is a social media manager at Company X, and all social media managers at Company X use Website A. Thus, Henry uses Website A. This is the only thing you can definitely know through deductive reasoning.

84. **D**   *Understand the Question/Key Words*: Circle *anger* and *resistance. Predict the Answer:* What happens when we feel like we're being forced to go along with something against our will? Psychological reactance, so (D) is the correct answer. If you don't remember, use POE. Choice (A) may seem tempting because anger is linked with aggression, but this has nothing to do with resistance to any kind of store's behavior. Choice (B) is a compliance technique in which a large request is made first, to soften you up for smaller requests; eliminate it. Conflicting motives, (C), may seem tempting if you read this situation as one of "want to buy/don't want to jump through the store's hoops." Remember your key words, though; conflicting motives have nothing to do with anger or resistance. Choice (E), systematic desensitization, is a method of gradually minimizing responses via repeated small exposures to a stimulus: it's got nothing to do with anger or resistance, so eliminate it.

85. **A**   *Understand the Question/Key Words:* You're looking for what a cognitive therapist would think about a psychoanalyst. Cognitive = focused on thinking. Eliminate anything that doesn't focus on thinking. Choice (A) looks really good on that score, but quickly make sure you're on the right track. Choice (B) is about behavior—that's more likely to be from a behaviorist. Choice (C) isn't relevant to thoughts. Choice (D) is a likely criticism from a humanistic therapist. Choice (E) focuses on desensitization, a behavioral technique. Choice (A) is correct.

86. **C**   *Understand the Question/Key Words*: Megan may have felt the test was too daunting and Zach didn't care. Tamika was in the middle. *Predict the Answer*: The Yerkes-Dodson law indicates that tasks of moderate difficulty will elicit the best performance, rather than tasks that are too hard or too easy: (C) is the answer. Choice (B) is about methods of influencing behavior and (E) is about assessing temperament, and neither apply to this situation. POE should have led you to eliminate them. Did (A) or (D) seem appealing? Type B behavior is easy-going, but doesn't apply to the scenario under which the other two students don't perform as well. Choice (D) refers to belief in one's self, but (C) explains better why she performed well, rather than just feeling like she would.

87. **B**   *Understand the Question/Key Words*: Circle *gustatory*. It's taste, right? *Predict the Answer*: And our tastes are…(B) is the correct answer. POE should lead you to eliminate (C) and (D) immediately, because (C) lists the way foods feel, and (D) lists food groups. Neither is related to taste. Then, if you don't remember what the 5 tastes are, look carefully at each component in your choices. In (A), tangy gives the game away. That's not a taste by itself. In (E), acidic gives the game away. It's not a taste by itself either. Both can be eliminated.

88. **D**   *Understand the Question/Key Words*: Circle *Content validity* and *test. Predict the Answer*: Content validity in a standardized test is how much it actually measures what it is said to measure: (D) is the answer. Use POE if you don't remember the definition: (A) isn't relevant; (B) defines predictive validity; and (C) and (E) are both measures of reliability rather than validity.

89. **C**   *Understand the Question/Key Words*: Circle *remembers*. Which type of memory aid relies on rhymes or short phrases? *Predict the Answer:* Choice (C), mnemonic device, is what you're looking for! If

in doubt, use POE. It's definitely not (B), procedural memory, because that's memory of tasks and skills. Nor is it (E), framing, because that's a method of creating false memories. The self-reference effect, (D), is the tendency to remember stuff that's relevant to us personally. That doesn't fit. Modal memory, (A), is too broad to be the answer.

90. **C** *Understand the Question/Key Words:* Circle *behavior of the subjects. Predict the Answer*: The control and independent variables here are the learning of words with and without picture cues; the behavior is that which is being measured. The behavior will *depend* on which way the subjects learn the words, so it's the dependent variable, (C). Turn to POE if you need to: (A), the correlation coefficient, doesn't apply here; (B) refers to how the subjects learn the words; and while there may be categorical variables, (D), here, they wouldn't be the subject's behavior. Choice (E), the working hypothesis, is something the experimenter sets, but is not the behavior of the subjects.

91. **B** *Understand the Question/Key Words*: Circle *Gestalt* and *symmetry. Predict the Answer*: What did Gestalt folks have to say about symmetry? Choice (B) is correct; that we have a tendency to perceive forms that are mirror images. Use POE to help if you need it. Reading carefully would have caused you to eliminate (A) because it's, well, the Gestalt concept of similarity. Choice (C) is related to the Gestalt concept of closure. Choice (D) is the Gestalt concept of proximity. And (E) refers to a central tenet of Gestalt psychology generally, but is not specific to symmetry.

92. **D** *Understand the Question/Key Words*: Circle *Maslow* and *Rogers. Predict the Answer*: Both were humanistic psychologists, so (D), self-actualization, fits the bill. If (E) seems familiar, it's because it's associated with Rogers—but not with Maslow, so it's a trap answer. Choice (A) is associated with Jung; (B) is associated with Freud and with a psychoanalytic approach. Choice (C) is associated with Alfred Adler, who was also a psychoanalyst.

93. **E** *Understand the Question/Key Words*: Circle *dream. Predict the Answer:* What explains why some things in dreams seem to symbolize, or stand for, things happening in our lives, even though they're not directly related? It's (E), latent content. If you don't remember, use POE. You can eliminate (A) immediately because, even though REM is the stage where most dreams occur, it has nothing to do with one thing meaning another. Neither does (D), which is a sleep disorder in which a person wakes up periodically. Choice (C), night terror, refers to a sleep disorder that takes place during slow-wave sleep. This is totally different from a nightmare! Did (B), paradoxical sleep, give you pause? This term refers to the paradoxical nature of REM sleep, in which our bodies aren't moving but our brain waves resemble those when we're awake.

94. **A** *Understand the Question/Key Words*: Circle *negative reinforcement. Predict the Answer*: Negative reinforcement is the removal of an unpleasant stimulus to increase a behavior. In the world of operant conditioning, *negative* means something is being removed and *positive* is adding something. What fits the bill? Choice (A) does: Tom doesn't have to do the negative stimulus, washing the dishes, if he gets a good grade, a positive development. Choice (B) is negative punishment, while in (E) it seems like there's a reward that isn't being implemented; (C) might be considered positive punishment, if a stern, calm talking-to counts as a negative stimulus; and (D) is positive reinforcement, a reward for an achievement.

95. **D** *Predict the Answer:* Tamara's belief that she isn't very good at math indicates low self-efficacy, so get rid of (A) and (C). But she also believes that she's in control of raising her grades—and that's an internal locus of control. That eliminates (B) and also (E). Choice (D) is the answer.

96. **E** *Understand the Question/Key Words:* Circle *IQ score* and *normal score distribution.* Where does a score of 135 fall? *Predict the Answer:* Since the mean, median, and modal scores of IQ tests along a normal distribution curve are 100, 135 is high. The answer is (E). You could have used POE to immediately eliminate (B) and (D). The standard deviation is approximately 15–16 points on IQ tests; (C) thus wouldn't be high enough for Jenny's 135 score. Choice (A) is a trick, because it intends to make you think of the original definition of IQ tests, as mental age divided by physical age times 100.

97. **C** *Understand the Question/Key Words:* Five-year-olds can't understand that differently arranged liquid is actually the same amount, but 10-year-olds can. What theory accounts for that? *Predict the Answer:* (C), Piaget's theory of conservation! We can only understand that what looks like different amounts are the same once we understand conservation, which happens once we reach Piaget's concrete operational stage, which occurs from roughly ages 7 to 11. The 10-year-olds are in it; the kindergarteners aren't. Don't remember? POE should lead you to eliminate (B), (D), and (E), which are all irrelevant to the situation. Choice (A) comes later than understanding conservation, so eliminate it too.

98. **D** *Understand the Question/Key Words:* Carmen will be punished if she does something, so she doesn't. Why? *Predict the Answer:* Choice (D), Kohlberg's theory of preconventional morality, says children *don't* do prohibited things out of fear of punishment (no trip to Grandma's) or desire to benefit in some way (going to Grandma's). Ding, ding, ding! But what if you don't know? Well, (B) is about when we realize that objects are still there even if we can't see them, as with a ball rolling under a bed; that definitely doesn't match. If (C) were correct, you'd expect to see some kind of avoidance in the scenario, but calling this avoidance would be a stretch. So would seeing initiative or guilt, (E). Cross them both off. Choice (A) might seem tempting, but Gilligan is all about caring relationships as the basis for moral decisions, *not* punishment, so she's out.

99. **E** *Understand the Question/Key Words:* Circle *test* and *standardized. Predict the Answer:* Standardization of tests involves determining norms for a given population, which are then utilized to compare test results. To define norms, the test is given to a sample thought to be representative of the population. The answer is thus (E). Use POE if you can't recall. Standardization is all about populations. The other answers aren't, and can be eliminated. Choice (A) describes the measurement of validity, not standardization. Choice (B) has more to do with consistency, not standardization (and *graders* means the scoring is not done via computer). Choice (C) is about format rather than standardization, and (D) has to do with the types of questions and answers.

100. **E** *Understand the Question/Key Words:* Circle *temperament, assessed, Rothbart. Predict the Answer:* Rothbart assessed temperament on a child's surgency (positive affect/activity), negative affect (frustration/sadness), and effortful control (ability to self-regulate). The answer is (E). All the other answers include one of her scales, but mix them up with terms that are *not* related to temperament scales, so they can all be eliminated.

Section II: Free Response

1. Essay number one is worth seven points. Points are given based on a student's ability to explain behavior and apply theories and perspectives in authentic contexts. Each essay is unique, but here is our run-down of what a student should definitely address in the Free Response Essay for this question:

Part A

- A correlational study observes the degree of association between two or more variables that occur naturally, such as 1) plans to go to college and 2) siblings with student loan debt. It's worth noting, however, that correlation does not equal causation.

- Approach-avoidance is a concept in motivation: a given element has both pluses and minuses that need to be considered, such as the value of a college education in gaining certain types of employment and the cost of that education.

- Type I error is what occurs when a study concludes that a difference exists when it in fact doesn't. Jonas's research design may be vulnerable to Type I error, due to confounding differences between his two samples and/or observer bias (he may subtly influence the results of his study to see what he expects to see).

Part B

When the seminar discusses the research design, here is a rundown of what needs to be addressed:

- Self-selection bias exists when the subjects of a study control whether they are included, such as when people very interested in an issue desire inclusion—potentially, for example, the students who see the ad online. Students whose motivation *is* affected may be much more prone to respond than those whose motivation isn't affected.

- The elaboration likelihood model refers to the tendency of people to be persuaded either by the logic of an argument or by some more superficial characteristic, such as looks or clothes. Seminar participants might be persuaded by several different aspects of Jonas's presentation.

- Type II error is what occurs when a study concludes no difference exists when in fact it does. It's also possible that Jonas's research design may be vulnerable to Type II error: since the group whose siblings have debt will be recruited from a college advice site, they may be more motivated to go to college than the average high school student, making the results more similar between the two groups than they would otherwise be.

- A confounding variable is an unknown variable that might play a role in the experiment. For example, each group of students might have multiple motivations to attend college (or not), besides just the existence of a sibling's student loan debt. The experiment may not be valid if potential confounding variables aren't addressed.

2. Essay number two is worth seven points. One point is awarded for explaining each term and giving a relevant example of each. Points are given based on students' ability to analyze psychological research studies, including analyzing and interpreting quantitative data. This is what our "student" chose to do for her essay. Use this as a sample of a high-scoring essay.

Sample Essay

A frightening experience can leave people with a <u>phobia</u>, which is anxiety about the threat of danger, rather than the actual presence of danger itself. Melody's anxiety indicates she has a phobia. It also means that her <u>amygdala</u>, the portion of the brain that processes negative emotions like fear, is activated.

Phobias can be treated with several different forms of psychological therapy. Behaviorist approaches such as <u>systematic desensitization</u>, for example, might help Melody. Systematic desensitization occurs when one response (such as Melody's anxiety) is replaced with another, such as a feeling of deep relaxation, while being exposed to anxiety-provoking stimuli in manageable doses.

A behaviorist therapist, for example, might suggest that they begin with pictures of an airplane on the ground. Melody will look at them and breathe deeply to relax. This will continue until she can look at them calmly. Then they might progress to a picture of an airplane in the sky and repeat the process. Then they might go to an airport to look at planes taking off and landing. Here, too, Melody will practice deep breathing until she is calm in a busy airport.

A therapist using a <u>cognitive</u> approach seeks to replace unrealistic thinking with more constructive thinking. The therapist might suggest, for example, that every time Melody thinks "It's going to crash!" when seeing a plane, she immediately replace the thought with "Very few planes actually crash. Planes are safer than cars."

A <u>psychoanalytic</u> therapist, on the other hand, might help Melody by providing insight into her fear. Psychoanalytic practitioners believe that the unconscious mind exerts a significant influence over our waking life. Psychoanalysts are highly interested in dreams, for example, because they use dreams to gain insight into what is making phobic patients anxious.

Melody might be asked to free associate to see whether she thinks a plane crash has any symbolic relationship to anything in her life. It's a potentially great thing (a trip) suddenly turning negative, after all. A psychoanalyst might, for instance, believe it relates to the fact that Melody came in fourth in a choir competition last year, which resulted in her just missing out on a scholarship. The therapist will work to affect her behavior more positively with the insight she gains through dream analysis.

All these therapists could also work with medications to affect behavior. Melody might be prescribed <u>anxiolytics</u>, anti-anxiety medication, to help relieve her fear when she flies.

There are positive sides to all these approaches. But for Melody to be able to fly again, cognitive therapy approaches might be too easy, because she's anxious, and they may not desensitize her to fear enough. Psychoanalytic therapy might be too hard, in the sense that this type of therapy can take a long period of time to reach an insight that will actually affect behavior.

The <u>Yerkes-Dodson Law</u> says that moderately difficult tasks are more likely to succeed than tasks that are either too easy or too hard. It could be that the behaviorist approach of desensitization is that moderately difficult task. Ultimately, the behaviorist approach, combined with anxiolytics to actually make Melody feel less anxious, might be the middle ground between all the approaches, and thus most likely to succeed.

HOW TO SCORE PRACTICE TEST 3
Section I: Multiple Choice

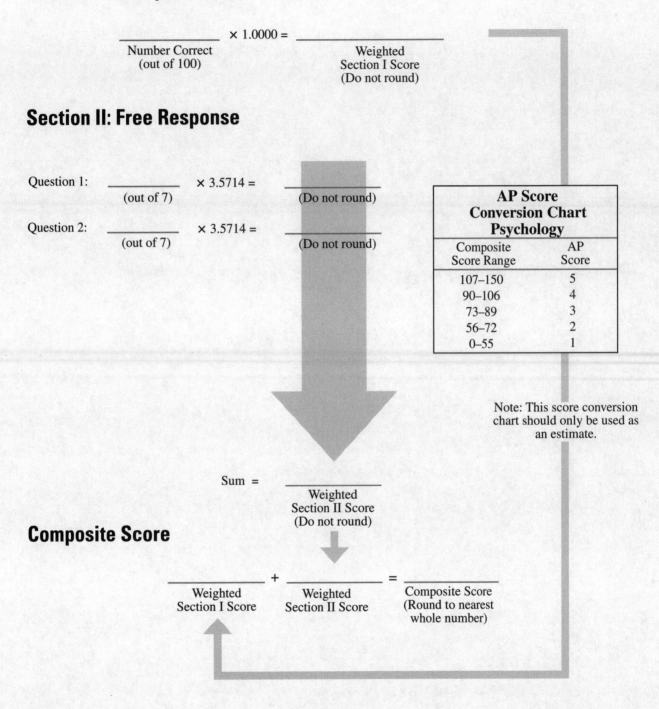

$$\frac{}{\text{Number Correct} \atop \text{(out of 100)}} \times 1.0000 = \frac{}{\text{Weighted} \atop \text{Section I Score} \atop \text{(Do not round)}}$$

Section II: Free Response

Question 1: $\dfrac{}{\text{(out of 7)}} \times 3.5714 = \dfrac{}{\text{(Do not round)}}$

Question 2: $\dfrac{}{\text{(out of 7)}} \times 3.5714 = \dfrac{}{\text{(Do not round)}}$

AP Score Conversion Chart Psychology

Composite Score Range	AP Score
107–150	5
90–106	4
73–89	3
56–72	2
0–55	1

Note: This score conversion chart should only be used as an estimate.

Sum = $\dfrac{}{\text{Weighted} \atop \text{Section II Score} \atop \text{(Do not round)}}$

Composite Score

$$\frac{}{\text{Weighted} \atop \text{Section I Score}} + \frac{}{\text{Weighted} \atop \text{Section II Score}} = \frac{}{\text{Composite Score} \atop \text{(Round to nearest} \atop \text{whole number)}}$$

Practice Test 4

AP® Psychology Exam

SECTION I: Multiple-Choice Questions

DO NOT OPEN THIS BOOKLET UNTIL YOU ARE TOLD TO DO SO.

Instructions

> ### At a Glance
>
> **Total Time**
> 1 hour and 10 minutes
> **Number of Questions**
> 100
> **Percent of Total Score**
> 66.6%
> **Writing Instrument**
> Pencil required

Section I of this exam contains 100 multiple-choice questions. Fill in only the ovals for numbers 1 through 100 on your answer sheet.

Indicate all of your answers to the multiple-choice questions on the answer sheet. No credit will be given for anything written in this exam booklet, but you may use the booklet for notes or scratch work. After you have decided which of the suggested answers is best, completely fill in the corresponding oval on the answer sheet. Give only one answer to each question. If you change an answer, be sure that the previous mark is erased completely. Here is a sample question and answer.

Sample Question   Sample Answer

Omaha is a

(A) state
(B) city
(C) country
(D) continent
(E) village

Use your time effectively, working as quickly as you can without losing accuracy. Do not spend too much time on any one question. Go on to other questions and come back to the ones you have not answered if you have time. It is not expected that everyone will know the answers to all of the multiple-choice questions.

About Guessing

Many candidates wonder whether or not to guess the answers to questions about which they are not certain. Multiple-choice scores are based on the number of questions answered correctly. Points are not deducted for incorrect answers, and no points are awarded for unanswered questions. Because points are not deducted for incorrect answers, you are encouraged to answer all multiple-choice questions. On any questions you do not know the answer to, you should eliminate as many choices as you can and then select the best answer among the remaining choices.

GO ON TO THE NEXT PAGE.

This page intentionally left blank.

GO ON TO THE NEXT PAGE.

PSYCHOLOGY
Section I
Time—1 hour and 10 minutes
100 Questions

Directions: Each of the questions or incomplete statements below is followed by five answer choices. Select the one that is best in each case and then completely fill in the corresponding oval on the answer sheet.

1. When she was in elementary school, Matilda became quite good at playing the recorder. She is a teenager now and has not picked up a recorder in many years. When she tries to resume playing the instrument, she finds it very difficult to locate the correct finger positions. This is an example of

   (A) constructive memory
   (B) retroactive interference
   (C) pruning of neural networks
   (D) proactive interference
   (E) source monitoring errors

2. The primary research method used by developmental psychologists is

   (A) case study
   (B) cross-sectional research
   (C) naturalistic observation
   (D) experimentation
   (E) correlational research

3. Which of the following types of scientists works from the perspective that an animal's behavior in its natural environment is adaptive, the result of an evolutionary process to promote survival?

   (A) Structuralists
   (B) Functionalists
   (C) Ethologists
   (D) Behaviorists
   (E) Empiricists

4. Which of the following is the best example of an attribute that is culturally based rather than primarily psychologically based?

   (A) Caring for one's children
   (B) Arriving on time for work
   (C) Having the desire to reproduce
   (D) Seeking food and water
   (E) Smiling

5. Every time you buy ice cream from the Yellow Brick Road ice cream parlor, you get your over-the-rainbow card stamped. Once you purchase ten items, you get your next item free. The Yellow Brick Road ice cream parlor has you on which of the following reinforcement schedules?

   (A) Variable-ratio
   (B) Variable-interval
   (C) Fixed-ratio
   (D) Fixed-interval
   (E) Continuous

6. Which of the following neurotransmitters is most explicitly associated with the experience of pleasure?

   (A) GABA
   (B) Acetylcholine
   (C) Serotonin
   (D) Dopamine
   (E) Adrenaline

7. As he was passing out math tests to his class, the teacher mentioned that, traditionally, females had done worse on this test than males. When he looked at the results of this test, not only had the females done worse than males, they had done worse than their performance on recent assessments. The teacher may have contributed to these results by way of

   (A) cross-section bias
   (B) availability heuristic
   (C) stereotype boost
   (D) stereotype threat
   (E) representativeness heuristic

GO ON TO THE NEXT PAGE.

8. An educational psychologist is administering a basic skills exam to second-graders of two different schools in order to compare the students' performance. The researcher administers the exam to the students of the Antrim School on a Wednesday morning and then administers the same exam in exactly the same fashion on that same Wednesday afternoon to the second-graders of the Barton School. Which of the following best identifies a confounding variable in the psychologist's research?

   (A) The psychologist is comparing two different schools.
   (B) The psychologist is comparing the same grade in each school.
   (C) The psychologist is testing the students in the two schools at two different times.
   (D) The psychologist is testing the students in the two schools on the same day.
   (E) The psychologist is administering a basic skills exam.

9. Pruning refers to

   (A) loss of hippocampus activity due to Alzheimer's disease
   (B) reduced sensory organ stimulation in response to an unchanging stimulus
   (C) activation of the ventromedial hypothalamus when someone is full
   (D) cutting back of unused neural networks during adolescence
   (E) heightened metabolism due to malfunction of the thyroid

10. Narcotics work because they are chemically very similar to

   (A) endorphins
   (B) hormones
   (C) secretions
   (D) GABA
   (E) acetylcholine

11. Research indicates that test performance will be enhanced if the test-taker

   (A) is told that members of his demographic group often do poorly on this test
   (B) is tested in the same room where the information on the test was taught
   (C) is in a much better mood than he or she was in when taught the test material
   (D) studies material from a different class before going to bed the night before the test
   (E) crams for the test, as opposed to spacing out review of the material

12. The minimum amount of physical energy needed for a person to notice a stimulus is called a(n)

   (A) JND
   (B) difference threshold
   (C) absolute threshold
   (D) median difference
   (E) hit threshold

13. As a result of a blasting cap accident, Phineas Gage had a metal rod pass through his head, damaging his frontal lobes. Which of the following was NOT a problem he experienced in the aftermath of this accident?

   (A) He could not adequately regulate his emotions.
   (B) He could no longer adequately supervise workers on his railroad gang.
   (C) He could not plan activities as expected of a railroad foreman.
   (D) He could not remember anything about the circumstances of the accident.
   (E) He had occasions when he could not control his anger.

14. A person who sustains major injuries that involve the destruction of the medulla oblongata will

   (A) be paralyzed
   (B) fall into a coma
   (C) suffer severe speech impairment
   (D) experience total loss of vision
   (E) die

15. In a crisis, the adrenal glands of the body secrete "emergency" hormones, while the body prepares for fight or flight, directed by

   (A) the central nervous system
   (B) the somatic nervous system
   (C) the sensorimotor nervous system
   (D) the sympathetic nervous system
   (E) the parasympathetic nervous system

16. In the Harlow study of emotional attachment, infant monkeys were placed in a cage and given both a "wire" mother and a "cloth" mother. Researchers then moved a bottle of milk from one mother to the other while introducing various stimuli to see whether the monkeys would form an attachment to either of the "mothers." In this experiment, the independent variable is

   (A) with which "mother" the bottle of milk is placed
   (B) the "wire" mother versus the "cloth" mother
   (C) the preference of the infants for the source of milk
   (D) the preference of the infants for the "wire" mother
   (E) the preference of the infants for the "cloth" mother

GO ON TO THE NEXT PAGE.

17. As an experiment, a group of newborn kittens was allowed to see through only one eye at a time. Each day, one of the eyes would be covered, switching between the two eyes on subsequent days. Which of the following best describes the visual limitations experienced by these cats as adults?

    (A) They were unable to make use of interposition depth perception.
    (B) They were unable to maintain perceptual constancy.
    (C) They were unable to distinguish left from right monocular cues.
    (D) They were unable to use binocular cues for depth perception.
    (E) They were unable to extinguish their visual blind spot.

Questions 18–19 refer to the situation described below.

A researcher wished to study the impact of classical music on memory in children. She therefore randomly selected two groups of children. One group was asked to read and later to recall lists of words while soft classical music played in the background. The second group was asked to read and recall lists of words with no background music playing.

18. The control group in this experiment is the group that

    (A) the researcher expected to demonstrate greater memory
    (B) demonstrated greater memory through recalling more words
    (C) demonstrated lesser memory through recalling fewer words
    (D) read the lists of words while classical music played in the background
    (E) read the lists of words with no background music playing

19. The dependent variable in this experiment is the

    (A) number of words recalled by the children
    (B) amount of time each child needs to recall the words
    (C) amount of music each child can recall
    (D) classical music playing in the background
    (E) lack of classical music playing in the background

20. Students diagnosed with attention-deficit hyperactivity disorder (ADHD) are four to nine times more likely to be

    (A) females than males
    (B) males than females
    (C) children than adults
    (D) Caucasian children than African American children
    (E) urban area children than rural area children

21. Which of the following best summarizes the psychoanalytic perspective's view of behavior?

    (A) Behavior is motivated by inner, unconscious forces.
    (B) Behavior is a response to external reward and punishment.
    (C) Behavior is a product of genetic programming and evolution.
    (D) Behavior is a compilation of the ways in which people think and interact.
    (E) Behavior is the act of striving to reach one's full potential.

22. Which of the following is the best example of a categorical variable?

    (A) Intelligence
    (B) Heart rate
    (C) Height
    (D) Occupation
    (E) Age

23. Donia was soaked by an unexpected cloudburst while walking to her car from the office. The fact that she failed to realize that the newspaper she was carrying would have made a great makeshift umbrella is an example of

    (A) confirmation bias
    (B) limited visualization
    (C) functional fixedness
    (D) conceptual constriction
    (E) negative variation

24. While driving to school, Elise hears about a concert ticket giveaway on the radio. She has to be the seventh caller to win. While pulling over so that she can call in, she repeats the phone number to herself several times. Elise was using which of the following to remember the phone number?

    (A) Iconic memory
    (B) Elaborative rehearsal
    (C) Chunking
    (D) Maintenance rehearsal
    (E) Retrieval

25. A participant in a single-trial free-recall task is presented with a list of words, one at a time, in the following order: house, flower, dog, table, license, water, computer, salad. In accord with the serial position curve, which of the following words is the participant most likely to forget?

    (A) House
    (B) Computer
    (C) Flower
    (D) Salad
    (E) License

GO ON TO THE NEXT PAGE.

26. The smallest units of meaning in a language are

    (A) phonemes
    (B) phenotypes
    (C) semantics
    (D) morphemes
    (E) syntactical rules

27. Which of the following psychological disorders is characterized by an abnormally elevated or expansive mood?

    (A) Depression
    (B) Schizophrenia
    (C) OCD
    (D) Dysthymia
    (E) Mania

28. During periods of darkness, the pineal gland in the middle of the brain produces which of the following hormones that is essential to sleep regulation?

    (A) Estrogen
    (B) Adrenaline
    (C) Testosterone
    (D) Melatonin
    (E) Dopamine

29. Jacob cries uncontrollably every time his mother takes him down the candy aisle in the supermarket and refuses to let him buy anything. Eventually, Jacob's mother gives in and lets him choose one candy item to buy if he stops crying. By his mother's action, Jacob's crying behavior is

    (A) punished
    (B) associated
    (C) reinforced
    (D) extinguished
    (E) shaped

30. Which of the following scientists was among the first to study the relationship between reinforcement and learning?

    (A) Sigmund Freud
    (B) B.F. Skinner
    (C) Carl Rogers
    (D) Mary Ainsworth
    (E) Charles Darwin

31. Jonathan's IQ score is in the 97th percentile. Of the following, which score is most likely his?

    (A) 85
    (B) 100
    (C) 130
    (D) 150
    (E) 170

32. When Ivan Pavlov consistently rang a bell before feeding the dogs in his laboratory, such that he got the dogs to salivate to just the sound of the bell ringing, he was

    (A) extinguishing a conditioned response
    (B) converting a neutral stimulus into a conditioned stimulus
    (C) converting an unconditioned stimulus into a conditioned stimulus
    (D) extinguishing an unconditioned stimulus
    (E) prompting spontaneous recovery of a conditioned response

33. Grounding a child for two weeks after the child has misbehaved is an example of

    (A) avoidant attachment
    (B) negative punishment
    (C) compliance learning
    (D) negative reinforcement
    (E) attentional neglect

34. Which of the following best summarizes why people tend to stay in a slightly elevated state of arousal after a crisis has occurred?

    (A) Their neurons remain in a state of graded potentiality even after they have fired.
    (B) Their neurons continue to keep the body in an alert state.
    (C) Their adrenal glands continue to secrete epinephrine even after the crisis is over.
    (D) Their parasympathetic nervous system remains in a state of fight or flight.
    (E) Their bloodstream continues to contain elevated levels of adrenaline.

GO ON TO THE NEXT PAGE.

35. Which of the following subsystems of the autonomic nervous system helps the body return to "business-as-usual" after an emergency?

   (A) Somatic nervous system
   (B) Peripheral nervous system
   (C) Sympathetic nervous system
   (D) Parasympathetic nervous system
   (E) Central nervous system

36. Tina is a very good student: Her grades are high, she is involved in extracurricular activities, and she typically excels at anything she tries. Therefore, when she caused an accident her second day of driver's ed., her instructor was shocked. The instructor's disbelief is most probably a result of

   (A) stereotype threat
   (B) stereotype boost
   (C) halo effect
   (D) assimilation
   (E) functional fixedness

37. The organ in the auditory process where transduction takes place is the

   (A) tympanic membrane
   (B) malleus
   (C) cochlea
   (D) pinna
   (E) stapes

38. You enter a bakery and are delighted by the aroma. After a short time, however, you no longer notice the odors because of sensory

   (A) perception
   (B) adaptation
   (C) transduction
   (D) detection
   (E) attrition

39. Carlotta is coming into therapy while in college because, although she does well in her courses and follows all of the rules, she is unhappy and lacking in self-esteem. According to Diana Baumrind, which parenting style did Carlotta's parents most likely follow?

   (A) Authoritative
   (B) Authoritarian
   (C) Permissive
   (D) Negligent
   (E) Helicopter

40. As a gymnast strives to keep herself upright on the balance beam, she is primarily making use of her

   (A) tactile sense
   (B) somatosensory cortex
   (C) vestibular sense
   (D) olfactory sense
   (E) inertial capacity

41. The fact that snow appears white in moonlight as well as in sunlight, even though sunlight is 800,000 times as bright, is an illustration of

   (A) an optical illusion
   (B) opponent process theory
   (C) perceptual constancy
   (D) an afterimage
   (E) the trichromatic theory

42. Stimulation of norepinephrine receptors appears to produce

   (A) euphoria
   (B) increased motor activity
   (C) alertness
   (D) anxiety
   (E) hypertension

43. Research using the visual cliff suggests that human infants

   (A) have little capacity for depth perception until they learn to walk
   (B) learn depth perception as they crawl, but may have some innate depth perception as well
   (C) would go "over the cliff" if their mothers were the ones calling them
   (D) use monocular but not binocular cues for vision
   (E) were thrown off by the checkerboard pattern used to simulate depth

44. All of the following are conditions sanctioned by the APA regarding the use of deception in a study EXCEPT

   (A) the research is of great importance and cannot be conducted without the use of deception
   (B) participants are expected to find the procedures reasonable upon being informed of them
   (C) participants must be allowed to withdraw from the experiment at any time
   (D) the research must be conducted as a double-blind study
   (E) experimenters must debrief the participants after the study is concluded

GO ON TO THE NEXT PAGE.

45. In visual perception, the brain's ability to organize incoming sensory information and simultaneously consider the abstract implications of that information is referred to as

    (A) serial processing
    (B) parallel processing
    (C) retinal processing
    (D) executive function
    (E) memory consolidation

46. Which of the following best summarizes a view of classical behaviorism?

    (A) Behavior is under the control of external stimuli that either reinforce or punish actions, thereby affecting the likelihood of the occurrence of these behaviors.
    (B) Behavior can be controlled by introspection.
    (C) Behavior is the result of competing motives that result from mental events that occur outside of one's awareness.
    (D) Behavior is influenced by internal drives and motivation.
    (E) Although behavior can be influenced by environmental factors, most actions and reactions occur as a result of genetic influence.

47. For which perspective is the quest to reach one's full potential and to achieve a differentiated self most central?

    (A) Psychoanalytic
    (B) Humanistic
    (C) Cognitive
    (D) Behaviorist
    (E) Social learning theory

48. A professional who develops tests to measure various psychological phenomena is called a

    (A) developmental psychologist
    (B) organizational psychologist
    (C) psychometrician
    (D) cognitive theorist
    (E) behaviorist

49. One's ability to make inferences about the behavior of a population from the behavior of a sample of that population is referred to as

    (A) reliability
    (B) external validity
    (C) internal validity
    (D) inter-rater reliability
    (E) correlational statistical inference

50. A study designed to investigate the friendship patterns of abused children was conducted by filming the interactions of the children and later having three raters view the footage and rate each child's pattern of behavior on a conflictual-behavior scale with values ranging from "constant conflict" to "minimal conflict." Which of the following kinds of reliability is most critical to this study, given the methodology used to measure the variables?

    (A) Coefficient-alpha reliability
    (B) Alternate-forms reliability
    (C) Inter-rater reliability
    (D) Test-retest reliability
    (E) Correlational statistical reliability

51. Hunger and eating are primarily regulated by the

    (A) somatosensory cortex
    (B) hypothalamus
    (C) medulla oblongata
    (D) occipital lobes
    (E) amygdala

52. The peg-word mnemonic system is a memory aid that relies upon

    (A) smell and taste cues
    (B) visualization and rhymes
    (C) semantic and episodic memory
    (D) muscle memory and spaced repetition
    (E) convergent and divergent thinking

53. Which of the following are most directly designed to help determine whether the findings of a study reflect a truly replicable phenomenon rather than the outcomes of chance processes?

    (A) Inferential statistics
    (B) Descriptive statistics
    (C) Standard deviation
    (D) Extraneous variables
    (E) Correlation coefficients

GO ON TO THE NEXT PAGE.

54. If a person has normal REM sleep behavior, what occurs during this sleep stage?

    (A) The person is prevented from dreaming because the brain is recalibrating and is largely inactive.
    (B) The person is emitting long, slow, delta waves.
    (C) The person is probably dreaming, but not acting out these dreams.
    (D) The person is dreaming and moving vigorously in bed so as to act out the plots of the dreams.
    (E) The person is physically recuperating from the day through the release of human growth hormone.

55. The gland sometimes referred to as the "master gland," which regulates much of the action of the other endocrine glands, is called the

    (A) thyroid gland
    (B) pancreas
    (C) pituitary gland
    (D) adrenal gland
    (E) lymph system

56. The tendency of young children learning language to overuse the rules of syntax is referred to as

    (A) overconfidence
    (B) confirmation bias
    (C) overgeneralization
    (D) overjustification
    (E) the two-factor theory

57. To demonstrate causation, a researcher must

    (A) manipulate the way a participant responds to some aspect of a situation
    (B) operationalize dependent and independent variables
    (C) develop a hypothesis that predicts the relationship between variables
    (D) show that the manipulation of one variable invariably leads to predicted changes in another
    (E) demonstrate a positive rather than a negative correlation between variables

58. The concept of learned helplessness was developed to explain the results of experiments in which dogs were confronted with electric shocks, an aversive stimulus. In control group situations, the dogs could perform a behavior that allowed them to escape the shocks. In experimental group situations, this behavior was often insufficient to allow the dogs to escape the shocks. Many of the dogs in the experimental group stopped trying to escape and would not return to the behavior even when it once again would have allowed for escape. The independent variable in this experiment was

    (A) whether or not the dogs felt they had control over their environment
    (B) the electric shocks
    (C) whether or not the dogs continued performing the behavior that had once worked
    (D) the dogs' natural reactions to electric shocks
    (E) the number of dogs participating in the experiment

59. Jose is talkative and likes to engage in pretend play. When offered two identical balls of putty, he insists on having the one that has been rolled out into a long snake instead of the one that remains in the shape of a ball. He is probably in which of Piaget's stages of cognitive development?

    (A) Sensorimotor
    (B) Preoperational
    (C) Conservation
    (D) Conventional
    (E) Formal operations

60. Georgia works in the local hospital because she wishes to help others, while Kathy works in the hospital strictly to make money. Their individual motivations demonstrate the difference between

    (A) drive-reduction and instinctive motivation
    (B) internal and external locus of control
    (C) sympathetic and parasympathetic nervous system
    (D) positive and negative reinforcement
    (E) intrinsic and extrinsic motivation

61. People who struggle with depression are thought to have trouble sleeping in part because of

    (A) elevated endorphin levels
    (B) decreased GABA levels
    (C) depleted epinephrine levels
    (D) increased dopamine levels
    (E) low serotonin levels

GO ON TO THE NEXT PAGE.

62. Vivian is watching her college's football team play on television. A riot breaks out among the crowd and she spots her friend Rudy, who is usually mild-mannered and obedient, assaulting people and destroying property as many others are doing. This is an example of

    (A) deindividuation
    (B) group polarization
    (C) groupthink
    (D) social facilitation
    (E) mere exposure effect

63. Through reinforcement, pigeons are taught to peck at paintings by a particular artist. The fact that pigeons do not peck at the paintings of other artists represents

    (A) modeling response
    (B) reflexive response
    (C) distinctive stimulus
    (D) stimulus generalization
    (E) stimulus discrimination

64. While browsing in a bookstore, Vhamala is drawn to a particular book title. After a moment, she realizes that this book is one that a friend had been talking about at lunch the other day. The fact that Vhamala remembers that the book was mentioned at a recent lunch is an example of which of the following types of memory?

    (A) Phonemic
    (B) Procedural
    (C) Semantic
    (D) Priming
    (E) Episodic

65. The process of converting physical energy from the environment into neural impulses is known as

    (A) sensation
    (B) priming
    (C) transduction
    (D) encoding
    (E) detection

66. An experiment that presents participants with a stimulus and then, at a later interval, presents them with incomplete perceptual information related to the initial stimulus to see whether they recognize the incomplete information more quickly is most likely studying the effects of

    (A) retroactivity
    (B) mnemonic devices
    (C) declarative memory
    (D) iconic memory
    (E) priming

67. Alfred Binet was primarily concerned with

    (A) discussing the role of genetics in levels of intelligence
    (B) measuring intelligence levels in children
    (C) measuring personality in children
    (D) measuring personality in adults
    (E) showing how adult personality can be modified

68. Hunter excels at mastering new vocabulary, learning a foreign language, answering trivia questions, adjusting to virtual reality video games, and painting. Which of these strengths most clearly demonstrates his fluid intelligence?

    (A) Mastering new vocabulary
    (B) Learning a foreign language
    (C) Answering trivia questions
    (D) Adjusting to virtual reality video games
    (E) Painting

69. In psychoanalytic theory, which of the following statements most accurately explains the purpose of repression?

    (A) It allows individuals to indirectly express their anger toward others.
    (B) It encourages clients to shift difficult feelings about loved ones onto their therapists.
    (C) It is a means of dealing with thoughts that are very anxiety-provoking.
    (D) It allows individuals to explain away acts to avoid uncomfortable feelings.
    (E) It is an unconscious model that allows people to describe the way things work.

70. If genetic factors play an important role in the development of intelligence as measured by an IQ test, then which of the following statements is most likely to be true?

    (A) The IQ scores of parents and their offspring will be more nearly alike than the IQ scores of fraternal twins reared together.
    (B) The IQ scores of fraternal twins reared together will be more nearly alike than the IQ scores of identical twins reared together.
    (C) The IQ scores of fraternal twins reared together will be more nearly alike than the IQ scores of identical twins reared apart.
    (D) The IQ scores of fraternal twins will be equivalent in similarity to the IQ scores of identical twins.
    (E) The IQ scores of identical twins reared apart will be more nearly alike than the IQ scores of fraternal twins reared together.

GO ON TO THE NEXT PAGE.

71. Negative symptoms of schizophrenia include which of the following?

    (A) Visual hallucinations
    (B) Auditory hallucinations
    (C) Blunted emotional responses
    (D) Delusions
    (E) Excessive motor activity

72. Three students are going in to take the SAT. Felice is not sure that she wants to go to college, is lackadaisical about the test, and is half asleep as she enters the test center. Skip is very concerned about the test; he sees his score as determining his entire future and he can be seen pacing nervously as he prepares to enter the test center. Armando takes the test seriously, but he knows that he will have additional chances to take it and that there are other factors that affect college admission. He has a mild case of nerves as he enters the test center. When Armando outperforms Felice and Skip, this supports which of the following?

    (A) Cannon-Bard theory
    (B) Piaget's formal operations stage
    (C) Yerkes-Dodson law
    (D) Selye's general adaptation syndrome
    (E) Gardner's multiple intelligences

73. Which of the following is NOT an example of the use of crystallized intelligence?

    (A) Learning how to use a new software program
    (B) Understanding the differences between an alligator and a crocodile
    (C) Recognizing immediately that a particular map represents Europe
    (D) Knowing that Queen Elizabeth I was born in 1533
    (E) Being able to recite Shakespeare's sonnets upon request

74. For which of the following would drive-reduction theories NOT provide a reasonable explanation?

    (A) In the middle of his five-mile race, Jerome grabs water from the water station to quench his thirst.
    (B) Ernest gobbles a few cookies on his way to class because he did not have time for lunch.
    (C) Tish decides to skip lunch because she is still full from eating a very large breakfast.
    (D) Cameron drives ten minutes out of her way to a fast-food place because she is hungry and has only two dollars.
    (E) Kezia is very full after eating dinner but decides to order the strawberry cheesecake anyway.

75. Abraham Maslow proposed the idea that some motives are more imperative to survival than others. Which of the following approaches expresses this?

    (A) Homeostatic regulation
    (B) Goal-setting
    (C) Expectancy-value
    (D) Cognitive dissonance
    (E) Hierarchy of needs

76. Which of the following is an example of a person who suffers from anterograde amnesia?

    (A) A six-year-old child who can't remember events related to her second birthday party
    (B) A twenty-year-old woman who can't remember the details of a traumatic event that occurred six months ago
    (C) A thirty-six-year-old man who experiences damage to his hippocampus and can't transfer information into his long-term memory
    (D) A fifteen-year-old boy who fell off his bicycle without his helmet and can't remember the events right before his accident
    (E) A forty-year-old woman who is recounting a story but can't remember where she first heard the story

77. Which of the following responses was most likely acquired through classical conditioning?

    (A) The anxiety reaction of a woman who is driving on the highway for the first time after being involved in a major accident on that highway
    (B) The frightened cry of a baby who is disoriented upon waking up from a nap
    (C) The uncontrollable blinking of a contact lens wearer who has just gotten something in his eye
    (D) The startled cry of a child who has just been awakened in the middle of the night by a loud clap of thunder
    (E) The salivation of a laboratory rat who has begun to eat the treat that awaited her at the end of a T-maze

78. Which of the following would be most useful in understanding a neighbor's interpretation of a certain family's recent crisis as being due to extreme financial distress?

    (A) Reinforcement theory
    (B) Classical behaviorism
    (C) Attribution theory
    (D) Hierarchy of needs
    (E) Cognitive dissonance

GO ON TO THE NEXT PAGE.

79. Children develop internal representational systems that allow them to describe people, events, and feelings verbally during which of Piaget's stages of cognitive development?

(A) Sensorimotor
(B) Preoperational
(C) Symbolic
(D) Concrete operational
(E) Formal operational

80. According to Kohlberg, at the third (postconventional) level of moral development, individuals

(A) follow rules in order to obtain reward
(B) follow rules in order to avoid punishment
(C) define what is right by what they have learned from others, especially authority figures
(D) justify their moral action based on the need to maintain law and order
(E) self-define principles that may or may not match the dominant morals of the times

81. Which of the following represents the correct order of auditory transmission from the time the sound is first heard to when it is processed in the brain?

(A) Oval window → cochlea → tympanic membrane → auditory nerve → auditory canal
(B) Auditory canal → auditory nerve → cochlea → tympanic membrane → ossicles
(C) Tympanic membrane → oval window → cochlea → auditory nerve → auditory canal
(D) Auditory canal → ossicles → oval window → cochlea → auditory nerve
(E) Cochlea → ossicles → oval window → auditory canal → auditory nerve

82. A tribe has been found that has no past tense in its language. Researchers have also found that the members of this tribe spend less time thinking about the past than other people. This finding is consistent with which theory?

(A) The behaviorist model for language development
(B) Chomsky's language acquisition device
(C) Selye's general adaptation syndrome
(D) Schachter-Singer two-factor theory
(E) Whorf's linguistic relativity

83. Heidi and Claus are in their 60s. They recently retired from their jobs and are planning to spend their time traveling and seeing their grandchildren. They enjoy looking back on their lives and counting their blessings. They are in Erikson's stage of

(A) intimacy versus isolation
(B) initiative versus guilt
(C) integrity versus despair
(D) autonomy versus shame
(E) generativity versus stagnation

84. Which of the following clinicians most likely follows Carl Rogers's approach to psychotherapy?

(A) Sy Jones, who emphasizes the need for modification of undesirable behaviors in his patients
(B) Terence Springer, who counsels individuals to find their inner spirituality and develop their relationship with a supreme being
(C) Cathy Cooper, who is an empathic counselor who encourages clients through unconditional support to find their own path to better health and growth
(D) Utrese Leed, who creates a framework for her patients that defines ideal psychological growth and development, and who supports their efforts toward professional achievement
(E) Ute Shrom, who takes a physiological approach to recovery through strenuous physical challenges that break down and subsequently build up one's character

85. An obese individual with a breathing-related sleep disorder most likely suffers from which of the following?

(A) Narcolepsy
(B) Hypersomnia
(C) Insomnia
(D) Sleep apnea
(E) Hypnotic susceptibility

86. Certain cross-cultural studies have suggested that six facial expressions are recognized by people of virtually every culture. Which of the following correctly lists these expressions?

(A) Happiness, sadness, anger, loathing, lust, and surprise
(B) Happiness, sadness, indifference, fright, surprise, and dislike
(C) Happiness, sadness, desire, repulsion, fear, and surprise
(D) Happiness, sadness, fight, flight, indifference, and anger
(E) Happiness, sadness, fear, anger, surprise, and disgust

GO ON TO THE NEXT PAGE.

87. Which of the following is primarily a chemical sense?

   (A) Touch
   (B) Vision
   (C) Taste
   (D) Hearing
   (E) Kinesthesis

88. All of the following are classified as feeding and eating disorders EXCEPT

   (A) pica
   (B) binge-eating disorder
   (C) bulimia nervosa
   (D) body dysmorphic disorder
   (E) anorexia nervosa

89. Which of the following behaviors is most likely to lead to health problems as a result of disrupted circadian rhythms?

   (A) Fasting several days per week
   (B) Visiting all-you-can-eat buffets several times a week
   (C) Constant worrying about work deadlines
   (D) Daydreaming about an upcoming vacation
   (E) Keeping an irregular sleep schedule

90. When Cordelia was a child, she was abused and she has been angry about it ever since. She is now a choreographer. When she creates dance routines for theatrical productions, critics and audiences often praise her realistic portrayals of anger and aggression. This would fit under the Freudian defense mechanism of

   (A) projection
   (B) reaction formation
   (C) repression
   (D) denial
   (E) sublimation

91. While visiting a museum, you study a statue by walking around it and examining it from many different places in the room. The retinal images of the statue change, but you maintain a consistent overall view of the statue because of

   (A) convergence
   (B) motion parallax
   (C) perceptual constancy
   (D) interpositioning
   (E) perceptual acuity

92. REM sleep is considered to be paradoxical sleep because

   (A) brain patterns change from alpha waves to delta waves over the course of a night's sleep
   (B) people can always act out the content of their dreams
   (C) people will try to increase REM sleep if deprived of REM sleep for a period of time
   (D) sleep cycles may change with age
   (E) the mind is very active, but the body is in a state of paralysis

93. Carmella has experienced a stroke. She now needs to use a communication board because her speech is difficult to understand. Carmella has probably sustained damage to her

   (A) Wernicke's area
   (B) hippocampus
   (C) amygdala
   (D) Broca's area
   (E) medulla oblongata

94. Probabilistic reasoning from specific observations to general propositions is known as

   (A) deductive reasoning
   (B) inductive reasoning
   (C) intuitive reasoning
   (D) statistical reasoning
   (E) observational reasoning

GO ON TO THE NEXT PAGE.

95. Claudio lives in an area with a few college students and several retirement communities. He is trying to start a computer consulting business that will make home visits to deal with customers' technology problems. He does all of his marketing for the business in a hip coffeehouse and on a dating website because he assumes that the elderly are relatively uninterested in technology. His business is not doing well. What obstacle to effective problem-solving may be interfering with his success?

(A) Availability heuristic
(B) Representativeness heuristic
(C) Functional fixedness
(D) Optimism bias
(E) Confirmation bias

96. Which of the following accurately states the order of the transmission of visual information?

(A) Optic nerve; ganglion cells; bipolar cells; rods and cones
(B) Bipolar cells; ganglion cells; fovea; optic nerve
(C) Rods and cones; retina; optic nerve; ganglion cells
(D) Bipolar cells; rods and cones; fovea; optic disk
(E) Rods and cones; bipolar cells; ganglion cells; optic nerve

97. Which of the following best summarizes Carl Rogers's view of personality?

(A) Personality traits such as inhibition, extroversion, and conscientiousness are constant over time.
(B) People's personality traits are overwhelmingly positive and goal-directed.
(C) Personality is mainly formed by behavioral expectations.
(D) Individual personalities vary based on differences in traits, emotions, and thought processes.
(E) Situational variables are more important in determining the way a person will act than are broad personality dispositions.

98. Research has shown a possible connection between the neurotransmitter acetylcholine and which of the following mental disorders?

(A) Parkinson's disease
(B) Alzheimer's disease
(C) Schizophrenia
(D) Mania
(E) Depression

99. Which of the following best explains why babies have poor vision for the first few weeks of life?

(A) The nodes of Ranvier have not yet formed.
(B) The neural connections to the primary visual cortex are not fully formed.
(C) The axons are covered in tight coats of lipids, which impede neural firing.
(D) The synaptic cleft of the neuron is filled with an aqueous humor.
(E) The glial cells are absent at birth.

100. Scientists have long sought a physical manifestation of learning and memory in the brain. Perhaps the closest they have come is in identifying strengthened synaptic connections. This is referred to as

(A) long-term potentiation (LTP)
(B) tip-of-the-tongue phenomenon
(C) cortical conditioning
(D) myelinization
(E) reuptake

END OF SECTION I

IF YOU FINISH BEFORE TIME IS CALLED, YOU MAY CHECK YOUR WORK ON THIS SECTION. DO NOT GO ON TO SECTION II UNTIL YOU ARE TOLD TO DO SO.

PSYCHOLOGY
Section II
Time—50 minutes

Percent of total score—33$\frac{1}{3}$

Directions: You have 50 minutes to answer BOTH of the following questions. It is not enough to answer a question by merely listing facts. You should present a cogent argument based on your critical analysis of the question posed, using appropriate psychological terminology.

1. Kai is the field-goal kicker for his high school's football team and he has been invited to a college evaluation clinic where coaches will watch him perform along with other kickers looking for scholarship opportunities. Two things that have made Kai a good kicker are great self-confidence and careful preparation for whatever conditions he will face in a game. However, he has concerns about this clinic because of three things:

   1. Only his teammates who snap and hold the ball will be on the field with him. All of the evaluators will be in the press box and he will not see them.
   2. The field is an artificial surface and he has never played or practiced on such a field.
   3. Several days ago, he sustained an eye injury and he will be wearing a patch over his left eye. He has been unable to practice since this accident.

   Explain how each of the following factors could influence Kai's performance at the clinic:

   • The "Big Five" trait of openness to experience
   • Convergence (depth perception)
   • Cognitive dissonance
   • Social facilitation
   • Sympathetic nervous system
   • Non-declarative memory
   • Self-efficacy

GO ON TO THE NEXT PAGE.

2. Scientists recently created a genetically modified (GMO) berry that is supposed to be good for improving physical health. Felix, a psychology researcher, has heard anecdotal reports that people eating the berry are reporting enhanced emotional health as well. He decides to design an experiment to test whether this berry might be a useful antidepressant. In cooperation with a university treatment center, he randomly selects fifty individuals who have been diagnosed with a major depressive disorder based on scores on the Beck Depression Inventory (BDI) and who have expressed willingness to participate in this study at his lab. He then randomly assigns twenty-five subjects to the experimental group: they will receive this berry, as well as other berries, with their meals, which are standardized for all of the subjects. The other twenty-five, the control group, will have berries with their meals, but not the GMO berry. In addition to keeping their diets regulated, the subjects will have the same wake-up and go-to-bed times during the six weeks that they are living in the lab. Otherwise, they are free to structure their days and activities as they please and they have access to the gym, library, and entertainment center at the lab.

At the end of the six weeks, the subjects again take the BDI and their scores are compared with the scores they had prior to the experiment. Felix finds that the subjects in the experimental group had lower scores on their second BDI, whereas the scores of subjects in the control group stayed the same. The p-value for this data was 0.05. Felix is preparing to submit his findings to a professional journal for publication in order to show that the GMO berry is a potent antidepressant.

Part A

- Identify the independent variable in this experiment.
- Identify a possible threat to the internal validity of this experiment.
- Explain the difference in assessing the reliability versus the validity of the BDI.
- Explain what would be involved in making this experiment double-blind and why that might be necessary.
- Describe the impact of the p-value in assessing the quality of this data.

Part B

- Describe the focus of cognitive therapy for depression.
- Describe the focus of humanistic therapy for depression.

STOP

END OF EXAM

Practice Test 4:
Answers and
Explanations

PRACTICE TEST 4: ANSWER KEY

1.	C	26.	D	51.	B	76.	C
2.	B	27.	E	52.	B	77.	A
3.	C	28.	D	53.	A	78.	C
4.	B	29.	C	54.	C	79.	B
5.	C	30.	B	55.	C	80.	E
6.	D	31.	C	56.	C	81.	D
7.	D	32.	B	57.	D	82.	E
8.	C	33.	B	58.	A	83.	C
9.	D	34.	E	59.	B	84.	C
10.	A	35.	D	60.	E	85.	D
11.	B	36.	C	61.	E	86.	E
12.	C	37.	C	62.	A	87.	C
13.	D	38.	B	63.	E	88.	D
14.	E	39.	B	64.	E	89.	E
15.	D	40.	C	65.	C	90.	E
16.	A	41.	C	66.	E	91.	C
17.	D	42.	C	67.	B	92.	E
18.	E	43.	B	68.	D	93.	D
19.	A	44.	D	69.	C	94.	B
20.	B	45.	B	70.	E	95.	B
21.	A	46.	A	71.	C	96.	E
22.	D	47.	B	72.	C	97.	B
23.	C	48.	C	73.	A	98.	B
24.	D	49.	B	74.	E	99.	B
25.	E	50.	C	75.	E	100.	A

PRACTICE TEST 4: ANSWERS AND EXPLANATIONS

Section I: Multiple Choice

1. **C** *Understand the Question/Key Words:* Why is Matilda struggling to play an instrument that she has not played for many years? *Predict the Answer:* Think about what type of memory phenomenon is at play here, and note Matilda's age. Teenagers strengthen neural connections for activities in which they continue to engage, but these connections weaken with disuse ("pruning"). There is no indication of learning another instrument or anything else that would "interfere" with her prior knowledge, so (B) and (D) do not apply. She has not altered her memory, so (A) is out. This is not a situation in which she recalls information, but cannot recall from what source she received it, so (E) does not apply.

2. **B** *Understand the Question/Key Words:* Developmental psychologists do what kind of research? *Predict the Answer:* Cross-sectional research. If you don't know this, review Chapter 13. Use POE to eliminate the rest of the choices.

3. **C** *Understand the Question/Key Words:* Which kind of scientist emphasizes the importance of adaptation in an "evolutionary process to promote survival"? *Predict the Answer:* Adaptation and survival should suggest ethology to you. If not, get reviewing, and use POE. Are structuralists, (A), the kind of scientists that emphasize these concepts? Even if you don't remember what structuralists are, the name does not imply evolution or adaptation. Functionalists represented another early perspective in psychology, but also one not emphasizing these concepts, so eliminate (B). Both behaviorists and empiricists emphasize learning experiences, so eliminate (D) and (E). That leaves (C) as the correct answer.

4. **B** *Understand the Question/Key Words:* Culturally based versus psychologically based? *Predict the Answer:* Look for something that is not considered "innate." Is (A), caring for one's children, cultural? It seems that most cultures do it in some form, but if you are unsure, leave it. Choice (B), arriving on time for work, is not something that is done in every culture, so this looks good. Choices (C), having the desire to reproduce, and (D), seeking food and water, are primary drives present in all cultures, and (E), smiling, has also been found as a universal facial expression. Choice (B) is clearly something that occurs only in time-oriented cultures.

5. **C** *Understand the Question/Key Words:* Which of the following means "reward after a specific number of purchases"? *Predict the Answer:* Fixed-ratio. If you don't remember, anything like "fixed number" will get you to your answer using POE. Get rid of (A), variable-ratio, and (B), variable-interval, because they are variable, and (E), continuous, because you are not being continuously rewarded. Choice (C), fixed-ratio, refers to a ratio or number, whereas (D), fixed-interval, refers to an *interval* or *time*.

6. **D** *Understand the Question/Key Words:* Circle *neurotransmitters* and *pleasure*. *Predict the Answer:* Dopamine. If you don't remember, use POE to get rid of the ones you do recognize. Is (A), GABA, associated with pleasure? No, so cross it off. Is (B), acetylcholine, associated with pleasure? No, it has something to do with memory. Choice (C), serotonin, may throw you off, so leave it if you are unsure. Seretonin affects mood (along with arousal, sleep, and pain sensitivity), but dopamine

more directly affects pleasure (and reward, movement, and attention). Choice (E), adrenaline, is not a neurotransmitter, so cross it off.

7. **D** *Understand the Question/Key Words:* What in the teacher's behavior may have caused the girls to perform so badly? *Predict the Answer:* This is an example of a stereotype (that girls are bad at math) and it's not a positive thing, so it cannot be a boost. Telling a group of people that it is expected to underperform compared to other groups on a task may produce a self-fulfilling prophecy. Choice (C) is the opposite: telling the group that it is expected to do particularly well. Choices (B) and (E) are obstacles to effective problem-solving because they cause people to ignore base rates.

8. **C** *Understand the Question/Key Words:* What in this study is making the psychologist's research impossible to accurately interpret? *Predict the Answer:* She gives the test in the morning at one school and in the afternoon at another. If you missed this point, use your definition of confounding variable to evaluate each answer choice. Is (A), the fact that the research is done at two *different schools*, a potential problem with the study? No, that is part of what she is comparing. Is (B), the fact that she is comparing the *same grade*, a potential problem? Definitely not. Is (C), the fact that the students are tested at *different times*, a potential problem? Bingo. Is (D), the fact that she is testing the students *on the same day*, a potential problem? No. Is (E), the fact that she is administering a *basic skills exam*, a potential problem? No.

9. **D** Choice (D) is the correct definition. Choice (A) is what Alzheimer's does. Choice (B) is sensory adaptation. Choice (C) is satiety. Choice (E) is hyperthyroidism.

10. **A** *Understand the Question/Key Words:* How do narcotics work? *Predict the Answer:* They imitate endorphins. If you are not sure exactly how they work but know they imitate a chemical substance in the brain, use POE. Do narcotics imitate (A), endorphins? Endorphins are chemicals in the brain that have to do with pleasure, so this could be it. Do narcotics imitate (B), hormones? This is less likely because hormones are secreted throughout the body and for a wide variety of purposes. Cross it off. Do narcotics imitate (C), secretions? What secretions? This is too broad, so cross it off. Do narcotics imitate (D), GABA? This is a specific neurotransmitter—an inhibitory one. Alcohol, not narcotics, acts on GABA receptors. Cross it off. Choice (E), acetylcholine, affects memory function and muscle contraction. The answer must be (A).

11. **B** *Understand the Question/Key Words:* What is likely to improve test performance? If you aren't sure, go ahead and use POE. Choice (A) describes stereotype threat and would tend to detract from test performance—eliminate it. Choice (C) contradicts what research shows about state-dependent memory: that it is best to be in the same frame of mind as when learning the material. Eliminate it. Choice (D) would cause interference with recalling the information needed for this test—eliminate it. Choice (E) contradicts the Ebbinghaus research about the benefits of spaced repetition—eliminate it. Choice (B) is consistent with what we know about context-dependent memory, so select it!

12. **C** *Understand the Question/Key Words:* Circle *minimum amount of physical energy. Predict the Answer:* Absolute threshold. If you don't remember, use POE. Would (A), the JND (just noticeable difference), be the amount of energy needed to notice a stimulus? No, the JND involves noticing

the difference between two stimuli. Cross it off. The same is true of (B), difference threshold. Choices (D), median difference, and (E), hit threshold, are both made-up terms, and sound like it.

13. **D** The frontal lobes are involved with decision-making, planning, and emotional regulation, so (A), (B), (C), and (E) are all problems that Gage had. The frontal lobes are not a specific repository of memories.

14. **E** *Understand the Question/Key Words:* Circle *medulla oblongata*. The medulla oblongata is critical for basic life functions, such as respiration. *Predict the Answer*: If the medulla oblongata is destroyed, it's all over. If you don't remember, you can probably still get rid of a few choices with POE. Choices (C) and (D) involve speech and vision, which are clearly tied to other areas of the brain. Be sure to review the major components of the brain if you missed this item.

15. **D** *Understand the Question/Key Words:* Which system prepares the body for fight or flight? *Predict the Answer:* Sympathetic nervous system. If you have trouble remembering whether it's the sympathetic, (D), or parasympathetic, (E), try this mnemonic: the sympathetic nervous system is *sympathetic* to your problems, so it responds. POE should have gotten rid of (A), the central nervous system, (B), the somatic nervous system, and (C), the sensorimotor nervous system, even if you couldn't remember whether it was (D) or (E).

16. **A** *Understand the Question/Key Words:* Which aspect of this study is the independent variable? *Predict the Answer*: The placement of the bottle of milk. The milk is being moved back and forth to see whether the monkeys attach to the food or to the mothers. In other words, the milk is being manipulated to see what response will occur—it is therefore the independent variable. If you don't remember, POE your way to the answer using your common sense. Choice (B) is close, but it's with which of these mothers the milk is placed that matters. Choices (D) and (E) are essentially the same answer, so they can't be right, and (C), (D), and (E) all talk about preferences, meaning responses, meaning dependent variables. Choice (A) has to be it.

17. **D** *Understand the Question/Key Words:* Cats that were allowed to see through only one eye at a time will have what kind of vision problems? *Predict the Answer*: Using both eyes together. Which answer choice means using both eyes together? Binocular vision. Choice (D) is the only answer that mentions binocular cues. Choice (A), interposition depth perception, would be hard to evaluate in a cat, as would be (B), perceptual constancy. Be careful of (C)—just because it mentions left and right doesn't mean it contains the full answer; it is still talking about monocular cues. Choice (E) would again be hard to evaluate because it involves perception.

18. **E** *Understand the Question/Key Words:* Circle the words *control group*, and then go to the experiment and label the control group. *Predict the Answer:* Because the study is about the effects of music on memory, the second group, which had no music, is the control group. Use POE to get rid of the other choices.

19. **A** *Understand the Question/Key Words*: Circle *dependent variable*; then go find it. *Predict the Answer*: The dependent variable is the thing being tested, so the number of words recalled is the dependent variable. Use POE to get rid of the other choices.

20. **B** *Understand the Question/Key Words:* Who is most often diagnosed with ADHD? *Predict the Answer:* Boys. This is something you should know.

21. **A** *Understand the Question/Key Words:* Circle *psychoanalytic. Predict the Answer:* Psychoanalytic = Freud = unconscious forces. Use POE: Does (A), unconscious forces, mean unconscious forces? Yup. Choice (B) refers to the behaviorist perspective; (C) to the evolutionary perspective; (D) to the cognitive perspective; and (E) to the humanist perspective, so eliminate those. The answer must be (A).

22. **D** *Understand the Question/Key Words:* Circle *categorical. Predict the Answer:* A categorical variable is something that falls into categories (as opposed to a continuous variable, which has a numerical range). Occupation, (D), looks like a categorical variable, but you can use POE to be sure. Choices (A) and (B) are both continuous variables measured by ranges of numbers, so eliminate them. Does (C), height, fall into categories? No, it's continuous. Cross it off. Does (D), occupation, fall into categories? Yes. Does (E), age, fall into categories? No, and that leaves (D) as your correct answer.

23. **C** *Understand the Question/Key Words:* The fact that she didn't see alternative uses for the paper is known as.... *Predict the Answer:* Functional fixedness. Choices (B), (D), and (E) are made up, and (A), confirmation bias, refers to something else.

24. **D** *Understand the Question/Key Words:* What was Elise doing to remember the number? *Predict the Answer:* Rehearsing it over and over. Use POE. Because you know she is rehearsing, you can get rid of (A), (C), and (E). Does it seem like a rehearsal that is elaborative or based on maintenance? Your answer must be (D), maintenance rehearsal.

25. **E** *Understand the Question/Key Words:* The serial position curve has to do with the positions of the words with regard to recall. Which of the words would the person be most likely to forget, given the position of the word in the list? *Predict the Answer:* The serial position phenomenon actually says people tend to forget items in the middle of a list, so the answer must be (E), license, because it is in the center of the list: all the other choices are close to the beginning ((A) and (C)) or end ((B) and (D)).

26. **D** *Understand the Question/Key Words:* Circle *smallest units of meaning. Predict the Answer:* Morphemes. If you don't remember, use POE to get rid of (B), phenotypes, and (E), syntactical rules.

27. **E** *Understand the Question/Key Words:* Circle *abnormally elevated or expansive mood.* Which disorder involves extreme happiness or "bigness"? *Predict the Answer:* Mania. If you don't remember, use POE. Does (A), depression, manifest itself in extreme happiness? No. Does (B), schizophrenia, manifest itself in extreme happiness? Extreme happiness is not a defining characteristic of schizophrenia. Does (C), OCD, or obsessive-compulsive disorder, manifest itself in extreme happiness? No, it's characterized by obsessions and compulsions. Does (D), dysthymia, manifest itself in extreme happiness? If you don't know, leave it. Does (E), mania, manifest itself in extreme happiness? Yes. Your answer is (E).

28. **D** *Understand the Question/Key Words:* Which hormone is essential for sleep regulation? *Predict the Answer:* Melatonin. If you don't remember, use POE. Is (A), estrogen, essential for sleep regulation? No. Cross it off. Is (B), adrenaline, essential for sleep regulation? No. Is (C), testosterone, essential for sleep regulation? No. Is (D), melatonin, essential for sleep regulation? If you don't remember, leave it. Is (E), dopamine, essential for sleep regulation? No, and it's not a hormone. The answer has to be (D).

29. **C** *Understand the Question/Key Words:* How does Jacob's mother influence his behavior? *Predict the Answer:* She gives in to his demands, thereby reinforcing his behavior. The other terms (associated, extinguished, shaped) are all relevant to learning theory, but not relevant to answering this question.

30. **B** *Understand the Question/Key Words:* Circle the words *reinforcement* and *learning.* Both of these terms mean you want to modify behavior. *Predict the Answer:* B.F. Skinner is the only behaviorist in this list. If you don't remember his name, use POE to get rid of the ones you know are not behaviorists: (A), Freud, (C), Rogers, (D), Ainsworth, and (E), Darwin.

31. **C** *Understand the Question/Key Words:* Circle *97th percentile.* The mean of IQ scores on a normal distribution is usually 100, and the standard deviation is around 15 points. The 97th percentile is two standard deviations above the mean, so his score should be around 100 + 15 + 15 = 130. Choice (C) is correct.

32. **B** *Understand the Question/Key Words:* What did Pavlov produce by means of his experiment? *Predict the Answer:* By pairing the food, an unconditioned stimulus, with the bell, a previously neutral stimulus, Pavlov classically conditioned the dogs to salivate (an unconditioned response when done in response to the food) to the bell alone (the salivation is now a conditioned response). This looks like (B), but use POE to be sure. Pavlov was creating a conditioned response, not extinguishing it, so eliminate (A). Pavlov wasn't converting the unconditioned stimulus (food) into the conditioned stimulus (bell); rather he was getting the same response to each. So eliminate (C). Pavlov wasn't extinguishing the food, which was the unconditioned stimulus and which continued to produce the natural response of salivation in the dogs. Eliminate (D). Before spontaneous recovery can occur, the conditioned response must be extinguished. Here, Pavlov was producing a conditioned response. Eliminate (E).

33. **B** *Understand the Question/Key Words:* Which concept relates to grounding someone for misbehaving? *Predict the Answer:* It's a form of punishment. Choices (A) and (E) are irrelevant to learning theory, and (C) is made up. Only (B) and (D) are concepts of learning theory, and only (B) fits the prediction. Choice (B) is the correct answer.

34. **E** *Understand the Question/Key Words:* Why do people stay aroused after an emergency? *Predict the Answer:* Adrenaline is still in their blood. Use POE. Cross off both (A) and (B) because they deal with neurons. Choice (A) is also a false statement—neurons do not remain graded after they fire. Watch out for (C): adrenal glands do secrete epinephrine but they would not continue to do so after the crisis has passed. This is the trap answer. Be sure to read each choice completely. Choice (D) is false because it is the sympathetic system that puts the body in a state of fight or flight. Choice (E) is the closest to your answer.

35. **D** *Understand the Question/Key Words:* Which system returns the body to normal after an emergency? *Predict the Answer*: Parasympathetic nervous system. Choices (B), peripheral nervous system, and (E), central nervous system, are not part of the autonomic system. Remember our mnemonic for distinguishing between (C) and (D): the *sympathetic* nervous system is *sympathetic* to your stress, so it responds.

36. **C** *Understand the Question/Key Words:* The teacher is shocked at her bad driving because…. *Predict the Answer:* Tina is always good = halo effect, (C). If you don't remember the term, use POE. Both (A) and (B) deal with assumptions being made about the performance of certain demographic groups. This is an individual and no such assumptions are mentioned. Eliminate (A) and (B). If the teacher had a schema involving Tina, it would have been a positive one, so he would not have assimilated the bad driving information into that schema. Eliminate (D). Functional fixedness refers to a mental set whereby someone cannot see uses for an object other than its traditional uses. Eliminate (E).

37. **C** This is where wave energy is transformed into a nerve impulse, so the correct answer is (C).

38. **B** *Understand the Question/Key Words:* Why don't you notice the way a bakery smells after a while? *Predict the Answer*: Adaptation. You get used to the smell, and your senses don't pay attention to it as much because it is constant and not a critical piece of information. Use POE to get rid of (A), (C), and (D) because they wouldn't explain why you would no longer notice the aroma. Choice (E) is not a real psychological term.

39. **B** *Understand the Question/Key Words:* Circle *Baumrind* and *parenting style*. *Predict the Answer:* This will be a style that prizes obedience and high performance at the expense of positive feelings. If you can't zero in on the style, use POE! Authoritative is Baumrind's preferred style and would not lead to sadness and low self-esteem, so eliminate (A). The child of permissive parents would not likely be a rule-follower, so eliminate (C). Choices (D) and (E) were not among Baumrind's three styles, though (D) was added by other researchers. In any case, neither predicts these qualities, so eliminate them. The correct answer is (B).

40. **C** *Understand the Question/Key Words:* The important concept here is *balance*. If you can't remember the choice that relates to balance, you can use POE. Choices (A) and (B) reference incoming touch sensations, which could be relevant, but are very similar and not specifically related to balance. They are not the primary factors here, so eliminate them. Olfaction is the sense of smell, so eliminate (D). Inertia relates to mass and movement, but not to balance, so eliminate (E). The correct answer is (C), vestibular sense.

41. **C** *Understand the Question/Key Words:* The important idea is that color is perceived as the same in very different conditions. *Predict the Answer:* This will be a concept that relates to sameness. If the answer is not immediately apparent, try using POE. This would only be an illusion if the snow were not actually white. Eliminate (A). Choices (B) and (D) both relate to opponent process and suggest that, if one were to look at a white object for a time, the opponent color would emerge. That did not occur here, so eliminate (B) and (D). Choice (E) relates to a different theory of color vision that describes three different types of cones. It is not geared to perception of the color white, so eliminate it. The correct answer is (C), perceptual constancy.

42. **C** *Understand the Question/Key Words:* Circle *norepinephrine receptors*. What happens when they are stimulated? *Predict the Answer*: A person experiences increased alertness. Does (A), euphoria, mean increased alertness? No. Cross it off. Does (B), increased motor activity, mean increased alertness? No. Does (C), alertness, mean increased alertness? Yup. Does (D), anxiety, mean increased alertness? Not exactly. Does (E), hypertension, mean increased alertness? No.

43. **B** *Understand the Question/Key Words:* Circle *visual cliff*. This is a study in which infants are subjected to an optical illusion of a drop. *Predict the Answer:* The infants would not crawl into the area that looked like a drop. Using POE, you can eliminate (A), (C), (D), and (E) as they all suggest that the infants could not perceive depth. You're left with the correct answer, (B).

44. **D** *Understand the Question/Key Words:* Which of the answers is NOT one of the conditions of the APA (American Psychological Association) regarding deception? Be careful—four of the five answer choices here are "right," while only one is "wrong." *Predict the Answer*: A study must be very important, unable to be done without deception, not objectionable to the participant, and it must both allow a participant to stop at any time and inform the participant at the end of the study. Cross off any answer that matches these. The one remaining is your answer.

45. **B** *Understand the Question/Key Words:* The important point here is the brain's ability to do things "simultaneously." *Predict the Answer:* Find processes that are occurring simultaneously. If you're unsure of the answer, try using POE. Choice (A) refers to the sort of step-by-step processing that a computer does, so eliminate it. In (C), would the retina be involved in abstract thought? Eliminate it. This does not involve executive functioning or memory, so eliminate (D) and (E). The correct answer is (B), parallel processing.

46. **A** *Understand the Question/Key Words:* Circle *behaviorism*. *Predict the Answer*: Behaviorists believe that behavior is the result of learning and consequences. Find an answer that exemplifies this tenet, and use POE. "Introspection" makes (B) wrong. Choice (C) is psychodynamic, (D) is almost the opposite, and (E) is way off.

47. **B** *Understand the Question/Key Words:* Circle *potential* and *differentiated self*. If these ideas don't trigger thoughts of Carl Rogers and the humanists, (B), rely on POE. These ideas are not central to (A), which emphasizes the role of childhood traumas and the unconscious mind, nor to (C), which emphasizes thinking strategies, nor (D), which emphasizes learning and conditioning, nor (E), which emphasizes interactive learning and modeling.

48. **C** *Understand the Question/Key Words:* This is someone who "develops tests." *Predict the Answer:* (C), Psychometrician. If you don't know the term for a test developer, use POE. Developmental psychologists study progression through the life span, so eliminate (A). Organizational psychologists study human behavior in organizations, and not necessarily by testing: eliminate (B). Cognitive theorists try to explain human behavior through either strategic thinking or dysfunctional thinking, while behaviorists try to explain it as a function of conditioning; neither is focused on creating tests. So eliminate (D) and (E).

49. **B**   *Understand the Question/Key Words:* If a relationship shown in a sample can be generalized so as to apply to the population from which it was taken, you can say the relationship is…. *Predict the Answer:* Generalizable. Use your work to POE the other choices. Reliability, (A) and (D), refers to whether a test produces consistent results, not whether the results themselves are valid, so you can eliminate these choices. Validity, on the other hand, deals with those conclusions. External validity, (B), specifically refers to whether results can be generalized to deal with situations outside the sample or test conditions. Internal validity, (C), looks only at whether a causal relationship can be drawn between the tested variables, and can be eliminated, along with (E), which is looking for correlation, not validity.

50. **C**   *Understand the Question/Key Words:* What would make this study reliable? The methodology used involves researchers evaluating various behavior patterns of children. Therefore, the evaluators need to do an unbiased, accurate job. *Predict the Answer:* Inter-rater reliability. Use POE if you don't remember the term. Choices (A) and (B) are made-up terms. Does (C), inter-rater reliability, address the accuracy of the evaluators? Yes. Does (D), test-retest reliability, address the accuracy of the evaluators? No. Does (E), correlational statistical reliability, address the accuracy of the evaluators? No.

51. **B**   *Understand the Question/Key Words:* What area of the brain regulates hunger and eating? *Predict the Answer:* Hypothalamus. If you don't remember, use POE. Does (A), the somatosensory cortex, regulate hunger and eating? Probably not—it is a cortex and somehow involves "sensory" stuff, and hunger is a primary drive. Cross this off. Does (C), the medulla oblongata, regulate hunger and eating? Probably not, because you know it is a part of vital organ functioning. Do the occipital lobes, (D), regulate hunger and eating? No, they involve vision. Does (E), the amygdala, regulate hunger and eating? No, it is involved in emotions. The answer must be (B).

52. **B**   *Understand the Question/Key Words:* Circle *peg-word mnemonic system. Predict the Answer:* This should be a strategy that enables recall of an ordered list, which is (B), visualization and rhymes. However, if that doesn't suggest an answer, use POE. This is a verbal technique and there are no smell or taste sensations involved, so eliminate (A). Neither meaning of the items (semantic) nor prior events (episodic) are part of the system, so eliminate (C). The system is verbal, not physical, so eliminate (D). Choice (E) describes problem-solving styles, not a mnemonic device, so eliminate it.

53. **A**   *Understand the Question/Key Words:* Which helps determine whether the findings of a study mean something or were a fluke? *Predict the Answer:* Inferential statistics. If you don't remember, use POE to evaluate the answer choices. Could (A), inferential statistics, help determine whether the findings of a study mean something? They help to infer stuff, so probably. Keep it, and read the others. Could (B), descriptive statistics, help determine whether the findings of a study mean something? They only describe, so probably not. Cross it off. Could (C), standard deviation, help determine whether the findings of a study mean something? Cross it off. Same goes for (D), extraneous variables. Could (E), correlation coefficients, help determine whether the findings of a study mean something? No, so the answer must be (A).

54. **C** *Understand the Question/Key Words:* "Normal REM sleep behavior" is the key. *Predict the Answer:* People will be active mentally and physiologically (e.g. increased heart rate, respiration, etc.), but, paradoxically, they will be virtually paralyzed. This leads you to (C), but you can double-check by using POE. The person is probably dreaming and the brain is quite active, so eliminate (A). Both (B) and (E) are characteristic of deep sleep, whereas REM is a light-sleep phenomenon, so eliminate them. Eliminate (D) because the person is unable to move much during REM.

55. **C** *Understand the Question/Key Words:* Which gland is called the master gland? *Predict the Answer:* Pituitary gland. If you don't remember, use POE to get rid of (B) and (E) because they are not glands. You also know that (D), the adrenal gland, isn't responsible for much more than adrenaline, so cross it off, too.

56. **C** *Understand the Question/Key Words:* What types of mistakes do all children make when learning language? *Predict the Answer:* They learn to use the rules of grammar, but they apply them too generally. Use POE. It must be (C), overgeneralization.

57. **D** *Understand the Question/Key Words:* What does a researcher have to do to show that one thing causes another? *Predict the Answer:* Show that manipulating one variable consistently leads to changes in another variable. Use POE to find the answer that is closest to yours. Choice (A) is unethical, and, along with (B) and (C), would do nothing to show causation. Regarding (E), remember that correlation does not mean causation!

58. **A** *Understand the Question/Key Words:* The idea here is that some of the dogs learned to be helpless when their efforts were repeatedly unsuccessful in allowing them to escape the shocks. The question is looking for the independent variable. *Predict the Answer:* The independent variable is what the experimenter manipulates, and here it should relate to whether or not the dog's behavior will be successful, which is (A). If you can't home in on this directly, use POE. The electric shocks are the aversive stimulus, not a variable by themselves, so eliminate (B). Choice (C) represents the dependent variable, so eliminate it. Choice (D) indicates why the shocks would be unpleasant for the dogs, but it is not a variable—eliminate it. Choice (E) relates to sample size, but is not being manipulated by the experimenter—eliminate it.

59. **B** Jose demonstrates characteristics of the preoperational stage, including the fact that he has yet to learn principles of conservation of matter. Choice (C) is not a stage in Piaget's theory. Choice (A) involves infants and toddlers who are just learning to walk and talk. Choice (D) is the stage during which children learn principles of conservation. Choice (E) is the stage when children become capable of abstract and higher-level thinking.

60. **E** *Understand the Question/Key Words:* Georgia is motivated by internal issues or emotions, while Kathy is motivated by money. How are these motivations different? *Predict the Answer:* Georgia is motivated intrinsically; that is, she is rewarded by the work itself. Kathy is motivated extrinsically; that is, by an external reward—money. If you don't remember the terms, use POE. For (A), neither helping behavior nor making money is homeostatic for drive-reduction, nor is either instinctive, so eliminate this. Choice (B) does not apply because locus of control refers to whether or not people

feel that they determine the outcomes in their lives. The concepts in (C) relate to arousal and calming states, not motivation, so cross it off. The satisfaction one derives from helping others and the money one makes from doing a job are both positive reinforcers, so eliminate (D).

61. **E** *Understand the Question/Key Words:* Circle *depression*. What chemicals in the brain are traditionally thought to be involved in depression? *Predict the Answer*: Depression should make you think "serotonin." If it doesn't, use POE to get rid of a few choices. Get rid of (A) and (D) due to elevated levels (not likely with depression). Review disorders and their relationships to chemicals in the brain.

62. **A** Deindividuation applies to situations of high arousal and low perceived personal identification, when individuals might succumb to mob mentality. Choice (B) involves group members becoming more extreme in their preexisting views as time goes on. Choice (C) occurs in a group that prizes consensus over free exchange of competing views. Choice (D) involves performing better when other people are around. Choice (E) involves people forming more positive views of something simply because they have encountered it repeatedly.

63. **E** *Understand the Question/Key Words:* Why do the pigeons not peck at other artists' paintings? *Predict the Answer*: Stimulus discrimination. They peck at the one they have learned and can distinguish from the others. With this information, use POE to cross off (A), modeling response, (B), reflexive response, and (D), stimulus generalization, because it is the opposite idea.

64. **E** *Understand the Question/Key Words:* She recalls the book by also recalling the lunch. What type of memory is she calling up? *Predict the Answer*: Episodic memory. She relates the memory to a recent episode. Use POE to get rid of the other four choices.

65. **C** *Understand the Question/Key Words:* Converting physical energy into neural impulses is called…. *Predict the Answer:* Transduction. If you don't remember, use POE. Choice (A), sensation, is out because it involves only detection of energy, not conversion. The same is true of (E), detection. You can also eliminate (D), encoding, because it is not involved in energy conversion.

66. **E** *Understand the Question/Key Words:* A person is shown something. Later, she is shown incomplete information related to the first thing she was shown. The experimenter watches to see whether she recognizes the incomplete information more quickly than usual. In other words, does the fact that she saw related stimuli make identifying the second set easier? *Predict the Answer*: The researcher is studying the effects of priming. If you don't remember the term, use POE. Cross off (B) because no mnemonic devices are used. Choice (C), declarative memory, is out because it deals with retrieved and "declared" information. Choice (D), iconic memory, is out because we don't know whether these are visual images or other types of information.

67. **B** *Understand the Question/Key Words:* What did Binet study? *Predict the Answer*: Binet = intelligence. He studied intellectual potential in children. Knowing he studied intelligence and not personality will help you cross off (C) through (E). Then take your best guess. You know he developed some kind of test, and most intelligence testing is done on children. Choice (B) is correct.

68. **D** *Understand the Question/Key Words:* Circle *fluid intelligence*. *Fluid* refers to real-time, flexible information-processing intelligence, whereas *crystallized* intelligence refers to acquired factual knowledge. Which of the subjects involves real-time, flexible intelligence? *Predict the Answer:* Adjusting to virtual reality video games, (D), requires fluid intelligence. Choices (A), (B), and (C) require primarily crystallized intelligence, so eliminate them. Choice (E), painting, involves some fluid intelligence, but it is not as clear an example as (D), so eliminate it.

69. **C** *Understand the Question/Key Words:* Circle *repression*. Repression means keeping stressful thoughts out of conscious awareness. *Predict the Answer:* Repression is a defense mechanism that keeps anxiety-producing information out of conscious awareness for our protection. Use POE to find the answer that is closest to yours. Choice (A) is the definition of displacement, (B) is transference, and (D) is rationalization. Choice (E) doesn't make any sense—people can't describe what is unconscious.

70. **E** *Understand the Question/Key Words:* Which answer shows that genetics, as opposed to environment, has a direct effect on intelligence? *Predict the Answer:* Find an answer that shows genes/biology as more important than environment. Use POE. Choices (B) and (C) say the opposite. Choice (D) also would not support genetics. In (A), fraternal twins have the same average genetic similarity as parents and their offspring, so this answer does not support genetics. The answer must be (E).

71. **C** *Understand the Question/Key Words:* Circle *negative symptoms*. Remember that "negative" means the absence of something. *Predict the Answer:* Lack of normal emotional responses. If you don't remember, POE will get rid of all the other choices because each describes the presence, not the absence, of something.

72. **C** The Yerkes-Dodson law posits that, for most people, most of the time, in most activities, a moderate level of arousal is best. Choice (A) is about sequencing of emotion and physiological arousal. Choice (B) is about when children become capable of abstract thinking. Choice (D) is about how people tolerate stress. Choice (E) is about different types of intelligence.

73. **A** *Understand the Question/Key Words:* Circle *NOT* and *crystallized intelligence*. *Predict the Answer:* Remember that crystallized intelligence refers to accumulated knowledge, while fluid intelligence is the ability to learn new tasks, process information quickly, and think abstractly. Look for the answer choice that describes the use of fluid intelligence, such as learning a new software program— (A) is correct. Choices (B), (C), and (D) are all examples of concrete factual knowledge that one acquires throughout life. Choice (E) is a bit tricky because it refers to Shakespeare's sonnets, which require abstract and symbolic thinking to understand. Note, however, that (E) specifies the ability to recite the sonnets, not necessarily understand them, and is therefore simply acquired knowledge.

74. **E** *Understand the Question/Key Words:* Circle *drive-reduction theories*. *Predict the Answer:* Cross off all the answers that show a response that reduces a drive. The remaining choice will be the answer. In (A), Jerome is thirsty and quenches his thirst, thus satisfying his drive. Cross off this response. In (B), Ernest didn't eat lunch, implying hunger, so he eats cookies, trying to reduce his hunger drive.

Cross it off. In (C), Tish is not hungry, so she doesn't eat. Although this is not drive *reduction*, it is not against natural drives. Leave it, and see whether there is a better choice. In (D), Cameron is hungry and needs food, so she goes out of her way to get it. This is drive reduction, so cross it off. In (E), Kezia orders more food even though she is very full. This desire goes against drive reduction, so this is your answer.

75. **E** *Understand the Question/Key Words*: Circle *Maslow* and *motives*. *Predict the Answer*: Maslow theorized that needs are arranged hierarchically, from physiological needs to self-actualization needs. Use POE. Does (A), homeostatic regulation, have to do with hierarchy? No. Cross it off. Does (B), goal-setting, have to do with hierarchy? No. Does (C), expectancy-value, or (D), cognitive dissonance, have to do with hierarchy? No. Choice (E), hierarchy of needs, is it.

76. **C** *Understand the Question/Key Words:* Circle *anterograde amnesia*. *Predict the Answer*: Look for an example of someone who can't form new memories. Get rid of (B) and (D) because they are clearly "after" memories. Choice (A) involves infantile amnesia, and (E) is an example of source amnesia.

77. **A** *Understand the Question/Key Words:* Circle *classical conditioning*. *Predict the Answer*: Find a choice that demonstrates a conditioned response to a stimulus. Choices (B), (C), and (D) are not conditioned responses. Beware of (E); it's a trap because it uses rats and salivation, but notice that the rat salivates only after it begins to eat. Choice (A) demonstrates a conditioned fear response after experiencing an accident on the highway.

78. **C** *Understand the Question/Key Words:* Which will help you understand how a person or persons interpret the behavior of others? *Predict the Answer*: Attribution theory. Attribution theory addresses how one person or group attributes certain things to another person or group in order to understand the other person's or group's actions or behaviors. If you don't remember this, use POE. Could (A), reinforcement theory, help explain how one group interprets the actions of another? Reinforcement has nothing to do with how groups interrelate. Cross it off. Could (B), classical behaviorism, help explain how one group interprets the actions of another? No. Could (C), attribution theory, help explain how one group interprets the actions of another? How they attribute things to others? Could be. Leave it. Could (D), hierarchy of needs, help explain how one group interprets the actions of another? No. Could (E), cognitive dissonance, help explain how one group interprets the actions of another? No. Your answer must be (C).

79. **B** *Understand the Question/Key Words:* During which of Piaget's stages of development do children develop symbolic and verbal representations? *Predict the Answer*: Preoperational. If you don't remember, think about the age at which this behavior occurs. You may recall the order of the stages and their approximate ages: sensorimotor, ages zero to two; preoperational, ages two to seven; concrete operational, ages seven to eleven; formal operational, ages twelve and up. The development of language and symbolic thinking occurs between the ages of two and seven. Use POE to get rid of (A) because *sensorimotor* definitely does not imply symbolic thought and (C) because *symbolic* is not one of Piaget's stages.

80. **E** *Understand the Question/Key Words:* Circle *Kohlberg* and *third (postconventional) level. Predict the Answer:* As "postconventional" implies, this stage of morality centers on carefully weighed principles that may or may not be conventional—they are determined by the individual. You may remember that Kohlberg posited only three stages, and this third one is the most advanced, so look for an answer that encompasses the most advanced form of moral thinking. Choices (A) and (B) illustrate the first or preconventional stage of development. Choices (C) and (D) represent the second or conventional stage of development.

81. **D** *Understand the Question/Key Words:* Circle *order of auditory transmission. Predict the Answer:* Use POE to assess the correct order based on what you know about this process.

82. **E** This is Whorf's theory: Thinking doesn't just affect language—the language used affects thinking. The behaviorist theory of language development is that children produce language that is reinforced. Chomsky's theory is that people have an innate capacity for learning language rules, especially grammar. Selye's theory involves stress. The Schachter-Singer theory involves emotion.

83. **C** According to Erikson, when looking back on their lives, elderly individuals hope to find that they have gained wisdom. Choice (A) applies to young adults, (B) to children in the three-to-six age range, (D) to children in the one-to-three range, and (E) to middle-aged adults.

84. **C** *Understand the Question/Key Words:* Circle *Carl Rogers.* How did he approach psychotherapy? *Predict the Answer:* Rogers believed in empathy and unconditional support that would promote self-discovery. If you don't remember, you know that Rogers is a big name in psychology, so get rid of the clearly un-psychological answer choices—(B) and (E)—and (D), due to the "professional achievement" goal.

85. **D** *Understand the Question/Key Words:* Circle *breathing-related sleep disorder. Predict the Answer:* Apnea. Your clue is "breathing-related." If you don't remember, you can still cross off (B), (C), and (E) because they are not breathing-related.

86. **E** *Understand the Question/Key Words:* What facial expressions are found in all cultures? *Predict the Answer:* List the ones you can think of: happiness, sadness, anger, fear, and surprise, for example. Then use POE. You can also use POE to get rid of lists that have inappropriate choices: (A) is out because of "lust," (C) is out because of "desire," and (D) is out because of both "fight" and "flight." "Indifference" is the problem with (B).

87. **C** *Understand the Question/Key Words:* Circle *chemical sense. Predict the Answer:* Find something that is a result of chemical interaction. Even if you don't remember that taste is a chemical sense, use POE to get rid of the answers that are definitely physical properties: (A), (B), (D), and (E) are all physical or mechanical processes.

88. **D** Though body dysmorphic disorder can be interrelated with other diagnoses, such as anorexia nervosa, it is not categorized as a feeding disorder because it does not involve eating. Rather, it is characterized by obsessive thoughts about body parts the person believes are disproportionate or abnormally shaped. This may lead to disordered eating, but it is in the category of obsessive compulsive and related disorders.

89. **E** *Understand the Question/Key Words:* Circle *circadian rhythms*. These involve sleep patterns. *Predict the Answer:* Choose what's most directly related to sleep, which is (E).

90. **E** Cordelia has harnessed what might otherwise be socially unacceptable impulses and turned them into something positive. She has not imagined these impulses in other people, (A); treated someone the opposite of how she truly feels about them, (B); fully buried her traumatic experiences, (C); or denied those experiences, (D).

91. **C** *Understand the Question/Key Words:* Why don't you see the different images of the statue as you view it from different places as distinct? Why does the image remain constant? *Predict the Answer*: Perceptual constancy. If you don't remember the term, use POE and your common sense. Choice (E) is definitely out. Could (A), convergence, mean that the image remains constant? "Convergence" means coming together, so not really. Cross it off. The same is true of (D), interpositioning. You may not be sure about (B), motion parallax, but (C), perceptual constancy, makes the most sense because the image remains constant.

92. **E** *Understand the Question/Key Words:* Circle *paradoxical sleep. Predict the Answer*: A paradox is a contradiction. Paradoxical sleep doesn't involve a true paradox, but rather an apparent paradox: the body is in deep sleep and immobile, but the brain waves present resemble those in near wakefulness. Choices (A), (B), (C), and (D) are properties of sleep, but no apparent paradox is noted. Choices (A) and (B) are untrue, while (C) and (D) contain correct information, but do not address the question.

93. **D** Broca's area is responsible for the production of fluent speech. Choice (A) is about speech, but it is about comprehension and meaning rather than fluency. Choice (B) is responsible for consolidating memory in the brain. Choice (C) is the "fear center" in the brain. Choice (E) controls basic processes like breathing and swallowing.

94. **B** *Understand the Question/Key Words:* Inferring from an observation to a generalization is what kind of reasoning? *Predict the Answer*: Inductive reasoning. If you don't remember, use POE where you can. Be careful on (A); deductive reasoning is something that can be clearly deduced, rather than being inferred or simply probable. Choice (D), statistical reasoning, is also out. Choices (C) and (E) are not the correct psychological terms.

95. **B**   Claudio has created a prototypical, or stereotypical, idea of an elderly person who is not interested in technology and this may conflict with the actual number of elderly individuals who are interested in his services. Choice (A) is also an obstacle, but it involves Claudio having more information about one group than others, which isn't supported in the question stem. Choice (C) involves being unable to see novel uses for familiar objects. Choice (D) is an attribution bias that causes people to view their own prospects too favorably. Choice (E) is an obstacle that involves seeking only evidence to support one's predetermined views or ignoring evidence that conflicts with those views: we don't have evidence Claudio does any of these.

96. **E**   *Understand the Question/Key Words:* What's the route visual information takes? *Predict the Answer*: Retina, bipolar cells, ganglion cells, and optic nerve. If you don't remember, you probably know that transduction starts in the retina, so rods and cones are first. Cross off (A), (B), and (D). Rods and cones are in the retina, so that takes care of (C).

97. **B**   *Understand the Question/Key Words:* Circle *Rogers* and *view of personality*. What did Rogers say about personality? *Predict the Answer*: Rogers believed in the goodness of the individual. If you are not sure, use POE. Cross off (A) because it is extreme and untrue (is that always the case?), and (C) because it is a behavioral explanation of personality. Choices (D) and (E) were not views of Rogers.

98. **B**   *Understand the Question/Key Words:* Circle *acetylcholine*. It's related to what disease? *Predict the Answer*: Alzheimer's. If you don't remember, you may remember that dopamine is somehow tied to Parkinson's, so you can cross off (A). If you have reviewed disorders enough, you will also know that it is not tied to (C), (D), or (E), so the answer must be (B).

99. **B**   *Understand the Question/Key Words:* Why do babies lack clear vision shortly after birth? *Predict the Answer*: Not all neural connections are in place at birth. If you don't know, use POE to get rid of what you can. Choice (D) is way off (aqueous humor is in the eye). Glial cells do not detect messages so (E) is out, and myelination is a tight coat of lipids, so watch out for (C).

100. **A**   Choice (A) is the correct term. If you didn't remember it, use POE. The tip-of-the-tongue phenomenon, (B), is when we try to recall something, but it is not easily available for conscious awareness. Cortical conditioning, (C), is a mashup of other terms, while myelinization, (D), and reuptake, (E), are features of neurons, not brain functions.

Section II: Free Response

1. Essay number one is worth seven points. Points are given based on a student's ability to explain behavior and apply theories and perspectives in authentic contexts. Each essay is unique, but here is our run-down of what a student should definitely address in their Free Response Essay for this question:

- The "Big Five" trait of openness to experience: If Kai ranks high in this trait, he will enjoy the opportunity to perform in a new environment and do well; if he ranks low, he would prefer his usual environment and this might negatively affect his performance.

- Convergence (depth perception): Kai may have difficulty judging depth in the mid-distance; for example, following the snap to the holder, or seeing where the holder places the ball. But remember that he should be okay judging depth to the goalposts, because that is too far for convergence to be a factor.

- Cognitive dissonance: He believes in the importance of careful preparation, yet he was unable to practice. This discordance will cause him tension and this might negatively affect his performance. He could cope by changing his attitude; for example, he could rationalize that his excitement will overcome the lack of preparation.

- Social facilitation: Since this is a simple, well-practiced skill, having other people around could enhance his performance. Not having others around will deprive him of this benefit. But the other side of that coin is that his knowing that the evaluators are around, even if he cannot see them, will still enhance his performance.

- Sympathetic nervous system: This arousal mechanism activates the fight-or-flight response. If he is nervous, this could negatively affect his performance. But you may wish to take this answer a step further and admit that his success as a kicker in the past has demonstrated that he is able to control this response in stressful situations, so he should do well in this situation.

- Non-declarative memory: Kicking a football is a procedural memory that is relatively resistant to decay. Also worth noting is the fact that "muscle memory" should remain intact in a stressful situation.

- Self-efficacy: He believes that he is a capable kicker and this belief makes it more likely that he will succeed in a stressful situation.

2.   Essay number two is worth seven points. Points are given based on students' ability to analyze psychological research studies, including analyzing and interpreting quantitative data. One point is given for each point addressed in each part of the question.

This is what our student chose to do for her essay. She scored a seven out of seven on this essay. Use this as a sample of a high-scoring essay.

Sample Essay

The independent variable is the GMO berry. That is what the experimenter is manipulating: the experimental group gets it and the control group does not.

A possible threat to internal validity is the lack of control of the subjects' lives while living at the lab. Only diet and sleep are being controlled. This might cause there to be confounding variables. For example, it is well-known that exercise can have an effect on mood. However, subjects may exercise or not at their discretion, thereby creating an alternative explanation for changes in mood. Exercise should have been controlled. Similarly, what the subjects do for entertainment could affect mood and should, therefore, be controlled as much as possible.

Reliability for an instrument like the BDI involves whether consistent scores are obtained for a subject when the instrument is given a second time. Absent some major intervention or trauma, a subject's score should not change very much from one administration to another if they are separated by just a few weeks. On the other hand, validity is about whether the BDI truly measures depression. One way to assess this might be to compare the BDI results with those obtained by professionals doing clinical interviews.

This experiment is single-blind because subjects don't know whether they are in the experimental group or the control group. To make it double-blind, you would need to make sure that the lab staff, the people running the experiment, don't know who is in which group. This could be important if they might treat the subjects differently knowing who was in which group, and this might in turn affect mood.

The p-value of 0.05 indicates that there is a ninety-five percent likelihood that the changes in mood between the experimental and control groups are due to consumption of the GMO berry. If there is less than a five percent chance that these differences were due to randomness, then the results can be considered significant.

Cognitive therapy would focus on the way people's thinking might be maladaptive and might cause them to be depressed. For example, some individuals might "catastrophize": that is, they might view relatively small problems as overwhelming and unmanageable. The therapy would try to get them to take a more realistic view of their problems.

Humanistic therapy would focus on an individual's search for a clear self-identity and to become a self-actualized human being. Obstacles to these efforts would be seen as significant contributors to depression. The therapist might assist the person in differentiating their senses of identity from those of their parents. The therapist might also look for ways to enhance self-image.

HOW TO SCORE PRACTICE TEST 4

Section I: Multiple Choice

$$\underset{\substack{\text{Number Correct} \\ \text{(out of 100)}}}{\underline{\hspace{3cm}}} \times 1.0000 = \underset{\substack{\text{Weighted} \\ \text{Section I Score} \\ \text{(Do not round)}}}{\underline{\hspace{4cm}}}$$

Section II: Free Response

Question 1: $\underset{\text{(out of 7)}}{\underline{\hspace{2cm}}} \times 3.5714 = \underset{\text{(Do not round)}}{\underline{\hspace{2.5cm}}}$

Question 2: $\underset{\text{(out of 7)}}{\underline{\hspace{2cm}}} \times 3.5714 = \underset{\text{(Do not round)}}{\underline{\hspace{2.5cm}}}$

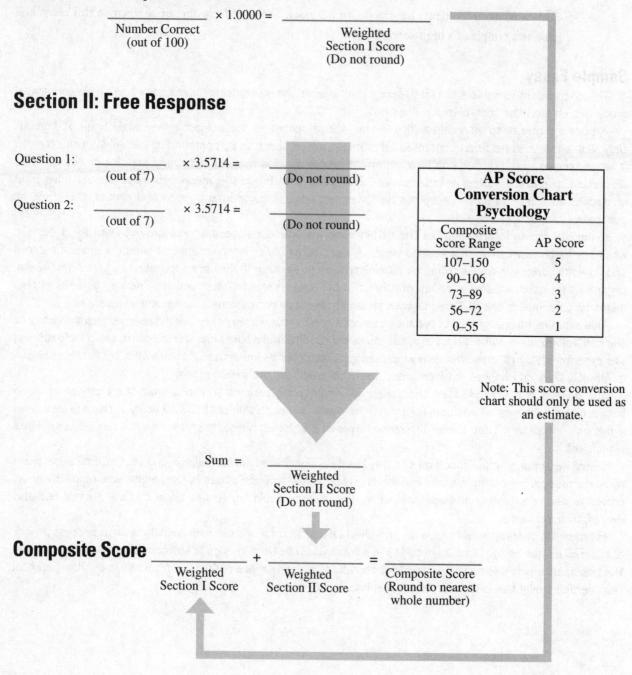

AP Score Conversion Chart Psychology	
Composite Score Range	AP Score
107–150	5
90–106	4
73–89	3
56–72	2
0–55	1

Note: This score conversion chart should only be used as an estimate.

$$\text{Sum} = \underset{\substack{\text{Weighted} \\ \text{Section II Score} \\ \text{(Do not round)}}}{\underline{\hspace{4cm}}}$$

Composite Score

$$\underset{\substack{\text{Weighted} \\ \text{Section I Score}}}{\underline{\hspace{2.5cm}}} + \underset{\substack{\text{Weighted} \\ \text{Section II Score}}}{\underline{\hspace{2.5cm}}} = \underset{\substack{\text{Composite Score} \\ \text{(Round to nearest} \\ \text{whole number)}}}{\underline{\hspace{2.5cm}}}$$

The Princeton Review®

1. YOUR NAME: _____
(Print) Last First M.I.

SIGNATURE: _____ DATE: __ / __ / __ .

HOME ADDRESS: _____
(Print) Number and Street

_____
City State Zip Code

PHONE NO. : _____
(Print)

IMPORTANT: Please fill in these boxes exactly as shown on the back cover of your test book.

2. TEST FORM

6. DATE OF BIRTH

Month		Day		Year	
○ JAN					
○ FEB					
○ MAR	⓪	⓪	⓪	⓪	
○ APR	①	①	①	①	
○ MAY	②	②	②	②	
○ JUN	③	③	③	③	
○ JUL		④	④	④	
○ AUG		⑤	⑤	⑤	
○ SEP		⑥	⑥	⑥	
○ OCT		⑦	⑦	⑦	
○ NOV		⑧	⑧	⑧	
○ DEC		⑨	⑨	⑨	

3. TEST CODE   4. REGISTRATION NUMBER

⓪	Ⓐ	⓪	⓪	⓪	⓪	⓪	⓪	⓪	⓪	⓪
①	Ⓑ	①	①	①	①	①	①	①	①	①
②	Ⓒ	②	②	②	②	②	②	②	②	②
③	Ⓓ	③	③	③	③	③	③	③	③	③
④	Ⓔ	④	④	④	④	④	④	④	④	④
⑤	Ⓕ	⑤	⑤	⑤	⑤	⑤	⑤	⑤	⑤	⑤
⑥	Ⓖ	⑥	⑥	⑥	⑥	⑥	⑥	⑥	⑥	⑥
⑦		⑦	⑦	⑦	⑦	⑦	⑦	⑦	⑦	⑦
⑧		⑧	⑧	⑧	⑧	⑧	⑧	⑧	⑧	⑧
⑨		⑨	⑨	⑨	⑨	⑨	⑨	⑨	⑨	⑨

The Princeton Review®

5. YOUR NAME

First 4 letters of last name				FIRST INIT	MID INIT
Ⓐ	Ⓐ	Ⓐ	Ⓐ	Ⓐ	Ⓐ
Ⓑ	Ⓑ	Ⓑ	Ⓑ	Ⓑ	Ⓑ
Ⓒ	Ⓒ	Ⓒ	Ⓒ	Ⓒ	Ⓒ
Ⓓ	Ⓓ	Ⓓ	Ⓓ	Ⓓ	Ⓓ
Ⓔ	Ⓔ	Ⓔ	Ⓔ	Ⓔ	Ⓔ
Ⓕ	Ⓕ	Ⓕ	Ⓕ	Ⓕ	Ⓕ
Ⓖ	Ⓖ	Ⓖ	Ⓖ	Ⓖ	Ⓖ
Ⓗ	Ⓗ	Ⓗ	Ⓗ	Ⓗ	Ⓗ
Ⓘ	Ⓘ	Ⓘ	Ⓘ	Ⓘ	Ⓘ
Ⓙ	Ⓙ	Ⓙ	Ⓙ	Ⓙ	Ⓙ
Ⓚ	Ⓚ	Ⓚ	Ⓚ	Ⓚ	Ⓚ
Ⓛ	Ⓛ	Ⓛ	Ⓛ	Ⓛ	Ⓛ
Ⓜ	Ⓜ	Ⓜ	Ⓜ	Ⓜ	Ⓜ
Ⓝ	Ⓝ	Ⓝ	Ⓝ	Ⓝ	Ⓝ
Ⓞ	Ⓞ	Ⓞ	Ⓞ	Ⓞ	Ⓞ
Ⓟ	Ⓟ	Ⓟ	Ⓟ	Ⓟ	Ⓟ
Ⓠ	Ⓠ	Ⓠ	Ⓠ	Ⓠ	Ⓠ
Ⓡ	Ⓡ	Ⓡ	Ⓡ	Ⓡ	Ⓡ
Ⓢ	Ⓢ	Ⓢ	Ⓢ	Ⓢ	Ⓢ
Ⓣ	Ⓣ	Ⓣ	Ⓣ	Ⓣ	Ⓣ
Ⓤ	Ⓤ	Ⓤ	Ⓤ	Ⓤ	Ⓤ
Ⓥ	Ⓥ	Ⓥ	Ⓥ	Ⓥ	Ⓥ
Ⓦ	Ⓦ	Ⓦ	Ⓦ	Ⓦ	Ⓦ
Ⓧ	Ⓧ	Ⓧ	Ⓧ	Ⓧ	Ⓧ
Ⓨ	Ⓨ	Ⓨ	Ⓨ	Ⓨ	Ⓨ
Ⓩ	Ⓩ	Ⓩ	Ⓩ	Ⓩ	Ⓩ

1. Ⓐ Ⓑ Ⓒ Ⓓ Ⓔ
2. Ⓐ Ⓑ Ⓒ Ⓓ Ⓔ
3. Ⓐ Ⓑ Ⓒ Ⓓ Ⓔ
4. Ⓐ Ⓑ Ⓒ Ⓓ Ⓔ
5. Ⓐ Ⓑ Ⓒ Ⓓ Ⓔ
6. Ⓐ Ⓑ Ⓒ Ⓓ Ⓔ
7. Ⓐ Ⓑ Ⓒ Ⓓ Ⓔ
8. Ⓐ Ⓑ Ⓒ Ⓓ Ⓔ
9. Ⓐ Ⓑ Ⓒ Ⓓ Ⓔ
10. Ⓐ Ⓑ Ⓒ Ⓓ Ⓔ
11. Ⓐ Ⓑ Ⓒ Ⓓ Ⓔ
12. Ⓐ Ⓑ Ⓒ Ⓓ Ⓔ
13. Ⓐ Ⓑ Ⓒ Ⓓ Ⓔ
14. Ⓐ Ⓑ Ⓒ Ⓓ Ⓔ
15. Ⓐ Ⓑ Ⓒ Ⓓ Ⓔ
16. Ⓐ Ⓑ Ⓒ Ⓓ Ⓔ
17. Ⓐ Ⓑ Ⓒ Ⓓ Ⓔ
18. Ⓐ Ⓑ Ⓒ Ⓓ Ⓔ
19. Ⓐ Ⓑ Ⓒ Ⓓ Ⓔ
20. Ⓐ Ⓑ Ⓒ Ⓓ Ⓔ
21. Ⓐ Ⓑ Ⓒ Ⓓ Ⓔ
22. Ⓐ Ⓑ Ⓒ Ⓓ Ⓔ
23. Ⓐ Ⓑ Ⓒ Ⓓ Ⓔ
24. Ⓐ Ⓑ Ⓒ Ⓓ Ⓔ
25. Ⓐ Ⓑ Ⓒ Ⓓ Ⓔ

26. Ⓐ Ⓑ Ⓒ Ⓓ Ⓔ
27. Ⓐ Ⓑ Ⓒ Ⓓ Ⓔ
28. Ⓐ Ⓑ Ⓒ Ⓓ Ⓔ
29. Ⓐ Ⓑ Ⓒ Ⓓ Ⓔ
30. Ⓐ Ⓑ Ⓒ Ⓓ Ⓔ
31. Ⓐ Ⓑ Ⓒ Ⓓ Ⓔ
32. Ⓐ Ⓑ Ⓒ Ⓓ Ⓔ
33. Ⓐ Ⓑ Ⓒ Ⓓ Ⓔ
34. Ⓐ Ⓑ Ⓒ Ⓓ Ⓔ
35. Ⓐ Ⓑ Ⓒ Ⓓ Ⓔ
36. Ⓐ Ⓑ Ⓒ Ⓓ Ⓔ
37. Ⓐ Ⓑ Ⓒ Ⓓ Ⓔ
38. Ⓐ Ⓑ Ⓒ Ⓓ Ⓔ
39. Ⓐ Ⓑ Ⓒ Ⓓ Ⓔ
40. Ⓐ Ⓑ Ⓒ Ⓓ Ⓔ
41. Ⓐ Ⓑ Ⓒ Ⓓ Ⓔ
42. Ⓐ Ⓑ Ⓒ Ⓓ Ⓔ
43. Ⓐ Ⓑ Ⓒ Ⓓ Ⓔ
44. Ⓐ Ⓑ Ⓒ Ⓓ Ⓔ
45. Ⓐ Ⓑ Ⓒ Ⓓ Ⓔ
46. Ⓐ Ⓑ Ⓒ Ⓓ Ⓔ
47. Ⓐ Ⓑ Ⓒ Ⓓ Ⓔ
48. Ⓐ Ⓑ Ⓒ Ⓓ Ⓔ
49. Ⓐ Ⓑ Ⓒ Ⓓ Ⓔ
50. Ⓐ Ⓑ Ⓒ Ⓓ Ⓔ

51. Ⓐ Ⓑ Ⓒ Ⓓ Ⓔ
52. Ⓐ Ⓑ Ⓒ Ⓓ Ⓔ
53. Ⓐ Ⓑ Ⓒ Ⓓ Ⓔ
54. Ⓐ Ⓑ Ⓒ Ⓓ Ⓔ
55. Ⓐ Ⓑ Ⓒ Ⓓ Ⓔ
56. Ⓐ Ⓑ Ⓒ Ⓓ Ⓔ
57. Ⓐ Ⓑ Ⓒ Ⓓ Ⓔ
58. Ⓐ Ⓑ Ⓒ Ⓓ Ⓔ
59. Ⓐ Ⓑ Ⓒ Ⓓ Ⓔ
60. Ⓐ Ⓑ Ⓒ Ⓓ Ⓔ
61. Ⓐ Ⓑ Ⓒ Ⓓ Ⓔ
62. Ⓐ Ⓑ Ⓒ Ⓓ Ⓔ
63. Ⓐ Ⓑ Ⓒ Ⓓ Ⓔ
64. Ⓐ Ⓑ Ⓒ Ⓓ Ⓔ
65. Ⓐ Ⓑ Ⓒ Ⓓ Ⓔ
66. Ⓐ Ⓑ Ⓒ Ⓓ Ⓔ
67. Ⓐ Ⓑ Ⓒ Ⓓ Ⓔ
68. Ⓐ Ⓑ Ⓒ Ⓓ Ⓔ
69. Ⓐ Ⓑ Ⓒ Ⓓ Ⓔ
70. Ⓐ Ⓑ Ⓒ Ⓓ Ⓔ
71. Ⓐ Ⓑ Ⓒ Ⓓ Ⓔ
72. Ⓐ Ⓑ Ⓒ Ⓓ Ⓔ
73. Ⓐ Ⓑ Ⓒ Ⓓ Ⓔ
74. Ⓐ Ⓑ Ⓒ Ⓓ Ⓔ
75. Ⓐ Ⓑ Ⓒ Ⓓ Ⓔ

76. Ⓐ Ⓑ Ⓒ Ⓓ Ⓔ
77. Ⓐ Ⓑ Ⓒ Ⓓ Ⓔ
78. Ⓐ Ⓑ Ⓒ Ⓓ Ⓔ
79. Ⓐ Ⓑ Ⓒ Ⓓ Ⓔ
80. Ⓐ Ⓑ Ⓒ Ⓓ Ⓔ
81. Ⓐ Ⓑ Ⓒ Ⓓ Ⓔ
82. Ⓐ Ⓑ Ⓒ Ⓓ Ⓔ
83. Ⓐ Ⓑ Ⓒ Ⓓ Ⓔ
84. Ⓐ Ⓑ Ⓒ Ⓓ Ⓔ
85. Ⓐ Ⓑ Ⓒ Ⓓ Ⓔ
86. Ⓐ Ⓑ Ⓒ Ⓓ Ⓔ
87. Ⓐ Ⓑ Ⓒ Ⓓ Ⓔ
88. Ⓐ Ⓑ Ⓒ Ⓓ Ⓔ
89. Ⓐ Ⓑ Ⓒ Ⓓ Ⓔ
90. Ⓐ Ⓑ Ⓒ Ⓓ Ⓔ
91. Ⓐ Ⓑ Ⓒ Ⓓ Ⓔ
92. Ⓐ Ⓑ Ⓒ Ⓓ Ⓔ
93. Ⓐ Ⓑ Ⓒ Ⓓ Ⓔ
94. Ⓐ Ⓑ Ⓒ Ⓓ Ⓔ
95. Ⓐ Ⓑ Ⓒ Ⓓ Ⓔ
96. Ⓐ Ⓑ Ⓒ Ⓓ Ⓔ
97. Ⓐ Ⓑ Ⓒ Ⓓ Ⓔ
98. Ⓐ Ⓑ Ⓒ Ⓓ Ⓔ
99. Ⓐ Ⓑ Ⓒ Ⓓ Ⓔ
100. Ⓐ Ⓑ Ⓒ Ⓓ Ⓔ

The Princeton Review®

1. YOUR NAME:
(Print)   Last   First   M.I.

SIGNATURE: _____   DATE: __ / __ / __

HOME ADDRESS: _____
(Print)   Number and Street

_____
City   State   Zip Code

PHONE NO. : _____
(Print)

IMPORTANT: Please fill in these boxes exactly as shown on the back cover of your test book.

2. TEST FORM

3. TEST CODE

4. REGISTRATION NUMBER

5. YOUR NAME

First 4 letters of last name					FIRST INIT	MID INIT

A B C D E F G H I J K L M N O P Q R S T U V W X Y Z

6. DATE OF BIRTH

Month	Day	Year
JAN		
FEB		
MAR		
APR		
MAY		
JUN		
JUL		
AUG		
SEP		
OCT		
NOV		
DEC		

The Princeton Review®

1. A B C D E
2. A B C D E
3. A B C D E
4. A B C D E
5. A B C D E
6. A B C D E
7. A B C D E
8. A B C D E
9. A B C D E
10. A B C D E
11. A B C D E
12. A B C D E
13. A B C D E
14. A B C D E
15. A B C D E
16. A B C D E
17. A B C D E
18. A B C D E
19. A B C D E
20. A B C D E
21. A B C D E
22. A B C D E
23. A B C D E
24. A B C D E
25. A B C D E

26. A B C D E
27. A B C D E
28. A B C D E
29. A B C D E
30. A B C D E
31. A B C D E
32. A B C D E
33. A B C D E
34. A B C D E
35. A B C D E
36. A B C D E
37. A B C D E
38. A B C D E
39. A B C D E
40. A B C D E
41. A B C D E
42. A B C D E
43. A B C D E
44. A B C D E
45. A B C D E
46. A B C D E
47. A B C D E
48. A B C D E
49. A B C D E
50. A B C D E

51. A B C D E
52. A B C D E
53. A B C D E
54. A B C D E
55. A B C D E
56. A B C D E
57. A B C D E
58. A B C D E
59. A B C D E
60. A B C D E
61. A B C D E
62. A B C D E
63. A B C D E
64. A B C D E
65. A B C D E
66. A B C D E
67. A B C D E
68. A B C D E
69. A B C D E
70. A B C D E
71. A B C D E
72. A B C D E
73. A B C D E
74. A B C D E
75. A B C D E

76. A B C D E
77. A B C D E
78. A B C D E
79. A B C D E
80. A B C D E
81. A B C D E
82. A B C D E
83. A B C D E
84. A B C D E
85. A B C D E
86. A B C D E
87. A B C D E
88. A B C D E
89. A B C D E
90. A B C D E
91. A B C D E
92. A B C D E
93. A B C D E
94. A B C D E
95. A B C D E
96. A B C D E
97. A B C D E
98. A B C D E
99. A B C D E
100. A B C D E

The **Princeton** Review®

1. YOUR NAME:
(Print)   Last   First   M.I.

SIGNATURE: _____   DATE: ___ / ___ / ___

HOME ADDRESS: _____
(Print)   Number and Street

_____
City   State   Zip Code

PHONE NO. : _____
(Print)

IMPORTANT: Please fill in these boxes exactly as shown on the back cover of your test book.

2. TEST FORM

3. TEST CODE

4. REGISTRATION NUMBER

5. YOUR NAME

First 4 letters of last name				FIRST INIT	MID INIT

A B C D E F G H I J K L M N O P Q R S T U V W X Y Z (columns)

6. DATE OF BIRTH

Month	Day	Year
JAN		
FEB		
MAR		
APR		
MAY		
JUN		
JUL		
AUG		
SEP		
OCT		
NOV		
DEC		

The **Princeton** Review®

1. A B C D E
2. A B C D E
3. A B C D E
4. A B C D E
5. A B C D E
6. A B C D E
7. A B C D E
8. A B C D E
9. A B C D E
10. A B C D E
11. A B C D E
12. A B C D E
13. A B C D E
14. A B C D E
15. A B C D E
16. A B C D E
17. A B C D E
18. A B C D E
19. A B C D E
20. A B C D E
21. A B C D E
22. A B C D E
23. A B C D E
24. A B C D E
25. A B C D E

26. A B C D E
27. A B C D E
28. A B C D E
29. A B C D E
30. A B C D E
31. A B C D E
32. A B C D E
33. A B C D E
34. A B C D E
35. A B C D E
36. A B C D E
37. A B C D E
38. A B C D E
39. A B C D E
40. A B C D E
41. A B C D E
42. A B C D E
43. A B C D E
44. A B C D E
45. A B C D E
46. A B C D E
47. A B C D E
48. A B C D E
49. A B C D E
50. A B C D E

51. A B C D E
52. A B C D E
53. A B C D E
54. A B C D E
55. A B C D E
56. A B C D E
57. A B C D E
58. A B C D E
59. A B C D E
60. A B C D E
61. A B C D E
62. A B C D E
63. A B C D E
64. A B C D E
65. A B C D E
66. A B C D E
67. A B C D E
68. A B C D E
69. A B C D E
70. A B C D E
71. A B C D E
72. A B C D E
73. A B C D E
74. A B C D E
75. A B C D E

76. A B C D E
77. A B C D E
78. A B C D E
79. A B C D E
80. A B C D E
81. A B C D E
82. A B C D E
83. A B C D E
84. A B C D E
85. A B C D E
86. A B C D E
87. A B C D E
88. A B C D E
89. A B C D E
90. A B C D E
91. A B C D E
92. A B C D E
93. A B C D E
94. A B C D E
95. A B C D E
96. A B C D E
97. A B C D E
98. A B C D E
99. A B C D E
100. A B C D E

Completely darken bubbles with a No. 2 pencil. If you make a mistake, be sure to erase mark completely. Erase all stray marks.

1. YOUR NAME: _____
(Print)   Last   First   M.I.

SIGNATURE: _____   **DATE:** ___ / ___ / ___

HOME ADDRESS: _____
(Print)   Number and Street

_____
City   State   Zip Code

PHONE NO. : _____
(Print)

IMPORTANT: Please fill in these boxes exactly as shown on the back cover of your test book.

2. TEST FORM

3. TEST CODE

4. REGISTRATION NUMBER

5. YOUR NAME
First 4 letters of last name | FIRST INIT | MID INIT

6. DATE OF BIRTH

Month	Day	Year
JAN		
FEB		
MAR	0 0 0 0	
APR	1 1 1 1	
MAY	2 2 2 2	
JUN	3 3 3 3	
JUL	4 4 4	
AUG	5 5 5	
SEP	6 6 6	
OCT	7 7 7	
NOV	8 8 8	
DEC	9 9 9	

1. Ⓐ Ⓑ Ⓒ Ⓓ Ⓔ
2. Ⓐ Ⓑ Ⓒ Ⓓ Ⓔ
3. Ⓐ Ⓑ Ⓒ Ⓓ Ⓔ
4. Ⓐ Ⓑ Ⓒ Ⓓ Ⓔ
5. Ⓐ Ⓑ Ⓒ Ⓓ Ⓔ
6. Ⓐ Ⓑ Ⓒ Ⓓ Ⓔ
7. Ⓐ Ⓑ Ⓒ Ⓓ Ⓔ
8. Ⓐ Ⓑ Ⓒ Ⓓ Ⓔ
9. Ⓐ Ⓑ Ⓒ Ⓓ Ⓔ
10. Ⓐ Ⓑ Ⓒ Ⓓ Ⓔ
11. Ⓐ Ⓑ Ⓒ Ⓓ Ⓔ
12. Ⓐ Ⓑ Ⓒ Ⓓ Ⓔ
13. Ⓐ Ⓑ Ⓒ Ⓓ Ⓔ
14. Ⓐ Ⓑ Ⓒ Ⓓ Ⓔ
15. Ⓐ Ⓑ Ⓒ Ⓓ Ⓔ
16. Ⓐ Ⓑ Ⓒ Ⓓ Ⓔ
17. Ⓐ Ⓑ Ⓒ Ⓓ Ⓔ
18. Ⓐ Ⓑ Ⓒ Ⓓ Ⓔ
19. Ⓐ Ⓑ Ⓒ Ⓓ Ⓔ
20. Ⓐ Ⓑ Ⓒ Ⓓ Ⓔ
21. Ⓐ Ⓑ Ⓒ Ⓓ Ⓔ
22. Ⓐ Ⓑ Ⓒ Ⓓ Ⓔ
23. Ⓐ Ⓑ Ⓒ Ⓓ Ⓔ
24. Ⓐ Ⓑ Ⓒ Ⓓ Ⓔ
25. Ⓐ Ⓑ Ⓒ Ⓓ Ⓔ

26. Ⓐ Ⓑ Ⓒ Ⓓ Ⓔ
27. Ⓐ Ⓑ Ⓒ Ⓓ Ⓔ
28. Ⓐ Ⓑ Ⓒ Ⓓ Ⓔ
29. Ⓐ Ⓑ Ⓒ Ⓓ Ⓔ
30. Ⓐ Ⓑ Ⓒ Ⓓ Ⓔ
31. Ⓐ Ⓑ Ⓒ Ⓓ Ⓔ
32. Ⓐ Ⓑ Ⓒ Ⓓ Ⓔ
33. Ⓐ Ⓑ Ⓒ Ⓓ Ⓔ
34. Ⓐ Ⓑ Ⓒ Ⓓ Ⓔ
35. Ⓐ Ⓑ Ⓒ Ⓓ Ⓔ
36. Ⓐ Ⓑ Ⓒ Ⓓ Ⓔ
37. Ⓐ Ⓑ Ⓒ Ⓓ Ⓔ
38. Ⓐ Ⓑ Ⓒ Ⓓ Ⓔ
39. Ⓐ Ⓑ Ⓒ Ⓓ Ⓔ
40. Ⓐ Ⓑ Ⓒ Ⓓ Ⓔ
41. Ⓐ Ⓑ Ⓒ Ⓓ Ⓔ
42. Ⓐ Ⓑ Ⓒ Ⓓ Ⓔ
43. Ⓐ Ⓑ Ⓒ Ⓓ Ⓔ
44. Ⓐ Ⓑ Ⓒ Ⓓ Ⓔ
45. Ⓐ Ⓑ Ⓒ Ⓓ Ⓔ
46. Ⓐ Ⓑ Ⓒ Ⓓ Ⓔ
47. Ⓐ Ⓑ Ⓒ Ⓓ Ⓔ
48. Ⓐ Ⓑ Ⓒ Ⓓ Ⓔ
49. Ⓐ Ⓑ Ⓒ Ⓓ Ⓔ
50. Ⓐ Ⓑ Ⓒ Ⓓ Ⓔ

51. Ⓐ Ⓑ Ⓒ Ⓓ Ⓔ
52. Ⓐ Ⓑ Ⓒ Ⓓ Ⓔ
53. Ⓐ Ⓑ Ⓒ Ⓓ Ⓔ
54. Ⓐ Ⓑ Ⓒ Ⓓ Ⓔ
55. Ⓐ Ⓑ Ⓒ Ⓓ Ⓔ
56. Ⓐ Ⓑ Ⓒ Ⓓ Ⓔ
57. Ⓐ Ⓑ Ⓒ Ⓓ Ⓔ
58. Ⓐ Ⓑ Ⓒ Ⓓ Ⓔ
59. Ⓐ Ⓑ Ⓒ Ⓓ Ⓔ
60. Ⓐ Ⓑ Ⓒ Ⓓ Ⓔ
61. Ⓐ Ⓑ Ⓒ Ⓓ Ⓔ
62. Ⓐ Ⓑ Ⓒ Ⓓ Ⓔ
63. Ⓐ Ⓑ Ⓒ Ⓓ Ⓔ
64. Ⓐ Ⓑ Ⓒ Ⓓ Ⓔ
65. Ⓐ Ⓑ Ⓒ Ⓓ Ⓔ
66. Ⓐ Ⓑ Ⓒ Ⓓ Ⓔ
67. Ⓐ Ⓑ Ⓒ Ⓓ Ⓔ
68. Ⓐ Ⓑ Ⓒ Ⓓ Ⓔ
69. Ⓐ Ⓑ Ⓒ Ⓓ Ⓔ
70. Ⓐ Ⓑ Ⓒ Ⓓ Ⓔ
71. Ⓐ Ⓑ Ⓒ Ⓓ Ⓔ
72. Ⓐ Ⓑ Ⓒ Ⓓ Ⓔ
73. Ⓐ Ⓑ Ⓒ Ⓓ Ⓔ
74. Ⓐ Ⓑ Ⓒ Ⓓ Ⓔ
75. Ⓐ Ⓑ Ⓒ Ⓓ Ⓔ

76. Ⓐ Ⓑ Ⓒ Ⓓ Ⓔ
77. Ⓐ Ⓑ Ⓒ Ⓓ Ⓔ
78. Ⓐ Ⓑ Ⓒ Ⓓ Ⓔ
79. Ⓐ Ⓑ Ⓒ Ⓓ Ⓔ
80. Ⓐ Ⓑ Ⓒ Ⓓ Ⓔ
81. Ⓐ Ⓑ Ⓒ Ⓓ Ⓔ
82. Ⓐ Ⓑ Ⓒ Ⓓ Ⓔ
83. Ⓐ Ⓑ Ⓒ Ⓓ Ⓔ
84. Ⓐ Ⓑ Ⓒ Ⓓ Ⓔ
85. Ⓐ Ⓑ Ⓒ Ⓓ Ⓔ
86. Ⓐ Ⓑ Ⓒ Ⓓ Ⓔ
87. Ⓐ Ⓑ Ⓒ Ⓓ Ⓔ
88. Ⓐ Ⓑ Ⓒ Ⓓ Ⓔ
89. Ⓐ Ⓑ Ⓒ Ⓓ Ⓔ
90. Ⓐ Ⓑ Ⓒ Ⓓ Ⓔ
91. Ⓐ Ⓑ Ⓒ Ⓓ Ⓔ
92. Ⓐ Ⓑ Ⓒ Ⓓ Ⓔ
93. Ⓐ Ⓑ Ⓒ Ⓓ Ⓔ
94. Ⓐ Ⓑ Ⓒ Ⓓ Ⓔ
95. Ⓐ Ⓑ Ⓒ Ⓓ Ⓔ
96. Ⓐ Ⓑ Ⓒ Ⓓ Ⓔ
97. Ⓐ Ⓑ Ⓒ Ⓓ Ⓔ
98. Ⓐ Ⓑ Ⓒ Ⓓ Ⓔ
99. Ⓐ Ⓑ Ⓒ Ⓓ Ⓔ
100. Ⓐ Ⓑ Ⓒ Ⓓ Ⓔ

NOTES

NOTES

NOTES